First World W[']
and Army of Occupatic
War Diary
France, Belgium and Germany

50 DIVISION
151 Infantry Brigade
Durham Light Infantry
1/5th, 1/6th, 1/7th and 1/9th Battalion
19 April 1915 - 31 January 1918

WO95/2840

The Naval & Military Press Ltd
www.nmarchive.com
Published in association with The National Archives

Published by

The Naval & Military Press Ltd

Unit 10 Ridgewood Industrial Park,

Uckfield, East Sussex,

TN22 5QE England

Tel: +44 (0) 1825 749494

www.naval-military-press.com

www.nmarchive.com

Contents

Document type	Place/Title	Date From	Date To
Heading	50th Division 151st Infy Bde 5th Bn Durham Lt Infy 1918 Feb To Oct 1918 From 150 Bde Same Div		
Heading	War Diary Vol 32 5th Bn The Durham Light Infantry February 1918		
War Diary	The Line	01/02/1918	06/02/1918
War Diary	Potijze	07/02/1918	07/02/1918
War Diary	Ypres	09/02/1918	14/02/1918
War Diary	Line	14/02/1918	18/02/1918
War Diary	St Jean Camp	19/02/1918	20/02/1918
War Diary	Tattinghem	21/02/1918	28/02/1918
Heading	151st Brigade 50th Division 5th Battalion Durham Light Infantry March 1918		
Heading	War Diary 5th Bn. Durham Light Infantry March 1918 Volume XXXVI		
War Diary	Tatingham	01/03/1918	08/03/1918
War Diary	Villers Bretonneux	09/03/1918	11/03/1918
War Diary	Marcelcave	12/03/1918	14/03/1918
War Diary	Bayonvillers	15/03/1918	21/03/1918
War Diary	In The Field	22/03/1918	31/03/1918
Heading	151st Brigade 50th Division 1/5th Battalion Durham Light Infantry April 1918		
War Diary	Line	01/04/1918	03/04/1918
War Diary	Villiers Mt Bernenchon	04/04/1918	07/04/1918
War Diary	Neuf Berquin	08/04/1918	08/04/1918
War Diary	Estaires	09/04/1918	09/04/1918
War Diary	Line	10/04/1918	16/04/1918
War Diary	Les Ciseaux	17/04/1918	30/04/1918
Heading	War Diary 5th D.L.I. May 1918 Volume XXXVIII		
War Diary	Arcis Le Ponsart	01/05/1918	05/05/1918
War Diary	Line	06/05/1918	13/05/1918
War Diary	Chaudardes	14/05/1918	19/05/1918
War Diary	Line	20/05/1918	25/05/1918
War Diary	Chaudardes	25/05/1918	27/05/1918
War Diary	Assumbly P	27/05/1918	31/05/1918
Heading	War Diary 5th Bn. Durham Light Infantry June 1918 Volume XXXIX		
War Diary	Vert Le Gravelle	01/06/1918	08/06/1918
War Diary	Line	06/06/1918	07/06/1918
War Diary	Chamozy	08/06/1918	13/06/1918
War Diary	Bois De Courton	13/06/1918	19/06/1918
War Diary	Broyes	20/06/1918	02/07/1918
War Diary	Connantre	03/07/1918	03/07/1918
War Diary	Huchenneville	04/07/1918	19/07/1918
War Diary	Rouxmesnil	20/07/1918	31/07/1918
Heading	Training Cadre 39th Division 117th Infy Bde 50 Division 151 Bde 5th Bn Durham Lt Infy Aug-Oct 1918 Demobilised Nov 1918		
War Diary	Dieppe	01/08/1918	01/08/1918
War Diary	Rouxmesnil Camp	02/08/1918	16/08/1918
War Diary	Rouen	17/08/1918	31/10/1918

Heading	50th Division 151st Infy Bde 6th Bn Durham Lt. Infy. Jun 1915-1918 Nov		
Heading	151st Inf. Bde. 50th Div. War Diary 6th Battn. The Durham Light Infantry June (8/30.6.15) 1915		
Heading	6th Battalion The Durham Light Infantry June 1915 (8/30.6.15)		
War Diary		08/06/1915	16/06/1915
War Diary	Hooge	17/06/1915	23/06/1915
War Diary	Lindenhoek Trenches	24/06/1915	27/06/1915
War Diary	Locre	28/06/1915	30/06/1915
Heading	151st Inf. Bde. 50th Div. 6th Battn. The Durham Light Infantry July 1915		
War Diary	Locre	01/07/1915	03/07/1915
War Diary	Trenches At Locre	04/07/1915	04/07/1915
War Diary	Trenches	05/07/1915	09/07/1915
War Diary	Kemmel	09/07/1915	16/07/1915
War Diary	Armentieres	17/07/1915	31/07/1915
Heading	151st Inf. Bde. 50th Div. 6th Battn. The Durham Light Infantry August (11/31.8.15) 1915		
Heading	6th Battalion The Durham Light Infantry August 1915 (11/31.8.15)		
War Diary	D'Armentieres	11/08/1915	13/08/1915
War Diary	Trenches	14/08/1915	19/08/1915
War Diary	Pont De Nieppe	20/08/1915	30/08/1915
War Diary	Trenches	31/08/1915	31/08/1915
Heading	151st Inf. Bde. 50th Div. 6th Battn The Durham Light Infantry September 1915		
War Diary		02/09/1915	06/09/1915
War Diary	Armentieres	07/09/1915	20/09/1915
War Diary	Trenches	20/09/1915	24/09/1915
War Diary	Armentiers	25/09/1915	25/09/1915
War Diary	Trenches	26/09/1915	29/09/1915
War Diary	Tissage	30/09/1915	30/09/1915
Miscellaneous	Messages And Signals		
War Diary		25/09/1915	30/09/1915
Heading	151st Inf. Bde. 50th Div. 6th Battn. The Durham Light Infantry October 1915		
War Diary		01/10/1915	09/10/1915
War Diary	81-82-83	09/10/1915	21/10/1915
War Diary	Trenches	22/10/1915	31/10/1915
Miscellaneous	Messages		
War Diary		06/10/1915	20/10/1915
Heading	151st Inf. Bde. 50th Div. 6th Battn. The Durham Light Infantry November 1915		
War Diary	Trenches	01/11/1915	07/11/1915
War Diary	Armentieres	08/11/1915	09/11/1915
War Diary	La Creche	10/11/1915	30/11/1915
Heading	151st Inf. Bde. 50th Div. 6th Battn. The Durham Light Infantry December 1915		
War Diary	Mount Sorril	01/12/1915	02/12/1915
War Diary	Dickebuch Huts	03/12/1915	05/12/1915
War Diary	Mount Sorril	06/12/1915	08/12/1915
War Diary	Dickebuch Huts	09/12/1915	14/12/1915
War Diary	Mount Sorril	15/12/1915	18/12/1915
War Diary	Poperinghe	19/12/1915	23/12/1915
War Diary	Bluff Sector	24/12/1915	31/12/1915

War Diary	La Blanche Maison	01/12/1915	17/12/1915
War Diary	Dickebusch	17/12/1915	17/12/1915
War Diary	Ypres	18/12/1915	22/12/1915
War Diary	Dickebusch	22/12/1915	31/12/1915
Miscellaneous	Appendix		
Miscellaneous	Appendix	18/12/1915	19/12/1915
Miscellaneous	Field Return		
Miscellaneous	Sanctuary Wood	24/12/1915	24/12/1915
Miscellaneous	Sanctuary Wood	30/12/1915	30/12/1915
Miscellaneous	Field Return		
Miscellaneous	Sanctuary Wood	31/12/1915	31/12/1915
War Diary	Ypres	01/01/1916	04/01/1916
War Diary	I24d 7.0	05/01/1916	09/01/1916
War Diary	Dickebusch (H 26 B2)	10/01/1916	12/01/1916
War Diary	Ypres I 24 D7.0	13/01/1916	17/01/1916
War Diary	Ypres I 24a 3.2	18/01/1916	20/01/1916
War Diary	A7-A12 Yprs	21/01/1916	25/01/1916
War Diary	Dickebusch	26/01/1916	29/01/1916
War Diary	A-7-A12 Yprs	30/01/1916	31/01/1916
Miscellaneous	6th Durham H.1.	07/01/1916	07/01/1916
Miscellaneous	In The Field	07/01/1916	07/01/1916
Miscellaneous	Field Return		
Miscellaneous	The Field	14/01/1916	14/01/1916
Miscellaneous	6th Divisional Ypres	21/01/1916	21/01/1916
Miscellaneous	The Field	21/01/1916	21/01/1916
Miscellaneous	Battalion Orders by Major G.A. Stevens Comdg 6th Durham L I	16/01/1916	16/01/1916
War Diary	Ypres I 24 B	01/02/1916	01/02/1916
War Diary	Ypres	02/02/1916	12/02/1916
War Diary	Dickebusch	13/02/1916	18/02/1916
War Diary	Ypres	19/02/1916	29/02/1916
Heading	War Diary March 1916 6th Durham Light Infantry Volume 12		
War Diary		01/03/1916	01/03/1916
War Diary	Ypres	02/03/1916	02/03/1916
War Diary	Dickebusch	03/03/1916	05/03/1916
War Diary	Ypres	06/03/1916	08/03/1916
War Diary	Dickebusch	09/03/1916	14/03/1916
War Diary	Ypres I 30 B	15/03/1916	17/03/1916
War Diary	Ypres	19/03/1916	01/04/1916
Miscellaneous	Lo Col Stevens D.S.O. Col 6th D.L.I.	01/03/1916	01/03/1916
Miscellaneous	In The Field	04/02/1916	04/02/1916
Miscellaneous	In The Field	11/02/1916	11/02/1916
Miscellaneous	Field Return		
Miscellaneous	In The Field	11/02/1916	11/02/1916
Miscellaneous	Field	18/02/1916	18/02/1916
Miscellaneous	Field Return	18/02/1916	18/02/1916
Miscellaneous	The Field	25/02/1916	25/02/1916
Miscellaneous	In The Field	28/01/1916	28/01/1916
Miscellaneous	6th Durham L.I.	28/01/1916	28/01/1916
Miscellaneous	In The Field	28/01/1916	28/01/1916
Heading	War Diary Of The 6 Batt. The Durham Light Infantry For The Month Of April 1916		
War Diary	Ypres Salient I.34.b. c & d Bean Pollock, International Trenches The Bluff & The New Year Trenches Gordon Post & Reserve Wood	01/04/1916	01/04/1916

War Diary	Ypres I.34.b C. & D. Bean Polluck & International Trenches & The "Bluff"	02/04/1916	02/04/1916
War Diary	Dickebusch Huts H.26.b Central	03/04/1916	03/04/1916
War Diary	Scottish Lines G. 17.d.3.3	04/04/1916	04/04/1916
War Diary	La Clytte M.12.9.9.	05/04/1916	07/04/1916
War Diary	N-Otenches N.6.c. 1/2.9.	08/04/1916	11/04/1916
Miscellaneous	Public Record Office		
War Diary	N.5.a.7.2.	11/04/1916	14/04/1916
War Diary	La Clytte	15/04/1916	30/04/1916
War Diary	Ypres (I 30 B)	01/05/1916	31/05/1916
War Diary	La Clytte	01/06/1916	30/06/1916
Heading	6 Bu The Durham Light Infantry War Diary July 1916 Volume Number 16		
War Diary	La Clytte	01/07/1916	18/07/1916
War Diary	Brulooze	18/07/1916	19/07/1916
War Diary	Aircraft	20/07/1916	22/07/1916
War Diary	Aircraft Farm	22/07/1916	27/07/1916
War Diary	Kemmel	27/07/1916	31/07/1916
Heading	War Diary 1/6th Battn The Durham Light Infantry August 1916 Volume No. 17		
War Diary	Kemmel	01/08/1916	04/08/1916
War Diary	Locre	04/08/1916	10/08/1916
War Diary	Berthen	10/08/1916	10/08/1916
War Diary	Fleinvillers Candas	11/08/1916	15/08/1916
War Diary	Heauzecourt	15/08/1916	20/08/1916
War Diary	Baizieux	21/08/1916	31/08/1916
Heading	151st Infantry Brigade 50th Division 6th Durham Light Infantry 151st Infantry Brigade September 1916		
Heading	Volume 18 War Diary Of 6 Bn The Durham Light Infantry For The Month September 1916		
War Diary	Baizieux	01/09/1916	15/09/1916
War Diary	Mametz Wood	15/09/1916	30/09/1916
Heading	War Diary October 1916 6th Durham Light Infy Volume 19		
War Diary	Somme	01/10/1916	01/10/1916
War Diary	Somme Trenches	01/10/1916	06/10/1916
War Diary	Henencourt	07/10/1916	23/10/1916
War Diary	Becourt	24/10/1916	25/10/1916
War Diary	Mametz Wood	26/10/1916	31/10/1916
Heading	War Diary 6 Bn Durham L.I. November 1916 Volume 20		
War Diary	Mametz Wood	01/11/1916	02/11/1916
War Diary	In The Trenches	03/11/1916	06/11/1916
War Diary	Mametz Wood	07/11/1916	30/11/1916
Heading	War Diary Volume No. 21 6 Durham Light Infantry December 1916		
War Diary	Becourt	01/12/1916	01/12/1916
War Diary	Warloy	01/12/1916	28/12/1916
War Diary	Albert	29/12/1916	31/12/1916
War Diary	Bazentin	31/12/1916	31/12/1916
Heading	6th Durham Light Infantry War Diary For January 1917 Volume No. 22		
War Diary	Bazentin	01/01/1917	03/01/1917
War Diary	High Wood West	03/01/1917	04/01/1917
War Diary	In The Trenches	04/01/1917	08/01/1917
War Diary	High Wood West	09/01/1917	12/01/1917

War Diary	In The Trenches	13/01/1917	16/01/1917
War Diary	Bazentin	17/01/1917	20/01/1917
War Diary	In The Trenches	21/01/1917	24/01/1917
War Diary	Bazentin	25/01/1917	25/01/1917
War Diary	Becourt	26/01/1917	29/01/1917
War Diary	Ribemont	30/01/1917	31/01/1917
Heading	6th Bn The Durham Light Infy. War Diary For February 1917 Volume 23		
War Diary	Ribemont	01/02/1917	10/02/1917
War Diary	Hamel	11/02/1917	12/02/1917
War Diary	Proyart	13/02/1917	19/02/1917
War Diary	Foucaucourt	20/02/1917	20/02/1917
War Diary	In The Trenches	21/02/1917	28/02/1917
Heading	6th Bn. Durham Light Infantry March 1917 Volume 21		
War Diary	Trenches	01/03/1917	01/03/1917
War Diary	Front Line	01/03/1917	04/03/1917
War Diary	Berny	04/03/1917	08/03/1917
War Diary	Foucaucourt	08/03/1917	08/03/1917
War Diary	Morcourt	09/03/1917	31/03/1917
War Diary	Wargnies	31/03/1917	31/03/1917
War Diary	Havernas	31/03/1917	31/03/1917
Heading	6th Bn. Durham Light Infantry War Diary For April 1917 Volume No. 25		
War Diary	Wargnies and Havernas	01/04/1917	01/04/1917
War Diary	Longuevillette	02/04/1917	02/04/1917
War Diary	Vacquerie Le Boucq	03/04/1917	03/04/1917
War Diary	Blangerval and Blangermont	04/04/1917	06/04/1917
War Diary	Neuville-Au-Cornet	07/04/1917	07/04/1917
War Diary	Villers-Sire-Simon	08/04/1917	10/04/1917
War Diary	Montenes Court	11/04/1917	11/04/1917
War Diary	Ronville	12/04/1917	13/04/1917
War Diary	Gojeul	14/04/1917	14/04/1917
War Diary	Warncourt Tower	14/04/1917	14/04/1917
War Diary	Warncourt	14/04/1917	14/04/1917
War Diary	Nr. Ronville	15/04/1917	15/04/1917
War Diary	Ronville	16/04/1917	22/04/1917
War Diary	Harp Line	23/04/1917	24/04/1917
War Diary	Nepal	25/04/1917	26/04/1917
War Diary	Arras	27/04/1917	27/04/1917
War Diary	Humbercourt	28/04/1917	30/04/1917
Heading	War Diary 6th Bn. The Durham Light Infantry May 1917 Volume 26		
Heading	War Diary Vol 26 6th Battalion The Durham Light Infantry May 1917		
War Diary	Berles-Au-Bois	01/05/1917	01/05/1917
War Diary	Riviere-Grossville	02/05/1917	03/05/1917
War Diary	Humbercourt	04/05/1917	18/05/1917
War Diary	Monchy-Au-Bois	19/05/1917	22/05/1917
War Diary	Laherliere	23/05/1917	23/05/1917
War Diary	Souastre	24/05/1917	31/05/1917
Heading	War Diary 6th Bn. The Durham Light Infantry T.F. June 1917 Volume 27		
Heading	War Diary 6th Battalion The Durham Light Infantry Volume 27 June 1-30. 1917		
War Diary	Souastre	01/06/1917	15/06/1917
War Diary	Line	16/06/1917	23/06/1917

War Diary	Boiry-Becquerelle	24/06/1917	30/06/1917
Heading	War Diary 6th Durham Light Infty July 1917 Volume No. XXVIII		
War Diary	Nr. Boiry	01/07/1917	01/07/1917
War Diary	Becquerelle	01/07/1917	01/07/1917
War Diary	Near Henin	02/07/1917	02/07/1917
War Diary	Support	03/07/1917	06/07/1917
War Diary	Line	07/07/1917	10/07/1917
War Diary	Neuville Vitasse	11/07/1917	11/07/1917
War Diary	Line	15/07/1917	19/07/1917
War Diary	Neuville Vitasse	19/07/1917	27/07/1917
War Diary	Support	28/07/1917	30/07/1917
War Diary	Front Line	31/07/1917	31/07/1917
Heading	War Diary 6th Bn. Durham Light Infantry August 1917 Volume XXIX		
War Diary	Front Line	01/08/1917	03/08/1917
War Diary	Brigade Reserve	04/08/1917	07/08/1917
War Diary	Front Line	08/08/1917	11/08/1917
War Diary	Divnl Reserve	12/08/1917	19/08/1917
War Diary	Front Line	20/08/1917	28/08/1917
War Diary	Brigade Reserve	28/08/1917	31/08/1917
Heading	War Diary 6th Bn. The Durham Light Infantry September 1917 Volume XXX		
War Diary	Front Line	01/09/1917	02/09/1917
War Diary	Sheet 1.B.S.W.	02/09/1917	12/09/1917
War Diary	Cherisy Sector	13/09/1917	17/09/1917
War Diary	Near Henin	18/09/1917	20/09/1917
War Diary	Front Line	21/09/1917	25/09/1917
War Diary	Cherisy Sector	26/09/1917	30/09/1917
Heading	War Diary 6th Durham Light Infantry October 1917 Volume XXXI		
War Diary	Beaurains	01/10/1917	03/10/1917
War Diary	Gomiecourt	04/10/1917	17/10/1917
War Diary	Eringhem	17/10/1917	19/10/1917
War Diary	Arneke	20/10/1917	20/10/1917
War Diary	Proven Area	21/10/1917	24/10/1917
War Diary	Hulls Farm Boesinge	25/10/1917	31/10/1917
Heading	War Diary 6th Bn. The Durham Light Infy. November 1917 Volume XXXII		
War Diary	Egypt Ho. (Bn Hqrs)	01/11/1917	04/11/1917
War Diary	Marsouin Fm	05/11/1917	06/11/1917
War Diary	Elverdinghe	07/11/1917	10/11/1917
War Diary	Houlle	11/11/1917	30/11/1917
Heading	War Diary 6th Bn. The Durham Light Infantry December 1917 Volume No XXXIII		
War Diary	Houlle	01/12/1917	12/12/1917
War Diary	Erie Camp Near Brandhoek	13/12/1917	17/12/1917
War Diary	Potijze	18/12/1917	18/12/1917
War Diary	Seine	19/12/1917	20/12/1917
War Diary	Passchendaele Sector	21/12/1917	24/12/1917
War Diary	Potijze	25/12/1917	25/12/1917
War Diary	Erie Camp	26/12/1917	30/12/1917
War Diary	St Jean Camp	30/12/1917	31/12/1917
Heading	War Diary 6th Bn. The Durham Light Infantry January 1918 Volume XXXIV		
War Diary	St Jean Camp	01/01/1918	08/01/1918

War Diary	Steenvoorde	09/01/1918	17/01/1918
War Diary	Aquin	18/01/1918	29/01/1918
War Diary	Acquin-Brandhoek	30/01/1918	31/01/1918
Heading	1/6th Div. L.I. Jan Vol VII		
Heading	War Diary 6th Bn. The Durham Light Infantry February 1918 Volume XXXV		
War Diary	Brandhoek	01/02/1918	01/02/1918
War Diary	Sunderland Camp Nr Potize	02/02/1918	03/02/1918
War Diary	Ypres	03/02/1918	04/02/1918
War Diary	Support Area	05/02/1918	05/02/1918
War Diary	Ham Bourg	06/02/1918	06/02/1918
War Diary	Passchendaele	07/02/1918	10/02/1918
War Diary	Sunderland Camp Nr. Potize	11/02/1918	14/02/1918
War Diary	Habourg Support Area	15/02/1918	28/02/1918
Heading	151st Brigade 50th Division 6th Battalion Durham Light Infantry March 1918		
Heading	War Diary 6th Bn. Durham Light Infantry March 1918 Volume XXXVI		
War Diary	St Martin	01/03/1918	08/03/1918
War Diary	Le Neuville	09/03/1918	17/03/1918
War Diary	Marcelcave	18/03/1918	31/03/1918
Heading	151st Brigade 50th Division 1/6th Battalion Durham Light Infantry April 1918		
War Diary	6 D.L.I.	01/04/1918	16/04/1918
War Diary	Cohem	17/04/1918	30/04/1918
Heading	6th Bn Durham Light Infantry May To June 1918 War Diary		
Heading	War Diary 6th D.L.I. May 1918 Volume XXXVIII		
War Diary	Arcis-Le-Ponsart	01/05/1918	03/05/1918
War Diary	Glennes	04/05/1918	06/05/1918
War Diary	Line	07/05/1918	18/05/1918
War Diary	Chaudardes	19/05/1918	23/05/1918
War Diary	Line	24/05/1918	31/05/1918
Heading	War Diary 6th Bn. Durham Light Infantry June 1918 Volume XXXIX		
War Diary	Vert La Gravelle	01/06/1918	01/06/1918
War Diary	Gravelle	02/06/1918	04/06/1918
War Diary	Nanteuil	05/06/1918	05/06/1918
War Diary	Line	06/06/1918	18/06/1918
War Diary	Broyes (Marne)	19/06/1918	30/06/1918
Heading	6th Bn. The Durham L.I. War Diary Volume No. July 1918		
War Diary	Broyes	01/07/1918	01/07/1918
War Diary	St. Sophie Farm	02/07/1918	03/07/1918
War Diary	Caumont	04/07/1918	11/07/1918
War Diary	Warcheville	12/07/1918	18/07/1918
War Diary	Rouxmesnil	19/07/1918	31/07/1918
Heading	Training Cadre 39th Division 117th Infy Bde 50 Division 151 Bde 6th Bn Durham Lt Infy Aug-Nov 1918		
Heading	Vol 33 6th Bn. The Durham Light Infantry War Diary August 1918		
War Diary	Rouxmesnil	01/08/1918	15/08/1918
War Diary	Roven	16/08/1918	31/08/1918
Heading	Vol 39 6th Bn. The Durham Light Infy War Diary September 1918		

War Diary	Roven	01/09/1918	30/09/1918
Heading	6th Bn. The Durham L.I. War Diary October 1918		
War Diary	Roven	01/10/1918	31/10/1918
Heading	6th Bn The Durham Light Infantry War Diary November 1918		
War Diary	Roven	01/11/1918	06/11/1918
Heading	50th Division 151st Infy Bde 7th Bn Durham Lt. Infy. Apr-Nov 1915		
Heading	151st Inf. Bde. 50th Div. Battn. Disembarked Boulogne From England 19.4.15 War Diary 7th Battn. The Durham Light Infantry April And May (19.4.15-31.5.15) 1915		
War Diary	Gateshead Boulogne	19/04/1915	19/04/1915
War Diary	Bavinchove	20/04/1915	20/04/1915
War Diary	Ryveld	21/04/1915	22/04/1915
War Diary	Vlamertinghe	23/04/1915	24/04/1915
War Diary	Verlorenhoek	25/04/1915	03/05/1915
War Diary	Nr. Ypres	03/05/1915	03/05/1915
War Diary	Watou	04/05/1915	07/05/1915
War Diary	Brandhoek	08/05/1915	10/05/1915
War Diary	Zillebeke	11/05/1915	16/05/1915
War Diary	Brielen	17/05/1915	21/05/1915
War Diary	Ypres	21/05/1915	24/05/1915
War Diary	Potijze	25/05/1915	26/05/1915
War Diary	Brielen	27/05/1915	31/05/1915
Heading	151st Inf. Bde. 50th Div. War Diary 7th Battn The Durham Light Infantry June 1915		
War Diary	Poperinghe	01/06/1915	03/06/1915
War Diary	Ouderdom	04/06/1915	05/06/1915
War Diary	Ypres	06/06/1915	08/06/1915
War Diary	Ouderdom	09/06/1915	11/06/1915
War Diary	Ypres	12/06/1915	20/06/1915
War Diary	Ouderdom	21/06/1915	21/06/1915
War Diary	Dranoutre	22/06/1915	24/06/1915
War Diary	Kemmel	25/06/1915	30/06/1915
Heading	151st Inf. Bde. 50th Div. 7th Battn. The Durham Light Infantry July 1915		
War Diary	Kemmel	01/07/1915	15/07/1915
War Diary	Locre	16/07/1915	16/07/1915
War Diary	Pont De Nieppe	17/07/1915	17/07/1915
War Diary	Armentieres	18/07/1915	31/07/1915
Heading	151st Inf. Bde. 50th Div. 7th Battn. The Durham Light Infantry August 1915		
War Diary	Armentieres	01/08/1915	01/08/1915
War Diary	Pont De Nieppe	02/08/1915	07/08/1915
War Diary	Armentieres	08/08/1915	31/08/1915
Heading	151st Inf. Bde. 50th Div. 7th Battn. The Durham Light Infantry September 1915		
War Diary	Armentieres	01/09/1915	26/09/1915
War Diary	Houplines	27/09/1915	30/09/1915
Heading	151st Inf. Bde. 50th Div. 7th Battn. The Durham Light Infantry October 1915		
War Diary	Houplines	01/10/1915	08/10/1915
War Diary	Armentieres	08/10/1915	14/10/1915
War Diary	Houplines	15/10/1915	22/10/1915
War Diary	Armentieres	23/10/1915	25/10/1915

War Diary	Houplines	26/10/1915	31/10/1915
Heading	151st Inf. Bde. 50th Div. Battn. Became Pioneers 50th Division 16.11.15 7th Battn. The Durham Light Infantry November 1915		
War Diary	Houplines	01/11/1915	04/11/1915
War Diary	Armentieres	05/11/1915	06/11/1915
War Diary	Houplines	07/11/1915	12/11/1915
War Diary	Armentieres Bailleul	13/11/1915	18/11/1915
War Diary	Bailleul	19/11/1915	30/11/1915
Heading	50th Division 151st Infy Bde 9th Bn Durham Lt. Infy. Apr 1915-Jan 1918		
Heading	151st Inf. Bde. 50th Div. Battn. Disembarked Boulogne From England From England 20.4.15 War Diary 9th Battn. The Durham Light Infantry April And May (20.4.15-31.5.15) 1915		
War Diary	Boulogne	20/04/1915	20/04/1915
War Diary	Terdeghem	21/04/1915	23/04/1915
War Diary	Vlamertinghe	24/04/1915	24/04/1915
War Diary	Potijze	25/04/1915	25/04/1915
War Diary	Verlorenhoek	26/04/1915	03/05/1915
War Diary	St Janter Biezen	04/05/1915	11/05/1915
War Diary	G H Q Lines	12/05/1915	18/05/1915
War Diary	Brielen	19/05/1915	24/05/1915
War Diary	G.H.Q. & lines in Tranches	24/05/1915	31/05/1915
Heading	151st Inf. Bde. 50th Div. War Diary 9th Battn. The Durham Light Infantry June 1915		
War Diary		01/06/1915	02/06/1915
War Diary	Brandhoek	02/06/1915	04/06/1915
War Diary	Huts NE Of Ouderdom S. H. 19	05/06/1915	06/06/1915
War Diary	Huts NE Of Ouderdom	07/06/1915	09/06/1915
War Diary	Kruisstradt & Zillebeke	10/06/1915	17/06/1915
War Diary	Dug Outs Kruisstraat	17/06/1915	18/06/1915
War Diary	Ouderdom	19/06/1915	21/06/1915
War Diary	Kemmel	22/06/1915	30/06/1915
Heading	151st Inf. Bde. 50th Div. 9th Battn. The Durham Light Infantry July 1915		
War Diary	Kemmel (Billets)	01/07/1915	05/07/1915
War Diary	Trenches Kemmel	05/07/1915	08/07/1915
War Diary	Kemmel	09/07/1915	09/07/1915
War Diary	Locre	10/07/1915	16/07/1915
War Diary	Armentieres	17/07/1915	31/07/1915
Heading	151st Inf. Bde. 50th Div. 9th Battn. The Durham Light Infantry August 1915		
War Diary	Armentieres	01/08/1915	31/08/1915
Heading	151st Inf. Bde. 50th Div. 9th Battn. The Durham Light Infantry September 1915		
War Diary	Armentieres	01/09/1915	30/09/1915
Miscellaneous	Distribution In Trenches	01/09/1915	01/09/1915
Map	Map		
Heading	151st Inf. Bde. 50th Div. 9th Battn. The Durham Light Infantry October 1915		
War Diary	Le Touquet	01/10/1915	05/10/1915
War Diary	Armentieres	06/10/1915	08/10/1915
War Diary	Houplines	09/10/1915	18/10/1915
War Diary	Armentieres	19/10/1915	31/10/1915
Miscellaneous	9th Bn. D.L.I.	29/10/1915	29/10/1915

Heading	151st Inf. Bde. 50th Div. 9th Battn. The Durham Light Infantry November 1915		
War Diary	Armentieres	01/11/1915	01/11/1915
War Diary	Houplines	03/11/1915	13/11/1915
War Diary	Steenwerck	15/11/1915	30/11/1915
Miscellaneous	9th D.L.I.	05/11/1915	05/11/1915
Miscellaneous	9th Bn. D.L.I.	12/11/1915	12/11/1915
Miscellaneous	9th Bn. Durh. Lt. Infy	19/11/1915	19/11/1915
Miscellaneous	9th Bn. Durh. Lt. Infy	26/11/1915	26/11/1915
Heading	151st Inf. Bde. 50th Div. 9th Battn. The Durham Light Infantry December 1915		
War Diary	Steenwerck	01/12/1915	19/12/1915
War Diary	Dickebusch	20/12/1915	29/12/1915
War Diary	Sanctuary Wood	31/12/1915	31/12/1915
Miscellaneous	9th Bn. Durh. Lt. Infy.	03/12/1915	03/12/1915
Miscellaneous	B E F	03/12/1915	03/12/1915
War Diary	9th Bn. Durh. Lt. Infy	10/12/1915	10/12/1915
Miscellaneous	B.E.F.	10/12/1915	10/12/1915
Miscellaneous	9th Bn. Durh. Lt. Infy.	17/12/1915	17/12/1915
Miscellaneous	B.E.F.	17/12/1915	17/12/1915
Miscellaneous	9th Bn. Durh. L.I.	24/12/1915	24/12/1915
Miscellaneous	9th Bn. Durh Light Inf.	31/12/1915	31/12/1915
Miscellaneous	B.E.F.	31/12/1915	31/12/1915
Heading	1/9th Bde Jan Vol VII 151 Inf Bde		
War Diary	Sanctuary Wood (Sheet 28 1.24 B)	01/01/1916	03/01/1916
War Diary	Maple Copse (1.28 Rd)	04/01/1916	06/01/1916
War Diary	Sanctuary Wood	09/01/1916	13/01/1916
War Diary	Dickebusch Huts (H. 26. B.3.9)	14/01/1916	14/01/1916
War Diary	Sanctuary Wood (28.1.24)	17/01/1916	20/01/1916
War Diary	Maple Copse (28.1.28 B & D)	21/01/1916	23/01/1916
War Diary	Sanctuary Wood	25/01/1916	25/01/1916
War Diary	Sanctuary Wood (28.1.24.6)	25/01/1916	29/01/1916
War Diary	Dickebusch	30/01/1916	31/01/1916
Miscellaneous	Temporary Promotions of Officers of Infantry Battalions to Complete Establishment (No. M.S 3522/1)		
Miscellaneous	9th Bn. Durh Light. Infy.	28/01/1916	28/01/1916
Miscellaneous	B.E.F.	28/01/1916	28/01/1916
Miscellaneous	9th Bn Durh. Light. Inf.	14/01/1916	14/01/1916
Miscellaneous	B.E.F.	14/01/1916	14/01/1916
Miscellaneous	9th Bn. Durh L. Infy.	07/01/1916	07/01/1916
Miscellaneous	B.E.F.	07/01/1916	07/01/1916
Miscellaneous	9th Bn. Durh. Light Inf.	21/01/1916	21/01/1916
Miscellaneous	B.E.F.	21/01/1916	21/01/1916
War Diary	Railway Dugouts 28.I.20.C.10.D Sanctuary Wood	01/02/1916	06/02/1916
War Diary	Sanctuary Wood	06/02/1916	06/02/1916
War Diary	Maple Copse	07/02/1916	08/02/1916
War Diary	Sanctuary Wood Maple Copse	08/02/1916	10/02/1916
War Diary	Sanctuary Wood	10/02/1916	13/02/1916
War Diary	Scottish Lines	13/02/1916	15/02/1916
War Diary	Bedford Ho. (28.1.26.a.7.4)	18/02/1916	29/02/1916
Miscellaneous	9th Bn. Durham Light Infantry	04/02/1916	04/02/1916
Miscellaneous	B.E.F.	04/02/1916	04/02/1916
Miscellaneous	9th Bn. Durham Light Infantry	11/02/1916	11/02/1916
Miscellaneous	B.E.F.	11/02/1916	11/02/1916
Miscellaneous	9th Bn. Durh. Lt Infy.	25/02/1916	25/02/1916
Miscellaneous	B.E.F.	25/02/1916	25/02/1916

War Diary		01/03/1916	31/03/1916
War Diary	B.E.F.	01/04/1916	14/04/1916
War Diary	L. Sub. Sector	15/04/1916	15/04/1916
War Diary	Vierstraat Area	15/04/1916	20/04/1916
War Diary	Left-L-Sector	20/04/1916	31/05/1916
Miscellaneous	9th Bn. Durh. Light Infy.	02/04/1916	02/04/1916
Miscellaneous	B.E.F.	21/04/1916	21/04/1916
Miscellaneous	9th Durham Light Infantry	07/04/1916	07/04/1916
Miscellaneous	B.E.F.	07/04/1916	07/04/1916
Miscellaneous	9th Bn. Durham Light Inf.	14/04/1916	14/04/1916
Miscellaneous	B.E.F.	14/04/1916	14/04/1916
Miscellaneous	9th Bn. Durham Light Inf.	28/04/1916	28/04/1916
Miscellaneous	B.E.F.	28/04/1916	28/04/1916
Miscellaneous	9th Bn. Durham Light Inf.	05/05/1916	05/05/1916
Miscellaneous	B.E.F.	05/05/1916	05/05/1916
Miscellaneous	9th Bn. Durham Light Infy.	12/05/1916	12/05/1916
Miscellaneous	B.E.F.	12/05/1916	12/05/1916
Miscellaneous	9th Bn. Durham Light Infy.	19/05/1916	19/05/1916
Miscellaneous	B.E.F.	19/05/1916	19/05/1916
Miscellaneous	9th Bn. Durham Light Inf.	26/05/1916	26/05/1916
Miscellaneous	B.E.F.	26/05/1916	26/05/1916
War Diary		01/06/1916	30/06/1916
Heading	9th Bn. Durham L.I. War Diary July 1916 Volume No. 12		
Miscellaneous	9th Bn. Durham Light Infy.	02/06/1916	02/06/1916
Miscellaneous	B.E.F.	02/06/1916	02/06/1916
Miscellaneous	9th Bn. Durham Light Infy.	09/06/1916	09/06/1916
Miscellaneous	B.E.F.	09/06/1916	09/06/1916
Miscellaneous	9th Bn. Durham Light Infy.	16/06/1916	16/06/1916
Miscellaneous	B.E.F.	16/06/1916	16/06/1916
Miscellaneous	9th Bn. Durham Light Infantry	23/06/1916	23/06/1916
Miscellaneous	B.E.F.	23/06/1916	23/06/1916
Miscellaneous	9th Bn. Durham Light Infantry	30/06/1916	30/06/1916
Miscellaneous	B.E.F.	30/06/1916	30/06/1916
War Diary		01/07/1916	31/07/1916
Miscellaneous	Special Order Of The Day By General Sir Douglas Haig K.T. G.C.B. K.C.I.E. G.C.V.O. A.D.C. Commander-In Chief British Armies In France	29/07/1916	29/07/1916
Miscellaneous	Special Order Of The Day By General Sir Douglas Haig K.T. G.C.B. K.C.I.E. G.C.V.O. A.D.C. Commander-In Chief British Armies In France	18/07/1916	18/07/1916
Miscellaneous	Special Order Of The Day By General Sir Douglas Haig K.T. G.C.B. K.C.I.E. G.C.V.O. A.D.C. Commander-In Chief British Armies In France	17/07/1916	17/07/1916
Miscellaneous	9th Bn. Durham Light Infy.	07/07/1916	07/07/1916
Miscellaneous	9th Bn. Durham Light Infy.	14/07/1916	14/07/1916
Miscellaneous	B.E.F.	14/07/1916	14/07/1916
Heading	War Diary 1/9th Batt. The Durham Light Infantry August 1916 Volume No 17		
War Diary		01/08/1916	08/08/1916
War Diary	Locre	08/08/1916	08/08/1916
War Diary	Berthen	09/08/1916	09/08/1916
War Diary	Prouville	11/08/1916	11/08/1916
War Diary	Vignacourt	15/08/1916	15/08/1916
War Diary	Raineville	16/08/1916	16/08/1916
War Diary	Raizeux	17/08/1916	30/08/1916

Type	Description	Start	End
Heading	151st Infantry Brigade 50th Division 9th Durham Light Infantry 151st Infantry Brigade September 1916		
Heading	9th Bn. Durham L. I. September 1916 Volume No 14		
War Diary		01/09/1916	30/09/1916
Heading	War Diary October 1916 9th Durham Light Infantry Vol 19		
War Diary		01/10/1916	31/10/1916
Heading	War Diary 9th Bn. Durham L.I. November 1916 Volume 20		
War Diary		01/11/1916	03/11/1916
War Diary	Map 57.c. S.W. 1/10000	03/11/1916	07/11/1916
War Diary	Mametz Wood	07/11/1916	30/11/1916
Heading	War Diary 9th Bn. Durham Light Infantry Nov. 30th To Dec. 31st 1916 Volume 17		
War Diary		01/12/1916	01/12/1916
War Diary	Warloy	02/12/1916	28/12/1916
War Diary	Albert	29/12/1916	30/12/1916
War Diary	Bazentin Le Petit	30/12/1916	31/12/1916
War Diary	Factory Corner Sh 57 C SW N 19c 71/2 2	31/12/1916	31/12/1916
Heading	War Diary 9th Bn. The Durham Light Infantry January 1917 Volume No 18		
War Diary	Bazentin Le Petit	31/12/1916	01/01/1917
War Diary	Factory Corner	03/01/1917	05/01/1917
War Diary	Bazentin Le Petit	07/01/1917	09/01/1917
War Diary	Support Trenches	09/01/1917	13/01/1917
War Diary	High Wood West Camp	15/01/1917	17/01/1917
War Diary	Front System Of Trenches	17/01/1917	21/01/1917
War Diary	Bazentin Le Petit	21/01/1917	24/01/1917
War Diary	Support Trenches	25/01/1917	27/01/1917
War Diary	Camp Site 4-Bazentin Le Petit	27/01/1917	27/01/1917
War Diary	Becourt	28/01/1917	29/01/1917
War Diary	Ribemont	30/01/1917	31/01/1917
Heading	War Diary 9th Bn. The Durham Light Infantry February 1917 Volume 23		
War Diary	Ribemont	01/02/1917	04/02/1917
War Diary	Ribemont Sh 62 D	05/02/1917	10/02/1917
War Diary	Hamel	11/02/1917	12/02/1917
War Diary	Foucaucourt Sh 62 C	13/02/1917	17/02/1917
War Diary	Foucaucourt	18/02/1917	20/02/1917
War Diary	Berny N 32 D	21/02/1917	23/02/1917
War Diary	Berny	23/02/1917	24/02/1917
War Diary	Front Line	25/02/1917	28/02/1917
War Diary	Foucaucourt	28/02/1917	28/02/1917
Heading	9th Bn. Durham Light Infantry March 1917 Volume 24		
War Diary	Foucaucourt	01/03/1917	04/03/1917
War Diary	Front System Of Trenches	04/03/1917	07/03/1917
War Diary	Foucaucourt	07/03/1917	07/03/1917
War Diary	Mericourt Sur Somme	07/03/1917	31/03/1917
Heading	War Diary 9th Bn. Durham L.I. Volume No. 25 For April 1917		
War Diary	Naours	01/04/1917	02/04/1917
War Diary	Gezaincourt	03/04/1917	03/04/1917
War Diary	Sibiville	04/04/1917	04/04/1917
War Diary	Croix	05/04/1917	07/04/1917
War Diary	Averdoingt	08/04/1917	15/04/1917
War Diary	Ronville	16/04/1917	28/04/1917

War Diary	Warluzel	28/04/1917	30/04/1917
Heading	War Diary 9th Bn. The Durh L.I. Volume 22 May 1917		
War Diary	Warluzel	01/05/1917	02/05/1917
War Diary	Bailleulval	03/05/1917	04/05/1917
War Diary	Warluzel	05/05/1917	22/05/1917
War Diary	St Amand	23/05/1917	31/05/1917
Heading	War Diary 9th Bn. The Durham Light Infantry T.F. June 1917 Volume 27		
War Diary	St Amand	01/06/1917	16/06/1917
War Diary	Henin-Sur-Cojeul	17/06/1917	24/06/1917
War Diary	Boisleux-Au-Mont	25/06/1917	30/06/1917
Heading	War Diary 9th Durham Light Infty July 1917 Volume No XXVIII		
War Diary	Boisleux-Au-Mont	01/07/1917	02/07/1917
War Diary	Henin-Sur-Cojeul	03/07/1917	03/07/1917
War Diary	Trenches Opp. Vis-En Artois Near R. Cojeul Bn H.Q. At O.19.a.2.4 Front Line From O.26.a.4.5 O 20 A 8. 5 149 Inf Bde on Our Right 5th Borders & 8th D.L.I. On Left	04/07/1917	07/07/1917
War Diary	We relived 1st Bn London Scottish	08/07/1917	10/07/1917
War Diary	150 Bde On Own Right	11/07/1917	15/07/1917
War Diary	Neuville Vitasse	16/07/1917	19/07/1917
War Diary	Mercatez	20/07/1917	26/07/1917
War Diary	Trenches H.Q. N. 36.b.4.0 149 Inf Bde on Own Right 5th Borders 8th D.L.I. On Left	27/07/1917	27/07/1917
War Diary	Right Flank O.31.d.6.7.	28/07/1917	28/07/1917
War Diary	Left Flank O.25.D.9.4.	29/07/1917	31/07/1917
Heading	War Diary 9th Bn. Durham Light Infantry August 1917 Volume XXIX		
War Diary	Trenches In Support H.Q. N.29.b.9.4. (SR 51 B Sw)	01/08/1917	03/08/1917
War Diary	Group Line	04/08/1917	07/08/1917
War Diary	Henin	08/08/1917	08/08/1917
War Diary	In Concrete Tr	09/08/1917	19/08/1917
War Diary	Trenches Bn H.Q. O.19.3.4	20/08/1917	20/08/1917
War Diary	Front Line O.26.a.3.5 to Coteulr	21/08/1917	24/08/1917
War Diary	Support Bn H.Q. N. 24.c.1.7	24/08/1917	27/08/1917
War Diary	Front Line	28/08/1917	31/08/1917
Heading	War Diary 9th Bn. The Durham Light Infy. September 1917 Volume XXX		
War Diary	Bn. H.Q. N.21.a	01/09/1917	04/09/1917
War Diary	Bn. H.Q. S.12.a	05/09/1917	12/09/1917
War Diary	Henin	13/09/1917	13/09/1917
War Diary	Bn. H.Q. N.25.d.5.4.	14/09/1917	15/09/1917
War Diary	Henin	15/09/1917	16/09/1917
War Diary	H.Q. N.36.B.4.0.	17/09/1917	20/09/1917
War Diary	Bn. H.Q. Nest N.30.a.5.3.	21/09/1917	28/09/1917
War Diary	Durham Lines S.H.A.	29/09/1917	30/09/1917
Heading	War Diary 9th Durham Light Infantry October 1917 Volume XXXI		
War Diary	Durham Lines Boisleux-Au-Mont (S 11 A)	01/10/1917	04/10/1917
War Diary	Gomiecourt	04/10/1917	17/10/1917
War Diary	Padde Veldt	18/10/1917	19/10/1917
War Diary	Arneke	20/10/1917	20/10/1917
War Diary	Proven (Pitchcot Camp)	21/10/1917	24/10/1917
War Diary	Saragossa Fm. Camp	25/10/1917	27/10/1917
War Diary	Marsouin Farm	28/10/1917	30/10/1917

War Diary	Hulls Farm	31/10/1917	31/10/1917
Heading	War Diary 9th Bn. The Durham Light Infy. November 1917 Volume XXXII		
War Diary	Hulls Farm	01/11/1917	01/11/1917
War Diary	Marsouin Farm	02/11/1917	04/11/1917
War Diary	Line	04/11/1917	07/11/1917
War Diary	Saragossa Camp	07/11/1917	09/11/1917
War Diary	Moulle	10/11/1917	30/11/1917
Heading	War Diary 9th Bn. The Durham Light Infantry December 1917 Volume No. XXXIII		
War Diary	Moulle	01/12/1917	11/12/1917
War Diary	Toronto Camp Brandhoek	12/12/1917	21/12/1917
War Diary	Toronto Camp	22/12/1917	29/12/1917
War Diary	Whitby Camp	30/12/1917	30/12/1917
War Diary	Seine	31/12/1917	31/12/1917
Heading	War Diary 9th Bn. The Durham Light Infantry January 1918 Volume XXXIV		
War Diary	Seine Th 28	01/01/1918	01/01/1918
War Diary	Hamburg	01/01/1918	04/01/1918
War Diary	Potijze	05/01/1918	17/01/1918
War Diary	Boisdinghem V.4. Sh 27a S.E.	18/01/1918	29/01/1918
War Diary	Toronto Camp Brandhoek	30/01/1918	31/01/1918

5TH BN DURHAM LT INFY

~~FEB — JLY 1918~~

1918 FEB TO OCT 1918

FROM 150 Bde
SAME DIV.

15th Note

WAR DIARY   Vol 32

5th Bn. "The Durham Light Infantry"

February 1918.

Volume — XXXV.

VOLUME 35

FEBRUARY 1915

5th DURHAM LIGHT INF.   Army Form C. 2118.

WAR DIARY
or
INTELLIGENCE SUMMARY.

(Erase heading not required.)

Instructions regarding War Diaries and Intelligence
Summaries are contained in F. S. Regs., Part II.
and the Staff Manual respectively. Title pages
will be prepared in manuscript.

Place	Date	Hour	Summary of Events and Information	Remarks and references to Appendices
The Line	Feb 1/	16/18	Battalion in line. Passchendaele Sector. Went up into close support on the evening of the 1st and then took over the left battalion front to the East of the village of Passchendaele. Here two Companies were in the front line, one in support at Crest Farm and the other in reserve on roads on Hamlin Spur. On entire Company relief was carried out half way through the tour. The tour of duty was a much pleasanter one than last time. The communications were far better. "Duck-board" tracks having been laid past Crest Farm into the village and our Hamlen Spur. A large dug out to hold 150 men had been made under Crest Farm and four reserves and deep bomb posts to accommodate a garrison each had been almost completed on Hamlen Spur. Numerous shells of wire had been made. The weather was very good and the shelling was very slight. Our casualties were only 2 killed and 2 wounded. The night of Feb 6/7 was spent at "Huddy Camp" P.07.32.e.	
P.07.32.e.	7th		Moved on light railway to Brandhoek and thence on Toronto Camp where we remained until 9th when the G.O.C. on which day the Batln moved to Ypres on light railway train from before the town moved to Brandhoek we received a draft of 7 sub officers and 150 men from 10th D.L.I. whilst had been broken up.	

Ab7092) Wt. W12859/M1293. 750,000. 1/17. D, D & L., Ltd. Forms/C2118/14.

Army Form C. 2118.

WAR DIARY
or
INTELLIGENCE SUMMARY.

(Erase heading not required.)

Instructions regarding War Diaries and Intelligence
Summaries are contained in F. S. Regs., Part II.
and the Staff Manual respectively. Title pages
will be prepared in manuscript.

Place	Date	Hour	Summary of Events and Information	Remarks and references to Appendices
YPRES	Feb 9		Battn acted as one of the Coys during Battn. We carried the same duties as before except that one company was at "SEAFIN CAMP" POTIJZE. We furnished large carrying and working parties each day.	
do.	14/15		Transfer to 151st Inf Brigade. At midnight 13/14 Night we agreed to belong to the 150 Inf Bde (York + Durham) of which we had formed a part since 1908 and were transferred to the 151st Brigade (5th 6th & 8th DLI) This change was on account of re-organization of Divisions on this brigade case of 3 Battns instead of 4 to 3 hitherto. The 9th DLI and 8th Brdws were sent away so previous battalions and we were transferred so as to make the 150th Bde to 3 Battns, and B complet. The new establishment of the 151st brigade on Feb 11 and was a fareweel speech. General Peat retired and made her good-byes under his command and stocking her good luck in the future. Battn in time, again and left battalion in the PASSCHENDAELE sector. The Battn was taken up in trucks at the light railway and detrained near the ZONNEBEKE – LANGEMARCK road. The front line was not quite the same as before as some of our left posts had been taken over by Division on our left and we had them from moves forward to the south. Coy to CREST FARM and 'A' Coy had two platoons at CREST FARM and 2 platoons close to the blockhouse. Bn Hdqs in the same spot as before as before as before BROODSEINDE – PASSCHENDAELE Rd. 4 Platoons C + D returned D''	
LINE	15/9/?			

Army Form C. 2118.

WAR DIARY

or

INTELLIGENCE SUMMARY.

(Erase heading not required.)

Instructions regarding War Diaries and Intelligence Summaries are contained in F. S. Regs., Part II. and the Staff Manual respectively. Title pages will be prepared in manuscript.

Place	Date	Hour	Summary of Events and Information	Remarks and references to Appendices
LINE	18th Apr	night	Relieved by 8th Yorks Regt, moved out by light railway to St Jean Camp.	
St Jean Camp	20	2	1 officer and 3 O.R. were sent forward to recce area. Moved into C.M.O. Camp. Billets at Tattinghem. Entrained at Yers at 1.10pm and detrained at WINNEZEELE.	
Tattinghem	21/22		Refitting and cleaning up. Battn altered its distinguishing patches to yellow diamonds.	
"	23		Church parade. Inspection by C.O.	
"	24		On Range	
"	25		Training interfered with by rain. Lecture by C.O. to all officers & N.C.O's on the training. Received draft of 108 O.R.	108 O.R.
	26		Company Drawing. Battalion attended demonstration by Corps Cadre who present. Div. Demonstration bay.	
	27		On Range. Cross country Running in afternoon.	
	28		Company Training. Cross country Running in the afternoon.	

O.R. 2nd Lieut
Capt & Adjt
Commdg 8th Bn Dorset R

A7093. Wt. w12839/M1293. 750,000. 1/17. D, D & L, Ltd. Forms/C2118/14.

151st Brigade.

50th Division

5th BATTALION

DURHAM LIGHT INFANTRY

M A R C H   1 9 1 8

Vol 33

151/50

WAR DIARY

5th Bn. Durham Light Infantry

151 Bde.

March, 1918.

Volume — XXXVI.

Army Form C. 2118.

WAR DIARY
or
INTELLIGENCE SUMMARY.

(Erase heading not required.)

VOLUME 36

MARCH 1918

Instructions regarding War Diaries and Intelligence Summaries are contained in F.S. Regs., Part II. and the Staff Manual respectively. Title pages will be prepared in manuscript.

Place	Date	Hour	Summary of Events and Information	Remarks and references to Appendices
TATINGHAM	1st		Batt Parade in rest area at TATINGHAM. Lt. G. F. Rowe rejoined Batt from leave	
"	2nd		Range practice for ARA Competition. TMB was posted to B Coy.	
"	3rd		Church Parade	
"	4th		Inspection of Batt by C.O. who was temporarily acting B & C. 157 Inf Bde. Inspection of transport in afternoon.	
"	5th		Elimination by Coys in ARA Competition. Range. Baths at ST OMER.	
"	6th		Coys at disposal of O.C. Coys. Baths at ST OMER.	
"	7th		Coy training. TATINGHAM area leaving TATINGHAM 11 PM.	
"	8th		Bn moved from TATINGHAM area. Bn entrained at ARQUES 1 van 9 in. detrained at LONGEAU about 11 am marched to VILLERS BRÉTONNEUX	
VILLERS BRETONNEUX	9th		Bn training. Service Cards by acquolast Chaplain. General of Cavalry Corps. A & B Coys & MARCELCAVE, C & D Coys	
"	10th		Church Parade. A & B Coys at MARCELCAVE area.	
"	11th		Bn moved to MARCELCAVE area	
MARCELCAVE	12th		at WIENCOURT. Coys at disposal of O.C. Coys.	
"	13th		Coys at disposal him Reserve. Coy Commanders reconnoitred the forward Batt Parade area	
"	14th		Batt Parade.	
BAYONVILLERS	15th		Batt moved to BAYONVILLERS by march route	
"	16th		Batt Parade. Baths at HARBONNIERES.	
"	17th		CHURCH PARADE. Inspection of all rifles by C.O. Bn Eliminating of ARA Competition	

A7092). Wt. W12839/M1298. 750,000. 1/17. D. D & L., Ltd. Forms/C2118/14.

Army Form C. 2118.

Instructions regarding War Diaries and Intelligence
Summaries are contained in F. S. Regs., Part II.
and the Staff Manual respectively. Title pages
will be prepared in manuscript.

WAR DIARY
or
INTELLIGENCE SUMMARY.

(Erase heading not required.)

VOLUME 36

MARCH 1918

Place	Date	Hour	Summary of Events and Information	Remarks and references to Appendices
BAYONVILLERS	19th		Batt. Training. Practice of Counter attacks	
"	20th		Batt. retained.	
"	21st		Batt. paraded in morning at very short notice. Bn had order to move to forward area & entrained at GUILLAUCOURT at abt 4 PM. Bn detrained at BRIE & to huts between	
IN FIELD	22nd		In early hours of morning the Bn. Batt. moved up to forward dispositions. At 9 am MANCOURT & TINCOURT. At 9 am by Bde with following dispositions:- D Coy in road, C Coy in road — D Coy A & B Coys forward between ROISEL & HERVILLY. About 2pm Bn were at NOBESCOURT FARM. The men in our to retire through an line & front of A & B C Coys 9/to in retreat to GREEN "LINE". Bn held line with 180 Sep Bde on the the 66th Div had orders to retire through an attacked covering their withdrawal to GREEN line with every night c remainder 151 on our left. At abt 5 PM Bn to hold withdrawn in front the line in our right covering the c ... B Coy being wounded withdraw to the attack of NOBESCOURT FARM. 1 or 2 2nd Lt	W SCOTT behind the front. Capt. J.H.M. was killed. When were received from Bns Hdqts wounded line. Bn hung on here the attack of a few to stay in front at 3 a.m. a withdrawal was order'd for a few hours never having re-gained CART, G.NY. this portion was only attempted West of the SOMME & taking at 7 am to be withdrawn to the break	
	23rd		A rear guard action. While the men of the Batt withdrew to LE MESNIL. Bn held LE CATELET the rear guard to the Batt when it had to withdraw force A Coy forming LE MESNIL and whe. to be 85 Div again took over West of the Bn. Bn withdrew towards ETHAM PIGNY.	

A7092). Wt. W1289/M1293. 750,000. 1/17. D, D & L., Ltd. Form6/C2118/12.

Army Form C. 2118.

WAR DIARY

or

INTELLIGENCE SUMMARY.

(Erase heading not required.)

VOLUME 36

MARCH 1918

Instructions regarding War Diaries and Intelligence Summaries are contained in F. S. Regs., Part II. and the Staff Manual respectively. Title pages will be prepared in manuscript.

Place	Date	Hour	Summary of Events and Information	Remarks and references to Appendices
	23rd		C Coy were in detail to high the high Summit East of the Somme while the rear of the Bn. crossed the Somme & then fell back across the river themselves. The Bridges were then blown up at ETERPIGNY at about 3 P.M. S.E. of BARLEUX. At about 4.0 P.M. the Bn. moved to the open ground S.E. of BARLEUX. At about 10 m.P.M. a further order came that the Bn. was again to come under orders of 66th Div. Batt. was moved G.N. of BARLEUX. A & B Coys. moved forward to the west to counter attack on the other head of BIACHES & bechrow, C Coy was in reserve. D was in support. About 10.0 a.m. the C & D Coys. were moved to S. of LAMAISONETTE & A & B went back to their old position S.E. of BARLEUX & as night of 23rd A & B went forward to the road East of 2/8 of L.Ft. About 6 P.M. D Coy was sent forward to the counter attack on bridge heads at PERONNE & required & the position to counter attack was occupied by A & B Coys. evacuated by D was occupied by A & B Coys.	
	24th		At 4.0 a.m. C Coy was moved to high ground S. of LA MAISONETTE to as to be in reserve up & required to counter attack. In the early morning the enemy crossed the bridge heads at ETERPIGNY & A & B Coys were ordered to counter attack. The high ground N.W of ETERPIGNY was occupied by them. The enemy held up to time. The Bn. was wounded in this fighting & about 4 P.M. A & B Coys were forced to withdraw the hill Slack was forced to be missing. A & B Coys withdrew to a redoubt E of BARLEUX & here C & D Coys again formed line.	
	25th			

WAR DIARY

or

INTELLIGENCE SUMMARY.

(Erase heading not required.)

Place	Date	Hour	Summary of Events and Information	Remarks and references to Appendices
	25th		The enemy's attack was held up here but at 10 P.M. fresh orders came to withdraw to the line ASSEVILLERS — ESTREES. When the following dispositions were taken up. A. on the right, B Coke, C left. D in reserve. This portion was only occupied until 10 P.M. when the orders were again altered to withdraw to the RISIERES - VMVILLERS line.	
	26th		But we again withdrew to SOYECOURT, VERMANDOZ PRS, LIHONS, RUSIERES line. The SOYECOURT line was to a position in front of RUSIERES Station. A. B Coys took up a line on the 8th Div on their right. C & B Coys & position in an the night having the left in the centre of the line to the VMVILLERS. About 9 P.M. C & B Coys were moved to support the RUSIERES - VMVILLERS line.	RUSIERES - VMVILLERS
	27th		A. B Coys held on in the RUSIERES but until about 11 when orders were received to try withdraw to the junction between RUSIERES & GUILLUCOURT. The secured a railway bridge which was later on place C Coy were ordered to the C line withdrawal to delay the enemy. Counter attack. H. SLOCOMBE - LIEUT. LATHAM were wounded in This. Majr Rawnsley, Lt. SLOCOMBE - Lt LATHAM were wounded in These action - Majr - BLUNER who had C Coy to take Command of the Batt.	
	28th		During the afternoon the enemy were driven back by a counter attack. At about 7 P.M. orders were received to the Australia division, at about 7 P.M. orders were received to the Australia division, to withdraw again into position. But to hold up again into position North of RUSIERES Station. During the Early morning the enemy broke through on the left of the Batt & about 9 a.m. orders came to withdraw again from the railway line & position. With orders to withdraw into the French on the left.	

Army Form C. 2118.

WAR DIARY

or

INTELLIGENCE SUMMARY.

(Erase heading *not* required.)

VOLUME 36   MARCH 1915

Instructions regarding War Diaries and Intelligence Summaries are contained in F. S. Regs., Part II. and the Staff Manual respectively. Title pages will be prepared in manuscript.

Place	Date	Hour	Summary of Events and Information	Remarks and references to Appendices
	2.95		Capt. & Lieut. Taylor became wounded & having & 2 Oths killed & others wounded in this withdrawal. D Coy has held the bridgehead at Cras while a further withdrawal of the unit took place.	
	29.		Orders were received that the Bn. would assemble in Morcuil & the Bn. proceeded there via Beaucourt ~ Mezieres. The night was spent in billets in Morcuil.	
			About 8 a.m. orders came to the Bn. & these we again went into action & at 11 a.m. the Bn. was moved east of the Bois de Demuin WD & a position in front of Demuin. Forward again to a position we remained till ordered at about 8 P.M. to withdraw again. Here they proceeded to a position in front of Hourges Wd. in support of they proceeded to a position in front of Hourges Wd. to the French. Parts of the 14 & Bde.	
	3.0.		Bn. in position in front of Hourges Wd. with French on the left. Bn. in position in front of Hourges Wd. 150 Bde. on right.	
	3.0.		Still in front of Hourges Wd. This position was heavily shelled. Had a 2 Oths. W. Williams wounded.	

151st Brigade.

50th Division.

1/5th BATTALION

DURHAM LIGHT INFANTRY

APRIL 1918.

WAR DIARY

or

INTELLIGENCE SUMMARY.

(Erase heading not required.)

Army Form C. 2118.

5th Bn. Durham Loyt Infantry

Instructions regarding War Diaries and Intelligence
Summaries are contained in F. S. Regs. Part II.
and the Staff Manual respectively. Title pages
will be prepared in manuscript.

Place	Date	Hour	Summary of Events and Information	Remarks and references to Appendices
LINE	1st		Battn in positions in front of NOURGES WOOD. Very heavy shelling. 2Lt Newby and Thompson wounded.	
	2.	1 am	Battn retired. Entrained at SERQUEUX for RUE 9th & ABBEVILLE area. Arrived at RUE, marched to VILLIERS 200 BUTTE.	
VILLIERS	4		Moved by Bus to BETHUNE area to RILLES at MT BERNENCHON.	
Mt Bernenchon	5		Draft of 155 O.R. arrived.	
do.	6		Batta. Draft of 70 O.R. arrived. 'A' Coy Commands parked forward area.	
do.	7		Moved by light railway to NEUF BERQUIN.	
NEUF BERQUIN	8		Marched to ESTAIRES accommodated in huts.	
ESTAIRES	9.	7.30 am	During B attack on Estaires defences, Battn was ordered to man the defences. Battn came into action during the morning and were heavily engaged during the afternoon in defence of the bridges over the river Lys, south of ESTAIRES. 2Lt G. wilkinson was killed. Capt. Peacock D.S.O. and 2Lt Marshall wounded. Lieut B.H. Carruthers missing.	
LINE	10 L.		Battn still holding bridgeheads until Divsn when it was withdrawn to NEUF BERQUIN where it dug in and took over from the 2nd Bte R.F. 29th Division. The Fawcett wounded.	
	11 L	10. ap	Enemy attacked and WE line was pushed back on to the NEUF BERQUIN. MERVILLE ROAD at Spur NE BERQUIN to a position S.E. of VIERHOUCK and dug in.	
			Lt. Col. G.O. Spence D.S.O. 2Lt. O.R. Byhears & Grant were wounded. Lieut. Y. Paul & L. Hodson missing.	

WAR DIARY
or
-2-
INTELLIGENCE SUMMARY.
(Erase heading not required.)

Instructions regarding War Diaries and Intelligence
Summaries are contained in F. S. Regs., Part II.
and the Staff Manual respectively. Title pages
will be prepared in manuscript.

Place	Date	Hour	Summary of Events and Information	Remarks and references to Appendices
LINE	12	4.9p.	Battn was relieved by a company of the 3o Bn COLDSTREAM GUARDS 3/31 Divn. The Bn then joined the remainder of the 15th 17 Bde and dug in N.E. of MERVILLE. Owing to the Division on the right retiring the Bn was withdrawn to the S.E edge of BOIS MOYEN.	
	13	2p.m.	Relieved by the 1st Bn WARWICKS, 15 Divn and marched to LA MOTTE CHATEAU, at 5 A.M. Bn was shelled out of CHATEAU and grounds and moved to PAPOTE district where they bivouaced.	
	14		Bn supplied 100 men to dig support line S.W of BOIS des VACHES Dug 88 yds of support line obtained. Brigade re organised	
	15		Dug up battalion and sally the 15th INF BDE BATTN on one battalion during action 9/12, all ranks. Casualties during action 9/12—	
			25 Killed. 112 Wounded 286 Missing	
	16	9.30p	Battn marched to LES CISEAUX and went into billets.	
LES CISEAUX	17 18/19 20		Coys at disposal for refitting & reorganization. address by G.O.C. Divn. Ditto. Capt W.J. Gwyther M.C. assumed temp command of Bn. Ditto. Draft of 4 officers 15" arrived Dato allotted	
do	21		Church parade	
do	22		Training continued. Range. Transport inspected by G.O.C. Divn.	
do	23		Lt Col. B.B. Robinson D.S.O. No4/L assumed temp command of Battn.	
do	24		Draft of 4 officers R.W.R 106. O.R arrived.	
do	25		Draft of 4 officers WEST YORKS arrived.	
do	26	11am	Battn commenced moving South, marched to WITTES, taken by Rail Rear to LA PUGNOY and at 10.O.P.M entrained.	

A7092). Wt. W28/39/M129a 730,000. 1/17.   D. D & L., Ltd.   Forms/C2118/14.

WAR DIARY
or
INTELLIGENCE SUMMARY.

(Erase heading not required.)

Place	Date	Hour	Summary of Events and Information	Remarks and references to Appendices
	27/28	10.a.m.	In train. Arrived at detraining station, marched to ARRAS – LE PONT SCOUT and took over huts of French Troops	
	29/30		Training. Baths allotted, Lecture to all officers by B.G. G.S. IX Corps.	

M MWnum Lieut. Col.
Commanding 1st Line 5th. Bn. Durham L. Infy.

No 35

1st/50

WAR DIARY

5th D. L. I.

May, 1916.

Volume — XXXVIII.

Army Form C. 2118.

VOLUME 35

WAR DIARY
or
INTELLIGENCE SUMMARY. 3rd Bn. Durham Light Infantry.
(Erase heading not required.)

MAY 1918

Instructions regarding War Diaries and Intelligence
Summaries are contained in F. S. Regs., Part II.
and the Staff Manual respectively. Title pages
will be prepared in manuscript.

Place	Date	Hour	Summary of Events and Information	Remarks and references to Appendices
ARRAS LA PENSART	1/4		Training to programme.	
	5th	5.15 am	Moved into forward area. marched to GONNYS. billeted in huts.	
			Reconnoitring party proceeded by bus to the line.	
LINE	6th		Moved into front line and relieved the 3rd Bn 73rd Bde Infy (French) in Sector S of CORBENY.	
do	7/11		Sector very quiet. 2 French soldiers escaped from the German	
			lines and came into our lines.	
			Reinforcements arrived. 7 officers	
	12		On relief. the line was very quiet.	
			Nos 1 & 2 Bn B and C4 Coys forward were relieved in the night by	
do	13		Relieved by 8th DLI and moved into reserve at CHAUDARDES when	
			Bn was billeted in caves.	
CHAUDARDES	14/15		Training continued.	
do	16		C.O. Coy Comdrs reconnoitred Support line &	
do	17		Coy moved to GUIRY le CHAUDARDES.	
do	18/19	night	Relieved 6th DLI in right sub section active action.	
LINE	20/21		Quiet.	
do	22		Reorganization of dispositions in the line.	
do	24/25	night	Relieved by 6th DLI and moved into Reserve at CHAUDARDES and	
			GUIRY le CHAUDARDES.	
CHAUDARDES	26		Training continued.	
	26	4.30 pm	Orders received to move immediately to assembly positions	
			with rations on. Patr began an attack by the enemy was anticipated.	
			It was then ascertained that an attack by the enemy was commenced. Companies	
			ordered to remain in the assembly positions and	
			await orders.	
	27	1 am	Terrific enemy barrage conducted of every calibre of shells	
			and burst mortars accompanied by Gas and Tear shells	

WAR DIARY

or

INTELLIGENCE SUMMARY.

(Erase heading not required.)

Instructions regarding War Diaries and Intelligence Summaries are contained in F. S. Regs., Part II. and the Staff Manual respectively. Title pages will be prepared in manuscript.

Place	Date	Hour	Summary of Events and Information	Remarks and references to Appendices

A7093). Wt. W2269/M1298 750,000. 1/17. D. D & L., Ltd. Forms/C2118/14.

WAR DIARY

or

INTELLIGENCE SUMMARY.

(Erase heading not required.)

- 3 -

Instructions regarding War Diaries and Intelligence Summaries are contained in F. S. Regs., Part II. and the Staff Manual respectively. Title pages will be prepared in manuscript.

Place	Date	Hour	Summary of Events and Information	Remarks and references to Appendices
	30		Remnant of 10th moved to ROYE crossing the Meuse at PONT a BINSIN; where Divn concentrated	
	31.		Moved to VERT LE GRANELLE	

Commdg 5 Divn Detachment

A7093). Wt. w18539/M1298 750,000. 1/17. D. D & L., Ltd. Forms/C2118/11.

WAR DIARY.

5th Bn. Durham Light Infantry.

June, 1918.

Volume — XXXIX.

Instructions regarding War Diaries and Intelligence Summaries are contained in F. S. Regs., Part II. and the Staff Manual respectively. Title pages will be prepared in manuscript.

VOLUME 39.

JUNE 1918

WAR DIARY
or
INTELLIGENCE SUMMARY.
(*Erase heading not required.*)

1/5th Bn. DURHAM LIGHT INFANTRY

Army Form C. 2118.

Place	Date	Hour	Summary of Events and Information	Remarks and references to Appendices
VERT LE GRAVELLE	1st		Remainder of Battn organised into a Company and formed part of a composite Bn with remainder of 151 Bde. Company under command of Capt E G Jones M.C. Owing to the death in action of the B.G.C. Lt Col B.D. Robinson D.S.O. assumed temp. command of Bde. Comp. Battn inspected by G.O.C. Division.	
	2		Equipping of Comp Company.	
	4		Following (immediate) Honours awarded:- SOMME & LYS engagements.	
			Bar to M.C. Capt M J Morrison M.C.	
			" Lieut H Green M.C.	
			D.S.O. Major A L Raimes.	
			M.C. Lieut E West: Capt G F Rowe: Lieut R W G Robinson: Lt R J Stockdale.	
			D.C.M. 201479 Pte T Tweedle. 27695 Pte E Dean 203422 Pte G McAskill.	
			" 202466 Pte H Laverick	
			M.M. 200060 Sgt J Fisher. 202935 Cpl W Weatherill. 200446 Pte West A.	
			200330 Pte Connolly P. 248039 Pte J Newby. 27009 Sgt White ...	
			200384 Pte Raffell E. 202990 Sgt Chester H. 201138 Pte Stephenson ...	
			200892 L/Sgt Graham G. 201073 Cpl Summerbell S.	
			200086 L/Cpl Dinsdale E. 201044 Pte Nicholson W.	
			320017 Sgt Davy W. 203082 Sgt Firth C.	
			Birthday Honours:-	
			D.C.M. 200097 CSM Kirby R (London Gazette 3/6/18).	
	5		Comp Battn moved by Bus to CORMOYEUX arriving about 1 am 6th. Spent day in Reserve and then moved into front line at MONTAGNE DE BLIGNY on night of 6/7th.	
	7		Dispositions 5th DLI Coy (Front line) 6th DLI Coy (Support) 8th DLI Coy (Reserve)	

A7092). Wt. W12839/M1293 750,000. 1/17. D. D & L., Ltd. Forms/C2118/14.

Army Form C. 2118.

WAR DIARY

or

INTELLIGENCE SUMMARY.

(Erase heading not required.)

Instructions regarding War Diaries and Intelligence Summaries are contained in F. S. Regs., Part II. and the Staff Manual respectively. Title pages will be prepared in manuscript.

Place	Date	Hour	Summary of Events and Information	Remarks and references to Appendices
KING	6/9.	18.00		
CAMP N.21	8/9.	18.00		
	9			
	10			
	11			
	12			
	13/14	18.15		
Base Camp N.21				
	15			
	19			
	20			
BRAYES.	21			
	22			

A7092. Wt. W1289/M1295. 750,000. 1/17. D. D & L. Ltd. Forms/C218/14.

WAR DIARY

or

INTELLIGENCE SUMMARY.

(Erase heading not required.)

Instructions regarding War Diaries and Intelligence
Summaries are contained in F. S. Regs., Part II.
and the Staff Manual respectively. Title pages
will be prepared in manuscript.

Place	Date	Hour	Summary of Events and Information	Remarks and references to Appendices
Bryas	24. 26.			
	27.			
	28.			
	29.			
	30.			

Commanding 151st Inf. Bde.

A7093). Wt. w18859/M1298 750,000. 1/17. D, D & L. Ltd. Forms/C2118/12.

WAR DIARY

or

INTELLIGENCE SUMMARY.

(Erase heading not required.)

5TH DURHAM. L.I.

JULY 1915

Instructions regarding War Diaries and Intelligence Summaries are contained in F. S. Regs., Part II. and the Staff Manual respectively. Title pages will be prepared in manuscript.

Place	Date	Hour	Summary of Events and Information	Remarks and references to Appendices
BROYES	1st	—	Training under Coy arrangements. Baths alloted to Coys. Lt-Col. G.G. Stapleton took over temporary command of 151st Inf. Brigade & Major H.L.J. Eyre assumed command of Battalion.	
"	2nd	—	Battn. moved from BROYES by march route to CONNANTRE en route for Entraining Station. CONNANTRE en route for Entraining Station. N.W. of	
CONNANTRE	3rd	—	Battn. marched to FERE CHAMPENOISE to entrain for British Zone. Entrained at FERE CHAMPENOISE at 3.33 p.m.	
HUCHENNEVILLE	4th	—	Detrained at LONGPRE at 3.30 p.m. Marched to HUCHENNEVILLE, a distance of 12 miles. No men fell out. Took over Billets. Settled in by about 11.30 p.m.	
"	5th	—	Coys at disposal of O.C. Coys.	
"	6th	—	Coys at disposal of O.C. Coys. Sgt. W. Graham M.M. awarded Bar to Military Medal for bravery and good work with the transport when saving the Battn. Stores from CHABDARDES [?] at the commencement of the German Offensive 27th May. 20020 Sgt. Gaze awarded an bung awarded the Meritorious Service Medal on 11th Yearly Honours June 1918.	
"	7th	—	Joint Church Parade with W.A.A.C. in Chateau Grounds HUCHENNEVILLE.	

D. D. & L., London, E.C.
(A10256) Wt W5300/1715 750,000 2/18 Sch. 62 Forms/C2118/16.

WAR DIARY

or

INTELLIGENCE SUMMARY.

(Erase heading not required.)

Army-Form C. 2118.

5TH. DURHAM L.I.

VOLUME 40

JULY 1915

Instructions regarding War Diaries and Intelligence
Summaries are contained in F. S. Regs., Part II.
and the Staff Manual respectively. Title pages
will be prepared in manuscript.

Place	Date	Hour	Summary of Events and Information	Remarks and references to Appendices
HUCHENNEVILLE	8th	—	8th March. Lt. Col. J.A. Stapleton re-assumes Command of Battn on Brig. Gen. Angelas re-assuming command of 151 Infty Bde. Specialist Classes the Musketry, Lewis Gun, etc.	
"	9th	—	Brig. Gen. Angelas inspected Battn at 12 noon at HUCHENNEVILLE. Orders received for a Training Cadre to be formed out of Battn. Remainder of Battn to proceed to Base at a date to be notified later. Training Cadre selected as follows:—	

D. D. & L., London, E.C.

(A10266) Wt W3900/P713 750,000 2/18 Sch. 52 Forms/C2118/16.

Army Form C. 2118.

WAR DIARY
or
INTELLIGENCE SUMMARY.
(Erase heading not required.)

5TH DURHAM L.I.

VOLUME 40

JULY 1918

Instructions regarding War Diaries and Intelligence Summaries are contained in F.S. Regs., Part II. and the Staff Manual respectively. Title pages will be prepared in manuscript.

Place	Date	Hour	Summary of Events and Information	Remarks and references to Appendices
HUCHENNEVILLE	9th	—	P.T. Instructor 204185 Sgt. Donnelly J. Major Duty	200157 Pte. Bougott J.
			Bombing Inst. 32007 " Berry H. Sanitary Duty	200288 L/Cpl. Burnicle J.
			Gas Instructors 200533 " Stockley R.	200090 Cpl. Fisk J.H.
			200030 Cpl. Bell G.D.	200269 Pte. Harding H.
			200256 " Pybus J.B.	200474 " McEwan B.
			200055 " Little F.	200512 " Bamber W.
			200052 " Kirkpatrick G.	200349 " Smith G.
			2.n Store 200013 A/Cpl. Fenton C.J.	325848 " Segarell E.T.
			200004 " Johnston J.H.	200206 " Turner J.B.
			200312 Pte. Benton J.B.	200121 " Smith J.
			Orderly Room 200269 Cpl. Roper R.	200053 " Millar J.H.
			Police 200110 A/Cpl. Spoors R.	200663 " Wilkinson J.F.
			Cook 200003 Pte.	200295 Cpl. Salmony H. Grooms
			Drivers 200007 " Gold H.	200241 Pte. Kelly J.
			200174 " Bannister L. Armourer Sgt.	A/S2 A/Sgt. Clark H.
			Sgt. A/T. Morrison D.C.M. awarded second bar.	
			2nd Lieut. Sarah C awarded M.C	
			295040 Pte. Bradley W.H. awarded M.M.	
	10th	—	Kit Inspection of Personnel proceeding to Base by M.O.	
			200354 Sgt. Luke J.H. awarded D.C.M.	

WAR DIARY

or

INTELLIGENCE SUMMARY.

(Erase heading not required.)

Instructions regarding War Diaries and Intelligence Summaries are contained in F. S. Regs., Part II. and the Staff Manual respectively. Title pages will be prepared in manuscript.

Place	Date	Hour	Summary of Events and Information	Remarks and references to Appendices
HOCHENN EVILLE	11th	—	Coys at disposal of Bdes. Specialist Training. G.O.C. Division addressed 15, Inf. Brigade at LIMERCOURT and presented medal ribbons	
"	12th	—	Coys at disposal of Inf. Bde. Specialist Training	
"	13th	—	Specialists Training	
"	14th	—	Divine Service. Parade cancelled owing to rain	
"	15th	—	All Officers R.O.'s and men not selected for Training Cadre proceeded to Base	
"	16th to 18th	—	Specialist Classes	
"	19th	—	Battn. moved to L.B.C. (DIEPPE) area by Lorry. Went into camp at ROUXMESNIL with other Cadres of 50th Div.	
ROUXMESNIL	20th	—	Inspections. Parade up to 25% of strength issued daily for DIEPPE	
"	21st	—	Church Parade on Y.M.C.A. Hut in Camp	
"	22nd	—	Battn. supplied Div. Guards duties. Training for all Officers R.O.'s in Musketry, Lewis Gun, & tactical handling of Platoon	
"	23rd	—	Training as above. 9672 L/Cpl. Hodson W. awarded D.C.M. 27612 Pte Curbin W awarded M.M. 325309 Pte Kerr J.T. awarded M.M.	
"	24th 26th 27th 28th 30th 31st	—	Training continued as above	
		—	R. Church Parade. Training continued as above	

(signature)
Lieut. Col
Commanding 1st Line 5th Bn. Durham L. Infty.

(A0966) W1 W3300/P713 750,000 7/18 Sch. 52 Forms/C2118/16
D.D. & L., London, E.C. above

Attached) TRAINING CADRE
39TH DIVISION
117TH INFY BDE

50 DIVISION

151 BDE

5TH BN DURHAM LT INFY

AUG - OCT 1918

DEMOBILISED NOV 1918

2686

5th Bn Durham Light Infantry

VOLUME 4.1

Army Form C. 2118.

WAR DIARY

or

INTELLIGENCE SUMMARY.

(Erase heading not required.)

AUGUST 1918.

Instructions regarding War Diaries and Intelligence Summaries are contained in F. S. Regs., Part II. and the Staff Manual respectively. Title pages will be prepared in manuscript.

117
39

Vol 33

Place	Date	Hour	Summary of Events and Information	Remarks and references to Appendices
Bight: Roundwood Camp.	1st		NCO and Officers Training in Tactical Scheme.	
	2nd 3rd		Training continued as above.	
	4th		Officers + 5 Sgts attended Divisional Church Parade at Martin Eglise representing 5 DLI	
	5th		NCOs and Officers training in tactical scheme. Weekly amusement held in Coys lines	
	6th 7th 8th		NCO and Officers training in tactical scheme.	
	9th		Commanding Officer, Mo. to ARC Sgt Pursuit - now Div School of training. Cadre.	
	10th		Officers + NCOs training as above.	
	11th		Church Parade.	
	12th		All 5 DLI parades for inspection by Commanding Officer	
	13th		Employed men rejoined Battalion from GHQ Division. NCOs + Officers training in tactical scheme.	
	14th		Inspection of Battalion by Commanding Officer. Remained on lines for hour.	
	15th		Battalion march from ROUXMESNIL to ROUEN.	
	16th		Battalion entrained at ROUEN + left en route to Gyfele	

D. D. & L., London, E.C.
Wt W5300/P773 750,000 2/18 Sch. 52 Forms/C2118/16.
(A10266) Wt W5300/P773 750,000 2/18 Sch. 52 Forms/C2118/16.

Army Form C. 2118.

WAR DIARY

or

INTELLIGENCE SUMMARY.

(Erase heading not required.)

Instructions regarding War Diaries and Intelligence
Summaries are contained in F. S. Regs., Part II.
and the Staff Manual respectively. Title pages
will be prepared in manuscript.

Place	Date	Hour	Summary of Events and Information	Remarks and references to Appendices

D. D. & L., London, E.C.
(A10266) Wt W3500/P713 750,000 2/18 Sch, 52 Forms/C2118/16.

Army Form C. 2118.

WAR DIARY
or
INTELLIGENCE SUMMARY.

(Erase heading not required.)

Instructions regarding War Diaries and Intelligence Summaries are contained in F. S. Regs., Part II. and the Staff Manual respectively. Title pages will be prepared in manuscript.

Place	Date	Hour	Summary of Events and Information	Remarks and references to Appendices
Rouen	30"		Battalion inspection by the Commanding Officer, a field Marshal Montgomery. M.O. — Report of work of sanitation officers made to C.O.	
	31		Clearance inspection by Company officers. M.O. — Removal of sick & clearance to C.O.	

Lieut. Col.

Commanding 14, Line 5th. Bn. Durham Infantry.

(A10266) W1 W5300/P713 750,000 2/18 Sch. 52 Forms/C2118/16.

D. D. & L., London, E.C.

5TH DURHAM. L.I.

Army Form C 2118.

VOLUME 42

SEPTEMBER 1918

WAR DIARY

or

INTELLIGENCE SUMMARY.

(Erase heading not required.)

Instructions regarding War Diaries and Intelligence Summaries are contained in F. S. Regs., Part II. and the Staff Manual respectively. Title pages will be prepared in manuscript.

39

Place	Date	Hour	Summary of Events and Information	Remarks and references to Appendices
ROUEN	1st	—	Voluntary Church Service	
"	2nd	—	Officers taking Officers from I.B.D. in Tactical Exercises. N.C.Os at disposal of R.S.M.	39
"	3rd		N.C.O. & Officers doing tactical exercises with Commanding Officer.	
"	4 d		N.C.O. & men working on new Officers Training Camp in Bull Ring. Officers preparing tactical exercise with C.O.	
"	5 th		Officers taking Officers from I.B.D. on tactical exercises. All N.C.Os & men continuing talks on new camp.	
"	6 th		C.Os inspection of Band. Officers preparing tactical exercise with C.O. N.C.Os, men working on new camp.	
"	7 th		C.Os inspection of Transport. Officers completing tactical exercise with C.O. N.C.Os, men working on New Camp. Baths on afternoon.	
"	8 d		Church Parade.	
"	9 th		Officers taking I.B.D. Officers in Tactical Exercise. Batln. moved from Camp near Rythol I.B.D. to new temporary Camp N.W. side Bull Ring near site for new Officers Training Camp.	

(A 10266) W. W. 3300/P713 750,000 2/18 Sch. 52 Forms/C2118/16.

D. D. & L., London, E.C.

Army Form C. 2118.

Instructions regarding War Diaries and Intelligence Summaries are contained in F. S. Regs., Part II. and the Staff Manual respectively. Title pages will be prepared in manuscript.

5TH DURHAM L.I.

VOLUME No 2

SEPTEMBER 1918

WAR DIARY
or
INTELLIGENCE SUMMARY.

(Erase heading not required.)

Places	Date	Hour	Summary of Events and Information	Remarks and references to Appendices
ROUEN.	10th 9 11th	-	Officers preparing tactical exercise with C.O. N.C.O.s & men continuing work on new Officers Training camp.	
"	12th		Officers & men attending lectures by Lt. Col. Campbell, Deputy Inspector of R.S. & B.T. N.C.O.s & men working on new camp.	
"	13th		Officers taking I.B.D. Officers on tactical exercise. N.C.O.s & men continuing work on new camp.	
"	14th		Officers preparing tactical exercise with C.O. N.C.O.s & men working on new camp. Voluntary church services.	
"	15th			
"	16th		Officers taking I.B.D. Officers in Tactical Exercise. N.C.O.s & men working on new camp.	
"	17th 18th		Officers preparing tactical exercise with C.O. N.C.O.s & men working on new camp.	
"	19th		Officers taking I.B.D. Officers in Tactical Exercise. N.C.O.s & men working on new camp.	
"	20th		Officers preparing Tactical Exercise with C.O. N.C.O.s & men working on new camp. Lt. T. Best reports for duty from 19th D.L.I.	

D. D. & L., London, E.C.
(A10256) Wt W3300/1713 750,000 2/18 Sch. 52 Forms/C2118/6.

Army Form C. 2118.

WAR DIARY
or
INTELLIGENCE SUMMARY.

(Erase heading not required.)

Instructions regarding War Diaries and Intelligence Summaries are contained in F. S. Regs., Part II. and the Staff Manual respectively. Title pages will be prepared in manuscript.

Place	Date	Hour	Summary of Events and Information	Remarks and references to Appendices
ROUEN	21st		C.Os inspection of Transport. N.C.Os & men working on new camp. Officers preparing tactical scheme with C.O.	
"	22nd		C.Os inspection of Batn. in full marching order. Voluntary Church Services. Batn. XI played and drew with ROUEN TOWN XI, 2 all.	
"	23rd		Officers taking F.S.D. Officers in tactical exercise. N.C.Os & men working on new camp.	
"	24/25		Officers preparing tactical exercise. N.C.Os & men working on new camp.	
"	26th		Officers taking F.S.D. Officers in Tactical Exercise. N.C.Os & men working on new camp.	
"	27th		Officers preparing tactical exercise with C.O. N.C.Os & men working on new camp.	
"	28th		C.Os inspection of Lewis Gun teams etc. No. 26 & 39 at Gen. exercise Brigade and inspected camp. Officers preparing tactical Exercise. N.C.Os & men working on new camp.	
"	29th		C.Os inspection of rate of Batn. Voluntary Church Services.	
"	30th		Officers taking F.S.D. Officers in tactical exercise. N.C.Os & men working on new camp.	

Lieut. Col.
Commanding 1st Line 5th Bn. Durham L. Infy.

Army Form C. 2118.

WAR DIARY

or

INTELLIGENCE SUMMARY.

(Erase heading not required.)

Instructions regarding War Diaries and Intelligence
Summaries are contained in F. S. Regs., Part II.
and the Staff Manual respectively. Title pages
will be prepared in manuscript.

Place	Date	Hour	Summary of Events and Information	Remarks and references to Appendices
ROUEN	1st		N.C.O.s & men working on new camp. Officers preparing Tactical Exercise with E.O.	
	2nd		N.C.O.s & men working on new camp. Officers completing Tactical Exercise with E.O.	
	3rd		N.C.O.s & men working on new camp. Officers taking N.C.O.s in Tactical of Exercise	
	4th		N.C.O.s & men working on new camp. Officers preparing Tactical Exercise with E.O.	
	5th		N.C.O.s & men Inspection of Battn Lewis Gunners, tool houses & Transport by E.O. Officers completing Tactical Exercise J.E.O.s & men working on new camp.	
	6th		E.O. inspection of Battn in Drill Order. Band changes	
	7th		N.C.O.s & men working on new camp. Officers taking J.B.G Officers in Tactical Exercise	
	8th		Officers preparing Tactical Exercise	
	9th		N.C.O.s & men working on new camp. Officers preparing Tactical Exercise	
	10th		N.C.O.s & men working on new camp. Officers taking J.B.G Officers in Tactical Exercise.	
	11th		N.C.O.s & men working on new camp. Officers preparing Tactical Exercise	
	12th		E.O. inspection of Battn Lewis Gunners, tool houses N.C.O.s & men working on new camp. Officers preparing Tactical Exercise	
	13th		E.O. inspection of Battn in Drill Order. Church Services.	
	14th		N.C.O.s & men working on new camp. Officers carrying out Tactical Exercise with J.B.G.	
			Band left for DIEPPE to play the Tattoo there. Officers met.	
	15th		N.C.O.s & men working on new camp. Officers & N.C.O. completing Tactical Exercise	
	16th			
	17th		N.C.O.s & men working on new camp. Officers taking J.B.G Officers in Tactical Exercise	

(A10366) Wt W5500/P713 750,000 2/8 96h. S2 Forms/C218/36.

D. D. & L., London, E.C.

WAR DIARY

or

INTELLIGENCE SUMMARY.

(Erase heading not required.)

Instructions regarding War Diaries and Intelligence Summaries are contained in F. S. Regs., Part II. and the Staff Manual respectively. Title pages will be prepared in manuscript.

Place	Date	Hour	Summary of Events and Information	Remarks and references to Appendices
ROUEN	18th		N.C.O.s & Men carrying out Tactical Exercise under Coys. Weeks. Remainder of Officers following Tactical Exercise with Bn.	
	19th		C.O. inspection of Salun Lines & coys. Tactical etc. N.C.O.s & Men carrying out Tactical exercise with Officers.	
	20th		Church Parade.	
	21st		Officers taking N.C.O.s & Men in Tactical Exercise. N.C.O.s & Men working on New Camp.	
	22nd		N.C.O.s carrying out Tactical Exercise under Coys. Weeks. Remainder of Officers following Tactical Exercise under C.O. Band returned from DIEPPE.	
	23rd		Officers following Tactical Exercise with Coys. N.C.O.s & Men working. Officers taking N.C.O.s & Men on Tactical exercise. N.C.O.s & Men working on new camp.	
	24th		N.C.O.s & Men carrying out Tactical Exercise. Officers following Tactical Exercise.	
	25th		Officers attending Lecture by Brig. Gen. Boggon. N.C.O.s & Men working on new camp.	
	26th		Officers taking N.C.O.s & Men in Tactical Exercise. N.C.O.s & Men working on new camp.	
	27th		Battn. working a Bde. guard, and mounting guards by Brig. N.C.O.s & Men working on new camp. Lt. Col. E.V. Wildman Lushington arrived to take over command of Bn. Lt. Col. E.V. Wildman Lushington assumes command of Bn.	
	28th		N.C.O.s & Men carrying out Tactical Exercise with coys with N.C.O. Officers. Officers carrying out ...	
	29th		Officers working a ... Tactical Exercise. N.C.O.s & Men on Miniature Range.	
	30th		Officers carrying Tactical Exercise. N.C.O.s & Men working on new camp.	
	31st		Officers taking N.C.O.s & Men in Tactical Exercise. N.C.O.s & Men working on new camp.	

E.V. Wildman Lushington
Lieut. Col.

D. D. & L., London, E.C.

(A10560) Wt W3500/1713 750,000 2/18 Sch. 52 Forms/C2118/16.

WAR
DIARY

6th BATTN. THE DURHAM LIGHT INFANTRY.

J U N E

(8/30.6.15)

1 9 1 5

WAR DIARY

or

INTELLIGENCE SUMMARY.

(Erase heading not required.)

Instructions regarding War Diaries and Intelligence Summaries are contained in F. S. Regs., Part II. and the Staff Manual respectively. Title pages will be prepared in manuscript.

Place	Date	Hour	Summary of Events and Information	Remarks and references to Appendices
			6th Battalion The Durham Light Infantry.	
			June 1915	
			(8/30.6.15)	
			(Note: The 6th and 8th D.L.I. were amalgamated into a Composite Battalion on 8th June, 1915. Independent formations resumed 11th August. 1915).	
			During the period of amalgamation separate diaries were kept by the two units.	

(19175) Wt W2358/F360 600,000 12/7 D. D. & L. Sch. 87a. Forms/C2118/15

6th Durh. L.I
amalgamated with
8th Durh. L.I

Instructions regarding War Diaries and Intelligence Summaries are contained in F. S. Regs., Part II. and the Staff Manual respectively. Title pages will be prepared in manuscript.

INTELLIGENCE SUMMARY.
(Erase heading not required.)

Place	Date	Hour	Summary of Events and Information	Remarks and references to Appendices
	June 8th		Tuesday. The 6th DURH: L.I. & the 8th D.L.I were this day amalgamated into a composite Bn; Lt Col J. TURNBULL V.D was appointed C.O Capt G.A. STEVENS (Roy Fus) Adjutant. Lt HOPE Quartermaster. The Bn: was organized into 4 companies A Coy (6th Durk:men) under Capt T.A. BRADFORD with Capt JAS.RITSON his 2nd in command. B Coy under Lt GILL (6th Durk. men) C Coy 6th Durk. under Lt HESLOP. D Coy under Capt LIVESAY 6th Durho; The Bn: retained 4 machine guns which were placed under Lt HOWE 6th Durho. The Transport (to be reduced to the establishment of 1 Bn:) was placed under Lt RAMSAY 8th Durho. All supernumerary staff were to be sent to the Base. The two Bns: remained in their separate Billets which were quite close to each other	
	9th		Wednesday. Remained in Bivouacs near BASSE BOUM. The organization of the composite Bn: continued with.	
	10th		Thursday. At Bivouacs at BASSEBOUM.	
	11th		Friday. In the evening the Bn: marched by companies from the bivouacs at BASSE BOUM to some dugouts with grounds of the CHATEAU of KRUISSTRAAT. S of YPRES. Head Qrs was established in a cellar. Here the 9th D.L.I. who were at the same place	

1577. Wt. W1091/1773. 500,000 1/15. D. D. & L. A.D.S.S./Forms/C. 2118.

Army Form C. 2118.

WAR DIARY

Vol 3

Instructions regarding War Diaries and Intelligence Summaries are contained in F.S. Regs., Part II. and the Staff Manual respectively. Title pages will be prepared in manuscript.

~~INTELLIGENCE SUMMARY.~~
(Erase heading not required.)

6th Durh. L.I.
(amalgamated with 8th Durh. L.I.) (58)

June 1915

Place	Date	Hour	Summary of Events and Information	Remarks and references to Appendices
	June 12th		**SANCTUARY WOOD.** Saturday. In the evening the Bn. was ordered to proceed to SANCTUARY WOOD. The route taken (both going independently) was through KRUISSTRAAT. The bridge over [canal just S.] of YPRES, thence along the town as far as the LILLE gate, then S. to the ETANG at ZILLEBEKE from there by MAPLE COPSE to SANCTUARY WOOD. It was a very dark night, there was a certain amount of shelling & a lot of bullets flying about. In the darkness - after arrival it was very difficult to find the dug outs & a large number of men had to stay out until morning. 2466 Pte FLETCHER T.H. was wounded 8th Durhs.	
	13th		Sunday. The Bn. remained in SANCTUARY WOOD. We were now under the orders of the 14th Inf. Bde. to whom we had been lent. Working parties were found chiefly for work in the HOOGE defences. There was very little sniper shelling in SANCTUARY WOOD but there were a great many bullets coming over from the front line. The "dump" for rations was at MAPLE COPSE which could only be approached by transport at night. Hd. Qrs: dug out was a very bad one. 2416 Pte CHARLTON 6th Durham was wounded & Pte ... in SANCTUARY WOOD; men employed on working parties. Casualties 13th B. Lce Cpl NEASHAM. 6th D.L.I. & 2944 Cpl LONGRIDGE both wounded etc	
	14th		Monday.	

1577 Wt. W10791/1773 500,000 1/15 D.D. & L.   A.D.S.S./Forms/C. 2118.

Army Form C. 2118.

WAR DIARY
or
INTELLIGENCE SUMMARY.
(Erase heading not required.)

Instructions regarding War Diaries and Intelligence
Summaries are contained in F. S. Regs., Part II.
and the Staff Manual respectively. Title pages
will be prepared in manuscript.

Vol. 3

June 1915

6th Durh. L.I.
amalgamated with
8th DLI

Place	Date	Hour	Summary of Events and Information	Remarks and references to Appendices
	June 15th		Tuesday the Bn. remained at SANCTUARY WOOD. Casualties 10-12 noon 1210 P/Sgt PITT 8th Durhs, 2610 Pte SHELTON 8th Durhs, 2634 Pte METCALF 6th Durhs. Copies of orders issued as regards the defence of HOOGE are annexed as an appendix. Orders were also received confidentially in connection with the attack proposed to be delivered against the Germans on the 16th. Copy of orders are attached. Officers commdg. companies examined the horizon they were to take up during the night. No lines were allowed in SANCTUARY WOOD for cooking as not to disclose the presence of troops there.	
	June 16th	2.30 a.m.	Wednesday. By 2.30 a.m. the Bn. moved into the 2nd line trenches running E & W through SANCTUARY WOOD. At 2.50 a.m.	
		2.50 a.m.	the bombardment commenced & was immediately replied to by the Germans. The bombardment was very intense & the noise of it was deafening, it lasted until 4.15 a.m. when the infantry advanced took place, that part of this ended between from Sanctuary Wood & appeared to make excellent progress	
		6.30 a.m.	At 6.30 a.m. a message (verbal) was received from O.C. ZOUAVE WOOD that he was about to attack the Germans near from N. of HOOGE asking for support. The Germans were reported to be evacuating their trenches. Two companies were at once sent off under Major HAWDON of the 6th DLI & the other two companies were ordered as rapidly as possible nearly 167 yellow on into ZOUAVE WOOD	

Army Form C. 2118.

WAR DIARY
or
INTELLIGENCE SUMMARY.

(Erase heading not required.)

Instructions regarding War Diaries and Intelligence Summaries are contained in F. S. Regs., Part II. and the Staff Manual respectively. Title pages will be prepared in manuscript.

6 /Durk L I
amalgamated with
8/DL1

Vol 3
June 1915

Place	Date	Hour	Summary of Events and Information	Remarks and references to Appendices
	June 16 (cont)	4 a.m	At 4.a.m verbal message received from O.C ZOUAVE WOOD to stop the Bn: fire. The present who was engaged in wiring in regard at 7.20 a.m. The Bn then returned into the trenches previous occupied. Heavy artillery	
		3.0 p.m	fire continued all day increasing in intensity between 3 & 4 p.m when the Germans appeared 10 down a counter attack. At such the firing died away almost completely. Working parties were ordered for work in HOOGE	
		9 p.m	About 8 p.m orders were received countermanding the working parties ordering the Bn: to stand by ready to man trenches at short notice. About the same time Maj J.H. SMEDDLE (who was then with the Bn:) received orders from the 151st Bde to proceed to BASSEBOOM & take charge of the Bde Transport	
			At 9 p.m orders were received from K.149 & K Bde: to relieve the trenches in K. HOOGE afternoon now held by the Y.K.N.F.	
		10 p.m	By 10 p.m arrangements for the relief were completed, the O.C Border Regt Y.K.N.F coming into SANCTUARY WOOD to arrange the details. The Bn: was disposed as follows :- B.Coy under Lt GILL (6th Durk) occupied B.9 trench A 60: (leave me platoon) under Capt T BRADFORD occupied H.13 & H.14 trenches up to the stables. Lt HESLOP occupied H.15 to the ISLAND POST. D.60: under Capt LIVESAY took the H.16 in support D.60: under Capt LIVESAY remained in support. A great deal of work had been done during the night in wiring the damage caused by the enemy's shelling during the day this was completely by the dawn with B.9 trench. Headqrs were established in ZOUAVE WOOD. Lt MILES with A Coy was kept in support in SANCTUARY WOOD. The Maloon from A Coy was were :- Lt HAWTHORN-THWAITE (6th Durk: gun shot wound) casualties during the day 6 other ranks gun shot wound night shoulder	

1577 Wt. W10791/1773 500,000 1/15 D. D. & L. A.D.S.S./Forms/C. 2118 no.1

Army Form C. 2118.

WAR DIARY
or
INTELLIGENCE SUMMARY.
(Erase heading not required.)

Instructions regarding War Diaries and Intelligence
Summaries are contained in F.S. Regs., Part II.
and the Staff Manual respectively. Title pages
will be prepared in manuscript.

Vol. 3

June 1915

6 K.O.S.L.I.
amalgamated with
8th K.S.L.I.

Place	Date	Hour	Summary of Events and Information	Remarks and references to Appendices
HOOGE	June 17th		Thursday the Bn: remained in HOOGE defences, there was some heavy shelling but extraordinary little damage was done. Part of T39 was untenable by daylight owing to being blown in the main communication trench from ZOUAVE WOOD was a bit knocked about. The day was spent in carrying on work repairs & work getting stores and ammunition up to the defences. At night Lt SAINT 8th Durhams carried out an excellent bombing enterprise against the German sap in front of H 15. This was worked in conjunction with the machine guns of the Bn; on our left and attained very successful, great credit being due to Lt SAINT. During the night the Germans were very active shelling & tried notwithstanding the position. During the afternoon the position of a German machine gun which fired on men passing to the N of ZOUAVE WOOD & in SANCTUARY WOOD was located by sound & information sent to the artillery who shelled the position with H.E. shell effectually putting the hostile machine gun out of action. The casualties this day were 1 man killed & 1 man wounded. Working party of 150 men was sent up during the night from the K.R.I.E. Rifles on work on the defences.	

Army Form C. 2118.

WAR DIARY

or

INTELLIGENCE SUMMARY.

(Erase heading not required.)

6th Durh L.I
8th DLI

Vol 3 June 1915

Instructions regarding War Diaries and Intelligence Summaries are contained in F. S. Regs., Part II. and the Staff Manual respectively. Title pages will be prepared in manuscript.

Place	Date	Hour	Summary of Events and Information	Remarks and references to Appendices
	June 18th		Friday Work was continued on the defences preparations were carried up sufficient for a garrison of 450 men. The second communication trench from ZOUAVE WOOD to HOOGE was partly excavated throughout but in places was still very shallow and only just practicable. The Bn: was relieved after dark 7.3.9 by the 9th N Fus the remainder of the works by the WILTSHIRE REGT. On relief the Bn: proceeded via KRUISSTRAAT to the F Hutments S. of VLAMERTINGE. There was very heavy rifle fire when passing through MAPLE COPSE but was sheltering from enemal. Two men were wounded + one man killed leaving ZOUAVE WOOD.	
	19th		Saturday The Bn: remained at F Hutments resting.	
	20th		Sunday The 151st Bde: moved today from the V Corps to the II Corps under Sir Charles Ferguson. The Bn: moves off from the hutments at 8.30 a m via OUDERDOM & LOCRE to DRANOUTRE when they went into Bivouacs at Corunna FARM W. of the village.	

1577 Wt. W10791/1773 500,000 1/15 D. D. & L. A.D.S.S./Forms/C. 2118.

Army Form C. 2118.

WAR DIARY
or
INTELLIGENCE SUMMARY.
(Erase heading not required.)

Vol 3

Title pages June 1915

Instructions regarding War Diaries and Intelligence Summaries are contained in F. S. Regs., Part II. and the Staff Manual respectively. Title pages will be prepared in manuscript.

Place	Date	Hour	Summary of Events and Information	Remarks and references to Appendices
	June 21st		Monday In the morning the Bn. who paraded in a field near the Brigade together with the 9th Durhams were addressed by Br General Ferguson on joining his Corps. In the evening the Bn. proceeded to relieve the trenches at LINDENHOEK cross roads. The trenches from E1 right to the farmland across the KEMMEL – WYTSCHAETE road went taken over from the 4 Lincolns HQ also being established in the street just WqThe LINDENHOEK cross roads. Relief was completed at 12.15 a.m on the 22nd	
	22nd		Tuesday In the trenches the enemy were generally quiet tho' there was a good deal of sniping. In the early hours the Germans turned a machine gun on our parapet. 288 SPRATTERSON A & KDLI C Co: (Lt HESLOP) was holding E.1 rt & left E.2 and support trenches. A Coy: under Capt BRADFORD was holding F.2. B Coy under Lt BLENKINSOP was holding F.5 & the barricade. The strength of the Bn: this day was 29 officers & 626 other ranks exclusive of details	
	23rd		Wednesday In the trenches. The situation was generally quiet with a fair amount of hostile artillery fire, some 5" in last night the German held up a noise board South "LEMBERG no taken on d. There was much cheering strong Germans in the German lines, we gave them 5 rounds rapid for luck. Work was commenced on the mines	

1577   Wt. W10701/1773   500,000   1/15   D. D. & L.   A.D.S.S./Forms/C. 2118.

WAR DIARY
or
INTELLIGENCE SUMMARY.
(Erase heading not required.)

Instructions regarding War Diaries and Intelligence Summaries are contained in F. S. Regs., Part II. and the Staff Manual respectively. Title pages will be prepared in manuscript.

Vol 3

June 1915

Place	Date	Hour	Summary of Events and Information	Remarks and references to Appendices
LINDENHOEK Trenches	24th.		Thursday. In the trenches. The night passed quietly another was very hard firing on the enemy's part. We bombed the enemy from E.1. & the right. Grenades into him, the Germans retaliated but did not harm. Our orders had a good day. In the morning a large number of rifles were found to jam; the ammunition was sent for, it was found the ammunition carried out into the chamber of the rifle which caused the jamming. The want of sufficient care was felt, if men let their carry smoke in the back lines, I immediately drew attention.	
	25th		Friday, In the trenches, everything was normal.	
	26th		Saturday. In the trenches. There was some heavy shelling between 12 noon & 2 pm especially in the outpost line. 2nd Lt. GELSTHORPE proceeded to WISQUES to attend a machine gun course.	
	27th.		Sunday. The day passed quietly. At night the Bn; was relieved with the evacuation of E by. The 9th D.L.I took over from the right of E.2 inclusive to the left of F.4. The 5th Loyal North Lancs took over from the right of F.5 along into G section On relief the Bn; proceeded to the Bde's huts near LOCRE. The mining company (which had been formed from the men of the 6th & 9th under 2nd Lt GUTHRIE) remained as a separate unit and the trenches coves be obtained for them in KEMMEL	

1577   Wt.W10791/1773   500,000   1/15   D.D.&L.   A.D.S.S./Forms/C. 2118.

Army Form C. 2118.

WAR DIARY

or

INTELLIGENCE SUMMARY.

(Erase heading not required.)

Instructions regarding War Diaries and Intelligence Summaries are contained in F. S. Regs., Part II. and the Staff Manual respectively. Title pages will be prepared in manuscript.

Vol 3

June 1915

6th Durh LI
amalgamated with
8th DLI

Place	Date	Hour	Summary of Events and Information	Remarks and references to Appendices
LOCRE	June 28th		Monday The Bn; remained in the hutments at LOCRE. During the evening 6. Co. was relieved by a (Bn) of the 150th KBde in the trenches & moved headquarters at the Hutments. The mining company went into Butts at KEMMEL.	
	29th		Tuesday. Remained at the hutments at LOCRE. General routine & drill carried out	
	30th		Wednesday Bn; remained at the hutments at LOCRE. General routine & drill carried out.	

1577 Wt.W10791/1773 500,000 1/15 D. D. & L. A.D.S.S./Forms/C. 2118.

6th BATTN. THE DURHAM LIGHT INFANTRY.

J U L Y

1 9 1 5

WAR DIARY

~~INTELLIGENCE SUMMARY~~

(Erase heading not required.)

6th Durh. L.I
(amalgamated with
8th Durh. L.I.)

Vol. 4

①

Instructions regarding War Diaries and Intelligence Summaries are contained in F. S. Regs., Part II. and the Staff Manual respectively. Title pages will be prepared in manuscript.

Place	Date	Hour	Summary of Events and Information	Remarks and references to Appendices
LOCRE	July 1st		The Battalion remained at LOCRE	
	July 2nd		Friday Remained at LOCRE, drill and Route marches.	
	3	8.30	Saturday The Bn went to the KEMMEL trenches. Headquarters were at the sheet at LINDENHOEK crossroads. The trenches occupied were from E.1 right right (at Pt N.36.a.4.10) 10th barricade on the KEMMEL - WYTSCHAETE road (-at Pt N.29.b.9.6). The German trenches were about 200 x off on the left of the line and about 40 x from E.1 right. The Germans held the higher ground and also held a commanding strong point at SPANBROEKMOLEN. The front line trenches were approached by a long communication trench known as REGENT STREET, about three quarters way up this branches off into VIGO STREET and PICCADILLY on the right, and to PALL MALL on the left. C Coy under Lt Hodon held E.1. right and left went supports. A Coy under Capt J.A.S. RITSON.held E 2 & E 4. B Coy under Lt. BLENKINSOP held F 5. Capt Riveaways Coy (D) held REGENT STREET dugouts and supporting points 8, 9, & 10. The strength of the Bn on this day was Officers 27, other ranks 872 (made up 8 D.L.I. 13 Off. 320 other ranks; 6 K.O.Y.L.I. 13 Off. 552 other ranks) 1 medical officer The relief of the trenches was completed about midnight.	

1577 Wt. W10791/1773 500,000 1/15 D. D. & L.   A.D.S.S./Forms/C. 2118.

Army Form C. 2118.

6th Bn Durh. L.I.
(Amalgamated)
8th D.L.I.

WAR DIARY

INTELLIGENCE SUMMARY.
(Erase heading not required.)

Instructions regarding War Diaries and Intelligence Summaries are contained in F.S. Regs., Part II. and the Staff Manual respectively. Title pages will be prepared in manuscript.

Place	Date	Hour	Summary of Events and Information	Remarks and references to Appendices
Trenches at LOCRE	Sunday July 4th		In trenches E1 to F5. The Bn relieved the 9th D.L.I. last night in the trenches. The day was normal. Information was received from the Artillery that KEMMEL HILL had they had observed a new work in front of the right of F.5. and they thought the Germans were heading gas cylinders. A special look out was kept. Large working parties were used at night.	
	5th		Monday In the trenches. Brigadier General SHEA. C.B. D.S.O. the new Brigadier inspected the trenches. The situation remained normal No 1242 Pte: L/Cpl: ROBINSON 6th D.L.I. was wounded.	
Trenches	6th		Tuesday In the trenches. Situation remained normal No. 3016 Pte SCOTT. H.J. 8th D.L.I. was wounded.	
	7th		Wednesday In the trenches. Situation normal, no casualties	
	8th		Thursday In the trenches. Situation normal, no casualties	
	9th		Friday The Bn was relieved from the trenches by the Y.D.L.I. On relief A.Y.D. Coys went to commencing at 9.30 p.m.	

1577 Wt.W10791/1773 500,000 1/15 D.D.&L. A.D.S.S./Forms/C.2118.

6th Durh.L.I.
(amalgamated with
8th D.L.I

Vol. 4

WAR DIARY

~~INTELLIGENCE~~ SUMMARY.

(Erase heading not required.)

Instructions regarding War Diaries and Intelligence Summaries are contained in F. S. Regs., Part II. and the Staff Manual respectively. Title pages will be prepared in manuscript.

Place	Date	Hour	Summary of Events and Information	Remarks and references to Appendices
KEMMEL	July 9th (Con)		August out in N.19.a. & B. & C bays tookeleno at N.20.6. (reference NEUVE EGLISE - ST.ELOI sheet. The Bn was now in support of the trenches, the bivvés being just behind KEMMEL HILL, the other Bn relieved from the trenches going to LOCRE. 91 was a very dark night and the relief was carried out without casualties. All men of the amalgamated 13th who were killed in action in their trenches were buried into grounds of the CHALET at LINDENHOEK (N.27.a.6.7).	
KEMMEL	10th		Saturday. The Bn remained in support, working parties being found for work in the trenches at night. The strength of the Bn this day was officers 24, other ranks 877 (made up 6th DLI 13 off. 563 other ranks 8th DLI 11 off. 314 other ranks) KEMMEL HILL was the highest ground in this neighbourhood & commanded an excellent view of the German lines from WYTSCHAETE to MESSINES (or rather the ruins of these places as they had been much shelled). KEMMEL HILL was well wooded and gave good cover. The nature of the fighting in this part of the line was the usual morning and evening bombardment on either side, a fair amount of anything through the day which increased at night with raids varied by bursts of fire when working parties were discovered. There was also a certain amount of bombing, rifle grenading & trench mortar warfare.	

1577 Wt. W10791/1773 500,000 1/15 D. D. & L. A.D.S.S./Forms/C. 2118.

WAR DIARY

Instructions regarding War Diaries and Intelligence Summaries are contained in F.S. Regs., Part II. and the Staff Manual respectively. Title pages will be prepared in manuscript.

INTELLIGENCE SUMMARY.

(Erase heading not required.)

④

6th Durh L.I. amalgamated with 8th D.L.I.

Vol 4

Place	Date	Hour	Summary of Events and Information	Remarks and references to Appendices
KEMMEL	July 11th		Sunday The Bn remained at the bivouacs finding working parties	
do	12th		Monday The Bn. remained at the bivouacs.	
do	13th		Tuesday The Bn. remained at the bivouacs. The officers reconnoitred the G.H.Q lines "switch" in case of having to occupy the line. There were many rumours of a concentration of German forces to our front. In the evening the following working parties through shell fire near LINDENHOEK crossroads. Killed 2109 Pte MASON. Wounded 1840 Pte HOLMES, 1855 Bug WEATHERALL, 973 Pte JACKSON. 2575 Pte MANN. 606 Sgt HEPENSTALL.	
do	14th		Wednesday The Bn. remained at the bivouacs finding working parties north of the sector (wood?) The Germans sprang a mine in L sector of the line (I was was raining heavy). 5 men of the 9th Durhams mining section were buried. A heavy bombardment with a lot of rifle fire follows for about an hour when affairs quietened down to normal.	
do	15th		Thursday The Bn. remained at KEMMEL. Part of the XXVIII Divn. arrived in the area in relief of the 50th Divn. Leave to the United Kingdom started this day, 2 officers & 3 men being allowed away together. Officers 6 days leave, other ranks 4 days	

1577 Wt. W10791/1773 500,000 1/15 D. D. & L. A.D.S.S./Forms/C. 2118.

Army Form C. 2118.

WAR DIARY

~~INTELLIGENCE SUMMARY~~

(Erase heading not required.)

Instructions regarding War Diaries and Intelligence Summaries are contained in F. S. Regs., Part II. and the Staff Manual respectively. Title pages will be prepared in manuscript.

Vol. 4

(5)

6 Durh. L.I.
amalgamated with
8 KDLI

Place	Date	Hour	Summary of Events and Information	Remarks and references to Appendices
KEMMEL	July '16		Friday The Bn. moved from KEMMEL to ARMENTIERES, marching off with the Bns: at 7:30 p.m. the night was very close and it was raining. The route taken was via DRANOUTRE & BAILLEUL. ARMENTIERES was reached at 1.a.m on the 14th the Bn; going into billets at the Blue Shed factory. HQ Coy in the RUE SADI CARNOT.	
ARMENTIERES	July '16		At 4.40 p.m the Bn marched off from the factory to relieve trenches in the vicinity of CHAPELLE d'ARMENTIERES. Trenches 67 & 68 were taken over from the Royal Scots & trench 69 from the Monmouths (T.F.) B Coy under Lt HARE took over 67; C Coy under Lt HESLOP took over 68. A Coy under Capt RITSON took over 69 & D Coy under Capt LIVESAY took over LILLE POST. The trenches went NW from the ARMENTIERES-LILLE road. HQ were established at a farm house a quarter mile N of Ra. There were two communication trenches leading to the front line LEITH WALK AVENUE & LOTHIAN AVENUE. The German trenches were from 250 to 300 yards away. The Bn strength the day was: officers 33 other ranks 863 made up 8 KDLI 17/17 other ranks 312, 6 KDLI off. 16 other ranks 551	

6 Durh. L.I.   Army Form C. 2118.

amalgamated with 8th DLI

WAR DIARY
~~INTELLIGENCE SUMMARY~~
(Erase heading not required.)

Instructions regarding War Diaries and Intelligence Summaries are contained in F.S. Regs., Part II. and the Staff Manual respectively. Title pages will be prepared in manuscript.

Vol 4

Place	Date	Hour	Summary of Events and Information	Remarks and references to Appendices
ARMENTIERES	July 18		Sunday In trenches 67 to 69. Situation normal, the work in hand is improvement of front line trenches. Provision of selected trenches, strengthening a string of strline & supporting trench at tactical points.	
	19th		Monday In trenches 67 to 69. Situation normal, the Cameron Highlanders are on our right	
	20th		Tuesday In trenches 67 to 69. No 1642 Gue TUCK.R.B. & 1485 Pte TAYLOR.H. both 6th D.L.I. wounded. Situation remained normal	
	21st		Wednesday In trenches 67 to 69. Situation remained normal, a good deal of gunning. 2 wt Lt ROBERTSON.G.C. 6th DLI Killed in Action.	
	22nd		Thursday In trenches 67 to 69. Situation normal. Good progress has been made with the work in hand. A good deal of shelling at Chapelle d'Armentieres. 2739 Pte FLETCHER.J. & 2758 Pte PINKNEY 8th DLI wounded	
	23rd		Friday In trenches 67 to 69. Situation normal.	
	24th		Saturday During the night the Bn was relieved by the 5th Loyal North Lancs. The situation was normal during the day. 2 coys remained, 1 in the subsidiary line & one at Rue Post. 2L 13 Br moved to billets at the HOSPICE ARMENTIERES with 16 14 Bn in the RUE NATIONALE. Strength of Bn this day was 6th DLI officers 39 other ranks 313. 8th DLI off 22 other ranks 556 off 17 other ranks	

1577 Wt.W10791/1773 500,000 1/15 D.D.&L. A.D.S.S./Form8/C.2118.

WAR DIARY

~~INTELLIGENCE SUMMARY~~

(Erase heading not required.)

Instructions regarding War Diaries and Intelligence
Summaries are contained in F. S. Regs., Part II.
and the Staff Manual respectively. Title pages
will be prepared in manuscript.

Vol 4

6th Durh. L.I.
amalgamated with
8th DLI

Place	Date	Hour	Summary of Events and Information	Remarks and references to Appendices
ARMENTIERES	July '15 25		Sunday In billets at the HOSPICE. Divine service was held. No 1611 Pte THOMAS 6th DLI. Killed in action.	
	26th		Monday In billets at the HOSPICE. General routine, drill & working parties. 2806 Pte HAYTON J. 6 DLI wounded. Lt GORDON R.A.M.C. left to join the 2nd Northumbrian Field Ambulance. Lt J.A. STENHOUSE RAMC who had been taken prisoner by the Germans on the 26th Aprl '15 who was subsequently released by them, rejoined for duty. A statement of his experiences is attached for record.	
	27th		Tuesday In billets at the HOSPICE. 2nd Lt J.C. MILLER, machine gun officer 6 DLI who was on duty in the trenches was killed in action. This officer was shot through the head, through a loophole, while engaged. Lt CASE, the R.E. officer in charge of work in our sector 1/15 line was killed by h snipers the same day. No 1710 Pte ROURKE was wounded when on a working party 6 DLI.	
	28th		Wednesday The two companies in the enemy line were relieved by the two companies from the HOSPICE. The companies changing over.	
	29th		Thursday The two companies O/K O/8 in the ordinary line went relieved by two companies O/K 9th DLI & the were 15n was collected at the Hospice	

1577 Wt.W16771/1773 500,000 1/15 D. D. & L. A.D.S.S./Forms/C. 2118.

WAR DIARY

~~INTELLIGENCE SUMMARY.~~

(Erase heading not required.)

6th Durh L.I. amalgamated with
8th DLI

Instructions regarding War Diaries and Intelligence Summaries are contained in F. S. Regs., Part II. and the Staff Manual respectively. Title pages will be prepared in manuscript.

Vol 4

Place	Date	Hour	Summary of Events and Information	Remarks and references to Appendices
ARMENTIERES	July 30		Friday. The Bn remained in Billets at the HOSPICE. General routine, drill, working parties.	
	31		Saturday. Bn remained at the HOSPICE. The strength of the Bn this day was :- officers 43 other ranks 864 (made up 6th KDLI off 20 other ranks 548, 8th DL.1 off 23 other ranks 316) ARMENTIERES has a few shells put into it daily, chiefly chapel. There are a large number of civilians left but some of them go nearly every day. Shops & armourers remain open & most requirements can be purchased but at war prices.	

1577   Wt.W10791/1773   500,000   1/15   D. D. & L.   A.D.S.S./Forms/C. 2118.

6th BATTN. THE DURHAM LIGHT INFANTRY.

A U G U S T

(11/31.8.15)

1 9 1 5

Army Form C. 2118.

WAR DIARY

or

INTELLIGENCE SUMMARY.

(Erase heading not required.)

Instructions regarding War Diaries and Intelligence Summaries are contained in F. S. Regs., Part II. and the Staff Manual respectively. Title pages will be prepared in manuscript.

Place	Date	Hour	Summary of Events and Information	Remarks and references to Appendices
			6th Battalion The Durham Light Infantry.	
			August 1915	
			(11/31.8.15).	
			(Note: The 6th and 8th D.L.I. were amalgamated	
			into a Composite Battalion on 8th June,	
			1915. Independent formations resumed	
			11th August, 1915).	
			During the period of amalgamation separate diaries	
			were kept by the two units.	

(1975) Wt W2358/P/60 60,000 12/7 D. D. & L. Sch. 53a. Forms/C2118/15

Army Form C. 2118

WAR DIARY
or
INTELLIGENCE SUMMARY 6th Durham L.I.
(Erase heading not required.)

Instructions regarding War Diaries and Intelligence
Summaries are contained in F. S. Regs., Part II.
and the Staff Manual respectively. Title Pages
will be prepared in manuscript.

Place	Date	Hour	Summary of Events and Information	Remarks and references to Appendices
Armentières	August 11	-	Major BORRETT D.S.O. The Kings Own Regiment, took over command of the Battalion, then in Billets at the Asylum.	
	12	-	Customary parade and considerable Routine Work.	
	13.	-	Captain J.W. JEFFREYS returned from the 2/5 Lancashire Fusiliers and resumed his duties as Adjutant. The Battalion proceeded to the trenches at night and relieved the 5th K.Battalion in trenches 4b six bays 45, 45, 445. SPX and SPZ. Capt. Heslops company held the front line, with the assistance of one platoon from "D" Company.	
Trenches.	14	-	Brigadier-General SHEA visited the Trenches. Much work in progress.	
	15	-	Major Borrett left to take over command of the 5th Shropshire Light Infantry. Captain Jeffreys took over command of the Battalion.	
	16	-	Much work done in all trenches, the main Y. Company was killed by a shell while cooking just behind the parados. 2 Lieut. P. H. B. LYON appointed Adjutant.	
	17.	-	Continued digging, making loopholes and putting up wire.	
	18	-	Comparative quiet, continued down the front. A Patrol went out at night endeavoured to reach the German wire which is about 200 yards away, but the Patrol was in charge but failed to reach the wire.	
	19	-	A quiet day at 8.30 p.m. the battalion was relieved by the 9th Batt. Northumberland Fusiliers, and proceeded into Billets at PONT DE NIEPPE Head quarters were established in a large house standing in its own grounds.	

WAR DIARY
or
INTELLIGENCE SUMMARY
(Erase heading not required.)

Instructions regarding War Diaries and Intelligence Summaries are contained in F. S. Regs., Part II. and the Staff Manual respectively. Title Pages will be prepared in manuscript.

Place	Date	Hour	Summary of Events and Information	Remarks and references to Appendices
PONT DE NIEPPE	20	—	Billets found to be rather crowded. Companies at disposal of their commanders.	
	21	—	Work of re-organising Battalion commenced. Formidable number of N.C.O's to be filled. Physical Drill, Commanding Officers parades etc.	
	22.	—	Divine Service at Pont De Nieppe	
	23	—	Second Lieut C.L. Elvey and J.P. Elliott reported from the 16th Batt. Durham Light Infantry, and reinforcements draft of 95 N.C.O's and men arrived from ...	
	24	—	Brigadier General inspected the billets.	
	25	—	Second Lieuts L.H.B. Gaford, O. Hay, H. Blackman, H. McKellar, P.S. Mann and C.E. Galdwin joined the Battalion from the 16th Durham and the complement of officers became something like complete again	
	25	—	Billets taken up in Rectory lane where the Battalion remained for a few days in reserve, finding working parties at night.	
	27	—	Major G.B. Hawdon went to Hospital. Battalion continued usual routine out of the trenches.	
	29.	—	Lieut W.F.E. Badcock returned from Hospital. The effective strength of the unit at this date was 25 officers and 962 other ranks.	
	30.	—	65 men killed a little and Hue on four of the R.E's billeted here were wounded	
Trenches	31	—	Proceeded to trenches 68, 69 and 70 and relieved the 5th Royal North Lancashire	

1875 Wt. W593/826 1,000,000 4/15 J.B.C. & A. A.D.S.S./Forms/C. 2118.

Army Form C. 2118.

WAR DIARY
or
INTELLIGENCE SUMMARY.

(Erase heading not required.)

Instructions regarding War Diaries and Intelligence
Summaries are contained in F. S. Regs., Part II.
and the Staff Manual respectively. Title pages
will be prepared in manuscript.

Place	Date	Hour	Summary of Events and Information	Remarks and references to Appendices

Army Form C. 2118

WAR DIARY
or
INTELLIGENCE SUMMARY

(Erase heading not required.)

Instructions regarding War Diaries and Intelligence
Summaries are contained in F. S. Regs., Part II.
and the Staff Manual respectively. Title Pages
will be prepared in manuscript.

Place	Date	Hour	Summary of Events and Information	Remarks and references to Appendices
Jancken	21		Regiment Headquarters being at HAYSTACK FARM. The Soft was reported that there was a likelihood of the French 70 - the "mushroom" being blown up by the Germans. Accordingly Major Patter's company of the 5th Lancers remained in here for that night while the line. re(?) lieved early next morning by "B" Company under Lieut. Badcock. Left Garden held 68 Lieut N..... 69 and Capt Nelltop ...... while occidiary line .... The whole occidiary line	

(19175) Wt W2383/P360 600,000 12/7 D. D. & L. Sch 52a. Forms/C2118/12

6th BATTN. THE DURHAM LIGHT INFANTRY.

S E P T E M B E R

1 9 1 5

Attached:

Messages.

Instructions regarding War Diaries and Intelligence
Summaries are contained in F. S. Regs, Part II.
and the Staff Manual respectively. Title pages
will be prepared in manuscript.

Place	Date	Hour	Summary of Events and Information	Remarks and references to Appendices
	Sept 2.		Scare about the firing still rampant. Trenches very bad during the wet weather, however, made his usual inspection. Lt Dent wounded.	
	4.		Brigade scheme to test communications whilst in the Trenches. No mistakes were made by the Battalion messengers or wireless operators. Lieut Badcock's company dealt with drawn partly from the mushroom leaving only three groups of sentries in the right entry and left of the French. These together with patrols out all night were considered sufficient to of guard this part of the line.	
	5.		1/R Coy. R.E. (Mining boy took over the mine from the newly-formed 1/8 W.Rig Brigade eliefing company c/buck. better weather	
	6.		The Battalion was relieved by the 5 Border Regiment and the K. Northumberland Fusiliers and marched down to billets in the Noyce Civil and the Grand College. Headquarters were established at 35 Rue National. Goodbillets Lt Colt Gen d Lieut Genl Au Herbert Plumer A.O.C. inspected the Battalion on parade and expressed himself highly pleased with its appearance. Brigadier General Shea also sent congratulatory message as follows — "I congratulate you upon the appearance of your	

1875. Wt. W593/826 1,000,000 4/15 J.B.C. & A. A.D.S.S./Forms/C.2118.

(39073) Wt. W235/P560 600,000 12/7 D.D. & L. Sch 51a. Forms/C.2118/15

Army Form C. 2118

WAR DIARY

or

INTELLIGENCE SUMMARY

(Erase heading not required.)

Instructions regarding War Diaries and Intelligence Summaries are contained in F. S. Regs., Part II. and the Staff Manual respectively. Title Pages will be prepared in manuscript.

Place	Date	Hour	Summary of Events and Information	Remarks and references to Appendices
Armentières	9.	-	Battalion today. Sir Herbert Plumer was very pleased. Kindly let all ranks know how pleased I am with the trouble they took to turn out well". In billets.	
	10.	-	Close order parades and cleaning up about 50 shells were put into the town during the afternoon but though they were incendiary, only two fires were caused, and these were soon extinguished. Very fine weather and comparatively quiet down the front. Spasmodic bombardment of Blarel at Chincteries. Our own working parties engaged with the R.E's on the Subsidiary Line was hit by a shell and fourteen men were wounded. Six of them were sever and one Private E. Brown, died on the Casualty Clearing Station.	
	11.	1	In billets, close order drill, company inspections &c.	
	12.	1	Church parade in the grounds of the Hospice being the R Battalion also attending, at night two platoons of Z company went up to garrison S.R.Y. and SP2 under the command of Lieut Hodra.	
	13.	-	One man wounded in the wrist by a machine gun bullet while on sentry go at 3 a.m. Very little of note transpired.	
	14.	-	A letter was received from Brigade asking for a fresh report of gallant action around Ypres 11th April and 1st May.	
	15.	-	The following names were sent in, along with a short statement of the credit obtained, with a view to being recommended:- Capt Welsh, Lieut Gee, Lieut R.V. Hart, Lieut R. of L. Blenkinsopp, and the following N.C.O's and men, Private Robinson, Pte Osborne, Cpl Hardy, G.A. & S.M. Bousfield	

1875 Wt. W593/826 1,000,000 4/15 J.B.C. & A. A.D.S.S./Forms/C.2118.

Army Form C. 2118

WAR DIARY
or
INTELLIGENCE SUMMARY

(Erase heading not required.)

Instructions regarding War Diaries and Intelligence Summaries are contained in F. S. Regs., Part II. and the Staff Manual respectively. Title Pages will be prepared in manuscript.

Place	Date	Hour	Summary of Events and Information	Remarks and references to Appendices
Chuilnelles	16.	-	Cpl. Hinton Sgt. Belbalpass. Sgt. Wall.	
	17.	-	Nothing of importance. For the list of names in of Officers, N.C.O's and men who have arrived goodservice since arrival in France. He listincluded Capt. Hislop, Lt. Angus, Lt. Lyon, Lt. Badcock, Sergt. Major Parry, C.S.M. McNair, Sergt. Curley, Ple. Taylor, Lt. Sgt. Bland, Sgt. & Q'Sgt. Johnson, B.Q.M.S. Walton, B.Q.M.S. Bohniser.	
	18.	-	The Battalion took over French 44 and six bays of French 43 trench 44.5, 3 bays of French 45 and 45 from the 8th Durham light Infantry. The leading platoon left their billets at 4 p.m. and the relief completed 9 p.m. fine, dry weather and a quiet night.	
	19.	-	The Battalion was disributed as follows — French 44 and six bays of French 43 — one company, and one platoon of Z. Coy. 155 rifles. trenches 44.5, 45.5 and 45.5 — X company and one platoon of Z. Company, 152 rifles. S. P. Y. and S. P. Z — two platoons of Z Company 80 rifles, Subsidiary Line, "O." Coy. 156 rifles.	
	20.	-	Arrangements having been carefully made, the Divisional artillery bombarded the enemy trench opposite French 44 and especially the Black Redoubt. The firing was timed to commence at 4 p.m. According to the front trench 44 and one bay of French 45 were vacated for a shall shelter remove, our sentries being left in craters.	

WAR DIARY
or
INTELLIGENCE SUMMARY

(Erase heading not required.)

Instructions regarding War Diaries and Intelligence Summaries are contained in F.S. Regs., Part II. and the Staff Manual respectively. Title Pages will be prepared in manuscript.

Place	Date	Hour	Summary of Events and Information	Remarks and references to Appendices
Trenches	20		Troops in dug-shelters in front line. Cyfte free minutes the enemy replied by bombarding heavily and dropping several of their shells. A Stokey box burying the Sentry. Private Readshaw. He was taken out suffering severely from shock and with a broken leg. He is now of course still went pretty Private Harwood while leads standing in a shell a latter trench. Casualties are one killed - one man severely wounded.	
	21		Last night a party from W. Company made up the damaged parapet on the right of trench 45 et. Communication trench was commenced from Battalion Headquarters to the new drawing station being theeg in "W" Company. Private Redshaw died at Casualty Clearing Station.	
	22		A fairly quiet day in trenches. Very fine weather, wind Easterly which had not yet brought any gas.	
	23.		Relieved one day early by the 5th K.N.F under Lieut Col. Sliver, Capt. Yates. Owing to moonlight the Infantry is extremely late. The 151st Brigade was relieved one day earlier by the 149th Brigade on account of a proposed general attack on the 25th. He whole show was brought up which in front of the front in before that the wind may blow Smoke over. Relief completed at the station near Chamaer Dressing station.	
	24.		Day spent cleaning up billets.	

WAR DIARY
or
INTELLIGENCE SUMMARY
(Erase heading not required)

6th Durham L.I.

Instructions regarding War Diaries and Intelligence Summaries are contained in F. S. Regs., Part II. and the Staff Manual respectively. Title Pages will be prepared in manuscript.

Place	Date	Hour	Summary of Events and Information	Remarks and references to Appendices
Armentières	Sep 25	—	Battalion in billets near the Station in Armentières. Formed a reserve for the VI Corps. O'Roung fire was commenced by our divisional artillery at 4.30 am. At 5.30 am fires were lighted of damp straw all along our front line trenches. Bombs were thrown and an effort made to cause the Germans to keep reserves behind this part of the line. Heavy firing heard to the north and south. has arrived of successful attacks made by the V Corps north of YPRES, and by the First Army to the south of LA BASSEE.	
Jraulle	26	—	the Battalion relieved the 11th Batt. Middlesex Regiment in trenches 81, 82, and 83, and supports Headquarters were established in a house at HOUPLINES. the Battalion relieved former part of 12th Division which is being withdrawn from the front of the line.	
	27	—	In trenches taken over from Middlesex Regiment. Much work to be done in cleaning up and improving our fighting positions in the front line.	
	28	—	In trenches 81, 82, 83 east of HOUPLINES.	
	29		Brigadier-General Shea visited the trenches, and expressed himself pleased with the work done there considering of a very considerable success by the X French Army on an immediate front by other	

1875 Wt. W593/826 1,000,000 4/15 J.B.C.&A. A.D.S.S./Forms/C.2118.

WAR DIARY
or
INTELLIGENCE SUMMARY

(Erase heading not required.)

Instructions regarding War Diaries and Intelligence Summaries are contained in F. S. Regs., Part II. and the Staff Manual respectively. Title Pages will be prepared in manuscript.

6

Place	Date	Hour	Summary of Events and Information
TISSAGE	Sept 30	–	Three companies of the Battalion relieved by the 8th Batt D.L.I. and proceeded into billets at the TISSAGE in HOUPLINES. "Y" Company under Capt Wardrop remained in trenches 81 and 82 outpost. the Battalion was continual only to have two minor casualties during this turn at the trenches.

M E S S A G E S .

WAR DIARY
or
INTELLIGENCE SUMMARY

(Erase heading not required.)

6th Durham L.I.

Place	Date	Hour	Summary of Events and Information	Remarks and references to Appendices
	Sept 25	10-14 am	The following message regarding the offensive commenced in the early hours of 25th September were received by the 6th Durham Light Infantry. "Report from 1st Army timed 6.45 AM begins ... gas and smoke appeared to have been effective in front of first and Indian Corps ... 5th Brigade in front of GIVENCHY have gained advanced German trenches apparently without much opposition ... meant German Division ... captured German front line & report parties of enemy surrendering ... 8th Division have captured second line German trenches in their front are ... Ends. — 151 Bde 10.14 am"	
		11 am	Wires 8 am ... 47th, 15th, 1st and 7th Divisions' attacks all crossed front line of German trenches, but troops are obscured from view by smoke ... Gas is hanging in front of 15th Division enemy advance to be close ... 9th Division have reached German second line on right and front line on left. — 151 Bde 11 am	
		11.20 am	2nd Corps wires 10 am ... 1st and 4th Gordons in German trenches in France at I.18.c.8.4. 4th Gordons have captured third line trenches and are consolidating. Right of 4th Gordons in touch with Royal Scots in German front line. J.13 c.5.5 ... Our route on Hill 60 road to Rendering enemy observation ...	

WAR DIARY

INTELLIGENCE SUMMARY

(Erase heading not required.)

Instructions regarding War Diaries and Intelligence Summaries are contained in F.S. Regs., Part II. and the Staff Manual respectively. Title Pages will be prepared in manuscript.

Place	Date	Hour	Summary of Events and Information	Remarks and references to Appendices
	Sept. 25.	(1)	1st Army wire 8.45 a.m. begins: all reserves north of BETHUNE – LA BASSEE road have either reached our front line, trenches or moving. None are below LA BASSEE road gained on troops are checked on 1st Bns checked temporarily by gas. 7th and 9th progressing on two brigades 15th disappeared in smoke. Germans north of Loos are following places reported overlaid by our troops. Enclosure north of LOOS CEMETARY, west of LOOS FOSSE No. 8. – 1st Bde 11.30 p.m.	
	25	2-4.0pm	V Corps wire 10.55 begins 42nd Brigade 8.25 report 9 R.B. checked in II.II B. Germans attacking. Had troops ordered to counter-attack on H. II B. German second line from I.12.7.2 to N.W. corner of BELLEWARDE LAKE on Royal Scots hold German second line trench from I.13 & 7.9 & I.19 & 9.9 and are in touch with Battalion on right, on total prisoners reported by Third Division – 2 officers, 140 men are 1st Army wire begun 10 am Loos and PUITS – 14 B 13 on Roads. Guns infantry advancing on HULLOCK and has captured CITE ST ELIE and reserve brigade of 9th Division ordered on HAISNES are 2nd Division held up near LES BRIQUE on London.	
		3.20	Corps report capture of MOULIN DU PIETRE and 142 prisoners – 1st Bde – 2.40 pm. Reported that 1st Army has captured LOOS HILL 70 and HULLOCK RIDGE & prisoners the enemy. 1st Army reports 11.15 am – 4/1st Division held front of 1st ETASSIER and have taken two guns are 15th Division on a HILL 70 and have retaken Road are brigade ordered to attack on ST. AUGUSTE. Right brigade	

Army Form C. 2118.

WAR DIARY
~~or~~

INTELLIGENCE SUMMARY.

(Erase heading not required.)

Instructions regarding War Diaries and Intelligence
Summaries are contained in F. S. Regs., Part II.
and the Staff Manual respectively. Title pages
will be prepared in manuscript.

Place	Date	Hour	Summary of Events and Information	Remarks and references to Appendices

of 1st Division was held up in front of German 1st line left has
prepared well ... as HULLOCK has been taken by us enemy are
retiring rapidly from HULLOCK and 1st Division pushing on in pursuit as
2nd Division north of canal has been brought back and has suffered
heavily ... as Indian Corps Roll Ross east of MOULIN DU PIETRE M30a. and e.
... brigade has been ordered to HAUTE POMMEREAU as 3rd Cavalry Division
has its head at VAUDRICOURT and has been ordered to continue its march to
NOYELLES LES VERMELLES as France G.H.Q. reports as follows as everything
continues to go well in CHAMPAGNE as Ar in front the cavalry have crossed
the German line . — 151 Bde 3.40 —

4/m The following reports received as 8th Division have been strongly counter
attacked and now only Roll CORNER FORT with Rifle Brigade, rest of old brigade
driven back to original position, as right battalion of 20th Division have
also been driven back to their original position as V Corps report that
German counter attacks have retaken all trenches except main front line
from J19 a c & L J13 c.s.s. We also still held croix at N.E. corner of
RAILWAY WOOD have consolidated those positions, as G.H.Q. report following
information from France officer as those of MINAUCOURT
the French have reached MAISON DE CHAMPAGNE main redoubt line

1577 Wt.W10791/1773 50,000 1/15 D. D. & L.   A.D.S.S./Forms/C. 2118.

Instructions regarding War Diaries and Intelligence
Summaries are contained in F. S. Regs., Part II.
and the Staff Manual respectively. Title pages
will be prepared in manuscript.

WAR DIARY
or
INTELLIGENCE SUMMARY.

(Erase heading not required.)

Place	Date	Hour	Summary of Events and Information	Remarks and references to Appendices
	25		Air squadrons have had but through the line as the advance has been carried half way between PERTHES and TAHURE and at SOUAIN the advance is about 1500 yards and at SOUAIN a half kilometre. X French Army reports that first line of enemy has recoiled or retreated on whole front as 21st Corps is progressing east of SOUCHEZ on the further news has reached from 1st Army — 151 Bde 1f	
	26	12.15p	Second Corps report begins as As far as we know at present the French made a good advance yesterday in CHAMPAGNE along a front of 12 miles in some cases pushing forward three or more miles, capturing 7,000 prisoners. The First Army also advanced north of LENS about two miles on their right. Their line last night running through HILL 70 to the west of HULLOCK and thence to an original line at CUINCHY, capturing 1,500 prisoners, 5 guns, and 4 machine guns — 240 prisoners were also captured yesterday on the heads of the British line are — 151 Bde 12.15f	
	27	10.25 am	G.H.Q. wires as follows Reports as the French attack in CHAMPAGNE is making good progress on the total number of prisoners taken now n. 14,000 and so guns on the French X Army have taken LES TILLEULS, which is astride the ARRAS-LENS road, as well as SOUCHEZ — and then 151 Bde 10.25f	
		10.6 am	Following from GHQ. 10-10 Reports as Liaison Officer with French G.H.Q. reports.	

1577 Wt.W10791/1773 500,000 1/15 D. D. & L. A.D.S.S./Forms/C. 2118.

Army Form C. 2118

WAR DIARY
or
INTELLIGENCE SUMMARY
(Erase heading not required.)

Instructions regarding War Diaries and Intelligence Summaries are contained in F. S. Regs., Part II. and the Staff Manual respectively. Title Pages will be prepared in manuscript.

Place	Date	Hour	Summary of Events and Information	Remarks and references to Appendices
	Sep. 27	10.15	as follows :- The French attack yesterday in CHAMPAGNE captured remarkable of German first & second line trenches on a front of 21 kilometres. That this morning prevailed an attack on the 2nd line before 2 p.m. The attack started at that hour. Result not yet known. Number of French prisoners captured yesterday in CHAMPAGNE are 18,000 prisoners & 31 guns. — 15th Febe 10.2 a.m.	
		11.20	Following from G.H.Q. timed 9.25 begins. There has been severe fighting today on the ground won by us yesterday, the enemy making determined counter-attacks east and north east of LOOS. The result of this fighting is that except that north of LOOS we hold all the ground gained yesterday, including the whole of Loos. This evening we retook the whole of the ground north-east of HULLOCH while we won a lot yesterday. We have in an effort drawn in reserves covering the French. An effort to make further progress. The number of prisoners collected after yesterday's fighting now amounts to 2,600. This field guns have been taken. A considerable number of machine guns. Our aeroplanes today bombarded and derailed a train near LOFFEKE, east of DOUAI, and another which was full of troops at ROSUT near STAMAND. VALENCIENNES station was blown up. — 15th Febe 10-20.	
	28	1-1.29 pm	Situation report from G.H.Q. begins. Thirty second corps of 10th French Army made progress during the night. French H.Q. report a further advance.	

1875 Wt. W593/826 1,000,000 4/15 J.B.C. & A. A.D.S.S./Forms/C. 2118.

Instructions regarding War Diaries and Intelligence
Summaries are contained in F. S. Regs., Part II.
and the Staff Manual respectively. Title pages
will be prepared in manuscript.

WAR DIARY

INTELLIGENCE SUMMARY.

(Erase heading not required.)

Place	Date	Hour	Summary of Events and Information	Remarks and references to Appendices
	37	a.m.	in CHAMPAGNE, where a still larger number of prisoners have been taken, but definite numbers are not available. the messages add — 151 P.W. 1-29p.	
			Second Army anno [?] total number of guns captured by French in CHAMPAGNE was amounts to 46 with our Second army anno — add 11-58 begins — following received from G.H.Q. an hour west of HULLOCH have repulsed a number of counter attacks over East of LOOS we are preparing our own reportive new arms of to 53 officers, 2,000 as [?] it was 81 machine guns are — 151 P.W. 1-7 p	
			1st Army have reported presence of 17th Bavarian Regiment note of LA BASSEE as this may herald extended to 3rd Bavarian Regiment from WYTSCHAETE sector as it is most important that you should infer that there is little or no movement of enemy in your front.	
	29	1.25	Approximate situation of 10 French army morning of 29th 10 trench army have taken Germans second line on a front of twelve hundred yards. line now runs from West of ANGRES due North and South to about midway between SOUCHEZ and GIVENCHY hence in a South Easterly direction to about 500 yards East of NEVILLE. This line gives the French a footing on the highest point of the ridge west of VIMY. I.G.H.Q. wired 12-55 p.m. begins. Mass French divisions have broken through last German line in CHAMPAGNE	
	30.	9-15 P.M.	Second Army 29th begins. First Army reports. Enemy has made several attacks in the neighbourhood of HOSSE No.8. All these have been	

1577 Wt.W10791/1773 500,000 1/15 D.D.&L. A.D.S.S./Forms/C. 2118

Army Form C. 2118.

Instructions regarding War Diaries and Intelligence
Summaries are contained in F. S. Regs., Part II.
and the Staff Manual respectively. Title pages
will be prepared in manuscript.

WAR DIARY
or
INTELLIGENCE SUMMARY.

(Erase heading not required.)

Place	Date	Hour	Summary of Events and Information	Remarks and references to Appendices
	30.	11.45 P.M.	repulsed and the latest reports state that severe fighting is going on in the neighbourhood of HOHENZOLLERN and FOSSE No. 8. Heavy shelling on the rest of first and fourth corp. nothing to report north of this.	

Second army wire 11.45 P.M. 29th begins: French have made further progress in Champagne. In the Ka main position 1000 prisoners were taken belonging to twenty one battalions of 16 different regiments. Total captured by French to date reckoned at one hundred guns and twenty five thousand prisoners. There is as yet no further news of the three divisions broke through the second line ends

Special Order of the Day By Field-Marshal Sir John French K.6.M.G., Commander-in Chief, British Army, in the field.

We have now reached a definite stage in the great battle which commenced on the 25 inst.

One of Allies in the south have pierced the enemy's last line of entrenchments and effected large captures of prisoners and guns.

The X. French Army on our immediate right has been heavily opposed but has brilliantly succeeded in securing the important position known as the VIMY RIDGE.

The operations of the British forces have been most successful and have had great and important results.

On the morning of the 25 instant the I. and IV. corps attacked and carried the enemy's first and most powerful line of entrenchments extending from our extreme right flank at GRENAY to a point North of the HOHENZOLLERN REDOUBT - a distance of 6,500 yards.

WAR DIARY
or
INTELLIGENCE SUMMARY.
(Erase heading not required.)

Instructions regarding War Diaries and Intelligence Summaries are contained in F. S. Regs., Part II. and the Staff Manual respectively. Title pages will be prepared in manuscript.

Place	Date	Hour	Summary of Events and Information	Remarks and references to Appendices
	30.		This position was exceptionally strong consisting of a double line which included some large redoubts and a network of trenches and bomb proof shelters. Dug-outs were constructed at intervals all along the line, some of them being large enough to shelter below the ground.	

This position was exceptionally strong consisting of a double line which included some large redoubts and a network of trenches and bomb proof shelters. Dug-outs were constructed at intervals all along the line, some of them being large enough to shelter below the ground.

The XI. Corps in general reserve and the 3rd cavalry Division were subsequently thrown into the fight, and finally the 28th Division.

After the exceedingly attendant upon every great fight, the enemy's second line was were taken, he commanding position known as Hill 69 in advance of Loos, was finally captured and a strong line was established and consolidated, inclose proximity to the German third and last line.

The main operations south of the La Bassée Canal were much facilitated and assisted by the subsidiary attacks delivered by the III. and Indian Corps and the troops of the N. Army.

Great help was also rendered by the operations of the V. Corps East of YPRES during which some important captures were made.

We are also much indebted to Vice Admiral Bacon and our naval comrades for the valuable co-operation of the Fleet.

Our captures have amounted to over 3000 prisoners and some 25 guns, besides many machine guns and a quantity of war material.

The enemy has suffered heavy losses, particularly in the many counter attacks by which he has vainly endeavoured to win back the captured positions but which have been gallantly repulsed by our troops.

Army Form C. 2118.

WAR DIARY
or
INTELLIGENCE SUMMARY.

(Erase heading not required.)

Instructions regarding War Diaries and Intelligence
Summaries are contained in F. S. Regs., Part II.
and the Staff Manual respectively. Title pages
will be prepared in manuscript.

Place	Date	Hour	Summary of Events and Information	Remarks and references to Appendices

I desire to express to the Army under my command my deep appreciation of the splendid work they have accomplished, and my heartfelt thanks for the brilliant leadership displayed by General Sir Douglas Haig and the Corps and Divisional Commanders who acted under his orders in the main attack,

In the same spirit of admiration and gratitude I wish particularly to comment upon the magnificent spirit & indomitable courage and dogged tenacity displayed by the troops.

Old Army, New Army and Territorials have vied with one another in the heroic conduct displayed throughout the battle by officers, non-commissioned officers and men,

I feel the utmost confidence and assurance that the same glorious spirit which has been so marked a feature throughout the first phase of this great battle will continue until our efforts are crowned by final and complete victory.

Special Orders of the day by the Field - Marshal commanding-in-Chief has received the following message from His Majesty the King:-
Field Marshal Sir John French G.C.B. &c., &c. Commander-in-Chief British Expeditionary Force. I heartily congratulate you and all ranks of my Army under your command upon which the success which has attended their gallant effort since the commencement of the combined attack, I recognize that his strenuous and determined fighting is but the

1577 Wt. W 10791/1773 500,000 1/15 D. D. & L. A.D.S.S./Forms/C. 2118.

WAR DIARY

INTELLIGENCE SUMMARY.

(Erase heading not required.)

Instructions regarding War Diaries and Intelligence Summaries are contained in F. S. Regs., Part II. and the Staff Manual respectively. Title pages will be prepared in manuscript.

Place	Date	Hour	Summary of Events and Information	Remarks references to Appendices
	Sep. 30		prelude to greater deeds and further victories.	
			Trust the sick and wounded are doing well.	
			The following reply has been sent	
			To. HIS MAJESTY THE KING.	
			Buckingham Palace.	
			Yourself Majestys forces in France are deeply grateful for your Majesty's most gracious message. AAA, There is no sacrifice the troops are not prepared to make to uphold the honour and traditions of your Majesty's Army and to secure final and complete victory. J.D.P. French Field Marshal	

6th BATTN. THE DURHAM LIGHT INFANTRY.

O C T O B E R

1 9 1 5

Attached:

Messages.

WAR DIARY

or

INTELLIGENCE SUMMARY. 6/D.L.I.

(Erase heading not required.)

Instructions regarding War Diaries and Intelligence Summaries are contained in F. S. Regs., Part II. and the Staff Manual respectively. Title pages will be prepared in manuscript.

October 1915

Date	Hour	Summary of Events and Information	Remarks and references to Appendices
Oct 1		Much cleaning, fitting up carried out in the new billets at TISSAGE. A special order of the day by Field-Marshal Sir John French (quoted in the Intelligence Summary) reached the Battalion.	
2		In private soldiers reported been arrived from the Base. All company commanders marched into Armentieres for further instruction in handling the strength of the Battalion on this date, including all details was:– Officers 28, Other Ranks 798.	
3		In billets in the TISSAGE, HOUPLINES.	
4		Instructions received that every man in the Battalion should be taught to throw bombs and to fire them, the many different patterns now in use in the Army render this a very difficult matter. About 7 p.m. some men of the Battalion brought bottles of brandy, eau de vie, absinthe etc, which they had found in a large cellar in HOUPLINES VILLAGE, into billets. Some stores of	

1875 Wt. W593/826 1,000,000 4/15 J.B.C. & A. A.D.S.S./Forms/C. 2118.

(A9175) Wt. W2355/P360 620,003 12/7 D. D. & L. Sch 52n. Forms/C2118/15

WAR DIARY
or
INTELLIGENCE SUMMARY.

(Erase heading not required.)

Instructions regarding War Diaries and Intelligence
Summaries are contained in F. S. Regs., Part II.
and the Staff Manual respectively. Title pages
will be prepared in manuscript.

Place	Date	Hour	Summary of Events and Information	Remarks and references to Appendices
	5 Oct.		of spirit had not been handed over to us by the 12th Division. On relief, there was a certain amount of trouble, which was soon checked by the Battalion & Company Sergeant-Majors. The Battalion relieved the 8th Battalion R.I. in trenches 81, 82, and 83.	
	6	-	Brigadier-General Segg explained that the Brigade was taking over trench 80. The 8th Battalion was to take trench 80 and relieve itself. The 6th, 7th, and 9th Battalions were to hold trenches 81 to 89 and relieve one another. The Loyal North Lancashire Regiment to hold trenches 88, 89, and relieve itself. Trenches 81, 82, and 83.	
	7	-	Private Winterson "Z" Company fell over unexpectedly the fire trench.	
	8	-	C patrol consisting of Corporal Hoyle, & Private Brown and Fairhurst, all of "W" Company went out at midnight. Corporal Pyburn	
	9	-	called at the listening post of 82 trench, and on to find the left listening post of 82 trench, but have not been seen since.	

WAR DIARY

or

INTELLIGENCE SUMMARY.

(Erase heading not required.)

Instructions regarding War Diaries and Intelligence Summaries are contained in F. S. Regs., Part II. and the Staff Manual respectively. Title pages will be prepared in manuscript.

Place	Date	Hour	Summary of Events and Information	Remarks and references to Appendices
81-82	9 Oct (Sta)		It is likely that they walled until the German trenches up the lines in, believing they were returning to their own trench.	
	10 (Sunday)		One company of the 15th D.L.I., which had been relieving to the 31st Division and which had been cut up at Loos on 26th September was attached to the Battalion for instruction in trench warfare. This company is only about 100 strong, is commanded by first Sergeant Francis, who is the only officer with the company.	
	11 =		Brigadier-General Seeco informed Co's that another attack was prepared by the first Army. When it took place the Barrels would make a demonstration by smoke bombs and artillery fire. Lieut.-General Sir Charles Fergusson in command of the II Corps. It were the Battalion forms a part, invited to the trenches.	
	12	—	Much repair work done in the trenches, the parapet being rebuilt and revetted in many places.	
	13	—	At 12.30 Battalion Headquarters moved to the Battle Port Station, while the 8th Battalion...	

1577 Wt.W10791/1773 500,000 1/15 D. D. & L. A.D.S.S./Forms/C. 2118.

WAR DIARY

or

INTELLIGENCE SUMMARY.

(Erase heading not required.)

Place	Date	Hour	Summary of Events and Information	Remarks and references to Appendices
	Oct. 14th Thursday		At 2 p.m. all the Divisional guns opened fire on German wire and trenches until 2.30 p.m. This keen raised and smoke shells were thrown over the parapet by British troops. the wind was northwards. The smoke was generally blown over the German trenches. Very few of it came back & as on previous shots up rockets repeatedly. "Enemy shirking" & very many rifle shots were fired over our trenches but little damage was done & there were no casualties. Fire from the parapet was kept up during the night & about midnight the enemy slightly wounded four there on fatigue duty at 61 Trench one man. A very misty morning. At 7.30 a.m. a patrol was sent out by O.C. Z Company from 63 Trench to examine the German wire and ascertain what damage had been done yesterday. The patrol consisted of 2nd Lieut. McMillan, Sergt. Ewbank & Private Waterman. He two first named personnel were now & German wire then on attempting to approach an new loophole plate only a few yards from the German parapet	

Instructions regarding War Diaries and Intelligence
Summaries are contained in F. S. Regs., Part II.
and the Staff Manual respectively. Title pages
will be prepared in manuscript.

Place	Date	Hour	Summary of Events and Information	Remarks and references to Appendices
	Oct. 15	—	were fired on. Sergt. Tunbridge was killed instantaneously. 2nd Lieut. Thelfallon made a very plucky escape to find Private Waterman returned. Sergt. Tunbridge's body was left inside the German wire.	
	16	—	The Battalion were relieved by the 7th D.L.I. and returned to billets in the Huebrecourt Ville and the College des Garçons, in Armentières. Relief complete at 7.15 p.m.	
	17	—	In billets in Armentières	
	18	—	Do	
	19	—	Do	
	20	—	Took over trenches 84, 85, 86, and 87 from the 9th D.L.I.; Headquarters being established in Château de la Rose, in Houplines.	
	21	—	In trenches 84, 85, 86, and 87	
			Do.	

1577 Wt. W10791/773 50,000 1/15 D.D. & L.   A.D.S.S./Forms/C. 2118.

WAR DIARY
or
INTELLIGENCE SUMMARY.

(Erase heading not required.)

Instructions regarding War Diaries and Intelligence Summaries are contained in F. S. Regs., Part II. and the Staff Manual respectively. Title pages will be prepared in manuscript.

Place	Date	Hour	Summary of Events and Information	Remarks and references to Appendices
Trenches	Oct 22	—	In Trenches 84, 85, 86 and 87	
	23	،	Do-	
	24	،	Do-	
	25	،	Do-	
	26	—	Relieved by the 9th D.L.I. Relief not complete until 9.40pm. Returned to billets in Armentières.	
	27	5.30am	Wd. The Brigade renewed a detachment of the Division at BAILLEUL. Sergt-Major Ferry Lieut. Nahau, Lieut. Brock and 51 men of the Battalion were present. Billets in Armentières.	
	28	،	Remained in billets.	
	29	،	To NIEPPE. The ground there is very wet and cut up, and the men are in tents.	
	30	—	The Battalion took over trenches 81, 82, and 83 from the 9th Battalion which is temporarily commanded by Major E.R. Clayton, the Brigade-Major of the 151st Brigade taking the Battalion forward as part.	

WAR DIARY

or

INTELLIGENCE SUMMARY.

(*Erase heading not required.*)

Instructions regarding War Diaries and Intelligence Summaries are contained in F. S. Regs., Part II. and the Staff Manual respectively. Title pages will be prepared in manuscript.

Place	Date	Hour	Summary of Events and Information	Remarks and references to Appendices
Trenches	Oct 3		to Trenches 81, 82, and 83. Six Platoons of the 6th Somerset Light Infantry attached to the Battalion for instruction. Major Howard commanding and his Headquarters attached to Battalion Headquarters. Four platoons of the C. Bn. under Lieut. Angier, were withdrawn from the trenches, and billetted in HOUPLINES.	

1577 Wt.W107791/1773 500,000 1/15 D. D. & L. A.D.S.S./Forms/C. 2118.

M E S S A G E S .

Oct 6	6.40pm	British troops with French G.H.Q. wires on French attack in Champagne progressing well but it is too early to give any details except that TAHURE has been captured on 15' Bde.
	8—	The following message has been received from G.H.Q. — enemy attacked in strength on the 1st Army front from east of LOOS to HOHENZOLLERN REDOUBT after a heavy bombardment on all attacks reported to have been made in force and all were repulsed at once except that the Germans captured a trench in the HOHENZOLLERN Redoubt which was held by two companies on the ...
	9.30pm	This afternoon the ... G.H.Q. — "This afternoon the east of LOOS ... latest report timed 9.30pm states that the Coldstream have companies driven the Germans out of ...

1577 (Wt.W.10791/1773 50,000 1/15 D. D. & L.   A.D.S.S./Forms/C. 2118.

WAR DIARY
or
INTELLIGENCE SUMMARY.

(Erase heading not required.)

Instructions regarding War Diaries and Intelligence
Summaries are contained in F. S. Regs., Part II.
and the Staff Manual respectively. Title pages
will be prepared in manuscript.

Place	Date	Hour	Summary of Events and Information	Remarks and references to Appendices
	Sept	1.30 p.m.	No front mentioned above and that all original trenches have been re-captured on Fricourt. 12th Division NW of HULLOCH have made a little ground from their original position.	
	13	5 p.m.	Further message from G.H.Q. — Repulse is confirmed of all German attacks on First Army front yesterday and during the night enemy made no attack except on line was subjected to artillery fire on the left at 12 noon. 12th Division who had made ground until counter attack were unable to maintain recaptured ground gained own line.	
	13	5 p.m.	First Army operations killed 5 p.m. on First Division gained enemy's trenches on right of S.W. of HULLOCH and are consolidating on Left. Battalion of First Division failed to get German trench on 12th Division have made progress on whole side of QUARRIES but fighting continues and attacks not yet clear on East Surrey of 12 Division have captured trench on left of 1st Division own 46th Division gained HOHENZOLLERN and Princes battalion are consolidating on FOSSE No 8 as in places and fighting continues there on 1st Dele 10.45 p.m.	
	14	11.40 a.m.	Following information received today on First Division failed to reach line Fricourt and no back to their old positions on 12th Division have recovered their positions on yesterday about GUN trench and near edge of QUARRIES St. HOHENZOLLERN Redoubt still	

1500 Wt. W10791/1773 500,000 1/15 D. D. & L. A.D.S.S./Forms/C. 2118.

WAR DIARY
or
INTELLIGENCE SUMMARY.

(Erase heading not required.)

Instructions regarding War Diaries and Intelligence Summaries are contained in F. S. Regs., Part II. and the Staff Manual respectively. Title pages will be prepared in manuscript.

Place	Date	Hour	Summary of Events and Information	Remarks and references to Appendices
	Oct 14	-	uncertain ... fighting continues in that area as on 151 Bde.	
	15	11·40 a.m.	Message from Saxon Army begins ... First Army report greater quieter ... HOHENZOLLERN redoubt held by 46th Division ... Germans still held small piece St. Elver at NW corner ... Qne deal of bombarding in front of First Corps ... enemie retaliation ...	

WAR DIARY
or

INTELLIGENCE SUMMARY.

(Erase heading not required.)

Instructions regarding War Diaries and Intelligence
Summaries are contained in F. S. Regs., Part II.
and the Staff Manual respectively. Title pages
will be prepared in manuscript.

Place	Date	Hour	Summary of Events and Information	Remarks and references to Appendices
	20 Oct	8.40am	Second Army wires timed 10.20pm begins First Army report 7.10 began. After heavy hostile bombardment of our trenches east of canal especially opposite HULLOCH the Quarries and HOHENZOLLERN. The enemy delivered an attack between the VERMELLES – HULLOCH road and the Quarries, and has been everywhere repulsed near situation is now quiet as heavy bombing on both sides at HOHENZOLLERN and normal shelling east of Canal as under — 1st Bde.	

1577 Wt. W10791/1773 500,000 1/15 D. D. & L. A.D.S.S./Forms/C. 2118.

5th BATTN. THE DURHAM LIGHT INFANTRY.

N O V E M B E R

1 9 1 5

Army Form C. 2118.

WAR DIARY

or

INTELLIGENCE SUMMARY.

(Erase heading not required.)

Instructions regarding War Diaries and Intelligence Summaries are contained in F. S. Regs., Part II. and the Staff Manual respectively. Title pages will be prepared in manuscript.

6th Durham Light Infantry

Place	Date	Hour	Summary of Events and Information	Remarks and references to Appendices
Trenches Host.			Lieut Hadcock and Lieut Stowe were granted temporary rank of Captains. Companies now commanded as follows:- 'W' Company, Capt. Little, Badger; 'X' Company, Capt. ?; ? 'Y' Company, Capt. ? B. Headcock; 'Z' Company, Capt. R. O. Stowe.	
	2 3	―	Rain began to fall and continued until evening. Continued to rain. The fire trench, the small culvert trenches and communicating trenches partially collapsed. Water was lying about 2 feet deep in some trenches. Most of the dug-outs fell in similar.	
	4	―	A fine day. All men at work clearing the trenches & rebuilding parapets, parados, traverses on a slope.	
	5	―	Another fine day. Three platoons of the 6th Battalion Durham Regiment who had been attached for instructions released by those other platoons of the same regiment which still work side in	

1577 Wt. W10791/1773 500,000 1/15 D. D. & L. A.D.S.S./Forms/C. 2118.

Army Form C. 2118.

WAR DIARY
or
INTELLIGENCE SUMMARY.

(Erase heading not required.)

Instructions regarding War Diaries and Intelligence Summaries are contained in F. S. Regs., Part II. and the Staff Manual respectively. Title pages will be prepared in manuscript.

Place	Date	Hour	Summary of Events and Information	Remarks and references to Appendices
	6		the trenches. General Capper have severely wounded in the Road. A man in the 8th Lincolns shot severely the brain. Lieut-Nehan was accidentally injured by stepping on a bayonet, & was taken to the field	
	7		Continued reforming of the trenches revetting and draining. Weather fine.	
			Battalion relieved in trenches 81, 82 & 83 by the 7th Battalion R.F. the Lincoln platoons accompanied the Battalion on relief & proceeded to their own billets. Relief complete at 6.40 pm. Returned to billets in Armentières. W and X companies living in the Hospice Civil, Y and Z Companies in the College des Garçons, and Headquarters in Rue Nationale.	
	8		General cleaning of arms, equipment, clothing &c.	
	9		Brick had been covered with the trenches.	

1577 Wt.W10791/1773 500,000 1/15 D. D. & L. A.D.S.S./Forms/C. 2118.

WAR DIARY

or

INTELLIGENCE SUMMARY.

(Erase heading not required.)

Instructions regarding War Diaries and Intelligence Summaries are contained in F. S. Regs., Part II. and the Staff Manual respectively. Title pages will be prepared in manuscript.

Place	Date	Hour	Summary of Events and Information	Remarks and references to Appendices
La Crèche	Nov 10	—	The Battalion marched out of Lemmenlaere at mid-day and reached La Crèche - a locality of Blancke, about 3¼ m from Bailleul about 1½ mile from Bailleul. The Billets had been vacated by the 14th Durham Light Infantry in the morning so that Battalion, however, had double the accommodation allotted to us, so that all ranks are crowded. There is no accommodation for sick, reynats or Quartermaster's Stores, medical inspection room, and recreation hut.	
	11	—	Stay transport is in the yard of La Grande Blancke. There there is a brick floor and fairly good accommodation. Officers are still in tents. Brigade Headquarters move to BAILLEUL and Divisional Headquarters to MERRIS.	
	12	—	Raining all day. Working party of five officers and 200 men digging drains at La Crèche till about 1 pm	
	13	—	Still raining, very strong wind, roads flooded.	

1577 Wt. W10791/1773 500,000 1/15 D.D. & L.   A.D.S.S./Forms/C. 2118.

WAR DIARY

or

INTELLIGENCE SUMMARY.

(*Erase heading not required.*)

Instructions regarding War Diaries and Intelligence Summaries are contained in F. S. Regs. Part II. and the Staff Manual respectively. Title pages will be prepared in manuscript.

Place	Date	Hour	Summary of Events and Information	Remarks and references to Appendices
La Cocke	14/15	—	Better weather. Platoon Training commenced. Started platoon football tournament. Ngmm.	
	15	—	Fine frosty weather. Training proceeding.	
	16	—	Fine frosty weather. More huts erected which relieves in some measure the crowding in billets. Petty heavy firing all day. A party from the Battalion attended a concert given by the Canadian Corps. Among the audience were eleven prisoners who had been captured during the day by one of the Canadian Divisions.	
	17	—	Platoon Training continues all the week. Weather still fine though cold.	
	18-19	—	Battalion Band has now been organized and is rehearsing very well under the conductorship of Cpl Bell. The instruments most needed are a bass drum, two clarinet and a B flat Cornet. Efforts are being made to secure these. The bugles have also been	

1577 Wt.W10791/1773 500,000 1/15 D. D. & L.   A.D.S.S./Forms/C. 2118.

WAR DIARY
or
INTELLIGENCE SUMMARY.
(Erase heading not required.)

Instructions regarding War Diaries and Intelligence Summaries are contained in F. S. Regs., Part II and the Staff Manual respectively. Title pages will be prepared in manuscript.

Place	Date	Hour	Summary of Events and Information	Remarks and references to Appendices
	29	—	re-started and Company-Quarter-master-master-Sergt Carle is acting as temporary Bugle-major. the Battalion drew (1- ? unit the 7th Battalion in the final game of the Principals Football League. the Band gave selection during the afternoon.	
	20	—	Church Parade in conjunction with the 5th Loyal North Lancashire Regiment. the Band was present, and afterwards in the afternoon rendered another programme in the field behind Headquarters. the Pioneers having erected a bandstand.	
	20	—	the Brigade moved past the Army Commander, Sir Herbert Plumer. All units were highly complimented by him and by Sir Charles ?? on their afternoon. In the afternoon the Battalion defeated the Loyal North Lancashire Regiment by five goals to nil in the second game of the Principals League.	

1577 Wt.W10791/1773 500,000 1/15 D.D. & L. A.D.S.S./Forms/C. 2118.

WAR DIARY

or

INTELLIGENCE SUMMARY.

(Erase heading not required.)

Instructions regarding War Diaries and Intelligence Summaries are contained in F. S. Regs., Part II. and the Staff Manual respectively. Title pages will be prepared in manuscript.

Place	Date	Hour	Summary of Events and Information	Remarks and references to Appendices
	Nov. 23	-	Company training began. 280 men of the Battalion attended a gas demonstration conducted by the Second Army Chemical Adviser, at which the Tube Helmet, Smoke Helmet proved extraordinarily efficacious.	
	24	-	Company training continued. The football match against the 8 Battalion resulted in a win for the 8th Battalion by three goals to one. Practice began on the short rifle range and was continued throughout the morning.	
	25	-	Battalion and Company training on the flying ground at BAILLEUL. Larger half of gifts arrived from Alexandria Fund and were distributed amongst the men of the Battalion.	
	26	-	Fine frosty weather.	
	27	-	A draft of 80 NCO's and men from the Second Line who had been temporarily posted to the 3rd Garrison Battalion, arrived from there and were taken on the strength.	

1577 Wt.W10791/1773 500,000 1/15 D.D.&L. A.D.S.S./Forms/C. 2118.

WAR DIARY

or

INTELLIGENCE SUMMARY.

(Erase heading not required.)

Instructions regarding War Diaries and Intelligence Summaries are contained in F. S. Regs., Part II. and the Staff Manual respectively. Title pages will be prepared in manuscript.

Place	Date	Hour	Summary of Events and Information	Remarks and references to Appendices
	27(da)	hor.	Practice with live grenades was commenced, a large pit having been dug for the purpose. Church Parade, with Brand and Bugles in the field. Battn Headquarters... the frosty fine weather still continued.	
	28	–	Battalion parade for field training had to be postponed owing to the frost ground, and rain setting in. A boxing contest, which created much interest, took place in Z Company Billet.	
	30	–	The Battalion football match with the 9th Durhams resulted in a win for the latter by three goals to one.	

6th BATTN. THE DURHAM LIGHT INFANTRY.

D E C E M B E R

1 9 1 5

Attached:

Appendix.

WAR DIARY
or
INTELLIGENCE SUMMARY
(Erase heading not required.)

Instructions regarding War Diaries and Intelligence
Summaries are contained in F. S. Regs., Part II.
and the Staff Manual respectively. Title Pages
will be prepared in manuscript.

Place	Date	Hour	Summary of Events and Information	Remarks and references to Appendices
MOUNT SORRIL	1.		Battalion in Trenches A.1 & A.2. nothing of importance happened during day. 5.9.m. Heavy Bombardment for 2 hours. 1 O.R. wounded.	
"	2		Heavy Bombardment at H.e.m, attack made on our left, enemy Shelling out Trenches all morning. No Casualties. Relieved at 9. p.m. and marched to Canada Huts near Dickybush, arriving at 3. a. m.	
DICKEBUSH HUTS	3.		Battalion resting all day.	
"	4		Cleaning Arms & Equipment. Gas inspection. Enemy Aeroplane dropped 4 Bombs in vicinity of Huts, no damage.	
"	5		Battalion went into A.1 A.2 A.3 & A.4 Trenches. Relief complete at 11. p. m. Successful relief.	
MOUNT SORRIL	6		Snowing heavily all morning, enemy quiet, very little shelling.	
"	7		Heavy Snowfall all day, enemy shelled Trenches from 3 - 5 3. 30 p. m. No Casualties.	

1875 Wt. W593/826 1,000,000 4/15 J.B.C. & A. A.D.S.S./Forms/C. 2118.

WAR DIARY
or
INTELLIGENCE SUMMARY

(Erase heading not required.)

Instructions regarding War Diaries and Intelligence Summaries are contained in F. S. Regs., Part II. and the Staff Manual respectively. Title Pages will be prepared in manuscript.

Place	Date	Hour	Summary of Events and Information	Remarks and references to Appendices
MOUNT SORRIL	8		Very quiet all day, snowing heavily, trenches very wet. Relieved at 9. p.m and marched to DICKEBUSH HUTS.	
DICKEBUSH HUTS.	9		Battalion resting all day.	
"	10.		Fine frosty day, men cleaning arms & Equipment, New clothing issued to men.	
"	11.		Route March from 10. a.m to 12.30 p.m.	
"	12		Fine frosty day. Divine Service at 10. a.m.	
"	13		Gas Helmet Drill. Kit inspection.	
"	14		Physical Drill 9. a.m. Inspection of arms & ammunition at 9 p.m to A 2 and 3 Trenches. Battalion marched off at 9 p.m to A 2 and 3 Trenches. Relief Completed at 11-30 p.m.	

1875 Wt. W593/826 1,000,000 4/15 J.B.C. & A. A.D.S.S./Forms/C. 2118.

WAR DIARY
or
INTELLIGENCE SUMMARY

(Erase heading not required.)

Instructions regarding War Diaries and Intelligence Summaries are contained in F. S. Regs., Part II. and the Staff Manual respectively. Title Pages will be prepared in manuscript.

Place	Date	Hour	Summary of Events and Information	Remarks and references to Appendices
MOUNT SORRIL	15		A 2 and 3 Trenches. Enemy shelled Trenches during morning. 3 O.Rank's killed & wounded. All night, Parted wire laid down Crater in front of Trench.	
"	16		Very fine day. Enemy Trenches shelled heavily during the afternoon by out Trench Mortars. Aeroplanes very active.	
"	17		Fine day. Very little shelling during the day. Patrols pushed out at 9.p.m. returned at 11·15 p.m, nothing of importance to report.	
"	18		Very quiet day. Relieved at 9. 30 p.m. and marched to VLRMERTINGHE and entrained for POPERINGHE.	
POPERINGHE	19.		Arrived at POPERINGHE at 2·30. a.m. and went into Billets. Battalion resting till noon, cleaning clothing during afternoon.	
"	20.		Inspection of arms and Equipment	
"	21		Very wet day. Lecture to N.C.Os by Commanding Officer.	

1875 Wt. W593/826 1,000,000 4/15 J.B.C. & A. A.D.S.S./Forms/C. 2118.

WAR DIARY
or
INTELLIGENCE SUMMARY
(Erase heading not required.)

Instructions regarding War Diaries and Intelligence Summaries are contained in F. S. Regs., Part II. and the Staff Manual respectively. Title Pages will be prepared in manuscript.

Place	Date	Hour	Summary of Events and Information	Remarks and references to Appendices
POPERINGHE	22.		Fine day. Route March 10.15 a.m. to 12.45 p.m. Gas defence Drill 2.30 to 3.30 p.m.	
"	23		Physical Drill 4.15 to 5 a.m. Battalion entrained at VLAMERTINGHE at 9 p.m. and marched to Bluff trenches and relieved a Battalion of South Wales Borderers. Relief completed at 11.30 p.m.	
BLUFF SECTOR.	24		Trenches in very bad condition; numerous bodies laid about mostly Germans. These we buried, & effected repairs to parapet's, working all day. Enemy heavily shelled the DEAN and INTERNATIONAL TRENCH all day.	
"	25		Fairly quiet day. Men on work to Parapet continually.	
"	26		Went back into Support. On out right (3rd Division) attacked and gained objective. (3 lines of trenches). MEDICAL OFFICER and Stretcher Bearers assisted bringing in and dressing wounded.	
	27			
	28		Still in Support. Shelled heavily all day. About 6 casualties.	

1875 Wt. W593/826 1,000,000 4/15 J.B.C. & A. A.D.S.S./Forms/C. 2118.

WAR DIARY

or

INTELLIGENCE SUMMARY

(*Erase heading not required.*)

Instructions regarding War Diaries and Intelligence Summaries are contained in F. S. Regs, Part II. and the Staff Manual respectively. Title Pages will be prepared in manuscript.

Place	Date	Hour	Summary of Events and Information	Remarks and references to Appendices
BLUFF SECTOR	29.		Enemy artillery active, working parties taking R.E. material to Ypres line.	
"	30.		Battalion took over Loop International and BEAM trenches. Relief completed without casualties.	
"	31.		Trenches heavily shelled all day, and parapets badly damaged. These were repaired at night.	

[signature]

Lieut Col.

Commanding 6th Durham L. Infy

1875 Wt. W593/826 1,000,000 4/15 J.B.C. & A. A.D.S.S./Forms/C. 2118.

WAR DIARY
or
INTELLIGENCE SUMMARY.
(Erase heading not required.)

Dec. 1915.

Instructions regarding War Diaries and Intelligence Summaries are contained in F. S. Regs., Part II. and the Staff Manual respectively. Title pages will be prepared in manuscript.

Place	Date	Hour	Summary of Events and Information	Remarks and references to Appendices
La Blanche Maison	Dec. 1.		Last day of Company Drill. Match with 7th Bn. Durham Light Infantry resulted in draw of 2 goals.	
"	2.		Battalion allotted to Battalion at Bailleul.	
"	3.		Parade in wet weather on the Flying Ground. A short attack was carried out in the presence of the General.	
"	4.		Cross country run arranged for this morning but off owing to bad weather. Still raining and all roads flooded.	
"	5.		Fine, but wet roads make Church parade impossible.	
"	6.		Football match with the 9th Bn. Durham Light Infantry resulted in a win for them by 2 goals to nil. Boxing competition was begun at 5 p.m. today.	
"	7.		Outpost scheme was carried out near Noote Boom between 9-30 a.m. and 3 p.m. More rain.	
"	8.		Lieut P.H.B. Lyon granted sick leave to England. 2 Lieut G.E. Baldwin temporary appointed Adjutant.	
"	9.		Battalion training on the Flying Ground, Bailleul. Party	

1577 Wt. W10791/1773 500,000 1/15 D. D. & L. A.D.S.S./Forms/C. 2118.

Army Form C. 2118.

WAR DIARY

or

INTELLIGENCE SUMMARY.

(Erase heading not required.)

Instructions regarding War Diaries and Intelligence Summaries are contained in F. S. Regs., Part II. and the Staff Manual respectively. Title pages will be prepared in manuscript.

Dec. 1915

Place	Date	Hour	Summary of Events and Information	Remarks and references to Appendices
La Blanche Maison	9.		The roads were all submerged and it was necessary for two companies of the Battalion to parade independently and march by a different route	
"	10.		Arrangements made for having the whole of the Blankets in the Battalion disinfected at Outterstiene	
"	11		Numerous cases of Scabies which had broken out in the a minor degree in the Battalion were evacuated to the Special Hospital at Pradelles Lieut A. Binley temporarily appointed Machine Gun Officer and 2nd Lieut Brock Scout and Sniping Officer.	
"	12		Divine Service under Company arrangements. Weather all very wet.	
"	13		Preparations began for the move into the 5th Corps area and intimation received that the Battalion would be the first Battalion in the Brigade to move on the 14 Kinst.	
"	14		Companies at the disposal of their commanders.	

1577 Wt. W10791/1773 500,000 1/15 D. D. & L.   A.D.S.S./Forms/C. 2118.

Army Form C. 2118.

WAR DIARY
or
INTELLIGENCE SUMMARY.
(Erase heading not required.)

Instructions regarding War Diaries and Intelligence
Summaries are contained in F. S. Regs., Part II.
and the Staff Manual respectively. Title pages
will be prepared in manuscript.

Dec. 1915.

Place	Date	Hour	Summary of Events and Information	Remarks and references to Appendices
La Blanche Maison	Dec 15		The Battalion formed up in field near Headquarters for inspection by Lieut General Sir Charles Ferguson 2nd Corps Commander who arrived at 9-15am. General Ferguson spoke in congratulatory terms of the 50th Division. The 151st Infantry Brigade and of the Battalion. Ranking all ranks for the splendid work they had done and the sterling soldierly qualities shown. He was intensely sorry to lose the 50th Division from his Corps and remarked that he would as soon have that Division under his command as any in the British Army.	
"	16.		The Machine Gun detachment under 2 Lieut A.L. Brock was appointed Machine Gun Officer proceeded to Dickebusch where they were billeted for one night prior to going into the trenches. 2 Lieut G.H.B. Catford appointed Scout and Intelligence Officer	
"	14.		Battalion paraded in full marching order at 11-15am.	

1577 Wt. W10791/1773 500,000 1/15 D.D. & L. A.D.S.S./Forms/C. 2118.

Army Form C. 2118.

WAR DIARY

or

INTELLIGENCE SUMMARY.

(Erase heading not required.)

Instructions regarding War Diaries and Intelligence Summaries are contained in F. S. Regs., Part II. and the Staff Manual respectively. Title pages will be prepared in manuscript.

Dec. 1915

Place	Date	Hour	Summary of Events and Information	Remarks and references to Appendices
DICKEBUSCH	Dec. 17		and marched to Steenwerck from where they entrained to Poperinghe on detrainment Battalion marched into camp at Dickebush huts arriving there about 5-30 pm at which time the transport which had come by road also arrived. The camp was in a disgraceful condition being knee deep in mud practically all over. Rain fell the whole of the day.	
YPRES	18.		The Battalion moved up into Brigade Reserve at Maple Copse relieving the 6 R. Royal Scots. H.Q. Sergeant & Lodge was accommodated on the railway going to Zillebeke. The distribution of the Battalion whilst in reserve was as follows:- "W" Company Canal Dugouts, "X" Company Maple Copse, "Y" Company Sanctuary Wood, "Z" Company Redoubts 2, 3 and H and the right of Sanctuary Wood.	
"	19		A fairly quiet day, all ranks aroused at 5am on account of a heavy	

1577 Wt. W10791/1773 500,000 1/15 D. D. & L. A.D.S.S./Forms/C. 2118.

WAR DIARY

or

INTELLIGENCE SUMMARY.

(Erase heading not required.)

Instructions regarding War Diaries and Intelligence Summaries are contained in F. S. Regs., Part II. and the Staff Manual respectively. Title pages will be prepared in manuscript.

Place	Date	Hour	Summary of Events and Information	Remarks and references to Appendices
YPRES	19	—	Bombardment on the left. Some little time later news was received [that] the Germans were making a gas attack on the 6 (R) Corps front north of Hooge. The artillery action spread down to our front. Our trenches were very hid by the 12 R. Royal Scots were heavily bombarded while the whole of Ypres salient was shelled with gas and lachrymatory shells. Sergeant Grainger and Private Gardner of "W" Company were killed and also Rfn 5 men wounded. Picket in Canal Dugouts. By order of the 24 R. Brigade (to which the Battalion was (temporary) attached) "W" Company had moved up to the Railway Dug-out, Capt Aislabie's Company moved into the Reserve trenches in Sanctuary Wood but were later ordered to return to the Dug-outs after suffering 3 or 4 casualties. The enemy put their 200 heavy shells into the support occupied/counterattacked and the right of Sanctuary Wood, considerable damage was done but fortunately the casualties were very few.	[initials] [initials] [initials] [initials] [initials]

1577 Wt. W6079/1773 500,000 1/15 D. D. & L. A.D.S.S./Forms/C. 2118.

Army Form C. 2118.

WAR DIARY
or
INTELLIGENCE SUMMARY.

(Erase heading not required.)

Instructions regarding War Diaries and Intelligence Summaries are contained in F. S. Regs., Part II. and the Staff Manual respectively. Title pages will be prepared in manuscript.

Place	Date	Hour	Summary of Events and Information	Remarks and references to Appendices
	19 1/2/5	7-30	Wire reports. — 27th Feb.	
	19 1/2/5		Prisoner report that information received that enemy has cylinders installed in front of 9th Division. Barrage from V Corps line from V Corps begins at ... VI Corps report that gas was very heavy over certain sectors but Relinds gave complete protection did not take any great confidence in them so hands are no information — 27 Feb.	

1577 Wt. W10791/1773 500,000 1/15 D. D. & L. A.D.S.S./Forms/C. 2118.

WAR DIARY

or

INTELLIGENCE SUMMARY.

(*Erase heading not required.*)

Army Form C. 2118.

Instructions regarding War Diaries and Intelligence
Summaries are contained in F. S. Regs. Part II.
and the Staff Manual respectively. Title pages
will be prepared in manuscript.

Dec. 1915

Place	Date	Hour	Summary of Events and Information	Remarks and references to Appendices
December 19 YPRES			few indeed. At night whilst the enemys artillery was still unusually active the Battalion relieved the 12th Royal Scots in trenches A.1 to A.12. These trenches were heavily bombarded throughout the whole of the night	W
"	20		Bombardment of our trenches still continued. Capt Cardwe[?] Company in A10 and A11 suffered heaviest losses, having been killed outright and about a dozen men wounded. In the same trenches Lieut Colonel (?) Jeffreys was wounded in both legs and the right hand. He shortly also wounded Major Simmons and a subaltern of the Royal Engineers and killed 3 men.	W
"	"		During the period it took to reinforce Lieut Colonel Jeffreys from the firing line over 400 high bangs went into the trench. Major Lcol Stevens, Adjutant of Batt. Durham Light Infantry assumed command of the Battalion	W
"	21		A rainy drizzly dreary day. Enemys artillery activity ceased and the situation in consequence became	W

WAR DIARY
or
INTELLIGENCE SUMMARY.

(Erase heading not required.)

Instructions regarding War Diaries and Intelligence Summaries are contained in F. S. Regs., Part II. and the Staff Manual respectively. Title pages will be prepared in manuscript.

Dec. 1915

Place	Date	Hour	Summary of Events and Information	Remarks and references to Appendices
YPRES	Dec. 21	1	Quieter. In the afternoon our Artillery commenced shelling the German trenches. Capt. R.B. Bradford 2nd Batt Durham Light Infantry temporarily appointed Adjutant to the Battalion.	
"	22		Considerable excitement was caused in trench A.12 by the sight of a man waving a white handkerchief and approaching our trench. Several shots were fired at him and one entered his shoulder. The man however managed to reach our trenches and turned out to be an escaped Russian prisoner. He had been employed by the Germans on their subsidiary line. A few minutes later another man was seen running towards the same trench which he managed to reach. He proved the greatest anxiety on finding that the occupants of the trench were British. He was sent to Brigade Headquarters under escort, whilst his comrade after being medically attended was sent on to the field	

1577 Wt. W10791/1773 500,000 1/15 D. D. & L. A.D.S.S./Forms/C. 2118.

Army Form C. 2118.

WAR DIARY

or

INTELLIGENCE SUMMARY.

(Erase heading not required.)

Instructions regarding War Diaries and Intelligence Summaries are contained in F. S. Regs., Part II. and the Staff Manual respectively. Title pages will be prepared in manuscript.

Place	Date	Hour	Summary of Events and Information	Remarks and references to Appendices
DICKEBUSCH	Dec. 22	—	Ambulance. 2 Lieut L.M. Peberdy was killed whilst out on patrol.	*(initials)*
"	23	—	Very quiet day. Relieved by the 5th Border Regiment which had been transferred from the 150th Brigade to the 151st Brigade. The Battalion moved into Divisional Reserve at Dickebusch huts. Total casualties during this Tour of the trenches — 1 Officer and 5 Other ranks killed, and 1 Officer and 45 Other ranks wounded.	
"	24th	—	In Hutments as above	*(initials)*
"	25th	—	In Hutments as above. Major Gen. Wilkinson, G.O.C. 50th Division — visited the Hutments and wished all ranks a Merry Xmas & a Happy New Year.	*(initials)*
"	26th	—	Very quiet day in Dickebusch Huts.	*(initials)*
"	27	—	Relieved the 5th Border Regiment in trenches A.7 to A.12. Relief completed without incident or casualties.	
"	28		Nothing of note beyond the usual artillery activity & strafe by	

1577 Wt. W10791/1773 500,000 1/15 D. D. & L.   A.D.S.S./Forms/C. 2118.

WAR DIARY

or

INTELLIGENCE SUMMARY.

(Erase heading not required.)

Instructions regarding War Diaries and Intelligence
Summaries are contained in F. S. Regs., Part II.
and the Staff Manual respectively. Title pages
will be prepared in manuscript.

Place	Date	Hour	Summary of Events and Information	Remarks and references to Appendices
	28.		A. strafe by our Guns north of Hooge.	
	29.		Wind favourable for gas, fine bright weather, of which the Artillery took advantage but no gas was sent over and the Men kept very quiet.	
	30		Continued work on trenches principally drainage. Some shelling of A.1. and one of our Machine Gun emplacements knocked in. Private Riley was killed and Private Greenwood wounded, both of whom were in Z Company. These were the only casualties during the tour of the trenches,	
	31		except for one man shot through the wrist of the ZILLEBEKE Dump. Relieved by the 5th Border Regiment and went into Brigade Reserve at Cafe Copse, Y Company Dugouts in Sanctuary Wood whilst X Company remained till Cafe Copse and "W" Company at the Canal Dugouts. The old year departed with a few minutes strafe from our Divisional Artillery.	

A P P E N D I X .

WAR DIARY

or

INTELLIGENCE SUMMARY.

(*Erase heading not required.*)

Instructions regarding War Diaries and Intelligence Summaries are contained in F. S. Regs., Part II. and the Staff Manual respectively. Title pages will be prepared in manuscript.

Place	Date	Hour	Summary of Events and Information	Remarks and references to Appendices
1	Dec 18.		APPENDIX

Special Order of the Day.

By Field-Marshall Sir J.D.P. French, G.C.B.,O.M.,G.C.V.O.,K.C.M.G., Commander-in-Chief British Army in the field.

In relinquishing the command of the British Army in France I desire to express to the Officers and men with whom I have been so closely associated during the last sixteen months, my heartfelt sorrow in parting with them before the campaign in which we have been so long engaged together has been brought to a victorious conclusion.

I have however the firmest conviction that such a glorious ending to their splendid and heroic efforts is not far distant and that what has cost their progress towards this final goal with intense interest but in the most complete and indomitable... | |

1577 Wt.W10791/1773 500,000 1/15 D. D. & L. A.D.S.S./Forms/C. 2118.

Army Form C. 2118.

WAR DIARY
or
INTELLIGENCE SUMMARY.

(Erase heading not required.)

Instructions regarding War Diaries and Intelligence Summaries are contained in F. S. Regs., Part II. and the Staff Manual respectively. Title pages will be prepared in manuscript.

Place	Date	Hour	Summary of Events and Information	Remarks and references to Appendices

spirit, dogged tenacity which knows no defeat and the heroic courage so abundantly displayed by the rank and file of the splendid army which it will ever remain the pride and glory of my life to have commanded during 3300 exciting months of ceaseless incessant fighting.

Regulars and Territorials, Old Army and New Army have ever shown these magnificent qualities in equal degree.

From my heart of hearts I thank them all.

At this sad moment of parting my heart goes out to those who have received life-long injury from wounds and I think with sorrow of that great and glorious host of my beloved comrades who have made the greatest sacrifice of all by laying down their lives for their country.

In saying good-bye ... to the British Army in France I ask them once again to accept his expression of ...

1577   Wt. W10791/1773   500,000   1/15   D. D. & L.   A.D.S.S./Forms/C. 2118.

WAR DIARY

or

INTELLIGENCE SUMMARY.

(Erase heading not required.)

Instructions regarding War Diaries and Intelligence Summaries are contained in F. S. Regs., Part II. and the Staff Manual respectively. Title pages will be prepared in manuscript.

Place	Date	Hour	Summary of Events and Information	Remarks and references to Appendices
			deepest gratitude and heartfelt devotion towards them and my earnest good wishes for the glorious future which of self to be assured. J.D.P. French. Field Marshal, Commanding in Chief the British Army in France,	
			1st December 1915.	
	1/12/15	2.10 a.m.	Message from 27th Brigade started at 2.0 a.m. Gas attack started on VI Corps front about 5-30 a.m. No news having are proceeding The two platoons of 6 D.I. from Canal Bng. Out are now in PROMENADE TRENCH by Brigade Headquarters All mines were broken at ZILLEBEKE but are being rapidly repaired. Until mines restored please send occasional orderlies	

1577 Wt.W10791/1773 500,000 1/15 D. D. & L.   A.D.S.S./Forms/C. 2118.

FIELD RETURN.

Army Form B. 213.

No. of Report _____

(To be furnished by all arms, services, and departments (except A.S.C. units) to the A. G.'s Office at the Base in accordance with Field Service Regulations, Part II.)

Date. _____

RETURN showing numbers RATIONED by, and Transport on charge of, _____ at _____

DETAIL	Personnel			Animals.									Guns, carriages, and limbers and transport vehicles.														REMARKS
				Horses			Mules										Horsed				Mechanical					
	Officers	Other ranks	Natives	Riding	Draught	Heavy Draught	Pack	Large	Small	Camels	Oxen	Guns, carriages and limbers, showing description	Ammunition wagons and limbers	Machine Guns	Aircraft, showing description	4 Wheeled	2 Wheeled	Motor Cars	Tractors	Lorries, showing description	Trucks, showing description	Trailers	Motor Bicycles	Bicycles	
Effective Strength of Unit																										
Details, by Arms attached to unit as in War Establishment :—																										
Total																										
War Establishment																										
Wanting to complete (Detail of Personnel and Horses below)																										
Surplus																										
*Attached (not to include the details shown above)																										
Civilians:— Employed with the Unit Accompanying the Unit																										
TOTAL RATIONED :—																										

* In the case of field ambulances, hospitals or depots, the number of patients are to be included here, the names being shown in A. F. A. 36.

_____ Signature of Commander.

Date of Despatch. _____

For information of the A.G.'s Office at the Base.

Officers and men who have become casuals, been transferred or joined since last report.

Place Sanctuary Wood   Date 24.. 12.. 15.

Regtl. Number	Rank	Name		Corps	Nature of casualty, or name of unit from or to which transferred	Date of being struck off or coming on the ration return	Remarks*
	Lt.Col	Jeffreys	A.C.	6 D.L.I.	Wounded	20-12-15	
	2Lt	Peberdy	L.M.	Do	Killed	22-12-15	
119	Sergt.	Lodge	T.	Do	Wounded	18-12-15	
665	L/cpl.	Gibson	C.	Do	Wounded	18-12-15	
1654	Sgt.	Hardy	H.H.	Do	Wounded	19-12-15	
2823	L/c	Jackson	W.	Do	Wounded	19-12-15	
1510	Sgt.	Grainger	J.	Do	Killed	19-12-15	
3439	Pte	Gardiner	J.	Do	Killed	19-12-15	
1779	Pte	German	G.	Do	Wounded	19-12-15	
1747	Pte	Chappell	G.	Do	Wounded	19-12-15	
2375	"	Catchpole	R.	Do	Wounded	19-12-15	
2299	Cpl.	Vickers	J.	Do	Wounded	19-12-15	
2634	Pte	Allen	J.	Do	Wounded	19-12-15	
1644	"	Clare	J.	Do	Wounded	19-12-15	
852	"	Stobbs	J.	Do	Wounded	19-12-15	
2345	"	Johnson	J.J.	Do	Wounded	19-12-15	
1768	L/cpl	Davies	W.	Do	Wounded	20-12-15	
1940	Bug	Sanderson	J.	Do	Wounded	20-12-15	
2523	L/cpl	Atkinson	J.	Do	Wounded	20-12-15	
3836	Pte	Allen	J.A.	Do	Wounded	20-12-15	
3824	"	Hardy	J.W.	Do	Killed	20-12-15	
3049	"	Newby	J.	Do	Killed	20-12-15	
2092	"	Lawson	J.W.	Do	Killed	20-12-15	
2481	"	Hudspeth	T.	Do	Wounded	20-12-15	
3692	"	Curry	R.E.	Do	Shock	20-12-15	
2201	Sgt.	Moore	J.T.	Do	Wounded	20-12-15	
3824	Pte	Nicholson	G.	Do	Wounded	20-12-15	
2331	"	Bowes	E.	Do	Killed	19-12-15	

* State whether absence is of a permanent or temporary nature, adding, in the case of casuals from wounds or disease, any available information for communication to the relatives.

For information of the A.G.'s Office at the Base.

Officers and men who have become casuals, been transferred or joined since last report.

Place _____ Date 24..12..15

Regtl. Number	Rank	Name	Corps	Nature of casualty, or name of unit from or to which transferred	Date of being struck off or coming on the ration return	Remarks*
2094	Pte	Marr 10	6 D.L.I.	Wounded	20-12-15	
3023	"	Elliott J.J.	Do	Killed	20-12-15	
3989	"	Hutchinson E.	Do	Killed	20-12-15	
1465	"	Short G.	Do	Wounded	20-12-15	
346	"	Jackson J.	Do	Wounded	20-12-15	
2567	"	Kirby J.	Do	Wounded	20-12-15	
3036	"	Metcalfe B.	Do	Wounded	20-12-15	
485	"	Walker J.B	Do	Wounded	20-12-15	
2009	"	Murray J.	Do	Evac. Sick	14-12-15	
2406	"	Sennett J.W.	Do	Do	14-12-15	
870	"	Carr J.J.	Do	Do	14-12-15	
4012	"	Oliver G.A	Do	Do	14-12-15	
2902	"	Robb W.	Do	Do	21-12-15	
3839	"	Evans E.	Do	Do	21-12-15	
1355	"	Hughes J.	Do	Do	21-12-15	
2084	"	Graham W.	Do	Do	21-12-15	
2514	"	Murphy J.	Do	Do	21-12-15	
1617	"	Lambert A.	Do	Do	21-12-15	
3024	"	Tarvey T.	Do	Do	21-12-15	
2431	"	Davies D	Do	Do	21-12-15	
3374	"	Byers J.G.	Do	Do	22-12-15	
1486	"	Fisher J.R.	Do	Do	22-12-15	
2889	"	Purbrick G.R.	Do	Do	22-12-15	
1284	"	Coughlin J.	Do	Do	22-12-15	
2976	"	Wray J.	Do	Do.	22-12-15	
3839	"	Evans. E.	Do	Re td to Duty	16-12-15	
2433	"	Dowson J.	Do	do	16-12-15	
3089	"	Howard J.J.	Do	do	16-12-15	

* State whether absence is of a permanent or temporary nature, adding, in the case of casuals from wounds or disease, any available information for communication to the relatives.

For information of the A.G.'s Office at the Base.

Officers and men who have become casuals, been transferred or joined since last report.

Place_____   Date_____

Regtl. Number	Rank	Name	Corps	Nature of casualty, or name of unit from or to which transferred	Date of being struck off or coming on the ration return	Remarks*
3965	Pte	Siddle J.E.	6 D.L.I.	Rtd to Duty	16-12-15	
3848	"	Johnson J.V.	Do	Do	16-12-15	
1494	"	Moffitt J.	Do	Do	16-12-15	
577	Sgt	Emmerson H.R.	Do	Do	16-12-15	
2058	Pte	Murphy J.	Do	Do	18-12-15	
1916	"	Wright H.	Do	Do	18-12-15	
2856	"	McGovern J.	Do	Do	18-12-15	
1903	"	McNally J.	Do	Do	18-12-15	
1633	"	Robert J.H.	Do	Do	18-12-15	
1259	"	Bell J.H.	Do	Do	18-12-15	
1654	"	Shannon J.	Do	Do	18-12-15	
1987	"	Carlton W.S.	Do	Do	18-12-15	
1452	"	Shaw H.	Do	Do	18-12-15	
1589	Cpl	Scisson R.R.	Do	Do	20-12-15	
665	A/c	Gibson W.	Do	Do	22-12-15	
—	2/Lt	Wilson S.M.	Do	Do	22-12-15	
954	L/Sgt	Bell J.	Do	Do	23-12-15	
2794	Pte	Howells J.W.	Do	Do	23-12-15	
3009	"	Parkin J.W.	Do	Do	23-12-15	
2012	"	McDonald J.	Do	Do	23-12-15	
2914	"	Reed G.R.	Do	Do	23-12-15	
1934	"	Shield H.	Do	Do	23-12-15	
1900	"	Robinson J.A	Do	Do	23-12-15	
2026	"	Bailey J.	Do	Do	23-12-15	
2167	"	Dunning J.	Do	Do	23-12-15	
3164	"	Blenkinsopp J.	Do	Do	23-12-15	
2586	"	Reed G.R.	Do	Do	23-12-15	
2875	"	McGinety J.	Do	Do	23-12-15	

* State whether absence is of a permanent or temporary nature, adding, in the case of casuals from wounds or disease, any available information for communication to the relatives.

For information of the A.G.'s Office at the Base.

Officers and men who have become casuals, been transferred or joined since last report.

Place_____   Date_____

Regtl. Number	Rank	Name	Corps	Nature of casualty, or name of unit from or to which transferred	Date of being struck off or coming on the ration return	Remarks*
2362	Cpl	Blenkinsopp	to 6 D.L.I.	Evac. Sick	18-12-15	
3818	Pte	Lumley J.	do	Do	18-12-15	
2839	"	Liddle B.	do	Do	22-12-15	
3352	"	Dobson J.R.	do	Do	20-12-15	
1866	"	Murphy J.	do	Do	18-12-15	
2026	"	Bailey H.	do	Do	18-12-15	
3881	L/c.	Hull R.	do	Do		
2167	Pte	Dunning G.	do	Do		
3041	"	Roxby R.	do	Do		
2791	"	Heighington T.	do	Retd to Duty		
3010	"	Bragg.	do	Do.		

* State whether absence is of a permanent or temporary nature, adding, in the case of casuals from wounds or disease, any available information for communication to the relatives.

Officers and men who have become casuals, been transferred or joined since last report.

Place _____ Date _3 0 . 12 . 15_

Regtl. Number	Rank	Name	Corps	Nature of casualty, or name of unit from or to which transferred	Date of being struck off or coming on the ration return	Remarks*
239	Pte	Elliott G.L.	6 D.L.I.	Ret to Duty	25.12.15	
3519	"	Robinson H.	6 D.L.I.	-Do-	25-12-15	
1469	"	Goddard H.	6 D.L.I.	-Do-	25-12-15	
5123	"	Bowman J.	6 D.L.I.	-Do-	25-12-15	
2614	"	Bowman J.G.	6 D.L.I.	-Do-	25-12-15	
2514	"	Geaphy J.	6 D.L.I.	-Do-	25-12-15	
2721	"	Hudson R.L.	6 D.L.I.	-Do-	25-12-15	
1231	"	Boyes C.	6 D.L.I.	-Do-	27-12-15	
3818	"	Armley J.	6 D.L.I.	-Do-	27-12-15	
1426	"	Foster J.R.	6 D.L.I.	-Do-	27-12-15	
2968	"	Thompson J.	6 D.L.I.	-Do-	27-12-15	
2060	L/C	McDonald	6 D.L.I.	-Do-	29-12-15	
994	Sgt	Race B.B.	6 D.L.I.	-Do-		
2889	Pte	Purbuck G.R.	6 D.L.I.	-Do-	24-12	
2604	"	Capp A.	6 D.L.I.	-Do-	27-12	
1250	"	Parkinson W.I.	6 D.L.I.	-Do-	25-12	
2338	A/C	Bateman	6 D.L.I.	-Do-	25-12	
2140	Pte	Storry	6 D.L.I.	-Do-		
1482	"	Gilchrist J.	6 D.L.I.	-Do-		
1328	"	Appleby J.H.	6 D.L.I.	-Do		
2953	"	Sample F.	6 D.L.I.	Wounded	30-12-15	
4074	"	Routledge J.W.	6 D.L.I.	Evac. Sick	25-12-15	
2303	"	Nelson J.S.	6 D.L.I.	-Do-	14-12-15	
2310	L/C	Shaw J.	6 D.L.I.	-Do-	24-12-15	
2516	Pte	Swinbank R.	6 D.L.I.	-Do-	24-12-15	

* State whether absence is of a permanent or temporary nature, adding, in the case of casuals from wounds or disease, any available information for communication to the relatives.

FIELD RETURN.

(To be furnished by all arms, services, and departments (except A.S.C. units) to the A. G.'s Office at the Base in accordance with Field Service Regulations, Part II.)

No. of Report.

Date.

RETURN showing numbers RATIONED by, and Transport on charge of, at

DETAIL	Personnel			Animals								Guns, carriages, and limbers and transport vehicles													REMARKS.
				Horses				Mules		Camels	Oxen				Horsed		Mechanical								
	Officers	Other ranks	Natives	Riding	Draught	Heavy Draught	Pack	Large	Small			Guns, carriages and limbers, showing description	Ammunition wagons and limbers	Machine guns	Aircraft, showing description	4 Wheeled	2 Wheeled	Motor Cars	Tractors	Lorries, showing description	Trucks, showing description	Trailers	Motor Bicycles	Bicycles	
Effective Strength of Unit																									
Details, by Arms attached to unit as in War Establishment:																									
Total																									
War Establishment																									
Wanting to complete (Detail of Personnel and Horses below)																									
Surplus																									
*Attached (not to include the details shown above)																									
Civilians:— Employed with the Unit																									
Accompanying the Unit																									
TOTAL RATIONED ...																									

* In the case of field ambulances, hospitals or depots, the number of patients are to be included here, the names being shown in A. F. A. 36.

Signature of Commander.

Date of Despatch.

Officers and men who have become casuals, been transferred or joined since last report.

Place __Sanctuary Wood__ Date __31.12.15.__

Regtl. Number	Rank	Name	Corps	Nature of casualty, or name of unit from or to which transferred	Date of being struck off or coming on the ration return	Remarks*
1994	Pte	Kelsey F	6 D.L.I.	Wounded	29-12-15	
1126	Cpl	Dunn A	-Do-	Gone Sick	27-12-15	
1939	Pte	Shields C	-Do-	-Do-	27-12-15	
3891	"	Kelly A	-Do-	-Do-	27-12-15	
786	Cpl	Malone	-Do-	-Do-	22-12-15	
2757	Pte	Elgie J A	-Do-	-Do-	19-12-15	
2044	"	Clark W	-Do-	-Do-	30-12-15	
2804	Pte	Hudson H	-Do-	-Do-	30-12-15	
3054	"	Waite J J	-Do-	-Do-	28-12-15	
4018	"	Marwood J	-Do-	-Do-	28-12-15	
994	Sgt	Race B.B	-Do-	-Do-	24-12-15	
1976	Pte	Dornley W	-Do-	-Do-	24-12-15	
3866	"	Clark J	-Do-	-Do-	24-12-15	
1831	"	Jobson T	-Do-	-Do-	22-12-15	
1652	"	Wooten J	-Do-	-Do-	22-12-15	
1432	"	Shaw	-Do-	-Do-	22-12-15	
2949	"	Thompson	-Do-	-Do-	25-12-15	
2154	Sgt	Hardacre	-Do-	-Do-	25-12-15	
2697	Pte	Capp W	-Do-	-Do-	27-12-15	
2067	Cpl	Brooks J	-Do-	-Do-	26-12-15	
370	Sgt	Brown M	-Do-	-Do-	26-12-15	
1848	Pte	Lambert	-Do-	-Do-	28-12-15	
242	Pte	Mackintosh W	-Do-	-Do-	26-12-15	
1448	"	Blades J M	-Do-	-Do-	26-12-15	
1915	"	Agar A P	Do	-Do-	23-12-15	
1908	"	Stevens N	-Do-	-Do-	24-12-15	
3328	Pte	Benson R	-Do-	Retd to Duty	1-11-15	
2197	"	Harrison	-Do-	-Do-	16-12-15	

* State whether absence is of a permanent or temporary nature, adding, in the case of casuals from wounds or disease, any available information for communication to the relatives.

WAR DIARY
or
INTELLIGENCE SUMMARY.

(Erase heading not required.)

Instructions regarding War Diaries and Intelligence Summaries are contained in F. S. Regs., Part II. and the Staff Manual respectively. Title pages will be prepared in manuscript.

C^o Durham L.I

Place	Date	Hour	Summary of Events and Information	Remarks and references to Appendices
Ypres	1916 Jany 1	—	The first day of the new Year was spent in Brigade Reserve at Kruple Copse (G 24 a 3.2) Our Divisional Artillery strafed at midnight provoking very little retaliation, and the artillery throughout the day was normally active. Captain R.B. Bradford appointed Brigade Major 151st Infantry Brigade. Brant Lt G. Yalawyn appointed Adjutant.	M.1
	2	1	A draft of 60 other ranks from the 3rd Entrenching Battalion was received. The majority of the men were generally good but—en casey of Scabies were sent to Hospital. The same day Capt. J. Walton rejoined the Battalion from England after an absence revived wounds of 6½ months. Lieut S.B. Shotte arrived at Bickelnock from England after a number absence.	
	3		Very quiet day, except for normal artillery activity in various parts of the front	

1577 Wt. W10791/1773 500,000 1/15 D. D. & L. A.D.S.S./Forms/C. 2118.

Army Form C. 2118.

WAR DIARY

or

INTELLIGENCE SUMMARY.

(Erase heading not required.)

Instructions regarding War Diaries and Intelligence
Summaries are contained in F. S. Regs., Part II.
and the Staff Manual respectively. Title pages
will be prepared in manuscript.

Place	Date	Hour	Summary of Events and Information	Remarks and references to Appendices
	4	—	We relieved the 5th Border Regiment in trenches A7–A12 T24d 7.0 to T24d 8.9, including its upper slopes of Sanctuary Wood immediately behind these trenches. Relief was carried out from 3.35 p.m. to about 6.30 p.m. Considerable work done in trenches principally drainage. Quiet day, with only one casualty. Private Robinson, R.J., slightly wounded and Private M. Vickerstaffe killed. The two officers appear to have one trenches at A7 (T24d 7.0) registered to a second.	
T24d 7.0	5	—	Quiet by day, with considerable artillery and aerial activity. It is noticeable that our guns have to stop strafing the moment the redoubtable FOKKER makes its appearance.	
	6	—	Enemy rather more active. Divisional artillery had a practice barrage of fire which was successfully carried out. The enemy retaliated with a few rounds behind	

WAR DIARY

or

INTELLIGENCE SUMMARY.

(*Erase heading not required.*)

Instructions regarding War Diaries and Intelligence
Summaries are contained in F. S. Regs., Part II.
and the Staff Manual respectively. Title pages
will be prepared in manuscript.

Place	Date	Hour	Summary of Events and Information	Remarks and references to Appendices
			Sanctuary Wood (I 2 4 d) and some interchange to A7-A9 – the same old place. Hit by Pte Whitfield & W. Coy wounded was the only casualty. We feel that we have checked, registered and relaid it traverses have spared many lives. Our artillery carried out bombardment of Hill 60 –	
	8	–	the Germans one – and considerable damage appeared to be done. During the retaliation 1375 Pte Rowe M. W. Coy was killed in A5.	
	9	–	A quieter day, the Battalion was relieved by the 5th Border Regiment and proceeded to Dickebusch Huts H 26 b. central at 4-25 pm.	
Dickebusch (4 2 6 b.)	10	–	In Huts at Dickebusch. 2242 Pte Anderson J accidentally killed with a revolver bullet. The general condition of the Camp very much improved since last visit. Inspection under company arrangements of clothing equipment – rifles [Lewis?] Helmets, socks and shirts. Rain to	
	11	–		

Army Form C. 2118.

WAR DIARY

or

INTELLIGENCE SUMMARY.

(Erase heading not required.)

Instructions regarding War Diaries and Intelligence Summaries are contained in F. S. Regs., Part II. and the Staff Manual respectively. Title pages will be prepared in manuscript.

Place	Date	Hour	Summary of Events and Information	Remarks and references to Appendices
	12	—	generally satisfactory. Church parade services for all denominations. Two German aeroplanes flew over the camp and dropped several shells or bombs in its vicinity, without however doing any damage. Our machines chased them away.	
	13	—	The Royal Artillery band gave selections in the camp during the morning. The Battalion of the 5th Border Regiment in trenches A.7 to A.12 (I.24.d.7.0 & I.24.d.8.9) four Lewis machine guns received from Brigade Store. The following officers arrived from England - Lieut W. P. Gill (re-joined) 2/Lieut Nicholas (re-joined) from the 3rd Batt - 2/Lieut [ ] reported for duty from England	
Ypres I.24.d.7.0	14	—	1479 Pte Coulthard [?] J. "C" Company, wounded by a civilian [ ] bearing down beyond [ ] accumulating [ ] this French is not protected from [ ] to his wounds.	

1577 Wt.W10791/1773 500,000 1/15 D. D. & L.   A.D.S.S./Forms/C. 2118.

Army Form C. 2118.

WAR DIARY

or

INTELLIGENCE SUMMARY.

(Erase heading not required.)

Instructions regarding War Diaries and Intelligence
Summaries are contained in F. S. Regs., Part II.
and the Staff Manual respectively. Title pages
will be prepared in manuscript.

Place	Date	Hour	Summary of Events and Information	Remarks and references to Appendices
	15	—	enemy lines in front of Stirling Castle, but is largely covered by the wood. Working parties were very busy repairing R.E.'s and considerable work was done in opening that Canal communication trench which was a long way after in December. The trenches as always the front line recommended trenches by this time nearly improved since the last tour of these trenches. Draft of one officer (Lieut. V.T.R. (Clarke) ?) the ranks arrived at Belgium hut.	
	16	—	Notification received through the medium of the times of several honours and awards for officers & men of the Battalion. These included four officers of whom the present Commanding officer Lieut Col G.W. Elflorp and Lieut-Col G.A. Stevens both of whom received the D.S.O. A copy of Battalion Orders for this date	

1577 Wt. W10791/1773 500,000 1/15 D. D. & L.   A.D.S.S./Forms/C. 2118.

WAR DIARY
or
INTELLIGENCE SUMMARY.

(Erase heading not required.)

Instructions regarding War Diaries and Intelligence Summaries are contained in F. S. Regs., Part II. and the Staff Manual respectively. Title pages will be prepared in manuscript.

Place	Date	Hour	Summary of Events and Information	Remarks and references to Appendices
	17		showing these awards is attached as an appendix. Official notification received of the promotion to Lieutenant of 2nd Lieut. R.F. Brock (Machine Gun Officer) 1st Lieut. J. Barron, with effect from 1st Dec. 1915. Official notification received of promotion to 2nd Lieut of Company Sergt-Major R. Bowman. Our artillery carried out a bombardment of the enemy's trenches and strong points on a considerable scale. Our trench mortars were trained in anticipation of enemy retaliation which proved to be vigorous. St Peters Street and Sanctuary Wood very heavily shelled with ring explosive and shrapnel. Our field guns again retaliated the ranges were larger and eight the enemy's gun eventually being silenced in the own fire from a howitzer.	

1577   Wt. W10791/1773   500,000   1/15   D. D. & L.   A.D.S.S./Forms/C. 2118.

Army Form C. 2118.

WAR DIARY

or

INTELLIGENCE SUMMARY.

(Erase heading not required.)

Instructions regarding War Diaries and Intelligence Summaries are contained in F. S. Regs., Part II. and the Staff Manual respectively. Title pages will be prepared in manuscript.

Place	Date	Hour	Summary of Events and Information	Remarks and references to Appendices
Ypres Ballaol 32	18		Capt. Watkins gallantly reorganged a little dribble of fire to draw from the enemy & essentially their engineers to adjacent Stuff building the heavy fire. The casualties of the officer & staff. The whole of the drug-out in St. Peter's Street were blown in, leaving the casualties considerably. The number of shells fired were remarkably slight. Stray evacuated of one man (Pte. Channing) being killed. Four stores of X Coy. wounded in I.24.d.9.0. the often confirmed had to casualties. Relieved by 5th Border Regt.	
	19		14 Brigade Reserve at Maple Copse. Fine weather. Normal artillery activity on both sides. The enemy commenced an organged bombardment of our trenches between A7 and A9. Particularly Redoubt 2 in I.24.d.3.3. the platoon of "M" Coy. in this strong point had a bad time. One man	

1577 Wt. W10791/1773 500,000 1/15 D.D. & L. A.D.S.S./Forms/C. 2118.

WAR DIARY

or

INTELLIGENCE SUMMARY.

(Erase heading not required.)

Instructions regarding War Diaries and Intelligence Summaries are contained in F. S. Regs., Part II. and the Staff Manual respectively. Title pages will be prepared in manuscript.

Place	Date	Hour	Summary of Events and Information	Remarks and references to Appendices
	20	—	Private Stephenson was killed. A few steers including Platoon Sergt Hogg. Fare-Cpl Dunsmore wounded. 2/Lieut. Wilson. Coy/Serj Major Walter and Bugler Scrafton behaved commendably during the bombardment which lasted until mid day. Our artillery was hampered by defective S's ammunition, yet dropped, not pronounced, continued by defective artillery activity through. Remained splendidly behaved until dusk.	
A.12 yds.	21	—	Very quiet day except for artillery. Relieved code by heard from other parts of the Line. Relieved 5th Border Regt— in the front line. A7 t/712.	
	22	—	Enemy registered wire entanglement over Sackville Street. Parts of the hill heavily shelled. Ammunition 13% Rifle Grenades Killed.	

1577 Wt. W10791/1773 500,000 1/15 D. D. & L. A.D.S.S./Forms/C. 2118.

Army Form C. 2118.

WAR DIARY

or

INTELLIGENCE SUMMARY.

(Erase heading not required.)

Instructions regarding War Diaries and Intelligence Summaries are contained in F. S. Regs., Part II. and the Staff Manual respectively. Title pages will be prepared in manuscript.

Place	Date	Hour	Summary of Events and Information	Remarks and references to Appendices
	23	—	In trenches A9 B9 A12 Continued work on front-line, support-line (reclaimed) and communication trenches	
	24	—	Relieved by 5th Border Regiment. Proceeded to Divisional Reserve at Dickebusch	
	25	—	Usual medical inspections and bathing at Poperinghe Baths. Two officers 74 men proceeded on leave during the four days. also 93 men were granted several one month's leave on re-engaging	
At Dickebusch	26	—	At Dickebusch Huts	
	27	.	Very quiet day	
	28	.	Relieved the 5th Border Regiment who reported having	
	29	—	had a very quiet four days.	
1-7-A12 Ypres.	30		Damp, foggy weather with an easterly wind blowing at about 5 miles per hour. Afternoon X Coy and Private Blackburne, Y Coy wounded with ...	

1577 Wt.W10791/1773 500,000 1/15 D. D. & L.   A.D.S.S./Forms/C. 2118.

WAR DIARY

or

INTELLIGENCE SUMMARY.

(Erase heading not required.)

Instructions regarding War Diaries and Intelligence
Summaries are contained in F. S. Regs., Part II.
and the Staff Manual respectively. Title pages
will be prepared in manuscript.

Place	Date	Hour	Summary of Events and Information	Remarks and references to Appendices
	31	—	out owing. Great precautions against gas attacks. The wind being still easterly gas guards to at 6 a.m. continued. Unusual gas precautions were strictly observed during the day but nothing of interest occurred during the day.	

4577 Wt. W10791/1773 500,000 1/15 D. D. & L.   A.D.S.S./Forms/C. 2118.

FIELD RETURN.

Army Form B. 213.

(To be furnished by all arms, services, and departments (except A.S.C. units) to the A. G.'s Office at the Base in accordance with Field Service Regulations, Part II.)

No. of Report. —

RETURN showing numbers RATIONED by, and Transport on charge of, 6ᵗʰ Durham R.L. at ———— Date. 1-1-16.

DETAIL	Personnel			Animals. Horses			Mules		Camels	Oxen	Guns, carriages, and limbers and transport vehicles					Horsed		Mechanical				
	Officers	Other ranks	Natives	Riding	Draught	Heavy Draught	Pack	Large	Small			Guns, carriages and limbers, showing description	Ammunition wagons and limbers	Machine Guns	Aircraft, showing description	4 Wheeled	2 Wheeled	Motor Cars	Tractors	Lorries, showing description	Trucks, showing description	Trailers	Motor Bicycles	Bicycles	REMARKS
Effective Strength of Unit	29/735																								
Details, by *Arms* attached to unit as in War Establishment:— Medical Office - 1 Armourer - 6																									
Total	28,742																								
War Establishment	30,800																								
Wanting to complete	2,58																								
(Detail of Personnel and Horses below) Surplus																									
*Attached (not to include the details shown above)																									
Civilians:— Employed with the Unit Accompanying the Unit																									
TOTAL RATIONED ...																									

* In the case of field ambulances, hospitals or depots, the number of patients are to be included here, the names being shown in A. F. A. 36.

———— Signature of Commander.

———— Date of Despatch.

For information of the A.G.'s Office at the Base.

Officers and men who have become casuals, been transferred or joined since last report.

Place _In the Field._   Date _7 – 1 – 16._

Regtl. Number	Rank	Name	Corps	Nature of casualty, or name of unit from or to which transferred	Date of being struck off or coming on the ration return	Remarks*
3893	Pte.	Riley G.	6 D.L.I.	Killed	31-12-15	
2043	"	Vickerstaffe G.	–Do–	–Do–	5-1-16	
2033	"	Greenwood S.	–Do–	Wounded	31-12-15	
1881	"	Place J.W.	–Do–	–Do–	31-12-15	
61	Sgt.	Smith E.	–Do–	–Do–	2-1-16	
1905	Pte.	German E.	–Do–	–Do–	2-1-16	
3089	Pte	Robinson R.	–Do–	–Do–	5-1-16	
1530	"	Green R.W.	–Do.	Evac. Sick	1-1-16	
3342	"	Sanderson J.	–Do–	–Do–	2-1-16	
3556	"	Robinson J.G.	–Do–	–Do–	2-1-16	
2998	"	Wallace W.H.	–Do–	–Do–	2-1-16	
4136	"	Wilson B.	–Do–	–Do–	2-1-16	
3982	"	Hickey H.	–Do–	–Do–	1-1-16	
3332	"	Bland	–Do–	–Do–	3-1-16	
577	Sgt	Emmerson	–Do–	–Do–	3-1-16	
1352	Pte	Wright J.N.	–Do–	–Do–	3-1-16	
4150	"	Russell G.	–Do–	–Do–	4-1-16	
2911	"	Richardson A.	–Do–	–Do–	4-1-16	
2017	"	Peadon W.	–Do–	–Do–	5-1-16	
1687	L/Sgt	Gill R.W.	–Do	–Do–	5-1-16	
2114	Pte	Patterson	–Do–	–Do–	5-1-16	
3566	"	McDonald	–Do–	–Do–	5-1-16	
1677	Cpl.	Turton W.	–Do.	–Do–	5-1-16	
18	Pte	Alderson W.	–Do–	–Do–	3-1-16	
2558	"	Hetherington A.	–Do	–Do–	3-1-16	
2354	"	Fraser	–Do–	Re'td to Duty	1-1-16	
1452	"	Shaw T.	–Do	–Do–	3-1-16	
1776	"	Bromley W.	–Do–	–Do–	4-1-16	

* State whether absence is of a permanent or temporary nature, adding, in the case of casuals from wounds or disease, any available information for communication to the relatives.

PUBLIC RECORD OFFICE

Officers and men who have become casuals, been transferred or joined since last report.

Place_____   Date_____

Regtl. Number	Rank	Name	Corps	Nature of casualty, or name of unit from or to which transferred	Date of being struck off or coming on the ration return	Remarks*
3866	Pte	Clarke J.	6 D.L.I.	Retd to Duty	4-1-16	
3024	"	Garvey T.	-Do-	-Do-	4-1-16	
1146	Cpl	Dunn A.	-Do-	-Do-	5-1-16	
3024	Pte	Waites	-Do-	-Do-	5-1-16	
2345	"	Catchpole R.	-Do-	-Do-	2-1-16	
2114	"	Patterson T.	-Do-	Evac Sick	6-1-16	
2120	"	Wood M.	-Do-	-Do-	6-1-16	

* State whether absence is of a permanent or temporary nature, adding, in the case of casuals from wounds or disease, any available information for communication to the relatives.

FIELD RETURN.

Army Form B. 213.

No. of Report _____

(To be furnished by all arms, services, and departments (except A.S.C. units) to the A. G.'s Office at the Base in accordance with Field Service Regulations, Part II.)

RETURN showing numbers RATIONED by, and Transport on charge of, _____ at _____ Date. _____

DETAIL	Personnel			Animals								Guns, carriages, and limbers and transport vehicles													REMARKS
	Officers	Other ranks	Natives	Horses			Mules		Camels	Oxen	Guns, carriages, limbers, showing description	Ammunition wagons and limbers	Machine guns	Aircraft, showing description	Horsed		Motor Cars	Tractors	Mechanical			Motor Bicycles	Bicycles	
				Riding	Draught	Heavy Draught	Pack	Large	Small							4 Wheeled	2 Wheeled			Lorries, showing description	Trucks, showing description	Trailers			

Effective Strength of Unit

Details, *by Arms* attached to unit as in War Establishment :—

Total

War Establishment

Wanting to complete

Surplus

(Detail of Personnel and Horses below)

*Attached (not to include the details shown above)

Civilians :— Employed with the Unit Accompanying the Unit

TOTAL RATIONED ...

* In the case of field ambulances, hospitals or depots, the number of patients are to be included here, the names being shown in A. F. A. 36.

_____ Signature of Commander.

_____ Date of Despatch.

Officers and men who have become casuals, been transferred or joined since last report.

Place _The Field_   Date _14th January 1916_

Regtl. Number	Rank	Name	Corps	Nature of casualty, or name of unit from or to which transferred	Date of being struck off or coming on the ration return	Remarks*
2242	Pte	Anderson G.	6 D.L.I.	Accidentlly killed	10-1-16	W.boy.
4182	Pte	Whitfield G.W.	-Do-	Wounded	7-1-16	W.boy
1375	"	Lowes C.B.	-Do-	Killed	8-1-16	W.boy
2005	"	Huggins E.	-Do	Evac. Sick	7-1-16	665.
2120	"	Wood C.B.	-Do	-Do-	7-1-16	665
3041	"	Roxby R.	-Do-	-Do-	7-1-16	665
21	Cpl	Bell T.	-Do-	-Do-	8-1-16	
1250	Pte	Parkinson	-Do-	-Do-	8-1-16	665
2285	Sgt	Watson J	-Do-	-Do-	8-1-16	
2016	L/Sgt	O'Neil J	-Do-	-Do-	9-1-16	
3152	Pte	Burdon R.	-Do-	-Do	9-1-16	
3681	L/Cpl	Jefferson W.	-Do-	-Do-	9-1-16	
2445	Cpl	Elliott A.	-Do	-Do-	9-1-16	
2681	Pte	Thrower S.	-Do-	-Do-	9-1-16	
1789	Pte	Renahen J.	-Do-	-Do-	11-1-16	
1459	"	Emmerson S.	-Do-	-Do-	11-1-16	
2643	L/Cpl	Angus S.	-Do-	-Do-	12-1-16	
1548	L/Cpl	Nimmons W.J.	-Do-	-Do-	12-1-16	
1446	Pte	Rivers R.	-Do-	-Do-	12-1-16	
1900	"	Robinson J.A	-Do-	-Do-	12-1-16	
1540	"	Neasham B.	-Do-	-Do-	12-1-16	
2057	"	McKeene J.	-Do-	-Do-	12-1-16	
1798	"	Broadley J.	-Do-	-Do-	12-1-16	
1161	"	Lally. A.	-Do-	-Do-	13-1-16	
1260	"	Bell T.	-Do-	-Do-	13-1-16	
2438	"	Hunter T.	-Do-	-Do-	13-1-16	
709	"	Ridley	-Do-	-Do-	13-1-16	

* State whether absence is of a permanent or temporary nature, adding, in the case of casuals from wounds or disease, any available information for communication to the relatives.

For information of the A.G.'s Office at the Base.

Officers and men who have become casuals, been transferred or joined since last report.

Place _The Field_ Date _14 Jany. 1916_

Regtl. Number	Rank	Name	Corps	Nature of casualty, or name of unit from or to which transferred	Date of being struck off or coming on the ration return	Remarks*
3099	Pte	Parkin J.W	6 D.L.I	Evac Sick	13-1-16	
3210	"	Simpson G	-Do-	-Do	13-1-16	
1284	"	Coughlin J.	-Do-	Retd to Duty	7-1-16	
1958	"	Stevens N.	-Do-	-Do	7-1-16	
1352	"	Wright J.W.	-Do-	-Do-	7-1-16	
3839	"	Evans E.	-Do-	-Do-	8-1-16	
1530	"	Green R.W.	-Do-	-Do-	8-1-16	
2995	"	Wallace W.H	-Do-	-Do-	8-1-16	
2114	"	Pattison J.	-Do-	-Do-	9-1-16	
2608	"	Clarke J	-Do-	-Do-	9-1-16	
1687	L/Sgt	Gill R.W	-Do-	-Do-	9-1-16	
736	Cpl	Malone J.	-Do-	-Do-	9-1-16	
1355	Pte	Hughes J	-Do-	-Do-	8-1-16	
3232	Pte	Bland N	-Do-	-Do-	9-1-16	
547	Sgt	Emmerson R.H.	-Do-	-Do-	11-1-16	
21	Cpl	Bell J.	-Do-	-Do-	11-1-16	
2976	Pte	Wray J.	-Do-	-Do-	11-1-16	
1848	"	Lambert J.T	-Do-	-Do-	11-1-16	
1618	"	Lambert A	-Do-	-Do-	11-1-16	
2806	"	Hudson H	-Do-	-Do-	13-1-16	
1939	"	Shield J.	-Do-	-Do-	8-1-16	
1458	"	Blads R	-Do-	-Do-	8-1-16	
4182	"	Westfield G.W.	-Do-	-Do-	11-1-16	
1843	"	Peacock W.J.	-Do-	-Do-	9-1-16	
3158	"	Hill C.	-Do-	Evac Sick	11-1-16	
3213	"	Evans Q	-Do-	-Do-	11-1-16	

* State whether absence is of a permanent or temporary nature, adding, in the case of casuals from wounds or disease, any available information for communication to the relatives.

Army Form B. 213.

FIELD RETURN.

(To be furnished by all arms, services, and departments (except A.S.C. units) to the A. G.'s Office at the Base in accordance with Field Service Regulations, Part II.)

No. of Report.

RETURN showing numbers RATIONED by, and Transport on charge of, 6th Bn Buffs at Ypres 21 Nov 1916 Date.

DETAIL	Personnel			Horses			Mules		Camels	Oxen	Guns, carriages and limbers, showing description	Ammunition wagons and limbers	Machine Guns	Aircraft, showing description	Horsed		Mechanical					Motor Bicycles	Bicycles	REMARKS
	Officers	Other ranks	Natives	Riding	Draught	Heavy Draught	Pack	Large	Small							4 Wheeled	2 Wheeled	Motor Cars	Tractors	Lorries, showing description	Trucks, showing description	Trailers			
Effective Strength of Unit																								
Details, by Arms attached to unit as in War Establishment:—	29	744	—	13	22	13	9	9																
Special Officer	1																							
Rank &	1	6																						
memor																								
Total	28	751		13	22	13	9	9																
War Establishment	30	1017																						
Wanting to complete	2	266																						
Surplus																								
*Attached (not to include the details shown above)	2	8																						
Civilians:— Employed with the Unit Accompanying the Unit																								
TOTAL RATIONED ...	28	780																						

(Detail of Personnel and Horses below)

* In the case of field ambulances, hospitals or depots, the number of patients are to be included here, the names being shown in A. F. A. 36.

————— Signature of Commander.

————— Date of Despatch.

For information of the A.G.'s Office at the Base.

Officers and men who have become casuals, been transferred or joined since last report.

Place __The Field__   Date __21 Jany. 1916.__

Regtl. Number	Rank	Name	Corps 609	Nature of casualty, or name of unit from or to which transferred	Date of being struck off or coming on the ration return	Remarks*
		Capt Cardew.	6 D.L.I.	Wounded	17-1-16	
1479	Pte	Coulthard H.	6 D.L.I. y	Killed	14-1-16	
1886	"	Cranney J.	Do z	Killed	19-1-16	
3056	"	Ellison G.	Do z	Wounded	19-1-16	
2732	"	Dryden J.	Do y	Wounded	17-1-16	
2031	"	Donaghy O	Do z	Wounded	17-1-16	
2981	"	Ward G.	Do z	Wounded	17-1-16	
5372	"	Stephenson W.	Do W	Killed	19-1-16	
1071	Sgt	Hogg R.V.	Do W	Wounded	19-1-16	
2581	L/Cpl	Quilchmire J.	Do W	Wounded	19-1-16	
3119	Pte	Sunter A.	Do W	Wounded	19-1-16	
1705	"	Allison J.	Do W	Wounded	19-1-16	
2903	Pte	Rodgers	Do	Evac Sick	15-1-16	
2765	"	Graham J.	Do	Do	12-1-16	
3383	"	Stewart R.	Do	Do	19-1-16	
5287	"	Rodmell G.	Do	Do	19-1-16	
2775	"	Gowton J.W.	Do	Do	19-1-16	
2093	"	Payne G.	Do	Do	19-1-16	
2564	"	Jardine J.B.	Do	Do	19-1-16	
4112	"	Simpson J.	Do	Do	19-1-16	
1971	"	Gooding J.	Do	Do	20-1-16	
3871	"	Kelly J.	Do	Do	20-1-16	
1014	"	Hepple H.	Do	Do	15-1-16	
2005	"	Huggins E.	Do	Re'td to Duty	15-1-16	
2017	"	Peadon W.	Do	Do	15-1-16	
2911	"	Richardson H	Do	Do	17-1-16	
2765	"	Graham J.	Do	Do	18-1-16	

* State whether absence is of a permanent or temporary nature, adding, in the case of casuals from wounds or disease, any available information for communication to the relatives.

2.

Officers and men who have become casuals, been transferred or joined since last report.

Place __The Field__   Date __21 Jany 1916.__

Regtl. Number	Rank	Name	Corps	Nature of casualty, or name of unit from or to which transferred	Date of being struck off or coming on the ration return	Remarks*
1540	Pte	Neasham J	6 D.L.I.	Ret'd to Duty	18-1-16	
3210	"	Simpson G.	Do	Do	19-1-16	
2902	"	Robb W.	Do	Do	20-1-16	
3982	"	Hickey H.	Do	Do	18-1-16	
3152	"	Burdon R P	Do	Do	14-1-16	
2041	"	Roxby R	Do	Do	17-1-16	
3871	"	Kelly J.	Do	Do	19-1-16	
1459	"	Emmerson	Do	Do	20-1-16	

* State whether absence is of a permanent or temporary nature, adding, in the case of casuals from wounds or disease, any available information for communication to the relatives.

Battalion Orders
by
Major G. A. Stevens. Cmdg 6th Durham L.I.
16-1-16

<u>1</u> Honours.

The "King has been graciously pleased to approve of the under-mentioned Honours and Awards for distinguished service in the Field, with effect from 1 January 1916. —

To be Companion of the Distinguished Service Order—
Major (temp. Lieut-Col.) John William Jeffreys. Durham Light Infantry.
Major George Archibald Stevens, Royal Fusiliers.
Awarded Military Cross. —
2Lieut (temp. Lieut) William Perceval Gill
Awarded Distinguished Conduct Medals. —
Regimental Sergt. Major G. Perry (Permanent Staff)
Company (now Regimental) Sergt. Major F. H. Bousfield
(Permanent Staff)
Company Sergt. Major (temp. Lieut) H. McNair
Lance-Corporal J. J. Robinson.

<u>2</u> Extract from "London Gazette."
To be Lieutenants (temporary). — 2 Lieut.
A. L. Brock and 2 Lieut. J. Barrow, Durham Light Infantry. dated 1 December 1915.

3 Officers.

The following Officers arrived from England on the dates stated and were posted to Companies as shewn.-

12 Jany 1916	Lieut. W.P. Gill	To Y Company
	2Lt. H.H. Nicholson	To X Company
	2Lt. A.W. Freeman	To W Company
16 Jany 1916	2Lt. V.H. Clark	To X Company.

4 Move.

On being relieved by 5ᵗʰ Border Regiment tomorrow night, Companies will proceed as follows.- "W" Company to Redoubts 2, 3, and 4; "X" Company to Canal Dug-Outs; "Y" Company to Sanctuary Wood Dug-Outs; "Z" Company to Maple Copse and Redoubt 6.

(Sgd) C.E. Yaldwyn.
2 Lieut & Adjutant
6ᵗʰ Durham L.I.

WAR DIARY
or
INTELLIGENCE SUMMARY.
(Erase heading not required.)

Instructions regarding War Diaries and Intelligence Summaries are contained in F. S. Regs., Part II. and the Staff Manual respectively. Title pages will be prepared in manuscript.

Place	Date	Hour	Summary of Events and Information	Remarks and references to Appendices
Ypres I.24.c.	1.2.16		In trenches A7 to A12. At dusk Battalion took over rearrangement of line. X Company remained in trenches A10 and A11 which now became the left of our line. Z Company vacated trench A12 which was taken over by the 8th DURHAMS and took over trenches A6 and A7. Y Company retained trenches A8 and A9. W Company took over two entirely new trenches A4 and A5. The Battalion on the right was the 5th YORKSHIRE REGT. Our Battalion Headquarters remained in the same place. These reliefs were completed about 7pm and the night passed very quietly. The Battalion front now extended from trench A4 to A11.	
Ypres	2.2.16		In trenches as above. The guns were busy as usual. The Battalion was relieved by the 5th BORDER REGT. and proceeded into close support, companies being distributed as follows:— W Coy. one platoon in R1 and one platoon in dug-outs I.30.b.; X Coy. in dug-outs at I.24.b.; Y Coy. in dug-outs at VIGO STREET end of SANCTUARY WOOD I.24.; Z Coy. one platoon in SANCTUARY WOOD I.24., one platoon BORDER LANE end of SANCTUARY WOOD in R3 I.24., one platoon in R3 I.24. two platoons in R2 I.24., one platoon in R4 I.24. W and X companies	

1577 Wt. W10791/1773 500,000 1/15 D. D. & L. A.D.SS./Forms/C. 2118.

Army Form C. 2118.

WAR DIARY

or

INTELLIGENCE SUMMARY.

(Erase heading not required.)

Instructions regarding War Diaries and Intelligence Summaries are contained in F. S. Regs., Part II. and the Staff Manual respectively. Title pages will be prepared in manuscript.

Place	Date	Hour	Summary of Events and Information	Remarks and references to Appendices
			were under the Command of O.C. Right Sub. Sector (Col. HEDLEY) 5th BORDER REGT and Y Company under the Command of the O.C. Left Sub. Sector (Col. HENDERSON) 9th DURHAM L.I. Battalion Headquarters were in MAPLE COPSE. The Lewis Gunners remained with their companies and the Battalion Grenadiers were in MAPLE COPSE, I,2,4, & amb r.	
Ypres	3.2.16		In close support as above the enemys artillery was early active. About 8.30 am. quite a number of ?? were put onto MAPLE LODGE and during the morning and up till late in the afternoon OBSERVATORY RIDGE received considerable attention from whizz-bangs, shrapnel + champer.	
Ypres	4.2.16		In close support as above. Working parties found during the day and at night. 2638 L/c BROWN T Z Company and 3779 Pte LONG A W Company wounded on working parties.	
Ypres	5.2.16		In close support as above. Fine warm weather. Enemys artillery still active and enemy aeroplanes very busy about. 2647 Sergt BAINBRIDGE AR shot by a sniper who had been causing considerable trouble yesterday and today. 887 Pte STAFFORD JR Z Company shot through the head	

1577 Wt. W10791/1773 500,000 1/15 D. D. & L. A.D.S.S./Forms/C. 2118.

WAR DIARY

or

INTELLIGENCE SUMMARY.

(Erase heading not required.)

Instructions regarding War Diaries and Intelligence Summaries are contained in F. S. Regs., Part II. and the Staff Manual respectively. Title pages will be prepared in manuscript.

Place	Date	Hour	Summary of Events and Information	Remarks and references to Appendices
Ypres	6th Feb.		at MAPLE COPSE DUMP, I.24.a.3.3. whilst working on the light railway, 2779 Pte Grant R. 2340 Pte Rutherford & 3848 Pte Forrest Q.T. and 1512 Pte Read A. wounded details in Sanctuary Wood, I.24.d.1.9, whilst from their billets to close support as above. Damp, foggy, not misty weather. Our divisional artillery arranged a bombardment of Hill 60 which was carried out effectively. The enemy were vigorous in their retaliation, but fortunately did very little damage to Battalion relieved the 5th Border Regt. in the same trenches at dusk, companies being distributed as follows:– "W" Coy A4 – A5; "Z" Coy A6 – A7; "Y" Company A8 – A9; "X" Coy A10 – A11.	
Ypres	7th Feb.		In trenches as above. the enemy wirflanged our trenches particularly A6 and A7, at intervals during the day. 1956 Pte Adamson R.H. "Y" Coy was killed and 9473 Cpl Denham T.3340 Pte Courtland W, wounded, in A.8. just on the left of St PETER ST., C.T. trenches as above. A wire barrier day Roy's naval the enemy appeared to be having a practice barrage	

1577 Wt. W10791/1773 500,000 1/15 D. D. & L. A.D.S.S./Forms/C. 2118.

Army Form C. 2118.

WAR DIARY

or

INTELLIGENCE SUMMARY.

(Erase heading not required.)

Instructions regarding War Diaries and Intelligence Summaries are contained in F. S. Regs., Part II. and the Staff Manual respectively. Title pages will be prepared in manuscript.

Place	Date	Hour	Summary of Events and Information	Remarks and references to Appendices
Ypres	9th		In trenches as above. A fine day with the aeroplanes early on its move. Some of our planes proceeded over the enemy lines on reconnaissance were about 8 am. Our guns bombarded enemy's battery positions at 7-30 am and 8 am. There was some retaliatory shelling from the other side during the day. It was noted that the enemy had turned two (?) rifts from the left front of CLONMEL COPSE (TIT c 3.2). Gun sounds were directed to these during the afternoon, and at night rifle and machine gun fire was concentrated on these points. [A6 and A7] were treated to several rounds of ammunition during the afternoon. The German artillery was again very busy shelling over roads behind our lines.	
Ypres	10th		In trenches as above. Another very heavy day. Our artillery made a very early and determined start and	

1577 Wt.W10791/1773 500,000 1/15 D. D. & L. A.D.S.S./Forms/C. 2118.

WAR DIARY

or

INTELLIGENCE SUMMARY.

(Erase heading not required.)

Instructions regarding War Diaries and Intelligence Summaries are contained in F. S. Regs., Part II. and the Staff Manual respectively. Title pages will be prepared in manuscript.

Place	Date	Hour	Summary of Events and Information	Remarks and references to Appendices
			of fire over the support line the whole support area. The front line was practically left untouched but about 1,500 ... were sent into Sanctuary Wood and the Vigo St and Sackville St area (I 24 b.). The enemy heavy artillery was also very active & shelled very heavily the Fosseway – Krinkhaat road (H 33 b to H 24 a) during the day, and at night gas shells were sent over into Ypres and Zillebeke. 2423- Pte Gee T.J. y Coy and 2879 Pte Marley D X Coy were killed whilst sitting in a dug-out in Sanctuary Wood, and 2642 Pte Angus wounded. 1490 Pte Parry W.H. was wounded in Sackville St K, the artillery activity continued throughout the night and until daybreak. An enemy aeroplane came over our lines about 3.30 p.m. flying very low, and remained in close vicinity until ... rifle and machine gun fire were quite ineffective in driving it away.	

WAR DIARY

or

INTELLIGENCE SUMMARY.

(Erase heading not required.)

Instructions regarding War Diaries and Intelligence
Summaries are contained in F. S. Regs., Part II.
and the Staff Manual respectively. Title pages
will be prepared in manuscript.

Place	Date	Hour	Summary of Events and Information	Remarks and references to Appendices
			~~reconstruction done~~ considerable damage since to the environs of the enemy into consequential retaliated. Reference was again shown for the area behind the lines, and no damage was done to the front line, nor were any casualties sustained the Batt= was relieved by the 5th Border Regt, & proceeded into Brigade Reserve, the distribution of Companies was as follows:- "W" & "Z" Coys (I.23d) "X" & "Y" Coys (I.20a) and Battalion Headquarters at Railway Dug-Outs. "I" Brigade Reserve as above. A very quiet day. Small working parties found to Sanctuary Wood and Brigade Headquarters. "Silent Susie" had some unwelcome attention to Battalion H.Q.; the burst of one shell narrowly missed a batman, pieces flying between himself and the	
Ypres.	11th			Regimental Sgt Major
Ypres.	12th		"I" Brigade Reserve as above. In the afternoon a rendezvous artillery bombardment developed on the left of HOOGE. The engagement appeared to reach its most intense point about 6 pm but it was a good	

WAR DIARY

or

INTELLIGENCE SUMMARY.

(Erase heading not required.)

Instructions regarding War Diaries and Intelligence
Summaries are contained in F. S. Regs., Part II.
and the Staff Manual respectively. Title pages
will be prepared in manuscript.

Place	Date	Hour	Summary of Events and Information	Remarks and references to Appendices
			while after dusk before it began to subside. There was no infantry attack on either side. The Battalion was relieved by the Newfoundland Fusiliers in accordance with the relief scheme of the 152nd Brigade by the 149th Brigade. Proceeded to Canada Hut, at-	
Brielen 13 Feb.			Brielen H. 32.a. In Huts as above. Enemy aeroplanes came over and dropped bombs, severely injuring the Commanding Officer, who brought in front case. It proved to be a 13-pdr. bomb. Our aeroplanes attempted to chase them away, but they rose to a great height & continued in the neighbourhood for about an hour. In the enemy we received the order to "Stand by" to move at half-an-hours notice, as the enemy were attacking at various points along a front of about 4,000 yards. Our "lot" carefully afloat in enraypmen	
"	14 Feb.		In Huts as above. The 151 Brigade still Standing by on the before being sent to retake the " International Trench" 800 yard o/forbet the enemy had taken by a mine explosion which made it unfit the forses and 800 yard	
	15 "			
	16 "			
	17 "			
	18 "			

Refresh 14th Brigade. Onslo 149th Brigade by order and Supplies 48-4-9-50+A16A5 inclusive, on line E30.a, I30.a, I30.8. MAPPARAGH WED by order 1300
1577 Wt. W10791/1773 500,000 1/15 D. D. & L. A/D.S.S./Forms/C. 2118.

Army Form C. 2118.

WAR DIARY

or

INTELLIGENCE SUMMARY.

(Erase heading not required.)

Instructions regarding War Diaries and Intelligence Summaries are contained in F. S. Regs., Part II. and the Staff Manual respectively. Title pages will be prepared in manuscript.

8/

Place	Date	Hour	Summary of Events and Information	Remarks and references to Appendices
Ypres	19.		On the night of the 18/19th relieved 4th Yorks on about Sorrel in trenches A9 to A3. Established bombing posts on either sides of the crater opposite A.1 and 50, and commenced a tunnel from 50 to the nearer sector about 5 yards long.	
	20		Some shelling of Armagh Wood and a few whizz bangs in A.1. to A.3. Capt Gill was slightly wounded by a piece of periscope glass struck by a snipers bullet. Much aeroplane activity during the day. The health of the men showed signs of deterioration. About 7-30 pm the enemy made a liberal distribution of whizz bangs over a very scattered area. Principal attention being paid to the different dumps.	

1577 Wt.W10791/1773 500,000 1/15 D. D. & L. A.D.S.S./Forms/C. 2118.

Army Form C. 2118.

WAR DIARY
or
INTELLIGENCE SUMMARY.
(Erase heading not required.)

Instructions regarding War Diaries and Intelligence Summaries are contained in F. S. Regs., Part II. and the Staff Manual respectively. Title pages will be prepared in manuscript.

9

Place	Date	Hour	Summary of Events and Information	Remarks and references to Appendices
Ypres	Feby 21		In trenches as above. Very little activity of any description. 4052 Pte Scott W Lewis gunner wounded.	
Ypres	" 22		In trenches as above. Another quiet day on our part of the front. No 11 Platoon were relieved but there remained in the afternoon, but the enemy remained so far as we were concerned quiet. A few remarkable ground flashes. 3136 Pte Gibson wounded. Enemy Gunnery left attacks were ordered on the [...] Border Regiment. Proceeded into close support, the raiders having[?] retreated[?] as follows:— "W" Company — Trenches (I 29 b & central). X Company in Sanctuary Wood Avenue, Cul'd (I 29 b central); X Company two platoons in R1 and R6 (I 28 b) and one platoon in Lovers Wood (I 98 b) "Y" Company [...] Glazgow Cross (I 29 d) two platoons and one platoon in Armagh "X" trench; "Z" Company two platoons in Armagh Wood (I 30 a central) and two platoons at Sanctuary [...]	

1577 Wt. W10791/1773 500,000 1/15 D. D. & L. A.D.S.S./Forms/C. 2118.

WAR DIARY

or

INTELLIGENCE SUMMARY.

(Erase heading not required.)

Instructions regarding War Diaries and Intelligence Summaries are contained in F. S. Regs., Part II. and the Staff Manual respectively. Title pages will be prepared in manuscript.

Place	Date	Hour	Summary of Events and Information	Remarks and references to Appendices
Ypres	23rd July	—	Ross (I 28 d 2.2). Battalion Headquarters were established at Leicester Square (I 29 b 1.9). One Lewis gun accompanied each company. A gas attack N.E. thence as above. The Brigadier decided upon a re-distribution accordingly at dusk. He drew two platoons of "X" Company in Sunken Road over into Armagh Wood and the two platoons of "X" Company in Sunken Road moved into Sunken Road in the G. of Durham h.i. "X" took over Armagh Wood. The officer commanding "X" Company (Lieut. Barnes) reported that Railway & Company (Lieut. Barnes) reported that Redoubt Yard & were in a pretty bad state of repair, particularly the latter where required practically re-building. Sunken Road was also a very unsatisfactory place, & unfortunately the activity of the enemy's aeroplanes prevented much improvement being effected.	
Ypres	24th July	—	A close support as above. Another quiet day, except	

Army Form C. 2118.

WAR DIARY

or

INTELLIGENCE SUMMARY.

(*Erase heading not required.*)

Instructions regarding War Diaries and Intelligence Summaries are contained in F. S. Regs., Part II. and the Staff Manual respectively. Title pages will be prepared in manuscript.

Place	Date	Hour	Summary of Events and Information	Remarks and references to Appendices
Ypres	25th Feby.		for the 179th Division strafe towards dusk. 2519 Lance Cpl Edwards W.S. of the Grenade Section wounded by a Rifle grenade whilst doing duty at a bombing post. Weather continued cold & frosty. La considerable amount of snow fell during the night. In close support as above. Lieut. C. R. Angus returned from Hospital & brought with him a draft of 41 other ranks from the Reare. About 15 of these men were sick wounded returned from Base Hospital and England. The physique of the men was generally pretty good. Only one man being sent to Hospital since. Sectors, the fighting strength of Battalion was now 24 officers and 742 other ranks.	
Ypres	26th Feby.		In close support as above. Slight afternoon strafe on our right was Reavier than normal, & must have soon caused considerable damage after it	

1577 Wt. W10791/1773 500,000 1/15 D. D. & L. A.D.S.S./Forms/C. 2118.

WAR DIARY

or

INTELLIGENCE SUMMARY.

(Erase heading not required.)

Instructions regarding War Diaries and Intelligence
Summaries are contained in F. S. Regs., Part II
and the Staff Manual respectively. Title pages
will be prepared in manuscript.

Place	Date	Hour	Summary of Events and Information	Remarks and references to Appendices
			ceased the enemy attempted a harassing attack by way of retaliation but our artillery barrage was completely repulsed it. The enemy flares were sent up for artillery support. Intense fire coming from Glencorse during the unmaintained trenches were by really shelled but "Y" Company escaped with no casualties. "X" Trench was also bombarded by fire men of T.R.T. R8. Company were wounded. The area named R.T., R8, and Surrah Road were heavily shelled but (9th Kon were no casualties. the night Battalion (9th R.H.) were not so fortunate suffered rather more 5th Border Frances (149 & A3) were practically wiped out. Resting some attacks was found the minenwerfer on Mount Sorrell and Observatory Ridge the bombardment ceased at 11 pm. the situation	 12

WAR DIARY

or

INTELLIGENCE SUMMARY.

(Erase heading not required.)

Instructions regarding War Diaries and Intelligence
Summaries are contained in F. S. Regs., Part II.
and the Staff Manual respectively. Title pages
will be prepared in manuscript.

Place	Date	Hour	Summary of Events and Information	Remarks and references to Appendices
Ypres			again became normal. The Brigade relief were eventually carried out owing on account of the late start, it was the early hours of the morning before completed. The battalion relieved the 5th Border Regiment in the front. Several french (I30L 54 & I30L 6 & ...) ... conference during discussed the battalion of the ... on the night the ... was to left the ... at York. Official information received regarding the great German offensive near Verdun. Enemy trench ... patrol action at the ... were being taken. The whole ... was remarkably quiet. A few whizz bangs received at VERDUN. The enemy losses inflicted ... or the enemy attacked furiously ... of the rifle fire. The situation continued normal on our part	
Ypres 24th Feby				

1577   Wt. W10791/1773   500,000   1/15   D. D. & L.   A.D.S.S./Forms/C. 2118.

WAR DIARY
or
INTELLIGENCE SUMMARY.
(Erase heading not required.)

Instructions regarding War Diaries and Intelligence
Summaries are contained in F. S. Regs., Part II.
and the Staff Manual respectively. Title pages
will be prepared in manuscript.

Place	Date	Hour	Summary of Events and Information	Remarks and references to Appendices
Ypres	25/5/15	—	Of the front. Trenches as above. The enemy early displayed activity by giving some of his heavy trench mortar bombs which caused a great deal of trouble to trenches 49, 50, and 41 were damaged most and the casualties include the following killed. — 1423 Sergt. W.E. Stinson 401 Pte. Duffy (last draft), 1516 Pte. C.H. Gee (grenadier) and 2609 Pte R. Coleman. The following were wounded during the afternoon. 2126 Pte. Long 3 (grenadier) 4823 Pte Rutherford, 653 Sergt Dinon R, 2008 Pte Fitzgerald 243r Pte Hunter Ja., 3999 Pte Hunter Wm, and 3523 R.H. Winter F.A. Mill 5. These casualties were sustained in trenches 49, 50 and 41 trenches were shelled & bombarded but the situation was eventually restored. Finally with the exception of shell fire, the situation cleared towards evening 8-30 pm a most	

WAR DIARY

or

INTELLIGENCE SUMMARY.

(Erase heading not required.)

Instructions regarding War Diaries and Intelligence
Summaries are contained in F. S. Regs., Part II.
and the Staff Manual respectively. Title pages
will be prepared in manuscript.

Place	Date	Hour	Summary of Events and Information	Remarks and references to Appendices

lively cannonade. Second Army intelligence
that enemy was manifesting considerable activity
behind SANCTUARY WOOD (I.13 and I.9) and might be
contemplating an attack. The shelling which
commenced at ⸳⸳⸳ was were at first thought to be the
prelude for the firing was a sweeping fire and
spread over a wide area. ZILLEBEKE and its
went ⸳⸳⸳ seemed to be the principal object of
attack. But the light railway between I.30 & the
dump at I.24 & I.14. The wood from ZILLEBEKE
was heavily strafed about midnight. 1603 Pte
⸳⸳⸳ "J" Company was killed whilst working on
the light railway. 3611 Pte Carter J. Z. Company
wounded. Other casualties were sustained by parties
from other Battalions. The burial parties at
I.22 b. just outside ZILLEBEKE were several times

1577   Wt.W10791/1773   500,000   1/15   D. D. & L.   A.D.S.S./Forms/C. 2118.

Army Form C. 2118.

WAR DIARY

or

INTELLIGENCE SUMMARY.

(Erase heading not required.)

Instructions regarding War Diaries and Intelligence Summaries are contained in F. S. Regs., Part II. and the Staff Manual respectively. Title pages will be prepared in manuscript.

16.

Place	Date	Hour	Summary of Events and Information	Remarks and references to Appendices
Ypres	23/24		disturbed owing to the cemetery being shelled. Orders were received that the Battalion would be relieved tomorrow night, but these were cancelled later, as also were orders subsequently raised for the relief of half of the Brigade. Nothing unusual occurred later. In trenches as above. Our artillery early got to work did considerable damage to trenches and dugouts. There was very little retaliation on our trenches, but our batteries particularly those round I 20 and I 31 were subjected to a great deal of attention. In the afternoon wire-cutting was recommenced & involved retaliation on MOUNT SORREL & I 30. a. received shrapnel & rifle grenades. His wire endured a practice barrage of rifle & m.m. which ceased his enemy shelled no further activity on either side the rest of the night.	

1577 Wt.W10791/1773 500,000 1/15 D. D. & L. A.D.S.S./Forms/C. 2118.

Lt. Col.

Comd. 6th Battalion

Army Form C. 2118.

WAR DIARY
or
INTELLIGENCE SUMMARY.
(Erase heading not required.)

Instructions regarding War Diaries and Intelligence Summaries are contained in F. S. Regs., Part II. and the Staff Manual respectively. Title pages will be prepared in manuscript.

Place	Date	Hour	Summary of Events and Information	Remarks and references to Appendices
			Wire received from 151 Infantry Brigade 27-2-16. following from 2nd Army Headquarters German wireless stn. message sent in English stated that Germans had captured fort of DOUAUMONT north east of VERDUN — France — state that the fort has been re-taken — It appears that only a small party of the enemy ever got into it and were quickly turned out again — on the WOEVRE front between ORNES and WORCK (KUERY) WARCU two miles east of ETAIN have been evacuated, the troops being withdrawn to the west of the COTES DE MEUSE — without any interference from enemy — carried out without any movement. Enemy raid to be attacking from enemy — reported any — Summary — movement in — securing be on —	Appendix I

1577 Wt.W10791/1773 500,000 1/15 D. D. & L.   A.D.S.S./Forms/C. 2118.

WAR DIARY

MARCH. 1916

6TH DURHAM LIGHT INFANTRY

VOLUME 12

151/50

WAR DIARY
or
INTELLIGENCE SUMMARY
(Erase heading not required.)

Instructions regarding War Diaries and Intelligence
Summaries are contained in F.S. Regs., Part II.
and the Staff Manual respectively. Title Pages
will be prepared in manuscript.

Place	Date	Hour	Summary of Events and Information	Remarks and references to Appendices
	March		Turned out again xxx On the WOEVRE front French trenches between ORNES and WORCK(K)ERY (Warcu 2 miles south east of ETAIN) have been evacuated the troops being withdrawn to the ridge of the COTES DE MEUSE xxx This morning it was carried out without any interference from xxx, xxx Enemy raid to be attacking without any regard to overative he is xxx xxxxxxxxx 52nd bde is making a demonstration this morning xxx Rapid fire will be opened with classs & c at 5-10am and grenades will be thrown into enemys trenches this will continue till 5-20pm xxx xxx by which favourable smoke clouds will be formed from trenches 35, 36 and 37 xxx	
		1		

1875 Wt. W593/826 1,000,000 4/15 J.B.C. & A. A.D.S.S./Forms/C. 2118.

Army Form C. 2118.

WAR DIARY
or
INTELLIGENCE SUMMARY.

(Erase heading *not required*.)

Instructions regarding War Diaries and Intelligence Summaries are contained in F. S. Regs. Part II. and the Staff Manual respectively. Title pages will be prepared in manuscript.

Place	Date	Hour	Summary of Events and Information	Remarks and references to Appendices
			I30 c ?. & I30 c 6.6. The Kansas Island The mine in front. It had been intended to employ a smoke damage, but the mine being unfavourable its project was abandoned. The remainder of the programme was carried out so arranged. The object on a very large degree attained. The fires was lavish in its expenditure of ammunition in reply, but our casualties totally only one killed and '13 wounded what the damage to an trenches was inconsiderable.' By 7 am all was quiet again, + nothing occurred during the remainder of the night.	
Ypres.	Mar 2.		On trench Served as above. Yesterday's demonstration was repeated, to draw attention from the practice relieve the 14th Division were to attack. All ranks stood-to at 3.45 a.m. and the final intense bombardment commenced shortly after 4 a.m. the front I30 c ?.)	

1577 Wt. W10791/1773 500,000 1/15 D. D.& L. A.D.S.S./Forms/C. 2118.

WAR DIARY
or
INTELLIGENCE SUMMARY

(Erase heading not required.)

Instructions regarding War Diaries and Intelligence Summaries are contained in F. S. Regs., Part II. and the Staff Manual respectively. Title Pages will be prepared in manuscript.

Place	Date	Hour	Summary of Events and Information	Remarks and references to Appendices
Ypres	March 2		9th Infy Brigade wire and OC has held what we have gained up till now but has had a hard knocking and Enemy attempted counter attacks which failed	
		2	Following message received from liason officer with 1st Duke of Wellington's regt. on situation along Battalion front as follows and work of consolidating going on well in front of our support line 335 in our old front trench and barricades and complete communication with 1st Gordons on right and R.E. party came up to help in work and A company has moved along to replace C company working party and 12 Manchester regt. has moved up two platoons to fill gap between our A and D companies and communication complete throughout and with you on our left and Not many casualties and not much damage to our lines and Ends	

Army Form C. 2118

WAR DIARY
or
INTELLIGENCE SUMMARY

(Erase heading not required.)

Instructions regarding War Diaries and Intelligence
Summaries are contained in F. S. Regs., Part II.
and the Staff Manual respectively. Title Pages
will be prepared in manuscript.

Place	Date . Hour	Summary of Events and Information	Remarks and references to Appendices
	March 2	O.C. 5th Yorks reports enemy exploded a mine under B3 soon after start of demonstration on French at bissut blocked but being carefully watched and will get fuller report later.	

1875 Wt. W593/826 1,000,000 4/15 J.B.C. & A. A.D.S.S./Forms/C. 2118.

WAR DIARY

or

INTELLIGENCE SUMMARY.

(*Erase heading not required.*)

Instructions regarding War Diaries and Intelligence Summaries are contained in F. S. Regs., Part II. and the Staff Manual respectively. Title pages will be prepared in manuscript.

Place	Date	Hour	Summary of Events and Information	Remarks and references to Appendices
			to 6.6. and the trenches in rear were literally sprayed with H.E. and shrapnel for half an hour, after which the batteries switched on to their normal zone." Our trench mortars also had a very busy time on targets such as German salient at I 30 d, the spront, the Caterpillar and Hill 60. Reports as to progress of 17th Division attack are given in Appendix I. There was a good deal of retaliation on our sector, but we were even more fortunate than on the previous evening; only three men being wounded comparatively slight damage caused to our trenches, the area behind our lines was pretty constantly shelled during the morning. Dance Wood & "X" trench particularly coming in for a deal of enfilade fire. At night by the 6th Northumberland Fusiliers relieved at midnight by the Battalion was very active, & transport etc. moving on Hooge road was very active & transport	

Army Form C. 2118.

WAR DIARY

or

INTELLIGENCE SUMMARY.

(Erase heading not required.)

Instructions regarding War Diaries and Intelligence
Summaries are contained in F. S. Regs., Part II.
and the Staff Manual respectively. Title pages
will be prepared in manuscript.

Place	Date	Hour	Summary of Events and Information	Remarks and references to Appendices
Dickebusch	Mar 3rd		and troops on the road were considerably throttled. The Battalion arrived at Canada Huts ( ) Dickebusch	
Dickebusch	Mar 4th		Strength 11.30 pm. Strength close as above. Orders received that one company(?) and later two companies were to be held in readiness to move to Armagh Wood tomorrow night. Parties sent to dele at Popringhe.	
Dickebusch	Mar 6th		Strength as above. Orders received that the whole Battalion was to move into close support, being distributed as follows:— Battalion Headquarters and W Coy Carriage Wood (I 2 d 2 ?); a (I 3 o c); X Coy Blauwepoort farm (I 3 o c); Y & X Coy to Railway Dug-Outs (I 30 d.); Z Company to dug-outs at H 3 o o.	
Ypres	Mar 6th		In close support as above. Situation generally very quiet. Cold dry weather and fairly numerous	
Ypres	Mar 7th		In close support as above. Nothing unusual occurred.	

WAR DIARY

or

INTELLIGENCE SUMMARY.

(Erase heading not required.)

Instructions regarding War Diaries and Intelligence Summaries are contained in F. S. Regs., Part II. and the Staff Manual respectively. Title pages will be prepared in manuscript.

Place	Date	Hour	Summary of Events and Information	Remarks and references to Appendices
Ypres	Mar 8th		The Battalion was relieved by the 6th Durham L.I. and proceeded to "B" Shaft huts at Dickebusch.	
Dickebusch	Mar 9th		In huts as above. A very quiet day, with nothing of interest occurring.	
Dickebusch	Mar 10th	10½	In huts as above. Capt. H. Harland and Capt. G. Parker returned to duty from England.	
Dickebusch	Mar 11th	11½	In huts as above. A bombing demonstration was arranged to take place at the Grenade Pit and the Battalion was paraded as strong as possible for this purpose. Capt. Parker and a party of 21 men went as guides but returned at 2½ pm without having found any trace of the demonstrators. The Battalion remained on parade about an hour and was then dismissed. "C" Company he half had Water.	
Dickebusch	Mar 12th		In huts as above. Church Spring morning. Church Parades for all denominations in the Y.M.C.A.	

1577 Wt. W10791/1773 500,000 1/15 D. D. & L. A.D.S.S./Forms/C. 2118.

WAR DIARY

or

INTELLIGENCE SUMMARY

(Erase heading not required.)

Instructions regarding War Diaries and Intelligence
Summaries are contained in F. S. Regs., Part II.
and the Staff Manual respectively. Title Pages
will be prepared in manuscript.

Place	Date	Hour	Summary of Events and Information	Remarks and references to Appendices
Buckchurch	13th March		In huts as above. The remainder of the Battalion had huts at Buckchurch. Considerable aerial activity over the village. 9 counts, but no bombs dropped or damage done. A very successful concert, attended by the Brigadier & staff-officers of the Brigade, took place in the Y.M.C.A. the 1st Battalion provided the first-half of the programme. The 8th Battalion the second-half. Heavy Battalion band gave several items at intervals during the evening.	
Buckchurch	14th March		In huts as above. Relieved the 5th Battalion Fakenhalands Fusiliers in the front-line trenches. Several trenches in a bad state of repair owing to (I.30.) recent-bombardment. A1. occupied by "X" Company were particularly bad received a great-deal of work doing to make it firgetable.	

1875 Wt. W 593/826 1,000,000 4/15 J.B.C. & A. A.D.S.S./Forms/C. 2118.

WAR DIARY

or

INTELLIGENCE SUMMARY

(*Erase heading not required.*)

Instructions regarding War Diaries and Intelligence
Summaries are contained in F. S. Regs., Part II.
and the Staff Manual respectively. Title Pages
will be prepared in manuscript.

Place	Date	Hour	Summary of Events and Information	Remarks and references to Appendices
Ypres J.30.b	15th March		In trenches as above. Fine weather & comparatively no artillery activity on either side Enabled a restatement of work to be done.	
Ypres J.30.d	16th March		In trenches as above. Enemy artillery showed considerable activity and shelled the area behind our line throughout most of the day, but left the trenches quite untouched. One or two rifle grenades were sent over during the afternoon but did no damage falling between A.1 and the enfront line.	
Ypres J.30.b	17th March		In trenches as above. Rifle fire weather continued Spasmodic rifle & machine-gun activity on either side led to a violent battle on our left. I—s balance that this enemy plans were forced to descend ... but we managed to	

1875 Wt. W593/826 1,000,000 4/15 J.B.C. & A. A.D.S.S./Forms/C. 2118.

Army Form C. 2118

WAR DIARY

INTELLIGENCE SUMMARY
(Erase heading not required.)

Instructions regarding War Diaries and Intelligence
Summaries are contained in F. S. Regs., Part II.
and the Staff Manual respectively. Title Pages
will be prepared in manuscript.

Place	Date	Hour	Summary of Events and Information	Remarks and references to Appendices
Ypres	Mar 19.		Operations at the Brows?

Wind easterly light. Situation normal. Ensuing fired a shallow mine at 11-15 am, in front of Trench 37. No damage nor casualties. At 3.32 PM enemy fired camouflet at 9.30 C.7.8 making winding cavity 66.12 yards long. No damage to trenches. 1 Man wounded by falling bricks | |
| | 25 | | French less. 3 PM today starts successful French enterprise carried out in ARGONNE and E and W Meuse. All quiet | |
| | 24 | | Following from 2nd Army dated 26th begins. German wireless this morning sent in English stated that Germans had captured fort of DOUAUMONT NE of Verdun. Fouch state that the fort has been recaptured. It appears that only armed party of the enemy got into it and was quickly | |

1875 Wt. W593/826 1,000,000 4/15 J.B.C. & A. A.D.S.S./Forms/C. 2118.

Army Form C. 2118

WAR DIARY
or
INTELLIGENCE SUMMARY

(Erase heading not required.)

Instructions regarding War Diaries and Intelligence Summaries are contained in F. S. Regs., Part II. and the Staff Manual respectively. Title Pages will be prepared in manuscript.

Place	Date	Hour	Summary of Events and Information	Remarks and references to Appendices
Ypres.	March 17.		... aeroplane over our own line, probably algeting near Brandhoek. Later 1 of our planes ... flew over the German lines ... on further reconnaissance work.	
	18.		The situation continued quiet, and the only incident of note was 3 trench Mortar Bombs. ... our front and support lines. The Battalion was relieved by the 5th Yorkshire Regiment and proceeded to Hill central whence it entrained for Poperinghe. This tour in the trenches was the Quietest experienced by the Battn. in the Ypres salient. The Batts billets in Poperinghe were Rue de Ypres, Rue de Ossings, Rue de Cornette.	
	19.		The billets as above. Rue de Ossings, Rue de ... Day was spent in general cleaning up of equipment rifles etc and all billets.	
	20.		The billets as above. Fine weather continued and parties were sent all day to the Divisional Baths at Poperinghe.	
	21.		The billets as above.	
	22		The billets as above.	

1875 Wt. W593/826 1,000,000 4/15 J.B.C. & A. A.D.S.S./Forms/C. 2118.

Army Form C. 2118

WAR DIARY
or
INTELLIGENCE SUMMARY
(*Erase heading not required.*)

Instructions regarding War Diaries and Intelligence
Summaries are contained in F. S. Regs., Part II.
and the Staff Manual respectively. Title Pages
will be prepared in manuscript.

Place	Date	Hour	Summary of Events and Information	Remarks and references to Appendices
Ypres.	March 23		in billets as above. Battalion entrained at Poperinghe at 6.45 p.m. and detrained at the Asylum, Ypres. H.12.B. and proceeded to relieve the 10 R Royal Welsh Fusiliers in the BLUFF trenches. The relief was completed about 11 p.m. The position of the trenches was I.34.c.6 to I.34.c.9.8. The disposition of trenches was as follows:— THE BEAN (captured German section) I.34.c.g.3 to I.34.d1.6. X Company; INTERNATIONAL New Year Trench, X Company; THE LOOP, W Company, Y Company, the Lt. O.S.H.T. was on	
	24.		Scupport line and Gordon Post, Y Company. W Company. The whole of the St Border Regt. on the left. The trenches was about 200x. The trenches were found to be in a pretty bad state and required a good deal of repairing, consolidating and cleaning up. Several dead bodies which were lying about were buried and others were discovered during the tour. A great deal of work was done by all Companies on the trenches. The grenading lads an exciting time in the crater which these were some bombing posts which it was impossible to ... during darkness. A great quantity of derelict material both Boschland and	

WAR DIARY

or

INTELLIGENCE SUMMARY

(Erase heading not required.)

Instructions regarding War Diaries and Intelligence Summaries are contained in F. S. Regs., Part II. and the Staff Manual respectively. Title Pages will be prepared in manuscript.

Place	Date	Hour	Summary of Events and Information	Remarks and references to Appendices
	March 24		British was relieved from the crater. The wire business in the whole was continued and passed to possess to engage. Enemy more than us repairing his trenches	
	25.		In trenches as above. Work continued. Enemy's activity confined to sniping which was however kept well in hand.	
	26.		In trenches as above. The Bath less Y Coy was relieved by the Durham L.I. in the BLUFF SECTOR and proceeded into brigade reserve at KINGSWAY and GORDON TERRACE	
			Aug 6th. Y. Company was transferred to the command of the O.C. & Bn. Durham L.I. who ordered them to take over from X Company.	
	27.		0011 NEW YEAR TRENCH NEW YEAR SUPPORTS and the higher posts	
			Pm Brigade reserve as above. At 4.30 p.m. our Artillery commenced a vigorous bombardment of the enemy's trenches on a frontage of 300 yards, S.14-15 near St ELOI. Our Artillery commenced a vigorous bombardment of the enemy's trenches and laid a barrage over his support line. The Royal Fusiliers and Northumberland Fusiliers of the 3rd Division attacked from front right	

WAR DIARY

or

INTELLIGENCE SUMMARY

(Erase heading not required.)

Instructions regarding War Diaries and Intelligence
Summaries are contained in F. S. Regs., Part II.
and the Staff Manual respectively. Title Pages
will be prepared in manuscript.

Place	Date	Hour	Summary of Events and Information	Remarks and references to Appendices
	MARCH 26		easily secured their objective. The left was not quite so successful but managed to establish a line on the other side of the crater. Our casualties were remarkably few. The German prisoners captured numbered 200 and 5 Officers, by whom it was stated that the X Company was completely involved in the explosion. Artillery activity continued throughout the day. 1 or 2 dumps and some shrapnel were sniped in the vicinity of our dugout. Some particularly close in Kingsway. In consequence X and Z companies were ordered to move and take over dugouts with K.W Company.	
	27		Nothing further of note occurred during the day.	
	28		The Brigade Assroc as above. Very quiet day and this weather.	
	29		The Brigade Assroc as above.	
	30.		The Battalion returned to the front line and was distributed exactly the same as before. Y Company moving	

1875. Wt. W593/826 1,000,000 4/15 J.B.C. & A. A.D.S.S./Forms/C. 2118.

WAR DIARY

or

INTELLIGENCE SUMMARY

(Erase heading not required.)

Instructions regarding War Diaries and Intelligence
Summaries are contained in F. S. Regs, Part II.
and the Staff Manual respectively. Title Pages
will be prepared in manuscript.

Place	Date	Hour	Summary of Events and Information	Remarks and references to Appendices
Ypres	March 30		back into support line and X Company taking over NEW YEAR TRENCH and supports. The relief was carried out without interruption and was completed about 8 p.m.	
	31.			
	April 1.		In trenches as above.	

J. Warren Major.

1875 Wt. W593/826 1,000,000 4/15 J.B.C. & A. A.D.S.S./Forms/C. 2118.

Lt Col Stevens
D.S.O.
Co/. 6th D.L.I.

I congratulate you on the
admirable spirit which
is being displayed by your
battalion under very trying
circumstances.
Please tell all ranks
how very pleased I am
with them all round.

J H Shea B.g.
Co/. 157 Bde

1/3/16.

For information of the A.G.'s Office at the Base.

Officers and men who have become casuals, been transferred or joined since last report.

Place _Satsfield_   Date _4-2-16_

Regtl. Number	Rank	Name	Corps	Nature of casualty, or name of unit from or to which transferred	Date of being struck off or coming on the ration return	Remarks*
3385	Pte	Robinson Q. O	L D I			
3756	Pte	Blackburn J	-Do-	Wounded	30-1-16	
3783	"	Atkinson	-Do-	-Do-	30-1-16	
3809	"	Bainbridge J.	-Do-	-Do-	31-1-16	
2268	"	Stephenson E.	-Do-	-Do-	31-1-16	
3385		Robinson W.	-Do-	Evac sick	28-1-16	
1887	L/Sgt	Bell R.W	-Do-	-Do-	28-1-16	
446	Pte	Pattinson J.	-Do-	-Do-	25-1-16	
115	"	Edmonson A.	-Do-	-Do-	28-1-16	
407	"	Hope W. E.	-Do-	-Do-	28-1-16	
2860	"	McDonald	-Do-	-Do-	28-1-16	
5211	"	Birch W.	-Do-	-Do-	28-1-16	
4033	"	Fox H.	-Do-	-Do-	31-1-16	
2944	"	Simpson C.	-Do-	-Do-	31-1-16	
3699	"	Underwood T	-Do-	-Do-	1-2-16	
3382	"	Stewart D.	-Do-	-Do-	1-2-16	
3349	"	Dobson J.	-Do-	-Do-	1-2-16	
1776	"	Bromley W.	-Do-	-Do-	1-2-16	
2363	"	McKenzie C.	909	-Do-	1-2-16	
3003	"	West	900	-Do-	1-2-16	
3321	"	Temple A.	-Do-	-Do-	1-2-16	
2246	"	Carroll A.	-Do-	-Do-	1-2-16	
2446	"	Dodds G.	-Do-	-Do-	2-2-16	
2184	"	Norman N.	-Do-	-Do-	2-2-16	
3085	"	Clarke H.	-Do-	-Do-	3-2-16	
2494	"	Stelling M.	-Do-	-Do-	3-2-16	
559	Cpl	Bails J.	-Do-	-Do-	1-2-16	
5213	P	Evans H.	-Do-	-Do-	31-1-16	

* State whether absence is of a permanent or temporary nature, adding, in the case of casuals from wounds or disease, any available information for communication to the relatives.

6

For information of the A.G.'s Office at the Base.

Officers and men who have become casuals, been transferred or joined since last report.

Place ___In the field___   Date ___11-2-16___

Regtl. Number	Rank	Name	Corps	Nature of casualty, or name of unit from or to which transferred	Date of being struck off or coming on the ration return	Remarks*
2014	Sgt	Bainbridge A.R.	6 D.L.I.	Killed	5-2-16	Z Coy
889	Pte	Stafford T.R.	-Do-	-Do-	5-2-16	Z Coy
1956	"	Adamson R.H.	-Do-	-Do-	7-2-16	Y Coy
2435	"	Gill J.J.	-Do-	-Do-	8-2-16	X Coy
2874	"	Markey W.	-Do-	-Do-	8-2-16	X Coy
3302	"	Brown P.	-Do-	-Do-	9-2-16	Y Coy
2488	L/Cpl	Brown J.	-Do-	Wounded	4-2-16	Z Coy
3179	Pte	Long A.	-Do-	-Do-	4-2-16	W Coy
2119	"	Grant R.	-Do-	-Do-	5-2-16	Y Coy
2360	"	Rutherford J.	-Do-	-Do-	5-2-16	X Coy
3868	"	Johnson J.T.	-Do-	-Do-	5-2-16	X Coy
1512	"	Reed H.	-Do-	-Do-	5-2-16	X Coy
1412	Cpl	Denham N.	-Do-	-Do-	7-2-16	Y Coy
3340	Pte	Coulthard D.	-Do-	-Do-	7-2-16	Y Coy
1479	"	Parry W.R.	-Do-	-Do-	8-2-16	X Coy
2692	"	Angus J.	-Do-	-Do-	8-2-16	Z Coy
2117	"	Patterson T.	-Do-	-Do-	10-2-16	X Coy
2001	"	Bainbridge P.	-Do-	-Do-	9-2-16	Y Coy
2075	"	Walker J.W.	-Do-	-Do-	9-2-16	Y Coy
2971	"	Taylor R.	-Do-	-Do-	9-2-16	Y Coy
1866	"	Murphy T.	-Do-	-Do-	9-2-16	Y Coy
3588	L/Cpl	Newton R.	-Do-	Evac Sick	4-2-16	Z Coy
3226	Pte	Lewis J.	-Do-	-Do-	3-2-16	
1976	"	Kane H.	-Do-	-Do-	5-2-16	
2643	L/Cpl	Hepplethwaite S.	-Do-	-Do-	5-2-16	
3718	"	Mayers J.	-Do-	-Do-	5-2-16	
3288	Pte	Girling E.	-Do-	-Do-	5-2-16	
2199	"	Kelly J.	-Do-	-Do-	5-2-16	

* State whether absence is of a permanent or temporary nature, adding, in the case of casuals from wounds or disease, any available information for communication to the relatives.

FIELD RETURN.

Army Form B. 213.

No. of Report ————

(To be furnished by all arms, services, and departments (except A.S.C. units) to the A. G.'s Office at the Base in accordance with Field Service Regulations, Part II.)

RETURN showing numbers RATIONED by, and Transport on charge of, ———— at ———— Date. ————

DETAIL	Personnel			Animals.										Guns, carriages, and limbers and transport vehicles.										Mechanical						REMARKS
	Officers	Other ranks	Natives	Horses			Mules		Camels	Oxen				Guns, carriages and limbers, showing description	Ammunition wagons and limbers	Machine guns	Aircraft, showing description	Horsed		Motor Cars	Tractors		Lorries, showing description	Trucks, showing description	Trailers	Motor Bicycles	Bicycles	
				Riding	Draught	Heavy Draught	Pack	Large	Small									4 Wheeled	2 Wheeled									
Effective Strength of Unit	28	691																										Not included
Details, by Arms attached to unit as in War Establishment:— M.O. R.A.M.C. Division.	1	6																										T.M.B. 15
																												T.G. 15
																												Included
																												Div. Employ
																												Corp. Police 6
																												Field
Total	29	698																										
War Establishment	31	107																										
Wanting to complete (Detail of Personnel and Horses below)	2	373																										
Surplus																												
*Attached (not to include the details shown above)		18																										
Civilians:— Employed with the Unit Accompanying the Unit																												
TOTAL RATIONED ...		633																										

* In the case of field ambulances, hospitals or depots, the number of patients are to be included here, the names being shown in A. F. A. 36.

———— Signature of Commander.

———— Date of Despatch.

For information of the A.G.'s Office at the Base.

Officers and men who have become casuals, been transferred or joined since last report.

Place _In the Field_   Date _11-2-16_

Regti. Number	Rank	Name	Corps	Nature of casualty, or name of unit from or to which transferred	Date of being struck off or coming on the ration return	Remarks*
1900	Pte	Robinson J.H.	D.L.I.R	1st to Duty	6-2-16	
1776	"	Bromly W	Do	-Do-	9-2-16	
2944	"	Scopon C	-Do-	-Do-	10-2-16	
2006	Cpl	Bryant A.	-Do-	-Do-	10-2-16	
2103	Pte	McKinyn C	Do	-Do-	10-2-16	
2284	"	Cowling C.	-Do-	-Do-	10-2-16	
	Lieut	Angus	Do	Wounded	6-2-16	
2800	Pte	Hodgson D	Do	Killed	9-2-16	

* State whether absence is of a permanent or temporary nature, adding, in the case of casuals from wounds or disease, any available information for communication to the relatives.

For information of the A.G.'s Office at the Base.

Officers and men who have become casuals, been transferred or joined since last report.

Place _____ Date _____

Regtl. Number	Rank	Name	Corps	Nature of casualty, or name of unit from or to which transferred	Date of being struck off or coming on the ration return	Remarks*
				E. oot. Sick	5-2-16	
		Pollock R.	-Do-	-Do-	7-2-16	
		Herts T.	-Do-	-Do-	7-2-16	
1806			-Do-	-Do-	7-2-16	
			-Do-	-Do-	7-2-16	
		Sergeant T.	-Do-	-Do-	7-2-16	
		Appleton W.	-Do-	-Do-	7-2-16	
			-Do-	-Do-	7-2-16	
		Hutchinson	-Do-	-Do-	6-2-16	
		Rothwell	-Do-	-Do-	7-2-16	
			-Do-	-Do-	7-2-16	
1700			-Do-	-Do-	7-2-16	
1708			-Do-	-Do-	7-2-16	
		Nelly T.	-Do-	-Do-	9-2-16	
2116			-Do-	-Do-	9-2-16	
1907		Daughterson J.E.	-Do-	-Do-	5-2-16	
2000			-Do-	-Do-	10-2-16	
		Appleton Arnold	-Do-		6-2-16	
24			-Do-	-Do-	11-2-16	
1142			-Do-	-Do-	4-2-16	
			-Do-	-Do-	6-2-16	
		Carroll A.	-Do-	-Do-	7-2-16	
			-Do-	-Do-	7-2-16	
2369		Martin R.	-Do-	-Do-	7-2-16	
2316	Sgt	Gill R.W.	-Do-	-Do-	29-1-16	
1275	Pte	Williams	-Do-	-Do-	6-2-16	
1400		Morton F.J.	-Do-	-Do-	6-2-16	
1652			-Do-	-Do-	6-2-16	

* State whether absence is of a permanent or temporary nature, adding, in the case of casuals from wounds or disease, any available information for communication to the relatives.

For information of the A.G.'s Office at the Base.

Officers and men who have become casuals, been transferred or joined since last report.

Place _____ Field _____ Date _____ 18·2·16 _____

Regtl. Number	Rank	Name	Corps	Nature of casualty, or name of unit from or to which transferred	Date of being struck off or coming on the ration return	Remarks*
2110	L/Cpl	Murray J	6 DLI	Evac Sick	13·2·16	✓
2441	pte	Spedding S	"	"	13·2·16	
1873	L.Cpl	Hasting	"	"	13·2·16	
2921	pte	Readman E	"	"	14·2·16	✓
2834	"	Fenwick J	"	"	15·2·16	✓
2856	"	McGovern	"	"	15·2·16	✓
2120	"	Wood M	"	"	15·2·16	
3073	"	Bell J	"	"	15·2·16	✓
4262	"	Chambers J	"	"	16·2·16	✓
2649	"	Angus J	"	"	18·2·16	✓
1729	Sgt.	Leighton JR	"	"	18·2·16	✓
1406	Corpl	Howell J	"	"	18·2·16	✓
972	pte	Clark AE	"	"	18·2·16	✓
3213	"	Evans A	"	"	18·2·16	✓
1540	"	Masham R	"	"	18·2·16	✓
3699	"	Underwood J	"	Returned to duty	15·2·16	
2779	"	Grant R	"	"	13·2·16	
4071	"	Hope E	"	"	13·2·16	
2746	"	Edward NF	"	"	20·2·16	
3297	"	Stones RE	"	"	14·2·16	
2971	"	Taylor R	"	"	14·2·16	
2432	"	Robson JW	"	"	17·2·16	

* State whether absence is of a permanent or temporary nature, adding, in the case of casuals from wounds or disease, any available information for communication to the relatives.

No. of Report _____

Army Form B. 213.

FIELD RETURN.

(To be furnished by all arms, services, and departments (except A.S.C. units) to the A. G.'s Office at the Base in accordance with Field Service Regulations, Part II.)

RETURN showing numbers RATIONED by, and Transport on charge of, _____ at _____ Date. 18-2-16.

DETAIL.	Personnel			Animals.									Guns, carriages, and limbers and transport vehicles					Horsed		Mechanical					REMARKS
	Officers	Other ranks	Natives	Horses			Mules		Camels	Oxen			Guns, carriages and limbers, showing description	Ammunition wagons and limbers	Machine Guns	Aircraft, showing description	4 Wheeled	2 Wheeled	Motor Cars	Tractors	Lorries, showing description	Trucks, showing description	Trailers	Motor Bicycles	Bicycles
				Riding	Draught	Heavy Draught	Pack	Large	Small																
Effective Strength of Unit	2175			13	11	2	154	9	9																
Details, by Arms attached to unit as in War Establishment:—																									
MO	1																								
RAMC		6																							
Armourer		1																							
Total	98,722																								
War Establishment	31,1017																								
Wanting to complete (Detail of Personnel and Horses below)	32,295																								
Surplus		18																							
*Attached (not to include the details shown above)																									
Civilians:— Employed with the Unit Accompanying the Unit																									
TOTAL RATIONED ...	703																								

* In the case of field ambulances, hospitals or depots, the number of patients are to be included here, the names being shown in A. F. A. 36.

_____ Signature of Commander.

_____ Date of Despatch.

For information of the A.G.'s Office at the Base.

Officers and men who have become casuals, been transferred or joined since last report.

Place _The Field_   Date _25-2-16_

Regtl. Number	Rank	Name	Corps	Nature of casualty, or name of unit from or to which transferred	Date of being struck off or coming on the ration return	Remarks*
	Capt	Gill W.P.	6 L.T.I.	Wounded	19-2-16	
	Capt	Gill W.P.	do.	Rej. to Duty	22-2-16	
3333	Pte	Bland H.	do.	Wounded	19-2-16	z Coy
3880	Pte	Walker C.	do.	Killed	22-2-16	x "
4052	Pte	Best A.	do.	Wounded	21-2-16	y "
3427	Pte	Gibson H.	do.	Wounded	22-2-16	y "
2519	Sgt	Edmed W.S.	do.	Wounded	24-2-16	z "
	2 Lt.	C.M.B. Catford	Do.	Evac. Sick	18-2-16.	
	2 Lt.	V.J.R. Clarke	Do.	do.	17-2-16	
	2 Lt.	A.W. Freeman	Do.	do.	17-2-16.	
	Lt	M. Mahar	Do	Rej. to Duty	4-2-16	
1337	Pte	Coughlin J.	Do.	do -	11-2-16.	
4188	Pte	Clayton J.	Do.	do -	11-2-16	
2782	Pte	Hickey H.	Do.	do -	11-2-16	
1263	Pte	Straker T.	Do.	do -	11-2-16	
2068	Pte	Maughan W.	Do.	do -	9-2-16	
3240	Pte	Varey J.J.	Do.	do -	9-2-16	
2849	Pte	Leonard J.	Do.	do -	10-2-16	
2110	L/Cpl	Murray J.	Do.	do -	13-2-16	
4052	Pte	Fox A.	Do.	do -	13-2-16	
1873	L/Cpl	Hastie J.W.	Do.	do -	13-2-16.	
3551	Pte	Appleton W.	Do.	do -	13-2-16.	
2432	Pte	Robson T.W.	Do.	do -	14-2-16.	
2479	Pte	Heels J.	Do.	do.	14-2-16	
	Pte	Spedding S.	Do.	do -	14-2-16	
120	Pte	Dodd H.	Do.	do.	14-2-16	

* State whether absence is of a permanent or temporary nature, adding, in the case of casuals from wounds or disease, any available information for communication to the relatives.

Officers and men who have become casuals, been transferred or joined since last report.

Place _Hatfield_   Date _21-2-16._

Regtl. Number	Rank	Name	Corps	Nature of casualty, or name of unit from or to which transferred	Date of being struck off or coming on the ration return	Remarks*
1761	Pte	Dickinson T.N.	6/D.L.I.	Evac Sick	20-2-16	
1476	"	Bromley W.	Do-	do-	17-2-16	
2459	"	Caverond R.H	Do-	do-	17-2-16	
3182	"	Blackett T.	Do-	do-	17-2-16	
3288	"	Girling E.	Do-	do-	17-2-16	
1870	"	Shannon M	Do-	do-	17-2-16	
2007	"	Booth A	Do-	do-	17-2-16	
21	C/A	Ball J	Do-	do-	17-2-16	
2928	Pte	Roberts W	Do-	do-	17-2-16	
2346	"	Gillings D	Do-	do-	20-2-16	
3088	"	Grundy W.	Do-	do-	20-2-16	
3199	"	Underwood J.	Do-	do-	21-2-16	
3400	"	Suddes H	Do-	do-	21-2-16	
1999	"	Relay T.	Do-	do-	21-2-16	
3392	"	Jeffray G.	Do-	do-	22-2-16	
2910	"	Richardson T.	Do-	do-	23-2-16	
3250	"	Anderson A.	Do-	do-	19-2-16	
2410	"	Martin R	Do-	do-	6-2-16	
2760	"	Goodfellow	Do-	Rec'd Duty	30-1-16	
1568	"	Malcom J.R.	Do-	do-	29-1-16	
3200	"	Teasdale T.W.	Do-	do-	4-1-16	
2226	"	Lewis T.	Do-	do-	12-2-16	
3324	"	Temple A.	Do-	do-	12-2-16	
2558	"	Hetherington A	Do	do-	10-2-16	
1727	"	Ripley F.	Do-	do-	10-2-16	
2642	"	Angus J	Do-	do-	17-2-16	
2557	"	Bainbridge J	Do-	do-	18-2-16	
2818	"	Jackson H	Do-	do-	17-2-16	
2559	"	Waterman J	Do-	do-	20-2-16	

* State whether absence is of a permanent or temporary nature, adding, in the case of casuals from wounds or disease, any available information for communication to the relatives.

The Field   25-2-16

4262	Pte	Chambers A	6 D.L.I.	Ret'd to Duty	19-2-16
2942	"	Stelling J.	Do	do	22-2-16
3263	"	Chapman J	Do	do	22-2-16
3187	"	Rothwell J	-Do	do	23-2-16
2243	"	Palmer J	-Do-	do	19-2-16
2120	"	Wood M.	-Do-	do	24-2-16
1170	"	McCutcheon E.	-Do-	Evac. Sick	17-2-16
1146	Cpl	Dunn A.	-Do-	To Base	9-2-16
1844	Pte	Robson 6.	-Do-	-Do-	10-2-16
1341	L/Cpl	Davidson R.	-Do	-Do-	16-2-16
1154	Pte	Stockdale H.	-Do-	-Do-	21-2-16
2564	"	Jardine G.B.	-Do-	Re (d to Duty	24-2-16
3874	L/Cpl	Sanderson J.	-Do-	Rvnts to Pte	16-2-16
3041	Pte	Roseby R.	-Do-	Div. Sam. Sect'n	22-2-16
3187	"	Gardiner J.	-Do-	-Do-	22-2-16
1170	"	McCutcheon E.	-Do-	Re'd to Duty	22-2-16
1170	"	McCutcheon E.	-Do-	To Base	25-2-16
1352	"	Thompson J	-Do-	Do	25-2-16
3207	"	Savage J.J.	-Do-	Evac. Sick	23-2-16

4

For information of the A.G.'s Office at the Base.

Officers and men who have become casuals, been transferred or joined since last report.

Place _In the Field_   Date _28-1-16_

Regtl. Number	Rank	Name	Corps	Nature of casualty, or name of unit from or to which transferred	Date of being struck off or coming on the ration return	Remarks*
W.604.1328	Pte	Appleby. R.H	6th D.L.I	Wounded	22-1-16	
3304	L/c	Thompson	6th D.L.I	Evac. Sick	22-1-16	
2184	Pte	Norman J.G	6th D.L.I	-Do-	22-1-16	
2744	„	Howells A.	-Do-	-Do-	22-1-16	
1888	„	Urquhart H.	-Do-	-Do-	25-1-16	
2942	„	Stelling	-Do-	-Do-	25-1-16	
1724	„	Ripley. F	-Do-	-Do-	23-1-16	
1964	„	Sanderson J.	-Do-	-Do-	23-1-16	
3142	„	Ferguson J.	-Do-	-Do-	26-1-16	
724	„	Turnbull A	-Do-	-Do-	26-1-16	
24	L/c	Bonner W	-Do-	-Do-	26-1-16	
1659	„	Dixon J.	-Do-	-Do-	26-1-16	
1949	Pte	Bolam J.G.	-Do-	-Do-	26-1-16	
1444	„	Walton	-Do-	-Do-	27-1-16	
3371	„	Smith A.	-Do-	-Do-	27-1-16	
1677	„	Williams	-Do-	-Do-	27-1-16	
2243	„	Palmer H.	-Do-	-Do-	27-1-16	
2079	„	Parkinson J.	-Do-	Rel to Duty	21-1-16	
3871	„	Kelly. J.	-Do-	-Do-	22-1-16	
3383	„	Stewart A.	-Do-	-Do-	22-1-16	
2732	„	Dryden J.	-Do-	-Do-	22-1-16	
1446	„	Rivers R.	-Do-	-Do-	23-1-16	
3213	„	Evans A.	-Do-	-Do-	18-1-16	
1798	„	Broadley J.	-Do-	-Do-	21-1-16	
623	„	Watson G	-Do-	-Do-	23-1-16	
2057	„	McKean J.	-Do-	-Do-	24-1-16	
2643	L/c	Angus S	-Do-	-Do-	25-1-16	

* State whether absence is of a permanent or temporary nature, adding, in the case of casuals from wounds or disease, any available information for communication to the relatives.

FIELD RETURN.

Army Form B. 213.

No. of Report _4_

(To be furnished by all arms, services and departments (except A.S.C. units) to the A. G.'s Office at the Base in accordance with Field Service Regulations, Part II.)

RETURN showing numbers RATIONED by, and Transport on charge of, _6ne D'un Roop N.Y._ at _____ Date. _26 Jany 191_.

DETAIL	Personnel			Animals										Guns, carriages, and limbers, and transport vehicles.													REMARKS
	Officers	Other ranks	Natives	Horses			Mules		Camels	Oxen						Horsed		Mechanical							Motor Bicycles	Bicycles	
				Riding	Draught	Heavy Draught	Pack	Large	Small			Guns, carriages and limbers, showing description	Ammunition wagons and limbers	Machine guns	Aircraft, showing description	4 Wheeled	2 Wheeled	Motor Cars	Tractors	Lorries, showing description	Trucks, showing description	Trailers				
Effective Strength of Unit	27	143	1	13	22	13	9	9	1	1	1																
Details, by *Arms* attached to unit as in War Establishment:—	1	6																									
Total	28			13	22	13	9	9	1	1	1																
War Establishment	30	101		11	22	15	9	9	1	1	1																
Wanting to complete (Detail of Personnel and Horses below)	2	25																									
Surplus																											
*Attached (not to include the details shown above)																											
Civilians:— Employed with the Unit Accompanying the Unit																											
TOTAL RATIONED ...																											

* In the case of field ambulances, hospitals or depots, the number of patients are to be included here, the names being shown in A. F. A. 36.

Signature of Commander. _____

Date of Despatch. _____

Officers and men who have become casuals, been transferred or joined since last report.

Place **In the Field**   Date **28-1-16**

Regtl. Number	Rank	Name	Corps	Nature of casualty, or name of unit from or to which transferred	Date of being struck off or coming on the ration return	Remarks*
3382	Pte	Bland N	6th D.L.I.	Retd to Duty	25-1-16	
1260	„	Bell J	—Do—	—Do—	25-1-16	
3187	„	Rodwell G	—Do—	—Do—	25-1-16	
4112	„	Simpson A	—Do—	—Do—	25-1-16	

* State whether absence is of a permanent or temporary nature, adding, in the case of casuals from wounds or disease, any available information for communication to the relatives.

For information of the A.G.'s Office at the Base.

Officers and men who have become casuals, been transferred or joined since last report.

Place_____   Date_____

Regtl. Number	Rank	Name	Corps	Nature of casualty, or name of unit from or to which transferred	Date of being struck off or coming on the ration return	Remarks*
2326	Pte	Thompson G	Do.	Retd. to 6 coo. Std	3-2-16	
3041	"	Pooley R.	Do	-Do-	30-1-16	
2	2Lt	Aiken F.A.S	-Do	Retd to Duty	3-2-16	
2775	Pte	Houghton S.W	-Do-	-Do-	28-1-16	
2090	"	Payne G.	-Do-	-Do-	28-1-16	
2902	"	Stelling N.	-Do-	-Do-	28-1-16	
2184	"	Rerman T.J	-Do-	-Do-	29-1-16	
623	"	Ward S.	-Do	-Do-	28-1-16	
2016	L/Sgt	O'Neill T.	-Do-	-Do-	31-1-16	
2445	Cpl.	Elliott A.	-Do-	L/Do-	28-1-16	
1659	A/c	Dixon J.	-Do-	-Do-	2-2-16	
1888	Pte	Urquhart G.H.	-Do-	-Ro-	2-2-16	
2760	"	Goodfellow J.B.	-Do-	-Do-	29-1-16	
1512	"	Calpass T.R.	-Do	-Do-	29-1-16	

* State whether absence is of a permanent or temporary nature, adding, in the case of casuals from wounds or disease, any available information for communication to the relatives.

Army Form C. 2118

Vol 10

WAR DIARY

or

INTELLIGENCE SUMMARY

(Erase heading not required.)

Instructions regarding War Diaries and Intelligence Summaries are contained in F. S. Regs., Part II. and the Staff Manual respectively. Title Pages will be prepared in manuscript.

Place	Date	Hour	Summary of Events and Information	Remarks and references to Appendices

War Diary of The
6 Batt. the Durham Light Infantry

for the month of

April, 1916.

Appendix. Trench Plan of the BLUFF, BEAN, POLLOCK
and neighbouring trenches

1875 Wt. W593/826 1,000,000 4/15 J.B.C. & A. A.D.S.S./Forms/C. 2118.

WAR DIARY

or

INTELLIGENCE SUMMARY

(*Erase heading not required.*)

Instructions regarding War Diaries and Intelligence Summaries are contained in F. S. Regs., Part II. and the Staff Manual respectively. Title Pages will be prepared in manuscript.

Place	Date	Hour	Summary of Events and Information	Remarks and references to Appendices
YPRES SALIENT	1/4/16		There was a good deal of hostile shelling to-day, particularly in the shape of *howitzer* & *field gun* on and near the *south-west* lundry from the front of GORDON POST past Bn. Hqrs, the front of GORDON POST past Bn. Hqrs, Bn. Dump, to Bde. H.Q. at foot of the SPOIL BANK. Our outposts at 30 S.t & 31.S were likewise severely "crumped". The 8th Bn. D.L.I. were obliged to evacuate & came up in GORDON TERRACE men obliged to evacuate & came up to our lines, they had a few casualties.	
BEAN, POLLOCK & INTER-NATIONAL trenches, to BLUFF & to NEW YEARtrench GORDON POST, & RESERVE WOOD	I.3.W.b.c.d			

Army Form C. 2118

WAR DIARY

or

INTELLIGENCE SUMMARY

(Erase heading not required.)

Instructions regarding War Diaries and Intelligence
Summaries are contained in F. S. Regs., Part II.
and the Staff Manual respectively. Title Pages
will be prepared in manuscript.

Place	Date	Hour	Summary of Events and Information	Remarks and references to Appendices
YPRES I.34.b. c & d. Beem, Polluck, Salvationnel Trenches & the "13 Buff"	2/4/16		The 6 Batt. the Durham Light Infantry were relieved at about midday by 2/3 by the 1st Batt., 1st Division, Canadian Corps. During the day the enemy subjected N.S. to a severe shelling particularly between GORDON POST and BRIGADE H.Q. The latter came in for a severe bombardment with "crumps" and field-guns from 2 p.m. onwards. The enemy had the range exactly and knocked in all our dug-outs except, fortunately, the signalling station and the dressing station. Capt. Harker, Brigade Major, was mortally wounded by shell-fire, displaying the greatest courage able was accompanied by Brigadier - General J. Shea, C.B., etc, who was fortunately at the time by 13 orders the 8 Batt. the Durham Light In- accompanied. The headquarters of the 13th battalion being Sentry were reoccupied up by heavy shell, They being the spoil Bank in GORDON TERRACE in Brigade Reserve at the time on the KINGSWAY, but above Batt. H.P. in I.33.a. They suffered 5-6 casualties, into Trench Tramway, from near LAN G.HOF CHATEAU, I.32.6. central, and to CHESTER FARM, I.33.a. 7.6.1 was completely wrecked I.26.d. 1/2. 1/2. to Company Commanders got their com- 13y exceptionally skilful manœuvring however we had 6 killed wounded at	

Army Form C. 2118

WAR DIARY
or
INTELLIGENCE SUMMARY
(Erase heading not required.)

Instructions regarding War Diaries and Intelligence Summaries are contained in F. S. Regs., Part II. and the Staff Manual respectively. Title Pages will be prepared in manuscript.

Place	Date	Hour	Summary of Events and Information	Remarks and references to Appendices
DICKEBUSCH HUTS. H.26.b. Central.	3/4/16		of the group near LANGHOF CHATEAU & a great deal of it was lost, some by being shortly hit by shells, & others by the swamping of them carrying it on the impossibility of seeing it under the circumstances. Although Companies & specialists managed to get away by about midnight, the Headquarter Staff of the 1st/13 Batt, 1st Div, Light Infantry H.P. Canadian Corps did not get here to 6th Durham till the small hours of the morning of the 3rd April. Lt Colonel 2nd in Command, Capt. —, Major J. Walton, — D.S.O, with the acting Adjutant, left at — White, R.A.M.C. Medical Officer, & the — the most down part the about 5. a.m. & worked their way through & what we left of the trench wrecked dug-out of KINGSWAY — before morning cut tramway to — LANGHOF CHATEAU. just — the hard — back in DICKEBUSCH.	

1875 Wt. W593/826 1,000,000 4/15 J.B.C. & A. A.D.S.S./Forms/C. 2118.

WAR DIARY

or

INTELLIGENCE SUMMARY

(Erase heading not required.)

Instructions regarding War Diaries and Intelligence Summaries are contained in F. S. Regs., Part II. and the Staff Manual respectively. Title Pages will be prepared in manuscript.

Place	Date	Hour	Summary of Events and Information	Remarks and references to Appendices
SCOTTISH LINES G.17.a.5.3.	4/4/16		This morning the Battalion left for the SCOTTISH LINES where it arrived at 10. a.m., but found a Canadian Scottish Battalion in possession. The latter left shortly after. At 11.15 a.m. Brigadier found J. Shea arrived & addressed the Battalion, which he congratulated on its behaviour during the time it has been in the YPRES Salient. He said he would give them the highest compliment which any soldier could present — "Men, you are good soldiers". The Battalion had been in the Salient since 17/12/15.	
LA CLYTTE M.12.9.9.	5/4/16		The Battalion left for the new area (N & O lincales) & arrived at LA CLYTTE (Divisional Rest) at 10.30.a.m. The camp is situated about halfway between RENINGHELST & KEMMEL on the main road. Considering the severe strain which they have had to bear the health & spirits of the men are splendid	
	6/4/16 7/4/16		Resting at LA CLYTTE. Nothing to report beyond customary kit inspections.	

1875. Wt. W593/826 1,000,000 4/15 J.B.C. & A. A.D.S.S./Forms/C. 2118.

WAR DIARY ⑤

or

INTELLIGENCE SUMMARY

(Erase heading not required.)

Instructions regarding War Diaries and Intelligence Summaries are contained in F. S. Regs., Part II. and the Staff Manual respectively. Title Pages will be prepared in manuscript.

Place	Date	Hour	Summary of Events and Information	Remarks and references to Appendices
N-9 Trenches N.6.C. 1/2.9.	8/4/16		Took over trenches N-3 to O.4.), Sheet 2 8, O.7. a. 2½.½. to O.7.b.6.9. Also S.P.7. at O.7.a 1¼. 8½, BOIS CARRÉ, O.7.b.c.+d., and the BRASERIE DEFENCES com- menced in the squares N. 12., N.5.6.4.0, N.5.6.7½.1., N.6.C.1.8 and N.6.a.4.2. Bn. H.Q. at N.6.C.1½.9. The 8th Batt. the DURH. L.I. took over the trenches on our right, whilst our left was held by the 8th battalion of the Canadians about ST. ELOI. The trenches are in bad condition communication trenches being few + in rather bad condition, support either derelict or few + in rather bad condition; front line either too low or not bullet= lacking; parapets in front line either too low or not bullet= proof; paradoes practically non-existent; dug-outs few + hardly protected.	
"	9/4/16		Between 12.0 midnight = 1.0 a.m. this morning the Canadians attacked ST. ELOI ridge + craters, with what success is not known. Our own line joined in the general scheme + swept enemy trenches O.7.b.central to O.7. c. s. 6. We had no casualties. A few	

Army Form C. 2118

WAR DIARY
or
INTELLIGENCE SUMMARY
(*Erase heading not required.*)

Instructions regarding War Diaries and Intelligence
Summaries are contained in F. S. Regs., Part II.
and the Staff Manual respectively. Title Pages
will be prepared in manuscript.

Place	Date	Hour	Summary of Events and Information	Remarks and references to Appendices
	9/4/16		Shells were thrown at & behind O.4., apparently meant for the P. & O. communication Trench. During the morning the enemy began a continuous shelling of our whole front line support & communication trench mortars & projectiles from Trench mortars & no front caused considerable damage in O.2. We had a few wounded during this & a similar shelling in the afternoon. Our artillery retaliated with good effect on enemy's front line & supports.	
	10/4/16		Germans still making unsuccessful night attack on the craters with great courage & obstinacy. Shelling of our trenches particularly in the region of Bois carré continued. One shell fell in front of the hedge before Batt. H.Q.	
	11/4/16		Enemy artillery still busy on the same registers as before. Their trench mortars, rum-jars, fish-tailed bombs caused a time & more inconvenience than their artillery. We were relieved by the 9th Batt. Devons. L.I., & marched
Relieved about 11 p.m.	

1875 Wt. W593/826 1,000,000 4/15 J.B.C. & A. A.D.S.S./Forms/C. 2118.

Document reference:.. WO95/2840. ◇END.

Document(s). being *a map*

'Secret. Trench Diagram', parts of 33B, D; 34A, B, C,D; parts of 35A,C.   1 Apr to 10 Apr 1916.

has been removed to the Map Room, reference: ...... MFQ 1387 ....

Date: .... 13 January 1997 .... Signed: ....

WAR DIARY

or

INTELLIGENCE SUMMARY

(Erase heading not required.)

Instructions regarding War Diaries and Intelligence Summaries are contained in F. S. Regs., Part II. and the Staff Manual respectively. Title Pages will be prepared in manuscript.

Place	Date	Hour	Summary of Events and Information	Remarks and references to Appendices
N. 5. a. 7. 2.	11/4/16	Quoted	to Brigade Reserve in RIDGEWOOD (N. 5. a & b.) wit one Company, under Capt. L. Thorpe, in dug-outs, between G.H.Q LINE & DICKEBUSCH — VIERSTRAAT ROAD, at N. 10. b. 6½. 7. — We are also responsible for defence of CAPTAIN'S POST (N. 5: d. 6. 3.) + MAJOR'S COPSE. (N. 11. a. 9. 9.)	Map Ref: Sheet 28.
"	12/4/16		Quiet day on the whole. Our dug-outs occasionally shelled by field-guns South - west of the RIDGEWOOD — BRASSERIE road. Considerable aeroplane activity.	
"	13/4/16		Glorious weather. No more shelling of our dug-outs. Great aeroplane activity, ours easily predominating	
"	14/4/16		Our aeroplanes completely predominated. Enemy chased away. Enemy dropped about 200 5.9 shells near GORDON FARM in var: search for a very heavy field-gun battery of ours which kept on all day.	

Army Form C. 2118

WAR DIARY
or
INTELLIGENCE SUMMARY

(Erase heading not required.)

Instructions regarding War Diaries and Intelligence Summaries are contained in F. S. Regs., Part II. and the Staff Manual respectively. Title Pages will be prepared in manuscript.

Place	Date	Hour	Summary of Events and Information	Remarks and references to Appendices
(contin)	14/4/16		At 9 p.m. we were relieved by the 8th Batt. Durh. L.I. and proceeded to DIVISIONAL RESERVE at LA CLYTTE	
LA CLYTTE	15/4/16		Here we remained 3 days resting, nothing happening from	
	16/4/16		importance so far as we were concerned. On the night of	
	17/4/16		17/18 April we returned to RIDGEWOOD where we remained	
			till night of the 20th April.	
	20/4/6		Night of 20/21 April we relieved 9 D.L.I. in the N-S trenches	
			At 9 p.m., 20/4/16, Battalion H.Q. near BRASSERIE received	
			some dozen crumps; one fell 18 feet east of the mess-	
			room + another 12 feet west of it, + about 18 feet from	
			orderly room. (The latter) W.Sergeant W. O'Dair was dangerously	
			wounded + the Orderly Room set on fire, some documents being	
			destroyed. Stretcher-bearer Ryder bound the O.R. Sergeant's	
			wounds + took him to Dressing Station. He had about	

1875 Wt. W593/826 1,000,000 4/15 J.B.C. & A. A.D.S.S./Forms/C. 2118.

Army Form C. 2118

WAR DIARY (9)
or
INTELLIGENCE SUMMARY
(Erase heading not required.)

Instructions regarding War Diaries and Intelligence Summaries are contained in F. S. Regs., Part II. and the Staff Manual respectively. Title Pages will be prepared in manuscript.

Place	Date	Hour	Summary of Events and Information	Remarks and references to Appendices
(continued)	20/4/16		9 casualties, mostly from a shell which hit the BRASSERIE, & 2 or 3 from field-gun shells fired across the field between BOIS CARRÉ & the BRASSERIE. The 9th Battalion D.L.I. also suffered some casualties.	
	21/4/16		Enemy artillery shelled BOIS CARRÉ & M.N.O. trenches with 5.9, & 2, & 18-pdr shells. The trenches have now lost the whole of the ridge at ST ELOI formerly won by 3rd. Division with possible exception of one crater. They suffered terrific shelling & themselves caused enemy heavy casualties.	
	22/4/16		Enemy shelling heavy. Our retaliation heavy. On night of 22/23 April battalion was relieved by 7th K.O. Shropshire Light Infantry, 3rd Division & proceeded to RIDGEWOOD.	
	23/4/16		A quiet day in RIDGEWOOD. On night of 23/24 we were relieved by 8 Batt. East Yorkshire Regiment, 3rd Division and marched to billets in Potijze, East & south-east of BERTHEN.	

WAR DIARY
or
INTELLIGENCE SUMMARY (10)
(Erase heading not required.)

Instructions regarding War Diaries and Intelligence
Summaries are contained in F. S. Regs., Part II.
and the Staff Manual respectively. Title Pages
will be prepared in manuscript.

Place	Date	Hour	Summary of Events and Information	Remarks and references to Appendices
	24/4/16		In next Programme of training issued.	
	25/4/16		Training began. Lt. Riddesdale R.A.M.C. acted as M.O. during illness of Capt. P. WHITE, R.A.M.C.	
	26/4/16		Lt. Colonel G. A. Stevens, D.S.O., who had been in command of the Battalion since the recovery of Lt. Colonel J. W. Jeffreys D.S.O., on	
			SANCTUARY WOOD, 20/12/16, was transferred as Brigadier - Major to the 8th Canadian Brigade.	
			Lieut. Colonel J. W. Jeffreys D.S.O. returned from sick leave and resumed command of the Battalion	
	27/4/16		The 151 Inf. Bde. was inspected at Brigade Headquarters by the Commander-in-Chief of the British Expeditionary Forces, General Sir Douglas Haig.	
	28/4/16 to 30/4/16		Programme of training continued.	

J. C. [signature] Lt. Colonel
Commanding the 8th Batt. the Durham Light Infantry

1875 Wt. W593/826 1,000,000 4/15 J.B.C. & A. A.D.S.S./Forms/C. 2118.

Army Form C. 2118.

WAR DIARY

or

INTELLIGENCE SUMMARY.

(Erase heading not required.)

Instructions regarding War Diaries and Intelligence
Summaries are contained in F. S. Regs., Part II.
and the Staff Manual respectively. Title pages
will be prepared in manuscript.

Place	Date	Hour	Summary of Events and Information	Remarks and references to Appendices
Ypres (I 30 b).	March	?	In accordance with the 50th Divisional scheme for assisting the 14th Division in their attack upon the Yser trench, the Bluff, the German salient I 34 & 10.6 known as the Bean, the Battalion concentrated during the night in Thomas Savel (I 30 b). the companies in the front-line remained as before. "Y" Company moved up from Armagh Wood (I 30 a) into the support-line. the Battalion on the left was the 4th Yorkshire Regiment and the 9th Durham L.I. occupied Lightyears Cross and "X" Trench. Other movements took place within the Brigade in order to carry out the pre-arranged rôle of making the enemy believe that an assault was intended on the Brigade front. the day was splendidly fine but there was remarkably little activity on our part. It was confined to a preliminary bombardment of the trenches from

WAR DIARY
or
INTELLIGENCE SUMMARY
(*Erase heading not required.*)

Army Form C. 2118

Instructions regarding War Diaries and Intelligence
Summaries are contained in F. S. Regs., Part II.
and the Staff Manual respectively. Title Pages
will be prepared in manuscript.

Place	Date	Hour	Summary of Events and Information	Remarks and references to Appendices
	May 1		—	
	2		Battalion route march of about 5 miles. In the middle of the march there where about 2 miles of a cobbled main road and for y men fell out. A very hot day. Oldest 3 b months in the trenches the business the Battalion is not fit for marching.	
	3.		—	
	4.		A draft of 8 ...... (1 Corpl and 1 Lance-corpl) forward.) A Pte across absorbed himself.	

1875 Wt. W593/826 1,000,000 4/15 J.B.C. & A. A.D.S.S./Forms/C. 2118.

Army Form C. 2118

WAR DIARY
or
INTELLIGENCE SUMMARY

(Erase heading not required.)

Instructions regarding War Diaries and Intelligence Summaries are contained in F.S. Regs., Part II. and the Staff Manual respectively. Title Pages will be prepared in manuscript.

Place	Date	Hour	Summary of Events and Information	Remarks and references to Appendices
P	May 5.		Brigadier General Shea inspected the billets of the Battalion and the men at drill and found them clean.	
	6.		Few officers visited the Lewis & Vickers Howitzer School at Berthen to see a demonstration. The school is under the command of Major Sir John Keane. Some Officers went to Terdeghem to see a demonstration of the Grenade School. Brig. Gen. Shea inspected the transport and was pleased with it. Lieut Kirkhouse took over the Adjutancy from 2 Lieut Galdwyn.	
	7.		Church parade at 11am. Brig. General Shea attended the parade ground and afterwards addressed the officers of the Battalion with those of the 8 D.L.I. and the Border Regiment.	
	8.		The Battalion rendezvoused at Bn Hdrs at 9.4 am and marched to KA Clyttenoor to be vacated by the 9 D.L.I. after arrival rain commenced by and then was not sufficient to dig.	

1875 Wt. W593/826 1,000,000 4/15 J.B.C. & A. A.D.S.S./Forms/C. 2118.

Army Form C. 2118

WAR DIARY
or
INTELLIGENCE SUMMARY
(Erase heading not required.)

Instructions regarding War Diaries and Intelligence Summaries are contained in F. S. Regs., Part II. and the Staff Manual respectively. Title Pages will be prepared in manuscript.

Place	Date	Hour	Summary of Events and Information	Remarks and references to Appendices
	May 9.		In camp at LA CLYTTE. 2 parties of 130 men each paraded at 7-30 a.m. and marched to VIERSTRAAT for work on the VIERSTRAAT Switch. Returned at 2-30 a.m. Bad cold wet day.	
	10.		Two parties for work as last night. 2 Lieut Peacock and 4 N.C.O's, returned from Bayonet fighting course.	
	11.		Two parties for work on Vierstraat Switch at 7-30 a.m. (Capt McQueen of the 7th Field Coy. R.E. having relieved 2nd Northumberland Field (Coys) Reserparties worked under his orders.	
	12		Paraded at 11 a.m. Marched 8 miles back to CICC.Ls near Mont des Cats close to Bailleu district. Et hot day, and 15 men fell out. All officers attended a Brigade Riding School.	

1875 Wt. W593/826 1,000,000 4/15 J.B.C. & A. A.D.S.S./Forms/C. 2118.

Army Form C. 2118

WAR DIARY
or
INTELLIGENCE SUMMARY
(Erase heading not required.)

Instructions regarding War Diaries and Intelligence Summaries are contained in F. S. Regs., Part II. and the Staff Manual respectively. Title Pages will be prepared in manuscript.

Place	Date	Hour	Summary of Events and Information	Remarks and references to Appendices
	May 13.		of wet days of forwards Brigadier General at Slsa returned to all officers, on the method of advancing against strong positions.	
	14.		Church parade after in Z Company's field	
	15		All officers attended a lecture by Capt Fraser (Brigade Major) on the tactical Gordon Highlanders employment of the Lewis and Machine Guns. 2 Lieut Maine left the Battalion to command a Trench Mortar Battery. (non country) run for the Brigade. Major or General Wilkinson (Comdg 60 Division) called at Battalion Hdqrs.	
	16.		The Brigade paraded opposite Brigade Headqrs and Brigadier General Slsa said farewell leaving to command the 30th Division.	
	17			

1875 Wt. W593/826 1,000,000 4/15 J.B.C. & A. A.D.S.S./Forms/C.2118.

Army Form C. 2118

WAR DIARY
or
INTELLIGENCE SUMMARY
(Erase heading not required.)

Instructions regarding War Diaries and Intelligence Summaries are contained in F. S. Regs., Part II. and the Staff Manual respectively. Title Pages will be prepared in manuscript.

Place	Date	Hour	Summary of Events and Information	Remarks and references to Appendices
	May 18.		of football match against the 8 Durham L.I. Result 11 goals to nil in our favour.	
	19.		A route march of 9 miles and 6 min fall out. The day was very hot	
	20.		Brigade Boxing tournament. Sergt Smith won the heavyweight. Sergt Halpin the middleweight. Oslivorland has now taken over	
	21		Brig. Gen. ... command of the Brigade.	
	22		All officers attended a short attack of the capture of an imaginary trench laid out by Sandbags after the instr Rod had been considered 2 Company leader Capt McNair carried out an assault on this practice trench.	
	23		The Battalion paraded with the 50 Division for Lieut-General Sir Herbert Plumer, Cmdg 2nd Army	

1875 Wt. W593/826 1,000,000 4/15 J.B.C. & A. A.D.S.S./Forms/C. 2118.

Army Form C. 2118

WAR DIARY
or
INTELLIGENCE SUMMARY

(Erase heading not required.)

Instructions regarding War Diaries and Intelligence Summaries are contained in F. S. Regs., Part II. and the Staff Manual respectively. Title Pages will be prepared in manuscript.

Place	Date	Hour	Summary of Events and Information	Remarks and references to Appendices
	May 23.		Officers N.C.Os and men who had been granted medals for distinguished conduct in the field were paraded before the general and received the medals from him. The Battalion football team beat the Border Regiment in the Brigade League football match by 2 goals to 1.	
	24.		The Director of Medical Services inspected the Battalion on the 25	
	25.		The Battalion played its last match in the Brigade Football League and beat the 9 D.L.I. by 4 goals to 3. Their in all probability winning the league	
	26.		Capt Thorpe to hospital(sick. Capt Bodcock took over command of X Company.	
	27.			

1875 Wt. W593/826 1,000,000 4/15 J.B.C. & A. A.D.S.S./Forms/C. 2118.

Army Form C. 2118

WAR DIARY
or
INTELLIGENCE SUMMARY
(Erase heading not required.)

Instructions regarding War Diaries and Intelligence Summaries are contained in F. S. Regs., Part II. and the Staff Manual respectively. Title Pages will be prepared in manuscript.

Place	Date	Hour	Summary of Events and Information	Remarks and references to Appendices
	May 28		The Battalion moved to Scherpenberg in the morning and had dinner and tea. At 7.30 pm left Scherpenberg and marched to Ridgewood where it relieved the Y.K.S.L.I. Brigade reserve. The Brigade now holds trenches from near St Eloi to opposite Vierstraat	
	29.		Provided parties at 9 pm of about 350 to work in the trenches	
	30.		In Ridgewood as Brigade Reserve. The men are in huts which protect them from the weather but are not bullet proof. This Ridgewood is about 4 miles from the German line.	
	31.		Working parties as usual. Private Brown and Pte Chapman were wounded whilst out on a working party in Nil Trench. Several good dug-outs have been erected by the Battalion in	

1875 Wt. W 593/826 1,000,000 4/15 J.B.C. & A. A.D.S.S./Forms/C. 2118.

WAR DIARY

or

INTELLIGENCE SUMMARY

(Erase heading not required.)

Instructions regarding War Diaries and Intelligence Summaries are contained in F. S. Regs., Part II. and the Staff Manual respectively. Title Pages will be prepared in manuscript.

Place	Date	Hour	Summary of Events and Information	Remarks and references to Appendices
	May 31		Ridgewood. Attack Trench afel frame-work has been used	

J. L. ....
Lieut Colonel
Commandg Birkhall

Army Form C. 2118.

WAR DIARY
or
INTELLIGENCE SUMMARY

(Erase heading not required.)

Instructions regarding War Diaries and Intelligence Summaries are contained in F. S. Regs., Part II. and the Staff Manual respectively. Title Pages will be prepared in manuscript.

Place	Date	Hour	Summary of Events and Information	Remarks and references to Appendices
1A. CONT.	Aug 1		In Ridgewood as Brigade reserve.	
	2		A very heavy artillery bombardment commenced in the Ypres salient about 8.30 a.m., died down about 1-30 p.m. The Battalion was ordered to Ridgewood by the 5th Border Regiment and relieved the 9. Durham L.I. in front line trenches N3 to O4 inclusive. Headquarters close to the Brasserie. Y Company N3 to O1 with 1 platoon in N12, bombers retreat. X Company in O1A to O4 with 1 platoon in N12 left. W Company in Bois Carré. Z Company in the Brasserie and N11 and S.P.4. Very heavy bombardment started again in the salient just after about midnight and continued for about 1 hour.	
	3		News received that the Canadians had lost Sanctuary Wood and Mount Sorrell. The following 2nd Lieutenants arrived from England and came on the Battalion strength 2 Lieuts Barnet, Du Motch, Appleby	

W. A. Charlton, Major, 19th Mar (?)

2449 Wt. W14957/M90 750,000 1/16 J.B.C. & A. Forms/C.2118/12.

WAR DIARY

or

INTELLIGENCE SUMMARY

(Erase heading not required.)

Instructions regarding War Diaries and Intelligence Summaries are contained in F. S. Regs., Part II. and the Staff Manual respectively. Title Pages will be prepared in manuscript.

Place	Date	Hour	Summary of Events and Information	Remarks and references to Appendices
LA CLYTTE	JUNE 4		2/Lieut A. Edwards East Lancashire Regiment arrived to take over Adjutant of the Battalion. Aeroplane was organised by the 24th Division on our right. Our Division co-operated by heavily shelling the HOLLANDSCHESCHUUR salient. No news of the success or otherwise of the show.	
	5		Quiet day. Corporal Dean from the 2nd Battn King Edwards Horse on appointment to the Battalion as 2nd Lieutenant. He left for England to get Officers clothes. The 12 Battn West Yorkshire Regiment relieved the 20th Battn (Canadians) [Hussars (Canadians)] on our left.	
	6		2/Lieut G. B. Wilson who arrived 2 days ago carried for duty in H.Q. Battalion report his arrival. It has been stopping at the R.M. Stores. A good aeroplane at 4 p.m. by our	
	7		4.5 Howitzers and 18 pounders, with a little assistance from the 6 inch guns against the sector in front of N.S. was satisfactory.	

Army Form C. 2118.

WAR DIARY
or
INTELLIGENCE SUMMARY
(*Erase heading not required.*)

Instructions regarding War Diaries and Intelligence Summaries are contained in F. S. Regs., Part II and the Staff Manual respectively. Title Pages will be prepared in manuscript.

Place	Date	Hour	Summary of Events and Information	Remarks and references to Appendices
La Clytte	June. 8.		The 9 Durham L.I. relieved the Battalion. Relief completed 10-30 p.m. Companies marched to La Clytte and the last arrived at 1 a.m. Billets(?) in Durham Huts in La Clytte. A wet night.	
	9.		Resting. Ashworth's Company gave an entertainment to the Battalion in the Recreation hut at La Clytte	
	10.		Rest. The Battalion each night whilst here at rest finds a working party for the front line of between 140 and 240 strong. This is however hard on the men. 2 Lieut Meyer who arrived with the Battalion on the 6th last Tuesday was killed by a rifle(?) bullet whilst in charge of a working party just behind the front line.	
	11.		2 Lieut Meyer was buried in the soldiers cemetery at 4-30 p.m. cd firing party was detailed and 2 buglers sounded last post	

WAR DIARY

or

INTELLIGENCE SUMMARY

(Erase heading not required.)

Instructions regarding War Diaries and Intelligence
Summaries are contained in F. S. Regs., Part II
and the Staff Manual respectively. Title Pages
will be prepared in manuscript.

Place	Date	Hour	Summary of Events and Information	Remarks and references to Appendices
LA(LYTTE	June 12.		General Wilkinson C.B. C.M.G. Commanding 50th Division dined at Headqrs.	
	13		—	
	14		The Battalion relieved 9. O.K.L. in the trenches N3, N4, N5, N6, O1, O1A, O2, O3, O4, In Southern redoubt, Wieltje redoubt and Eastern Redoubt, SP.Y, Bois Carré dugouts and Brassins defences. Relief completed at 10.30 pm. At 11 pm the DAYLIGHT Saving bill and all watches put forward one hour.	
	15.		In trenches	
	16.		2 Lieut Yaldwyn and 2 Lt Kau returned from leave. At 10-30 pm a sudden heavy bombardment to the south. This presently died down and a very heavy bombardment continued in the Ypres salient. This continued till 11-30am.	
	17.		Fine day. Wind North East.	

2449 Wt. W14957/M90 750,000 1/16 J.B.C. & A. Forms/C.2118/12.

Instructions regarding War Diaries and Intelligence
Summaries are contained in F. S. Regs., Part II.
and the Staff Manual respectively. Title Pages
will be prepared in manuscript.

Place	Date	Hour	Summary of Events and Information	Remarks and references to Appendices
LACUYTTE	June 18.		Sergt O'Neill left for a course of instruction prior to being commissioned a officer. At 6 p.m. the enemy began a fairly heavy bombardment by "N and Trench Mortars of the ground just behind "N and O. trenches and of N 12 and bombers retreat. 4 men of the Battalion wounded but not seriously. 5 of the East Yorkshire regiment joining our left were blown to pieces by a "Rum Jar", and Trench Mortar. Corpl Dawson dangerously wounded as is in Chicory C.T. about midnight. Sergt O'Neill left tomorrow.	
	19.		At mid-day the enemy opened accurate & fire with Whizz-bangs and Howitzers on our front line and Communication Trenches. This lasted for 10 minutes. Very little damage being done and no casualties.	

WAR DIARY

or

INTELLIGENCE SUMMARY

(Erase heading not required.)

Instructions regarding War Diaries and Intelligence Summaries are contained in F. S. Regs., Part II. and the Staff Manual respectively. Title Pages will be prepared in manuscript.

Place	Date	Hour	Summary of Events and Information	Remarks and references to Appendices
LA CLYTTE	JUNE 20		The Battalion was relieved by the 9 Durham L.I. in the trenches and returned to RIDGEWOOD. Relief complete at 12 midnight (summer time) Brig Scrafton severely wounded. The Battalion has had only 5 casualties, During the last tour in the trenches, it has been a trying time for all ranks, on account of the Trench Mortars which present sleep by day.	
	21		In Ridgewood. Z Coy at LA CLYTTE under Captain McNair. 240 men on working parties under the R.E's at night.	
	22		In dugouts at RIDGEWOOD 1½ miles from the German lines. Wind East and South East. "Gas Alert" declared at 9-30 pm. Working parties as last night.	

2449   Wt. W14957/M90 759,000 1/16 J.B.C. & A.   Forms/C.2118/12.

WAR DIARY

or

INTELLIGENCE SUMMARY

(Erase heading not required.)

Instructions regarding War Diaries and Intelligence
Summaries are contained in F. S. Regs., Part II.
and the Staff Manual respectively. Title Pages
will be prepared in manuscript.

Place	Date	Hour	Summary of Events and Information	Remarks and references to Appendices
LA (C1776)	June 23.		Brig. General. T. P. Westmorland. C.M.G. D.S.O. commanding the Brigade was thrown from his horse and badly bruised and cut.	
	24		—	
	25		Pte. Rouse W (Company was killed whilst on a working party). Pte Lawson and Pte Wilson (died of wounds) badly wounded. "Minor Operations" are now proceeding. Our guns did a good deal of wire cutting and destroying of the enemies front line	
	26		Battalion relieved by Durham L.I. in Trenches N3 to O4. Relief completed at 11.50 pm (summer time).	
	27.		At 1-30 am our Division (artillery) put up a barrage behind enemies front line, continued	

WAR DIARY

or

INTELLIGENCE SUMMARY

(Erase heading not required.)

Instructions regarding War Diaries and Intelligence Summaries are contained in F. S. Regs., Part II. and the Staff Manual respectively. Title Pages will be prepared in manuscript.

Place	Date	Hour	Summary of Events and Information	Remarks and references to Appendices
La (AYTE)	June 27.		till 2-30 am, at 2-45 am began again and continued till 3-15 pm. Enemy only retaliated slightly. 150 Brigade carried out a raid (or wrinkle)	
	28.		Our guns continued to shell German wire and front line heavily. The enemy made little or no reply. 2 Lieut' Nicholson and 21 Other Ranks arrived at R. M. Stores in the evening.	
	29		Good deal of Trench Mortar activity on both sides	
	30.		The wind has for some time been South or South West. No danger therefore of gas attack.	

J. Holyworth
Lieut & ADJUTANT for Lieut Colonel
Cmdg 6 Durham L.I.

Army Form C. 2118.

WAR DIARY

or

INTELLIGENCE SUMMARY

(Erase heading not required.)

Vol 13

Instructions regarding War Diaries and Intelligence Summaries are contained in F. S. Regs., Part II. and the Staff Manual respectively. Title Pages will be prepared in manuscript.

Place	Date	Hour	Summary of Events and Information	Remarks and references to Appendices

6 Bn THE DURHAM LIGHT INFANTRY.

WAR DIARY.

July. 1916.

Volume Number 16.

2449 Wt. W14957/M90 750,000 1/16 J.B.C. & A. Forms/C.2118/12.

WAR DIARY
or
INTELLIGENCE SUMMARY

(Erase heading not required.)

Instructions regarding War Diaries and Intelligence Summaries are contained in F. S. Regs., Part II and the Staff Manual respectively. Title Pages will be prepared in manuscript.

Place	Date	Hour	Summary of Events and Information	Remarks and references to Appendices
LA CLYTTE	July 1		ed good deal of Trench Mortar activity on both sides. 2 Lieut F.W. Little and 2 Lieut S.R. Little who are not related joined the battalion.	
	2		A quiet day. News arrived of an attack by the 3rd Division Army on a 16 mile front. Somme district. The Battalion relieved by the 9 Durham L.I. and returned to LA CLYTTE. Relief complete before mid night and all Companies reached Durham Huts before 2am on the 3rd.	
	3.		No digging parties required. The Battalion has now been settled in the trenches of finding working parties of 200 or 300 men for 36 days.	

2449 Wt. W14957/Mgo 750,000 1/16 J.B.C. & A. Forms/C.2118/12.

WAR DIARY

or

INTELLIGENCE SUMMARY

(Erase heading not required.)

Instructions regarding War Diaries and Intelligence Summaries are contained in F. S. Regs., Part II. and the Staff Manual respectively. Title Pages will be prepared in manuscript.

Place	Date	Hour	Summary of Events and Information	Remarks and references to Appendices
La U[...]July 4	4		6 days ago the General privately informed the C.O. that he wished him to make a raid on the enemy trenches opposite NH trench. The trenches are here about 80 yards apart. The party was selected and 2 Lieut Auriett put in charge and the ground scouted. A twice has now been fixed for 11-30 pm on the 6th.	
	5.		General Westmorland (the Brigadier) came to see the raiding party at practice at 10-45 am.	
	6.		...ed raiding party, composed of 2 Lieut Auriett in command Lieut Aubin and 18 N.C.O's and men of Y Coy. and 14 bombers left NS trench at 11-15 pm. to surprise the enemy in the crater at west side of BOIS CARRE	

Army Form C. 2118.

WAR DIARY
or
INTELLIGENCE SUMMARY

(Erase heading not required.)

Instructions regarding War Diaries and Intelligence
Summaries are contained in F. S. Regs., Part II.
and the Staff Manual respectively.   Title Pages
will be prepared in manuscript.

Place	Date	Hour	Summary of Events and Information	Remarks and references to Appendices
LA (LITTE) July	7		At 2am the party returned having failed in their enterprise owing to the absence of previous on the parapet which prevented the possibility of surprise. Capt R.V. Hart had taken charge of all arrangements for the work.	
	7.		The Battn relieved the 9 Battalion D.L.I. in trenches N3 to O4. Relief complete at midnight (summer time). Owing to mistake in telephone message no report was received am.	
	9.		Capt Brinson and 3 men of W. Company wounded in N5 by minenwerfers. Signalling dugout was blown in and the occupants had a narrow escape. Corpl Dixon behaved with great coolness and gallantry. 2 Lieut Accworth's raiding party went out from NH at 11-20 pm to raid the crater opposite.	

WAR DIARY

or

INTELLIGENCE SUMMARY

(Erase heading not required.)

Instructions regarding War Diaries and Intelligence Summaries are contained in F. S. Regs., Part II. and the Staff Manual respectively. Title Pages will be prepared in manuscript.

Place	Date	Hour	Summary of Events and Information	Remarks and references to Appendices
Tally (?)	July 9		...d prisoner was captured near our wire and 2nd Lieut Minett thinking the rest of the patrol had forced part had given of which he withdrew his party. The prisoner the alarm he withdrew his party was a private soldier in the 215th Reserve Regiment and a bomber by trade.	
	10.		Telegrams of congratulation received from the 2nd Army, the Corps and the 50 Division upon the capture of a prisoner who is of great value in giving information as to troops on our front. 2 Lieuts W. R. Tattersall, F. C. D. Scott Sedgwick and Barton, Richardson, Smith & Richardson reported their arrival to the Battalion.	

2449 Wt. W14957/M90 750,000 1/16 J.B.C. & A. Forms/C.2118/12.

WAR DIARY

or

INTELLIGENCE SUMMARY

(Erase heading not required.)

Instructions regarding War Diaries and Intelligence Summaries are contained in F. S. Regs., Part II. and the Staff Manual respectively. Title Pages will be prepared in manuscript.

Place	Date	Hour	Summary of Events and Information	Remarks and references to Appendices
LA CLYTTE	July 11		Secret announcement was made to the Battalion that the Canadians on our left would make a raid tonight, with the aid of gas arrangements. The raid was cancelled. Capt & 2/c Main failed in the front line trench owing to the proximity of a heavy minnenwerfer fire close behind him.	
	12.		Following officers reported their arrival with the Battalion 2 Lieut Ramsay, McVickers, and Nelson.	
	13		—	
	14		Private Corns, Pte Lauder, and Pte Stokeld of Y Coy were killed in O4 trench, and Sergt Watson of Y Company was seriously wounded.	

WAR DIARY
or
INTELLIGENCE SUMMARY
(*Erase heading not required.*)

Instructions regarding War Diaries and Intelligence
Summaries are contained in F. S. Regs, Part II.
and the Staff Manual respectively. Title Pages
will be prepared in manuscript.

Place	Date	Hour	Summary of Events and Information	Remarks and references to Appendices
La Gytte	July 14		An officers patrol consisting of 2 Lieut Annett 2 Lieut Dubin Sergt Gough, Sgt Sinch, Sergt Bryant Lance Sergt Thirlwg. 10 bombers and 10 rifles effected an entry into the German trench opposite N5. The left under 2 Lieut Annett found the trench very much dilapidated and unoccupied. The right under 2 Lieut Dubin came into collision with some Germans in the trench and a short fight resulted with bombs and rifle fire. 2 Sgt Gough was slightly wounded. No other casualties on our side. Number of casualties of Germans 4 or 5.	
	15		The battalion relieved by 6 Northumberland Fusiliers and marched back to camp near	

WAR DIARY

or

INTELLIGENCE SUMMARY

(Erase heading not required.)

Instructions regarding War Diaries and Intelligence Summaries are contained in F. S. Regs., Part II. and the Staff Manual respectively. Title Pages will be prepared in manuscript.

Place	Date	Hour	Summary of Events and Information	Remarks and references to Appendices
LA (LYNE) July 15.			BROLOOZE and Scherpenberg, where the last platoon arrived about 3 a.m.	
	16.		A draft of 13 N.C.O.s and men arrived for the battalion from the Base. Throughout the last fortnight, there has been reinforcements consistantly good news of the Battalion in the South. Battalion in fine Bivouacs and tents. All ranks very comfortable. 3Bn of	
	17.		The Cmdg Officer left for 10 days leave on account of ill health. Major McGallow assumed temporary command in his absence. Working party of 4 Officers +50 Other Ranks at 7.15 p.m.	
	18.		Companies at disposal of Company Commanders	

2449 Wt. W1495?/Mg0 750,000 1/16 J.B.C. & A. Forms/C.2118/12.

WAR DIARY
or
INTELLIGENCE SUMMARY
(Erase heading not required.)

Instructions regarding War Diaries and Intelligence Summaries are contained in F. S. Regs., Part II and the Staff Manual respectively. Title Pages will be prepared in manuscript.

Place	Date	Hour	Summary of Events and Information	Remarks and references to Appendices
Brulooze	July 18		Brigade informed us No. 1569 Corpl Dixon (Butts Signal Section) had been awarded the Military Medal.	
	19.		Fine day. No working parties.	
AIRCRAFT.	20.		Battln relieved 3rd Battalion Rifle Brigade. Brigade and unit into Brigade Reserve. 35-333.34 (5ssw-25sw) N32b.2.3. Relief carried out in day light. The Battn marched past The Brigadier at Brigade Headqrs at DRANOUTRE - the Band and Bugles playing "Marching Through Georgia". The Battalion marched well and looked fit.	
	21.		Renovating huts and 35-333.34	
	22.		Ceased Parody and Lieut. McBay (re-inforcement.)	

WAR DIARY

or

INTELLIGENCE SUMMARY

(Erase heading not required.)

Instructions regarding War Diaries and Intelligence Summaries are contained in F. S. Regs., Part II. and the Staff Manual respectively. Title Pages will be prepared in manuscript.

Place	Date	Hour	Summary of Events and Information	Remarks and references to Appendices
AIRCRAFT FARM.	July 22.		Class of 21 for Lewis Gun began under instruction of 2 Lieut. Ramsay Batt. G. O.	
		23.	Still in Brigade reserve. 2 Lieut. Tate (re-inforcement) joined Battalion. Battalion paraded for Divine Service. Band furnished Music for Church of England. R. C's celebrated Mass at DRANOUTRE. Z Company relieved a Company of 9 D.L.I. in Fort Victoria, Fort Regina, Fort Edward and Mortuary and came under order of G. O. C. 151 Infy Bde. Relief complete 11 pm (Runners)	
	24.		Supplied 170 men for working parties	
	25.		Quiet day.	

2449 Wt. W14957/M90 750,000 1/16 J.B.C. & A. Forms/C.2118/12.

Army Form C. 2118.

WAR DIARY
or
INTELLIGENCE SUMMARY
(*Erase heading not required.*)

Instructions regarding War Diaries and Intelligence Summaries are contained in F. S. Regs., Part II. and the Staff Manual respectively. Title Pages will be prepared in manuscript.

Place	Date	Hour	Summary of Events and Information	Remarks and references to Appendices
AIRCRAFT FARM	1916 July 26.		Corps Commander visited Battalion while in Brigade Reserve. Relieved 7 Durham L.I. in Trenches 5.1 to 5.4.	
	27		The Battalion is disposed as follows:- holding 51 to 54 trenches. Z Company in front line, X Coy in S. P.11 — 2 platoons of W. Company in Fort Saskatchewan and 2 platoons of W. Coy. and the whole of Y Company in Reserve. Chateau at 2 pm Capt McNair went to hospital suffering from shock and collapse. At 2-4.5 pm the Germans began to heavily bombard the 9 trenches with heavy Trench Mortars. This	

2449 Wt. W14957/M90 750,000 1/16 J.B.C. & A. Forms/C.2118/12.

Army Form C. 2118.

WAR DIARY
or
INTELLIGENCE SUMMARY
(Erase heading not required.)

Instructions regarding War Diaries and Intelligence
Summaries are contained in F. S. Regs., Part II.
and the Staff Manual respectively. Title Pages
will be prepared in manuscript.

Place	Date	Hour	Summary of Events and Information	Remarks and references to Appendices
KEMMEL July	24.		continued. Fell 5-15 p.m. Pte Goodfellow of Z company and Pte Pears of X Coy (Lewis Gunner) were killed and Corpl Jackson, Pte Mulholland and Lance-corpl Doolds were wounded. The close support positions were utterly knocked to pieces but the actual fire trench not very much damaged. Company H.Q. were blown in	
	28.		Z Company was withdrawn from the front line leaving only 2 Lewis Gunners 1 bombing post 1 sniping post and 1 sentry group in the front line. The remainder withdrawn to Kitchen Avenue as reserve of Young's Street. At night X Company	

WAR DIARY

or

INTELLIGENCE SUMMARY

(Erase heading not required.)

Instructions regarding War Diaries and Intelligence
Summaries are contained in F. S. Regs., Part II.
and the Staff Manual respectively. Title Pages
will be prepared in manuscript.

Place	Date	Hour	Summary of Events and Information	Remarks and references to Appendices
Kemmel	1916 July 28		relieved by Y Company in the front line.	
	29.		Hot weather and a quiet day.	
	30.		A draft of 190 men were expected but did not arrive. There is a great deal of work to be done in repairing front line trenches. Pte Carter, a bomber of Y Company was killed by a rifle bullet when on battle[?] last night.	
	31.		The Company and two platoons which occupied Kemmel Chateau bathed every day in the moat which surrounds the house. A quiet day.	

H. E. Kennel
Lieut? Colonel
Cmdg 6 Durham L.I.

2449 Wt. W14957/M90 750,000 1/16 J.B.C. & A. Forms/C.2118/12.

Army Form C. 2118.

WAR DIARY

or

INTELLIGENCE SUMMARY

(Erase heading not required.)

Instructions regarding War Diaries and Intelligence Summaries are contained in F. S. Regs., Part II. and the Staff Manual respectively. Title Pages will be prepared in manuscript.

Place	Date	Hour	Summary of Events and Information	Remarks and references to Appendices

Vol 14

War Diary

1/6th Batt. The Durham Light Infantry

August 1916

Volume No 14.

2449 Wt. W14957/M90 750,000 1/16 J.B.C. & A. Forms/C.2118/12.

Army Form C. 2118.

WAR DIARY

or

INTELLIGENCE SUMMARY

(*Erase heading not required.*)

Instructions regarding War Diaries and Intelligence
Summaries are contained in F. S. Regs., Part II.
and the Staff Manual respectively. Title Pages
will be prepared in manuscript.

Place	Date	Hour	Summary of Events and Information	Remarks and references to Appendices
KEMMEL	1916 August 1		Battalion in trenches 91 to G 4. Relieved by the 5th Bn. Durham L. I. relief complete 11-45 p.m. Total casualties during 7 days in the trenches 3 killed 4 wounded. Several men suffering from Shell Shock, and from the heavy Trench Mortar Bombardment of 27th ult.	
	2.		On relief Battalion marched to WAKEFIELD HUTS between WESTOUTRE and LOCRE, were the last company arrived at 2-45 a.m. Draft of 190 men composed of men of the 2nd line of the 6th, 7th, 8th, and 9th Durham L. I. arrived.	
	3		The Brigadier inspected the last draft. Very hot weather.	
	4.		...ds strong as possible marching order parade.	

Army Form C. 2118.

WAR DIARY

or

INTELLIGENCE SUMMARY

(Erase heading not required.)

Instructions regarding War Diaries and Intelligence
Summaries are contained in F. S. Regs., Part II.
and the Staff Manual respectively. Title Pages
will be prepared in manuscript.

Place	Date	Hour	Summary of Events and Information	Remarks and references to Appendices
LOCRE.	1916. August 4.		As strong as possible marching order parade. Secret orders issued that the Division is going out to rest and probably down to the SOMME very shortly. A draft of 114 N.C.Os and men arrived for the Battalion, about 1/3 of them from our 2nd and 3rd line, and from 7th, 8th and 9th Durham L.I.	
	5.		Major General Wilkinson C.B. C.M.G. Commanding Division inspected the last line draft/s, 303 N.C.O's and men paraded. The draft was formed up ready for him at 4-25 am, and received the general with the Royal Salute, Band playing. At 10 am the Battalion marched out south of the DRANOUTRE— NEUVE EGISE Road to practice open attack operations as directed by the Division. The enemy were dropping shells pretty close and the Brigadier appeared, and remarked on the apparent danger, the Battalion marched back to huts.	

WAR DIARY

or

INTELLIGENCE SUMMARY

(Erase heading not required.)

Instructions regarding War Diaries and Intelligence Summaries are contained in F.S. Regs., Part II. and the Staff Manual respectively. Title Pages will be prepared in manuscript.

Place	Date	Hour	Summary of Events and Information	Remarks and references to Appendices
LOCRE	1916 Aug 6.		Church parade 10 a.m. at WAKEFIELD HUTS, Capt Astbury, Brigade Chaplain, officiated.	
	7.		The 7th Kings Own Lancashire Regiment arrived by train at BAILLEUL at 4 a.m. and relieved us in WAKEFIELD CAMP (huts) at 5 a.m. The B attalion then marched back to billets near MONT DES CATS and BERTHEM, where it lay last May. Arrived in billets about 10.30 a.m. There are now 43 officers with the Battalion.	
	8.		Companies in the same billets as last April and May. All ranks very happy and comfortable.	
	9.		2 Lieut Lean took over command of the Lewis Gun	
	10.		The Battalion entrained at GODWAERSVELDE Station at 10.30 p.m. and slow, dusty, march to the Railway Station in the dusk of the evening.	

2449 Wt. W14957/M90 750,000 1/16 J.B.C. & A. Forms/C.2118/12.

Army Form C. 2118.

WAR DIARY
or
INTELLIGENCE SUMMARY

(Erase heading not required.)

Instructions regarding War Diaries and Intelligence
Summaries are contained in F. S. Regs., Part II.
and the Staff Manual respectively. Title Pages
will be prepared in manuscript.

Place	Date	Hour	Summary of Events and Information	Remarks and references to Appendices
BERTHEN	1916 Aug 10.		All Transport accompanied the Battalion, in the truck of the training which marching out slung it was 39 Officers and 954 Other Ranks.	
FLEINVILLERS CANDAS	11.		arrived at FLEINVILLERS CANDAS Station about 9-30 am. The Battalion marched half a mile from the Station and halted. Marched afterwards to HEAUZECOURT, will the Battalion arrived at 3-15 pm and went into billets. A lot dusty day.	
	12.		In comfortable billets at HEAUZECOURT. Companies marched to baths in the River OUTHIE	
	13.		In billets at HEAUZE COURT.	
	14.		conference of C.Os with the Brigadier at Brigade Headqrs at Ribaucourt.	
	15.		paraded at 3am and marched to out of HEAUZE COURT. Took breakfast in the cookers. Boeing	

Army Form C. 2118

WAR DIARY

or

INTELLIGENCE SUMMARY

(Erase heading not required.)

Instructions regarding War Diaries and Intelligence
Summaries are contained in F. S. Regs., Part II
and the Staff Manual respectively. Title Pages
will be prepared in manuscript.

Place	Date	Hour	Summary of Events and Information	Remarks and references to Appendices
LOCRE	1916. Aug. 6.		Church parade 10 am at LOAKEFIELD HUTS, Capt Astbury, Brigade Chaplain, officiated.	
	7.		The 4th Kings Own Lancashire Regiment arrived by train at BAILLEUL at 11 am and relieved us in WAKEFIELD CAMP (huts) at 1am. The B attalion then marched back to billets near MONT DES CATS and BERTHEN, where it lay last May. Arrived in billets about 10-30 am. There are now 43 officers with the Battalion.	
	8.		Companies in the same billets as last April and May. All ranks very happy and comfortable	
	9.		2 Lieut Lean took over command of the Lewis Gun	
	10.		The Battalion entrained at GODWOERSVELDE Station at 10-30 pm, ed slow, dusty, march to the Railway Station in the dusk of the evening.	

WAR DIARY
or
INTELLIGENCE SUMMARY
(Erase heading not required.)

Instructions regarding War Diaries and Intelligence Summaries are contained in F. S. Regs, Part II. and the Staff Manual respectively. Title Pages will be prepared in manuscript.

Place	Date	Hour	Summary of Events and Information	Remarks and references to Appendices
BERTHEN	Aug¹ 1916 10.		All Transport accompanied the Battalion, the truck at the turning which marching out slinging it was 39 Officers and 954 Other Ranks.	
FLEINVILLERS CANDAS	11.		arrived at FLEINVILLERS CANDAS Station about 7-30 a.m. The Battalion marched half a mile from the Station and halted. Marched afterwards to HEAUZE COURT, via the Battalion arrived at 3-15 p.m. and went into billets. A hot dusty day.	
	12.		In comfortable billets at HEAUZE COURT. Companies marched to bathe in the River OUTHIE	
	13.		In billets at HEAUZE COURT.	
	14.		conference of C.Os with the Brigadier at Brigade Headqtrs at Ribaucourt.	
	15.		paraded at 3 am and marched to out of HEAUZE COURT. Took breakfast in the coolest of the evening	

2449 Wt. W14957/M90 750,000 1/16 J.B.C. & A. Forms/C.2118/12.

WAR DIARY
or
INTELLIGENCE SUMMARY
(Erase heading not required.)

Instructions regarding War Diaries and Intelligence Summaries are contained in F. S. Regs, Part II. and the Staff Manual respectively. Title Pages will be prepared in manuscript.

Place	Date	Hour	Summary of Events and Information	Remarks and references to Appendices
HÉAUZECOURT	Augst 13		and allowed 40 minutes for getting it. Owing to lack of proper arrangements this time was insufficient and only "Y" Company had tea before the battalion moved off. Reached VILLERS BOCAGE at 9-50 am after a march of 14½ miles, 14 men fell out on the road.	
	16.		Paraded at 9-30 am and marched 7 miles to where we found good billets	
	14.		Paraded at 7am and marched 11 miles to a wood opposite BAIZIEUX. Hot day and the steep hill at the end of the march, tired the men fairly hard, 9 fell out.	
	15		The BAIZIEUX wood about 12 mile east of Amiens. There is a fairly good training area here and platoons commenced training.	

WAR DIARY

or

INTELLIGENCE SUMMARY

(Erase heading not required.)

Instructions regarding War Diaries and Intelligence Summaries are contained in F. S. Regs., Part II. and the Staff Manual respectively. Title Pages will be prepared in manuscript.

Place	Date	Hour	Summary of Events and Information	Remarks and references to Appendices
	1916. August 18		tents have been allotted to the battalion. The men bivouaced by means of sticks and waterproof sheets. The Battalion is however very deficient in waterproof sheets.	
	19.		BAIZIEUX wood. (Companies of the platoon training went to battle at BEHENCOURT.	
	20.		Instead of Church parade in the morning the battalion was put under orders to continue training. General Wilkinson visited the battalion at training. Voluntary church parade in the afternoon.	

2449 Wt. W14957/M90 750,000 1/16 J.B.C. & A. Forms/C.2118/12.

WAR DIARY
or
INTELLIGENCE SUMMARY

(Erase heading not required.)

Instructions regarding War Diaries and Intelligence Summaries are contained in F. S. Regs., Part II. and the Staff Manual respectively. Title Pages will be prepared in manuscript.

Place	Date	Hour	Summary of Events and Information	Remarks and references to Appendices
BAIZIEUX August 21	21	—		
	22		The Brigade Commander and all Brigade C.O's assembled at FRICOURT DUMP at 6 am and were shown the approaches to the trenches now held by the Army.	
	23		The Brigade Major and the C.O's again visited the approaches to the line held by the 1st division.	
	24		In BAIZIEUX Wood. Battalion, Company and platoon training.	

2449 Wt. W14957/Mgo 750,000 1/16 J.B.C. & A. Forms/C.2118/12.

WAR DIARY

or

INTELLIGENCE SUMMARY

(Erase heading not required.)

Instructions regarding War Diaries and Intelligence Summaries are contained in F. S. Regs, Part II. and the Staff Manual respectively. Title Pages will be prepared in manuscript.

Place	Date	Hour	Summary of Events and Information	Remarks and references to Appendices
BAIZIEUX	19th August		Under a scheme drawn up by the Division. all Headqrs of Brigades and Battalions practiced sending messages and keeping communication by contact patrol Signalling.	
	26		The various small ranges in the neighbourhood of "BAIZIEUX" were allotted to the Battalion for musketry today. There are now 8 Lewis Gunners in the battalion and the teams are becoming fairly well trained.	
	29		Church parade with the 5th Border Regiment at 9.45 a.m. eft 10 am battalion paraded to practice the attack. Heavy rain.	

Army Form C. 2118.

WAR DIARY
or
INTELLIGENCE SUMMARY
(Erase heading not required.)

Instructions regarding War Diaries and Intelligence Summaries are contained in F. S. Regs., Part II. and the Staff Manual respectively. Title Pages will be prepared in manuscript.

Place	Date	Hour	Summary of Events and Information	Remarks and references to Appendices
BAIZIEUX	1916 August 27		The Adjutant, Lieut A E Burnett, East Lancashire Regiment went to hospital. His left arm had been crushed by his horse falling on the line on parade. 2 Lieut Kirkhouse now Acting Adjutant.	
	28		Lieut Gen. Sir W.P. Pulteney Commanding 3 Corps had arranged to review the Division and present Medals. The parade was cancelled on account of wet. Sergt Maun (Band Sergt) and Corporal Dixon (Signalling Corps) went to the 14g Brigade H.Q. and Sir W.P. Pulteney presented them with Medal ribbons of the Military Medal.	
	29		Rain prevented the practice of our attack on summer trenches by the Brigade.	

2449 Wt. W14957/Mg0 750,000 1/16 J.B.C. & A. Forms/C.2118/12.

WAR DIARY

or

INTELLIGENCE SUMMARY

(Erase heading not required.)

Instructions regarding War Diaries and Intelligence Summaries are contained in F. S. Regs., Part II. and the Staff Manual respectively. Title Pages will be prepared in manuscript.

Place	Date	Hour	Summary of Events and Information	Remarks and references to Appendices
BAIZIEUX	1916 August 30		A very wet morning. The Brigade (less 1 Battalion at Muckelty) carried out a practice assault on the trenches. The Battalion returned to "BAIZIEUX", all ranks wet through. There was no possibility of drying the clothes in the wood. In the evening billets for 6 platoons were allotted to the Battalion in "BAIZIEUX" village.	
	31		A fine morning. Range allotted to the Battalion for Musketry.	

J. J......
Lieut Colonel
Commanding Durham L.I.

2449   Wt. W14957/Mgo   750,000   1/16   J.B.C. & A.   Forms/C.2118/12.

6th. DURHAM LIGHT INFANTRY

151st. INFANTRY BRIGADE

S E P T E M B E R   1 9 1 6.

Army Form C. 2118.

WAR DIARY

or

INTELLIGENCE SUMMARY

(Erase heading not required.)

Instructions regarding War Diaries and Intelligence Summaries are contained in F. S. Regs., Part II. and the Staff Manual respectively. Title Pages will be prepared in manuscript.

Place	Date	Hour	Summary of Events and Information	Remarks and references to Appendices

VC 15

151/56

VOLUME 15

WAR DIARY

of the

DURHAM LIGHT INFANTRY

6 Bn The

SEPTEMBER. 1916

2449 Wt. W14957/M90 750,000 1/16 J.B.C. & A. Forms/C.2118/12.

Army Form C. 2118.

WAR DIARY
or
INTELLIGENCE SUMMARY
(Erase heading not required.)

Instructions regarding War Diaries and Intelligence Summaries are contained in F. S. Regs., Part II. and the Staff Manual respectively. Title Pages will be prepared in manuscript.

Place	Date 1916	Hour	Summary of Events and Information	Remarks and references to Appendices
BAIZIEUX	Sept. 1.		BAIXIEUX WOOD	
	2.		Battalion paraded for divine service. Capt. Hethery officiated	
	3.		Companies paraded for training.	
	4.		Battalion paraded for strong or possible to carry out a practice attack upon trenches	
	5.		Still in BAIZIEUX WOOD. All ranks very comfortable	
	6.		Company training. Lewis gunners, Bombers and Snipers training independently. Baths allotted to battalion.	
	7.		Quiet day.	

2449 Wt. W14957/Mg0 750,000 1/16 J.B.C. & A. Forms/C.2118/12.

WAR DIARY
or
INTELLIGENCE SUMMARY

(Erase heading not required.)

Instructions regarding War Diaries and Intelligence Summaries are contained in F. S. Regs., Part II. and the Staff Manual respectively. Title Pages will be prepared in manuscript.

Place	Date	Hour	Summary of Events and Information	Remarks and references to Appendices
BAIXIEUX	1916 Sept			
	9.	—	Battalion paraded to carry out another practice assault on Trujeter	
	10.		Battalion moved from BAIXIEUX Wood in to at 5 am. fine day.	
	11.		to BECOURT Wood. all ranks very busy making bivouacs.	
	12.		Battalion required for working party.	
	14.		On the night of the 14/15 the Battalion moved to SHELTER WOOD. the Only 20 Officers went in to action with the Battalion. Lieut & Adjutant H EBSWORTH returned from sick furlough from England cadre 650 other ranks	
	15.		the Battalion moved from SHELTER WOOD. to the South West corner of MAMETZ WOOD. Later in the Battalion moved further up to MAMETZ WOOD	

Army Form C. 2118.

WAR DIARY
or
INTELLIGENCE SUMMARY
(Erase heading not required.)

Instructions regarding War Diaries and Intelligence
Summaries are contained in F. S. Regs., Part II.
and the Staff Manual respectively. Title Pages
will be prepared in manuscript.

Place	Date	Hour	Summary of Events and Information	Remarks and references to Appendices
MAMETZ WOOD	1916 Sept 15.		About 4 pm word came that the Battalion would move at ____ fire at once. C O held a conference with all Company Commanders. Battalion attacked the German trenches STARFISH LINE — PRUE TRENCH. Relieved 6th Batts Northumberland Fusiliers. 2 Lieut Ethering H (O.C. Y(or) Co.) killed. Capt C W Badcock wounded, 2 Lts Harvey, D F Chilton, Tattersall wounded.	
	16.		A great account of Artillery activity on both sides. 2 Lieut Ramsay wounded. 2 Lieut R.J. Harris killed. The casualty left X Company with no officers, and the Senior N.C.O. took command.	
	17.		Capt T.D. Cook wounded. 4 Other ranks killed. No Other Ranks wounded about 4 fires up Fireclast by 5/6 Bn Durham L.J. Battalion received order to Brigade assault — 6th AVENUE, 6 AVENUE EAST, INTERMEDIATE TRENCH and JUTLAND AVENUE	

WAR DIARY
or
INTELLIGENCE SUMMARY
(*Erase heading not required.*)

Instructions regarding War Diaries and Intelligence Summaries are contained in F. S. Regs., Part II. and the Staff Manual respectively. Title Pages will be prepared in manuscript.

Place	Date	Hour	Summary of Events and Information	Remarks and references to Appendices
	1916 Sept. 18.		While in Brigade reserve battalion improved considerably dugouts.	
	19.		Parties out all day clearing up the battlefield, burying and collecting disjointed material. The Battalion in Mametz Wood.	
	20.		Moved from Brigade Support to North West corner of Mametz Wood.	
	21.		Draft of 50 Other Ranks arrived. Battalion now 350 men.	
	22.		Still in Mametz Wood.	
	23.		Fine weather. Working party of whole battalion on road just East of Bazentin Le Petit wood. Maj. on ... G.O.C. ... Brigade M.G. Company took over the appointment of 2nd in command.	
	24.		Moved to ... Avenue East over Intermediate line at 3pm. Whole Battalion on working party.	

WAR DIARY

or

INTELLIGENCE SUMMARY

(Erase heading not required.)

Instructions regarding War Diaries and Intelligence
Summaries are contained in F. S. Regs., Part II.
and the Staff Manual respectively. Title Pages
will be prepared in manuscript.

Place	Date	Hour	Summary of Events and Information	Remarks and references to Appendices
	1916 Sept 24.		at 4 a.m. to 12 noon.	
	25.		The French and 4th Army resumed the attack at 12-35 pm. Battalion in Dernancourt reserve. Billets bombarded by our artillery.	
	26.		Still in support. At 8 pm warned to be in readiness to support 5th Border Regt & 150 th Brigade. Lt. Col. J.W.S. ? proceeded to 150th Brigade H.Q. to reconnoitre.	
	27.		Moved into HOOK TRENCH at 3-15am. Trenches heavily shelled by enemy with high explosives.	
	28.		Moved to Starfish line. 2 Companies remained in Hook Trench. Enemy shelled heavily	
	29.		Enemy artillery very active.	

2449 Wt. W14957/M90 750,000 1/16 J.B.C. & A. Forms/C.2118/12

Army Form C. 2118.

WAR DIARY

or

INTELLIGENCE SUMMARY

(Erase heading not required.)

Instructions regarding War Diaries and Intelligence Summaries are contained in F. S. Regs., Part II. and the Staff Manual respectively. Title Pages will be prepared in manuscript.

Place	Date	Hour	Summary of Events and Information	Remarks and references to Appendices
	19/16 Sept 30.		Relieved 9 Durham L.I. in advanced trenches. Evening — shelled slightly.	

Helmold 9. 4. Ayr
Major
C. in C.g 6 Durham L.I.

30-9-16

2-49 Wt. W14957/M90 750,000 1/16 J.B.C. & A. Forms/C.2118/12.

War Diary

October. 1916

6th Durham Light Infy

Volume 19

151/50

WAR DIARY
or
INTELLIGENCE SUMMARY
(Erase heading not required.)

Instructions regarding War Diaries and Intelligence
Summaries are contained in F. S. Regs., Part II.
and the Staff Manual respectively. Title Pages
will be prepared in manuscript.

Place	Date	Hour	Summary of Events and Information	Remarks and references to Appendices
SOMME	1916		c/c Jam Summer time altered back to normal by putting clock back 1 hour. Kis 12 to 12 midnight. 2 Lieut Yaldwyn (Sniping Officer) attached to Y Company for duty. Commanding Officer saw all Company Commanders at 3am, to talk over details of the attack. Completed running of trenches about dawn and occupied Forming up battle order by 6am. 60 men (Draft and details) brought up from the Transport lines to act as Carrying Party for the Battalion. Artillery bombardment of German trenches from 7am to 3·15 p.m. 2 Lieut Yaldwyn wounded about noon. The Commanding Officer Major W'llrichson wounded about 1·30 p.m. Lt Colonel Bradford of the 9th Bn Durham L.I. took over command of the Battalion for the period of the operations.	724
		3·15pm	Assault delivered. 1st objective gained let on the left later on the right — also. 2nd Lieut 18 2·30, Cotching, Barnett & Appleby wounded.	

2449 Wt. W14957/M90 750,000 1/16 J.B.C. & A. Forms/C.2118/12.

Army Form C. 2118.

WAR DIARY
or
INTELLIGENCE SUMMARY
(Erase heading not required.)

Instructions regarding War Diaries and Intelligence Summaries are contained in F. S. Regs., Part II. and the Staff Manual respectively. Title Pages will be prepared in manuscript.

Place	Date	Hour	Summary of Events and Information	Remarks and references to Appendices
SOMME TRENCHES	1916 Oct 1.		Considerable amount of hostile Machine Gun fire from the right during the attack. German trenches not much damaged by Artillery fire. Block established on the right but as troops on the right had not obtained their objective. 1 Company of the 9 Durham L.I. sent up to re-inforce. About midnight 2nd objective was gained by combined assault.	
	2		German bombing attack on our 2nd line right repulsed in the early morning. Fairly quiet day but wet. During the night of the 2/3rd 6 Durham L.I. and 9 Durham L.I. relieved by 1 Northumberland Fusiliers.	
	3.		Relief complete about 4-30am. Lt. Colonel Bradford ceased to be in command and Lieut Ebnor assumed command of the battalion. Battalion moved to Starfish Line.	

2449 Wt. W14957/M90 759,000 1/16 J.B.C. & A. Forms/C.2118/12.

WAR DIARY

or

INTELLIGENCE SUMMARY

(Erase heading not required.)

Instructions regarding War Diaries and Intelligence Summaries are contained in F. S. Regs., Part II. and the Staff Manual respectively. Title Pages will be prepared in manuscript.

736-

Place	Date	Hour	Summary of Events and Information	Remarks and references to Appendices
SOMME TRENCHES	1916. Oct. 3		at 1 pm B attalion moved off by platoons, at 150 paces interval to "BECOURT" wood where it took up quarters it had previously occupied there.	
	4.		Wet morning - spent in packing up. Battalion moved at 11.45 am by platoons to HENENCOURT WOOD, arriving about 4 pm, having had dinners in route. Good camp. All battalion in tents.	
	5.		Quiet day spent in taking deficiencies, and cleaning rifles, equipment etc.	
	6.		More cleaning up. One hours physical drill and bayonet fighting. Specialists carried out training separately. Baths for all the battalion and issue of clothing afterwards.	

2449 Wt. W14957/M90 750,000 1/16 J.B.C. & A. Forms/C.2118/12.

WAR DIARY

or

INTELLIGENCE SUMMARY

(Erase heading not required.)

Instructions regarding War Diaries and Intelligence Summaries are contained in F. S. Regs., Part II. and the Staff Manual respectively. Title Pages will be prepared in manuscript.

Place	Date	Hour	Summary of Events and Information	Remarks and references to Appendices
HENENCOURT	1916 Oct 7		Physical drill, bayonet fighting, and short route march. O.C. Coys detailed 20 men per Coy for bombing instruction.	
	8		Church parade cancelled because of rain. Wet day. Specialists paraded separately + 120 men per Coy trained in throwing bombs. Medical Officer and Adjutant attended Divisional Gas School. also 2 N.C.Os per Company.	
	9		Physical training and bayonet fighting. Details trained separately	
	10.		Physical training and Bayonet fighting. Specialists trained separately.	
	11		Outposts by Coy. Night operation 7PM-9PM. Football match. 2 kut w Coy 7—2	
	12		Physical training & bayonet fighting. Artillery formation and last stage of attack. Specialists trained separately. Football match. 2 kut x Coy 3—1	

2449 Wt. W14937/Mg0 750,000 1/16 J.B.C. & A. Forms/C.2118/12.

Army Form C. 2118.

WAR DIARY

or

INTELLIGENCE SUMMARY

(Erase heading not required.)

Instructions regarding War Diaries and Intelligence Summaries are contained in F. S. Regs., Part II. and the Staff Manual respectively. Title Pages will be prepared in manuscript.

728

Place	Date	Hour	Summary of Events and Information	Remarks and references to Appendices
HENNENCOURT	13		Physical drill & bayonet fighting. Night outposts by day. Specialists trained separately. Whole battalion night digging. Lecture to all officers by C.O. Subject "Morale". 2/Lt H Sell reported he armed.	
	14.		Physical drill & bayonet fighting. Attack by Roving Party. Remainder of Battalion company drill. Specialists trained separately. Lecture to all officers by C.O. Subject - "Trench Attack". Holbrook match tie with 5th Bombs Regt again replayed. Match stopped - no score.	
	15		Church parade. Qt Mileson No 317A was promoted by the C.O. with the Military Medal. After parade fatigue parties of 100 and 45 detailed for woodcutting at an empire party respecting Ceremonial. night operations - night advance outcrament.	
	16.		Physical drill & bayonet fighting Ceremonial parade. Specialists trained separately, lecture to all NCOs by C.O. Subject "Morale" lecture to C.O. Adjutant and Company commanders by Major Holbrook at Brigade HQ Subject "Supplies".	
	17		No training. Whole Battalion on fatigue erecting huts and road making	
	18.		Physical drill & bayonet fighting. Bombing attack. Specialists trained separately. Working parties of 100 and 45 respectively - charge of 2/Lt Wheeler and 2/Lt Applegarth returned.	
	19		Wet. Very little training possible.	
	20		Battalion with the exception of specialists on fatigue erecting huts and road making. Specialists continued their training	

2449 Wt. W14957/M90 750,000 1/16 J.B.C. & A. Forms/C.2118/12.

Army Form C. 2118.

WAR DIARY
or
INTELLIGENCE SUMMARY

(Erase heading not required.)

Instructions regarding War Diaries and Intelligence Summaries are contained in F. S. Regs., Part II. and the Staff Manual respectively. Title Pages will be prepared in manuscript.

6th Durham Light Infy

October 1916

Place	Date	Hour	Summary of Events and Information	Remarks and references to Appendices
	21.	8.20 A.M.	Column drives out at 10 A.M. according to programme. Specialists training separately	
	22.		Bayonet fighting & Physical Drill. Attack scheme at 10 A.M by whole battalion.	
Beocourt	23.		Battalion moved to near Beocourt Wood marching off by platoons at 9.30 A.M. In the afternoon a tent camp was set up on ground that was "no man's land" on 1st July 1916.	
	24.		Battalion found working parties of 250 men on wiring & road making. Specialists were however kept wire training. In the afternoon Pte H.O. Thompson was accidentally killed by the explosion of a German bomb.	
	25.		Battalion moved to south-west corner of MAMETZ WOOD moving off by platoons at 9.30 A.M. entraining the 11th Bn Royal Scots. Tent camp very wet, dirty and muddy.	
MAMETZ WOOD	26.		2/Lt Tate sick and evacuated to hospital. C.O. and the four Company commanders and Signal officer reconnoitred the approach trenches on the right forward brigate. Battalion found working parties of support battalion on the right forward brigate. Battalion found working parties of 60 men under Lt G. Corbett for burying trucks.	
	27.		Battalion found working parties of 100 men under 2/Lt K.B. Stuart and 2/Lt Burton in the morning and another of 100 men under 2/Lt Lestgate in the morning and another of 30 men under an N.C.O.	

2449 Wt. W14957/M90 750,000 1/16 J.B.C. & A. Forms/C.2118/12.

WAR DIARY

or

INTELLIGENCE SUMMARY

(Erase heading not required.)

Instructions regarding War Diaries and Intelligence Summaries are contained in F.S. Regs., Part II. and the Staff Manual respectively. Title Pages will be prepared in manuscript.

Place	Date	Hour	Summary of Events and Information	Remarks and references to Appendices
MAMETZ WOOD	27		at 2-2/Lt Wharmer in the evening 2-/Lt Ritson at 2-Lt Costello confined to bed owing to the death of Pte H.B. Thompson	
	28		Battalion drew Box Respirators as Rastray Party. Officers and N.C.O.s reconnoitred the trenches. Working parties of 150 men returned	
	29		Commanding Officer and party of officers reconnoitred trenches. Draft of 20 N.C.O.s and men arrived, chiefly drawn from 5th D.L.I. and withdrawn mine signallers.	
	30		Working parties totalling 200 found by day and night. Very wet at night. Working parties returning in shells met with as mine ration. During the night 29/30th enemy dropped several very wet and very windy. Working parties totalling 370 found by Battalion. Men out on 30 nobles.	
	31.		Working parties totalling 370 found by Battalion. Men out on 30 nobles. Whole camp moved in the afternoon on to better ground.	
			near the camp — no damage done. Fine as very windy. Whole camp moved in the afternoon on to better ground.	

730—
EB

[signature]

Lieutenant

Commanding 6 Durh. L. I.

2449 Wt. W14957/M90 750,000 1/16 J.B.C. & A. Forms/C.2118/

WAR DIARY.

6" Bn. Durham L.I.

November. 1916.

Volume 20.

WAR DIARY

or

INTELLIGENCE SUMMARY

(Erase heading not required.)

Instructions regarding War Diaries and Intelligence Summaries are contained in F. S. Regs., Part II. and the Staff Manual respectively. Title Pages will be prepared in manuscript.

732-

Place	Date	Hour	Summary of Events and Information	Remarks and references to Appendices
MAMETZ WOOD.	1.11.16.		Wet morning but cleared up later. 320 men on working party.	
	2.11.16.		280 men on working party. Extra S.A.A. bombs, flares, etc issued.	
In THE TRENCHES	3.11.16.	1 P.M.	Battalion to moved into the line relieving 4th Yorkshire Regt 150th Brigade in Oatie Sector. W Company in front line, X and Y Companies in Star Line: "Z" Company and Lewis Party in Star Switch. Relief completed. Y Company but me killed and three wounded on way in; otherwise very successful relief:	
	4.11.16	10.5 PM	Except for few hits, men withdrawn from front line because of "strafe" with 9.2" guns on Boche front line.	
		3 P.M.	Conference between Commanding Officers at our Headquarters with Brigadier General commanding.	
		6 P.M.	Brigade took over our Headquarters as their advanced Headquarters. Hand to "W" Headquarters as our advanced Headquarters. Commanding Officer saw and explained details to Company commanders during the night.	
	5.11.16.	9.10 AM	Companies moved into battle position about dawn, being rather late in getting into position and it was daylight before "Z" Company arrived. Zero hour advance started well but to got held up by machine gun and rifle fire before getting very far.	
		10 A.M.	"D" Company sent up on right to reinforce X Company.	
		11.35 AM	Battalion placed under command of Col. Bradford of 9th Durham Light Infantry in order to ensure safety of his right flank.	

2449 (Wt. W14957) Mgo? 750,000 1/16 J.B.C. & A. Forms/C.2118/22.

WAR DIARY

or

INTELLIGENCE SUMMARY

(Erase heading not required.)

Instructions regarding War Diaries and Intelligence
Summaries are contained in F. S. Regs., Part II.
and the Staff Manual respectively. Title Pages
will be prepared in manuscript.

733-

Place	Date	Hour	Summary of Events and Information	Remarks and references to Appendices
IN THE TRENCHES	5.11.16	11.50 A.M.	2nd Lt G.W.Robson returned to bring up his working party and established a double block on the right of the Battalion in the GIRD LINE.	
		12.10 P.M.	2nd Lt McVickers went out with Private Parker and Private Dawson to reconnoitre.	
		12.30 P.M.	Commanding Officer (Major A.E.Ebsworth) went up to MAXWELL TRENCH and sent up men reinforcing the to reinforce companies in front.	
		4.20 P.M.	Sergeant Young reported at Headquarters with remainds of Raiding Party, 2nd Lt G.W.Robson having been killed. This party were given flare light to be taken to the QUARRY	
		8 P.M.	2nd Lt K.B. Stuart and 2nd Lt R.H.C. Wharam collected about 150 men from MAXWELL TRENCH and in endeavouring to get to THE BUTTE to reinforce 9th Durham Light Infantry, 2nd Lt K.B. Stuart was killed.	
		11 P.M.	German Counter-attack forced 9th Durham Light Infantry to retire from ground gained.	
	6.11.16.	1 A.M.	Orders to resume attack at 8 A.M. cancelled.	
		10 A.M.	Headquarters moved back to normal position. During the night 6/7th the Battalion was relieved by 5th Durham Light Infantry, and moved back to the old camp at MAMETZ WOOD. Casualties during the period in the front line :-	Casualties amongst Other Ranks — Approximately 150.

Officers

Killed
2nd Lt K.A Stuart.
2nd Lt G.W.Robson
2nd Lt A.S. Robson

Wounded
2nd Lt Tudgate
2nd Lt Tryerman
2nd Lt R.H. Stewart
Lt G. Corbett
2nd Lt F. Burton

Missing
2nd Lt H. Fell
2nd Lt A.H. Tudgate
2nd Lt A.S. Robson

Forms/C.2118/1/2

2449 Wt. W14957/M90 750,000 1/16 J.B.C. & A.

WAR DIARY
or
INTELLIGENCE SUMMARY
(Erase heading not required.)

Instructions regarding War Diaries and Intelligence Summaries are contained in F. S. Regs., Part II. and the Staff Manual respectively. Title Pages will be prepared in manuscript.

734E

Place	Date	Hour	Summary of Events and Information	Remarks and references to Appendices
MAMETZ WOOD	7.11.16.		Wet day. Lt. Col. H.M. Allen D.S.O. C.M.G 7th Bn Royal Scots (Black Watch) took over the command of the Battalion. Lt T.B. Heslop took over command of 'X' Company, and 2nd Lt McVickers took command of Y Company. Rifle inspection at 4 P.M.	
	8.11.16.		Somewhat finer day. Whole day spent in cleaning up and airing clothing, etc.	
	9.11.16.		Fine day. 180 men on working parties. 2nd Lt to R. Lewis joined Battalion.	
	10.11.16.		Fine day. 270 men on working parties. The following officers joined Battalion :- 2nd Lt T.J. Arnott, 2nd Lt L. Martin, 2nd Lt F.H. Ince. Draft of 9 men arrived. 2nd Lt H.J. McVickers went to hospital. Regimental canteen opened.	
	11.11.16.		Dull day. 250 men on working parties. Major-General Wilkinson visited the Camp and expressed himself as satisfied with the Camp.	
	12.11.16.		Dull day. Whole Battalion (160 men) employed as working party on the High West Road. Men remaining in camp (light duty men etc) employed in making paths and drains.	
	13.11.16.		Battalion furnished working parties of 200 men. Men remaining in camp employed on paths and drains.	
	14.11.16.		The following officers joined Battalion :- 2nd Lt J.H. Gaype, 2nd Lt J D. Barnes, 2nd Lt E.A. Ouchter, Capt R.S. Johnson, 2nd Lt R.B. Arnsworth, 2nd Lt C. Atkinson, 2nd Lt J Phillips. Anextenate B Hon Lt W.H. Hope went to hospital. Men in camp employed on drainage and betterment.	
	15.11.16.		Working parties of 157 men under 2nd Lt J D Barnes and 2nd Lt L. Martin furnished. At night Battalion furnished 100 men under two officers to assist stretcher bearers. 2nd Lt R.J. Phillips and one other rank wounded. During day Major Ellsworth conducted party of officers to front trenches.	
	16.11.16		No working parties furnished. Whole Battalion paraded for baths. Rifle, bayonet and ammunition inspection afterwards. Work on training camp continued. Specialists continued their training.	

WAR DIARY

or

INTELLIGENCE SUMMARY

(*Erase heading not required.*)

Instructions regarding War Diaries and Intelligence
Summaries are contained in F. S. Regs., Part II.
and the Staff Manual respectively. Title Pages
will be prepared in manuscript.

Remarks and references to Appendices
735

Place	Date	Hour	Summary of Events and Information
MAMETZ WOOD	17.11.16.		Took over working parties hitherto provided by 2nd Bn Welsh Regiment, 3rd Brigade, 1st Division on roads in MAMETZ WOOD. Major A Ebsworth went to convalescent hospital.
	18.11.16.		Snowfall but thaw and rain later. Whole battalion working on roads in MAMETZ WOOD.
	19.11.16.		Whole Battalion employed on fatigue. 2nd Lt J. Rushworth joined the Battalion.
	20.11.16.		Whole Battalion employed on fatigue.
	21.11.16		
	22.11.16		4 Military Medal to No 3408 Sgt H Cuddrea, No 3131 L/Cpl J Trindle, Pte J Thompson No 2969 and Pte T. Chapman No 3263 proceeded on ten days leave to England. Draft of 49 other ranks arrived. Notification of award and No 2298 Pte R Barker received. Draft of 27 other ranks arrived. No 2263 Q.M.S. J Rowland, No 2249 Sgt R J Walley, No 2321 C.S.M. J Standridge proceeded on ten days leave to ENGLAND. Draft of 27
	23.11.16		Whole Battalion employed on fatigue.
	24.11.16.		Whole Battalion employed on fatigue. Draft of 33 other ranks arrived. Reinforcements.
	25.11.16.		Whole Battalion on fatigue. The following officers joined the Battalion:- 2nd Lt J.A. Burrows, Craggs, 2nd Lt H.W. Shroud and 2nd Lt J.H. Lennox, 2nd Lt J.A. Burrows L. C. Reed. Still out.
	26.11.16		Whole Battalion employed on fatigue. 2nd Lt T.J. Arnott proceeded on ten days leave, also No 2120 Sgt H Wood No 3100 Pte J Hodgson. Very wet day No 3010 Corpl S.E. Bragge and No 3100 Pte J Hodgson.

WAR DIARY
or
INTELLIGENCE SUMMARY

(Erase heading not required.)

Instructions regarding War Diaries and Intelligence Summaries are contained in F. S. Regs., Part II. and the Staff Manual respectively. Title Pages will be prepared in manuscript.

736

Place	Date	Hour	Summary of Events and Information	Remarks and references to Appendices
MAMETZ WOOD.	27·11·16		Whole Battalion employed on fatigue. Dull day.	
	28·11·16.		Whole Battalion employed on fatigue. Dull, cold day	
	29·11·16.		Whole Battalion employed on fatigue.	
	30·11·16.		Whole Battalion employed on fatigue. After days' work Battalion moved to BECOURT arriving 6 P.M. being relieved by the 13th Royal Scots.	

W. Miller

Lt-Colonel

Comdg 6th Bn The Durham Light Infantry.

2449 Wt. W14957/M90 750,000 1/16 J.B.C. & A. Forms/C.2118/12.

WAR DIARY

VOLUME No 21

6 DURHAM LIGHT INFANTRY

DECEMBER 1916

WAR DIARY

or

INTELLIGENCE SUMMARY.

(Erase heading not required.)

Instructions regarding War Diaries and Intelligence Summaries are contained in F. S. Regs., Part II. and the Staff Manual respectively. Title pages will be prepared in manuscript.

Place	Date	Hour	Summary of Events and Information	Remarks and references to Appendices
BECOURT	1-12-16		The Battalion moved from huts where they had spent the night, passing the CHATEAU, BECOURT at 10 AM and marched to WARLOY via ALBERT — MILLENCOURT and HENENCOURT. Dinners were served on route. Part of the Battalion moved the way and marched round via BOUZINCOURT.	
WARLOY,	1.12.16	4 P.M.	Battalion arrived at WARLOY and went into billets which had already been allotted by the Billeting Officer (2nd Lt. F. Martin), Lt H. J. Bircham proceeded on leave.	
	2-12-16		Day spent in cleaning up, inspections, and taking deficiencies. Draft of N.C.O. and eleven other ranks arrived. Major A. Ebsworth rejoined from Rest Camp (EBARTS FARM).	
	3-12-16	10 A.M.	Battalion paraded for Divine Service. Remainder of day spent in cleaning up and taking deficiencies. Major A. Ebsworth proceeded on special leave for fourteen days.	
	4-12-16		Physical Training, Close order drill, Musketry, Bayonet Fighting and Bombing. ~~Physical Training? N.C.O.'s? Training~~ well.	
	5-12-16		Whole Battalion went to Brigade Baths during the day. Draft of 60 O.R. arrived. Battalion inspected by Corps Commander	
	6-12-16		Route March, Close Order Drill, and Bombing. Specialists trained separately	
	7-12-16		Route March, Close order & extended order drill, Bayonet Fighting, Musketry and Bombing, Specialists trained separately. Draft of 50 O.R. arrived. 2nd Lt. J. D. Barnes admitted to hospital from Fourth Army Signal School	
	8-12-16		Physical Training, Close Order & Extended Order, Bayonet Fighting, Musketry & Bombing. Specialists trained Separately. Draft of 5 N.C.O.'s and 18 O.R. arrived.	

WAR DIARY
or
INTELLIGENCE SUMMARY.

(Erase heading not required.)

Instructions regarding War Diaries and Intelligence Summaries are contained in F. S. Regs., Part II. and the Staff Manual respectively. Title pages will be prepared in manuscript.

Place	Date	Hour	Summary of Events and Information	Remarks and references to Appendices
WARLOY.	9-12-16		Physical Training - Close order & extended order drill. Musketry. Laying out & revetting of Trenches. Specialists trained separately. Lt J.A. Heslop promoted to be Acting Captain whilst Commanding a Company.	
	10-12-16.		Battalion paraded for Divine Service. Afterwards the Brigadier-General presented the Military Medal to the undermentioned N.C.O.s & men :- No. 4467 Sgt R. Smith. No. 3408 Sgt H. Caldwell. No. 1835 Pte T. Walters. No. 208 Pte R. Butler. No. 3131 Pte T. Foster. 2/Lt J.H. Payne went to hospital sick. ~~well.~~	
	11-12-16.		One Company on Range. Remainder; Physical Training Bayonet fighting: Close order drill and Musketry. 2/Lt R. Northanger evacuated sick to hospital.	
	12-12-16.		One Company on Range. Remainder; Physical Training, Bombing, Close order drill and Musketry.	
	13-12-16.		One Company on Range. One Company on route march; other two companies line bombing practice & Close order drill. 2/Lt E.A. Grubber evacuated sick to hospital.	
	14-12-16.		One company on Range. Remainder; Physical Training Bombing; Company drill and Musketry. Pte A. Radford No. 5698 committed suicide. 2/Lt & 9 D.Barnes returned to duty from hospital.	
	15-12-16.		Two companies on Route March, laying out and revetting of trenches and in the afternoon tactical exercise remaining two companies: Bombing, close & extended order drill : snipers on range. 2/Lt F.A. Brook and 2/Lt F.E. Robson joined Battalion and posted to Z Company. Draft of four other ranks arrived. 2/Lt H.A. Buck, 2/Lt G.W. Payne returned from hospital.	
	16-12-16.		One company on range: two companies used the baths remainder paraded for route march and practice in	

WAR DIARY
or
INTELLIGENCE SUMMARY.

(*Erase heading not required.*)

Instructions regarding War Diaries and Intelligence Summaries are contained in F. S. Regs., Part II. and the Staff Manual respectively. Title pages will be prepared in manuscript.

Place	Date	Hour	Summary of Events and Information	Remarks and references to Appendices
	17-12-16.		laying out and revetting trenches.	
	18-12-16.		Battalion paraded for Divine Service, with the exception of two companies who were the battn. 2nd & B D. Returned to Battalion after. One Company on Range. Remained. Physical Training, Bayonet fighting, Bombing & Company Drill.	
	19-12-16.		One Company on Range. Remainder Erecting wire entanglements, revetting & consolidating trenches & Company Drill.	
	20-12-16.		Physical Training. Battalion paraded for battalion drill & route march and in the afternoon for a battalion tactical exercise.	
	21-12-16.		One Company on the Range. Remainder; Bombing, erecting wire entanglements, revetting & consolidating trenches & Company Drill. In the afternoon two Companies carried out a Company exercise. Lt J.G. Jack R.A.M.S. evacuated sick to hospital.	
	22-12-16.		Physical training. Battalion paraded for battalion exercise - attack on trenches. Arrangements made for daily feet inspection as for men to be inspected by their Platoon Commander every time they go to the baths.	
	23-12-16.		One Company on Range: ten Companies bombing as one company carried out attack through a wood.	
	24-12-16.		Battalion paraded for Divine Service. Draft of 8 other ranks joined Battalion.	
	25-12-16.		Battalion paraded for Divine Service. In the afternoon Battalion Sports.	
	26-12-16.		Battalion paraded for Brigade Exercise. R.H.A. Garrison R.A.M.C. attached to Battalion vice Lt. J.G. Jack	

2353 Wt. W2544/1454 700,000 5/15 D. D. & L. A.D.S.S./Forms/C. 2118.

WAR DIARY
or
INTELLIGENCE SUMMARY.
(*Erase heading not required.*)

Instructions regarding War Diaries and Intelligence
Summaries are contained in F. S. Regs., Part II.
and the Staff Manual respectively. Title pages
will be prepared in manuscript.

Place	Date	Hour	Summary of Events and Information	Remarks and references to Appendices
	27-12-16		Battalion paraded for Brigade exercise — attack on trenches. 2/Lt [Hellyard appointed Signal Officer.	
	28-12-16		Battalion moved to billets in ALBERT marching via HENENCOURT & MILLENCOURT leaving WARLOY at 1.30 P.M. and arriving at ALBERT at about 4.30 P.M. relieving the 5th Warwickshire Regt. 2/Lt G A Roberts and 40 other ranks remained behind for the purpose of proceeding to training camp at BAIZIEUX.	
ALBERT.	29-12-16		Battalion provided working party of 200. for work on ALBERT—BAPAUME Road. Remainder paraded in marching order for inspection by Commanding Officer. 2/Lt F W Lennox evacuated sick to hospital.	
	30-12-16		Battalion provided working parties of 280 ; 200 for work on ALBERT—BAPAUME Road & 80 for laying pipes near BAZENTIN. Clothing & equipment inspected and deficiencies noted for wards to ensure that all new drafts to parade were in possession of a complete kit & equipment before proceeding into the forward area. Draft of 180 arrived to rejoin from BAIZIEUX training Camp.	
	31-12-16		Battalion provided working party of 80 men for laying pipes near BAZENTIN, party detailed on 30th remaining there. Battalion moved to huts at BAZENTIN marching via LA BOISSELLE & CONTALMAISON, leaving ALBERT at 12.30 P.M. and arriving at BAZENTIN. about 4 P.M. relieving the 8th Berkshire Regt.	
BAZENTIN.				

[signature]

Lt-Colonel
Commanding 6/B. The Durham Light Infantry

6th Durham Light Infantry.

War Diary
for
January, 1917.

Volume No. 22.

———— • ————

WAR DIARY
or
INTELLIGENCE SUMMARY

(Erase heading not required.)

Instructions regarding War Diaries and Intelligence Summaries are contained in F. S. Regs., Part II. and the Staff Manual respectively. Title Pages will be prepared in manuscript.

Place	Date	Hour	Summary of Events and Information	Remarks and references to Appendices
BAZENTIN.	1-1-17		Working party of 80 men provided by Battalion for laying water pipe. Drill day.	
	2-1-17.		Battalion, with the exception of specialists who continued their training employed in draining the camp. Working party of 80 provided for laying water pipe. 2nd Lt G. Markham appointed to command of "W" Company.	
	3-1-17.	3-15pm	Battalion, with the exception of specialists who continued this training, employed in draining camp in the morning. In the afternoon Battalion moved to HIGH WOOD WEST CAMP, relieving 4th East Yorkshire Regt.	
HIGH WOOD WEST.				
IN THE TRENCHES.	4-1-17.		The Battalion relieved the 5th Border Regt in the Support line; Relief being completed by about 7pm. Details remained at HIGH WOOD EAST Camp.	
	5-1-17.		Quiet day. Working party of 30 provided. Enemy's artillery active at night.	
	6-1-17		Enemy inactive in day. Commanding officer, O.C. "W" and "Y" Companies went up to new front line trenches. 2nd Lt R.H. Cleveland-Stevens appointed from hospital, and appointed at Battalion H.A. Quartermaster & Lt W.H. Hope rejoined from leave. Enemy artillery very active throughout the night.	
	7-1-17.		Quiet day. Adjutant and O.C. "X" and "Z" Companies went up to new front line trenches. Watkins ... parties totalling 270 O.R. provided. Fairly day but not good for observation. R.S.M. G. Perry rejoined from leave. Usual Enemy shelling at night.	
	8-1-17.		Battalion relieved by 9th Durham light infantry; relief being complete about 6-15pm and moved to huts at HIGH WOOD WEST Camp, incoming relief taking over from 5th Border Regt.	

2449 Wt. W14957/M90 750,000 1/16 J.B.C. & A. Forms/C.2118/12.

WAR DIARY

or

INTELLIGENCE SUMMARY

(Erase heading not required.)

Instructions regarding War Diaries and Intelligence
Summaries are contained in F. S. Regs., Part II.
and the Staff Manual respectively. Title Pages
will be prepared in manuscript.

Place	Date	Hour	Summary of Events and Information	Remarks and references to Appendices
HIGH WOOD WEST.	9-1-17.		Cold frosty day. Working Parties totalling 417 provided by Battalion during day and night. Enemy fired one round into camp stabling officers' latrine. Orders drawn up as to action in the event of the camp being shelled.	
	10-1-17.		Battalion paraded for baths. During day a practice "alarm" of enemy shelling took place	
	11-1-17.		Cold day with some rain and sleet. 30 yards rifle range commenced but stopped during its formation.	
	12-1-17.		Battalion moved into the front line trenches, Battalion H.Q. being at FACTORY CORNER, relieving the 5th Border Regt. Relief was complete by 7.55 p.m. Battalion moved above.	
IN THE TRENCHES	13-1-17.		Enemy artillery pretty active during day firing with 5·9n as Whizz-bags; as during night artillery as M.G. was very active. Searching Cross-roads near FACTORY CORNER and other approaches intermittently during morning. Our artillery carried out a "shoot" during a considerable amount of damage to enemy front line. Two casualties during day.	
	14-1-17.		Our artillery was fairly quiet. Several patrols went out reconnoitring at night. A German patrol was caught by our Lewis Guns as apparently wiped out. A wounded German officer was brought in but his men got away almost immediately. Enemy artillery was very active in the vicinity of FACTORY CORNER as the front line and back boards track being busy out of 2nd Lt. C. Reed took over command of 'Z' Company on Lt A.L. Brook's departure to "Detail" camp sick	
	15-1-17.		Throughout the Enemy shelled intermittently with guns of various calibres the vicinity of FACTORY CORNER. and french board track. "Natal" camp at HIGH WOOD was shelled, 1 O.R. killed and 8 O.R. wounded.	

WAR DIARY

or

INTELLIGENCE SUMMARY

(Erase heading not required.)

Instructions regarding War Diaries and Intelligence Summaries are contained in F. S. Regs., Part II. and the Staff Manual respectively. Title Pages will be prepared in manuscript.

Place	Date	Hour	Summary of Events and Information	Remarks and references to Appendices
IN THE TRENCHES	16-1-7.		Wiring of Battalion front completed. Enemy artillery shelled nearly of FACTORY CORNER, FISH WALK and area of left front company with H.E. and shrapnel. Battalion relieved by 9th D.L.I. and moved to huts at No. 1 site BAZENTIN-LE-PETIT.	
BAZENTIN.	17-1-7.		Battalion paraded for baths; the remainder of day being spent in cleaning up and taking defaulters.	
	18-1-7.		Battalion provided working parties totalling about 400 by day and by night.	
	19-1-7.		Battalion provided various working parties during day.	
	20-1-7.		Battalion relieved the 5th Border Regt in the Support line, "detail" moving to HIGH WOOD EAST. Camp. Capt A.S. Johnson evacuated sick to hospital.	
IN THE TRENCHES	21-1-7.		FLERS and the Tank behind our line were shelled during the day, also the Tramway. A working party laying duck boards was shelled by the Enemy in the morning and were recalled by order from the Brigade as they seemed to be drawing Enemy's fire. One man slightly wounded.	
	22-1-7.		Work of improving trenches and shelters continued, as parties employed in laying new duckboard track. Enemy artillery was quieter than usual.	
	23-1-7.		Work on trenches and new track continued. Various working parties provided for front line. Enemy's artillery very quiet.	

WAR DIARY

or

INTELLIGENCE SUMMARY

(Erase heading not required.)

Instructions regarding War Diaries and Intelligence Summaries are contained in F. S. Regs., Part II. and the Staff Manual respectively. Title Pages will be prepared in manuscript.

Place	Date	Hour	Summary of Events and Information	Remarks and references to Appendices
IN THE TRENCHES.	24-1-17.		Work on trenches continued. Enemy shelled the vicinity of FLERS LINE occasionally through the night as it was very active on this sector during the day. At 9A.M. enemy obtained a direct hit on one of our shelters which was blown in; five men being killed and four wounded.	
BAZENTIN	25-1-17.		Battalion was relieved by the 9th D.L.I. and moved to site 5 BAZENTIN. Capt. A.B. Ham and 2nd Lt. H. Stevens joined Battalion. Day spent in cleaning up. Cold frosty day.	
BECOURT	26-1-17.		Battalion marched to huts at BECOURT (site 5).	
	27-1-17.		Physical training and Running Drill, Inspection of Arms, Ammunition Equipment Clothing etc and deficiencies noted. 2nd Lt. H. Lennox evacuated sick to hospital.	
	28-1-17.		Battalion paraded for Divine Service. Physical Drill carried out from 6 the parade. 2nd Lt. J. Rushworth rejoined Battalion from Divisional Canteen.	
	29-1-17.		Battalion moved to billets in RIBEMONT arriving about 3.30 p.m. taking over from the 4th Australian Division.	
RIBEMONT.	30-1-17.		Physical Drills Bayonet Fighting, inspections.	
	31-1-17.		Physical Drill & Bayonet Fighting, Squad & Company Drill and Bombing Practice under the Supervision of the Bombing Officer (2nd Lt. C. Atkinson).	

CO 6 Bn. The Durham Light Infantry.

Lt. Colonel

2449 Wt. W14957/M90 750,000 1/16 J.B.C. & A. Forms/C.2118/12.

6th Bn. The Durham Light Infy.

WAR DIARY

FOR

FEBRUARY 1917.

VOLUME 23

WAR DIARY

or

INTELLIGENCE SUMMARY

(Erase heading not required.)

Instructions regarding War Diaries and Intelligence Summaries are contained in F. S. Regs., Part II. and the Staff Manual respectively. Title Pages will be prepared in manuscript.

Place	Date	Hour	Summary of Events and Information	Remarks and references to Appendices
RIBEMONT	1-2-17.		Training continued. Musketry practice, close & extended order drill, Specialists continued their training under their Specialist instructor. Platoons reorganised in four sections each under a N.C.O. as follows:- Section No 1 & 2 Rifles. Section No 3 Bombers & Section No 4 Lewis Gunners. Barbers shop established: staff consisting of the four company barbers. 2/Lt. F.C.D. Scott rejoined from Musketry Camp.	
	2-2-17.		Physical training, musketry practice, bayonet fighting, bomb throwing, close and extended order drill and practice patrols.	
	3-2-17.		Physical training. Bayonet fighting, practice bomb throwing, close & extended order drill & practice patrols. Specialists instructed in their specialist work separately. (5% D) Special Film drawn by the special publics game to return for Battalion pierrot for Divisional ... troupe.	
	4-2-17.		Physical training, musketry drill (progressive) to return for Battalion pierrot. Physical training & musketry drill (progressive) (Brigade public)	
	5-2-17.		Physical training. Bayonet fighting, practice bomb throwing, close drill & extended drill as practice patrols.	
	6-2-17.		Training under ... system. Brigade route March, via BAIZIEUX & FRANCVILLERS as so back to RIBEMONT.	
	7-2-17.		Physical training, musketry, bayonet fighting, practice bomb throwing, close & extended order drill as practice patrols.	
	8-2-17.		Training Circles to Trenches dug. Two Companies went for a short route march.	

Army Form.C. 2118.

WAR DIARY

or

INTELLIGENCE SUMMARY

(Erase heading not required.)

Instructions regarding War Diaries and Intelligence Summaries are contained in F.S. Regs., Part II. and the Staff Manual respectively. Title Pages will be prepared in manuscript.

Place	Date	Hour	Summary of Events and Information	Remarks and references to Appendices
RIBEMONT.	9-2-17.		Confusion exercised in practice attack; two companies working together at a time.	
	10-2-17.		Battalion paraded at 9 a.m. & marched to HAMEL via MERICOURT L'ABBÉ and SAILLY LAURETTE arriving about 12 noon. Battalion billeted in huts & billets.	
HAMEL.	11-2-17.		Battalion paraded for Divine Service.	
	12-2-17.		Battalion marched to PROYART leaving HAMEL at 10-40 a.m. arriving in PROYART at about 3. P.M.	
PROYART.	13-2-17.		Day spent in clearing billets & cleaning up. Two castle [?] were commenced to [?]	
	14-2-17.		Lt Col. J.W. Jeffrey D.S.O. assumed command of Battalion, proceeding to take command of his former major Battalion. Lt Col H.M. Allen C.M.G D.S.O. 1/7 Black Watch.	
PROYART	15-2-17		Battalion in Billets at Proyart.	
PROYART	16-2-17		do	
do	17-2-17		do	

2449 Wt. W14957/M90 750,000 1/16 J.B.C. & A. Forms/C.2118/12.

WAR DIARY
or
INTELLIGENCE SUMMARY

(Erase heading not required.)

Instructions regarding War Diaries and Intelligence Summaries are contained in F.S. Regs., Part II. and the Staff Manual respectively. Title Pages will be prepared in manuscript.

Place	Date	Hour	Summary of Events and Information	Remarks and references to Appendices
PROYART	18 2/4 to 19 2/4		Church Parade in Proyart Square	
			Battn left PROYART at 1.p.m and marched 4 miles to CAMP POMMIERS at FOUCAUCOURT. Arrived at 2.30 & had to wait on road till 3.p.m while the 10th Yorkshire Regt vacated huts. These are very good & men had electric light wire beds erected in them. Each hut contains a Company.	
FOUCAUCOURT	20 2/4		Thaw began on 18th & to-day it rained steadily. The Bn marched to ESTREES (2 miles) where the reserve platoon arrived at 6.p.m, & was met by guides of the 5th Yorkshire Regiment which Battalion we were to relieve in the trenches, as left Battn of the right Brigade of the Division. The C.T.s were knee deep in very heavy mud, the route & over the open were not known. By midnight no Company relief was complete.	
IN THE TRENCHES	21-2-17		Companies in the following order Z Coy on the right, Y Company in the centre, X Company on the left and W Company in support in LOUVET TRENCH. Completed the relief at 8.45 a.m. About 100 men had their boots in the mud and some their great coats and even their trousers.	
	22-2-17		A foggy morning, so that communication between H.Q. and Companies was possible over the open, without going into the trenches which we about impassable owing to heavy mud.	
	23-2-17		About 7 p.m hun artillery fire began on our own night; this gradually opened across our front and after very heavy fire for 40 minutes things again became quiet.	

2449 Wt. W14957/M90 750,000 1/16 J.B.C. & A. Forms/C.2118/12.

WAR DIARY
or
INTELLIGENCE SUMMARY
(Erase heading not required.)

Instructions regarding War Diaries and Intelligence Summaries are contained in F. S. Regs., Part II. and the Staff Manual respectively. Title Pages will be prepared in manuscript.

Place	Date	Hour	Summary of Events and Information	Remarks and references to Appendices
In the Trenches	23-2-17 (cont.)		The telephone wires to W, X and Y Companies were broken; that to Z Company held all right. 2/Lt F.C. Scott with one N.C.O. and 10 men made a complete reconnaissance of the German wire to the NORTH of CRAPAUD WOOD. He found it undamaged by our artillery fire.	
	24-2-17		Clear morning, so no movement possible on the TP. The C.T.s are still almost impossible owing to mud. 5th Border Regiment relieved us.	
	25-2-17		Relief complete at 1-30 a.m. A long and difficult march for tired men to POMMIERS CAMP, where are the rest billets for the Battalion. Two platoons of Z Company — the last to arrive — reached their huts about 4-30 a.m.	
			The Battalion was unfortunate in its casualties during its tour of the trenches losing 7 killed and 12 wounded.	
	26-2-17		Cleaning up. Companies paraded for baths beside transport lines. In the afternoon the band played beside the mens huts.	
	27-2-17		All made fitted with new small bore respirators. Battalion relieved 8th Bn The Border Light Infantry in BERNY Support trenches. Relief complete at 8-55 p.m.	

Army Form C. 2118.

WAR DIARY

or

INTELLIGENCE SUMMARY

(Erase heading not required.)

Instructions regarding War Diaries and Intelligence Summaries are contained in F. S. Regs., Part II. and the Staff Manual respectively. Title Pages will be prepared in manuscript.

Place	Date	Hour	Summary of Events and Information	Remarks and references to Appendices
IN THE TRENCHES	28·2·7.		Heavy artillery fire NORTH of SOMME at 1 a.m. At "stand to" there was also heavy artillery fire opposite the left Brigade of the Division. Relieved the 5th Border Regiment in the trenches in the front line which we had handed over to them four days ago. Relief complete at 10 p.m.	

J.L. Jeffreys
Lt. Colonel
Commanding 6th/B The Durham Light Infy.

2449   Wt. W14957/M90   750,000   1/16   J.B.C. & A.   Forms/C.2118/12.

WAR DIARY
or
INTELLIGENCE SUMMARY.

(Erase heading not required.)

Instructions regarding War Diaries and Intelligence
Summaries are contained in F. S. Regs., Part II.
and the Staff Manual respectively. Title pages
will be prepared in manuscript.

Place	Date	Hour	Summary of Events and Information	Remarks and references to Appendices

6ᵀᴴ Bɴ. Durham Light Inғaɴᴛʀʏ.

Marce, 1917.

Volume 24.

A5834   Wt. W4973 M687 750,000 8/16 D. D. & L. Ltd. Forms/C.2118/13.

Army Form C. 2118.

WAR DIARY
or
INTELLIGENCE SUMMARY.

(Erase heading not required.)

Instructions regarding War Diaries and Intelligence Summaries are contained in F.S. Regs., Part II. and the Staff Manual respectively. Title pages will be prepared in manuscript.

Place	Date	Hour	Summary of Events and Information	Remarks and references to Appendices
Trenches Front lines	1.3.17		Enemy's artillery much quieter, occasional shelling of Battalion Hd Qrs. Wire cutting continued by our artillery, several shells falling in our front trench and among our wire. Hostile aeroplanes active during the day. Lt. Col. J. W. Jeffreys D.S.O. evacuated to hospital. Major E. Branch, Durham Light Infantry, temporarily took over Command of the Battalion. The following officers joined the Battalion:- 2nd Lt. B.S. Harvey M.C., 2nd Lt. R.H. Stewart, 2nd Lt. A. Walton	
-"-	2.3.17		Enemy artillery quiet, only shelling at intervals. Wire cutting continued by our artillery. Continued work of deepening and cleaning of C.T.s.	
-"-	3.3.17		Wire cutting continued by our artillery. Enemy inactive. Major E. Branch proceeded to hospital. Major W.S. Lyttle M.C. East Lancs Regt. attd. 5th Border Regt. temporarily took over Command of the Battalion.	
-"-	4.3.17		Battalion relieved in front line by 5th Bn Border Regt. Battalion moved into Brigade Support at BERNY in relief of 5th Border Regt. 2nd Lt. W.H. Richardson joined.	
BERNY	5.3.17		Enemy artillery quiet. BERNY and vicinity shelled with 4.2s. Wire in	
-"-				

T2134. Wt. W708-776. 500000. 4/16. Sir J. C. & S.

WAR DIARY

or

INTELLIGENCE SUMMARY.

(*Erase heading not required.*)

Instructions regarding War Diaries and Intelligence Summaries are contained in F. S. Regs., Part II. and the Staff Manual respectively. Title pages will be prepared in manuscript.

Place	Date	Hour	Summary of Events and Information	Remarks and references to Appendices
BERNY.	6.3.17.		in front of Reserve Line strengthened. Major W.C. Hunt, M.C., 1st Bn. Durham L.I. temporarily took over Command of Battalion. Out:- 2 Lr. H. V. Taylor and 44 O.R. joined. Major W. Ho. Little, M.C., East Lancs Regt. proceeded to rejoin 5th Bn. Border Regt. Own artillery very active about 4.15 am, enemy in reply put up a heavy barrage. Throughout the day enemy artillery more active than usual. BERNY, the Sunken Road, and roads about BERNY frequently shelled. Enemy aeroplanes very active. Considerable amount of work done clearing and clearing of trenches.	
,,	7.3.17		Artillery quiet on both sides, except for customary shelling of BERNY and BERNY DUMP. There appeared to be only one enemy battery firing in this sector, of nine shells fired, five were "duds". Wire in front of Reserve Line made continuous. Work of clearing out trenches and re-claiming dug-outs continued.	
,,	8.3.17		Battalion relieved by 2nd Bn. South Staffordshire Regt. 59th Division, and	

WAR DIARY

or

INTELLIGENCE SUMMARY.

(Erase heading not required.)

Instructions regarding War Diaries and Intelligence Summaries are contained in F. S. Regs., Part II. and the Staff Manual respectively. Title pages will be prepared in manuscript.

Place	Date	Hour	Summary of Events and Information	Remarks and references to Appendices
FONCAUCOURT			Marched to FONCAUCOURT. Enemy quiet during relief. Lt. Col. J.W. Jeffreys, D.S.O. rejoined from hospital and took Battalion out of trenches.	
MORCOURT	9.3.17		Battalion marched to MORCOURT and accommodated in Camp 54.	
—"—	10.3.17		Day spent in cleaning of arms, clothing and equipment. Huts inspected by Commanding Officer.	
—"—	11.3.17		Battalion turned for Divine Service at 10.30 a.m. in Camp. Recreational Committee formed, consisting of Lt. W. Greener as President and one N.C.O. per Company as members, to supervise Recreational Training.	
—"—	12.3.17		Training commenced. Battalion paraded "as strong as possible" under Commanding Officer. Staff joined:- 2Lt. W.L. Newton and Y.O.R.	
—"—	13.3.17		Training Continued. Battalion paraded for Baths in MORCOURT in the afternoon.	

T./134. Wt. W708—776. 500000. 4/15. Sir J. C. & S.

WAR DIARY

or

INTELLIGENCE SUMMARY.

(*Erase heading not required.*)

Instructions regarding War Diaries and Intelligence
Summaries are contained in F. S. Regs., Part II.
and the Staff Manual respectively. Title pages
will be prepared in manuscript.

Place	Date	Hour	Summary of Events and Information	Remarks and references to Appendices
MORCOURT	14.3.17		Companies at disposal of Company Commander. Capt. J.B. Mealor evacuated sick. Capt. R.S. Johnson took over command of "A" Coy. Battalion Concert in the evening in Recreation Hut.	
—"—	15.3.17		Training continued in accordance with scheme drawn up by each Company Commander. Inter-platoon football competition commenced.	
—"—	16.3.17		Training continued in accordance with the several programmes of Company Commanders. Arrangements made for exercising Companies in the Rifle and Lewis Gun Ranges and Bombing Pit, and as far as possible every man in the Battalion to be exercised in musketry and the throwing of live hand grenades and rifle grenades and firing of Lewis Gun.	
—"—	17.3.17		Training continued according to programme. Trench board walks about Camp improved.	
—"—	18.3.17		Battalion paraded for Divine Service in the open at 10.20 a.m. 2Lt E.R. Appleton joined.	

T.1134. Wt. W708–776. 500000. 4/15. Sir J. C. & S.

WAR DIARY
or
INTELLIGENCE SUMMARY.

(*Erase heading not required.*)

Instructions regarding War Diaries and Intelligence Summaries are contained in F.S. Regs., Part II. and the Staff Manual respectively. Title pages will be prepared in manuscript.

Place	Date	Hour	Summary of Events and Information	Remarks and references to Appendices
MORCOURT	19.3.17		Training Continued.	
—"—	20.3.17		Platoon training continued. Arrangements made for platoons to practice wiring during their training.	
—"—	21.3.17		Training Continued	
—"—	22.3.17		Platoon training continued. All men who had not been inoculated during the last year paraded at medical hut for inoculation with T.A.B. Football match played with 8th Durham Light Infantry Bn. We lost by 2 goals to 1.	
—"—	23.3.17		Platoon training Continued. In addition to their usual work, Platoon Commanders instructed that they must exercise their platoons for 15 minutes each day in musketry, bomb throwing and bayonet fighting. 2nd Lt. H. V. Taylor to hospital.	
—"—	24.3.17		Battalion training Commenced. Lieut. R. Beberdy joined and posted to W Company.	
—"—	25.3.17		Battalion paraded for Divine Service at 11-15 a.m. In the afternoon the Brigade Boxing Tournament took place. Battalion entered	

WAR DIARY

or

INTELLIGENCE SUMMARY.

(Erase heading not required.)

Instructions regarding War Diaries and Intelligence Summaries are contained in F. S. Regs., Part. II. and the Staff Manual respectively. Title pages will be prepared in manuscript.

Place	Date	Hour	Summary of Events and Information	Remarks and references to Appendices
MORCOURT	26.3.17		three men all of whom won in the weight for which entered, viz: middleweight lightweight and featherweight.	
— ,, —	27.3.17		Battalion paraded at 7.55 am for a Divisional Field Day, but the exercise was abandoned owing to heavy rain. Battalion paraded for bath, each man receiving a clean change of clothing at the Baths. 06.15, SC & Y Coy marched their companies in deployment into Artillery formation. Col Jas Jeffreys DSO evacuated sick, also 2Lt Hts Irons. Major 16 D.b. Hunt M.C. assumed command of the Battalion.	
— ,, —	28.3.17		Z Company continued training in bombing, Lewis Gun and musketry. W Company continued training in bombing, Lewis Gun and musketry. Remainder of Battalion paraded 9.45 am for a Battalion exercise. Draft of 30 OR joined, they had a very good allowance.	
— ,, —	29.3.17		Platoons exercised by their Coy Commanders in attack. Night battalling by Platoons abandoned owing to very heavy rain. Capt J. Walton and 2Lt D.J. Charlton joined.	

T2134. Wt. W708—776. 500000. 4/15. Sir J. C. & S.

WAR DIARY

or

INTELLIGENCE SUMMARY.

(Erase heading not required.)

Instructions regarding War Diaries and Intelligence Summaries are contained in F. S. Regs., Part II. and the Staff Manual respectively. Title pages will be prepared in manuscript.

Place	Date	Hour	Summary of Events and Information	Remarks and references to Appendices
MORCOURT.	30.3.17		Inspection of feet, clothing, arms and equipment, and in marching order.	
			Transport proceeded by Road to ST. GRATIEN. leaving 9.15 am.	
—"—	31.3.17		Battalion paraded 7.30 am and marched to AMIENS – WARFUSEE Road where they got into busses and rode to TALMAS, where they detrucked and marched to WARGNIES, W., X & Y Coys continuing the march	
WARGNIES	—"—		to HAVERNAS where they billeted.	
HAVERNAS.	—"—		Transport marched from ST. GRATIEN to WARGNIES	

W.Hunt

Major

Commanding 6th Durham Light Infty

6TH BN. DURHAM LIGHT INFANTRY

Vol 22

151/50

WAR DIARY.

FOR

APRIL 1917.

VOLUME N° 25.

Army Form C. 2118.

WAR DIARY

or

INTELLIGENCE SUMMARY.

(Erase heading not required.)

Instructions regarding War Diaries and Intelligence Summaries are contained in F. S. Regs., Part II. and the Staff Manual respectively. Title pages will be prepared in manuscript.

Place	Date	Hour	Summary of Events and Information	Remarks and references to Appendices
WARGNIÉS and HAVERNAS	1-4-7		Battalion paraded for Divine Service in the open morning between the two village occupied by the Battalion.	
LONGUEVILLETTE	2-4-7.		Battalion marched to LONGUEVILLETTE via CANAPLES and FIENVILLERS arriving in billets about 12.45 p.m.	
VACQUERIE LE BOUCQ.	3-4-7		Battalion marched to VACQUERIE LE BOUCQ arriving about 1-10 p.m. as was billeted in the village. 2/Lt B.D.R. Durham joined Battalion from 7 D.L.I. to take up duties of adjutant.	
BLANGERVAL and BLANGERMONT	4-4-7.		Battalion marched to BLANGERVAL and BLANGERMONT as was billeted in these villages. There was some difficulty in securing billets as the villages were already partly full with troops.	
	4 & 5-4-17. 5-4-17.		Major A. Ellsworth rejoined from Commanding Officers' Course in ENGLAND and 2/Lt B. Kitchener also proceeded to Divisional Depot Battalion as Adjutant T.J. Arnott proceeded to Sig. Divisional Depot Battalion recently. Some to take up appointment as Quartermaster; 2/Lt B. Kitchener also proceeded to Divisional Depot Battalion as Assistant Instructor. Commanding Officer (Lt. Col. W.T. Cornwell-Hunt) destructed surveying whole memorising the formations.	
	6-4-7.		Funeral of Lt. Col. W.T. Cornwell-Hunt at St. Pol. All officers attended as a party representatives of the N.C.O.'s and the men of the Battalion. Command of Battalion devolved on Major A. Ellsworth.	
NEUVILLE-AU-CORNET.	7-4-7.		Battalion marched to NEUVILLE-AU-CORNET moving off at 10-15 a.m. where the Battalion was billeted in the village.	

T4134. Wt. W708—776. 500,000. 4/15. Sp.J. C.&S.

WAR DIARY

or

INTELLIGENCE SUMMARY.

(Erase heading not required.)

Instructions regarding War Diaries and Intelligence
Summaries are contained in F. S. Regs., Part II.
and the Staff Manual respectively. Title pages
will be prepared in manuscript.

Place	Date	Hour	Summary of Events and Information	Remarks and references to Appendices
VILLERS-SIRE-SIMON.	8-4-17.		Battalion marched to VILLERS-SIRE-SIMON via TERNAS, AVERDOINGT as PENIN as was billeted in the village.	
	9-4-7.		Companies were at disposal of Company Commanders for inspection of all equipment boots, box respirators etc.	
	10-4-7		Battalion marched to MONTENESCOURT cutting off at 2·50 p.m. Halt being carried on terms at 5·30 p.m. arrived being ... of the Battalion. Major H.F. Watson D.S.O. arrived to assume command. Battalion to Armored Depot Battalion to assume command.	
MONTENESCOURT	11-4-7.		Battalion marched to FAUBOURG de RONVILLE being 'MONTENESCOURT at 5 p.m. in fighting order with blankets; packs being brought together with any surplus kit. On arrival Battalion was billeted in the CAVES.	
RONVILLE.	12·4·17 13·4·17		The Batt" moved to NEPAL trench and remained during the 13th 4.17.	
GOJEUL WARNCOURT TOWER.	14.4.17		Batt. moved to COJEUL River bed to take up position in readiness for attack. The whole Batt". attacked at 5·20 a.m. WARNCOURT TOWER being the left flank. The 5th Division on our right flank attacked at the same time. The casualties suffered by the Batt" during the action were as under:—	

Army Form C. 2118.

WAR DIARY
or
INTELLIGENCE SUMMARY.

(Erase heading not required.)

Instructions regarding War Diaries and Intelligence Summaries are contained in F. S. Regs., Part II. and the Staff Manual respectively. Title pages will be prepared in manuscript.

Place	Date	Hour	Summary of Events and Information	Remarks and references to Appendices
WARNCOURT	14.4.17		Capt. A. L. Brook. 2nd Lieutenants W.L. Newton, H. Greener, Jw. Payne & W.H. Richardson. Killed in action. Capt. R.S. Johnson, 2nd Lieuts C. Reed, E.R Appleton, F.C.D Scott, D.F. Charlton, H.H. Nicholson. R. Ainsworth, G.R. Roberts - all wounded. Other ranks: 14 Killed. 92 Wounded. 66 Missing. The Batt. was relieved at 10 p.m when the 56th Div. took over that portion of the line. The Batt. returned to the O.G. line at O.G. line until relieved by 5th Yorks Rgt. at 7 p.m.	
RONVILLE	15.4.17		Battalion in Div. Reserve in Caves.	
RONVILLE	16.4.17		"	
	17.4.17		"	
	18.4.17		"	
	19.4.17		"	
	20.4.17		"	
	21.4.17		Returned to O.G. line supporting Brigade.	
	22.4.17		Supporting Brigade. O.G. Line. 2nd Lt. D.R. Lewis. Died of wounds, wounded same day in ARRAS.	
HARP LINE	23.4.17		moved to HARP LINE 4.45 a.m -	

2353 Wt. W2344/1454 700,000 5/15 D. D. & L. A.D.S.S./Forms/C.2118.

WAR DIARY

or

INTELLIGENCE SUMMARY.

(Erase heading not required.)

Instructions regarding War Diaries and Intelligence Summaries are contained in F. S. Regs., Part II. and the Staff Manual respectively. Title pages will be prepared in manuscript.

Place	Date	Hour	Summary of Events and Information	Remarks and references to Appendices
HARP LINE	24.4.17		Supporting Brigade HARP LINE until 2.a.m. - moved to NEPAL Trench.	
NEPAL	25.4.17		Supporting Brigade. Moved South of HARP Line at 7.30 pm.	
	26.4.17		Returned to O.G. Line at noon and relieved 7th N.F.	
ARRAS	27.4.17		10 a.m. Took over billets at ARRAS. 8 p.m. Batt. moved by train to rest area.	
RUMBERCOURT	28.4.17		Batt. arrived at HUMBERCOURT, 2 a.m.	
	29.4.17		Batt. in Rest.	
	30.4.17		Batt in Rest.	

Lt. Col.
Commdg 6th Batt: Durham Lt. Infty.

Vol 23

War Diary.

6th. Bn. The Durham Light Infantry.

May. 1917.

Volume 26.

WAR DIARY

VOL. 26.

6TH BATTALION

THE

DURHAM

LIGHT

INFANTRY.

MAY. 1917.

WAR DIARY
or
INTELLIGENCE SUMMARY.

(Erase heading not required.)

6 Durham L. 9.

Instructions regarding War Diaries and Intelligence
Summaries are contained in F. S. Regs., Part II.
and the Staff Manual respectively. Title pages
will be prepared in manuscript.

Place	Date	Hour	Summary of Events and Information	Remarks and references to Appendices
BERLES. AU. BOIS	1.5.17	3.15 p.m.	The Batt. moved to BERLES AU BOIS from HUMBERCOURT arriving at 7.30. p.m. Lieut. J.R. Roberton, joined as M.O. v. Capt. Hill J.G. Hill to hospital.	
RIVIÈRE - GROSSEVILLE	2.5.17		Battalion left BERLES - AU - BOIS at 5.25 p.m. and arrived in billets at RIVIÈRE - GROSSEVILLE 6.50 p.m.	
— do —	3.5.17		Batt. resting & re-organising under cay Bd arrangements. Capt. F. Walton & 2d A. S.R. Dobson to hos. sick.	
HUMBERCOURT	4.5.17	4.15 p.m.	Batt. moved off at short notice & marched to HUMBERCOURT arriving at 10.40 p.m.	
"	5.5.17		Batt. engaged in cleaning-up under Company Arrangements.	
"	6.5.17		Batt. resting and training Conference held by Commanding Officer.	
"	7.5.17		Training under Company arrangements and Route march. 2d Lt. T.J. BURTON joined Batt. from England	
"	8.5.17		— do —	
"	9.5.17		— do —	
"	10.5.17		Extensive field operations and field firing on LUCHEUX Range - from 11 a.m. to 9 p.m.	
"	11.5.17		General training continued.	
"	12.5.17		do	
"	13.5.17		(Sunday) Intelligent class exercised in LUCHEUX Range.	
"	14.5.17.		General field training.	

2353 Wt. W2514/1454 700,000 5/15 D. D. & L. A.D.S.S./Forms/C. 2118.

Army Form C. 2118.

WAR DIARY

or

INTELLIGENCE SUMMARY.

(Erase heading not required.)

Instructions regarding War Diaries and Intelligence
Summaries are contained in F. S. Regs., Part II.
and the Staff Manual respectively. Title pages
will be prepared in manuscript.

6th Duk. R.9,

Place	Date	Hour	Summary of Events and Information	Remarks and references to Appendices
HUMBERCOURT	15.5.17.		Field Firing Scheme under Div. arrangements at LUCHEUX. Appd. Commanders present 2nd Lt. J.T. RICHARDSON rejoined.	MAP. REF.
	16.5.17		General training in open war. fare under Coy arrangements.	LENS. 11.
	17.5.17		General training under Coy arrangements.	
	18.5.17	8.45am	The Battn. moved off to new area via COUTERELLE - GOMBREMETZ - HUMBERCAMP - POMMIER - BIENVILLERS	
MONCHY-AU-			arriving at MONCHY-AU-BOIS - 2.45 p.m. Ref. Map - 51.c. W.30.c. 6.9.	
BOIS.	19.5.17		Coy training.	
	20.5.17		(Sunday) Coy training after Church Parade. 2/Lts J.F. TINGLE and N.PETTER joined.	
	21.5.17		Brigade Operations in Old German line — morning & night.	
	22.5.17		Training under Company arrangements.	
LAHERLIERE	23.5.17	9 a.m.	Battn. moved to new area via BIENVILLERS — POMMIER arriving at 12.20. p.m. Map. ref. 51.c. V.10.c.	
SOUASTRE	24.5.17	4.15pm	Battn. moved to new area via HUMBERCAMP - ST. AMAND arriving at 5.50 p.m. Map. ref. Reer. 11.	
	25.5.17		Training under Coy arrangements. LT. C.N. WAWN, 2/Lieuts. R.E. WATSON, J.G. RANT & T.G. DRUE R.Y joined Battn.	
	26.5.17		Training under Coy arrangements	
	27.5.17		(Sunday). Divine Services & usual Sunday Routine.	
	28.5.17		Coy training : Infantrmin received that the MILITARY CROSS has been awarded Capt. R.S. Johnson & Capt. H. Smith .	
	29.5.17		Coy arrangements for theoretical instruction (specialists; training for 2/Lt. G.P. Runge & 2/Lt. I.O. Watson joined Bn. Commanding Officer inspected full parade of the Battalion.	

WAR DIARY

or

INTELLIGENCE SUMMARY.

(Erase heading not required.)

6 Durham L.I.

Instructions regarding War Diaries and Intelligence
Summaries are contained in F. S. Regs., Part II.
and the Staff Manual respectively. Title pages
will be prepared in manuscript.

Place	Date	Hour	Summary of Events and Information	Remarks and references to Appendices
SOUASTRE	30.5.17		Battalion training in attack. Information re'd that 250,417 Cpl BETTS had been awarded French Croix de Guerre.	
"	31.5.17		Coy training in the morning. Battalion Sports during the afternoon. Night operations under Company arrangements in O.G. trenches; coys returning about 5 a.m. following morning.	
SOUASTRE.				
1.6.17.				

J. Ribson, Lt Col.
Commanding, 6th Durh: Lt. Infty

WAR DIARY

or

INTELLIGENCE SUMMARY.

(Erase heading not required.)

Instructions regarding War Diaries and Intelligence Summaries are contained in F. S. Regs., Part II. and the Staff Manual respectively. Title pages will be prepared in manuscript.

Place	Date	Hour	Summary of Events and Information	Remarks and references to Appendices

WAR DIARY.

6th Bn. The Durham Light Infantry, T.F.

June 1917.

Volume 27.

2353   Wt. W.2544/t454 700,000 5/15 D. D. & L.   A.D.S.S./Forms/C. 2118.

WAR DIARY

6TH BATTALION
THE
DURHAM
LIGHT
INFANTRY.

VOLUME 29. 27.

JUNE 1 — 30. 1917.

Army Form C. 2118.

WAR DIARY
or
INTELLIGENCE SUMMARY.

(Erase heading not required.)

Instructions regarding War Diaries and Intelligence Summaries are contained in F. S. Regs., Part II. and the Staff Manual respectively. Title pages will be prepared in manuscript.

Volume 29.

Place	Date	Hour	Summary of Events and Information	Remarks and references to Appendices
SOUASTRE	1.6.17	5 a.m.	Battalion returned from night operations. Blankets with drawn.	
"	2.6.17	7.45 a.m.	Party of 8 officers & 12 other ranks, under Bde arrangements visited the BUTTE de WARLENCOURT & the parts of the Somme front on which the Division fought in 1916.	
"	3.6.17		Usual Sunday Routine.	
"	4.6.17		Musketry on SOUASTRE range. - All coys completed grouping, rapid & application at 200 yds.	
"	5.6.17		Bde operations. C.O. of 6 Durh: L.I. in command (6 & 8 D.L.I. representing Blue force. Ceremonial parade after operations. Extremely hot day & C.O. congratulated Batt on manner in which operations & ceremony were carried out.	
"	6.6.17		Training under Coy arrangements.	
"	7.6.17		W coy engaged in musketry - Remainder of coys - rapid wiring - Digging - bombing.	
"	8.6.17		Z coy engaged in musketry - Remainder training under coy arrangements. 2nd Lt. D/B Scott joined.	
"	9.6.17		Y coy - do - Remainder Route march.	
"	10.6.17 SUNDAY		Usual Sunday Routine.	
"	11.6.17		Musketry cancelled owing to bad weather. Coy inspections etc.	
"	12.6.17		Coy training. Parties at instruction in wiring under 7 Field Coy R.E. 2nd Lt. A.H. STEWART in charge of parties proceeding to BUTTE de WARLENCOURT to purpose of erecting memorial to fallen officers & men of the Batt?	

2353 Wt. W2544/1454 700,000 5/15 D.D.&L. A.D.S.S./Forms/C. 2118.

WAR DIARY

or

INTELLIGENCE SUMMARY.

(*Erase heading not required.*)

Instructions regarding War Diaries and Intelligence Summaries are contained in F. S. Regs. Part II. and the Staff Manual respectively. Title pages will be prepared in manuscript.

Place	Date	Hour	Summary of Events and Information	Remarks and references to Appendices
SOUASTRE	13.6.17		Explaining + instruction in wiring. The C.O., Captain A.B. Ware + Capt W.B. Bonsall, 2nd Lts B.J. Harrington + I.A. Miller visited new trench area to be taken over by Batt.	
	14.6.17		Coy training + equipment inspection. Draft of 58 joined Batt. (Canadian reinforcements.)	
	15.6.17	7.15am	Batt. moved to new area via BIENVILLERS-MONCHY-AU-BOIS-ADINFER, BOISLEAUX-MONT-BOIRY.	
			BECQUERELLE to HENIN (N.32.L.1.1.) During march Batt held to minor MADINFER. Arrived in Camp 8 p.m.	
LINE.	16/6/17	7.30pm	Batt moved into front line (O.26.a.6.8 to O.31.b.4.9) relieving 10th ESSEX REGT (53rd Inf Bde). Batton HQ were at N.30.b.6.2 + Coys held line as follows Right - Y Coy; Centre W Coy; Left - X Coy. Support (in MALLARD TRENCH) Z Coy.	Ref to Map 51.B.S.W. 1/20,000
	17/6/17	9.30 - 11.30am	Lens held by X + W Coys was heavily shelled by 10.5cm Battery	
		9.45pm	Patrol of 1 N.C.O & 13 men under 2/Lt RICHARDSON went out from coy at O.25.d.9.4 to obtain information about isolated trench about O.25.d.8.2. As soon as patrol left coy it was fired on + before it reached isolated trench a very light was fired from it + two of enemy ran along trench. The isolated trench was then examined + found to be in bad condition with few small dug outs. Patrol returned across shelled when approaching our line. Later enemy fired firesteinwerfer on to isolated trench.	
		10.20pm	Small patrol under 2/Lt D.B. SCOTT went out from coy at O.26.a.2.0 to examine a large shell hole shown on air photo 8.6.3286. Shell hole was found to be unoccupied.	

WAR DIARY

or

INTELLIGENCE SUMMARY.

(Erase heading not required.)

Instructions regarding War Diaries and Intelligence
Summaries are contained in F. S. Regs., Part II.
and the Staff Manual respectively. Title pages
will be prepared in manuscript.

Place	Date	Hour	Summary of Events and Information	Remarks and references to Appendices
	18/6/17	9 p.m.	Enemy began to shell MALLARD TRENCH & FOSTER AVENUE. About 9.30 the firing increased arms augmented by Flammal & M.G. fire. At the same time a party of about 30 of the enemy appeared all round the cup head at O.25.d.9.4 outside the wire. Volley of bombs were immediately thrown into the cup, apparently wounding the whole garrison, two of whom are missing. An immediate bombing counter attack up the cup failed as the enemy were too strong, meanwhile Stokes Mortar & Rifle grenades fired into cup head while Lewis guns & rifle were fired into No Mans Land on either side. Another counter attack was organised & led by 2/Lt AUBIN. M.C. & 2/Lt RICHARDSON, worked up the cup, with no opposition on either flank 25 yards away, no resisting cup head enemy was found & have reoccupied, leaving 1 dead (157th I.R.) in cup & two others from same Regt dead outside. Minor damage is claimed by Lewis gunners.	
		10.30 p.m.	Patrol of 2 N.C.Os & 4 men under 2/Lt DRURY went out from O.26.a.5.8 to examine shell hole at O.26.[b.1.7] [underlined] They saw an enemy covering party & head escorts (a working party) apparently consolidating shell holes in front of NARROW TRENCH (. They were fired at by M.G.s which also prevented an attempt to work round flank of enemy covering party, & returned.	
	19/6/17	12.30 a.m.	Patrol of 1 Sergt & 4 men under 2/Lt STEWART left cup at O.26.c.2.9 to examine shell hole at O.26.c.3.7. The forward members of the patrol had just reached the shell hole when they were challenged from left rear. They turned about & saw 4 of enemy in the rear. Shots were exchanged & bombs thrown from ?	

2353 Wt. W2544/1454 700,000 5/15 D. D. & L. A.D.S.S./Forms/C. 2118.

WAR DIARY
or
INTELLIGENCE SUMMARY.

(Erase heading not required.)

Instructions regarding War Diaries and Intelligence Summaries are contained in F. S. Regs., Part II. and the Staff Manual respectively. Title pages will be prepared in manuscript.

Place	Date	Hour	Summary of Events and Information	Remarks and references to Appendices
			patrol was mortally wounded. Remainder of patrol bringing in wounded man, returned at 1.30 am.	
		late	During the day Stokes Mortar fired on isolated cap at O25.d.82 which appeared to be occupied by enemy	
			Enemy fired light "Minnies" + "Fottale into our line intermittently during the day	
		10 pm.	Patrol left trench at O26.a.3.2. Towards S of working party was heard but nothing could be seen around. Patrol under 2/Lt P.B.SCOTT left BULLFINCH TRENCH at head large working party at about O26.c.47. This was immediately fired on by our Artillery both apparently good results.	
			Two patrols under N.C.O.s went out to reconnaissance isolated cap at O25.d.82 + finding it occupied SThen Mortars were turned on drove his channel.	
	20/6/17		Battn relieved by 8th D.L.I. at returned to camp as 2nd Reserve Battn to Brigade at N32.b.11	
			Casualties during tour of duty: Officers-nil. Other Ranks: Killed - One - 16654 Pte Hall W. Wounded - 15 -	
			Missing - two - 250591 Pte Garbutt H + 17265 Pte Dennett G.A.	
	21.6.17		Battalion resting in Camp as 2nd Bde Reserve.	
	22.6.17		-- do --	
	23.6.17		Battalion engaged in Coy Training + providing working parties for C.R.E.	
BOIRY - BECQUERELLE	24.6.17		Battalion - less Y coy - marched to Div. Res. area + was relieved by 7. N.F. taking over the billets camp in Div. Res. area. Y coy attached to Corps Artillery as working party.	

2353 Wt. W2544/1454 700,000 5/15 D. D. & L. A.D.S.S./Forms/C. 2118.

WAR DIARY

or

INTELLIGENCE SUMMARY

(Erase heading not required.)

Instructions regarding War Diaries and Intelligence Summaries are contained in F. S. Regs., Part II. and the Staff Manual respectively. Title Pages will be prepared in manuscript.

Place	Date	Hour	Summary of Events and Information	Remarks and references to Appendices
BOIRY-BECQUERELLE	25.6.17		Training under Coy arrangements. 2 Lts. T. PEAT and B.A. LEATHERBARROW joined Batt.	
	26.6.17		Coy Training.	
	27.6.17.		The Battalion (less Coy on detachment) was inspected by Maj. Gen. Sir P.S. Wilkinson, K.C.M.G., C.B. G.O.C. 50 Division. Lt. the Hon. W.L. VANE, etc. commenced in the Battalion	
	28.6.17		he was days visited the Battalion. Training under Coy arrangements.	
	29.6.17	3 am	Coy arrangements. Yeng returned from detachment. Commanding officer and Coy Commanders visited trenches which Battalion	
	30.6.17		spects to take over. Training under Coy arrangements. Training under Coy arrangements.	

June 30. 1917.

L. Robson

Lt. Col.

Cmdg 6th Durham L. I.

-: WAR DIARY :- 9625

6TH DURHAM LIGHT INFTY

JULY 1917

VOLUME No XXVIII

Army Form C. 2118.

Volume **30**

WAR DIARY
or
INTELLIGENCE SUMMARY
(Erase heading not required.)

Place	Date	Hour	Summary of Events and Information	Remarks and references to Appendices
Mt BOIRY BECQUERELLE	1.7.17	—	Normal Sunday Routine in Camp.	MAP REF. 51.0.5.W.
HENIN	2.7.17	10 am	Battn. moved to Brigade support - W and X coy camping at N.31.a.1.1.1. Y and Z coy camping at (N.31.f.1.1.) Stores and transport remains at East Camp ground. Lt WAWN and 2/Lt DRUERY evacuait sick.	
SUPPORT.	3.7.17	8 pm	Battn moved to support W coy in Egret EGRET TR O.19.c 8.9 - O.19.c 8.0. X coy in MARLIERE N.17.a.1.3. Y coy in DUCK TR N24.d.9.9 - N 24.d.9.5 and CURLEW TR N24.d.6.5 - N24.d.6.4. Z coy in LION TR and LION SWITCH O.19.a. H.Q. PUTTEE LANE N24.c.1.6. We relieved the (1st Bn 9th Rangers) 12 Bn the London Regt.	
	4.7.17		Enemy shelled areas to the left of EGRET TR including LION TR intermittently throughout the day.	
	5.7.17		Aerial Activity of the enemy was great over LION TR & LION SWITCH were swept by MG fire. Enemy's ... was ... trench enemy's line from LION SWITCH.	
	6.7.17	8.10am	H.E. was detonated on LION TR. Few were hurt but by no damage the night was not damaged. 2nd/Lt AUBIN J.F.G. evacuated sick. 2nd/Lt L.MARTIN rejoined from hospital.	
LINE	7.7.17		On the night 7/8th we relieved 9 R.I.L. in JACKDAW and APE TKS. O.20.a.9.5 to O.26.a.6.7. W left Z Brethe X right Y coy in support in BISON BOAR and BUCK TKS. O.20.a.C and O.19.6.	
	8.7.17		A patrol under 9/ Fanshaw Jaw and ... a scouting party near No 1 TR we encounter numbers 2/Lt ROBSON B.B.S. James the Barr Light flares aloft were terver over front line during the night. CAPT A.B HARE rejoined from leave.	
	9.7.17		A patrol under 2/Lt PEAT. T went out to examine the wire in front of Z Company and enemy patrol was sighted but disappeared before it could be engaged by ours.	

1875 Wt. W593/826 1,000,000 4/15 J.B.C. & A. A.D.S.S./Forms/C. 2118.

WAR DIARY

or

INTELLIGENCE SUMMARY

(Erase heading not required.)

Instructions regarding War Diaries and Intelligence Summaries are contained in F. S. Regs., Part II. and the Staff Manual respectively. Title Pages will be prepared in manuscript.

Place	Date	Hour	Summary of Events and Information	Remarks and references to Appendices
LINE	9:7:17		A patrol under 2/Lt Tingle. Went out from X Coy to examine BOSCHE SAP very little movement heard.	
		4-5pm	Our artillery put up a barrage in enemys front line and a smoke barrage in front of TRIANGLE WOOD many shells dropped near JACKDAW TR. during the barrage 5 men were seen to evacuate post at 021a 2.4	
	10:7:17		Patrol left our front but nothing was seen or heard of the enemy, these patrols were _____ for the purpose of covering parties to the companies at work in the trenches	
		8:30am	About 3 coys of the enemy moved towards St ROHART & FACTORY from BORY NOTTS DAME. 6ys were about 80 strong and moved in sections with connecting files	
NEUVILLE VITASSE.	11:7:17	11.10pm	We were relieved by the 9 B.L.I. and moved into camp occupied by the 9 B.L.I. at N 20 c	
			2/Lt G/c L.T.K. reported to the Batt: Canalteia during tour 3 O.Ra killed, 9 wounded	
			Batt in Brigade Reserve.	
			Lt C.N. Wann received from hospital. Capt H.Walton proceeded on leave	
	12:7:17		do do	M.C.
	13:7:17		do do	
	14:7:17		do	
	15:7:17		during the night 15 16 st took over from 9th D.L.I. in front line right section 0 20 a. 6.4 - 0 26 a. 5.8 Y Coy on the left & Coy right Z Centre W resident. During night small party of the enemy sighted coming towards X Coy front advanced by Lewis Gun fire one killed 2/Lt PEAT. took out patrol to examine wire on Z coy front 2/Lt LEATERBARROW B.R. wounded sick. Major F. Walton assumed command of 1 Bn nights Col F.W. Robson D.S.O.	

1875 Wt. W593/826 1,000,000 4/15 J.B.C. & A. A.D.S.S./Forms/C 18.

Army Form C. 2118

WAR DIARY
or
INTELLIGENCE SUMMARY

(Erase heading not required.)

Instructions regarding War Diaries and Intelligence Summaries are contained in F. S. Regs., Part II. and the Staff Manual respectively. Title Pages will be prepared in manuscript.

Place	Date	Hour	Summary of Events and Information	Remarks and references to Appendices
LINE	16/7/17		Y.C. bois front shelled intermittently throughout the day. Our artillery active between 3 & 4 am. our enemys front also 10 am & 1 am clemical shell bombardment. Patrol under 2/Lt MARTIN L to examine emplaced emplacements. No trace of work or wiring found.	
	17/7/17		Attacks by enemy vom 3 and throughout the day. N.C.O. Patrol examined 330 & of C6 & & Valley & towards enemy. No trace of enemy found. 2/Lt RICHARDSON J.I. took out patrol examined shell holes at 020 67.4 Nothing unusual found proceeded to 020 67.6 shell holes there found unoccupied. Enemys Trench & Scard towards S.E. at 11.30 p.m. 2/Lt G... T.H. took out a patrol about 40& enemy sighted wiring with covering parties on flanks. Lewis Guns turned on them enemy dispersed. 2/Lt TINGLE J.T. took out patrol to examine Boche road at 026 636 found & destroyed only a map of shell holes. Small working party & enemy seen & destroyed. Enemy sards went out Artillery on little more active than yesterday. There was no sights of enemy wiring working from our front during the night. No. 7 R. about 020 & 8.0 and at 026 & 8.7.	
	18/7/17			
	19/7/17		About 4 a.m. a heavy barrage started on the Brigade frontand on our right opening in intensity. Communication Trenches bombarded with shrapnel. Trench mortars bombarded our Trenches about 4.30 am Barrage ceased about 5.15 am. We were relieved in the sector & Capt by 4 Bn N.F. Relief starting at 10.30 p.m. 2/Lt AUBIN J.F.G. M.C. reported from hospital.	

1875 Wt. W593/826 1,000,000 4/15 J.B.C. & A. A.D.S.S./Forms/C. 2118.

WAR DIARY
or
INTELLIGENCE SUMMARY
(Erase heading not required.)

Instructions regarding War Diaries and Intelligence Summaries are contained in F.S. Regs., Part II. and the Staff Manual respectively. Title Pages will be prepared in manuscript.

Place	Date	Hour	Summary of Events and Information	Remarks, and references to Appendices
NEUVILLE VITASSE.	18.7.17		Moved to camp occupied by H.F. & M 24 64 3. Divisional Reserve.	
	20.7.17		Batn in Divisional Reserve.	
	21.7.17		do	
	22.7.17		Companies at the disposal of Coy Commanders, after church parade. 2/Lt LEATHERBARROW B.R. rejoined from Hospital. 2/Lt GRANT J evacuated sick ...	
	23.7.17		Companies at the disposal of Coy Commanders.	
	24.7.17		do 2/Lt W.F. DOWNE reported from England. 2/Lt J.T. RICHARDSON left Bn to join Flying Corps as Flying Corps probationer. Col. F.W. ROBSON D.S.O. resumed command of the Batn.	
	25.7.17		Companies at the disposal of Coy Commanders.	
	26.7.17		Companies at the disposal of Coy Commanders. Capt H. WALTON M.C. returned from leave.	
	27.7.17		Battalion relieved the 5th Bn Yorkshire Regt in Support; the disposition of Companies being as follows:- W Coy Right, EGRET LOOP, X Coy Centre EGRET TR., Y Coy Left EGRET LOOP, Z Coy in Support in THE NEST & ALBATROSS TR, Casualties during relief - one man wounded. Lt-Col. F.W. Robson D.S.O. proceeded on 1 month' leave and Major F. Walton assumed command of Battalion, Capt A.S. Shore 2nd in Command. 2nd Lt B.B.S. Robson evacuated sick to Hospital.	

Army Form C. 2118.

WAR DIARY
or
INTELLIGENCE SUMMARY.
(*Erase heading not required.*)

Instructions regarding War Diaries and Intelligence
Summaries are contained in F. S. Regs., Part II.
and the Staff Manual respectively. Title pages
will be prepared in manuscript.

Place	Date	Hour	Summary of Events and Information	Remarks and references to Appendices
SUPPORT FRONT	28.7.17		Batt.ⁿ in Support 2/Lt G.P.RUDGE reported back from Signalling course VII Army School.	
	29.7.17		Batt.ⁿ in Support	
	30.7.17		do.	
FRONT LINE.	31.7.17		R.L.D We relieved 9ᵗʰ Battalion in Front Line (SWIFT TRENCH and MARTIN TRENCH) from O.25 & O.5 to O.31 at 8.2. A Coy on the left, W we the centre & C Coy on the right, C Coy no reserve at Southern Road N36 & 6.5 H.Q. on AVENUE TRENCH N36dd.5.0	

J.W.Baxter Major
(Comdg 6ᵗʰ Bn The Durham Light Inf.)

T2134. Wt. W708 —776. 50f000. 4/15. Sir J. C. & S.

WAR DIARY.

6th Bn. Durham Light Infantry

August, 1917.

VOLUME XXIX

Army Form C. 2118.

WAR DIARY
or
INTELLIGENCE SUMMARY.
(Erase heading not required.)

Instructions regarding War Diaries and Intelligence
Summaries are contained in F. S. Regs., Part II.
and the Staff Manual respectively. Title pages
will be prepared in manuscript.

Place	Date	Hour	Summary of Events and Information	Remarks and references to Appendices
FRONT LINE	1.8.17		There were enemy patrols. Patrols went out from each Coy but no enemy activity was noted. 2/Lt W. F. DUNNE while conducting a covering party from	REF SHEET 51 b S.W.
	2.8.17		Hargan (?) Coy to the front line was wounded and evacuated to hospital. During the day there was little enemy activity. About 12 midnight gas shells were distributed. Built on our front. A retaliation by 2/B RIDGES G.P. was a	
			vertical Cone. (?) There was no mans land such a retaliation 2/Lt E. WATSON	
	3.8.17		.... enemy nothing very ... 2/Lt J.C. HESLOP joined the Batt:. Nothing unusual occurred during the day. A patrol under 2/Lt B.R. LEATHERBARROW .... was sent out .... cutting wires and engaged them, the ...... to our rifle fire, but the party were off before our patrol could again engage them. 2/Lt P.E. WATSON went out from HORSESHOE	
			POST (0.31.6.8.2) with a patrol to visit enemy listening post & if possible to capture occupier. After being out 1½ hours in .... Cun was ever turned on them, 2/Lt WATSON being wounded.	
BRIGADE RESERVE	4.8.17		At were relieved in the FRONT LINE by the 9th Sn D/s Durham Light Infantry during	
	5.8.17		the day and .... to Brigade Reserve Camp N 26 c 1 0 near HENIN SUR COJEUL. Major A. EBSWORTH rejoined the Batt: from So & Dy.t Depot Batt:. Batt: in Brigade Reserve. Usual Sunday Routine. 2/Lt AN BROWN joined the Batt:.	
	6.8.17		Batt: in Brigade Reserve. Boys at the disposal of Coy Commanders. 2 Coys moved to the front line, being Coys on base.(?) to South to the Batt: in the Line.	

T.1134. Wt. W708-776. 500,000. 4/15. Sir J. C. & S.

Instructions regarding War Diaries and Intelligence
Summaries are contained in F. S. Regs., Part II.
and the Staff Manual respectively. Title pages
will be prepared in manuscript.

Place	Date	Hour	Summary of Events and Information	Remarks and references to Appendices
BRIGADE RESERVE	7.8.17		Battn in Brigade Reserve. Instructions issued. Preparation for the line.	
FRONT LINE.	8.8.17		We relieved the 9th Battn The Durham Light Infantry in the frontline. Three companies in SWIFT TR, WOOD TR and DODD TR (0316 B.2 to U1 a 3.7) one X Coy on the left. Z Coy in support in SUNKEN W Coy in the centre and Y company on the right. Z Coy in support in SUNKEN ROAD N36 b central. Battn H.Q. in AVENUE TR N36 a 5.9. During the night two patrols left our lines but no movement of the enemy was noticeable.	
	9.8.17		During the day there was no activity. Three patrols left our lines but no enemy activity was observed.	
	10.8.17		About 5.45 a.m. a prisoner was captured by us in front of our lines at U16 7.9. He had been carrying rations and lost his way in NOMANSLAND. Three patrols left our lines during the night but nothing was seen of the enemy. Our patrol reported working wire found in FORWARD TR 032 c 2.9.	
	11.8.17		Throughout the day there was little enemy activity. To early morning 2/Lr B.R.LEATERBARROW carried enemy 031 69.9. It was found to be a series of shell holes connected up with no signs of fortification other than barbed wire. The party remained in and near the hole for 20 minutes but nothing of the enemy could be discovered.	

WAR DIARY

or

INTELLIGENCE SUMMARY.

(Erase heading not required.)

Instructions regarding War Diaries and Intelligence
Summaries are contained in F. S. Regs., Part II.
and the Staff Manual respectively. Title pages
will be prepared in manuscript.

Place	Date	Hour	Summary of Events and Information	Remarks and references to Appendices
FRONT LINE.	11.8.17		Three patrols left our lines during the night. One reported working on FORRARD TR... could be distinctly heard, as if revetting were being done. Another reported that the enemy occupied a post at U.6.5.? Otherwise nothing was seen or heard of the enemy.	
Div^n RESERVE	12.8.17.		During the morning there was little activity. We were relieved during the afternoon by the 4th Batt Northumberland Fusiliers and proceeded to Divisional Reserve Camp at M.24 61.9.	
	13.8.17		Coys at the disposal of Coy Commanders.	
	14.8.17		Training carried out in accordance with programme issued to Coy Commanders.	
	15.8.17		do	do
	16.8.17		do	do
	17.8.17		do	do
	18.8.17		do	do
	19.8.17		Bugler Sergt J. JACKSON in charge of massed buglers of the Corps at the VI. Corps Horse Show. Usual Sunday Routine.	
FRONTLINE	20.8.17		During the morning we relieved the 4th East Yorks Regt and two companies of the	

T2134. Wt. W708—776. 500000. 4/15. Sir J. C. & S.

WAR DIARY

or

INTELLIGENCE SUMMARY.

(Erase heading not required.)

Instructions regarding War Diaries and Intelligence
Summaries are contained in F. S. Regs., Part II.
and the Staff Manual respectively. Title pages
will be prepared in manuscript.

Place	Date	Hour	Summary of Events and Information	Remarks and references to Appendices
FRONT LINE	20:8:'17		H.M. YORKSHIRE REGT in support in the right sub sector, left sector. X Coy in LION TR and PANTHER TR. O19.a.1. X Coy in EGRET TR. O19.c. 8.9 - O19.c. 3.0. Y Coy in CURLEW TR. N24.a. 6.3 - N2Hd. 6.9. and W. Coy in Caves in MARLIERE VILLAGE. N17a. 1.3. Batt'o H.Q. at N24.a 1.6. 2/L. F.N. TEE reported to the Batt'o for duty from England.	
	21:8:'17		Batt'o in support. General attitude of the enemy quiet.	
	22:8:'17		do Nothing unusual occurred during the day	
	23:8:'17		do 2/L J.D. BARNES left Batt'o attached R.F.C. on probation. Lieut. C. N. WAWN dismissed His Majesty's service for conduct of G.C.16.	
	24:8:'17		During the afternoon we relieved the 9th Batt'o The DURHAM LIGHT INFANTRY in the front line of the right sub sector, left sector. Three companies in the front line. O20.a. 6.4. 4026a. 32. One company in close support in BISON RESERVE O20.C and BUCK RESERVE O19.D. 2/L. G.H. KING reported to the Batt'o for duty. 2/L. PEAT. T. evacuated sick to hospital. Three officer patrols left our lines during the night. 2/L. T. BURTON while on patrol being wounded at duty. Apart from a M.G. firing from O2663.5 and rounds of working parties in N'o TR at O20 d.9.3 nothing was seen of the enemy.	
	25:8:'17		General attitude of the enemy quiet. Our Lewis Guns fired at dispersed parties moving behind	

WAR DIARY

or

INTELLIGENCE SUMMARY.

(Erase heading not required.)

Instructions regarding War Diaries and Intelligence
Summaries are contained in F. S. Regs., Part II.
and the Staff Manual respectively. Title pages
will be prepared in manuscript.

Place	Date	Hour	Summary of Events and Information	Remarks and references to Appendices
FRONT LINE	25:8:17		enemy's lines. Three officer patrols left our lines during the night. One patrol reported eastern end of SPOOR LANE occupied by the enemy as listening post. There was no other enemy activity apart from occasional M.G. bursts.	
	26:8:17		from 0210 O.O. and working towards NIGHT Tr. Nothing unusual occurred during the day enemy very quiet. Three officer patrols left our lines. One patrol report very light fired from the end of SPOOR LANE and were heard there. A party of eight or ten of the enemy were sighted by another patrol leaving enemy's lines at about 026685 and patrolling parallel to their own lines.	
	27:8:17		Our Lewis Guns fired at intervals during the day into enemy's lines, enemy's activities still quiet. During the night two officer patrols left our lines, no signs of enemy were seen on terra with the exception of occasional bursts of No.5 ??. Our stokes mortars and Lewis Guns and rifle grenadiers fired intermittently during the night into SPOOR LANE reported occupied by the enemy.	
	28:8:17		During the afternoon we were relieved by the 9th Batt. The DURHAM LIGHT INFANTRY and moved to Brigade Reserve Camp at N25 b. 8/Lts E. ARMBRISTER, A.S. GREEN, C.W. REES, D.R. THOMSON R.T.H. ELLIFF, and C.G.R. LEWIS were attached for duty from the 8th DURHAM LIGHT INFANTRY.	
BRIGADE RESERVE	29:8:17		Battn. in Brigade Reserve. Cleaning up equipment & clothing.	

Army Form C. 2118.

WAR DIARY
or
INTELLIGENCE SUMMARY.

(Erase heading not required.)

Place	Date	Hour	Summary of Events and Information	Remarks and references to Appendices
Brigade Reserve	30th.		Battalion supplying working parties + remainder under coy arrangements.	
	31/8/17		do —	
			Lt Col Rigg DSO. returned from leave,	
			J. Sassoon	
			Major,	
			Commanding 6 Dub.; R.9.	

16th BATTALION
... ...
LIGHT INFANTRY.
31 - 8 - 17.
No. .... Date ....

T.2134. Wt. W708—776. 500000. 4/15. Sir J. C. & 8.

WAR DIARY

6. Bn. The Durham Light Infantry

September, 1917.

Volume — XXX

WAR DIARY
or
INTELLIGENCE SUMMARY

(Erase heading not required.)

Place	Date	Hour	Summary of Events and Information	Remarks and references to Appendices
FRONT LINE	1.9.17	-	During the afternoon the Battn. relieved the Q.V.R. in the Left Sector, Right Sub-sector. X, Y, Z Coys were in Front Line & W Coy in close support. Communication trenches were widened & deepened leading to 1,3 & 5 posts. Two patrols went out during the night. One from Jackdaw Trench reported that work was being carried on 200 yds S.E. of OTTO SAP. The second, after patrolling the length of the central Coy front reported that nothing was seen or heard of the enemy. There were very few casualties during the day.	
	2.9.17		General Improvement of trenches carried out during the period. A Stokes Mortar was taken up to a forward position & covered by two parties of ten men with an officer in charge. The mortar was fired on ROHART FACTORY. No signs of the enemy were seen. A patrol returned from opposite NIGHT TRENCH & reported that nothing had been seen or heard of the enemy.	
	3.7.17		Revetting carried on in BUCK RESERVE, BISON RES. BUFFALO & JACKDAW Trenches & No 10 Post. Patrols again reported that practically no movement was observed in enemy lines.	
	4.9.17		Trench improvement was carried on. Rifle grenades were fired from BIG SAP at night & sniping was carried out during the day.	
	5.9.17		The Battalion was relieved by the H.N.F., the relief being completed by 8.30 p.m. One N.C.O. was wounded during the relief. The Battn. moved to NORTHUMBERLAND LINES. (m.23.0.1.6.)	
	6.9.17 to 12.9.17		Battn. in Div Res. at NORTHUMBERLAND LINES. The majority of the Batt, was employed working parties, two whole coys in Hindenburg Line for two days under Major Wallin. They remaining men in Camp carried on training etc.	

WAR DIARY

or

INTELLIGENCE SUMMARY.

(Erase heading not required.)

Instructions regarding War Diaries and Intelligence
Summaries are contained in F.S. Regs., Part II.
and the Staff Manual respectively. Title pages
will be prepared in manuscript.

Place	Date	Hour	Summary of Events and Information	Remarks and references to Appendices
CHERISY SECTOR	13/9/17		Batt: relieved 5th Bn. the Duch: L.I. in the Right Section Right Sub-section. Relief complete by 5 a.m.	
	14/9/17		On the night 13/14th two patrols went out, one under 2nd Lieut. [?] and the other under 2nd Lieut. [?]. Both with[?] no result. Our wire was inspected along the whole Bn. Front. Nothing was seen or heard of enemy. Our Artillery continued cutting enemy wire on our right. About 4 a.m. our Light & Medium T.M's continued. They were cutting with good effect. Enemy T.M's retaliated obtaining a direct hit on our [?] [?] Front line trench. We had no casualties.	
	15/9/17		At 4 a.m. 3 coys of 9th Duch.L.I. on our left, raided enemy Front & support trenches supported by barrage of Artillery. M.G's & T.M's. Raid successful & 23 prisoners taken. Our front line trenches were cleared except for a few wounded.	

Army Form C. 2118.

WAR DIARY

or

INTELLIGENCE SUMMARY.

(Erase heading not required.)

Instructions regarding War Diaries and Intelligence Summaries are contained in F. S. Regs., Part II. and the Staff Manual respectively. Title pages will be prepared in manuscript.

Place	Date	Hour	Summary of Events and Information	Remarks and references to Appendices
CHERISY SECTOR.	15/9/17.		continued :—	
			2nd Lt Lotherhouse + 10 of our men worked "dummies"	
			which had been placed in position in No Man's Land the night	
			before. These drew a good deal of fire from enemy's artillery, M. guns	
			+ etc. Enemy barrage came down on our close support lines & C.T's.	
			Casualties :— 1 killed, + wounded + 4 men suffering from shell-	
			shock. One machine-gun + 17 M. captured by us.	
			At 4.40 pm a Coy of 8th D.L.I. again raided portion of same Enemy	
			trenches accompanied by barrages, dummies, etc.	
			Raid unsuccessful but very few of enemy found in trenches.	
			One wounded prisoner taken. Two machine guns captured.	
	16/9/17.		At 4 am locality of raids was subjected to projection of gas	
			accompanied by artillery & M.G. fire.	
			On the night 17/18th this patrol went out under 2nd Lt — Cook,	
			Lewis	
	17/9/17.		2nd Lt Lewis' patrol saw enemy wiring party out + got a	
			Lewis Gun on to them.	

T.2134. Wt. W708—776. 500000. 4/15. Sir J. C. & 8.

WAR DIARY
or
INTELLIGENCE SUMMARY.
(Erase heading not required.)

Place	Date	Hour	Summary of Events and Information	Remarks and references to Appendices
CHERISY	17/9/14		In the afternoon the 9th Bn. D.L.I. relieved us & we came	
SECTOR			back to Brigade Reserve, Hdr HENIN. X Coy moved to CONCRETE TR. Reserve to front line Battn.	
NEAR HENIN	18/9/17		3 Companies in Brigade Reserve at	Company cleaning equipment bathing changing clothing.
	19/9/17		3 Coys in Brigade Reserve at disposal of company commanders. X Coy relieved by S. Coy	
	20/9/17		3 Coys in Brigade Reserve. Training carried on until 11 am Church Parade 12 midday.	
FRONTLINE	21/9/17.		We relieved the 8th Bn. the Durham L.I. in support sector. Relieve came 9.11 am. and the 9th Bn. the Durham L.I. in right front Battn. 3.2 m. and 7 p.m. in the right sector H.A. in AVENUE TR. N 36 b 5 0. Z Coy in Lindui Road. N 36 b 4 6. X W & Y Coy in the	
			Frontline from 03168 3 to U1 a 4 9.	
			During the night 11 bombs left our line and reported the following trench at U1.66."; will enlist	
			Gap at U1 b 7½. 0 received. rocks were apparently being concealed. Hostile patrol were seen but	
			cleared off before action could be taken. Routing was reported in the enemy lines	
			Nothing unusual happened during the day. Our Lewis gunners strained shots. Two patrols left our	
	22/9/17		lines, nothing was seen of the enemy but sounds of working were easily distinguishable	
			no though working was being carried on.	
	22/9/17.		During the day there was no unusual activity. Two officer patrols left our lines the	

Army Form C. 2118.

WAR DIARY

or

INTELLIGENCE SUMMARY.

(Erase heading not required.)

Instructions regarding War Diaries and Intelligence
Summaries are contained in F. S. Regs., Part II.
and the Staff Manual respectively. Title pages
will be prepared in manuscript.

Place	Date	Hour	Summary of Events and Information	Remarks and references to Appendices
FRONTLINE	23/9/17		Patrol went along the enemys wire for 200 yards no gaps were found in it. Another patrol was fired on by machine guns but advanced quite close to the enemys wire which was very thickly wired. No front. No signs of enemy patrols were encountered.	
	24/9/17		Enemy Artillery a little more active than usual. Our officer went out to enemy's unregistered new trench at O32 a.0.4½ created. It crossed on a sunken tramway for 80 yards measured by telegraph wire paced out from our trenches. They got to within 35 yards of unfilled trench and found a large party digging there with covering party out. Two officers another other ranks went out to attempt to get into the enemys line but could not owing to wire which was confronted of two rows of concertina with 12 or 15 feet of wire about 18 inches high. At daybreak went to O1.63.5 found no trace of enemy foxhole or anything unusual.	
	25/9/17		During the morning we relieved the 9th Durham L.I. as support. Battn. night front sector. Y Coy in CUCKOO RESERVE. X Coy in EGRET LOOP W Coy in the NEST and ALBATROSS TR. Y Coy in CUCKOO RESERVE. X Coy in the NEST N30 a 5.4. H.Q. in the NEST N30 a 5.4.	

T.2134. Wt. W708—776. 500,000. 4/15. Sir J. C. & S.

WAR DIARY

or

INTELLIGENCE SUMMARY.

(Erase heading not required.)

Instructions regarding War Diaries and Intelligence
Summaries are contained in F. S. Regs., Part II.
and the Staff Manual respectively. Title pages
will be prepared in manuscript.

Place	Date	Hour	Summary of Events and Information	Remarks and references to Appendices
CHERISY	26/3/17	}	Work continued.	
SECTOR	27/3/17	}		
	28/3/17	}		
	29/3/17		4th Batt⁰ was relieved by 5 N.F. relief taking place between 1 pm & 3 pm. Battⁿ moved to Div Reserve at NORTHUMBERLAND LINES.	
	30/3/17		Working Party of 3 Officers and 180 men supplied to work on Horse Standings. Remainder of men cleaning up etc. Church Parade of men in Camp at 11.30 am.	

J. W. Robson Lt Col

Comdg 6 Durham L. I.

10/11

WAR DIARY.

6th Durham Light Infantry.

October 1914.

Volume XXI.

WAR DIARY

or

INTELLIGENCE SUMMARY.

6 D.L.I.

21

(*Erase heading not required.*)

Instructions regarding War Diaries and Intelligence Summaries are contained in F. S. Regs., Part II. and the Staff Manual respectively. Title pages will be prepared in manuscript.

Place	Date	Hour	Summary of Events and Information	Remarks and references to Appendices
BEAURAINS	1.10.17		Greater part of Bn at FICHEUX on working party. Remainder inspected by C.O. Capt A.B. HARE to 5th Div. Depot Batt.	
	2.10.17		Major F. WALTON to Senior Officers' Course, Aldershot. Inspection by C.O.	
	2.10.17		Working party rejoined from FICHEUX. Inspection of Batt. completed.	
GOMIECOURT	4.10.17		Batt. moved to GOMIECOURT. (Map sheet 5th Gordon Hdrs. A 28 d. Hut's [c]) (57c.) Leela Camp, relieving Batt.	
	5.10.17		Training - principally attack on strong points. 2nd Lt P.H.B. LYON joined Batt.	
	6.10.17.		2nd Lt K.W. TAYLOR to hospital. - Training in close order drill & Coy football matches.	
	7.10.17		Training under Coy arrangements.	
	8.10.17		Bn Ranks of Byde Ammunition Parade, followed by attack of Byde scheme Bn training at [ ] Wood under Bde arrangements.	
	9.10.17.		Brigade engaged in Operations viz Divisional attack on air objective Gommecourt Trench & Maul Post. Corps Commander (Lt. Gen. HALDANE) & Sqt. P. FINN, L/c NESBITT & Pte ALLISON. 2d. RUSHWORTH - to England for 6 months. (A.C. 2/209 (O.1) presented Military Medals to	
			Capt. SALMON. H. - to rejoin 10 D.L.I. (A.G. 4/481 (O.I).	
	10.10.17		Draft of 70 joined from 7 D.L.I. Training in accordance with Bde Orders - principally attack on strong points, etc. 2nd Lt DR THOMPSON - to hospital.	
	11.10.17		" " Annual training scheme under Coy arrangements. - do -	
	12.10.17		- do -	
	13.10.17		Ordinary training Routine. Batt. football team v. 5 Yks - 6 D.L.I - One - 5 Yks - nil. (Divisional Football Competition)	

WAR DIARY
or
INTELLIGENCE SUMMARY.

(Erase heading not required.)

Volume 31.

Instructions regarding War Diaries and Intelligence
Summaries are contained in F. S. Regs., Part II.
and the Staff Manual respectively. Title pages
will be prepared in manuscript.

Place	Date	Hour	Summary of Events and Information	Remarks and references to Appendices
GOMIECOURT.	14.10.17.		Usual Sunday Routine. Officers Football Match. 6ti Ll. Coy - 8 ti Ll. Coy.	
	15.10.17		Training under Coy arrangements.	
	16.10.17		— do —	
	17.10.17.		Battn. marched to BAPAUME (less 2 coys) leaving Camp at 1.45 a.m. Batt. entrained at	
			BAPAUME at 5 a.m. & detrained at ESQUELBECQ (NORTHN FRANCE) 2-4 5 p.m. & marched to	
ERINGHEM.			billets at ERINGHEM. During the morn, 50 Div Salvage Coy were attached to Battalion. 2 coys	
			remained in Camp at GOMIECOURT until 6 p.m. 17-10-17.	
	18.10.17		2 coys arrived in billets at ERINGHEM at 9.45 a.m.	
ERINGHEM.	19.10.19		Coys out - marching under Coy arrangements.	
ARNEKE	20.10.17		Battn marched to billets in ARNEKE via ERKELSBRUGGE arriving at 1-15 p.m.	
PROVEN]	21.10.17.		Battn. marched to WORMHOUDT, & entrained for PROVEN. Night spent in PIDDINGTON Camp.	
AREA.]	22.10.17		Battn. marched to SARAWAK Camp [X.29.C.7.2.] Map 19. Belgium & France.	
	23.10.17		Remained in SARAWAK Camp.	
	24.11.17		Battn. marched to PROVEN, entrained & proceeded to BOESINGHE. Marched to camp HULL'S FARM. (B18.C.8.4 Sheet 28)	
			About 9 p.m. whilst waiting in field near Camp to take over from F.N.F. Battn. was bombed by aeroplanes of	
			"Gotha" type. 2/Lt. R.W.RAGG and 16 other ranks wounded. (Including 1 wounded at duty).	

WAR DIARY

or

INTELLIGENCE SUMMARY.

(Erase heading not required.)

Instructions regarding War Diaries and Intelligence
Summaries are contained in F. S. Regs., Part II.
and the Staff Manual respectively. Title pages
will be prepared in manuscript.

Place	Date	Hour	Summary of Events and Information	Remarks and references to Appendices
HULLS FARM BOESINGE	25.10.17.		Batt^n engaged in carrying & working parties. 6 other ranks wounded whilst engaged on this work.	
	26.10.17		Seven other ranks wounded & 12 reported missing from Carrying party for M.G. Coy provided by Z coy. This party, under 2/Lt E.A.ARMBRISTER was called upon to attack with M.G. Coy & returned on 27.10.17.	
	27.10.17.		Battalion still engaged in carrying & working parties.	
	28.10.17		do.	
	29.10.17		do. 2/Lt F.W.TEE wounded.	
	30.10.17.		do.	
	31.10.17.		Battalion moved to front line & relieved 4 EAST YORKS R^ST with H.Q at EGYPT HOUSE.	

T.B.Hurlot Capt.
Captain, for
O.C. 6^" DURHAM LIGHT INFANTRY.

2353   Wt. W²544/1454   700,000   5/15   D. D. & L.   A.D.S.S./Forms/C. 2118.

Vol 29

WAR DIARY

6th Bn. The Durham Light Infantry

November — 1917.

Volume — XXXII

Army Form C. 2118.

WAR DIARY
or
INTELLIGENCE SUMMARY.
(Erase heading not required.)

Instructions regarding War Diaries and Intelligence
Summaries are contained in F. S. Regs., Part II.
and the Staff Manual respectively. Title pages
will be prepared in manuscript.

Place	Date	Hour	Summary of Events and Information	Remarks and references to Appendices
EGYPT HO. (8th Nghrs)	1-11-17		Holding the line approx. U6 central – VIC34 – VIC13 Including railway. 4th Yorkshire Regt on right. 15th Notts-Derby on left. Our line now held with X on right front & left front & left front W right support & 3 left support. Both our firing line covered by a screen of shell holes. Enemy infantry very quiet.	REF SCHAAP-BALIE Echln 2 hours
do	2-11-17		During the night our advanced our line which now is as follows U6 & 60 – VIC17 – VIC58 – VIC03. Casualties nil? Then fairly forward of frontline down in dark without the knowledge of the enemy. H.L.I. relieved Roller Derby in left. $\underline{\text{... to ... slightly improved}}$	
do	3-11-17		Again moved forward to following line U6&63 – U6&68 – VIC17 – VIC58 – VIC96 – VIC03½. Enemy flying our line continually apparently uncertain when we were. Hostile EGYPT HO with Verbess gutby own chosen Lute but no effect. Started the 9PM. rendezvous let 4 PM. Capt Howell 6 Inf land. 8th Br Durd P.S relieved 11th Yorks Regm right. Lieut Green went down suffering from exhaustion the	
do	4-11-17		Again shelled EGYPT HO most of the day. Relieved By 9th & Dk Durd P.S relief completed 11 PM. Put several hundred gas shells over at night. Otherwise everything quiet from 5 PM Onwards.	
MARSOUIN	5-11-17		Arrived about 3AM.	SHEET 25 EDITION 3 1/40000
	6-11-17		Steeling area of camps rather badly. Moved to Whisle Nell Camp ELVERDINGHE. Capt Miller rejoined from III Army School. 2/Lt. 03 off W reported to Bn. to Lea Rykhoorn Journal Bn	

WAR DIARY

or

INTELLIGENCE SUMMARY.

(*Erase heading not required.*)

Instructions regarding War Diaries and Intelligence
Summaries are contained in F. S. Regs., Part II.
and the Staff Manual respectively. Title pages
will be prepared in manuscript.

Place	Date	Hour	Summary of Events and Information	Remarks and references to Appendices
ELVERDINGHE	7-11-17		Refitting & cleaning up. Major Tindall DLI. joined Bn from 12th DLI.	Sheet 28 Edn 3 1/40000
do	8-11-17		do Lieut Fee rejoins from hospital	
	9-11-17		do Major Tindale proceeded on leave. Capt Livesey rejoins from Salvage Co.	
	10-11-17		Battalion left Elverdinghe by train. Detrained at Watten and marched to Houlle.	
HOULLE	11-11-17		Very wet. Settling down in billets. 2nd Lieut rejoins Brooks, Fletcher & Eccleston	
	12-11-17		Lieut Douglas reported from England. Route march. Church service.	
	13-11-17		Devoted to Kit inspection & route march. Afternoon to recreational train.	
	14-11-17		Training carried on at Bn area. All Coy had Cross country run in afternoon. 2nd Lieut Brigg rejoined from Sep'd Div. Capt P. Livesey left Battalion (Divisional services) by order B. G. C. M. Rejoined Sep'd Div.	
	15-11-17		On training area during morning. Cross country runs. Football in afternoon.	
	16-11-17		do Boxing & Cross country running.	

WAR DIARY

or

INTELLIGENCE SUMMARY.

(Erase heading not required.)

Instructions regarding War Diaries and Intelligence
Summaries are contained in F. S. Regs., Part II.
and the Staff Manual respectively. Title pages
will be prepared in manuscript.

Place	Date	Hour	Summary of Events and Information	Remarks and references to Appendices
HOO LÉ	17.11.17		On Training area in morning. Recreational training in afternoon. Lieut Doyle reported to B.L.9	
	18.11.17		Kit inspection interior economy. Church parade.	
	19.11.17		Whole Bn on range in morning. Divisional Football Tournament v 5th Durl L9 Lost 1-0	
	20.11.17		On Training area in morning. Recreational training in afternoon.	
	21.11.17		Training area in morning. Bn sports held. wet afternoon. 2/Lt Davidson joined Battalion.	
	22.11.17		Training in morning. Recreation at training in afternoon	
	23.11.17		2/Lts Orton & Sheldon joined Bn	
	24.11.17		Training. Brigade Scheme. v 5th DLI in Tug of War. 5th won	

2353 Wt. W2544/1454 700,000 5/15 D. D. & L.   A.D.S.S./Forms/C. 2118.

WAR DIARY

or

INTELLIGENCE SUMMARY.

(Erase heading not required.)

Instructions regarding War Diaries and Intelligence Summaries are contained in F. S. Regs., Part II. and the Staff Manual respectively. Title pages will be prepared in manuscript.

Place	Date	Hour	Summary of Events and Information	Remarks and references to Appendices
HOULLE	25·11·17 26·11·17		On Fatigue area. Brigade Divisional Boxing at night	
	27·11·17		Church Parade. Played 9th D.L.I in Final for Bde football Cup. Result 2o score. Capt· Peberdy joined from England.	
	28·11·17 29·11·17 30·11·17		Training area do do On team Brigade Cross Country Cup. Bayonet wrestling and Div Boxing fat. Men in Semi Final of Middle, Welter, Lightweight Weights	

T/Maj & Capt⸍r for
Cmdg 6 Durham L. I.

VII 30

WAR DIARY.

6th Bn. The Durham Light Infantry.

December, 1917.

Volume No XXXIII

WAR DIARY
or
INTELLIGENCE SUMMARY

(Erase heading not required.)

Instructions regarding War Diaries and Intelligence Summaries are contained in F. S. Regs., Part II. and the Staff Manual respectively. Title Pages will be prepared in manuscript.

Place	Date	Hour	Summary of Events and Information	Remarks and references to Appendices
HOULLE	1.12.17		Training under Coy arrangements in morning + recreation in afternoon. Capt. F.E. Cardew joined from England	
"	2.12.17		do	
"	3.12.17		do + ran the Divisional Cross country run in afternoon	
"	4.12.17		Lt T.R. Roberts R.A.M.C. went on leave. Lt O'Neill M.O. (R.A.M.C.) joined from 11th N.F.A. 67% 7th Bn furnished the course.	
"	5.12.17		Morning spent in hasty musketry. Afternoon free.	
"	6.12.17		Major Tyndale rejoined from leave. Training in morning. To wet in afternoon for recreation.	
"	7.12.17		Training in morning + Pn v. Pn Brigade Football Cup in afternoon by Brady the 9th Durh. L.I. Gone to field.	
"	8.12.17		Training in morning	
"	9.12.17		"	
"	10.12.17		Recreation training in afternoon	
"	11.12.17		DIVISIONAL SPORTS in afternoon	
			Training in morning Company tournament in afternoon night	2/Lt. A.C. Coad & R.T. & n. 10th R.S.M. Perry & & word to Hospital 2/Lt R.B. Uhlman joined from England
"	12.12.17		7th Battalion marched from HOULLE to WATTEN and entrained. Detrained at BRANDHOEK marched to WERIE CAMP into huts.	

WAR DIARY
or
INTELLIGENCE SUMMARY
(Erase heading not required.)

Instructions regarding War Diaries and Intelligence Summaries are contained in F. S. Regs., Part II and the Staff Manual respectively. Title Pages will be prepared in manuscript.

Place	Date	Hour	Summary of Events and Information	Remarks and references to Appendices
MERIE CAMP NEAR BRANDHOEK	13.12.17 14.12.17 15.12.17		Platoon & Company training.	G.11 C & D AREA 3.
BRANDHOEK	16.12.17		Preparing to go into line.	
	17.12.17		Moved into camp at POTIJZE by bus.	
POTIJZE	18.12.17		Battalion went into support at SEINE (D16d15) relieved 5th Border Regt. in Suffolk. (INDIARUBBER) Dug outs & batteries in pill box. Battalion going up Saut Ridge agreeably affected. There was a considerable amount of shelling in the afternoon & 2 men wounded. Evening but remarks & night was quiet.	D16d15
	19.12.17		2/Lieut. J.C. Hunlops evacuated sick from a cause. Quiet day except for occasional shell, but had no casualties.	
SEINE	19.12.17		Moved up & relieved 5th Northumberland Fusiliers in front line. 4 N.YORKS moved into SEINE	
	20.12.17		Battalion Headquarters at INDIGO (D16 & 23) Distributed as follows — 2 Coys in PASSCHENDAELE with posts approximately W2SC 05.60, E1a.14, D6 & 92, D6d.79, D6d.72. 3 Coy (Capt. Walton) in left & W Coy (Capt. Johnson) on right. The 14th Division were on the 1st left & 8th Seaforth R.S. on right. X Coy (Capt. Polmerly) were attached behind the front line at CREST FM & Y Coy (Capt. Anken) at HAALEN in rear of X Coy. Approx. D11d.	

1875 Wt. W593/826 1,000,000 4/15 J.B.C. & A. A.D.S.S./Forms/C. 2118.

Army Form C. 2118

WAR DIARY
or
INTELLIGENCE SUMMARY
(Erase heading not required.)

Instructions regarding War Diaries and Intelligence Summaries are contained in F. S. Regs., Part II. and the Staff Manual respectively. Title Pages will be prepared in manuscript.

Place	Date	Hour	Summary of Events and Information	Remarks and references to Appendices
PASSCHEN DAELE SECTOR	21.12.17		That [S'gt]. Fairly quiet day. Patrol reported the ground in front of our line to be very wet & marshy. Our posts dry.	
	22.12.17		Artillery on both sides very active noted. There [for] very deadful by Aeroplanes. Our posts opposite PASSCHENDAELE came in for a great deal of shelling, but fortunately there were no direct hits.	
	23.12.17		More quiet than the previous day nothing reported. S.O.S. seen to go up on left of our sector own shrapnel following a heavy bombardment.	
	24.12.17		Quiet day except for our shelling during the day. In evening we were relieved by the 2nd 10th YORKSHIRE REGT. Excellent relief carried out in record time without a casualty. Total casualties during tour actually in line 1 died of wounds, 1 Officer (Wilson) wounded but remained on duty & 7 men wounded. The Bn marched back by companies to POTIJZE CAMP — Headquarters arriving last at about 9 P.M. Men all in splendid spirits.	

1875 Wt. W593/826 1,000,000 4/15 J.B.C. & A. A.D.S.S./Forms/C. 2118.

Army Form C. 2118.

WAR DIARY
or
INTELLIGENCE SUMMARY

(Erase heading not required.)

Instructions regarding War Diaries and Intelligence Summaries are contained in F. S. Regs., Part II. and the Staff Manual respectively. Title Pages will be prepared in manuscript.

Place	Date	Hour	Summary of Events and Information	Remarks and references to Appendices
POTIJZE	25.12.17		Snowing all morning. Went to MERIE CAMP at BRANDHOEK by bus during during afternoon.	
MERIE. CAMP	26.12.17		Devoted to cleaning up etc & men had a splended Xmas dinner consisting of Turkey, roast beef, vegetables, fruit, plum pudding, beer &port wine tomatoes.	
	27.12.17		Church parade. Inspected by Corps Commander General Sir Hunter Weston who complimented the battalion on their smart appearance on parade particularly as they had only been out of the line at 2 days.	
	28.12.17		Part of Battalion went on working parties in trench area.	
	29.12.17		Received orders to move to ENGLISH FARM near St JEAN (Sheet 28 D 27 b) during afternoon found insufficient accomodation. Way had shelter.	
St-JEAN CAMP	30.12.17		Moved into St JEAN CAMP where the 5th Northumberland Fusiliers were. Everyone living in tents. Supplied working parties under 8th Corps C R E.	
	31.12.17		Supplied working parties.	

J. Robson Lt Col
commg 6th W.D.L.I.

2449 Wt. W14957/M90 750,000 1/16 J.B.C. & A. Forms/C.2118/12.

Vol 31'

WAR DIARY.

6th Bn. The Durham Light Infantry

January, 1918.

Volume — XXIV.

Army Form C. 2118.

WAR DIARY
or
INTELLIGENCE SUMMARY
(Erase heading not required.)

Instructions regarding War Diaries and Intelligence Summaries are contained in F. S. Regs., Part II. and the Staff Manual respectively. Title Pages will be prepared in manuscript.

Place	Date	Hour	Summary of Events and Information	Remarks and references to Appendices
S. JEAN CAMP.	1-1-18		Supplied working parties under 8th Corps. 5th Border Regt: up & D.R.9 went into front line relieving 4th & 7th North'n 7. respecting gas in support.	
	2-1-18		Supplied working parties.	
	3-1-18		do	
	4-1-18		do	
	5-1-18		do 5th Border Regt: 8th & 9th D.R.9 came out of line.	
	6-1-18		Moved into a camp by the side of MENIN ROAD. Relieved by 33rd Div complete.	
	7-1-18		On march to the GRAND PLACE, YPRES. Entrained at 10 A.M. Proceeded to STEENVOORDE area into billets. Bn. headquarters Q.4.C.27. EECKE. Bde. do STEENVOORDE Div do	SHEET 27 S.E.
	8-1-18		2/Lieut Watkin L.C. went to hospital from 9th Corps of course. Day spent in cleaning up & getting into billets through billets being unsatisfactory. Short route march allotted.	
STEENVOORDE	9-1-18		Snowy very hard. Lecture in barn even the only item of training possible.	

WAR DIARY
or
INTELLIGENCE SUMMARY
(Erase heading not required.)

Instructions regarding War Diaries and Intelligence Summaries are contained in F. S. Regs., Part II. and the Staff Manual respectively. Title Pages will be prepared in manuscript.

Place	Date	Hour	Summary of Events and Information	Remarks and references to Appendices
STEENVOORDE	10.1.18		Draft of 96 arrived from Depôt. Nearly all were aged 19–20 years. 2/Lieut Jenkerton A.E. joined Battalion. 2/Lieut Heslop J.C. rejoined from hospital. Major Walter 7. McCleft Battalion to command 18th/5th Manchester Regt.	
do	11.1.18		Battalion at baths. Training under company arrangements	
do	12.1.18		Training as per programme and attached for Chamber. Brigade Commander inspected billets. Lieut C.H. Symes joined to form a bombing Coy.	
do	13.1.18		Snowing all day — training restricted	
do	14.1.18		Training under Coy arrangements	
do	15.1.18		Very wet.	
do	16.1.18		Transport moved by road.	
do	17.1.18		Battalion marched to 'CAESTRE Station detraining at WIZERNE S about 6 p.m. Bn marched to AQUIN arriving about 5.30 pm after a trying march (Lt. C.H Symes to hospital).	
AQUIN	18.1.18		The day devoted to cleaning up, etc. Capt Strom M.C rejoined from leave.	
	19.1.18		One coy on musketrie Range (Wize) & the rest engaged in counter attack exercises & R.T + B.7.	

WAR DIARY

or

INTELLIGENCE SUMMARY

(Erase heading not required.)

Instructions regarding War Diaries and Intelligence
Summaries are contained in F. S. Regs., Part II.
and the Staff Manual respectively. Title Pages
will be prepared in manuscript.

Place	Date	Hour	Summary of Events and Information	Remarks and references to Appendices
A.QUIN.	20.1.18 Sunday		2nd Lt. J.L. GOTT, 2nd Lt. A. DOBSON & 2nd Lt. R. RAILTON joined Bn as reinforcements. Men who had completed Part III of S. Musketry Course were allotted range under Lt. Kirkdune Bns Adjt. The remainder of Bn at usual Divine Service.	
"	21.1.18		X coy allotted Miniature Range & rest of coys engaged in general training. Details & Specialists trained separately.	
"	22.1.18		2nd Lt. M.R. PINKNEY D.C.M. joined Bn as reinforcement. Part III of General Musketry Course continued under Lt. Kirkdune Miniature Range allotted to X coy. General training, including night firing & wiring by other coys.	
"	23rd		First Concert by Battalion Concert Party, "THE RED DIAMONDS" was given under the supern vision of Capt S.B. Carter & Lt. P.H.B. Logan M.C. this concert was repeated on two successive nights, usual training carried out.	
"	24th		As field day as practice.	
"	25		Worg on Miniature Range. X coy carrying up positions in skull holes for aeroplane photographs. Remainder of coys general training.	
"	26		Brigade Field Day on model of PASSCHENDAELE Ridge near MOORSLEDE.	
"	27th		Usual Divine Service.	
"	28th		General Training.	
"	29th		General training & wiring competition.	
ALQUIN– BRANDHOEK	30th		Battalion marched to WIZERNE, entraining at 12.20pm. Detraining at BRANDHOEK at 5.20pm, the	
	31st		Battalion into new TORONTO Camp. Kit & equipment inspection & general preparations for line.	

T.B. Hoolote Major ...
Cmdg 6th Durham Lt. Infty

2449 Wt. W14957/M90 750,000 1/16 J.B.C. & A. Forms/C.2118/12.

VII

151 151

WAR DIARY

6th Bn. The Durham Light Infantry

February, 1916.

Volume — XXXV.

Wo 32

WAR DIARY

or

INTELLIGENCE SUMMARY.

(Erase heading not required.)

Volume 35

Instructions regarding War Diaries and Intelligence Summaries are contained in F. S. Regs., Part II. and the Staff Manual respectively. Title pages will be prepared in manuscript.

Place	Date	Hour	Summary of Events and Information	Remarks and references to Appendices
BRANDHOEK	1.2.18		Bath in Toronto East Camp. Day spent in preparing to move up the line. At night a concert in conjunction with Divisional Cinema	
SUNDERLAND Camp POTIZE	2nd		Bath moved by three trains (light railway) at 9 am 9.15 + 9.30 am to SAVILLE Road after move to SUNDERLAND Camp for Dinner. At 2.30 pm moved into MAIDEN Camp Relieved 5th Border Regt in Brigade Reserve.	
YPRES	3rd		Working, early morning till start working. Relieved by 9 D.L.I.) went back to Cellars in Ypres near the Barracks.	
SUPPORT Area HAMBOURG	4th 5th 6th		Draft of 5 officers & 100 other ranks from 10th Bttn joined. Some employed on other detail. Bttn (?) moved up to HAMBOURG and relieved 4th York Regt as Support Bttn. Quiet day, at night the Bttn relieved 5th Durham Light Infantry as Left front Bttn. W cy as Right front by Z cy as Left front cy. X cy at CREST FARM and Y cy at HAZLE N Switch	
PASSCHEN- DAELE	7th		At night Z cy took over two LEFT posts of W cy and W cy took over two LEFT posts of 8 D.L.I. in our RIGHT	
	8th		Y cy moved up from HAZLE N and took over from too LEFT cy of 8 D.L.I. Three strong 3 cys in front line and one in support also the cy	

2353   Wt. W3544/1454 700,000 5/15 D. D. & L.   A.D.S.S./Forms/C. 2118.

Army Form C. 2118.

WAR DIARY
or
INTELLIGENCE SUMMARY

(Erase heading not required.)

Instructions regarding War Diaries and Intelligence Summaries are contained in F. S. Regs., Part II. and the Staff Manual respectively. Title Pages will be prepared in manuscript.

Place	Date	Hour	Summary of Events and Information	Remarks and references to Appendices
PASSCHENDAELE	9th		The 87th Inf Bde 29th Division took over from 2 coy who returned to CREST FARM relieved one coy 1/8 D.L.I. here. During the day 2/Lieut G.H. KING was slightly wounded. At night it is coy was raided by a small party of Germans who caught a party of 1 officer 1 NCO & 1 man who were taking return round the ... 1/2/Lieut W. WATKIN was wounded and No 12009. Pte ATTEWELL was taken prisoner.	
	10th		The Battn was relieved by 5th the Yorkshire Regt and came out to SUNDERLAND Camp.	
SUNDERLAND Camp nr. POTIZE	11.		Day spent cleaning up etc.	
	12.		Found 150 men for working parties. Bn to Baths in Ypres.	
	13.		Five hundred men working parties very wet day.	
	14.		Preparing to go up. Marched off 2.30 pm H and relieved 4 Bn East York in Support in HAMBURG area.	

2449 Wt. W14957/M90 750,000 1/16 J.B.C. & A. Forms/C.2118/12.

WAR DIARY

or

INTELLIGENCE SUMMARY

(Erase heading not required.)

Instructions regarding War Diaries and Intelligence Summaries are contained in F. S. Regs., Part II. and the Staff Manual respectively. Title Pages will be prepared in manuscript.

Place	Date	Hour	Summary of Events and Information	Remarks and references to Appendices
MARDUKE SUFFAT BALL	15. 16. 17. 18.		Supplied camp parties for front line Baths	
	19.		A great tria days.	
	9. 20.		Relieved by 64 + 5th R. Welsh Comp. Day spent cleaning up and preparing to move Entrenched 1 km at Wizernes. Detrained at Wizernes and marched to Lt Marton where regiment into Billets (Quistier)	
	21.		Cleaning up.	
	22.		Cleaning up and short march.	
	23.		Cleaning up and short march.	
	24.		Church Parade	
	25.		Wet. Interior Economy.	
	26.		Demonstration by Demonstration Platoon	
	27.		Training	
	28.		Range. C. Practical. C.R.E. Platoon Complete	

Lt Col _____ Lieut Col
Cmdg. 6 Durham L.I.

151st Brigade.

50th Division.

6th BATTALION

DURHAM LIGHT INFANTRY

M A R C H   1 9 1 8

No 33

WAR DIARY.

6th Bn. Durham Light Infantry

151 Bde.
50

March, 1918.

Volume — XXVI.

WAR DIARY
or
INTELLIGENCE SUMMARY
(Erase heading not required.)

Volume 36.

Instructions regarding War Diaries and Intelligence Summaries are contained in F. S. Regs., Part II. and the Staff Manual respectively. Title Pages will be prepared in manuscript.

Place	Date	Hour	Summary of Events and Information	Remarks and references to Appendices
ST. MARTIN	1.3.18		Training. Boxing match. In the evening a Concert by the R.E. Dramatic Sn.	
"	2nd.		Training and Baths. 2/Lt. Rhodes went to a Conference at IV Army Inf. School. Capt. G.E. Carden to the command.	
"	3rd.		Training cancelled owing Frenchmen existing.	
"	4th.		Training. The following Egypt commemorations published in G.R.O. 's / Feb. 29. A.M. of 14th Bn. to the Bn. of 4th Corps. 17.12.17.	
"	5th.		Training and Baths.	
"	6th.		A.R.A. Platoon Competition stage (a) fired on C. Range. the following No. 1 W. cy. Platoons were the best & their respective Companies. No. 6 in X cy. No. 14 in Z cy. No. 11 in Y cy.	
"	7th.		Training.	
"	8th.		Batt. moved at short notice by train from Argues to Ingram. Lewis St. Martin 1st 8.35 pm. arriving at Ingram to Corbie to 9.30 am. thence marched to La Neuville near Corbie to billets. Dinner en route arrived about 2.0 pm.	
Le NEUVILLE	9th.			
"	10th.		Church parade & various economy. The afternoon the band played in the square in Corbie.	

WAR DIARY
or
INTELLIGENCE SUMMARY
(Erase heading not required.)

Instructions regarding War Diaries and Intelligence Summaries are contained in F. S. Regs., Part II. and the Staff Manual respectively. Title Pages will be prepared in manuscript.

Place	Date	Hour	Summary of Events and Information	Remarks and references to Appendices
LA NEUVILLE	11.3.18		"Summer time" came into force at midnight 10/11th March. The Bath marched from the Neuville at 8.30 am to Marcel Cave arriving about 11.30 am	
	12th		Day spent on train scenery etc. the Bath was in turn in G.H.Q Reserve & 5th Army Reserve and were to move at 12 hrs notice by train in case of the latter being required. the Bath to be at the disposal of VII Corps for Counter attack purposes.	
	13th		Twenty (20) C.O. & D.O. for Counter attack companies selected points to Counter attacked warmly reconnoitred.	
	14th to 16th		Training continued in the MARCELCAVE & MORCOURT area, Battn turnpits in counter attack exercises in view of probable operations as a result of the German offensive.	
	17th		Stage "C" of A.R.A. Competition fired at MORCOURT drawn by No.6 Platoon which was subsequently beaten on the same range by 8th Bn in stage D. Chewd Punch in MARCELCAVE Square for men not firing	

MARŒELLCAVE.

18th.
20th.   Training continued & visits paid to potatoe area & potatoes issued by Officers.

21st.   Batta entrained at FULLAUCOURT about 5pm. & detrained at BRIE. Marched to BOUCLY where Batta occupied front line in support to 66th Div. who had been attacked in the morning. (XIX Corps.) Day movements to right.

22nd.   Remained in front line. Slight encounter with enemy patrols & fired & fired in masses of enemy at long range. Grenaded the line about 9 pm & withdrew to CARDISNY Ridge.

23rd.   Occupation of CARDISNY line completed by 7 am. then orders were received that the Army was withdrawing to the west of the Somme. Rearguard action fought from CARDISNY, which was entered by the enemy as the Batta left, to LE MESNIL & the afternoon when received to cover ETERPISNY Bridge. Batta embarked in LE MESNIL village, but enabled to successful rearguard action under Capt. AUBIN M.C. & Capt. CARDEN, the Batta crossed the bridge with very slight casualties. Lt. CHARLTON & 2/Lt DOBSON missing. Occupied line with 66th & 8th Divn on West bank of the river for the night.

24th.   Batta withdrew through BARLEUX to FOUCAUCOURT. & remained in camp for two hours. At 4 pm. it marched to ESTREES & occupied a line for the night N.E. of the village.

25th Moved hurriedly in the morning to GENERMONT & deployed for action with divisions of MARCHELEPOT under orders of 8th Div. on right of Belgian Bde. Battn on our left in support found a line on the railway & subsequently moved about a mile to the South. Div. on the right retiring, Kelly formed defensive flank through HYENCOURT front of PRESSOIRE. At 7 pm Battn withdrew to heart line in front of PRESSOIRE.

26th About 9 am after confused orders the whole line withdrew & the Battn in artillery formation passed through LIHONS to a line in front of ROSIERES. A line was dug here & the Battn remained for the night.

27th At 9.30 am owing to the withdrawal of a column by on the right, the Battn fell back, but 3 Coys (W.X.+Z) counter-attacked & restored the line. Capt. H. WALTON M.C. commanding Z Coy killed. Details of Battn who had been left at Valtues were sent from WARFUSÉE under Lt TYERMAN to counter-attack at HARBONNIERES. A further general withdrawal was ordered & the 13 Battn moved back to the CAIX line, during what operations Lt Col. F.W. ROBSON D.S.O. was

28th killed by machine gun fire. A further partial retirement was checked by a counter-attack organised by Capt CARDEW with the remnants of 3 Coys. Subsequently the whole Battn withdrew in the direction of MOREUIL, leaving the line held by other units. About 100 men of the Battn collected at AILLY-SUR-NOYE & stayed the night.

29th

Remnants of Bn. left AILLY under Major T.D. HESLOP ordered to proceed to ground 90.
S. of DEMUIN. On arrival were not required, but were shelled + suffered casualties. Returned to BERTEAUCOURT retrieving the night Transport. Then moved to BOVES + found about 200 men of the Bn. collected under Capt. AUBIN. M.C.

30th

Party under Major HESLOP moved to HOURGES + took up a support position on North of Village. Party under Capt. AUBIN marched to SAINS-EN-AMIENOIS with transport.

31st

Party under Major HESLOP retired after all troops in front had passed through + dug in in the front arts of the new LUCE hill right when ordered to consolidate at a farm on road N.W. of DOMART. when night was spent with remainder of Divl. troops in forward area. Party under Capt. AUBIN marched to SALEUX

During the fighting from 21st – 31st March the Bn. suffered the following casualties.
Killed : Officers 6 O.R. 35 . Wounded : Officers 5 O.R. 187
Missing : Officers 2 O.R. 87 . Wounded + Missing Officers Nil O.R. 3

T.B.Heslop Major.
Comdg. 6th DLI

151st Brigade.

50th Division.

1/6th BATTALION

DURHAM LIGHT INFANTRY

APRIL 1918.

6 D.L.I.

1st April — Party under Major HESLOP went back to bring S.9 GENTELLES & the stores concentrated in Bois de GENTELLES. Left at 9pm. marched to MONSEAU. Party under Capt. AUBIN entrained in the evening & arrived at RUE on morning of 2nd April.

2nd — Party under Major HESLOP marched to SALEUX & entrained for RUE & arrived at RUE on morning of 3rd. Capt AUBIN'S party marched to VRON.

3rd — Major HESLOP's party arrived at VRON.

4th — Battn entrained at 12 noon & proceeded to BEUVRY, arriving at night.

5th & 6th — Battn refitting & cleaning up.

7th — Battn moved by lorries to BILLIS nr ESTAIRES.

8th — Stand to at 4.30 a.m. in anticipation of attack on Portuguese on Battn right. Remainder of the day quiet.

9th — ESTAIRES heavily bombarded commencing about 4 a.m. Billet occupied by nearly all the officers struck & the following killed: Capt. J.J. AUBIN M.C. Capt G. KIRKHOUSE. Lt. Col. TYECMAN; Lt D.B. SCOTT; 2/Lt F. SHIRTLIFF. & Capt. R.A. MACKENZIE (R.A.M.C.) afterwards died of wounds.

- 9th (contd). Battn moved out with only 5 Officers. Battn positions were engaged about 9 a.m. Capt. S.E. CARDEN killed, 2/Lt. T.R. RAILTON missing. After fighting all day the Battn withdrew to line running North from LESTREM.

- 10th. Fighting continued, one Coy 87th Bn being attacked by 1st Batn. In readjusted towards night owing to withdrawal of troops on right.

- 11th. Fighting continued near BEAUPRE which subsequently developed into rearguard action towards MERVILLE. Line formed in front of MERVILLE. Subsequently withdrew through MERVILLE at night attack up line on W.& the town

- 12th. Troops on flanks having withdrawn. Battn withdrew to line through LE SART northwards. Line again withdrawn in the afternoon to within 1000 yards S. edge of FORET de NIEPPE through PONT TOURNANT.

- 13th. Battn relieved by 5th Div. at moved in the early morning to LA MOTTE Chateau where it was heavily shelled moved to STEEN BECQUE in close reserve.

- 14th & 15th. Remained in reserve, but sent forward working parties to dig trenches in FORET de NIEPPE.

- 16th. Marched to billets at COHEM near AIRE.

17th	CO HSM	Inspection by G.O.C. Divn who thank all ranks for their work in recent operations
18th-20th	"	Battn refitting. Training commenced. Draft 9 ORs + 9 officers arrived on 20th
21st	"	Church Parade
22nd	"	Inspection of new draft & transport by G.O.C. Divn & B.S.C.
23rd-25th	"	Training & refitting. Lt C.F. Walker M.C. took over Command on 23rd
26th	"	Battn moved by 'bus to LA PUGNOY (near BETHUNE) & entrained
27th	"	& to SERZY (near SOISSONS)
28th	"	Arrived at detraining station 8am & marched to camp at ARCIS-LE-PONSART
29th	"	Refitting & resting
30th	"	Training commenced

J. W. Saxton.
Lieut-Col.
Comdg 6th DLI

1st May 1918.

6TH BN DURHAM LIGHT INFANTRY

MAY & JUNE 1918

WAR DIARY

NR 35

151/50

WAR DIARY.

6th D.L.I.

May, 1918.

Volume — XXXVIII.

WAR DIARY

or

INTELLIGENCE SUMMARY.

(Erase heading not required.)

Instructions regarding War Diaries and Intelligence Summaries are contained in F. S. Regs., Part II. and the Staff Manual respectively. Title pages will be prepared in manuscript.

Place	Date	Hour	Summary of Events and Information	Remarks and references to Appendices
ARCIS - le - PONSART	May 1st & 3rd		Training continued in general in vicinity of Camp.	
GLENNES	4th		Battn marched to GLENNES into billets.	
	5th & 6th		Remained at GLENNES, preparing to the line.	
Line	7th		Battn moved into Support area of line. S & CORBENY, with CRAONNE on left flank	
	8th & 11th		Remained in Support area. relieving 73rd R.I. (French)	
	12th		Battn relieved 5th D.I. to right Front Battn with two Coys in Front line, one in Support & one in Reserve.	
	13th & 17th		Remained in line. Active patrolling each night.	
	18th		Battn relieved by 5th D.I. & moved to reserve in CHAUDARDES Village	
CHAUDARDES	19th & 23rd		Battn in reserve. Training carried out in morning. Concerts by General Jackson (Divl Troops) or Divl Band	
Line	24th		Battn relieved 5th D.I. in Front line. Dispositions changed to 3 Coys in Front line, with Precepts down in reserve.	

D. D. & L., London, E.C.
(A8col) Wt W1771/M2931 759,000 5/17 **Sch. 82** Forms/C2118/14

WAR DIARY
or
INTELLIGENCE SUMMARY.
(Erase heading not required.)

Instructions regarding War Diaries and Intelligence
Summaries are contained in F. S. Regs., Part II.
and the Staff Manual respectively. Title pages
will be prepared in manuscript.

Place	Date	Hour	Summary of Events and Information	Remarks and references to Appendices
Lne	25st & 26th		Battn in Line. Active patrolling.	
	27th		Enemy commenced very heavy bombardment at 1 am followed by attack at 4 am. Majority of Officers & men missing. Battn continued towards the AISNE where small parties of the Battn were collected at bridgeheads at CONCEVREUX. Lt Col. Walker MC in command of remnants of 149 & 151 Inf. Bde. Further retirement in the evening to bridge S of AISNE.	
	28th		Fighting continued by few survivors who became attached to 25th Division.	
	29th		Composite Battn formed of men of 9 Divn retirement from Concevreux east of bounds. THERY.	
	30th & 31st		Fighting continued by Composite Battn though not so intense. Major HESLOP wounded. Transport arrived at VERT la GRAVELLE where a few stragglers collected. Total Casualties of fighting 30 Officers, 499 OR killed Walker wounded Total Casualties wounded missing	

J. Sacron. Lieut Col.
Cmdg 6th DLI

WAR DIARY.

6th Bn. Durham Light Infantry

June, 1918.

Volume XXXIX.

WAR DIARY

or

INTELLIGENCE SUMMARY.

(Erase heading not required.)

Instructions regarding War Diaries and Intelligence Summaries are contained in F. S. Regs., Part II. and the Staff Manual respectively. Title pages will be prepared in manuscript.

Place	Date	Hour	Summary of Events and Information	Remarks and references to Appendices
VERT la GRAVELLE	June 1st		Remnants of Battn (about 35 fighting men) reported by SOc Div. About 35 men under Capt HARE were put in the line when in orders with the French near BOIS de BONVAL Composite Bde formed, Lt Col Walker to command 151 Bde Composite Battn.	
	2nd		Capt HARE'S party moved to BOIS de COURTON	
	3rd & 4th		Composite Battn remained at VERT la GRAVELLE ready to move	
NANTEUIL	5th		Composite Bde moved by 'bus to ORMOYEUX, from where they marched to remain near NANTEUIL	
Luis	6th		Battn to by Commander visited the line of the 151st Bde Comp Br moved to LES HAIES (2 Coy) + ESPILLY (1 Coy) At night the Battn relieved 9th Cheshire in MONTAGNE de BLIGNY	
	7th		Battn in the line which was reorganised to fill gaps.	
	8th		At dusk, the Battn moved back to CHAUMUZY, the line being taken over by 149th + 758th Bde Battn, where it was joined by Capt HARE'S party.	
	9th 10th 11th		Posts occupied on N. + W. of CHAUMUZY, Battn being under orders to counter attack if required.	
	12th		Battn relieved by 58th Comp Br ; 6th DLI Coy being relieved by Cheshires	
	13th		Relief completed at dawn + Battn moved to remain in BOIS de COURTON	

D. D. & L., London, E.C.
(A8c04)   Wt W1771/M2031 750,000 5/17   Sch. 83   Forms/C2118/14

WAR DIARY
or
INTELLIGENCE SUMMARY
(Erase heading not required.)

Instructions regarding War Diaries and Intelligence
Summaries are contained in F. S. Regs., Part II.
and the Staff Manual respectively. Title Pages
will be prepared in manuscript.

Place	Date	Hour	Summary of Events and Information	Remarks and references to Appendices
	14th June		Officers & NCOs reconnoitred routes for counter attack of regiment	
	15th		Some training carried on. Dispositions for counter attack complete	
	16th		Divine Service held for all denominations reinforced by supporting units.	
	17th		Training continued.	
	18th		Italian Officers of BRESCIA Division came to arrange relief. Batt. relieved at 9.30 & moved to BOIS de JOUFFRE.	
BROYES (MARNE)	19th		Batt. entrained at EPERNAY, detrained at SEZANNE & marched to billets at BROYES where the transport had been for some time.	
	20th		Cleaning of clothing & re-equipment	
	21st & 22nd		Re-equipment continued in preparation for formation of new Composite Bde.	
	23rd		Composite Bde formed consisting of 149th, 150th & 151st Bde Composite Battns, 151st Battn being Composite Battn. Commanded by Lt Col P. KIRKUP. DSO. MC. 8th Div. 6th Div. provided one Coy of transport.	
LES ESSARTS	24th & 25th		Training of Composite Battn. Details of 6th Div under Lt Col T Wellesley moved to LES ESSARTS	

2449 Wt. W14957/Mg0 750,000 1/16 J.B.C. & A. Forms/C.2118/12.

Army Form C. 2118

WAR DIARY

or

INTELLIGENCE SUMMARY

(Erase heading not required.)

Instructions regarding War Diaries and Intelligence
Summaries are contained in F. S. Regs., Part II
and the Staff Manual respectively. Title Pages
will be prepared in manuscript.

Place	Date	Hour	Summary of Events and Information	Remarks and references to Appendices
	26th		Training continued. Order received for transport to move to JANVILLERS, en route for forward area. Battn to follow by bus on 27th to which transport on the MARNE near DORMANS Transport left at 9 pm. Order cancelled in the evening.	
	27th		Training continued. Transport returned.	
	28th		Training continued.	
	29th		Corporate Bde assembled for presentation of medals by G.O.C. Division, who announced the possibility of the removal of the Battn being distributed.	
	30th		Church Parade. Details rejoined & the Battn was informed under command of Lt Col. F. Willson M.C.	

J. Warren Lieut Col.
Cmdg. 6th Bn. Durst. L.I.

30/6/18

6th BN. THE DURHAM L. I

WAR DIARY

VOLUME No. —

JULY 1918.

WAR DIARY
or
INTELLIGENCE SUMMARY.

(Erase heading not required.)

Instructions regarding War Diaries and Intelligence
Summaries are contained in F. S. Regs., Part II.
and the Staff Manual respectively. Title pages
will be prepared in manuscript.

Place	Date	Hour	Summary of Events and Information	Remarks and references to Appendices
BROYES	July 1918 1st		Preparations for move tomorrow.	
St SOPHIE FARM	2nd		Bath. marched to Provins & War Camp St SOPHIE FARM (CONNANTRE), staying area on the way to entraining station.	
	3rd		Marched to FERE CHAMPENOISE where the Battn entrained.	
CAUMONT	4th		Detrained at LONGPRE & marched to billets at CAUMONT (near ABBEVILLE), arriving about 9.30.	
	5th to 10th		Battn. remained at CAUMONT. & opened out training Cadre + surplus Personnel.	
	11th		Battn. addressed by Major General JACKSON Cmg 50th Divn from the repatriation.	
WARCHEVILLE	12th		Marched to billets at WARCHEVILLE.	
	13th & 14th		Reorganization completed.	
	15th		Surplus personnel (16 Off. 170 O.R.) marched to PONT REMY & entrained for Base (ETAPLES)	
	16th to 18th		Training Cadre remained at WARCHEVILLE.	
ROUXMESNIL	19th		Cadre moved by lorries to ROUXMESNIL Camp near DIEPPE.	
	20th to 31st		Instruction of Specialist Officers + NCOs carried on in Camp.	

J. C. Saxton Lt. Colonel
Comdg 5/6th Bn The Durham Light Infantry

D. D. & L., London, E.C.

(A10260) Wt W3000/1713 750,000 2/18 Sch. 52 Forms/C2118/16.

attached

50 DIVISION

151 BDE

6TH BN DURHAM LT INFY

AUG-NOV 1918

2686

6th Bn The Durham Light Infantry.

War. Diary.

August 1918.

WAR DIARY
or
INTELLIGENCE SUMMARY.

(Erase heading not required.)

Instructions regarding War Diaries and Intelligence Summaries are contained in F. S. Regs., Part II. and the Staff Manual respectively. Title pages will be prepared in manuscript.

Place	Date	Hour	Summary of Events and Information	Remarks and references to Appendices
ROUXMESNIL	Aug. 1916 1st - 3rd		Instruction of specialist Officers & N.C.Os. continued in camp.	
	4th		Representatives of the Battn. attended Service in 4th Anniversary of Declaration of War at MARTIN EGLISE Camp at which were present Divisional & Brigade Staffs on members of all Battns. of 50th was 50th Divn.	
	5th – 10th		Instruction of specialists continued.	
	11th		Church Parade in camp. Battn. had now been informed that on a Cadre they would proceed to ROUEN in a few days to administrate & train new Officers at reinforcement camp.	
	12th & 13th		Instruction of specialists continued.	
	14th		Advance party left for ROUEN.	
	15th		Cadre Battn. with band & bugles entrained at DIEPPE for ROUEN.	
ROUEN	16th		Battn. arrived at ROUEN in early morning marched to camp being now in 117th & (Bde. 39th Divn.	
	17th 18th		Classes held for N.C.Os. & Officers.	
	19th		Battn. inspected by Brig Genl. Armytage Cmg. D.O. Cmdg. 117th In. Bde.	
	20th to 31st		N.C.O. Classes continued. Officers engaged in preparation of tactical schemes.	

D. D. & L., London, E.C. (A10266) W. W5300/P713 750,000 2/16 Sch. 52 Forms/C2118/16.

6th Bn. The Durham Light Infy

War Diary

September, 1918.

Army Form C. 2118.

WAR DIARY
or
INTELLIGENCE SUMMARY.
(Erase heading not required.)

Instructions regarding War Diaries and Intelligence
Summaries are contained in F. S. Regs., Part II.
and the Staff Manual respectively. Title pages
will be prepared in manuscript.

Place	Date	Hour	Summary of Events and Information	Remarks and references to Appendices
ROUEN	1918 Sept. 1st – 8th		Batt. (less detachments) in camp near CHAMPS de COURSES. Officers engaged and running on preparation of Tactical Exercises for future Officers Training School. Remainder of Battn. working on making of new camp.	
	9th 10th – 21st		Moved 15 men temporary camp near site of camp in course of erection. Work on Tactical Exercise and new camp continued. Lt Col E.W. MONTGOMERIE M.C. (Norfolk Regt.) moved on 14th to take temporary command during absence on sick leave of Lt Col WALTON M.C.	
	22nd		(Sunday) Batt. took part in Fête at JARDIN des PLANTES.	
	23rd to 30th		Work on Tactical Exercise and new camp continued. Lt Col F WALTON M.C. returned on 28th.	

J. Sackson Lt Col.
Comdg. 6th Bn. Durh. L.I.

D. D. & L., London, E.C.
(A10460) W.t W.5100/P.713 750,000 2/18 **Sch. 52** Forms/C2118/6.

6th Bn. The Durham L.I.

WAR DIARY.

OCTOBER 1918.

WAR DIARY
or
INTELLIGENCE SUMMARY.

(Erase heading not required.)

Instructions regarding War Diaries and Intelligence
Summaries are contained in F. S. Regs., Part II.
and the Staff Manual respectively. Title pages
will be prepared in manuscript.

Place	Date	Hour	Summary of Events and Information	Remarks and references to Appendices
ROUEN	1/10/18		Officers engaged on preparation of Justice Bennaux, whil were carried out with Regiment & Officers on two days a week. Remainder of hds battalions on working parties on road camp.	
	5/10/18		As above. In the absence on special leave of Lt Col Watkins, Lt Col S.W. Montgomery mc (Norfolk	
	6/10/18		Regt) assumed command	
	8/10/18		As above. Lt Col Watkins mc commanding	
	8/10/18			
	10/10/18		As above. Lt Col Watkins mc left & 19th Bat: & assume command of 18th Bn Devils & Surrey	
	30/10/18		Capt WTE Bedrock in command	
	31/10/18		As above. Major A.L. MacMillan TD /5th Seaforth Highlanders) assumed command	

Williamson, Major
Cmdg 6th Bn Devl L.I.

(A10660) W: W5300/713. 250,000 2/15 Sch. 52 Forms/C218/10.

D. D. & L. London, E.C.

6th BN THE DURHAM LIGHT INFANTRY.

WAR DIARY.

NOVEMBER, 1918.

Army Form C. 2118.

WAR DIARY

or

INTELLIGENCE SUMMARY.

(Erase heading not required.)

Instructions regarding War Diaries and Intelligence Summaries are contained in F. S. Regs., Part II. and the Staff Manual respectively. Title pages will be prepared in manuscript.

Place	Date	Hour	Summary of Events and Information	Remarks and references to Appendices
ROUEN	1/11/18		Bttn: Cadre continued work on new wing & indents of Equipment & Stores	
	5/11/18			
	6/11/18		Bttn: demobilised & personnel despatched to Base.	

J. McMenemie, *Major*
Comg 6th Bn Dorset R.

D. D. & I., London, E.C.
(A10266) W† W5300/P713 250,000 2/18 Sch. 59 Forms/C2118/16.

7TH BN DURHAM LT. INFY.

APR - NOV 1915

50
TO DIV TROONS

Battn. disembarked
Boulogne from
England 19.4.15.

WAR
DIARY

7th BATTN. THE DURHAM LIGHT INFANTRY.

APRIL AND MAY

(19.4.15-31.5.15)

1 9 1 5

Army Form C. 2118.

WAR DIARY

or

INTELLIGENCE SUMMARY.

(Erase heading not required.)

Instructions regarding War Diaries and Intelligence Summaries are contained in F. S. Regs., Part II. and the Staff Manual respectively. Title pages will be prepared in manuscript.

Place	Date	Hour	Summary of Events and Information	Remarks and references to Appendices
Gateshead	19.4.15	9.20 / 9.50 a.m.	Battn. entrained at Gateshead. 3 officers and 86 other ranks left on 14¾, arrived at Boulogne that night stayed in rest camp and left by train at 5.10pm 20.4.15	RB
Boulogne			for BAVINCHOVE near CASSEL, billeted in village that night and kept 21.4.15 in	
ARNINCHOVE	20.4			
RYVELD	21.4		billeting area RYVELD - troops settled in early and quickly. weather fine some showers - water scarce in district, carts employed. drill & troops good	RB
"	22.4.		Medical inspection - arms orders & discipline read out to coys. all ranks warned by O.C. coys. to take special care of arms. S.A.A & equipment & iron rations where ration bags carried, contrary to orders received in this matter.	RB
KAMERTINGHE	23		Went into billets at KAMERTINGHE	RB.
"	24		Marched to the Chateau at POTIJZE via YPRES. The Battalion were under shell fire during this move. The Battalion bivouaced for the night in the Chateau grounds.	RB.
VERLORENHOEK	25		The Battalion rested during the day. At dusk the Battalion marched via the horn to VERLORENHOEK and bivouaced on the South side of road at that place	RB.

1577 Wt. W10791/1773 500,000 1/15 D. D. & L. A.D.S.S./Forms/C. 2118.

WAR DIARY
or
INTELLIGENCE SUMMARY.

(Erase heading not required.)

Instructions regarding War Diaries and Intelligence Summaries are contained in F. S. Regs., Part II. and the Staff Manual respectively. Title pages will be prepared in manuscript.

Place	Date	Hour	Summary of Events and Information	Remarks and references to Appendices
VERLOREN HOEK	26 & 27		At 2 p.m. the Battalion advanced towards ZEVENKOTE & GRAVENSTAFEL (the same under the command of the Brigadier). Brigade orders the Battalion to take up a position ← 21–22 D/? Reg. Belgium Sheet 28). The Battalion suffered considerably in the advance through heavy shell fire and on arriving at the ridges themselves (in this way, about 3 p.m. the Battalion was ordered to retire (by a strong order) which it did and proceeded to VERLOREN HOEK. He advanced rested here — many were made in good order, and much behind deliberately.	
	28 —		The Battalion was engaged each evening in digging near the first line trenches and doing other fatigue work, also the troops occupying the first line — N.E. of FREZENBERG.	
VERLOREN HOEK & YPRES	28 — 2nd 3rd		Left VERLOREN HOEK to go into huts near YPRES. Left huts and marched to WATOU (about 12 miles), arriving there at	

1577 Wt. W10791/1773 500,000 1/15 D. D. & L.   A.D.S.S./Forms/C. 2118.

Army Form C. 2118.

WAR DIARY

or

INTELLIGENCE SUMMARY.

(Erase heading not required.)

Instructions regarding War Diaries and Intelligence Summaries are contained in F.S. Regs., Part II. and the Staff Manual respectively. Title pages will be prepared in manuscript.

Place	Date	Hour	Summary of Events and Information	Remarks and references to Appendices
WATOU	4th.	1	about 1.30 a.m. on May 4th the Battalion went into Billets line. The men were somewhat footsore but were in excellent spirits.	R.S.
"	5th	1	Sir John French addressed the Battalion, said that they had done fine work.	R.S.
"	6th	1	Battalion had short Route Marches.	
"	7th	1	The ..... Recruits taken as regards route which was reported by N.O. to be improved	R.S.S.
BRANDHOEK	8th	1	Left WATOU and marched to BRANDHOEK and went into Bivouac in the woods there.	
"	9th	1	Remained in the woods at BRANDHOEK. Enemy aeroplane very active. Street ..... were take to conceal the men	
"	10th	1	Remained in woods at BRANDHOEK.	
ZILLEBEKE	11th.	1	Left BRANDHOEK woods about 2.30 p.m. and marched by a very circuitous rate to ZILLEBEKE and were issued and A.R.E. Officer met the G.O. This officer indicated a line of trench which had to be ..... out the Battalion was distributed along this line. The work was started and was discontinue at 2.30 a.m. (The men had been digging	R.S.S.

1577 Wt. W.12791/1773 500,000 1/15 D. D. & L. A.D.S.S./Forms/C. 2118.

Army Form C. 2118.

WAR DIARY
or
INTELLIGENCE SUMMARY.
(Erase heading not required.)

Instructions regarding War Diaries and Intelligence
Summaries are contained in F. S. Regs., Part II.
and the Staff Manual respectively. Title pages
will be prepared in manuscript.

Place	Date	Hour	Summary of Events and Information	Remarks and references to Appendices
ZILLEBEKE	11th	—	For 5½ hrs) and the Battalion went into the "G.H.Q. Line". This was a second line of trenches E. of YPRES.	R.S.S.
"	12th	—	The Battalion remained in the G.H.Q. line. We were heavily shelled all day and lost 12 men and an officer.	R.S.S.
"	13th	—	A digging party of 500 men was furnished. This party was working until the 9 in. Field boy. R.E. and dug another line of trench about 50 yards E. of the "G.H.Q. Line". The Battalion remained in the G.H.Q. line.	R.S.S.
"	14th	—	A digging party of 800 men was furnished to the 3rd field boy. R.E. They were occupied in straightening and tableting the line of trench dug the previous being The Battalion remained in the "G.H.Q. Line." We were in reserve to Gen. Kavanagh's Cavalry Division & Cavalry commands was to see the ground they would have to advance over in the event of the Battalion being required to make a counter attack.	Ill.
"	15th	—	The Battalion remained in the "G.H.Q. line" & was still in reserve to Gen Kavanagh's Cavalry Division.	Ill.

1577 Wt. W10791/1773 500,000 1/15 D.D. & L. A.D.S.S./Forms/C. 2118.

Army Form C. 2118.

WAR DIARY
or
INTELLIGENCE SUMMARY.

(Erase heading not required.)

Instructions regarding War Diaries and Intelligence Summaries are contained in F. S. Regs., Part II. and the Staff Manual respectively. Title pages will be prepared in manuscript.

Place	Date	Hour	Summary of Events and Information	Remarks and references to Appendices
ZILLEBEKE	17th	—	The Battalion remained in the "C.H.Q. line". A Digging Party of 450 men was furnished the 3rd Fields for R.E. This Party was employed in extending & deepening the trenches 60x in front of the G.H.Q. line just South of the MENIN road.	RR3
BRIELEN	18th	—	The Battalion arrived in the huts at BRIELEN about 4 a.m. (after flag ?)	ESS
"	18th	—	The Battalion remained in these huts. A Digging Party of 400 men was provided to the 3rd Field Coy. R.E. This Party was employed in improving the "C.H.Q. line" near POTIJZE.	
"	19th	—	The Battalion remained in these huts. A Digging Party of two men was furnished to the 3rd field Coy R.E. This Party dug a new line at THE ZILLEBEKE switch.	
"	20th	—	The Battalion remained in these huts. A Digging Party of 250 men was furnished to the 3rd R.E. Coy. This Party was employed in improving the line dug the previous evening.	RR3
RMT		—	The Battalion moved from the huts to the first line trenches.	

1577 Wt. W10791/1773   500,000 1/15   D. D. & L.   A.D.S.S./Forms/C. 2118.

WAR DIARY

or

INTELLIGENCE SUMMARY.

(Erase heading not required.)

Instructions regarding War Diaries and Intelligence Summaries are contained in F. S. Regs., Part II. and the Staff Manual respectively. Title pages will be prepared in manuscript.

Place	Date	Hour	Summary of Events and Information	Remarks and references to Appendices
YPRES	21st.	—	A 7 & 6 boys were attacked the 3 Royal Fusiliers (85th Brigade). The Battalion less two boys, was attached to the 3 Middlesex Regt (8th Brigade). A 7 & 6 boys were split up among these Royal Fusiliers. The Battalion (less two boys) took over a section of the line and relieved the 20th Hussars.	RCC.
"	22nd.	—	The Battalion remained in the trenches as above. C & D boys & the Machine Gun Section — why has never been in the front trenches before — adapted themselves to the circumstances splendidly.	RBB.
"	23rd.	—	The Battalion, less A & B boys, was withdrawn to YPRES (GRIELEN). At B boys' remained with 3 Royal Fusiliers in the front line east of YPRES. This	MSS.
"	24th 8am	—	was followed up, attacked by the battalion, being surrounded of the 3 Royal Fusiliers, with [ ] was our A & B boys, were [ ] to Royal Fusiliers to retire to a second line & a strong Infantry assault. The [ ] were orders to [ ] from [ ] (as [ ]) to men of the B boys. Behaved in the most valiant manner.	RBB.

1577 Wt. W10791/1773 500,000 1/15 D. D. & L. A.D.S.S./Forms/C, 2118.

Army Form C. 2118.

WAR DIARY

or

INTELLIGENCE SUMMARY.

(Erase heading not required.)

Instructions regarding War Diaries and Intelligence Summaries are contained in F.S. Regs., Part II and the Staff Manual respectively. Title pages will be prepared in manuscript.

Place	Date	Hour	Summary of Events and Information	Remarks and references to Appendices
YPRES	2nd	—	The Bn. had 2 or 3 days rest in the huts when the gas attack was first noticed. The steam roused the Battalion & preparations were at once made	MB3.
"		a.m	Gitten, the men were preparing by degree the gas.	
"			The Bn. (less 2 or 3 huts) left the huts at 9. a.m — minding the YPRES which were being Heavily Shelled — also moving to the G.H.Q line.	ff3.
POTIJZE	2nd	—	The Bn. was with the grits of the 50th Brigade	MB3.
"			The Battalion remained in the G.H.Q line. The men who were left	
"			from Ar 16 days returned at 9. p.m. They had attacked themselves	
"			to other units during the fighting	
"	26th	—	The Battalion left the G.H.Q line and bivouaced in a field	MB3.
"				
"	27th	—	The Bn. moved into huts at BRIELEN.	
BRIELEN	27th	—	The Battalion remained in bivouac as above.	MB3.
"	28th	—	The Battalion moved into the huts.	
"	29th	—	The Battalion remained in the huts.	
"	30th	—	The Battalion remained in the huts.	
"	3rd	—	The Battalion remained in the huts. The Brigadier (Gen. Martin) (the Battalion remained in the huts)	MB3.

1577 Wt. W10791/1773 500,000 1/15 D. D. & L.   A.D.S.S./Forms/C. 2118.

Army Form C. 2118.

WAR DIARY

or

INTELLIGENCE SUMMARY.

(Erase heading not required.)

Instructions regarding War Diaries and Intelligence Summaries are contained in F. S. Regs., Part II. and the Staff Manual respectively. Title pages will be prepared in manuscript.

Place	Date	Hour	Summary of Events and Information	Remarks and references to Appendices
BRELEN	contd	—	inspected the Battalion. He expressed himself as thoroughly satisfied with the state of the Arms, & everything else.	L.M.B.

1577 Wt. W10791/1773 500,000 1/15 D. D. & L.   A.D.S.S./Forms/C. 2118.

WAR
DIARY

7th BATTN. THE DURHAM LIGHT INFANTRY.

J U N E

1915

Army Form C. 2118.

WAR DIARY
or
INTELLIGENCE SUMMARY.
(Erase heading not required.)

Instructions regarding War Diaries and Intelligence
Summaries are contained in F. S. Regs., Part II.
and the Staff Manual respectively. Title pages
will be prepared in manuscript.

2

Place	Date	Hour	Summary of Events and Information	Remarks and references to Appendices
POPERINGHE	1st.	—	Left huts and marched to POPERINGHE, where we went into billets.	—
"	2nd.	—	In billets as above. Coys had that route March. The Battalion Bomb Throwers (36 in number) had some practice with live bombs	—
"	3rd.	—	In billets at POPERINGHE.	—
OUDERDOM	4th.	—	Marched to area one mile N.E. OUDERDOM where we went into bivouacs.	—
"	5th.	—	In bivouacs as above.	
YPRES	6th.	—	Left above bivouacs and went into dugouts 1½ miles W.S.W. of YPRES. The Battalion was in support to the 150th Brigade who were occupying the first line trenches.	—
"	7th.	—	In dugouts as above. All Officers reconnoitred the approach to the trenches.	—
"	8th.	—	In dugouts as above.	
OUDERDOM	9th.	—	Relieved by 9th D.L.I. and went back to huts near OUDERDOM.	
"	10th.	—	In huts as above. Six Officers & 50 selected N.C.Os. went to the first line trenches which the Battalion was to take over on 12/6/15	—
"	11th	—	In huts as above. C.O. & Adjutant visited the trenches	—

1577   Wt. W10791/1773   500,000   1/15   D. D. & L.   A.D.S.S./Forms/C. 2118.

WAR DIARY

or

INTELLIGENCE SUMMARY.

(Erase heading not required.)

Instructions regarding War Diaries and Intelligence Summaries are contained in F. S. Regs., Part II and the Staff Manual respectively. Title pages will be prepared in manuscript.

Place	Date	Hour	Summary of Events and Information	Remarks and references to Appendices
OUDERDOM YPRES	11th	—	which the Battalion came to take over 12/6. 15.	App.
	12th	—	Relieves the 4th Yorks Battalion who were in trenches two miles S.E. of YPRES near SANCTUARY WOOD. The relief was carried	App.3
	"	1	out quietly & well.	
	13th	—	In trenches as above. Men worked hard in improving the parapets & dugouts.	
	14th	—	In trenches as above.	
	15th	—	In trenches as above. The Ground	App.6
	16th	—	In trenches as above. The 3rd Division attacked the enemy's trenches on BELLEVARDE RIDGE about a mile to our left not to our own.	
			The Co-operated by bursts of rapid fire.	
			A Rifle Battery bringing fire to bear on the enemy's support trenches was obstructed about 100x in rear of their line	App.
YPRES	17th	—	Relieved by 5th Yorks. & moved into dugouts in SANCTUARY WOOD — in support to 5th Yorks.	
"	18th	—	In support to 5th Yorks. Was above. Furnished a digging	App.

WAR DIARY

or

INTELLIGENCE SUMMARY.

(*Erase heading not required.*)

Instructions regarding War Diaries and Intelligence
Summaries are contained in F. S. Regs., Part II.
and the Staff Manual respectively. Title pages
will be prepared in manuscript.

Place	Date	Hour	Summary of Events and Information	Remarks and references to Appendices
YPRES	18th	—	Working party to 5th Yorks for digging a new communication trench immediately in rear of the full fire trench.	Rbb
"	19th	—	In support to 5th Yorks as above. A working party of 350 men was furnished to complete the communication trench dug by the previous night.	Rbb
"	20th	—	Relieved by 4th Yorks & went into dugouts 1½ miles N.S.W. of YPRES	
CHATEAU & DRANOUTRE	2nd	—	Marched to huts N.E. of DRANOUTRE	Rbb
DRANOUTRE	3rd	—	Moved (with 149th Infty Brigade) to DRANOUTRE where we went into huts. In the evening two Coys went into supporting.	Rbb
"		—	Began to relieve the troops occupied by 5th D.L.I.	
"	23rd	—	The above Battalion. The two Coys remained in huts at DRANOUTRE.	
"	24th	—	As above.	
KEMMEL	25th	—	Battalion less two Coys moved to close billets near KEMMEL. Machine Gund were sent up to the trenches with 9th D.L.I.	Rbb
"	26th	—	In billets as above.	

Army Form C. 2118.

WAR DIARY

or

INTELLIGENCE SUMMARY.

(Erase heading not required.)

Instructions regarding War Diaries and Intelligence Summaries are contained in F. S. Regs., Part II. and the Staff Manual respectively. Title pages will be prepared in manuscript.

Place	Date	Hour	Summary of Events and Information	Remarks and references to Appendices
KEMMEL	27th	—	Relieved 6/8th D.L.I. in first line trenches. Relief began at dusk and took two hours.	E.M.B.
"	28th	—	In trenches as above. A considerable amount of work was done in registering the fronts. Enemy in front of our sector very quiet.	M.B.
"	29th	—	In trenches as above.	C.B.G.
"	30th	—	In trenches as above. A draft of 160 men arrived and was allotted to companies.	

R.B. Bradford

Captain & Adjutant
7th Bn. Durham Light Infantry

1577 Wt. W10791/1773 500,000 1/15 D. D. & L. A.D.S.S./Forms/C. 2118.

7th BATTN. THE DURHAM LIGHT INFANTRY.

J U L Y

1 9 1 5

Army Form C. 2118.

WAR DIARY
or
INTELLIGENCE SUMMARY.

(Erase heading not required.)

Instructions regarding War Diaries and Intelligence Summaries are contained in F. S. Regs., Part II. and the Staff Manual respectively. Title pages will be prepared in manuscript.

B

Place	Date	Hour	Summary of Events and Information	Remarks and references to Appendices
KEMMEL	1st	—	In trenches as above	WDB
”	2nd	—	In trenches as above	
”	3rd	—	Relieved by 6/8th Durham Light Infantry, and went into Bivouacs East of KEMMEL (above)	RWB
”	4th	—	In Bivouacs as above. Five parties of 50 men and 1 officer were furnished to R.E. for work on Supporting Points.	
”	5th	—	In Bivouacs as above.	
”	6th	—	In Bivouac as above. Furnished six parties of 50 men and 1 officer, just in rear of front line trench.	R.E.
”	7th	—	In Bivouac as above. Furnished seven parties of 50 men + officer	
”	8th	—	For work on new track in rear of front line trench. Furnished six parties of 50 men +	R.E.
”	9th	—	For Bivouacs as above. Furnished slsix parties of 50 men + officer for work on new track in rear of front line trench.	
”	10th	—	Relieved 6/8th Dh. L.I. in the trenches.	Rbs
”	11th	—	In trenches as above.	
		—	In trenches as above.	

1577 Wt. W10791/1773 500,000 1/15 D. D. & L. A.D.S.S./Forms/C. 2118.

Army Form C. 2118.

14

WAR DIARY

or

INTELLIGENCE SUMMARY.

(Erase heading not required.)

Instructions regarding War Diaries and Intelligence Summaries are contained in F.S. Regs., Part II. and the Staff Manual respectively. Title pages will be prepared in manuscript.

Place	Date	Hour	Summary of Events and Information	Remarks and references to Appendices
KEMMEL	12th	—	In trenches as above. Lord Bruce - G.O.C. 5th. Division - visited the trenches.	RBB.
"	13th.	—	In trenches as above. Enemy shewed great activity. A/O Lys &c. uncle + boys etc. were heavily bombarded throughout the day. We replied by firing rifle grenades, but had not enough to seriously economise enemy.	CBS.
"	14th	—	In trenches as above. Enemy exploded a large mine about 100' to our left, at the same time having rapid fire in our trenches for about 10 minutes. Believed they the Welsh Regt., and proceeded to LOCRE	RBB.
LOCRE	15th	—	Left LOCRE at 8.30 p.m. and marched to PONT DE NIEPPE	CBS.
"	16th	—	where we went into billets.	
PONT DE NIEPPE; NIEPPE; ARMENTIERES	17th.	—	Left PONT DE NIEPPE at 5 p.m. and marched to ARMENTIERES where we went into billets.	
"	18th	—	In Billets as above.	
"	19th	—	In Billets as above. The Brig. General visited the billets.	CBS.

1577 Wt. W10791/1773 500,000 1/15 D. D. & L. A.D.S.S./Forms/C. 2118.

WAR DIARY

or

INTELLIGENCE SUMMARY.

(Erase heading not required.)

Instructions regarding War Diaries and Intelligence Summaries are contained in F.S. Regs., Part II. and the Staff Manual respectively. Title pages will be prepared in manuscript.

Place	Date	Hour	Summary of Events and Information	Remarks and references to Appendices
ARMENTIÈRES	20th.	—	In Billets as above. A Platoon from each Company fired 30 rounds on the 30 yard Range.	Ekk
"	21st.	—	In Billets as above. The Brig. General inspected the Billets.	
"	22nd.	—	In Billets as above. Two Companies (C + B) went into the Reserve Trenches and became attached to 6/9th D.L.I.	ASB
"	23d.	—	In Billets as above.	
"	24th.	—	Relieved the 6/9th D.L.I. in the trenches. Relief was completed about midnight.	
"	25th.	—	In Trenches as above. Everything was quiet.	ELL
"	26th.	—	In Trenches as above. The G.O.C. — 2nd Army — visited the Trenches.	
"	27th.	—	In Trenches as above.	
"	28th.	—	In Trenches as above.	
"	29th.	—	In Trenches as above.	NN6
"	30th.	—	In Trenches as above. Capt. Hunt was appointed Intelligence Officer for the Battalion. His duties are to collect all information and send it to the Brigade by 12 noon daily.	ELL

1577 Wt. W10791/1773 500,000 1/15 D. D. & L. A.D.S.S./Forms/C. 2118.

WAR DIARY

or

INTELLIGENCE SUMMARY.

(*Erase heading not required.*)

Instructions regarding War Diaries and Intelligence Summaries are contained in F. S. Regs., Part II. and the Staff Manual respectively. Title pages will be prepared in manuscript.

Place	Date	Hour	Summary of Events and Information	Remarks and references to Appendices
ARMENTIERES	3rd	—	The C.O. had some of the thrifts house with our colors etc on our the trenches & and some done with cairns. This way one to enable the men to catch hold of the rifles after firing if required for a charge.	R.B.
"	Sat.	—	I thought as usual. Sir Charles Ferguson visited the trenches and was pleased with everything. Lord Plumer - the G.O.C. 5th Division - accompanied him. He expressed his appreciation of the work done by all ranks during the past week.	E.B.

R.B. Bradford.
Capt. & O.C. "C" Coy.

1577 Wt. W10791/1773 500,000 1/15 D. D. & L.   A.D.S.S./Forms/C. 2118.

7th BATTN. THE DURHAM LIGHT INFANTRY.

A U G U S T

1 9 1 5

WAR DIARY

or

INTELLIGENCE SUMMARY.

(Erase heading not required.)

17/

Instructions regarding War Diaries and Intelligence Summaries are contained in F. S. Regs., Part II. and the Staff Manual respectively. Title pages will be prepared in manuscript.

Place	Date	Hour	Summary of Events and Information	Remarks and references to Appendices
Armentières	1st	—	Relieved by the 5th Northumberland Fusiliers and 5th Border Regiment. The relief was complete at 7½ p.m. The Battalion moved to Billets at PONT DE NIEPPE.	RBB
PONT DE NIEPPE	2nd	—	In Billets as above.	RBB
	3rd	—	In Billets as above.	
	4th	—	One Officer and 20 men per Company were selected as Grenadiers and it was arranged for them to parade daily under the Grenadier Officer. Battalion.	RBB
	5th	—	Brigadier inspected the Battalion.	RBB
	6th	—	In Billets as above.	
	7th	—	In Billets as above.	RBB
ARMENT...	8th	—	Moved into Billets ARMENTIÈRES.	RBB
IÈRES	9th	—	In Billets as above. The Officers reconnoitred the subsidiary	
	10th	—	lines in rear of the trenches we are to move into the ARMENTIÈRES Billets. The Battalion Quiet & that sector in front of ARMENTIÈRES. 30 yards Bridge. The Brigadier visited the Billets.	RBB

1577 Wt. W 10791/1773 500,000 1/15 D. D. & L. A.D.S.S./Forms/C. 2118.

WAR DIARY

or

INTELLIGENCE SUMMARY.

(Erase heading not required.)

18.

Instructions regarding War Diaries and Intelligence Summaries are contained in F. S. Regs., Part II. and the Staff Manual respectively. Title pages will be prepared in manuscript.

Place	Date	Hour	Summary of Events and Information	Remarks and references to Appendices
ARMENTIÈRES	11th	—	In Billets as above	RWB
,,	12th	—	In Billets as above.	RWB
,,	13th	—	Relieved the 5th Loyal North Lancs. kept in the trenches. The new completer at 11 a.m.	
,,	14th	—	In trenches as above.	
,,	15th	—	In trenches as above.	
,,	16th	—	In trenches as above.	RWB
,,	17th	—	In trenches as above.	
,,	18th	—	In trenches as above.	
,,	19th	—	Relieved by 4th & 5th Northumberland Fusiliers. Moves to billets in ARMENTIÈRES.	RWB. Kirk
,,	20th	—	In billets as above.	
,,	21st	—	In billets as above. Brig. Gr. inspected the billets.	
,,	22nd	—	In billets as above.	
,,	23rd	—	In billets as above.	
,,	24th	—	In billets as above.	

1577 Wt. W10791/1773 500,000 1/15 D. D. & L. A.D.S.S./Forms/C. 2118.

WAR DIARY

or

INTELLIGENCE SUMMARY.

(*Erase heading not required.*)

Instructions regarding War Diaries and Intelligence
Summaries are contained in F. S. Regs., Part II.
and the Staff Manual respectively. Title pages
will be prepared in manuscript.

19

Place	Date	Hour	Summary of Events and Information	Remarks and references to Appendices
ARMENTIÈRES	25th	—	In billets as above.	RHB
"	26th	—	Relieved the 8th. Yorks. in the trenches. The relief was completed at 8.45 p.m.	RHB
"	27th	—	In trenches as above.	RHB
"	28th	—	In trenches as above. G.-O.-C. Division visited the trenches.	RHB
"	29th	—	In trenches as above.	
"	30th	—	In trenches as above.	
"	31st	—	Relieved by 9th Durham Light Infantry & moved into billets at Armentières.	RHB

R H Bradford

7th BATTN. THE DURHAM LIGHT INFANTRY.

S E P T E M B E R

1 9 1 5

Army Form C. 2118.

WAR DIARY

or

INTELLIGENCE SUMMARY.

(Erase heading not required.)

20.

September

Instructions regarding War Diaries and Intelligence Summaries are contained in F. S. Regs., Part II. and the Staff Manual respectively. Title pages will be prepared in manuscript.

Place	Date	Hour	Summary of Events and Information	Remarks and references to Appendices
ARMENTIÈRES	2nd.	—	In Billets as above	PBB
	2nd.	—	In Billets as above a lecture was given to N.C.Os of the Battalion on "Flies".	
	3rd.	—	In Billets as above.	
	4th.	—	In Billets as above. The practises getting up to support line assuming that our front line was attacked. The C.O. & Adjutant they	HBB
	5th.	—	In Billets as above. Sent up two hundred men at 8.30 p. m. to work on subsidiary line under R.E.	HBB
	6th.	—	In Billets as above	
	7th.	—	In Billets as above.	
	8th.	—	In Billets as above. The G.O.C. 50th Division inspected the Battalion's Standing Order.	BB
	9th.	—	In Billets as above Companies went for route Marches of 6 miles	BB
	10th.	—	In Billets as above	

1577   Wt. W10791/1773   500,000   1/15   D. D. & L.   A.D.S.S./Forms/C. 2118.

WAR DIARY
or
INTELLIGENCE SUMMARY.

(Erase heading not required.)

Army Form C. 2118.

2/-

Sept. 15.

Instructions regarding War Diaries and Intelligence Summaries are contained in F. S. Regs., Part II. and the Staff Manual respectively. Title pages will be prepared in manuscript.

Place	Date	Hour	Summary of Events and Information	Remarks and references to Appendices
ARMENTIÈRES	16th	—	In Billets as above.	AB
		—	In Billets as above. Relieved the 5th Yorks. in the trenches. The relief was completed at 9 a.m.	
	18th	—	In trenches as above. The Germans turned some liquid into their parapet which ignited the grass. The fire turned rapidly towards our obstacle but before it reached it its own fortunately relief to South West the fire stopped advance.	AB
		—	In trenches as above. Our line was heavily shelled by enemy.	AB
		—	In trenches as above. Four officers from the New Army were attached to us for the day. They were very fit.	RAB
		—	In trenches as above during the morning.	
	17th	—	In trenches as above.	
	18th	—	In trenches as above.	
	19th	—	In trenches as above. Relieved by the 5th. Loyal North Lancs. and moved to billets in ARMENTIÈRES. The relief was complete.	AB

1577 Wt. W10791/1773 500,000 1/15 D. D. & L. A.D.S.S./Forms/C. 2118.

WAR DIARY

or

INTELLIGENCE SUMMARY.

(Erase heading not required.)

Instructions regarding War Diaries and Intelligence Summaries are contained in F. S. Regs., Part II. and the Staff Manual respectively. Title pages will be prepared in manuscript.

Place	Date	Hour	Summary of Events and Information	Remarks and references to Appendices
ARMENTIÈRES	19th.	—	at 9 p.m.	RHS
"	20th.	—	In Billets as above. Furnished a Working Party of nine Officers 400 men total. Furnished by R.E. for work in Subsidiary Line.	
"	21st.	—	In Billets as above.	CHR
"	22nd.	—	In Billets as above. Furnished a Working Party of nine Officers and 450 men for work in Subsidiary Line	
"	23rd.	—	In Billets as above	RHS
"	24th.	—	In Billets as above. The Brigade was Army Corps Reserve. We had to remain in Billets and be ready to move at short notice.	
"	25th.	—	In Billets as above.	
"	26th.	—	In Billets as above. Relieved the 7th. Royal Sussex in trenches N.E. of HOUPLINES. The relief was completed at 9 p.m.	RHS
HOUPLINES	27th.	—	In trenches as above. A particularly quiet day	
"	28th.	—	In trenches as above. Great attention was paid to improving the damage. Our Patrols got right up to enemy's wire but could not detect anything of value	RHS

1577 Wt. W10791/1773 500,000 1/15 D. D. & L.   A.D.S.S./Forms/C. 2118.

WAR DIARY

or

INTELLIGENCE SUMMARY.

(Erase heading not required.)

Instructions regarding War Diaries and Intelligence
Summaries are contained in F. S. Regs., Part II.
and the Staff Manual respectively. Title pages
will be prepared in manuscript.

Place	Date	Hour	Summary of Events and Information	Remarks and references to Appendices
HOUPLINES	29th	—	In trenches as above. Sgt. Speight and Sgt. White crept up a ditch and reached the enemy wire entanglement. They brought back a piece of wire from it. Our Snipers were very active and broke [Your enemy [sniper?] principles.]	WBB.
▲	30th	—	In trenches as above. Every effort was made by energetic patrolling to obtain information about the enemy, but the enemy opposite us at present evidently do very little patrolling & but little we are extra [ordinarily cheerful]. The weather has [set in] very cold.	WBB.

1577 Wt. W10791/1773 500,000 1/15 D. D. & L. A.D.S.S./Forms/C. 2118.

7th BATTN. THE DURHAM LIGHT INFANTRY.

O C T O B E R

1 9 1 5

Instructions regarding War Diaries and Intelligence
Summaries are contained in F. S. Regs., Part II.
and the Staff Manual respectively. Title pages
will be prepared in manuscript.

24. ___

October 1915.

Place	Date	Hour	Summary of Events and Information	Remarks and references to Appendices
HOULPLINES REST	1st	—	In trenches as above.	RBB
"	2nd	—	In trenches as above. Our patrols acted with great energy and obtained some very useful information. The enemy evidently patrol very little.	RBB
"	3rd.	—	In trenches as above. Sgt. Birchall & Sgt. Thompson crept up a ditch and approached to about 10 yards from enemy's wire. They obtained some valuable information regarding the enemy's defences.	MB
"	4th	—	In trenches as above. Hostile patrols are still conspicuous by their absence, and our patrols have been up to the German wire at several points and have thoroughly reconnoitred it without attracting the enemy's attention.	RBB
"	5th.	—	In trenches as above.	
"	6th.	—	In trenches as above.	
"	7th.	—	In trenches as above.	
"	8th	—	Relieved by the 9 D.L.I. The relief was completed about 7.30 p.m.	GHB

1577   Wt. W10791/1773   500,000   1/15   D. D. & L.   A.D.S.S./Forms/C. 2118.

WAR DIARY

or

INTELLIGENCE SUMMARY.

(Erase heading not required.)

Instructions regarding War Diaries and Intelligence
Summaries are contained in F. S. Regs., Part II.
and the Staff Manual respectively. Title pages
will be prepared in manuscript.

Oct. 1915

Place	Date	Hour	Summary of Events and Information	Remarks and references to Appendices
ARMENTIÈRES	8th.	—	The Battalion returned to Billets in Armentières.	MR
"	9th.	—	In billets as above.	
"	10th.	—	In Billets as above. A&B Companies went for a six mile Route March. The men marched very well.	
"	11th.	—	In Billets as above. C & D Companies went for a six mile Route March. The men marched very well.	MR
"	12th.	—	In Billets as above. The Company bombs (36 pr. coy) threw live grenades at the Bomb School.	VRR
"	13th.	—	In billets as above.	
"	14th.	—	Relieved the 6 D.L.I. in the trenches N.E. of Houplines.	
HOUPLINES	15th.	—	In trenches as above. The enemy on our front are very quiet.	
"	16th.	—	In trenches as above. Three Platoons of the 1st Northumberland R.W.S Fusiliers were attached to the Battalion for instruction.	RWS
"	17th.	—	In trenches as above. Our patrols were out all night at various points of the front but were unable to get into touch with the enemy who confine his activity to working parties.	MR

1577 Wt.W10791/1773 500,000 1/15 D. D. & L. A.D.S.S./Forms/C. 2118.

WAR DIARY

or

INTELLIGENCE SUMMARY.

(Erase heading not required.)

Army Form C. 2118.

Instructions regarding War Diaries and Intelligence Summaries are contained in F. S. Regs., Part II. and the Staff Manual respectively. Title pages will be prepared in manuscript.

Oct. 1915.

Place	Date	Hour	Summary of Events and Information	Remarks and references to Appendices
HOUPLINES	18th	—	In trenches as above. Scout patrolling work has been done by all our companies and much useful information has been obtained.	R.B.B.
"	19th	—	In trenches as above. The Brigadier sent a special message to the Battalion expressing his appreciation of the high standard of work done during the time in the trenches.	Ldt.
"	20th	—	In trenches as above.	
"	21st	—	In trenches as above.	Ldt.
"	22nd	—	In trenches as above. Sir Charles Ferguson visited the trenches.	
ARMENTIÈRES	23rd	—	Relieved by the 9th D.L.I., and moved to billets in ARMENTIÈRES.	L.B.B.
"	24th	—	In billets as above.	
"	25th	—	In billets as above. 4 or 5 companies went for a route march of 6 miles.	
HOUPLINES	26th	—	Relieved the 6 D.L.I. in the trenches. The relief was completed at 6.8 p.m.	
"	27th	—	In trenches as above. 2Lt. W.F. Laing and a party Thomson were detailed to form part of a bombing men from the Battalion	

1577 Wt. W10791/1773 500,000 1/15 D. D. & L.   A.D.S.S./Forms/C. 2118.

WAR DIARY

or

INTELLIGENCE SUMMARY.

(Erase heading not required.)

Instructions regarding War Diaries and Intelligence
Summaries are contained in F.S. Regs., Part II.
and the Staff Manual respectively. Title pages
will be prepared in manuscript.

2/

Oct. 1915.

Place	Date	Hour	Summary of Events and Information	Remarks and references to Appendices
HOUPLINES.	27th.		Battalion formed from the 50th. Division. This Battalion, which was commanded by Lt. Col. Vaux D.S.O. was inspected at BAILLEUL by His Majesty King George V	Rbk.
″	28th.		In trenches as above. Our Patrols acted with great energy but were unable to secure any hostile patrols although much useful information was gained.	Rbk.
″	29th.		In trenches as above. Six Platoons of the 8th. Somersets were attached to the Battalion for instruction.	Rstr.
″	30th.		In trenches as above.	Rstr.
″	31st.		In trenches as above. A Draft of 25 men came to the Battalion from the 3rd. line R.C.L.	Rstr.

R.M.Bradford.
Capt
Comdg. 7/D.L.I.

151st Inf.Bde.
50th Div.

Battn. became
Pioneers 50th
Division 16.11.15.

7th BATTN. THE DURHAM LIGHT INFANTRY.

N O V E M B E R

1 9 1 5

WAR DIARY
or
INTELLIGENCE SUMMARY.

(Erase heading not required.)

Instructions regarding War Diaries and Intelligence Summaries are contained in F. S. Regs., Part II and the Staff Manual respectively. Title pages will be prepared in manuscript.

November 1915.

Place	Date	Hour	Summary of Events and Information	Remarks and references to Appendices
ARMPLINES	1st.	—	In trenches as above.	A65
"	2nd.	—	In trenches as above. Very heavy rain fell continuously throughout the day and the parapets & parados of the trenches collapsed in many places.	
"	3rd.	—	In trenches as above.	A66
"	4th.	—	Relieved by the 9th D.L.I. The relief was completed at 6.30pm. The Battalio. returned to Billets in Armentières.	
ARMENTIÈRES	5th.	—	In Billets as above.	A67
"	6th.	—	In billets as above. A working party of 350 men under Major Hunt was sent up to the trenches of the 6th Durham to work on the communication trenches. These were in a bad state owing to the heavy & continuous rain.	
HOUPLINES	7th.	—	Relieved the 6th Durham in the trenches N.E. of Houplines. The relief was completed at 6.45pm. The 9th Durham were on our left, N. Fusiliers on our right.	A68
"	8th.	—	In trenches as above. Our snipers were very active and	A69

1577 Wt. W10791/1773 500,000 1/15 D. D. & L. A.D.S.S./Forms/C. 2118.

Army Form C. 2118.

WAR DIARY
or
INTELLIGENCE SUMMARY.

(Erase heading not required.)

Nov. 1915. #9.

Place	Date	Hour	Summary of Events and Information	Remarks and references to Appendices
HOUPLINES	8th.	—	accounted for four German.	MBB
"	9th.	—	In trenches as above. Six Platoons of the 8th. Lincolnshire were attached to the Battalion.	MBB
"	10th.	—	In trenches as above. The six Platoons of the 8th Lincolnshire returned to their Billets in Armentières.	
"	11th.	—	In trenches as above.	
"	12th.	—	Relieved by 14th D.L.I. The relief was commenced at 6 a.m. and was completed at 7.30 a.m. Returned to Billets in Armentières.	ABB
ARMENTIÈRES BAILLEUL	13th.	—	Marched to Billets near BAILLEUL. The march carried out march (9 miles) in excellent style.	
"	14th.	—	In Billets as above.	
"	15th.	—	In Billets as above.	
"	16th.	—	In Billets as above. The Companies carried out Platoon & Company Drill	MBB
"	17th.	—	In Billets as above.	MBB
"	18th.	—	In Billets as above.	

WAR DIARY

or

INTELLIGENCE SUMMARY.

(*Erase heading not required.*)

Nov, 1915

30

Instructions regarding War Diaries and Intelligence Summaries are contained in F. S. Regs., Part II. and the Staff Manual respectively. Title pages will be prepared in manuscript.

Place	Date	Hour	Summary of Events and Information	Remarks and references to Appendices
BAILLEUL	19th	—	In billets as above.	HH
"	20th	—	In billets as above.	"
"	21st.	—	In billets as above.	"
"	22nd.	—	The Battalion marched past Sir Herbert Plumer.	"
"	"	—	The Battalion commenced training as a Pioneer Battalion. One Company (A) was sent to ARMENTIÈRES for a services attachment to 6th Division R.E.	HH
"	23rd	—	B, C, & D companies practised the attack on an Enemy system of trenches.	"
"	24th.	—	B, C, & D companies carried out Route Marches of 12 miles.	"
"	25th	—	In billets as above.	"
"	26th.	—	In billets as above.	"
"	"	—	B and D Coy carried out Route March of 12 miles A Coy relieved & marched into ARMENTIÈRES	"
"	27th	—	In billets as above. The Battalion (less 1 Coy) practised an Attack on a hostile system of trenches.	HH

1577 Wt. W10791/1773 500,000 1/15 D. D. & L. A.D.S.S./Forms/C. 2118.

WAR DIARY

or

INTELLIGENCE SUMMARY.

(*Erase heading not required.*)

Instructions regarding War Diaries and Intelligence
Summaries are contained in F. S. Regs., Part II.
and the Staff Manual respectively. Title pages
will be prepared in manuscript.

31.

Nov. 19 15

Place	Date	Hour	Summary of Events and Information	Remarks and references to Appendices
BAILLEUL	28th	—	In billets as above. Instruction was given to the men in Revetting, Knotting, Lashing, Slaughter of Battalion Drill.	R.M.
"	29th	—	A, B, & D Coys. carried out Route Marche of 12 miles.	
"	30th	—	In billets as above. The Battalion practised the attack on an enemy system of trenches	

9TH BN DURHAM LT. INFY.

APR 1915-JAN 1918

To 62 DIV TROOPS

Battn. disembarked
Boulogne from
England 20.4.15.

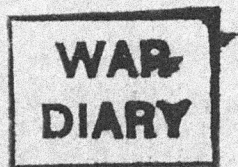

WAR
DIARY

9th BATTN. THE DURHAM LIGHT INFANTRY.

APRIL AND MAY

(20.4.15 - 31.5.15)

1 9 1 5

WAR DIARY

or

INTELLIGENCE SUMMARY.

(Erase heading not required.)

Instructions regarding War Diaries and Intelligence
Summaries are contained in F. S. Regs., Part II.
and the Staff Manual respectively. Title pages
will be prepared in manuscript.

Place	Date	Hour	Summary of Events and Information	Remarks and references to Appendices
BOULOGNE	20.4.15	6 a.m.	arrived Rest Camp. Strength 11. 27 officers 9.N other ranks. Strength of PONT & BELGUE STATION at H 10 pm. 3 officers 75 men 70 horses	X
TERDEGHEM	21.4.15		2.15 proceed. & the Baths. Even on this train arriving from HAVRE. Detrained at ST ALDEGONDE station at 9 am. marched to TERDEGHEM village. Went into billets. H.Q. in village. remainder in neighbouring FARMS. Settled in by firs.	X
do No	22.4.15		ordinary routine in billets at 6 p.m. two aeroscope Ventoon reported tanks and 10 horse dropped tomb. Intrepid troops report himself wished by fire	X
do No	23.4.15		Men from TERSENHEM to HAMMERTINGE strength K 31 officers 1028 other ranks	SM
HAMMERTINGE	24/4/15		Moved to POTIZE arrived at H 1 pm & bivouacked in wood. Killed all night. Cap. H.B. England missing in H-morning. Pt-Graham killed, several horses killed by shell fire.	SM
POTIJZE	25.4.15		At 4 pm moved main force faced Ridge VERLOREN HOEK and retired to high ground again C 24. L. at 2th A Little killed, wounded of other Cpl Porter severe Laund. Ordered Relieve from Rest pasition, sunk sub, faced E × S of VERLORENHOEK	SM.
VERLORENHOEK	26.4.15		to breech by the morrs attacked 1 85th Brigade	Appx
	27.4.15		1 head. Lt Grave wounded (Pilkem Kill) Gr.r 2 off report missing (wounds)	No
	28.4.15		... R.H.Field battery Capt. Pease Ch Thom. wounded. Barton & Worsley missing 2m.r Dodge wounded. Battery later laving alive	Appx
	29.4.15		On train 8 wounded to shell fire	Appx

Army Form C. 2118.

WAR DIARY

or

INTELLIGENCE SUMMARY.

(Erase heading not required.)

Instructions regarding War Diaries and Intelligence Summaries are contained in F. S. Regs., Part II. and the Staff Manual respectively. Title pages will be prepared in manuscript.

Place	Date	Hour	Summary of Events and Information	Remarks and references to Appendices

1577 Wt.W10791/1773 500,000 1/15 D.D.&L.   A.D.S.S./Forms/C. 2118.

Army Form C. 2118.

WAR DIARY
or
INTELLIGENCE SUMMARY.
(Erase heading not required.)

Instructions regarding War Diaries and Intelligence
Summaries are contained in F. S. Regs., Part II.
and the Staff Manual respectively. Title pages
will be prepared in manuscript.

Place	Date	Hour	Summary of Events and Information	Remarks and references to Appendices
G.H.Q. LINES	12/5/15		Heavy shelling all morning. Killed 19, wounded	442
	13/5/15		" " day. Killed 36, wounded. Summoned train	443
	14/5/15		Heavy rain. Digging in front of camp. 8 wounded. Onslow arrived of 8st Battalion	444
	15/5/15		Sir E.W. arrived. Party trenches front to ... Transferred to 6th B. Coy Cav Cmd	445
			into 6 ... of 8st Brigade	
	16/5/15		6th & 8th D.C.O. returned trench. Digging at night to wounded	
			Trench. Digging at night. Total wounded 102. Summer 1 man wounded	446
	17/5/15		Very bad rain. Happy. Arrived 11.30 ... 2 killed 12 wounded	447
	18/5/15		12.10 a.m. Marched off. arrived Les N. of YPRES at 1.30 a.m. past route	448
BRIELEN	19		In two. a few shells falling in field about 500 yds off	
	20		" Guns making party of 40 for trenches. 1 man wounded	449
			Rival Balloon close these shells with high explosives.	
	21st		Moved up to POTIJZE G.H.Q.	450
	22nd		Attached to 88th Brigade — G.H.Q. Cav	1003
	23rd		C.+D. Companies sent up into Front line trenches. 7 wounded	454
	24th		Whit Monday. Trenches gassed at 2.45 a.m. Guns in G.H.Q. lines ...	1008

1577   Wt. W10791/1773   500,000   1/15   D. D. & L.   A.D.S.S./Forms/C. 2118.

Army Form C. 2118.

WAR DIARY

or

INTELLIGENCE SUMMARY.

(Erase heading not required.)

Instructions regarding War Diaries and Intelligence
Summaries are contained in F. S. Regs., Part II.
and the Staff Manual respectively. Title pages
will be prepared in manuscript.

Place	Date	Hour	Summary of Events and Information	Remarks and references to Appendices
G.H.Q. & base *[illegible]*	May 25		For 3 hours Grenadier outposts to 13 hours shelled five from enemy *[illegible]*	
			of 9 a.m. engaged 1 Officer 1 S.A. Other Ranks shrapnel from gun	
			[illegible] E.O. rejoined by Officers at *[illegible]* to Central Area. *[illegible]*	
			[illegible] except Officers Capt heads, H.Mess, to Central Area. 1 wounded *[illegible]* guns	
				P.B.
	26		Quiet day except 2 hours shell fire. 9 wounded. 1 killed	P.B.
	27		Shelling of front & G.H.Q. lines commenced 9 a.m. 4 wounded	P.B.
	28		Quiet day except for Hdy Bangs about 4.30 p.m. 2 killed, 1 wounded	P.B.
			Orders received for relief of B.n from trenches. [Corp Pease Hospital	
			wounded died at midnight	
	29		Arrived in trench near BRANDHOEK 1 accidently wounded.	P.B.
	30		Church service at 11.45. Holy Communion. 12.45	P.B.
	31		Quiet day. Artillery relieving up to *[illegible]* 2 wounded *[illegible]* 7.8 morning shell	P.B.

WAR DIARY

9th BATTN. THE DURHAM LIGHT INFANTRY.

J U N E

1 9 1 5

WAR DIARY

or

INTELLIGENCE SUMMARY. 9/D.L.I.

(Erase heading not required.)

June 1915

Instructions regarding War Diaries and Intelligence Summaries are contained in F. S. Regs., Part II. and the Staff Manual respectively. Title pages will be prepared in manuscript.

Place	Date	Hour	Summary of Events and Information	Remarks and references to Appendices
	1		7 a.m. Rifle Inspection. 7.15 a.m. running off general drill, 10 a.m. Bayonet Fixing. Lectures on stoppages of *Lewis*, dealing with fractures &c. Practising quick adjustment of respirators, 1 Officer & 28 Men on 17 & 16 men sent to Base for front trench working course.	24
	2		7 a.m. Rifle Inspection 7.15 running drill 10 a.m. Respirators & respirators.	25

1577 Wt. W10791/1773 500,000 1/15 D. D. & L.   A.D.S.S./Forms/C. 2118.

(13975) Wt. W2355/F360 600,000 12/7 D. D. & L. Sch 52a. Forms/C2118/13.

WAR DIARY
or
INTELLIGENCE SUMMARY.

(Erase heading not required.)

Instructions regarding War Diaries and Intelligence
Summaries are contained in F. S. Regs., Part II.
and the Staff Manual respectively. Title pages
will be prepared in manuscript.

Place	Date	Hour	Summary of Events and Information	Remarks and references to Appendices
BRANDHOEK	1915 June 2		Reconnaissance from to of — t So of POPERINGHE. 11 a.m. cleared up trenches in mud. 12.30 p.m. Parade ordered for 2 p.t. 3.30 moved off to new billets. Sp. arrived in billets at 7 p.m. Estminet.	46
	3	7 a.m.	Inspection of arms. 7.15 Running shoes. 10 a.m. Remainder of Regiment to go Inspection & Bath for Ron's Baths.	43
	4	5.15 a.m.	Received orders from at 8 — 8 a.m. forward with Brigade to new ground. Arrived 10.30 a.m. relieved Etc — t for a Battalion moved out of Huts when we occupied Room. Shops been transport	44
Huts NE of DODERDOM 5.6.15	5	7 a.m.	Rifle Inspection	45
		7 a.m.	Running Drill	
		10.30	Litting repetition	
		11 a.m.	Inspected by Bde. East & Martin C.O.	
		5.30 p.	Rifle mark.	
	6	7.45	Holy Communion. 10.45 s. Parade for service at 11 a.m. Divine Service	46
		3.14 p.	Battalion inspected by Corps commander	

1577 Wt.W10791/1773 500,000 1/15 D.D.&L. A.D.S.S./Forms/C. 2118.

Army Form C. 2118.

WAR DIARY
or
INTELLIGENCE SUMMARY.

(*Erase heading not required.*)

Instructions regarding War Diaries and Intelligence Summaries are contained in F. S. Regs., Part II. and the Staff Manual respectively. Title pages will be prepared in manuscript.

Place	Date	Hour	Summary of Events and Information	Remarks and references to Appendices
HUTS NE of QUAEREDM	7/6/15	7 a.m.	Inspection of Rifles, ammunition, field dressings & identity discs	/b/
	7/6/15	7.30	Rifle inspection re. Filling of respirators.	
		5 p.m.	Route March	
			B Inns Brang & sund Berages IM 6 79 inc.	
			One Company one up & occupy MAPLE COPSE	
	8/6/15	7 a.	Rifle inspection re. Filling respirators	/c/
		10 a.	Companies at disposal of Coy Officers	
	9/6/15	7 a.	Rifles & ammunition inspection	/bb/
		8 p.m.	Whole Battalion up & dug out near KRUISSTRADT	/bb/
near KRUISSTRADT	10/6/15	5 p.	Tasted Company in Maple Copse and Carried on timber to Sanctuary Wood	/bb/
ZILLEBEKE	12/6/15	11.30	Attached of appointment of new Majs & N Market 2nd W.L.I.	/bb/
		4 p.	New adjutant arrived	
			Lieut at Canal Bridge	
			Guards at Canal Bridge	
	13/6/15	9.30 p	Relieved D Coy in MAPLE COPSE by sending up a Coy.	/bb/
	13/6/15		Standto	/bb/
	14/6/15		300 men digging during night under R.E. Bridge Front on Canal	/b/
	15/6/15		200 " " " " " " " "	/b/
	16/6/15		" " " " "	/bb/
	17/6/15		Sergt Major Crouch and several men arrived back from hospital	/bb/

1577 Wt.W10791/1773 500,000 1/15 D. D. & L. A.D.S.S./Forms/C. 2118.

Army Form C. 2118.

WAR DIARY
or
INTELLIGENCE SUMMARY.
(Erase heading not required.)

Instructions regarding War Diaries and Intelligence
Summaries are contained in F. S. Regs., Part II.
and the Staff Manual respectively. Title pages
will be prepared in manuscript.

Place	Date	Hour	Summary of Events and Information	Remarks and references to Appendices
DUG OUTS KRUISSTRAAT	17/6/15		200 men digging in ZILLEBEKE SWITCH Bridge guard for Canal	///
"	18/6/15		" " " " "	///
OUDERDOM	19/6/15		Moved from near OUDERDOM, withdrawing company from MAPLE COPSE. Bridge Guards returned.	//
	20/6/15		Moved to billets at farm near DRANOUTRE	//
	21/6/15		Took over trenches in front of KEMMEL Relief completed 12.50 am 22/6/15	///
KEMMEL	22/6/15		Coy Sjt Mjr Danson killed by sniper	//
	23/6/15		Pte Harrison killed. 2nd Lieut A.J. Haughton killed during night whilst out. A great loss to the Battn as he was a most reliable and energetic officer. reconnoitring wire in front of trenches.	//
	24/6/15		2nd Lt Haughton & Pte Harrison buried by Bn Chaplain Shadwick. Pte Bowman killed 4 men wounded (2 still on duty)	//
	25/6/15		Strength 27 Officers, 736 Other ranks. 4 men wounded (1 still on duty) Pte Bowman buried	//
	26/6/15		Slight shelling by enemy Our Artillery dropped one shell 15 yds short of our trench fell about 200 yds to front 5 Officers Enemy broke over trench	///

1577   Wt. W10791/1773   500,000   1/15   D. D. & L.   A.D.S.S./Forms/C. 2118.

WAR DIARY

or

INTELLIGENCE SUMMARY.

(Erase heading not required.)

Instructions regarding War Diaries and Intelligence Summaries are contained in F. S. Regs., Part II. and the Staff Manual respectively. Title pages will be prepared in manuscript.

1577 Wt.W10791/1773 500,000 1/15 D. D. & L.   A.D.S.S./Forms/C. 2118.

Place	Date	Hour	Summary of Events and Information	Remarks and references to Appendices
KEMMEL	27/6/15	9.15	Genl Lindsay Commanding Division came round through trenches returned 11.45	Am
		10	Adjt. of J.H. Lances called to see about shelter over of trenches	
		12. noon	Strength 27 Officers 730 Other ranks. Casualties one man wounded 26/6/15	
	28/6/15	11 p	Trenches taken over by 5th Loyal North Lancs	Ap
	29/6/15		Provided 2 men & 72 men for Brigade Level	Am
	30/6/15		Provided 180 men for digging trenches for RE	Am
			100 " " " " "	
			Draft of 50 arrivies from 2/9 D.L.I. on first Sept	

9th BATTN. THE DURHAM LIGHT INFANTRY.

J U L Y

1 9 1 5

Army Form C. 2118.

WAR DIARY
or
INTELLIGENCE SUMMARY.

(Erase heading not required.)

Instructions regarding War Diaries and Intelligence
Summaries are contained in F. S. Regs., Part II.
and the Staff Manual respectively. Title pages
will be prepared in manuscript.

Place	Date	Hour	Summary of Events and Information	Remarks and references to Appendices
KEMMEL (Billets)	1st July		Supplies digging parties 150. Ammunition & equipment all Bn rifles etc. Condemned 152 as unserviceable due to expansion of members on account of gas on cartridges which must have started at POTIJZE. Bn bivouacked on W slope of KEMMEL HILL, he obtained learn from Staff Capt of an order to use 4 farm huts in case of inclement weather.	Ref. 24 July ✕
	2nd July		We relieve 6 L'Nkamas at 9.30 p.m. The relief was complete by 11.15 p.m. 37 off. 786 men. Our mining section under Lieut GREENER is working in Gr [...] permanently and is busy making a gallery & front undermining	A/B
	4 July		Sketches surrendered. Army rates out sheights of trenches [...] is to be so as we are only 14 below sheights.	M.
			Strength 27 Officers 783 Other Ranks	
	6 July		Major English visits trenches G, G, G, G+ G+ B's Brs S.P's (rifle only) night 4-5 and went into mine at G. Br Gen J Slee CB. DSo on arrival as G.O.C. inspected trenches with Co. and direction that wiring of front line should be proceeded with before everything else.	A/B

WAR DIARY
or
INTELLIGENCE SUMMARY.

(Erase heading not required.)

Instructions regarding War Diaries and Intelligence
Summaries are contained in F. S. Regs., Part II.
and the Staff Manual respectively. Title pages
will be prepared in manuscript.

Place	Date	Hour	Summary of Events and Information	Remarks and references to Appendices
TRENCHES				
KEMMEL	6 July		All rations carried in carts at 9 p.m. are taken to and reach the Coys in trenches until 1 a.m.	M
	6 July		Our improved trenches is moving and Told each Coy Commander to arrange a plan in case he was unable to attack, for counter-attack and to have every detail ready for harassing fire at short notice. These are very troublesome in trenches and large quantities of C.O.Ly wire are worn daily.	M
	7 July		The II army desires to know how many rounds of S.A.A. we have then in the trenches in to Ponchaux 92,650. In Trenches & Reserve 97,000.	M

M.G.	3,000
2 S.A.A. Carts	78,000
M.O. "	11,785
Pack animals	16,000
Other	1,440
Trench	
Bn. Reserve	85,000
B.H.Q.	54,000

1577 Wt. W10791/1773 500,000 1/15 D. D. & L. A.D.S.S./Form/C. 2118.

4381 9/15

M6

Army Form C. 2118.

WAR DIARY
or
INTELLIGENCE SUMMARY.

(*Erase heading not required.*)

Instructions regarding War Diaries and Intelligence Summaries are contained in F. S. Regs., Part II. and the Staff Manual respectively. Title pages will be prepared in manuscript.

Place	Date	Hour	Summary of Events and Information	Remarks and references to Appendices
Trenches Kemmel	8.7/15		Strength 27 Officers 768 other ranks. — Casualties One man wounded 7/7/15	

We expect that there may be a German offensive movement our and the
B, is busily employing in making preparations to repel it. The wire by
right of 8¹ were made strongly cut and was laid by R.E. All front
platforms have been reference over. The parapet has been reference over.
Strengthening throughout and Officer Commanding & Company has known
orders apparent by B. for a counter attack each Coy has or platoon
ready in support of S.P.11. By 14 July a second line but in rear of
the Coy at S.P.11. This line will be complete to that of the front parapet is
blown in. the D.A.I line will be occupied. Enemys artillery shelled
HENNAPES from at 12 noon without is billeted on support log. The
farm has raged here from ground by fire from incendiary shells but
no Casualties occupied. Rifle Grenades 18 act of apparent and
new but. Relief Carts arrived at 9 pm. and relion Carrier
R.E. stor Carrie at front work at 2. am.

1577 Wt. W10791/1773 500,000 1/15 D. D. & L.   A.D.S.S./Forms/C. 2118.

Army Form C. 2118.

WAR DIARY

or

INTELLIGENCE SUMMARY.

(Erase heading not required.)

Instructions regarding War Diaries and Intelligence
Summaries are contained in F. S. Regs., Part II.
and the Staff Manual respectively. Title pages
will be prepared in manuscript.

Place	Date	Hour	Summary of Events and Information	Remarks and references to Appendices
KEMMEL	9 July		One man wounded. 27 officers 761 other ranks total strength. Bn. was relieved by 5th K.N.L. relief complete at 11 p.m., proceeded to LOCRE huts for 6 days rest. 4 + Coy is huts (20 per hut)	
KEMMEL LOCRE	10 July		Draft of 20 184 arrived from 3rd Line. The G.O.C. II Army, Sir Herbert Plumer, came C.O. at Bde. helpers are here a private interview with each. The Brigade General Gen. came round all Coy round the B.H.Q. Bns and Col. HENDERSON has instructed to make a survey and scheme for occupation of right section in case of necessity.	
LOCRE	11 July		C.of E. church parade 11 a.m. R.C. 9 a.m. service round G.H.Q. snider field G.O.C. 534 men on L afternoon C.W. and 2.1½ afternoon digging. 2 officers 140 men digging. 2 men wounded.	
	12 July		24 officers 967 other ranks 20 officers 4 officers digging.	
	13 July		1 officer 110 digging. Heavy bombardment at 8.30 p.m. in YPRES direction. Gas at Bde. (Wind & gas)	
LOCRE	14 July		C.+ D. bathing. Enemy blew up an defensive mine at 6.15 wrote 8.30 p.m. is worked by Lieut. GREENER 6 men missing 30 wounded.	

Army Form C. 2118.

WAR DIARY
or
INTELLIGENCE SUMMARY.
(Erase heading not required.)

Instructions regarding War Diaries and Intelligence Summaries are contained in F. S. Regs, Part II. and the Staff Manual respectively. Title pages will be prepared in manuscript.

Place	Date	Hour	Summary of Events and Information	Remarks and references to Appendices
LOCRE	16/7		Bde. left LOCRE at 8.15 p.m. and marched to ARMENTIERES via DRANOUTRE and BAILLEUL. 9/DLI and 8/8 DLI reached their billets at 1 a.m. 17 July.	Sgt
ARMENT[IERES]	17 July.		Officers and men MES. for Coy. visited trenches leaving billet at 9 a.m.	SM
			2 Officer & 6 other ranks in evening 9/DLI took over 70, 71, 72, & 73 trenches from 2/KSLI relief complete at 12 midnight. 4 Co. found of England at bridge known	SM
"	18 July		Lieut O. FIELD killed 5 other ranks wounded all except only by hand grenades.	SM
"	19 July		5 men wounded mostly by shells. mortars. the fire on our mortars and grenades by	SM
"	20 July		was of reprisal. 3 Germans over the killed by snipers. in trenches 3	SM
"	21 July		1 man killed 2 wounded. the rifles 1 German accounted to snipers. In German lines.	SM
"	22 July		after parade one 2 guns put bombs into German lines. Sgt Whitly killed, Pt. Kilbey on Pt. killed one wounded. Lieut Mauchlin slightly wounded.	SM
"	23 July.		Intelligence officers Army (Lieut STEPHENSON) saw small parties of enemy making about in PERENCHIES.	SM
"	24 July		one wounded. Intelligence officer reports having seen many German fatigue parties in PERENCHIES carrying various trenches towards German battery.	SM
"	25 July		one wounded. Intelligence officer reports various fatigue parties of German battery.	SM

1577 (Wt.W10791/1773 500,000 1/15 D. D. & L. 200ff 814 other Trench Stores A.D.S.S./Forms/C. 2118.

WAR DIARY

or

INTELLIGENCE SUMMARY.

(Erase heading not required.)

Instructions regarding War Diaries and Intelligence
Summaries are contained in F. S. Regs., Part II.
and the Staff Manual respectively. Title pages
will be prepared in manuscript.

Place	Date	Hour	Summary of Events and Information	Remarks and references to Appendices
ARMENTIERES	29/9		Position of battery finished, not t. R.A. staff. Releiving by 5/K.R.R. 70 hours 71, 72, 673, 6/3 7 / Dublin.	Sm
"	2.59/		E.D. returned from leave. Billets in town.	sg
"	26/9		Fatigue parts 9 pm. L.R.E. 120.	
"	29 "		Fatigue parts 9 pm. L.R.E. 2.4.5 Cpl. BETTISON, Lieut. SPENCER sm 26 Lieut. BELL + coming from 27 units sm	sm
"	28 "		Inspection of billets by Coe.	sm
"	29 "		30 officers 9.30 others. Fighting St. 27 90th. Trench Strength 23 & 811. A + B. went into support line behind 67 and 6.7 Trenches.	sm
"	31 "		Estra guard 1 N.C.O 15 men for Ash Baker	sm

9th BATTN. THE DURHAM LIGHT INFANTRY.

A U G U S T

1 9 1 5

WAR DIARY

or

INTELLIGENCE SUMMARY.

(Erase heading not required.)

Instructions regarding War Diaries and Intelligence
Summaries are contained in F. S. Regs., Part II.
and the Staff Manual respectively. Title pages
will be prepared in manuscript.

1/9 Denham L.

Place	Date	Hour	Summary of Events and Information	Remarks and references to Appendices
	1915			
ARMENTIERES	1/6 Aug		Billets (BLUE FACTORY)	
			Daily routine carried out whilst in billets.	
"	7 Aug		took over 78, 79, 80, 78 S, 79 S, 80 S from Yorks Dead Bois relief complete 11.30 p.m.	
"	9 "		Pte CLARK in billets.	
"	19		Relieve by 5 N.F. and 6 N.F. Proceed to Billets	
"	31		Relieve 7/Su 71, 72, 73 and supports.	

1577 Wt. W10791/1773 500,000 1/15 D. D. & L.   A.D.S.S./Forms/C. 2118.

95 Hants Capt adjt.

9th BATTN. THE DURHAM LIGHT INFANTRY.

S E P T E M B E R

1 9 1 5

Army Form C. 2118.

WAR DIARY

or

INTELLIGENCE SUMMARY.

(Erase heading not required.)

Instructions regarding War Diaries and Intelligence Summaries are contained in F. S. Regs., Part II. and the Staff Manual respectively. Title pages will be prepared in manuscript.

1/9 DLI

Place	Date 1915	Hour	Summary of Events and Information	Remarks and references to Appendices
ARMENTIERES	1 Sept.		We relieved 7/DLI Right 31 Aug/1 Sept, and took over 72, 73, 74 and supports. the garrison refit & much attacked.	
	2 Sept.		1 killed 2 wounded	
	8 Sept.		1 wounded	
	9 Sept.		We were relieved 9/11 by 6 N.F. and 72 + 73 by 4 N.F. relief complete 10.30 pm 8.9th. Billets 2 days. Corps Orders Retd learns the Pershing say Blue shooting. General L. Herbert PLUMER inspects DLI Bde on 9/DLI at 11 am. Clear fatigue etc charges & working parties 687 Rampart file 25 officers.	
	11 Sept.		Digging party 300 7 am. Trenches Salisbury his uncle R.E.	
"	12 Sept.		Relieved 4th YORKS and 5 YORKS and occupied 78, 79, 80, 785, 775, 805.	
	13 Sept.		4 Officers from 21st Bn (New army) attacked for 24 hrs instruction.	
	14 Sept.		1 man accidentally wounded. Capt. BAISTER Lieut MACK Jarvis, Col STUART General Staff accompanied our trenches for instruction.	
	15 "		our trenches for instruction.	
	17 "		Lieut Boys Stones wounded, also C.S.M. WRIGHT and one man all by Whizz bangs.	
	18 "		Enemy's guns very active. Painful blown away in 78 and 79.	
	20		Sgt Radley Pte Cummings wounded	

1577   Wt. W10791/1773   500,000   1/15   D. D. & L.   A.D.S.S./Forms/C. 2118.

Army Form C. 2118.

WAR DIARY
or
INTELLIGENCE SUMMARY.
(Erase heading not required.)

Instructions regarding War Diaries and Intelligence
Summaries are contained in F. S. Regs., Part II.
and the Staff Manual respectively. Title pages
will be prepared in manuscript.

1/9 Durh.L.I

151 Bde

Place	Date	Hour	Summary of Events and Information	Remarks and references to Appendices
ARMENTIERES	19/15 23 Spt		Sgt. J. Ridley, Pte Devlin bombade. Enemy very inactive. Officers' patrol worked up to enemy's knife rests by Day. Offsd 76 trench. (3/mn)	
" "	24 Spt.		Enemy shelled 79. to at 10 a.m. No casualties. Relieved by 4 N.F. and **6** N.F. at 8. P.M. D.L.I. Bde has placed in II Corps reserve for the coming attacke N + S.	
" "	25 "		Heard very heavy bombardment. S.	
" "	26		Moved to HOUPLINES in support to D.L. Bde. in trenches 81 - 89. (Billets)	
" "	27		Took over trench 90 - 94 from 6. Queens. on N. bank of River in am about LE TOUQUET. 92, 93 are very close enemy 93 being abut 45ʸ.	
" "	28		15 Officers 25 NCos. attacked from 13ᵗʰ CHESHIRE REGT. Pte RAINE killed in 93. Heavy Rain.	
" "	29		15 " 25 NCos. " "	Heavy Rain
" "	30		8 Platoons of other regt. attacked for 24 hrs. Incoming rations to Support line by means of my own border riders trolley way. There is a tram complete standing in LE TOUQUET station which has apparently abandoned in Oct 1914 by the church.	2 men
	30.		Sgt H. Ridley, Pte H. Devlin reg. appointed	1 man bombade

1577 Wt. W10791/1773 500,000 1/15 D. D. & L. A.D.S.S./Forms/C. 2118.

Distribution in Trenches

Trench	Officers	Others	Grenadiers	Machine Gunners	Stretcher Bearers	Signallers	Total
71	4	70	10	6			90.
71A	1	31	5	-	2	3	42.
71s.	1	37	4				42.
72	7	133	-	7	2	3	152.
72s	1	35	4				40.
73	3	144	5	6	2	3	163
73s	2	45	5		2		54.
74s	4	58	4	-	-	3	69.
Dump at end of Ponte Egal av.	1	36					37
Hdqrs.	2	4				19	25
							714

1/9/15

.... Capt & Adjt.
9th Bn. Durham Lt. Infy.

Fighting Strength	815
Trench Strength as shown 31. Aug.	714
In Trenches on 1st Sept.	714

Reference graph 36
7.3c.
SCALE 5"

LEITH WALK AVENUE

LEITH WALK AVENUE

KENRIGHT FARM

KIRKBRIDE AVENUE
HARTAKAS

PORT GEAN FARM (BARN)

69

69 S

70 S

70 A

70 D

71 A

71 A

71

72

72 S

73

73 S

To HENDERSON'S 2½ mi.

To LILLE 4 mi.

Subsidiary Central AVENUE

Green Lane

Br. House
5/20

Br. House
5/20

Subsidiary line

To STATION 1½ mi.

To Dane Coffee

Subsidiary line

74

75

9th BATTN. THE DURHAM LIGHT INFANTRY.

O C T O B E R

1 9 1 5

WAR DIARY

or

INTELLIGENCE SUMMARY.

(Erase heading not required.)

Instructions regarding War Diaries and Intelligence Summaries are contained in F. S. Regs., Part II. and the Staff Manual respectively. Title pages will be prepared in manuscript.

1/9 Durham L.I.

151. Beton,

Place	Date	Hour	Summary of Events and Information	Remarks and references to Appendices
	OCT. 15			
LE TOUQUET	1.		Half Bn. of 13/Cheshire Regt. 25th Div. ferr.Army attached. All R.E. and R.F.A. of same Div. are all special instruction in trench warfare.	
	2.		Pte. J. DOUGLAS handed in 93 whist trench in 35 yards from enemy.	
	4.		He handed over to 18th Cheshire Regt. and more to billets in LE BIZET.	
	5.		Received orders to train every man in bomb throwing. to the Coys were taught to use practice throwing bully beef tins allotted.	
			In afternoon at 2.30pm. Lieut CALLANDER was lecturing to D Coy on the G.S. II trench when he exploded the bomb he had in his hand killing himself and Pte Repfield, Lieut BOYS-STONES & Privates E DOAR were slightly wounded as also 17 NCOs & men of one platoon wounded. If the detonator had been previously removed this accident would have been averted.	
ARMENTIERES	6.		Bn. moved to ARMENTIERES billets in Rue NATIONALE.	
	7.		Finished fatigue trenches to R.E. we had left billet at 5.30 pm & returned at 2.20 a.m.	
HOUPLINES	8.		Took over 84, 85, 86, 87 trenches from 7/D.L.I. Hdqrs in Chateau HOUPLINES.	

1577 Wt.W10791/1773 500,000 1/15. D. D. & L. A.D.S.S./Forms/C. 2118.

J. S. Hawthorn Capt. Adjt

Army Form C. 2118.

WAR DIARY
or
INTELLIGENCE SUMMARY.

(Erase heading not required.)

Instructions regarding War Diaries and Intelligence Summaries are contained in F. S. Regs., Part II. and the Staff Manual respectively. Title pages will be prepared in manuscript.

Place	Date	Hour	Summary of Events and Information	Remarks and references to Appendices
	Oct.			1/9 Devil th
				157 Bdes
HOUPLINES	9.		1 coy from 15th Durll! attacked 21 Div. 2nd army. They had just come from LOOS & VERMELLES.	
"	13.		Enden to observe enemy out return his trul reserve, R.F.A. bombarded enemy's line heavily 2pm — 3.30pm. 3.30p.m. we lights [?] from bombs the centre of which rolled over to everywhere in our Choire Chord. Enemy open heavy rifle fire and sent up flares. Ohen M.O. and Artillery fortus opened on us. 110 shells fell in and round 86 hand alone. All men were in Shell hered in Sentry shelters in consequence. one man was brunk stying 3 slightly wounded in consequence. one man was brunk stying by a bomb thrown by a comrade. 15th D.L.I. lifted at 11.30 a.m. Two men slightly wounded. R.F.A. again bombarded enemy in afternoon but drew no reply.	
	14.			
	15.		1 man wounded.	
	17.		2 men wounded.	
	18.		Pte Arthur Ridley. Drowned. Buried. Bhoine by 2/D.L.I.	

J.S.Menle Capage [?]

1577 Wt.W10791/1773 500,000 1/15 D.D.&L. A.D.S.S./Forms/C. 2118.

Army Form C. 2118.

WAR DIARY

or

INTELLIGENCE SUMMARY.

(Erase heading not required.)

Instructions regarding War Diaries and Intelligence Summaries are contained in F. S. Regs., Part II. and the Staff Manual respectively. Title pages will be prepared in manuscript.

Place	Date	Hour	Summary of Events and Information	Remarks and references to Appendices
	Oct.			157 Bde.
ARMENTIERES	19. 22.		Billets Hopital Civil. Relieve 1/Rot. in B6 & 83, again Clayton Bde. again 7/167 Bde. Commenced Br 22 – 31.Oct while the Bn. Lieut Col Henderson has on leave.	
	28.		56. N.Col return under Capt Dryden, Lieut Boys-Stones and Sgt Tindall went to BAILLEUL to meet part the majesty King George V, stay former part of 5th/5th Complete Bn. The following letters was rec. from Sir Herbert PLUMER commanding II army clearer orders to say that he was very pleased with the soldierly bearing of the troops and all to rear.	
	31. 29. 30.		Relieve Wz by 6/Des. Casualties 24th. 1 man wounded Cpl. Kela, Pte Holloway killed Pte Spurr slightly wounded.	

J. Hastle Clark
Lieut Col
1577 Wt. W10791/1773 500,000 1/15 D. D. & L. A.D.S.S./Forms/C. 2118.

5

No. of Report _____

FIELD RETURN.

Army Form B. 213.

(To be furnished by all arms, services, and departments (except A.S.C. units) to the A. G.'s Office at the Base in accordance with Field Service Regulations, Part II.)

RETURN showing numbers RATIONED by, and Transport on charge of, _O.K.Ra.A.I.J._ at _H.B.G.J._ Date. _29th Oct. 1915_

DETAIL	Personnel			Animals							Guns, carriages, and limbers and transport vehicles												REMARKS
	Officers	Other ranks	Natives	Horses Riding	Draught	Heavy Draught	Pack	Mules Large	Small	Camels	Oxen	Guns, carriages and limbers, showing description	Ammunition wagons and limbers	Machine guns	Aircraft, showing description	Horsed 4 Wheeled	2 Wheeled	Motor Cars	Tractors	Lorries, showing description	Trucks, showing description	Trailers	Motor Bicycles	Bicycles	
Effective Strength of Unit	29	834		12	25	9	5	10	4					4		16	3							9	Not Rationed by Unit
Details, by Arms attached to unit as in War Establishment:—																									2/Goorpoo Willoks
																									Driv.
Rank	1																								San. Section
Interpreter		4																							Pigeon men
Commr. Sergt.		1																							M.G. employed
																									employed under Town Major
																									Railways fory
																									Attached 1/3 Co. A.S.C.
																									31st Fr. Co. R.E.
																									N.C.O. School
Total	30	840		12	25	9	5	10	4					4		16	3							9	Div. Band Masters
War Establishment	30	800		12	25	9	5	10	4					4		16	3							9	Pole "Steersman
Wanting to complete (Detail of Personnel and Horses below)																									M Du " School
Surplus		40																							O.R. Clerk at Base
*Attached (not to include the details shown above)																								51	Officers
Civilians:— Employed with the Unit Accompanying the Unit																									Hospital
																									Bks. Band Masters
TOTAL RATIONED:—	28	789		12	25	9	5	10	4															53	

* In the case of field ambulances, hospitals or depots, the number of patients are to be included here, the names being shown in A. F. A. 36.

29th Oct. 1915

Signature of Commander. _____

Date of Despatch.

9th BATTN. THE DURHAM LIGHT INFANTRY.

N O V E M B E R

1 9 1 5

WAR DIARY
or
INTELLIGENCE SUMMARY.

(Erase heading not required.)

Instructions regarding War Diaries and Intelligence Summaries are contained in F. S. Regs., Part II. and the Staff Manual respectively. Title pages will be prepared in manuscript.

1/9 Durham L.I.

B.E.F.   15th Bde

Place	Date	Hour	Summary of Events and Information	Remarks and references to Appendices
ARMENTIÈRES/Nov.	1916		Billeted in town, HOSPICE CIVILF, and ITITUT St JUDE. Bn Hdqrs at 35 Rue Nationale	
HOUPLINES	3	3 p.m.	Relieved 7/Bn. in 84, 85, 86, 87. — 8/Bn on our right, 6/N.F. on our left Div. 3 Platoons attacked from 8/Kirc 2.it Div. Trenches full of water owing rain on 1st & 2nd Bn.	
	7	7 p.m.	2/o Coy wounded. This NCo. did the Observation NCo. of B. Coy did excellent work sniping, patrolling etc. Never hit in front of our wire at 10. am a fog prevented but lifted suddenly. Lieut Palmer went No 200. Bell ran out and was brought him in.	
	8	8 a.m.	Pte. J. Inchan slightly wounded.	
"	12	12 p.m.	Relieved by 14/Dn. 16/Dn. & 3 Coy & 3 Security number in Chateau yard.	
"	11		1 wounded safely.	
	13		Marcher & killed N. of STEENWERCK	
STEENWERCK	15-20		1st Weeks training — squad drills, at all men in Routine Training home & down Monday.	
	19		Lieut WATSON arrived	
	20		S.M. CROUCH left the Scene in 10 /Dn after 7 years in the Bn.	

1577   Wt. W10791/1773   500,000   1/15   P. D. & L.   A.D.S.S./Forms/C. 2118.

WAR DIARY

or

INTELLIGENCE SUMMARY.

(Erase heading not required.)

Instructions regarding War Diaries and Intelligence
Summaries are contained in F. S. Regs., Part II.
and the Staff Manual respectively. Title pages
will be prepared in manuscript.

Place	Date	Hour	Summary of Events and Information	Remarks and references to Appendices
STEENWERCK	Jan/15		Sir Herbert PLUMER and SIR CHARLES FERGUSON inspected the Bat.	
STEENWERCK	22	23-30	Company training and rest period.	

1577 Wt. W10791/1773 500,000 1/15 D. D. & L.   A.D.S.S./Forms/C. 2118.

FIELD RETURN.

Army Form B. 213.

No. of Report._____

(To be furnished by all arms, services, and departments (except A.S.C. units) to the A. G.'s Office at the Base in accordance with Field Service Regulations, Part II.)

RETURN showing numbers RATIONED by, and Transport on charge of,_____ at_____ Date 5/11/15

Detail	Personnel			Horses			Mules			Camels	Oxen	Guns, carriages, and limbers and transport vehicles — Guns, carriages and limbers, showing description	Ammunition wagons and limbers	Machine guns	Aircraft, showing description	Horsed 4 Wheeled	Horsed 2 Wheeled	Motor Cars	Tractors	Lorries, showing description	Trucks, showing description	Trailers	Motor Bicycles	Bicycles	Remarks
	Officers	Other ranks	Natives	Riding	Draught	Heavy Draught	Pack	Large	Small																
Effective Strength of Unit	30	828		12	25	9	9	5	10	4					4		16	3							9	3 Not Rationed by Unit; 2 Horses Wdon; 13 Div.; 3 San Section; 8 Pigeon men; 1 Telde enlisted; 1 Emplyt under Town Major; 3 Labourer by; 12 Attchd (No 3) 64 ASC; 31st Inf Bn
Details, by Arms attached to unit as in War Establishment: R.A.M.C.	1	4																							2 "N.C.O. or School"; 2 at Grenade School; 1 "French Mor barrier"; 1 Di Rond instructor; 1 O/R Sick at home; 1 M.G. Course
Shoeingsmith		1																							
Armourer Sergt.		1																							
Total	31	834		12	25	9	9	5	10	4					4		16	3							9
War Establishment	30	800		12	25	9	9	5	10	4					4		16	3							9	54
Wanting to complete																									
Surplus	1	34																								Officers 1 In Hospital; 1 Pte Bomb thrower; 1 French How Course
*Attached (not to include the details shown above)																									
Civilians:— Employed with the Unit																									
Accompanying the Unit																									
Total Rationed	28	780		12	25	9	9	5	10	4															5 7

* In the case of field ambulances, hospitals or depots, the number of patients are to be included here, the names being shown in A. F. A. 36.

Signature of Commander._____

Date of Despatch._____ 5/11/15

Perforated Sheet giving detail of personnel and horses wanting to complete, shown on Army Form B. 218.

Number of Report ___

Detail of Wanting to Complete						
CAVALRY						
R. A.						
R. E.						
INFANTRY						
R. A. M. C.						
A. O. C.						
A. V. C.						

Drivers: R.A., R.E., A.S.C., Car, Lorry, Steam

Gunners

Smith Gunners

Range Takers

Farriers: Serjeants, Corporals, Shoeing, or Shoeing and Carriage Smiths, Cold Shoers

Wheelers: R.A., H.T., M.T.

Saddlers or Harness Makers

Blacksmiths

Bricklayers and Masons

Carpenters and Joiners

Fitters & Turners (R.H.): Wood, Iron

Fitters: R.A., Wireless

Electricians: Plumbers, Ordinary, W.T.

Signalmen

Engine Drivers: Loco., Field

Air Line Men

Permanent Line Men

Operators, Telegraph

Cablemen

Brigade Section Pioneers

General-duty Pioneers

Signallers

Instrument Repairers

Motor Cyclists

Motor Cyclist Artificers

Telephonists

Clerks

Machine Gunners

Armament Artificers: Fitters, Range Finders

Armourers

Storemen

Privates

W.O.'s and N.C.O's. (by ranks) not included in trade columns

TOTAL wanting to agree with complete: Officers, Other Ranks

Horses: Riding, Draught, Heavy Draught, Pack

Remarks :—

Signature of Commander.

_____ Unit.

151 st Infy Bde 50 th Div 2 Army Formation to which attached.

5/11/15 Date of Despatch.

[P.T.O.

(82434.) Wt. 4394/2217. 500,000. 6/15. B.M.&S. Forms/B. 213/6.

FIELD RETURN.

Army Form B. 213.

(To be furnished by all arms, services, and departments (except A.S.C. units) to the A. G.'s Office at the Base in accordance with Field Service Regulations, Part II.)

RETURN showing numbers RATIONED by, and Transport on charge of, 9th Nov. D.L.O. at B.E.F. Date 12th Nov. 1915.

DETAIL	Personnel			Animals. Horses			Mules		Camels	Oxen	Guns, carriages, and limbers and transport vehicles — Guns, carriages and limbers, showing description	Ammunition wagons and limbers	Machine Guns	Aircraft, showing description	Horsed 4 Wheeled	Horsed 2 Wheeled	Motor Cars	Mechanical Tractors	Lorries, showing description	Trucks, showing description	Trailers	Motor Bicycles	Bicycles	REMARKS
	Officers	Other ranks	Natives	Riding	Draught	Heavy Draught Pack	Large	Small																
Effective Strength of Unit	30	825		12	25	9 5	10	4					4		16	3							9	Not Rationed by Unit
Details, by Arms attached to unit as in War Establishment:—																								2 Bombo troops 3
																							Div. Section 2
N.A.M.C.	1	4																						Sig. Section 12
Armourer Sgt		1																						Brigade ammn 3
																								Pioneers Empl 8
																								with Train 1
																								Servants Civil 3
																								Attached 1932 ASC 3
																								31st T.M. battery 12
Total	31	830		12	25	9 5	10	4					4		16	3							9	N.C.O. or Schools 1
War Establishment	30	800		12	25	9 5	10	4					4		16	3							9	Div. Mount Instr. 1
Wanting to complete																								Grenade Schol 1
Surplus (Detail of Personnel and Horses below)	1	30																						Off Clerk at Base 1
*Attached (not to include the details shown above)																								Base School 2
Civilians:— Employed with the Unit Accompanying the Unit																								Officer ∑ 52
Total Rationed :—	30	778		12	25	9 5	10	4																Pte Brownbe 1 ∑ 53

* In the case of field ambulances, hospitals or depots, the number of patients are to be included here, the names being shown in A. F. A. 36.

_____ Signature of Commander.

12th Nov. 1915 Date of Despatch.

Perforated Sheet giving detail of personnel and horses wanting to complete, shown on Army Form B. 218.

Number of Report _____

Detail of Wanting to Complete	Drivers						Farriers				Wheelers			Fitters		Fitters & Turners (R.E.)							Electricians			Engine Drivers																	Armament Artificers						W.O's. and N.C.O's. (by ranks) not included in trade columns			TOTAL, to agree with columns		Horses			
	R.A.	R.E.	A.S.C.	Car	Lorry	Steam	Gunners	Smith Gunners	Range Takers	Serjeants	Corporals	Shoeing, or Shoeing and Carriage Smiths	Cold Shoers	R.A.	H.T.	M.T.	Saddlers or Harness Makers	Bricklayers and Masons	Carpenters and Joiners	Wood	Iron	R.A.	Wireless	Plumbers	Ordinary	W.T.	Signalmen	Locco.	Field	Air Line Men	Permanent Line Men	Operators, Telegraph	Cablemen	Brigade Section Pioneers	General-duty Pioneers	Signallers	Instrument Repairers	Motor Cyclists	Motor Cyclist Artificers	Telephonists	Clerks	Machine Gunners	Fitters	Range Finders	Armourers	Storemen	Privates			Officers	Other Ranks	Riding	Draught	Heavy Draught	Pack
CAVALRY																																																						
R.A.																																																					
R.E.																																																					
INFANTRY																																																					
R.A.M.C.																																																					
A.O.C.																																																					
A.V.C.																																																					

Remarks :—

O.C. B. Durham Lt Infy
151st Infy Bde 50 Div. 2nd Army

_____ Signature of Commander.

_____ Unit.

_____ Formation to which attached.

12 November 1915 Date of Despatch.

[P.T.O.

(89484.) Wt. 4394/2217. 500,000. 6/15. B.M.&S. Forms/B. 213/6.

Army Form B. 213.

FIELD RETURN.

No. of Report _____

(To be furnished by all arms, services, and departments (except A.S.C. units) to the A. G.'s Office at the Base, in accordance with Field Service Regulations, Part II.)

RETURN showing numbers RATIONED by, and Transport on charge of, _9th Bn Durh. Lt. Inft_ at _13 A. Y_ ____ 19 Nov 1915. Date.

DETAIL	Officers	Other ranks	Natives	Riding	Draught	Heavy Draught	Pack	Large	Small	Camels	Oxen	Guns, carriages, limbers, showing description	Ammunition wagons and limbers	Machine guns	Aircraft, showing description	4 Wheeled	2 Wheeled	Motor Cars	Tractors	Lorries, showing description	Trucks, showing description	Trailers	Motor Bicycles	Bicycles	REMARKS
Effective Strength of Unit	32	828		12	25	9	5	10	4					4		16	3							9	Not Returned by Unit
Details, by Arms attached to unit as in War Establishment:— R.A.M.C.	1	35																							3 2/bdrs Wksps 2
Armourer Sgt.	1																								11
Total	33	834		12	25	9	5	10	4					4		16	3							9	1 5 3 3 attached A.S.C.
War Establishment	30	800		12	25	9	5	10	4					4		16	3							9	2 2 1
Wanting to complete																									44
Surplus	3	34																							1 O.R. Clk at base
*Attached (not to include the details shown above) (Detail of Personnel and Horses below)																									Officer Bde Bomb
Civilians:— Employed with the Unit																									
Accompanying the Unit																									
Total Rationed	32	790		12	25	9	5	10	4																45

* In the case of field ambulances, hospitals or depots, the number of patients are to be included here, the names being shown in A. F. A. 36.

_____ Signature of Commander.

19/4/15 _____ Date of Despatch.

Perforated Sheet giving detail of personnel and horses wanting to complete, shown on Army Form B. 218.

Number of Report _____

Signature of Commander. _____

Unit. _____

Formation to which attached. _____

Date of Despatch. _____

[P.T.O.

Remarks :—

Detail of Wanting to Complete

CAVALRY
R. A.
R. E.
INFANTRY
R. A. M. C.
A. O. C.
A. V. C.

Drivers: R. A., R. E., A. S. C., Car, Lorry, Steam

Gunners
Smith Gunners
Range Takers

Farriers: Sergeants, Corporals, Shoeing, or Shoeing and Carriage Smiths, Cold Shoers

Wheelers: R. A., H. T., M. T.

Saddlers or Harness Makers
Blacksmiths
Bricklayers and Masons
Carpenters and Joiners

Fitters & Turners (R. E.): Wood, Iron

Fitters: R. A., Wireless

Plumbers

Electricians: Ordinary, W. T.

Signalmen

Engine Drivers: L.000., Field

Air Line Men
Permanent Line Men
Operators, Telegraph
Cablemen
Brigade Section Pioneers
General-duty Pioneers
Signallers
Instrument Repairers
Motor Cyclists
Motor Cyclist Artificers
Telephonists
Clerks
Machine Gunners

Armament Artificers: Fitters, Range Finders, Armourers

Storemen
Privates

W.O.'s and N.C.O's. (by rank) not included in trade columns

TOTAL wanting to agree with to complete: Officers, Other Ranks

Horses: Riding, Draught, Heavy Draught, Pack

(82434) Wt. 4894/2217. 500,000. 6/15. B.M.&S. Forms/B. 213/6.

FIELD RETURN.

Army Form B. 213.

No. of Report. _____

(To be furnished by all arms, services, and departments (except A.S.C. units) to the A. G.'s Office at the Base in accordance with Field Service Regulations, Part II.)

RETURN showing numbers RATIONED by, and Transport on charge of, _OK Dirt Sh Inf'y_ at _B.D.Z._ _10th Nov 1915_ Date.

DETAIL	Personnel			Animals — Horses			Pack	Mules		Camels	Oxen	Guns, carriages, limbers, description	Ammunition wagons and limbers	Machine guns	Aircraft, showing description	Horsed 4 Wheeled	Horsed 2 Wheeled	Motor Cars	Tractors	Lorries, showing description	Trucks, showing description	Trailers	Motor Bicycles	Bicycles	REMARKS
	Officers	Other ranks	Natives	Riding	Draught	Heavy Draught		Large	Small																
Effective Strength of Unit	32	826		12	25	9	9	5	10	4					4		16	3							9	Not Rationed by Unit
Details, by Arms attached to unit as in War Establishment:—	1	3																							9	2 Doctor Medical 2 Personnel Sanitary Sec Signal Section Field Ambulance Ex Lungs Co Attached ASC 3rd Type M.G. or Section Type
W.O. Mech Armourer Sgt		1																								3, 2, 6, 5, 1, 3, 12, 2
Total	33	826		12	25	9	9	5	10	4					4		16	3							9	2 Model Sekery Armourer Sgt JR Clerk, Nurse
War Establishment	30	800		12	25	9	9	5	10	4					4		16	3							9	Officer 1 39
Wanting to complete (Detail of Personnel and Horses below)																										
Surplus	3	26																								Offrs
*Attached (not to include the details shown above)																										Pte Brown 1 Grenade School Pte Transport 1
Civilians:— Employed with the Unit Accompanying the Unit																										42
TOTAL RATIONED :—	30	793		12	25	9		5	10	4																

* In the case of field ambulances, hospitals or depots, the number of patients are to be included here, the names being shown in A. F. A. 36.

_____ Signature of Commander.

26th Nov. 1915 Date of Despatch.

[P.T.O.]

Perforated Sheet giving detail of personnel and horses wanting to complete, shown on Army Form B. 218.

Number of Report _____

Detail of Wanting to Complete		CAVALRY	R.A.	R.E.	INFANTRY	R.A.M.C.	A.O.C.	A.V.C.
Drivers	R.A.							
	R.E.							
	A.S.C.							
	Car							
	Lorry							
	Steam							
Gunners								
Smith Gunners								
Range Takers								
Farriers	Sergeants							
	Corporals							
	Shoeing, or Shoeing and Carriage Smiths							
	Cold Shoers							
Wheelers	R.A.							
	H.T.							
	M.T.							
Saddlers or Harness Makers								
Blacksmiths								
Bricklayers and Masons								
Carpenters and Joiners								
Fitters & Turners (R. E.)	Wood							
	Iron							
Fitters	R.A.							
	Wireless							
Plumbers								
Electricians	Ordinary							
	W.T.							
Signalmen								
Engine Drivers	L.000.							
	Field							
Air Line Men								
Permanent Line Men								
Operators, Telegraph								
Cablemen								
Brigade Section Pioneers								
General-duty Pioneers								
Signalers								
Instrument Repairers								
Motor Cyclists								
Motor Cyclist Artificers								
Telephonists								
Clerks								
Machine Gunners								
Armament Artificers	Fitters							
	Range Finders							
	Armourers							
Storemen								
Privates								
W.O.'s and N.C.O's (by ranks) not included in trade columns								
TOTAL wanting to complete to agree with	Officers							
	Other Ranks							
Horses	Riding							
	Draught							
	Heavy Draught							
	Pack							

Remarks :—

Signature of Commander.

Unit.

Formation to which attached.

Date of Despatch.

Qr.Br. Anuh. Lt. Infy

157th. Bde. 50th Div. 2nd Army

26th Nov. 1915

(82434.) Wt. 4894/2217. 500,000. 6/15. B.M.&S. Forms/B. 213/6.

9th BATTN. THE DURHAM LIGHT INFANTRY.

D E C E M B E R

1 9 1 5

WAR DIARY
or
INTELLIGENCE SUMMARY.
(Erase heading not required.)

Instructions regarding War Diaries and Intelligence Summaries are contained in F. S. Regs., Part II. and the Staff Manual respectively. Title pages will be prepared in manuscript.

Place	Date	Hour	Summary of Events and Information	Remarks and references to Appendices
	DECEMBER.			
STEENWERCK	1-14		Still at rest. Company and Battalion training - practice of the attack etc.	
	15.		Inspection of Battalion by the Corps Commander Sir Charles Fergusson.	
	19		Battalion left STEENWERCK and arrived POPERINGHE at 3-24 P.M. by train. Thence it marched by BUSSEBOOM and OUDERDOM to DICKEBUSCHE Huts (Sheet 28.H.26.B."7)	
DICKEBUSCH	20.		Batt'n went up to dugouts in Maple Copse (I.23.d.10.16) taking over from 8th Durh. L.I. -	
	23.		Batt'n relieved 8th Durh. L.I. in SANCTUARY WOOD (I.24.B.), 17th Division being on our left, and 5 BORDER Regt. on our right. [Trenches B1 to B7 inclusive]	
	20.		"A" Coy. had 5 casualties in CANAL DUGOUTS (I.19.D.) 21 Dec. 2/Lt. A. Macmullin sick to hospital.	
	26.		Germans attempted unsuccessfully to explode mine in front of B3 held by 'C' Coy. No damage was done.	
	27.		Batt'n relieved in the trenches by 6th Batt'n Durh. L.I. and by 8th Batt'n Durh. L.I. -	
DICKEBUSCH	28		Batt'n at rest in DICKEBUSCH Huts.	
	29		Capt. Hunter (Adjutant) sick to hospital - also 2.h: Mr Challons, Transport officer Lt. Stafford. hospital.	
SANCTUARY Wood	31.		Batt'n relieved 8th Durh.L.I. in the trenches in SANCTUARY WOOD. Being New Year's Eve our artillery, machine guns and grenadiers 'strafed' the enemy at 10-55 P.M. and at 11-55 P.M.- with apparently good effect. They made no reply except with four bombs - one? which exploded in a	

Army Form C. 2118.

WAR DIARY

or

INTELLIGENCE SUMMARY.

(Erase heading not required.)

Instructions regarding War Diaries and Intelligence Summaries are contained in F. S. Regs., Part II. and the Staff Manual respectively. Title pages will be prepared in manuscript.

Place	Date	Hour	Summary of Events and Information	Remarks and references to Appendices
	DECEMBER.			
SANCTUARY Wood.	31	10·55 P.M.	Bay of B⁴. opposite to BIRDCAGE and killed one man and wounded three others.	

1577 Wt. W10791/1773 500,000 1/15 D. D. & L. S./Forms/C. 2118.

No. of Report _____

FIELD RETURN.

Army Form B. 213.

(To be furnished by all arms, services, and departments (except A.S.C. units) to the A. G.'s Office at the Base in accordance with Field Service Regulations, Part II.)

RETURN showing numbers RATIONED by, and Transport on charge of, ___ at ___ C.R.E. Date. 3/12/15

DETAIL	Personnel			Horses			Mules			Camels	Oxen	Guns, carriages, limbers, showing description	Ammunition wagons and limbers	Machine Guns	Aircraft, showing description	4 Wheeled	2 Wheeled	Motor Cars	Tractors	Lorries, showing description	Trucks, showing description	Trailers	Motor Bicycles	Bicycles	REMARKS
	Officers	Other ranks	Natives	Riding	Draught	Heavy Draught	Pack	Large	Small							Horsed									
Effective Strength of Unit	32 817			12	257	9	9	5	10	4					4			16	3						9	Not Rationed by Unit
Details, by Arms attached to unit as in War Establishment: R.A.M.C.	1	5																								2 Works Workshop ... 3
Armourer	1																									Divisional ... 2
																										Signalling Section ... 3
																										Divl. Train ... 6
																										Brigade Artillery ... 1
																										Sadlers Coy ... 3
																										Mobile A.S.C. ... 12
																										" 3rd Tk Battery ... 2
Total	33 833			12	257	9	9	5	10	4					4			16	3						9	N.C.O. School ... 2
War Establishment	30 800			12	257	9	9	5	10	4					4			16	3						9	M.G. School ... 4
Wanting to complete (Detail of Personnel and Horses below)																										In field Amb ... 1
Surplus	3	33																								O.R. above Estab ... 40
*Attached (not to include the details shown above)																										Officers ... 1
Civilians: Employed with the Unit Accompanying the Unit																										Prov. Tpt. H+ ... 1 ... 42
TOTAL RATIONED	31 793			12	257	9	9	5	10	4																

* In the case of field ambulances, hospitals or depots, the number of patients are to be included here, the names being shown in A.F.A. 36.

Signature of Commander. _____

Date of Despatch. 3/12/15

For information of the A.G.'s Office at the Base.

Officers and men who have become casuals, been transferred or joined since last report.

Place. B.E.F.   Date 3/12/15

Regtl. Number	Rank	Name	Corps	Nature of casualty, or name of unit from or to which transferred	Date of being struck off or coming on the ration return	Remarks*
1608	Capt	Hebron A.F.	9th L.I.	Granted	3-10	
721	Sergt	Dodds T.			12	
1820	L/S	Craig W.		Leave		
1203	Cpl	Aird T.		to	15	
1215	WO	Dixon J.H.				
969		Kirkley				
1576	Cpl	Scott R.J.		England		
1882	L/C	Munroe J.J.				
1484	Pte	Baker J.J.				
1517		Halliday J.				
1234		Pringle J.C.				
1246		Moffat J.C.				
		Paton J.				
1973	Pte	Lockey W.		forfeits 2 days pay for misconduct	2/12/15	
1444		Egan J.				
2093		Kerr J.		To pay for Smoke h'd and lost by negl	2/11	
2112		Pattinson J.				
2608		Bossom J.		Sick to hospital	27-11-15	
3467		Dixon C.			28-11-15	
3079		McGuirk Ch.			28-11-15	
3278		Turner H.			28-11-15	
2120	Pte	Reid C.A.		To duty from hospl	29-11-15	
1016	L/c Pipe	Munroe J.		To duty from A.S.C.	30-11-15	
2301	Bugle	Campbell Wm			30-11-15	
2425	Pte	Purvis J.C.		Div San	28-11-15	
1939		Dunwoodie J.			28-11-15	
3056	Sergt	Wilks Chk		from Grenade School	28-11-15	
	Pte	Gibson J.W.			28-11-15	
2129	Cpl	Padgett D.T.		To M.G. School	27-11-15	
1334	L/c	Gilson A.B.			27-11-15	
2172	Pte	Broomdale R.J.		Bde Bomb Officer servant	26-11-15	(Milling on leave)
1040	Pte	McKay J.		To Base from Div San	27-11-15	
1921		McCarthy J.C.		To N°3 A.S.C.	30-11-15	
1433		Kennyó C.				

* State whether absence is of a permanent or temporary nature, adding, in the case of casuals from wounds or disease, any available information for communication to the relatives.

Perforated Sheet giving detail of personnel and horses wanting to complete, shown on Army Form B. 213.

Number of Report _____

Detail of Wanting to Complete

Row labels: CAVALRY · R.A. · R.E. · INFANTRY · R.A.M.C. · A.O.C. · A.V.C.

Column headings:

Drivers: R.A., R.E., A.S.C., Car, Lorry, Steam

Gunners

Smith Gunners

Range Takers

Farriers: Sergeants, Corporals, Shoeing, or Shoeing and Carriage Smiths, Cold Shoers

Wheelers: R.A., H.T., M.T.

Saddlers or Harness Makers

Blacksmiths

Bricklayers and Masons

Carpenters and Joiners

Fitters & Turners (R.E.): Wood, Iron

Fitters: R.A., Wireless

Plumbers

Electricians: Ordinary, W.T.

Signalmen

Engine Drivers: Loco., Field

Air Line Men

Permanent Line Men

Operators, Telegraph

Cablemen

Brigade Section Pioneers

General-duty Pioneers

Signallers

Instrument Repairers

Motor Cyclists

Motor Cyclist Artificers

Telephonists

Clerks

Machine Gunners

Armament Artificers: Fitters, Range Finders

Armourers

Storemen

Privates

W.O.s and N.C.O.s (by rank) not included in trade columns

TOTAL to agree with complete: Officers, Other Ranks

Horses: Riding, Draught, Heavy Draught, Pack

Remarks :—

Signature of Commander. _____

Unit. _____

Formation to which attached. _____

Date of Despatch. _____

[P.T.O.

(82484.) Wt. 4394/2217. 500,000. 6/15. B.M.&S. Forms/B. 213/6.

FIELD RETURN.

Army Form B. 213.

(To be furnished by all arms, services, and departments (except A.S.C. units) to the A. G.'s Office at the Base in accordance with Field Service Regulations, Part II.)

RETURN showing numbers RATIONED by, and Transport on charge of, _____ at _____ Date. 10th Dec 1915

No. of Report _____

DETAIL	Personnel — Officers	Other ranks	Natives	Horses — Riding	Draught	Heavy Draught	Pack	Mules — Large	Small	Camels	Oxen	Guns, carriages and limbers, showing description	Ammunition wagons and limbers	Machine Guns	Aircraft, showing description	Horsed — 4 Wheeled	2 Wheeled	Motor Cars	Tractors	Lorries, showing description	Trucks, showing description	Trailers	Motor Bicycles	Bicycles	REMARKS
Effective Strength of Unit	32	829		12	25	9	5	10	4					4		16	3							9	
Details, by Arms attached to unit as in War Establishment:— RAMC	1	5																							2 Bonto Intelligence 3
Armourer		1																							Divisional ... 3
																									Sanitary Section 6
																									Brigade Signals 1
																									Railway bn. 3
																									Attached A.S.C. 12
																									3rd T.M. Battery 2
																									N.C.O's School 2
																									Field Cashier 1
Total	33	835		12	25	9	5	10	4					4		16	3							9	O.C. Sect. Para 36
War Establishment	30	800		12	25	9	5	10	4					4		16	3							9	Dept. Remount Officer 5
Wanting to complete																									Pds. Cavalry 1
Surplus	3	35																							" Signals 1
*Attached (not to include the details shown above)																									23
Civilians:— Employed with the Unit Accompanying the Unit																									
TOTAL RATIONED ...	2	1094		12	25	9	5	10	4																

(Detail of Personnel and Horses below)

* In the case of field ambulances, hospitals or depots, the number of patients are to be included here, the names being shown in A. F. A. 36.

_____ Signature of Commander.

10/12/15 Date of Despatch.

Officers and men who have become casuals, been transferred or joined since last report.

Place. _B.E.F_   Date _10th Decr. 1915_

Regtl. Number	Rank	Name	Corps	Nature of casualty, or name of unit from or to which transferred	Date of being struck off or coming on the ration return	Remarks*
	Capt.	Gibbon F.A.L.	9th D.L.I.	Granted	7-15/12/15	
28	Sergt	Farrier H.		}	4 w 12/15	
1291	Pte	Bainbridge L.		Leave to		
1245	"	Samham N.		England		
2574	Pte	Vallans J.		awarded 21 days F.P. No 1 for misconduct	14-12-15	
1754	"	Bell M.		do. do. do.	do.	6-12-15
2400	"	Scott W.		do. do. do.	do.	8-12-15
2142	"	Purvis Fg		do. do. do.	do.	8-12-15
2083	"	Henderson		do. do. do.	do.	8-12-15
1087	"	Goldsworthy W.		do. 28 days do.	do.	8-12-15
1498	"	Howles W.		do. 21 do. do.	do.	9-12-15
1270	"	Dunning W.		do. 21 do. do.	do.	10-12-15
2339	Bugl	Pickavance J.		To duty from hospital	4-12-15	
1028	Pte	Burke			3-11-15	reported to hosp 3/11 & was admitted 3/11/15
2067	"	Oxton J.			8-12-15	
1525	"	Jamieson J.T.			10-12-15	
470	"	Summerside R.R.		C.C.S.	4-12-15	
1944	Pte	Roberts J.H.		To Div. District Shoemaker	3-12-15	
1274	"	Hughes H.		" Post Office	3-12-15	
277	"	Cobbett J.				
	Capt	Dryden C.		" Bde. as Signalling Officer	7-12-15	
214	Pte	Dunning W.		" communical Centre		
30 b	Sgt	Craig A.H.		" Div. Pound	9-12-15	
207	Pte	McRae C.		"		
1003	"	Pegg J.		"		
2172	Pte	Borrowdale W.		" duty from Bde	3-12-15	
3129	Lapl	Padgett		" Officers M.G. School	4-12-15	
1357	2/c	Tyler N.B.		"		
	Lieut	Stafford J.C.		from Bde transport	5/12/15	

Perforated Sheet giving detail of personnel and horses wanting to complete, shown on Army Form B. 213.

Number of Report ——————

Detail of Wanting to Complete

CAVALRY
R. A.
R. E.
INFANTRY
R. A. M. C.
A. O. C.
A. V. C.

Drivers: R. A. | R. E. | A. S. C. | Car | Lorry | Steam

Gunners
Smith Gunners
Range Takers
Farriers: Sergeants | Corporals | Shoeing, or Shoeing and Carriage Smiths | Cold Shoers
Wheelers: R. A. | H. T. | M. T.
Saddlers or Harness Makers
Blacksmiths
Bricklayers and Masons
Carpenters and Joiners
Fitters & Turners (R. E.): Wood | Iron
Fitters: R. A. | Wireless
Plumbers
Electricians: Ordinary | W. T.
Signalmen
Engine Drivers: Loco. | Field
Air Line Men
Permanent Line Men
Operators, Telegraph
Cablemen
Brigade Section Pioneers
General-duty Pioneers
Signallers
Instrument Repairers
Motor Cyclists
Motor Cyclist Artificers
Telephonists
Clerks
Machine Gunners
Armament Artificers: Fitters | Range Finders | Armourers
Storemen
Privates

W.O.'s. and N.C.O's. (by ranks) not included in trade columns

TOTAL to agree with wanting to complete: Officers | Other Ranks

Horses: Riding | Draught | Heavy Draught | Pack

Remarks:—

Signature of Commander.

Lieut Col. ... G. Lockerby

15th Inf Bde. ... Formation to which attached. Unit.

Dec. 10. 1915 _Date of Despatch._

[P.T.O.

(82434.) Wt. 4394/2217. 500,000. 6/15. B.M.&S. Forms/B. 213/6.

FIELD RETURN.

Army Form B. 213.

No. of Report _____

(To be furnished by all arms, services, and departments (except A.S.C. units) to the A. G.'s Office at the Base in accordance with Field Service Regulations, Part II.)

RETURN showing numbers RATIONED by, and Transport on charge of, _9th The Duke of_ R.C.L.I _at_ _____ Date. _17 Dec. 1915._

DETAIL	Personnel			Animals — Horses			Mules			Camels	Oxen	Guns, carriages, limbers showing description	Ammunition wagons and limbers	Machine Guns	Aircraft showing description	Horsed 4 Wheeled	Horsed 2 Wheeled	Motor Cars	Tractors	Lorries, showing description	Trucks, showing description	Trailers	Motor Bicycles	Bicycles	REMARKS
	Officers	Other ranks	Natives	Riding	Draught	Heavy Draught / Pack	Large	Small																	
Effective Strength of Unit	32	24		12	25	9	5	10	4				1				16	3						9	Not Returned by Hand 5
Details, by Arms attached to unit as in War Establishment:																									26ja 6 ... 8
R A M C	1	6																							Div. ... 3
Armourer		1																							Sanitary Sec ... 1
																									Brigade Employ ... 7
																									Railw. y. C. ... 3
																									Attched A.S.C. ... 3
																									3.4. 7. H. C. 4. ... 12
																									N.C.O. & School ... 2
																									L. Field Amba ... 5
Total	33	834		12	25	9	5	10	4				4				16	3						9	Mudal School ... 2
War Establishment	30	800		12	25	9	5	10	4				4				16	3						9	W. & Bhishtis ... 1
Wanting to complete (Detail of Personnel and Horses below)																									Div. Employ ... 4
Surplus		36																							Officer ... 37
*Attached (not to include the details shown above)																									Other Ranks ...
Civilians:— Employed with the Unit Accompanying the Unit																									
TOTAL RATIONED ...	32	801		12	25	9	5	10	4																

* In the case of field ambulances, hospitals or depots, the number of patients are to be included here, the names being shown in A. F. A. 36.

_____ Signature of Commander.

17th Dec. 1915 Date of Despatch.

Officers and men who have become casuals, been transferred or joined since last report.

Place _____ B.E.F. _____ Date _17th Decr 1915_

Regtl. Number	Rank	Name	Corps	Nature of casualty, or name of unit from or to which transferred	Date of being struck off or coming on the ration return	Remarks*
	Sgt	Mack T.	9.D.L.I.		11-19/12/15	
	Capt	Lambert N.T.				
1977	Sgt	Gardiner G.			11-18/12/15	
2680	Cpl	MacNeil S.	(RAMC)		"	
1385	Pte	Cowper Sle			"	
1627		Kirk E.			"	
2709		Ayre J.			"	
C 1256		Feetham H.L.			"	
2866		McCue Sh.			"	
1516		Atkinson H.R.			"	
	Lt	Boys Stones R.			15-23/12/15	
	2/Lt	Palmer				
267	CSM	Bell R.H.			15-22/12/15	
1292	Sergt	Gilroy				
1470	2/Lt	Macmillan J.J.				
1857		Brown S.				
2075	Pte	Hawdon W.				
2713		Cain S.J.				
1854		Hamill				
1564	Cpl	Burton J.J.				
2196	Pte	Graham R.		awarded 7 days F.P. No 1 for misconduct		16/12/15
2618		Connelly D.		forfeits 1 days pay for misconduct	4/12/15	
1207		Dunnett W.		"		
2734		Simpson C.		"		
457		Lister		"		
1688		Wilkinson J.J.		"	5/12/15	
3439		Hunter R.		"	6/12/15	
D 2855	L/Corpl	Telford T.		To hospl. sick	12-12-15	
C 873	Pte	Teffen R.		"	13-12-15	
D 2000		Hartley R.		from Div. Sergt	19-9-15	(for information)
D 1297		Smiles G.S.		CCS	27-11-15	
C 1637		Cook J.		hospl injury to finger	15-12-15	
B 606	Sgt	Work S.T.N.		toe		
	Capt	Dryden E.		To duty from Bde	18-12-15	
C 2142	Pte	Dawson W.		Div. Band	15-12-15	
B 504	Sgt	Craig A.E.		"		
B 505	Pte	McNeal C.		"		
D 1023		Pegg J.		"		
A 1238		Knox J.W.	N.J.	Bde as Storeman		
C 1496		Hoyes		"		
A 1527		Watt R.W.		2/Army Wksps	16-12-15	
A 1344		Turner		"		
D 2857		Foster G.S.		"		
A	Pte	Wilkinson	(RAMC)	Attached Corps on leave		
	L/C	Devlin		to Eng from 2/Army		Wksps

* State whether absence is of a permanent or temporary nature, adding, in the case of casuals from wounds or disease, any available information for communication to the relatives.

Have you any knowledge of his men whereabouts please?

Perforated Sheet giving detail of personnel and horses wanting to complete, shown on Army Form B. 218.

Number of Report _____

Detail of Wanting to Complete	Drivers						Gunners	Smith Gunners	Range Takers	Farriers			Cold Shoes	Wheelers				Saddlers or Harness Makers	Blacksmiths	Bricklayers and Masons	Carpenters and Joiners	Fitters & Turners (R.E.)		Fitters			Plumbers	Electricians			Engine Drivers		Air Line Men	Permanent Line Men	Operators, Telegraph	Cablemen	Brigade Section Pioneers	General-duty Pioneers	Signallers	Instrument Repairers	Motor Cyclists	Motor Cyclist Artificers	Telephonists	Clerks	Machine Gunners	Armament Artificers			Storemen	Privates	W.O's. and N.C.O's. (by ranks) not included in trade columns			TOTAL to agree with wanting to complete		Horses			
	R.A.	R.E.	A.S.C.	Car	Lorry	Steam				Serjeants	Corporals	Shoeing, or Shoeing and Carriage Smiths	R.A.	H.T.	M.T.					Wood	Iron	R.A.	Wireless	Ordinary	W.T.	Signalmen	Loco.	Field																	Fitters	Range Finders	Armourers						Officers	Other Ranks	Riding	Draught	Heavy Draught	Pack

CAVALRY

R.A.

R.E.

INFANTRY

R.A.M.C.

A.O.C.

A.V.C.

Remarks :—

Signature of Commander. _____

Unit. _____

Formation to which attached. _____

Date of Despatch. _____

[P.T.O.

(82434.) Wt. 4894/2217. 500,000. 6/15. B.M.&S. Forms/B. 213/6.

FIELD RETURN.

Army Form B. 213.

(To be furnished by all arms, services, and departments (except A.S.C. units) to the A. G.'s Office at the Base in accordance with Field Service Regulations, Part II.)

No. of Report: _____

RETURN showing numbers RATIONED by, and Transport on charge of, _At. M. Duk 2._ at _B.E.F._ Date. _24/12/15_

DETAIL	Personnel: Officers	Other ranks	Natives	Horses: Riding	Draught	Heavy Draught	Mules: Pack	Large	Small	Camels	Oxen	Guns, carriages and limbers, showing description	Ammunition wagons and limbers	Machine Guns	Aircraft, showing description	Horsed 4 Wheeled	Horsed 2 Wheeled	Motor Cars	Tractors	Lorries	Trucks	Trailers	Motor Bicycles	Bicycles	REMARKS
Effective Strength of Unit	32	824		12	25	9	5	10	4					4		16	3							9	At Huts
Details, by Arms, attached to unit as in War Establishment: RAMC Armourer	16 1																							9	N.C.O's feb. 3; 2 Cylon wigdons 5; 3 Cylon wigdons 3; Smithy See 1; Pol. Rinekefs 7; Stores Cpy 1; Em R.L. A.S.C. 3; 31 7th Bty 12
Total	33	841		12	25	9	5	10	4					4		16	3							9	On Field Ambu. 23
War Establishment	30	800		12	25	9	5	10	4					4		16	3							9	Div. bombing 11 OK Co R.E. 1
Wanting to complete																									6 8
Surplus	3	31																							
*Attached (not to include the details shown above) (Detail of Personnel and Horses below)																									Officers: In Hosp 1; Rgt. Rombed 1; Rifle made School 3;
Civilians:— Employed with the Unit Accompanying the Unit																									
TOTAL RATIONED ..	30	773		12	25	9	5	10	4																

* In the case of field ambulances, hospitals or depots, the number of patients are to be included here, the names being shown in A. F. A. 36.

_____ Signature of Commander.

_24/12/15_ _____ Date of Despatch.

Perforated Sheet giving detail of personnel and horses wanting to complete, shown on Army Form B. 218.

Number of Report _____

Detail of Wanting to Complete			
CAVALRY			
R. A.			
R. E.			
INFANTRY			
R. A. M. C.			
A. O. C.			
A. V. C.			

Drivers: R.A. | R.E. | A.S.C. | Car | Lorry | Steam

Gunners | Smith Gunners | Range Takers

Farriers: Sergeants | Corporals | Shoeing, or Shoeing and Carriage Smiths | Cold Shoers

Wheelers: R.A. | H.T. | M.T.

Saddlers or Harness Makers | Blacksmiths | Bricklayers and Masons | Carpenters and Joiners

Fitters & Turners (R.E.): Wood | Iron

Fitters: R.A. | Wireless

Plumbers

Electricians: Ordinary | W.T.

Signalmen

Engine Drivers: Loco. | Field

Air Line Men | Permanent Line Men | Operators, Telegraph | Cablemen | Brigade Section Pioneers | General-duty Pioneers | Signallers | Instrument Repairers | Motor Cyclists | Motor Cyclist Artificers | Telephonists | Clerks | Machine Gunners

Armament Artificers: Fitters | Range Finders | Armourers

Storemen | Privates

W.O's. and N.C.O's. (by ranks) not included in trade columns

TOTAL to agree with wanting to complete: Officers | Other Ranks

Horses: Riding | Draught | Heavy Draught | Pack

Remarks :—

Signature of Commander. _____

151st Light Rail ... Formation to which attached.

24/2/18 ... Date of Despatch.

(82434.) Wt. 4394/2217. 500,000. 6/15. B.M.&S. Forms/B. 213/6.

FIELD RETURN.

No. of Report. _____

(To be furnished by all arms, services, and departments (except A.S.C. units) to the A. G.'s Office at the Base in accordance with Field Service Regulations, Part II.)

Date. _____

RETURN showing numbers RATIONED by, and Transport on charge of, _____ at. _____

DETAIL	Personnel			Horses			Mules			Camels	Oxen	Guns, carriages, and limbers and transport vehicles				Horsed		Mechanical				Motor Bicycles	Bicycles	REMARKS
	Officers	Other ranks	Natives	Riding	Draught	Heavy Draught	Pack	Large	Small			Guns, carriages and limbers, showing description	Ammunition wagons and limbers	Machine guns	Aircraft, showing description	4 Wheeled	2 Wheeled	Motor Cars	Tractors	Lorries, showing description	Trucks, showing description	Trailers			
Effective Strength of Unit				11	25	9	5	10	4					4		10	3							9	
Details, by Arms attached to unit as in War Establishment:— R.A.M.C.	7	5																							
Attached	1	1																							
Total	33	824		11	33	9	5	10	4					4		16	3						9	1	
War Establishment	30	800		12	25	9	5	10	4					14		16	3						3		
Wanting to complete																									
Surplus	3	24		1																					
*Attached (not to include the details shown above)																									
Civilians:— Employed with the Unit Accompanying the Unit																									
TOTAL RATIONED	75	720		11	25	9	5	10	4																

(Detail of Personnel and Horses below)

* In the case of field ambulances, hospitals or depots, the number of patients are to be included here, the names being shown in A. F. A. 36.

_____ Signature of Commander.

_____ Date of Despatch.

Officers and men who have become casuals, been transferred or joined since last report.

Place: _____ Date _31st December 1915_

Regtl. Number	Rank	Name	Corps	Nature of casualty, or name of unit from or to which transferred	Date of being struck off or coming on the ration return	Remarks*
A 705	Cpl	Allen J				
" 3186	Pte	Dempsey C		attached to		
C 2537	"	Dover J G		175th Tunnelling		
" 2653	"	Edwards W		Coy R.E.		
" 2448	L/Cpl	Edgar R		"		
" 1340	Pte	Carroll J		"		
" 2098	"	Tillery J		"	30/12/15	
" 2019	"	Lord W		"		
" 2047	"	Scott		"		
" 1251	"	Graham H		"		
" 2652	"	Revel J		"		
" 2681	"	Collinson T		"		
" 2670	"	Carr C W		"		
" 1361	"	Brown J		"		
" 1471	"	Armstrong W		"		
" 1199	"	Atkinson J		"		
" 1294	"	Williamson A	R.A.M.C.	Returned to Unit		
A 3803	"	Tanner J		To Divisional	20/12/15	
B 3450	"	Davis		"		
B 2401	"	Middlemas A		" Brewtk Shop	31/12/15	
D 2638	Sgt	Nelson		" Bombers	30/12/15	
B 357	Pte	Marsters R		" A.S.C, MT Section Base	25/12/15	
B 1424	A/Sgt	Serre J		To Machine		
A 1380	Pte	Reid J		Gun Course		
C 2323	"	McMillan J				
C 2096	"	Potts T W		WISGUES	26/12/15	
" 1198	"	Gault J R				
" 1488	"	Wilkinson J				
" 2923	"	Bilton				
D 1847	"	Laundry J				
A 2385	"	Lee P		To Hospital Sick	23/12/15	
" 2237	"	Dixon T		"	23/12/15	
" 3159	"	Bell R		"	23/12/15	
D 2717	"	Walker S H		"	25/12/15	
" 2594	"	Clarke J		"	25/12/15	
A 1919	Sgt	Carr		"	31/12/15	
" 2779	Pte	Carter J		"		
" 3066	Pte	Walker R E		"		
" 2172	"	Whittaker W		"		
D 1666	"	Annis W		"		
" 3004	"	Parres A		"		
A 2265	"	Nixon E		"		
C 3044	"	Duke L		"		
" 2663	"	Richardson J		"		
B 1649	Sgt	McCourt		" Venereal disease		
A 1203	Pte	Dixon C G		" Accidentally Wounded	22/12/15	
C 1616	"	Moran J		" Shell Shock		
D 2123	"	Phillipson H R		" Wounded	25/12/15	
B 2436	"	Watson J		"	21/12/15	

* State whether absence is of a permanent or temporary nature, adding, in the case of casuals from wounds or disease, any available information for communication to the relatives.

For information of the A.G.'s Office at the Base.

Officers and men who have become casuals, been transferred or joined since last report.

Place. B E F   Date 31st December 1915

Regtl. Number	Rank	Name	Corps	Nature of casualty, or name of unit from or to which transferred	Date of being struck off or coming on the ration return	Remarks*
C 448	Pte.	Moody H		From Hospital	23/12/15	
C 2660	"	Howe D		" "	24/12/15	
A 3150	"	Bell R		" "	25/12/15	
C 783	"	Deffen R		" "	28/12/15	
A 2187	Lc	Gregory J		From Bt Course	29/12/15	
D 1847	Pte	Lamonby J		" M G Course	31/12/15	
		Spencer H G		To M Gun Corse Wissans	26/12/15	
Lieut	Capt	Hartley J E		" Hospital Sick	28/12/15	
Lieut	"	Challons J E		" " Shell Shock	"	(Transport Officer)
		Stafford		" " Sick	31/12/15	
	Capt	Brisker S L		" 175th Tunnelling Coy R.E.	30/12/15	
	Lieut	Greener M		Adjt Transport Officer	28/12/15	
	2/Lieut	Bell R N		From Bombing Course	27/12/15	
	"	Mack F				

* State whether absence is of a permanent or temporary nature, adding, in the case of casuals from wounds or disease, any available information for communication to the relatives.

Perforated Sheet giving detail of personnel and horses wanting to complete, shown on Army Form B. 213.

Number of Report

Army Form B. 213.

Detail of Wanting to Complete		CAVALRY	R.A.	R.E.	INFANTRY	R.A.M.C.	A.O.C.	A.V.C.

Drivers:
- R.A.
- R.E.
- A.S.C.
- Car
- Lorry
- Steam

Gunners
Smith Gunners
Range Takers

Farriers:
- Serjeants
- Corporals
- Shoeing, or Shoeing and Carriage Smiths
- Cold Shoers

Wheelers:
- R.A.
- H.T.
- M.T.

Saddlers or Harness Makers
Blacksmiths
Bricklayers and Masons
Carpenters and Joiners

Fitters & Turners (R. E.):
- Wood
- Iron

Fitters:
- R.A.
- Wireless

Plumbers

Electricians:
- Ordinary
- W.T.

Signalmen

Engine Drivers:
- Loco.
- Field

Air Line Men
Permanent Line Men
Operators, Telegraph
Cablemen
Brigade Section Pioneers
General-duty Pioneers
Signallers
Instrument Repairers
Motor Cyclists
Motor Cyclist Artificers
Telephonists
Clerks
Machine Gunners

Armament Artificers:
- Fitters
- Range Finders

Armourers
Storemen
Privates

W.O.'s and N.C.O.'s (by ranks) not included in trade columns

TOTAL wanting to complete to agree with:
- Officers
- Other Ranks

Horses:
- Riding
- Draught
- Heavy Draught
- Pack

Remarks :—

Signature of Commander.

Unit.

Formation to which attached.

Date of Despatch.

3rd Dec. 1915

(8434.) Wt. 4394/2217. 500,000. 6/15. B.M.&S. Forms/B. 213/6.

[P.T.O.

WAR DIARY

or

INTELLIGENCE SUMMARY.

(Erase heading not required.)

Instructions regarding War Diaries and Intelligence
Summaries are contained in F. S. Regs., Part II.
and the Staff Manual respectively. Title pages
will be prepared in manuscript.

Place	Date	Hour	Summary of Events and Information	Remarks and references to Appendices
SANCTUARY WOOD (Sheet 28) I.24.B	Jan 1st	6 AM.	Heavy firing by two of our batteries in the direction of HOOGE. Enemy retaliated with some howitzer shells which fell near MAPLE COPSE (I.28.3RD). Some bombing took place in front of 3rd trench.	
	Jan. 2.		One man wounded (2995 Pte Dobson R 'B' coy) Enemy shelling rather accurate.	
	Jan 3	4.40 PM	Enemy blew in a mine opposite B'trench but no infantry attack followed.	
MAPLE COPSE (I.28.RD)	Jan 4th	6 P.M.	Bttn relieved in front line by 9th Battn Durh LI and moved in MAPLE COPSE. Capt. Dryden 'C' coy sick 1563 Sgt Jozeji? I. to hospital/shell shock. Capt Dryden 'C' coy (1.9.D.75) to hospital (measles) Companies disposed - A coy. MAPLE COPSE. 'B' coy. CANAL DUGOUTS (1.9.D.75). 'C' coy. DUGOUTS in SANCTUARY WOOD). 'C' coy. REDOUBTS (2.3.4.) SANCTUARY WOOD). No 2940 Pte Robinson D. accidentally killed.	
SANCTUARY WOOD	Jan 6th Jan 9	6 PM.	Relieved 8th Battn Durh LI in front line in SANCTUARY WOOD) (Trenches B'- B7 [I.19.a.5.3 to 9.1] Trench mortar bomb thrown in left 13 Bth but no damage done	
	Jan 10 Jan 10		3224 Pte Gibson J.W wounded. No.17794 Pte Sulley J. killed by sniper. No. 2720 Pte Reid. C. S. wounded.	
	Jan 11		No. 1582 Bennet J.H. wounded. No.1338 Mcpl Milmine C. wounded.	
	Jan 12 Jan. 12	7.30 AM	Enemy (mines) exploded mine in front of 'B' - nothing further happened During night of 12/13th our patrols visited crater formed by mine explosion - it is 10 feet deep - 15 across. - 15 yards from enemy, 10 from our own parapet. No enemy patrols were seen. Bttn relieved at night by 8th Battn Durh LI and moved back to rest at DICKEBUSCH HUTS.	
DICKEBUSCH HUTS (N.26 B.3.9)	Jan 14			

1577   Wt. W10791/1773   500,000   7/15   D. D. & L.   A.D.S.S./Forms/C. 2118.

WAR DIARY

or

INTELLIGENCE SUMMARY.

(*Erase heading not required.*)

Instructions regarding War Diaries and Intelligence
Summaries are contained in F. S. Regs., Part II.
and the Staff Manual respectively. Title pages
will be prepared in manuscript.

Place	Date	Hour	Summary of Events and Information	Remarks and references to Appendices
SANCTUARY WOOD (28.1.24 b)	17		Batt⁵ relieved 8ᵗʰ D.H.L.I in the front line B' to B7 (28.1.19 a 5's to 9/). Night passed quietly. Enemy threw bombs & offensive B⁴ in the object, it is thought, of covering noise made by working party which our patrol discovered in front of his trench. No 2779 Pte Shevelthick slightly wounded. Lieut. R.E. ATKINSON slightly wounded by anti-aircraft shrapnel.	
	18	9.30AM to 12 noon	Enemy started violent bombardment on our immediate left and right. Hill 62 on our right. This continued until after midday but nothing followed it.	
	20	12 noon	New Batt⁵ trolleys being built were shelled by a whizzbang gun — direction of Hill 60. Enemy aeroplanes must have spotted the new sandbags and caissons — one man of 7 Durh. L.I was killed. No. 1633 Pte Dixon wounded.	
MAPLE COPSE (28.1.28 B v)	21 23		Enemy sniper shot 1213 Pte Turbitt C.S.H who died of wounds; No 1463 Pte ARMSTRONG killed. Batt⁵ relieved by 85 Durh.L.I put away into Bde reserve in MAPLE COPSE on night 21/23 had Draft of 175 O.R. arrived in trenches. The draft has been some time in the country with an entrenching batt⁵ (Since August and October). The draft seems fairly good though about 6 have been discovered by M.O. to have scabies — and one man is blind in right eye and another lacks a trigger finger. Draft is from 2ⁿᵈ & Durh. L.I.	
SANCTUARY WOOD	25		Batt⁵ relieved 8ᵗʰ Durh L.I in front line B' to B7. One man (No 2053 MOORE R.S.) returning	

WAR DIARY

or

INTELLIGENCE SUMMARY.

(Erase heading not required.)

Instructions regarding War Diaries and Intelligence Summaries are contained in F. S. Regs., Part II. and the Staff Manual respectively. Title pages will be prepared in manuscript.

Place	Date	Hour	Summary of Events and Information	Remarks and references to Appendices
SANCTUARY Wood (28.1.24.b.)	25.		On leave wounded by anti-aircraft shrapnel. Night of 25 & 26 passed very quietly. Extremes.	
	26.		Explosive point discovered in enemy line at (28.S.13.C.4½/5¾). Enemy can be seen moving about in his trenches — working-carrying limbers etc.	
		9.30.P.M.	/Lt. MACK. T. killed, while out on patrol, by a stray bullet. He was with two men when shot — he told the men to go back as he was done for, but they got him in safely to the trench where he died almost immediately.	
	27.		Wind reported veering round to E and N.E. An attack possibly with gas expected, very sharp look out has been kept but nothing extraordinary (removing & were registering) artillery retired. Enemy artillery has been exceptionally quiet these last few days.	
			Lieut. T. MACK was buried at ZILLEBEKE Village (28.1.22.b. 8/3). Brigadier General /.S. SHEA took the service in place of the chaplain who did not arrive.	
	28.	4.P.M.	R4 trench crumped by 5.9 gun from HULL. 30 crumps put over but no casualties and very little damage done.	
	29.	3.P.M.	Wind E & N.E. very slight. Reg. on our left shelled very heavily for about half an hour. Our 8" guns must very well in retaliation.	

1577   Wt.W10791/1773   500,000   1/15   D. D. & L.   A.D.S.S./Forms/C. 2118.

Army Form C. 2118.

WAR DIARY

or

INTELLIGENCE SUMMARY.

(Erase heading not required.)

Instructions regarding War Diaries and Intelligence Summaries are contained in F. S. Regs., Part II. and the Staff Manual respectively. Title pages will be prepared in manuscript.

Place	Date	Hour	Summary of Events and Information	Remarks and references to Appendices
SANCTUARY Wood. (B11.24c.)	29	7-8p.m.	Batt: relieved by 8th Durh. L.I. moved back in Div.l Reserve at DICKEBUSCH Huts.	
DICKEBUSCH	30 } 31		Battn at rest in huts. Divis.l Reserve.	

1577 Wt. W10791/1773 500,000 1/15 D. D. & L.   A.D.S.S./Forms/C. 2118.

Temporary Promotions of Officers of Infantry Battalions to Complete Establishment
(Nº M.S 3522/1)

Name in full (Surname first)	Present Rank	Proposed Rank	Cause of Vacancy	Promotion to date from	Recommended by
BOYSTONES, RICHARD	Lieutenant	Temporary Captain	Temporary Captain E. Dryden to 2nd Bn. Durham Light Infantry (A.G/A.H.Q/a/845)		Henderson — Lieut Colonel Commanding 9th B" Durh. Light Infantry / Brig. General Commanding 151st Infantry Brigade / Major General Commanding 50th Division / General Commanding 5th Corps.

Temporary Promotions of Officers of Infantry Battalions to complete Establishment

(No M.S 3522/1)

Name in full (Surname first)	Present rank	Proposed rank	Cause of Vacancy	Promotion to date from	Recommended by
BOYSTONES, RICHARD	Lieutenant	Temporary Captain	Temporary Captain E. Dryden to 2nd Bn. Durham Light Infantry (A.G/4/A.G/a/845)		[signature] Lieut Colonel Commanding 9th/8th Durham Light Infantry. Brig General Commanding 151st Infantry Brigade. Major General Commanding 50th Division. General Commanding 5th Corps.

Temporary Promotions of Officers of Infantry Battalions to Complete Establishment

(No M.S 3522/1)

Name in full (Surname first)	Present Rank	Proposed Rank	Cause of Vacancy	Promotion to take from	Recommended by
Boys Stokes, Richard	Lieutenant	Temporary Captain	Infantry battalion & Brigade to 2nd Bt. 2nd Line Light Infantry (No 9/924 G/u/545)		[signature] have been commanding 1st to 4th Septr /915 Brig. General commanding 151 Infantry Brigade commanding 50th Division General commanding 5th Corps.

FIELD RETURN.

Army Form B. 213.

No. of Report _____

(To be furnished by all arms, services, and departments (except A.S.C. units) to the A. G.'s Office at the Base in accordance with Field Service Regulations, Part II.)

RETURN showing numbers RATIONED by, and Transport on charge of _____ at _____ Date _____

DETAIL	Personnel			Animals									Guns, carriages, and limbers and transport vehicles													REMARKS
	Officers	Other ranks	Natives	Horses			Mules		Camels	Oxen			Guns, carriages and limbers, showing description	Ammunition wagons and limbers	Machine Guns	Aircraft, showing description	Horsed		Motor Cars	Tractors	Lorries, showing description	Trucks, showing description	Trailers	Motor Bicycles	Bicycles	
				Riding	Draught	Heavy Draught	Pack	Large	Small								4 Wheeled	2 Wheeled								
Effective Strength of Unit	29	956		13	25	9	5	10	4						4		No. 3								9	
Details, by Arms attached to unit as in War Establishment:																										
Anne c	1	5																								
Attached		1																								
Total	30	962		13	25	9	5	10	4						4		No. 3		2053							
War Establishment	30	987		13	25	9	5	10	4						4		No. 3									
Wanting to complete		25																								
Surplus																										
*Attached (not to include the details shown above)																										
Civilians:— Employed with the Unit																										
Accompanying the Unit																										
TOTAL RATIONED ...				13	25	9	5	10	4																	

(Detail of Personnel and Horses below)

* In the case of field ambulances, hospitals or depots, the number of patients are to be included here, the names being shown in A. F. A. 36.

_____
Signature of Commander.

_____ 1916
Date of Despatch.

For information of the A.G.'s Office at the Base.

Officers and men who have become casuals, been transferred or joined since last report.

Place _B. E. F_   Date _28 January 1916_

Regtl. Number	Rank	Name	Corps	Nature of casualty, or name of unit from or to which transferred	Date of being struck off or coming on the ration return	Remarks*
		See daily Casualty Report				

* State whether absence is of a permanent or temporary nature, adding, in the case of casuals from wounds or disease, any available information for communication to the relatives.

Perforated Sheet giving detail of personnel and horses wanting to complete, shown on Army Form B. 213.

B. 213.

Number of Report _____

Detail of Wanting to Complete:

		CAVALRY	R.A.	R.E.	INFANTRY	R.A.M.C.	A.O.C.	A.V.C.

Drivers: H.A., R.E., A.S.C., Car, Lorry, Steam
Gunners
Smith Gunners
Range Takers
Farriers: Serjeants, Corporals, Shoeing, or Shoeing and Carriage Smiths
Cold Shoers
Wheelers: R.A., H.T., M.T.
Saddlers or Harness Makers
Blacksmiths
Bricklayers and Masons
Carpenters and Joiners
Fitters & Turners (R.E.): Wood, Iron
Fitters: R.A., Wireless
Plumbers
Electricians: Ordinary, W.T.
Signalmen
Engine Drivers: Loco., Field
Air Line Men
Permanent Line Men
Operators, Telegraph
Cablemen
Brigade Section Pioneers
General-duty Pioneers
Signallers
Instrument Repairers
Motor Cyclists
Motor Cyclist Artificers
Telephonists
Clerks
Machine Gunners
Armament Artificers: Fitters, Range Finders
Armourers
Storemen
Privates

W.O.'s and N.C.O.'s (by ranks not included in trade columns)

TOTAL to agree with wanting to complete: Officers, Other Ranks

Horses: Riding, Draught, Heavy Draught, Pack

INFANTRY — Other Ranks: *Nil*

Remarks :—

Signature of Commander. _[signature]_

Unit. _9 Bn Durham Light Infantry_

Formation to which attached. _157 Bg. 13 Bn 50 Div 2 Army_

Date of Despatch. _28th January 1916_

[P.T.O.

FIELD RETURN.

(To be furnished by all arms, services, and departments (except A.S.C. units) to the A. G.'s Office at the Base in accordance with Field Service Regulations, Part II.)

No. of Report _____

RETURN showing numbers RATIONED by, and Transport on charge of, _____ at _____ Date. _____

DETAIL	Personnel			Horses				Mules		Camels	Oxen	Guns, carriages, limbers, showing description	Ammunition wagons and limbers	Machine guns	Aircraft, showing description	Horsed		Motor Cars	Tractors	Lorries, showing description	Trucks, showing description	Trailers	Motor Bicycles	Bicycles	REMARKS
	Officers	Other ranks	Natives	Riding	Draught	Heavy Draught	Pack	Large	Small							4 Wheeled	2 Wheeled								
Effective Strength of Unit	20	726	2	11	25	9	5	10	4					4		16	3								
Details, by Arms attached to unit as in War Establishment:																									
R.A.M.C.	1	5																							
Armourer.		1																							
Total	21	802	2	11	25	9	5	10	4					4		16	3								
War Establishment	20	800		11	25	9	5	10	4					4		14	3								
Wanting to complete (Detail of Personnel and Horses below)																									
Surplus	1	2																							
*Attached (not to include the details shown above)																									
Civilians: Employed with the Unit Accompanying the Unit																									
TOTAL RATIONED	21	806	2	11	25	9	5	10	4																

* In the case of field ambulances, hospitals or depots, the number of patients are to be included here, the names being shown in A. F. A. 36.

_____ Signature of Commander.

_____ Date of Despatch.

Officers and men who have become casuals, been transferred or joined since last report.

Place _B.E.F._   Date _4th January 1916_

Regtl. Number	Rank	Name	Corps	Nature of casualty, or name of unit from or to which transferred	Date of being struck off or coming on the ration return	Remarks*
A 1994	Pte.	Tully A.		Killed in action	10/1/16	
C 3234	Pte.	Gibson J.W.		gunshot wound of leg	10/1/16	
B 2920	"	Reid G.S.		Wounded in thigh	10/1/16	
D 1580	"	Bennett J.H.		" " " cheek	11/1/16	
A 1338	L/C	Kilmine C.		" " " hand	11/1/16	
A 3701	Pte.	Scott W.E.		Slightly wounded	12/1/16	
C 1372	Col.	Carmichael R.		Shell Shock	10/1/16	Shell at duty
" 2996	Pte.	Casey		do do	10/1/16	" " "
B 1760	L/C	Murphy G.		Sick to Hospital	31/12/15	
B 2619	Pte.	Harbottle		" " "	6/1/16	
D 1524	"	Young A.		" " "	6/1/16	
C 3766	"	Atkinson W.		" " "	7/1/16	
A 1148	Sgt.	Storey R.		" " "	9/1/16	
C 1082	Pte.	Goldsworthy S.		" " "	10/1/16	
B 1653	"	Holden C.		" " "	11/1/16	
D 2546	"	Tulip L.		" " "	11/1/16	
A 2391	"	Birkett A.		" " "	12/1/16	
B 1289	"	McQueen J.		Accidentally injured to Hospital	13/1/16	
A 2380	Pte.	Startling E.		to Bde Bomb Store	28/12/15	
A 3026	"	Hall E.		Attached to R.E.	30/12/15	Carpenter
B 3976	"	Emmerson W.J.		" " "	"	"
B 2586	Pte.	Finlay W.		From Hospital	7/1/16	
B 1596	Sgt.	Riddell A.			10/1/16	
A 3267	Pte.	Richards R.		From Base	10/1/16	

* State whether absence is of a permanent or temporary nature, adding, in the case of casuals from wounds or disease, any available information for communication to the relatives.

As one Officer + 30 O.R. are being transferred to Brigade Machine Gun Company. I should like a reinforcement to cover this loss (The reinforcement should include a trained M.G. Officer.

Lt J.B. Jameson of this Bn is at present acting as an Instructor at a M.G. school at Portland in England but I should like him sent out again.

You will notice that I have 13 men away with Trench Howitzers + 16 attached to a tunnelling Company. These should also be replaced

A. Henderson Lt Col
1/9th Durham L.I.

14/1/16

Perforated Sheet giving detail of personnel and horses wanting to complete, shown on Army Form B. 213.

Number of Report ____

Detail of Wanting to Complete

CAVALRY
R. A.
R. E.
INFANTRY
R. A. M. C.
A. O. C.
A. V. C.

Drivers: H. A. | R. E. | A. S. C. | Car | Lorry | Steam
Gunners
Smith Gunners
Range Takers
Farriers: Serjeants | Corporals | Shoeing, or Shoeing and Carriage Smiths | Cold Shoers
Wheelers: R. A. | H. T. | M. T.
Saddlers or Harness Makers
Blacksmiths
Bricklayers and Masons
Carpenters and Joiners
Fitters & Turners (R. E.): Wood | Iron
Fitters: R. A. | Wireless
Plumbers
Electricians: Ordinary | W. T.
Signalmen
Engine Drivers: Loco. | Field
Air Line Men
Permanent Line Men
Operators, Telegraph
Cablemen
Brigade Section Pioneers
General-duty Pioneers
Signallers
Instrument Repairers
Motor Cyclists
Motor Cyclist Artificers
Telephonists
Clerks
Machine Gunners
Armament Artificers: Fitters | Range Finders
Armourers
Storemen
Privates

W.O.'s. and N.C.O.'s. (by ranks) not included in trade columns

TOTAL to agree with wanting to complete: Officers | Other Ranks

Horses: Riding | Draught | Heavy Draught | Pack

Remarks :—

Signature of Commander.

Unit.

Formation to which attached.

Date of Despatch.

[P.T.O.

(8434.) Wt. 4394/2217. 500,000. 6/15. B.M.&S. Forms/B. 213/6.

FIELD RETURN.

Army Form B. 213.

No. of Report. _____

(To be furnished by all arms, services, and departments (except A.S.C. units) to the A. G.'s Office at the Base in accordance with Field Service Regulations, Part II.)

RETURN showing numbers RATIONED by, and Transport on charge of, _G: 18. Dark. Dy at B.E.F._ ____ at ____ _7th Jan. 1916._ Date.

DETAIL	Personnel			Animals — Horses			Mules			Camels	Oxen	Guns, carriages and limbers, showing description	Ammunition wagons and limbers	Machine Guns	Aircraft, showing description	Horsed 4 Wheeled	Horsed 2 Wheeled	Motor Cars	Tractors	Lorries, showing description	Trucks, showing description	Trailers	Motor Bicycles	Bicycles	REMARKS
	Officers	Other ranks	Natives	Riding	Draught	Heavy Draught	Pack	Large	Small																
Effective Strength of Unit	32	841		11	25	0	6	10	4					4		16	3							9	At Home
Details, by Arms attached to unit as in War Establishment:— R.A.M.C. Armourer.	1	5 1																							Rd. A.S.C. M.T. Section 4 — 1 M.C.Co. Drivers 25 2 Corps Wk Shops 3 Div 12 Bde Employ 1 Salvage Coy 3 Att A.S.C 13 31 TH Bn 39 2 ... 6 Divisional Employ 16 O.R. Clerk R.E. 2 A.M.175 ... G 100.
Total	33	847		11	25	0	6	10	4					4		16	3							9	G.M.E. Corner
War Establishment	30	660		12	25	0	5	10	4					4		16	3							9	O. cars 1 P. Shop 5 B Bn Bombers 1 A.M.175 ... 7
Wanting to complete																									
Surplus (Detail of Personnel and Horses below)	3	17		1																					
*Attached (not to include the details shown above)																									
Civilians:— Employed with the Unit Accompanying the Unit																									
TOTAL RATIONED...	26	847		11	25	0	5	10	4																

* In the case of field ambulances, hospitals or depots, the number of patients are to be included here, the names being shown in A.F.A. 36.

_____ _J. J. Hartley Capt._ Signature of Commander.

1st March 1916. Date of Despatch.

Officers and men who have become casuals, been transferred or joined since last report.

Place. B.E.F.   Date 7th Jan'y 1916

Regtl. Number	Rank	Name	Corps	Nature of casualty, or name of unit from or to which transferred	Date of being struck off or coming on the ration return	Remarks*
C 1447	Pte	Dixon E.J.		Killed in action	31/12/15	✓
" 2846	"	Robinson W.		" (accidentally)	6/1/16	✓
A 3149	"	Black G.	To Hosp	Wounded (Shrapnel)	31/12/15	✓
B 1345	"	Hatton J.		" "	"	✓
" 2995	"	Dobson R.		" Bullet wound in arm	2/1/16	✓
C 1565	L/c	Fazey J.		Shell Shock	4/1/16	✓
D 2023	Pte	Armstrong E.		Wounded (Shrapnel)	31/12/15	✓
B 2586	"	Finlay W.		Sick to Hospital	"	✓
C 3331	"	White J.a.		" " "	1/1/16	✓
B 1576	Sgt	Riddell A.H.		" " "	"	✓
C 1275	Pte	Redley J.		" " "	2/1/16	✓
B 1310	Sgt	Johnson C.a.		" (Venereal) "	"	✓
" 2426	Pte	Smith W.		" to Hospital	3/1/16	✓
D 2909	"	Davidson J.		" " "	5/1/16	✓
B 1206	Cpl	Borthwick J.	To	Bde Orderly	21/12/15	✓
C 2939	Pte	Huddart W.	"	" "	"	✓
A 1004	Bugler	Scurfield J.	"	" "	"	✓
C 1377	Pte	Mallaburn A.	To	M.G. Course	1/1/16	✓
D 1725	"	Clark J.	"	" "	"	✓
A 2702	Pte	Morrow W.	To	31st French Howitzer	5/1/16	✓
B 1347	Pte	Baggaley J.	From	Hospital	1/1/16	✓
D 2555	A/Cpl	Gifford J.	"	"	"	✓
A 2229	Sgt	Carter J.	"	"	3/1/16	✓
A 3066	Cpl	Walker R.P.	"	"	"	✓
A 2265	Pte	Nixon E.	"	"	"	✓
A 1161	C.S.M	Wood W.	"	"	"	✓
D 2594	Pte	Clark J.	"	"	"	✓
C 2663	"	Richardson J.	"	"	4/1/16	✓
A 1203	"	Dixon J.B.	"	"	5/1/16	✓
B 2384	"	Coates G.	"	"	"	✓
D 3004	"	Purves H.	"	"	"	✓
B 1314	Pte	Hughes R.H.	"	Div. Post Office	4/1/16	✓
D 2773	"	Corbett J.	"	M.G. Comm. Wagon	1/1/16	✓
A 1380	"	Reid W.H.	"	" "	"	✓
B 1424	Arm/Sgt	Jervis J.	"	" "	"	✓
" 2323	Pte	McMillan J.	"	" "	"	✓
C 2096	"	Potts H.W.	"	" "	"	✓
" 1198	"	Gault J.D.	"	" "	"	✓
" 1488	"	Wilkinson J.	"	" "	"	✓
" 2923	"	Biller J.	"	" "	"	✓
Capt		Dryden E.		Sick to Hosp	4/1/16	✓
" + Adjt		Stacks J.C.		Retd from	5/1/16	✓
2/Lieut		Spencer N.G.		" M.G. Course	1/1/16	✓

* State whether absence is of a permanent or temporary nature, adding, in the case of casuals from wounds or disease, any available information for communication to the relatives.

Perforated Sheet giving detail of personnel and horses wanting to complete, shown on Army Form B. 218.

Number of Report _____

Detail of Wanting to Complete		CAVALRY	R.A.	R.E.	INFANTRY	R.A.M.C.	A.O.C.	A.V.C.
Drivers	R.A.							
	R.E.							
	A.S.C.							
	Car							
	Lorry							
	Steam							
Gunners								
Smith Gunners								
Range Takers								
Farriers	Serjeants							
	Corporals							
	Shoeing, or Shoeing and Carriage Smiths							
Cold Shoers								
Wheelers	R.A.							
	H.T.							
	M.T.							
Saddlers or Harness Makers								
Blacksmiths								
Bricklayers and Masons								
Carpenters and Joiners								
Fitters & Turners (R.E.)	Wood							
	Iron							
Fitters	R.A.							
	Wireless							
Plumbers								
Electricians	Ordinary							
	W.T.							
Signalmen								
Engine Drivers	Loco.							
	Field							
Air Line Men								
Permanent Line Men								
Operators, Telegraph								
Cablemen								
Brigade Section Pioneers								
General-duty Pioneers								
Signallers								
Instrument Repairers								
Motor Cyclists								
Motor Cyclist Artificers								
Telephonists								
Clerks								
Machine Gunners								
Armament Artificers	Fitters							
	Range Finders							
Armourers								
Storemen								
Privates								
W.O's. and N.C.O's. (by ranks) not included in trade columns								
TOTAL to agree with waiting to complete	Officers							
	Other Ranks							
Horses	Riding							
	Draught							
	Heavy Draught							
	Pack							

Remarks :—

Signature of Commander.

Unit.

Formation to which attached.

Date of Despatch.

[P.T.O.

(82484.) Wt. 4894/2924. 500,000. 6/15. R.M.&S. Forms/B. 213/6.

FIELD RETURN.

(To be furnished by all arms, services, and departments (except A.S.C. units) to the A. G.'s Office at the Base in accordance with Field Service Regulations, Part II.)

RETURN showing numbers RATIONED by, and Transport on charge of _____ at B.E.F. _____ Date.

DETAIL	Personnel			Animals									Guns, carriages, and limbers and transport vehicles					Mechanical					
	Officers	Other ranks	Natives	Horses Riding	Draught	Heavy Draught	Pack	Mules Large	Small	Camels	Oxen	Guns, carriages and limbers, showing description	Ammunition wagons and limbers	Machine Guns	Aircraft, showing description	Horsed 4 Wheeled	2 Wheeled	Motor Cars	Tractors	Lorries, showing description	Trucks, showing description	Trailers	Motor Bicycles	Bicycles	REMARKS
Effective Strength of Unit	30	704		12	25	9	5	10	4					4		16	3							8	
Details, by Arms attached to unit as in War Establishment:—	1	5		1													1								
R.A.M.C.		1																							
Total	31	802		12	25	9	5	10	4					4		16	3							9	
War Establishment	30	849		13	25	9	5	10	4					4		16	3							9	
Wanting to complete		1851																							
Surplus	1																								
*Attached (not to include the details shown above)																									
Civilians:— Employed with the Unit Accompanying the Unit																									
TOTAL RATIONED ...		1867		12	25	9	5	10	4					4											

* In the case of field ambulances, hospitals or depots, the number of patients are to be included here, the names being shown in A. F. A. 36.

Signature of Commander.

Date of Despatch.

Officers and men who have become casuals, been transferred or joined since last report.

Place. B E F   Date 31ˢᵗ January 1916

Regtl. Number	Rank	Name	Corps	Nature of casualty, or name of unit from or to which transferred	Date of being struck off or coming on the ration return	Remarks*
		For Casualties see Daily Report.				
72ᵗ		J. O. Jones		Joined unit	9/1/16	
"		F. T. Vasey		"	"	
"		A. C. Heslop		"	"	

* State whether absence is of a permanent or temporary nature, adding, in the case of casuals from wounds or disease, any available information for communication to the relatives.

There are needed to complete establishment 176 Other Ranks but a draft of 174 will join to-day.

There are however 131 other ranks away from Battn.

I should like a trained M.G. Officer if possible Lt Jameson of this Battn is employed at M.G. School Wisques England. I also require skilled workmen as Pioneers

S Henderson

Lt Col

1/9th Durham L.I.

2¹/₁/16

Perforated Sheet giving detail of personnel and horses wanting to complete, shown on Army Form B. 213.

Number of Report ____

Detail of Wanting to Complete	Drivers						Farriers						Wheelers										Fitters & Turners (R.E.)		Fitters		Electricians			Engine Drivers																						Armament Artificers								TOTAL to agree with columns		Horses				
	R.A.	R.E.	A.S.C.	Car	Lorry	Steam	Gunners	Smith Gunners	Range Takers	Serjeants	Corporals	Shoeing, or Shoeing and Carriage Smiths	Cold Shoers	R.A.	H.T.	M.T.	Saddlers or Harness Makers	Blacksmiths	Bricklayers and Masons	Carpenters and Joiners	Wood	Iron	R.A.	Wireless	Plumbers	Ordinary	W.T.	Signalmen	Loco.	Field	Air Line Men	Permanent Line Men	Operators, Telegraph	Cablemen	Brigade Section Pioneers	General-duty Pioneers	Signallers	Instrument Repairers	Motor Cyclists	Motor Cyclist Artificers	Telephonists	Clerks	Machine Gunners	Fitters	Range Finders	Armourers	Storemen	Privates	W.O.'s and N.C.O's. (by ranks) not included in trade columns	Officers	Other Ranks	Riding	Draught	Heavy Draught	Pack
CAVALRY																																																								
R.A.																																																		Nil					
R.E.																																																							
INFANTRY																																																							
R.A.M.C.																																																							
A.O.C.																																																							
A.V.C.																																																							

Remarks :—

Signature of Commander.

C'n 50th Durham Light Infantry   Unit.

151st Inf. Bde., 50th Div. Army   Formation to which attached.

21st January 1916.   Date of Despatch.

[P.T.O.

(82434.) Wt. 4394/2217. 500,000. 6/15. B.M.&S. Forms/B. 213/6.

Army Form C. 2118.

WAR DIARY
or
INTELLIGENCE SUMMARY.

(Erase heading not required.)

Instructions regarding War Diaries and Intelligence Summaries are contained in F. S. Regs., Part II. and the Staff Manual respectively. Title pages will be prepared in manuscript.

Place	Date	Hour	Summary of Events and Information	Remarks and references to Appendices
RAILWAY DUGOUT SANCTUARY WOOD. 28.I.20.c.10.D. SANCTUARY WOOD.	1/2 Feb.		Batt. relieved 2nd E. Yorks. on night of 1/2 February.	
	2/3		Batt. relieved the 8th Durh. L.I. in the front line A1 to B4.	
	3	11·15AM	Enemy field guns shelled all round Batts H.Q - hit some dugouts but no destruction. Capt. F.A.L. GIBBON went to BASE, HAVRE, on two months course of instruction.	
	5.		Sniping very active. No. 1848 Pte G. Auckland 'B' Coy. wounded in GOSROCK ROAD. 2Lt F.B. Innes, 2Lt F.I. Vasey, 2Lt E.R. Webster joined for duty from 3rd line on 5th January.	
	6	1AM	Working party of enemy near BIRR CROSS ROAD dispersed by our rifle fire. We French mortared the BIRR CROSS opposite right of B4 vigorously at 8AM, assisted by 18 pdrs. Enemy replied with rifle grenades and small trench mortars on B2 and supports. we had Seven casualties - two killed and five wounded.	
SANCTUARY WOOD and MAPLE COPSE.	6/7.		Relieved by 8th Durh. L.I. Batts H.Q. moved to MAPLE COPSE. Position of Coys. 'A' Coy. I.24.8.3.Y (dugouts) ; 'B' Coy R2,R3,R1,R1 ; 'C' Coy. I.24.6.4.5 (dugouts) ; 'D' Coy. R1 (one platoon) & I.24.C.8.2 (dugouts). (S.W. corner of ZILLEBEKE LAKE).	
	7		Large working parties on support line B. end SANCTUARY WOOD. Less men wounded.	
	8.		Brigade H.Q. hourly enumber owing to too much electric light. 2Lt W.H. STEPHENSON sick to hospital. Very hot day - shelling fairly continuous and desultory. Enemy aeroplane over Sanctuary Wood.	

WAR DIARY

or

INTELLIGENCE SUMMARY.

(Erase heading not required.)

Instructions regarding War Diaries and Intelligence
Summaries are contained in F. S. Regs., Part II.
and the Staff Manual respectively. Title pages
will be prepared in manuscript.

Place	Date	Hour	Summary of Events and Information	Remarks and references to Appendices
SANCTUARY WOOD MARIE CORPS.	8.	Noon	Noon all afternoon - keep low down and not fired upon at all by anti-aircraft guns. 2nd Lt. G. PALMER Seriously wounded - jaw broken in several places. C.S.M. H.R.Roll 567 ('E' coy) wounded in foot and Shoulder. Three men killed, 7 wounded.	
	9.		Shelling again - three men wounded. Capt. H.E.B. HEADS, A.R.O. GATHERALL, 2nd Lt A.G. HESLOP and Lt SLATER joined the Batt⁰ (the first two rejoined, second two from 3rd line).	
	10.		Three men wounded. 2nd Lt. TOMLINSON, 2nd Lt. G. ALLISON and 35 O.R. to B.H.E. in. G. company.	
SANCTUARY WOOD.	10/11		The Batt⁰ relieved 2nd Lieut. I.L.I. in the front line A⁰¹ to B⁰⁴	
	11.	1·6A.M.	B²·³. Crumped at intervals all night. Enemy have run out a sap opposite our line with L⁰ apparent object of making a new forward trench. One man slightly wounded.	
	12.		had night again B²·³ was Crumped at regular intervals - no damage was done	
		9·30A.M.	B²·³. Crumped and every three hours to half the day. About 4·45 p.m. shelling increased considerably. Clouds of smoke (at first thought to have been gas) blew over from direction of to 6th E. heavy rifle & artillery fire was open fire from N. Salient. Replied got attack on 11 - Corps front. Our front quiet except for heavy shell fire.	
	12/13	8·30 PM	Batt⁰ relieved by 6th N. F. moved up to Div²ⁿ reserve at SCOTTISH LINES (28.G.23.A.5.7). Three men killed at SHRAPNEL CORNER (28.1.20.A.52) - Six O.R. wounded	

1577   Wt. W10791/1773   500,000   1/15   D.D. & L.   A.D.S.S./Forms/C. 2118.

WAR DIARY
or
INTELLIGENCE SUMMARY.
(Erase heading not required.)

Instructions regarding War Diaries and Intelligence Summaries are contained in F. S. Regs., Part II. and the Staff Manual respectively. Title pages will be prepared in manuscript.

Place	Date	Hour	Summary of Events and Information	Remarks and references to Appendices
SCOTTISH LINES	13.		Batt" "at rest"	
	14.		Attack on 14th Div. front - trenches on the BLUFF taken - Batt ordered to "stand to" ready to move at half an hour's notice. Capt. M.F. Lambert (o.c. 'C' coy) sick to hospital.	
	15.		151 Bde - 'at rest' - put in Corps reserve - standing by. Bde relieved 150th Bde in right sector (Hill 60 sector). 9th Durh L.I. move to Bde reserve at BEDFORD Ho:	
BEDFORD Ho. 18/9. (29.1.26.a.7.4.)			Brigade Reserve	
	19th		— " — Lieut R.E. Atkinson, Brigade Bombing Officer, killed in action	
	20th		— " —	
	21st		— " —	
	22nd		Relieved 8th Bn D.L.I. in front line trenches T, 37 & 41 (Hill 60 sector) 12th transferring (14th division on our right) 6th D.L.I. on our left; one man wounded	
	23rd		One man killed, Lieut J.H. Edgar, died of wounds, 9 men wounded,	
	24th		Three men killed 2 died of wounds 22 men wounded	
	25th		Three men wounded	
	26th		Relieved from front line trenches by 8th Bn D.L.I. & went into close support relieving 6th Bn D.L.I. Bn Hqrs Coys SQUARE WOOD; 6 killed, 8 wounded.	

Army Form C. 2118.

WAR DIARY
or
INTELLIGENCE SUMMARY.

(*Erase heading not required.*)

9th Dn Durham L.I.

Place	Date	Hour	Summary of Events and Information	Remarks and references to Appendices
,, ,,	27/3/16		Close Support. 1 man wounded.	
	28/3/16		,, ,, 1 man wounded.	
	29/3/16		,, ,, 1 killed, 6 wounded	
			Strength 28 Officers 904 Other Ranks	

Henderson Lt Col
9th Durham L.I.

1577 Wt.W10791/1173 500,000 1/15 D. D. & L. A.D.S.S./Forms/C. 2118.

FIELD RETURN.

No. of Report _____

(To be furnished by all arms, services, and departments (except A.S.C. units) to the A. G.'s Office at the Base in accordance with Field Service Regulations, Part II.)

RETURN showing numbers RATIONED by, and Transport on charge of, _9th F. Durham Light Infantry_ at _B E F_

Date. _4th February 1916_

DETAIL	Personnel			Animals								Guns, carriages, and limbers and transport vehicles											REMARKS
	Officers	Other ranks	Natives	Horses: Riding	Draught	Heavy Draught	Mules: Pack	Large	Small	Camels	Oxen	Guns, carriages, limbers, showing description	Ammunition wagons and limbers	Machine Guns	Aircraft, showing description	Horsed: 4 Wheeled	2 Wheeled	Motor Cars	Mechanical: Tractors	Lorries, showing description	Trucks, showing description	Trailers	Motor Bicycles	Bicycles	
Effective Strength of Unit	35 9 32			12 25 9	5 10 4									4		16	3							9	9 Batt A.S.C.
Details, by Arms attached to unit as in War Establishment:— R.A.M.C.	1	5																							
Armourer	1																								Empty
Total	29,964			12 25 9	5 10 4									4		16	3								
War Establishment	30,457			12 25 9	5 10 4																				
Wanting to complete	1 23																								
Surplus																									Officers
*Attached (not to include the details shown above)																									At Base
Civilians:— Employed with the Unit																									
Accompanying the Unit																									
TOTAL RATIONED	24,831			12 25 9	5 10 4																				

* In the case of field ambulances, hospitals or depots, the number of patients are to be included here, the names being shown in A. F. A. 36.

_____ Signature of Commander.

4th February 1916 Date of Despatch.

Officers and men who have become casuals, been transferred or joined since last report.

Place _B E F_   Date _4th February 1916_

Regtl. Number	Rank	Name	Corps	Nature of casualty, or name of unit from or to which transferred	Date of being struck off or coming on the ration return	Remarks*
		See daily Casualty Report.				

* State whether absence is of a permanent or temporary nature, adding, in the case of casuals from wounds or disease, any available information for communication to the relatives.

I require 2 Officers to replace
2nd Lt Mack, killed & C McDougall
to England.

On 12th inst 2 Officers will be
taken off strength of this Bn & Bde
Machine Gun Coy. In replacing
these I should like one trained M.G.
Officer.

A Henderson
Lt Col

Number of Report —

Detail of Wanting to Complete			
CAVALRY			
R.A.			
R.E.			
INFANTRY			
R.A.M.C.			
A.O.C.			
A.V.C.			

Drivers: R.A. | R.E. | A.S.C. | Car | Lorry | Steam

Gunners — Smith Gunners — Range Takers

Farriers: Serjeants | Corporals | Shoeing, or Shoeing and Carriage Smiths | Cold Shoers

Wheelers: R.A. | H.T. | M.T.

Saddlers or Harness Makers — Blacksmiths — Bricklayers and Masons — Carpenters and Joiners

Fitters & Turners (R.E.): Wood | Iron

Fitters: R.A. | Wireless

Plumbers

Electricians: Ordinary | W.T. | Signalmen

Engine Drivers: L.000. | Field

Air Line Men — Permanent Line Men — Operators, Telegraph — Cablemen — Brigade Section Pioneers — General-duty Pioneers — Signallers — Instrument Repairers — Motor Cyclists — Motor Cyclist Artificers — Telephonists — Clerks — Machine Gunners

Armament Artificers: Fitters | Range Finders | Armourers

Storemen — Privates

W.O's. and N.C.O's. (by ranks) not included in trade columns

TOTAL to agree with wanting to complete

Horses: Officers | Other Ranks | Riding | Draught | Heavy Draught | Pack

Nil.

Remarks :—

Signature of Commander.

Unit. 9th B'n Durham Light Infantry

Formation to which attached. 151st Infy Bde, 50th Divn, 2nd Army

Date of Despatch. 4th February 1916

(32434.) Wt. 4894/2217. 500,000. 6/15. B.M.&S. Forms/B. 213/6.

[P.T.O.

FIELD RETURN.

No. of Report _____

(To be furnished by all arms, services, and departments (except A.S.C. units) to the A. G.'s Office at the Base in accordance with Field Service RETURN showing numbers RATIONED by, and Transport on charge of, _____ at _____ 12 2 7

DETAIL	Personnel			Animals.							Guns, carriages, and limbers and transport vehicles						
	Officers	Other ranks	Natives	Horses Riding	Draught	Horses Heavy Draught	Mules Pack	Large	Small	Camels	Oxen	Guns, carriages and limbers, showing description	Ammunition wagons and limbers	Machine guns	Aircraft, showing description	Horses 4 Wheeled
Effective Strength of Unit	3090			12	95	9	5	10	4							4
Details, by Arms attached to unit as in War Establishment:— RAMC	1	5														
ano		1														
Total	31906			12	95	9	5	10	4							
War Establishment	30989			12	25	9	5	10	4							
Wanting to complete	71				10											
Surplus (Detail of Personnel and Horses below)		1														
*Attached (not to include the details shown above)																
Civilians:— Employed with the Unit Accompanying the Unit																
TOTAL RATIONED ...	25772			12	125	9	5	10	4							

* In the case of field ambulances, hospitals or depots, the number of patients are to be included here, the numbers being shown in A. F. A. 36.

_____ Signature of Commander.

11th February 1916 Date of Despatch.

For information of the A.G.'s Office at the Base.

Officers and men who have become casuals, been transferred or joined since last report.

Place_ B.E.F   Date 17th February 1916.

Regtl. Number	Rank	Name	Corps	Nature of casualty, or name of unit from or to which transferred	Date of being struck off or coming on the ration return	Remarks*
1878	Pte	Ireland	G	9th Dub. L.I.	Wounded	5/2/16	Place of burial 922. b. 8.3. sheet 28
374	"	Evans	J.H.	"	Killed in action	"	
65"	"	Curry	H	"	Wounded	6/2/16	
3163	"	Ford	a	"			
2702	"	Birkett	E.J.	"		"	
2975	"	Searle	F	"	Slightly Wounded		
1795	"	Skelton		"	Wounded		
2075	"	Hawdon	G.W.	"	Died of wounds	"	Place of burial 922. b. 8.3. (sheet 28)
3056	"	Gipson	J.W.	"	Wounded		
1176	L/Sgt	Morgan	J.H.	"	Severely wounded		
567	Co M	Bell	G.W.R	"	Wounded	8/2/16	
2242	Sgt	Blakey	J.S.	"	Slightly wounded	"	Remaining at duty
2218	Cpl	Lauder	J.S.	"		"	
2742	Pte	Ormston	J.H.	"	Wounded	"	
2278	"	Brown	H	"	Killed in action	"	Place of burial 922. b. 8.3 (Sheet 28)
2763	"	Nicholson	J	"		"	
2201	"	Turnbull	J	"		"	
3240	"	Harwood	H	"	Severely Wounded	"	
	2/Lieut	Palmer	G	"		"	
2208	Pte	Morris	J.W.	"	Wounded	"	
2846	"	Reed	J.J.	"		"	
744	"	McNeil	L.D.	"	Severely Wounded	"	
1221	"	Yarey	I	"	Wounded	"	
2825	"	Gardner	E	"		"	
3593	"	Lynn	E.C.	"		9/2/16	
3470	"	Carter	J.W.	"		"	
1766	"	Robson	H	"		"	
1763	"	Swaddle	G	"		10/2/16	
1468	"	McGuinness		"		"	
2245	"	Curry	A.	"	Slightly wounded	"	Remaining at duty
1442	Pte	Dixon	E.J.				Place of burial
2845					Killed in action		922 b 8.3 (sheet 28)
1794							
1468							
1213							
	2/						
					Report.		
	Cpl		L.I.	Joined Bn. for England	9/2/16	
	2/				"	
				Transferred to Corps M.G. Coy	6/2/16	

case of casuals from wounds or disease,
e relatives.

71 Other Ranks are now required to complete establishment. If possible I should like a few joiners or fitters for Pioneers

[signature]

Perforated Sheet giving detail of personnel and horses wanting to complete, shown on Army Form B. 218.

Number of Report

Detail of Wanting Complete	Drivers						Gunners	Smith Gunners	Range Takers	Farriers			Shoeing, or Shoeing and Carriage Smith	Cold Shoes	Wheelers			Saddlers or Harness Makers	Blacksmiths	Bricklayers and Masons	Carpenters and Joiners	Fitters & Turners (R. E.)		Fitters		Plumbers	Electricians			Signalmen	Engine Drivers		Air Line Men	Permanent Line Men	Operators, Telegraph	Cablemen	Brigade Section Pioneers	General-duty Pioneers	Signallers	Instrument Repairers	Motor Cyclists	Motor Cyclist Artificers	Telephonists	Clerks	Machine Gunners	Fitters	Range Finders	Armourers	Storeman	Privates	W.O.'s and N.C.O.'s (by ranks) not included in trade columns					TOTAL to agree with wanting to complete			Horses				
	R. A.	R. E.	A. S. C.	Car	Lorry	Steam				Sergeants	Corporals			R. A.	H. T.	M. T.					Wood	Iron	R. A.	Wireless		Ordinary	W. T.		Field	L000c.																								Officers	Other Ranks		Riding	Draught	Heavy Draught	Pack
CAVALRY																																																											
R. A.																																																												
R. E.																																																												
INFANTRY																																																												
R. A. M. C.																																																												
A. D. C.																																																												
A. V. C.																																																												

Remarks :—

(S2434.) Wt. 4394/2217. 500,000. 6/15. B.M.&S. Form/B. 913/6.

Army Form B. 213.

FIELD RETURN.

(To be furnished by all arms, services and departments (except A.S.C. units) to the A. G.'s Office at the Base in accordance with Field Service Regulations, Part II.)

RETURN showing numbers RATIONED by, and Transport on charge of. _____ at _____ Date. _____

DETAIL	Personnel Officers	Personnel Other ranks	Personnel Natives	Horses Riding	Horses Draught	Horses Heavy Draught	Pack	Mules Large	Mules Small	Camels	Oxen	Guns, carriages and limbers, showing description	Ammunition wagons and limbers	Machine guns	Aircraft, showing description	Horsed 4 Wheeled	Horsed 2 Wheeled	Motor Cars	Tractors	Lorries, showing description	Trucks, showing description	Trailers	Motor Bicycles	Bicycles	REMARKS
Effective Strength of Unit	28 597																								
Details, by *Arms* attached to unit as in War Establishment:—																									
Total	29 903																								
War Establishment															4	16 3								9	
Wanting to complete (Detail of Personnel and Horses below)	1	34		10												2									
Surplus																									
*Attached (not to include the details shown above)																									
Civilians :— Employed with the Unit Accompanying the Unit																									
TOTAL RATIONED ...	21 733	12	15	9	5	10	4																		

* In the case of field ambulances, hospitals or depots, the number of patients are to be included here, the names being shown in A. F. A. 36.

_____
Signature of Commander.

_____
Date of Despatch.

Officers and men who have become casuals, been transferred or joined since last report.

Place _No 6 ?_   Date _2?-1? ?? 1916_

Regtl. Number	Rank	Name	Corps	Nature of casualty, or name of unit from or to which transferred	Date of being struck off or coming on the ration return	Remarks*
B 2476	Sgt	Beattie L ?	9th Durh L I	wounded	22-2-16	
C 3128	Pte	Kilpatrick C ?				
D 1998		Errington W			23-2-16	
D 2168		Roedke J			"	
C 103?		Donnelly J		Killed in Action	"	
B 208	L/Cpl	Negg H		Joined from F A	"	
D 1635	Sgt	Wilson J		F A	"	
B 2476	Pte	Chisholm R		wounded	24-2-16	
C 2447		Anderson R				
2651		Humphreys W		Shell Shock		
1444		Egan J		wounded		
14975		James J		Bruised leg & Shock		
		Rogers		back to F A		
		Roll of men attached to T V Coy				
A 2333	Pte	Gillap W			22-2-16	
D 1548	Cpl	Brinkerton R				
C 1155		Allison J				
C 1275		Kelly J F				
C 26?		Horsfield				

* State whether absence is of a permanent or temporary nature, adding, in the case of casuals from wounds or disease, any available information for communication to the relatives.

As I have 2 Officers employed at Base, 1 attached to a Travelling Coy who will shortly be transferred, 4 in hospital all of whom will be evacuated.

I shall be glad of a reinforcement of 4 Officers and 84 Other Ranks

(Sd) A Henderson Lt Col
1/4th D L I

Perforated Sheet giving detail of personnel and horses wanting to complete, shown on Army Form B. 213.

Number of Report

Detail of Wanting to Complete.	Drivers. R.A.	R.E.	A.S.C.	Car	Lorry	Steam	Gunners	Smith Gunners	Range Takers	Farriers Sergeants	Corporals	Shoe-ing, or Shoeing and Carriage Smiths	Cold Shoers	Wheelers R.A.	H.T.	M.T.	Saddlers or Harness Makers	Blacksmiths	Bricklayers and Masons	Carpenters and Joiners	Fitters & Turners (R.E.) Wood	Iron	Fitters R.A.	Wireless	Plumbers	Electricians Ordinary	W.T.	Signalmen	Engine Drivers Loco.	Field	Air Line Men	Permanent Line Men	Operators, Telegraph	Cablemen	Brigade Section Pioneers	General-duty Pioneers	Signallers	Instrument Repairers	Motor Cyclists	Motor Cyclist Artificers	Telephonists	Clerks	Machine Gunners	Armament Artificers Fitters	Range Finders	Armourers	Storemen	Privates	W.O.'s and N.C.O's (by ranks) not included in trade columns.	TOTAL to agree with waiting to complete Officers	Other Ranks	Horses Riding	Draught	Heavy Draught	Pack
CAVALRY																																																								
R. A.																																																								
R. E.																																																								
INFANTRY																																																								
R. A. M. C.																																																								
A. O. C.																																																								
A. V. C.																																																								

Remarks :—

Signature of Commander.

Unit.

Formation to which attached.

Date of Despatch.

[P.T.O.

(28149.) Wt. W. 10698/4046. 500,000. 10/15. M.R.Co.,Ltd. Forms/B. 213/6.

Army Form C. 2118.

WAR DIARY
or
INTELLIGENCE SUMMARY.
(Erase heading not required.)

Instructions regarding War Diaries and Intelligence
Summaries are contained in F. S. Regs., Part II.
and the Staff Manual respectively. Title pages
will be prepared in manuscript.

9th Bn Durham L.I.

Place	Date	Hour	Summary of Events and Information	Remarks and references to Appendices
	1st/3/16		In Bde Support to Trenches 31 & 41 S. Hill 60 Scot. Artillery Division made a demonstration on our front, cutting wire. D. Coy & his Gunners a Bombers who occupied a front line trench GLASGOW CROSS. assisted in demonstration by rapid fire, Bombs, etc., 4 men killed 5 wounded, 1 missing.	
	2nd "		Still in Bde support, 50th Division made a demonstration on our front. St Eloi's enemy who was attacked by 17th Division, on our right. The platoon of A. Coy who occurred up & attacked at West-Riding Regiment. Enemys Artillery replies vigorously, doing considerable damage to all our positions. Attack of 17th Division very successful. On B. Coys attacked to 149th Infy Brigade, 10 killed 24 wounded, 10 missing, on right of 2/3rd Hd Qrs 6 a D. Coys were retired a trunk to Rest Camp. DICKEBUSCH	
	3rd "		HQ 900 C & D. Companies Rest Camp DICKEBUSCH, on right of 3/4 A. Coy Bn retired to rest. HQ Qrs at Rest Camp 5 men wounded.	
	4th "		HQ Qrs. A, B & D. Coys, Rest Camp. B. Coy, in close support, BLEAUWPOORT FARM attacked 149th Infy Bde Coy. cos. front facing here in excellent health & spirits.	
	5th "		B. Company retire HQ Qrs. 4th " BLEAUWPOORT FARM, Enemys Aeroplane dropped 3 Bombs in vicinity of camp, No damage.	

1577 Wt.W10791/773 500,000 1/15 D. D. & L. A.D.S.S./Forms/C. 2118.

Army Form C. 2118.

WAR DIARY

or

INTELLIGENCE SUMMARY.

(Erase heading not required.)

Instructions regarding War Diaries and Intelligence
Summaries are contained in F. S. Regs., Part II.
and the Staff Manual respectively. Title pages
will be prepared in manuscript.

Place	Date	Hour	Summary of Events and Information	Remarks and references to Appendices
	6/3		Rest Camp. DICKEBUSCH.	
	7/3		"	
			The following message was received today on the operations of 1/2nd march 16.	
			HdQrs 50th Division 6/3/16.	
			* Dear Shea ✕ (Brigadier General 151st Infy Bde)	
			General Pilcher has written asking me to express his thanks to you, and the officers of the	
			5th Border & 9th D.L.I. concerned, for the quick & ready manner in which ambulances	
			were rendered to the 9th Duke of Wellington's Regt, on 2nd March, when they were sent out	
			to it. The Officer Commanding this informed General Pilcher that the prompt	
			help he received in being sent litters of different descriptions as well as troops was of	
			the greatest value. Will you let the troops found how their service were appreciated.	
			Yours Sincerely, ✕ P. S. Wilkinson ✕ (G.O.C. 50th Division T.F.).	
	8/3		Rest Camp. DICKEBUSCH, Lt. A. Hardman very kindly opened his castle by taking in a huge crump hole on 6th	
			✕ previous attack on 8th; all handy helpers to speedy necessary of so much buried furniture. To O.C. 9th 8th Inf one. 9	
	9/3		The following letter was received.	
			Dear Sir, Pleass accept my Thanks & appreciation for the two platoons of Your Regiment that	
			came to reinforce my Pol on March 2nd., You men were officered, they came up	

Army Form C. 2118.

WAR DIARY

or

INTELLIGENCE SUMMARY.

(Erase heading not required.)

Instructions regarding War Diaries and Intelligence
Summaries are contained in F. S. Regs., Part II.
and the Staff Manual respectively. Title pages
will be prepared in manuscript.

Place	Date	Hour	Summary of Events and Information	Remarks and references to Appendices
	9/3		Through the Barrage in perfect order, and behaved throughout with great gallantry. I hope you know were not too heavy. My men much appreciated this assistance.	
			G.S. Warner, Major, O.C. 9th Duke of Wellington's Regiment.	
	10/3		Relieved the 1st Bn Royal Scots Fusiliers in 3H — 3YR Trenches (Bluff area) K.O. Yorks Regt-	
			on Right- 4th N.F.s on Left. one man wounded.	
	11/3		Pretty quiet time, much both stop and sniping which very badly wounded abt on 1/2 Shaft, 3 wounded	
	12/3		Enemy very quiet on our front. There was a relief of the Enemy &c on night of 12th.	
	13/3		Sniping by enemy much more active, gave him liberal doses of Lewis Gun fire which peninsula him. one killed or wounded	
	14/3		Relieved by 4th Bn. Yorks Regt, and went into close support at Bedford Hows, Lantern Road & Swan Chateau, 3 men wounded.	
	15/3		Still in supports, 250 working Party under R.E. in Smithie, one wounded	
	16/3		— " — 100 — " — —	
	17/3		— " — 250 — " — — — Received a draft of 30 reinforcements.	
	18/3		Relieved from close support by 4th Bn Yorks trenches & proceeded to Rest Billets at Scottish Lines.	

1577 Wt. W10791/1773 500,000 1/15 D. D. & L. A.D.S.S./Forms/C. 2118.

4

Army Form C. 2118.

WAR DIARY

or

INTELLIGENCE SUMMARY.

(Erase heading not required.)

Instructions regarding War Diaries and Intelligence Summaries are contained in F. S. Regs., Part II. and the Staff Manual respectively. Title pages will be prepared in manuscript.

Place	Date	Hour	Summary of Events and Information	Remarks and references to Appendices
	19/3		Scottish Lines. Company training carried out, Draft of 94 Reinforcements arrived from England.	
	20/3		— '' —	
	21/3		— '' —	
	22/3		— '' —	
	23/3		(Bluff Sector) Relieved 6th K.O in Trenches 34 - 37 R. + 3rd Borders on our Right. 5th Dn. Durham L.I. on left. One man wounded.	
	24/3		Enemy fairly quiet. Woke him up with Trench Mortar a Bomb. 1 killed & 1 wounded 1 man wounded	
	25/8		Enemy very quiet. Draft of 63 arrived from England.	
	26/3		Afternoon H.Arn Trenches strip blown up by British on our Right in ST.E.L.O1 blew in our latrine immediately in our front. Opened out — but the enemy who had been taken completely by surprise took some few minutes before retaliating. Not video becoming very active, when enemy aeroplane came direction of attack his bombardment of our front practically ceased, during this Shrappe a German Factory from direction of Hill 60 made one attempt at enfilade on trenches but any Attnt lamp chopped 10 H.E. Shells into his own front line before they came to. Stopped doing considerable damage & this our front line above one killed & five wounded. An excellent trench M.Tr portfolio discovered.	

WAR DIARY

or

INTELLIGENCE SUMMARY.

(Erase heading not required.)

Instructions regarding War Diaries and Intelligence
Summaries are contained in F. S. Regs., Part II.
and the Staff Manual respectively. Title pages
will be prepared in manuscript.

Place	Date	Hour	Summary of Events and Information	Remarks and references to Appendices
			which enabled officers & men into enemy's communication Trench. Support line a Mine of their line from this point our Lewis Gun Officer (Lt-Germans) killed 6 Germans with a burst from Lewis Gun, fired into a party of enemy who stopped by Lewis Guns, who got valuable information from this observation Point. Shot was situated Map Ref: Sheet 28 1/40,000 I.34.6.6.3½.	
	28/3		Things much quieter, one man died of wounds. Enemy fire very active on our far right.	
	29/3		Our man wounded, enemy shell very active on most sub sector on our right.	
	30/3		Our man wounded. — " — — " — — " —	
	31/3		No Casualties, enemy very quiet on our front. A few Rifle Grenades & Trench Mortars were distributed among Trench but failed to bring any activity on their part.	

H. B. Moor
Lieut-Colonel.
Commanding, 9th Bn Durham Light Infantry.

WAR DIARY
or
INTELLIGENCE SUMMARY.

(Erase heading not required.)

Instructions regarding War Diaries and Intelligence
Summaries are contained in F. S. Regs., Part II.
and the Staff Manual respectively. Title pages
will be prepared in manuscript.

Place	Date	Hour	Summary of Events and Information	Remarks and references to Appendices
B.8.7.	1/4/16		Still in Bluff Sector. Trenches 34 – 37 R. Things very quiet. OR OM immediate front, reconnaitre.	
	2/4/16		Enemy's Artillery much more active today ranging in our trenches, several dug-outs & parapets damaged but very slight casualties, 3 wounded. Brigade H.Q O. came in for special attention. This afternoon being motionless, storm troopers, there were many casualties. Captain J.G. Hoile, 2nd. D.L.I. Brigade Major, fatally outpatient. 9th D.L.I. was hit. very badly & died of his wounds the following morning. He was loved & honoured by all ranks who deeply regret his early death. Battling & suffering great pain, his thoughts to the last were for others who were wounded on the same line. Relieved by 2nd Canadian Battalion and moved into Brigade Reserve occupying dug-outs at RIDGEWOOD near VIERSTRAAT. 2 men wounded, one died of wounds.	
	3/4		Still in Brigade Reserve.	
	4/4		Took over the Right Sub Section in VIERSTRAAT area opposite WYTSCHAOTE from 19th Bn. Canadian Regiment. 5th Bn. N.F.'s on Right. 5th Bn. Border Regt. on Left.	
	5/4		Enemy's enjoying fairly active. One casualties, one killed & 2 wounded. The following Special Order of the day was received from Brigadier General Jelf'sa, Commanding 151st Inf. Bde. "The G.O.C. looks at least the officers, N.C.O's & men of the Brigade for the good work done while the Brigade was in the YPRES SALIENT & to congratulate them on the good name which they have made	

1577 Wt. W10791/1773 500,000 1/15 D. D. & L. A.D.S.S./Forms/C. 2118.

WAR DIARY

or

INTELLIGENCE SUMMARY.

(Erase heading not required.)

Instructions regarding War Diaries and Intelligence Summaries are contained in F. S. Regs., Part II. and the Staff Manual respectively. Title pages will be prepared in manuscript.

Place	Date	Hour	Summary of Events and Information	Remarks and references to Appendices
			made	
	6/4		for themselves. He continuing wishes to thank? these in the ranks, for the ordinary & cheerful spirit in which they faced many difficulties & much discomfort. He is very proud & commands much these men.	
	7/4		Enemy quiet on our front but very activity on both sides round about at ST. ELOI section on our left to Comaretto	
	8/4		Enemy's artillery very active. H.E. & shrapnel these being placed in & in rear from front line on various localities. Casualties Killed 2 & 9 wounded	
	9/4		Enemy artillery still active. Barrage placed behind on front line. 1 died of wounds & 9 wounded. Relieved by 5th D.T.R. & proceeded to Rest billets at LA CLYTTE, being in divisional Reserve. Still in divisional Reserve, men got hot baths a clean underclothing.	
	10/4		" " Refitting with clothing arms etc	
	11/4		Proceed to RIDGEWOOD to form Brigade Reserve, relieving 5th Bn Border Regiment:	
	12/4		Enemy shelling RIDGEWOOD. 6 Casualties going in, furnished 300 working party. Still in Brigade Reserve. furnished 300 working party, 7 Casualties	
	13/4		" " "	
	14/4		Relieved 6th Bn D.T.R. & from Left sub-section in VIERSTRAAT area. Casualties 1 killed, 3 wounded. 2nd Bn Border Regt. on our right. 2 Officers & 41 OR. Reinforcements arrived	

577—Wt. W/6791/1473—500,000—4/15—D/D. & L.l. A.D.S.S. (forms) C. 2118. Bn. Border Regt.

WAR DIARY

or

INTELLIGENCE SUMMARY.

(Erase heading not required.)

Instructions regarding War Diaries and Intelligence Summaries are contained in F. S. Regs., Part II. and the Staff Manual respectively. Title pages will be prepared in manuscript.

Place	Date	Hour	Summary of Events and Information	Remarks and references to Appendices
Kants tedr̃	15/4		Enemy fairly active with their Artillery which caused 10 casualties, 1 killed, 9 wounded. Enemy Infantry	
VIERSTRAAT AREA			in trenches opposite very quiet & although Trench Mortars & to the Bombs were distributed among them it failed to bring any activity on their part; no Targets for our snipers	
	16/4		Enemy turning up a bit; sent out a great fatigue guard in early hours of morning; no opportunity of firing. Capt. M.H. Bolton, who only returned from leave the evening previous, to be buried in Suidslay Cemetery at Ridgewood, one man was wounded	
	17/4		Enemy quiet on our front; 1 man wounded	
	18/4		" " " " 1 " wounded	
	19/4		" " " " In Casualties, this being the Anniversary of our arrival in France, the Casualties for the Year have been heavy & are as follows:-	
			Other Ranks Killed 98	
			died of wounds 31	
			Wounded 560	
			Sick 575	
			1264	
			Officers Killed 4	
			" died of wounds 1	
			" Wounded 16	
			" Sick 26	
			50	
	22/4		Relieved by 6th Bn Durham Light Infantry & proceeded to RIDGEWOOD where Bivouac Return	

1577 Wt. W10791/1773 500,000 1/15 D. D. & L. A.D.S.S./Forms/C. 2118.

Army Form C. 2118.

WAR DIARY
or
INTELLIGENCE SUMMARY.

(Erase heading not required.)

Instructions regarding War Diaries and Intelligence Summaries are contained in F. S. Regs., Part II. and the Staff Manual respectively. Title pages will be prepared in manuscript.

Place	Date	Hour	Summary of Events and Information	Remarks and references to Appendices
Zepp. L. Rail	29/4		As the enemy first Poorr Arlery Enemy's Artillery became rather active. Aeroplanes very active and damaging aerial Dygouts including Oraey Front which was set on fire, one man wounded.	
	2/4		Relieved from Pat. Recamp by 7th K.O.S.L.I. 8th Brigade, 3rd Division. who are taking over our Brigade line, & proceeded to Briens near WESTROUTRE & from part of Brigade Reserve, at it a it remained until the 18th.	
	22/4 to		Still in Briens at rest. Programme Training being carried out.	
			On Friday 28th April the G in Chief, Sir Douglas Haig, inspected the Durham Light Infantry Brigade. On 29/4, 14 O.R. Reinforcements arrived 2 1 officer & 12 O.R. on 9/17/16.	
	3/5		Proceeded to LA CLYTTE and furnished 250 men nightly for working on VIERSTRAAT defences. On 7th 1 officer & 46 O.R. Reinforcements arrived	
	4/5 to 7/5		Relieved by 6th Bat. D.L.I. & proceeded from Poot Briens near WESTROUTRE	
	8/5 to 16th		Training being vigorously carried out. On 8/5 L.M. Gotry a 3 O.R. Reinforcements arrived. The Brigadier General, H.M. Office, has been promoted to Major General & left us to take Command of the 30th Division. All ranks were very sorry to part with him, & he had endeared himself to all.	
	17/5		Try Groceunghe Brigade Sports were held.	

WAR DIARY

or

INTELLIGENCE SUMMARY.

(Erase heading not required.)

Instructions regarding War Diaries and Intelligence Summaries are contained in F. S. Regs, Part II. and the Staff Manual respectively. Title pages will be prepared in manuscript.

Place	Date	Hour	Summary of Events and Information	Remarks and references to Appendices
	18/5		Held some very successful Regimental Sports.	
	23/5		Stiée in Rest-Billets. On Tuesday 23rd a Ceremonial parade of the 50th Division was held by Sir Herbert C. O. Plumer, G.O.C. 2nd Army, a number of honours were distributed at the same, mentioned the a Major & G. Brock Formey R.L.F. — Lieut. D. J. Ridley " C.L.F. — D.C.M. Pte. H. Lee, Holliday, Gibson, Clancey — Cpt. Headley, L/C Cannon — Military Medals. This was the first time the Northumbrian Division had paraded as a Division in a Ceremonial parade since mobilization and after 13 months of very hard active service they presented a very fine appearance & were complimented by the G.O.C. on their smart appearance & their steadiness on parade. Received reinforcements of 43 O.R. on 23rd.	
	24/5 25/5 26/5 27/5		Rest-Billets. Inter Coy. neat finished, relieved 8th Bn. East Yorks at Ridgewood, forming Bde in Bde Reserve. Took over the from 4th Shropshire L.I. the left sub-sector of VIERSTRAATE area, about 28.1.2000 N.7 a. B. a M.12. a. 5th Bn Broke in on night. A small barrage on our left. 1 man killed.	
	28th		Enemy very active with trench mortars & minniwerfers making left of our line practically untenable during	

Army Form C. 2118.

WAR DIARY

or

INTELLIGENCE SUMMARY.

(*Erase heading not required.*)

Instructions regarding War Diaries and Intelligence Summaries are contained in F. S. Regs., Part II. and the Staff Manual respectively. Title pages will be prepared in manuscript.

Place	Date	Hour	Summary of Events and Information	Remarks and references to Appendices
	29/5		Atte. days & try tactics damaging the Trenches. MG hostile & Rifles fire all evening with Enemy o Turkts [?] who at present have ships hand. 1. wounded	
	30/5		Still same bombing & trench mortaring. 1 Killed & 2 wounded	
	31/5		Enemy's artillery is rather quiet a there is no sniping by enemy every day. Whitley & 2 guns re Shrapnel from Empire. We are putting this Trend Trench under rest. 3 wounded 1 Killed 1 Killed. Practically repairing & recapture the whole of the line again by day. A wounded.	

J.G. Brewen Lieut & Adjt, M.O.C. [?]
9th Australian Light Infantry

1577   Wt.W10791/1773   500,000   1/15   D. D. & L.   A.D.S.S./Forms/C. 2118.

Army Form B. 213.

FIELD RETURN.

(To be furnished by all arms, services and departments (except A.S.C. units) to the A.G.'s Office at the Base in accordance with Field Service Regulations, Part II.)

No. of Report _____

RETURN showing numbers RATIONED by, and Transport on charge of _____ at _____ Date _____

DETAIL	Personnel			Animals										Guns, carriages, and limbers, and transport vehicles.													REMARKS
	Officers	Other ranks	Natives	Horses			Mules		Camels	Oxen				Guns, carriages and limbers, showing description	Ammunition wagons and limbers	Machine guns	Aircraft, showing description	Horsed		Motor Cars	Tractors	Lorries, showing description	Mechanical		Motor Bicycles	Bicycles	
				Riding	Draught	Heavy Draught	Pack	Large	Small									4 Wheeled	2 Wheeled				Trucks, showing description	Trailers			
Effective Strength of Unit	32 919			12	16	9	5	10	4							4		14	3								9	
Details, by *Arms* attached to unit as in War Establishment:—																											
R.A.M.C. Armoured.	1 5 1																										
Total	33 925		14	12	16	9	5	10	4							4		14	3								9	
War Establishment	35 987		14	12	15	9	5	10	4							4		14	3								9	
Wanting to complete *(Detail of Personnel and Horses below)*	62																											
Surplus																											
*Attached (not to include the details shown above)	2		2																								
Civilians:—																											
Employed with the Unit																											
Accompanying the Unit																											
TOTAL RATIONED ...	35 638			12	15	9	5	10	4							4		14	3								9	

* In the case of field ambulances, hospitals or depots, the number of patients are to be included here, the names being shown in A. F. A. 36.

Signature of Commander. _____

Date of Despatch. _____

Officers and men who have become casuals, been transferred or joined since last report.

Place _B.E.F._   Date _21st April 1916_

Regtl. Number	Rank	Name	Corps	Nature of casualty, or name of unit from or to which transferred	Date of being struck off or coming on the ration return	Remarks*
C 2142	Pte	Parnes J		Wounded	14-4-16	To Hospital
C 1533	"	Errington G		"	"	"
" 1617	"	Rogers C		"	"	"
" 1484	"	Parkin W.A	Killed in Action		"	
D 1318	Col	Armstrong R	" "	"	15-4-16	
A 2240	Pte	Bell J.B		Wounded	"	To Hospital
D 1304	"	Mason J		"	"	"
" 4737	"	Duffy J		"	"	"
" 354	"	Chilton E		"	"	"
" 1064	"	Hudson J		"	"	"
" 2198	"	Forks J.B		"	"	"
A 1021	"	Robson T		"	16-4-16	"
" 2087	Sgt	Campbell C		"	18-4-16	"
" 3112	Pte	Bell H		"	"	"
" 1203	"	Dixon J.B		"	20-4-16	"
B 2015	"	Copper J		"	"	"
	Captain	Batterson M.A		Killed in Action	18-4-16	
D 472	Pte	Baker J		Accidental injury to Ankle	17-4-16	To Hospital

Perforated Sheet giving detail of personnel and horses wanting to complete, shown on Army Form B. 213.

Number of Report _____

Detail of Wanting to Complete.				
CAVALRY				
R. A.				
R. E.				
INFANTRY				
R. A. M. C.				
A. O. C.				
A. V. C.				

Drivers. R. A. / R. E. / A. S. C. / Car / Lorry / Steam

Gunners / Smith Gunners / Range Takers

Farriers Serjeants / Corporals / Shoeing or Shoeing and Carriage Smiths / Cold Shoers

Wheelers R. A. / H. T. / M. T.

Saddlers or Harness Makers / Blacksmiths / Bricklayers and Masons / Carpenters and Joiners

Fitters & Turners (R. E.) Wood / Iron

Fitters R. A. / Wireless

Plumbers / **Electricians** Ordinary / W. T. / Signalmen

Engine Drivers Loco. / Field

Air Line Men / Permanent Line Men / Operators, Telegraph / Cablemen / Brigade Section Pioneers / General-duty Pioneers / Signallers / Instrument Repairers / Motor Cyclists / Motor Cyclist Artificers / Telephonists / Clerks / Machine Gunners

Armament Artificers Fitters / Range Finders / Armourers

Storemen / Privates

W.O.'s. and N.C.O.'s (by ranks) not included in trade columns.

TOTAL, to agree with waiting to complete Officers / Other Ranks

Horses Riding / Draught / Heavy Draught / Pack

Remarks :—

Signature of Commander. _____

Unit. _____

Formation to which attached. _____

Date of Despatch. _____

(handwritten): O. C. 5th Durham Light Infy.
151st Inf. Bde. 50th Div. 2nd Army.
21st April 1916

(26149.) Wt. W. 10698/4046. 500,000. 10/15. M.R.Co., Ltd. Forms/B. 213/6.

(26149.) Wt. W. 10698/4046. 500,000. 10/15. M.R.Co., Ltd. Forms/B. 213/6.

[P.T.O.

FIELD RETURN.

Army Form B. 213.

No. of Report _____

(To be furnished by all arms, services and departments (except A.S.C. units) to the A. G.'s Office at the Base in accordance with Field Service Regulations, Part II.)

RETURN showing numbers RATIONED by, and Transport on charge of, _9th Durham Light Infantry_ at _B.E.F._ Date _7th March 1916_

RETURN showing numbers RATIONED by, and Transport on charge of, and Transport vehicles.

DETAIL	Personnel Officers	Personnel Other ranks	Personnel Natives	Horses Riding	Horses Draught	Horses Heavy Draught	Mules Pack	Mules Large	Mules Small	Camels	Oxen	Guns, carriages and limbers, showing description	Ammunition wagons and limbers	Machine guns	Aircraft, showing description	Horsed 4 Wheeled	Horsed 2 Wheeled	Motor Cars	Tractors	Lorries, showing description	Trucks, showing description	Trailers	Motor Bicycles	Bicycles	REMARKS
Effective Strength of Unit	31	965		12	15	9	5	10	4					4		14	3							9	Not returned by Sergt.
Details, by Arms attached to unit as in War Establishment:—																									
R.A.M.C.	1	5																							
_____		1																							
Total	32	971		12	15	9	5	10	4					4		1								4	
War Establishment	35	987		12	15	9	5	10	4					4		16	3							4	146
Wanting to complete	3	16														2									Officers
Surplus																								1	
*Attached (not to include the details shown above)																								6	Repress
Civilians:—																									
Employed with the Unit																									
Accompanying the Unit																									
TOTAL RATIONED ...	25	825		12	15	9	5	10	4																

* In the case of field ambulances, hospitals or depots, the number of patients are to be included here, the names being shown in A. F. A. 36.

_____ Signature of Commander.

_____ Major.

7th April 1916 Date of Despatch.

Officers and men who have become casuals, been transferred or joined since last report.

Place _B. E. F._   Date _7th April 1916._

Coy	Regtl. Number	Rank	Name	Corps	Nature of casualty, or name of unit from or to which transferred	Date of being struck off or coming on the ration return	Remarks*
			Battle Casualties.				
C	2838	Pte	McNasty		Missing. reported wounded	3/4/16	
"	2098	"	McDonald		" "	"	
B	2157	"	Williams J		Wounded.	2/4/16	To hospital
"	2002	"	Bell H		"	"	"
"	2322	"	Dickson C		"	"	"
D	2595	"	Kendall J		"	5/4/16	"
"	1219	"	Maddison J		"	"	Remaining on duty
C	3228	"	Collins J.		Killed in Action	"	Buried place N.5.a.5.3
D	2883	"	Cawthorne W		" "	7/4/16	"

* State whether absence is of a permanent or temporary nature, adding, in the case of casuals from wounds or disease, any available information for communication to the relatives.

Perforated Sheet giving detail of personnel and horses wanting to complete, shown on Army Form B. 213.

Number of Report _____

Horses: Pack / Heavy Draught / Draught / Riding

TOTAL wanting to serve with to complete: Other Ranks / Officers

W.O's. and N.C.O's (by ranks) not included in trade columns.

Privates
Storemen
Armourers
Armament Artificers — Range Finders
Fitters
Machine Gunners
Clerks
Telephonists
Motor Cyclist Artificers
Motor Cyclists
Instrument Repairers
Signallers
General-duty Pioneers
Brigade Section Pioneers
Cablemen
Operators, Telegraph
Permanent Line Men
Air Line Men
Engine Drivers — Field / Loco.
Signalmen
Electricians — W. T. / Ordinary
Plumbers
Fitters — Wireless / R. A.
Fitters & Turners (R. E.) — Iron / Wood
Carpenters and Joiners
Bricklayers and Masons
Blacksmiths
Saddlers or Harness Makers
Wheelers — M. T. / H. T. / R. A.
Cold Shoers
Farriers — Shoeing, or Shoeing and Carriage Smiths / Corporals / Sergeants
Range Takers
Smith Gunners
Gunners
Drivers — Steam / Lorry / Car / A.S.C. / R. E. / R. A.

Detail of Wanting to Complete.		
CAVALRY		
R. A.		
R. E.		
INFANTRY		
R. A. M. C.		
A. O. C.		
A. V. C.		

Signature of Commander.

9th Bn. The Durham Light Infantry Unit.

151st Inftry Bde. 50th Divn. 2nd Army Formation to which attached.

7th April 1918 Date of Despatch.

Remarks:—

(26149.) Wt. W. 10698/4046. 500,000. 10/15. M.R.Co., Ltd. Forms/B. 213/6.

[P.T.O.]

Army Form B. 213.

FIELD RETURN.

No. of Report. _____

(To be furnished by all arms, services and departments (except A.S.C. units) to the A. G.'s Office at the Base in accordance with Field Service Regulations, Part II.)

RETURN showing numbers RATIONED by, and Transport on charge of, _____ at _____ Date. _____

DETAIL	Personnel			Animals									Guns, carriages, and limbers, and transport vehicles.				Horsed		Mechanical						REMARKS
	Officers	Other ranks	Natives	Horses Riding	Horses Draught	Horses Heavy Draught	Pack	Mules Large	Mules Small	Camels	Oxen		Guns, carriages and limbers, showing description	Ammunition wagons and limbers	Machine guns	Aircraft, showing description	4 Wheeled	2 Wheeled	Motor Cars	Tractors	Lorries, showing description	Trucks, showing description	Trailers	Motor Bicycles	Bicycles	
Effective Strength of Unit	2094																									
Details, by Arms attached to unit as in War Establishment:— R.A.M.C.	1 5																									
Armourer	1																									
Total	30 094																									
War Establishment	25 094																									
Wanting to complete (Detail of Personnel and Horses below)	33																									
Surplus																										
*Attached (not to include the details shown above)																										
Civilians:— Employed with the Unit Accompanying the Unit																										
TOTAL RATIONED																										

* In the case of field ambulances, hospitals or depots, the number of patients are to be included here, the names being shown in A. F. A. 36.

_____
Signature of Commander.

_____ Date of Despatch.

For information of the A.G.'s Office at the Base.

Officers and men who have become casuals, been transferred or joined since last report.

Place __B.E.F.__   Date __11ᵗʰ April 1916__

Regtl. Number	Rank	Name	Corps	Nature of casualty, or name of unit from or to which transferred	Date of being struck off or coming on the ration return	Remarks*
			— BATTLE CASUALTIE			
C 2630	Sgt	Oxenham W		Wounded	7.4.16	To Hospital
2661	Cpl	Couper J			"	Still at duty
2829	Pte	Wensch E.J.		Killed in action	"	
4416	"	Hooks E.J.		"	"	
3099	"	Maddison R.		"	"	
3645	"	Edwards C.		"	"	
511	CSM	Hope J.W.		Wounded	"	To Hospital
4292	Sgt	Gilroy J.		"	"	"
2388	Pte	Miller J.J.		"	"	"
2445	"	Gray		"	"	"
2694	Pte	Blake W		Shell Shock	"	Still at duty
2611	"	Little		Wounded	"	To Hospital
873	"	Liffin C		"	"	"
4011	"	Duke		"	"	"
4172	"	Billingham J.J.		"	"	"
D 865	"	Emery		"	"	"
2556	"	Howes J		"	"	"
2444	"	Morrow		Shell Shock	"	"
2518	"	Higgins J.J		Wounded	"	"
4152	"	Palmer			"	Still at Duty
C 2158	"	Boyd W		Shell Shock	"	"
2194	"	Fenwick J.W		Wounded	"	To Hospital
2065	"	Richards		"	"	"
2218	Cpl	Laidler R		"	8/4/16	"
B 2186	"	Gregory J		"	"	"
D 262	Pte	Doyle R.		"	"	"
2336	"	Sowerby J.G		Died of Wounds	"	"
4426	Cpl	Watty		Wounded	"	To Hospital
2550	Pte	Charlton J.G.		"	"	"
4255	"	Coulson		"	"	"
2995	"	Stewart J.J		"	"	"
C 1408	Cpl	Todd J		"	"	"
351	Pte	Cain J		"	"	"
4888	"	McKasty J.W		"	2/4/16	"
2098	"	McDonald S		"	"	"
A 7138	"	Crowley J		Shell Shock	29/2/16	"
D 2886	"	Convery W			26/2/16	"
A 1411	Cpl	Hall W		Wounded	11/4/16	"
3035	Pte	Fairbairn W			"	"
969	"	Scott R.G	(Posted the 13/4/16)		"	"
2450	"	Sweeney W	accidental fractured leg.		"	"
C 1633	"	Dixon		Wounded	"	"
2845	"	Gardner J.J		"	"	"
A 3555	"	McKay R			13/4/16	"

* State whether absence is of a permanent or temporary nature, adding, in the case of casuals from wounds or disease, any available information for communication to the relatives.

Perforated Sheet giving detail of personnel and horses wanting to complete, shown on Army Form B. 213.

Number of Report _____

Detail of Wanting to Complete.	Drivers.					Farriers				Wheelers					Fitters & Turners (R. E.)		Fitters				Electricians			Engine Drivers														Armament Artificers							W.O.'s. and N.C.O.'s (by ranks) not included in trade columns.	TOTAL, wanting to agree with complete		Horses			
	R. A.	R. E.	A.S.C.	Car	Lorry	Steam	Gunners	Smith Gunners	Range Takers	Sergeants	Corporals	Shoeing, or Shoeing and Carriage Smiths	Cold Shoers	R. A.	H. T.	M. T.	Saddlers or Harness Makers	Blacksmiths	Bricklayers and Masons	Carpenters and Joiners	Wood	Iron	R. A.	Wireless	Plumbers	Ordinary	W. T.	Signalmen	Loco.	Field	Air Line Men	Permanent Line Men	Operators, Telegraph	Cablemen	Brigade Section Pioneers	General-duty Pioneers	Signallers	Instrument Repairers	Motor Cyclists	Motor Cyclist Artificers	Telephonists	Clerks	Machine Gunners	Fitters	Range Finders	Armourers	Storemen	Privates		Officers	Other Ranks	Riding	Draught	Heavy Draught	Pack
CAVALRY																																																						
R. A.																																																						
R. E.																																																						
INFANTRY																																																						
R. A. M. C.																																																						
A. O. C.																																																						
A. V. C.																																																						

Remarks :—

Signature of Commander.

Ot 10th Durham Light Infantry Unit.

151st Inf. Bde. 50th Div. 2nd Army Formation to which attached.

14th March 1916 Date of Despatch.

(26149.) Wt. W. 10698/4046. 500,000. 10/15. M.R.Co., Ltd. Forms/B. 213/6.

P.T.O.

FIELD RETURN.

Army Form B. 213.
Field Service Regulations, Part II).

No. of Report _____

(To be furnished by all arms, services and departments (except A.S.C. units) to the A. G.'s Office at the Base in accordance with Field Service Regulations, Part II).

RETURN showing numbers RATIONED by, and Transport on charge of, _____ at _____ Date. _28th April 1916_

DETAIL	Personnel			Animals									Guns, carriages, and limbers, and transport vehicles.										Mechanical				REMARKS
	Officers	Other ranks	Natives	Horses Riding	Draught	Heavy Draught	Pack	Mules Large	Small	Camels	Oxen	Guns, carriages and limbers, showing description	Ammunition wagons and limbers	Machine guns	Aircraft, showing description	Horsed 4 Wheeled	2 Wheeled	Motor Cars	Tractors	Lorries, showing description	Trucks, showing description	Trailers	Motor Bicycles	Bicycles	
Effective Strength of Unit	54	887		14	16	10	4	10	5					4		14	3							9	Not replaced by others. 3
Details, by Arms attached to unit as in War Establishment:—																									
R.A.M.C.	1	5																							
Armourer.		1																							
Total	55	893		14	16	10	4	10	5					4		14	3							9	
War Establishment	55	887		14	16	10	4	10	5					4		14	3							9	
Wanting to complete		4																							
Surplus (Detail of Personnel and Horses below)		1																							
*Attached (not to include the details shown above)																									
Civilians:— Employed with the Unit																									
Accompanying the Unit																									
TOTAL RATIONED ...	58	934		14	16	4	10	5																	

* In the case of field ambulances, hospitals or depots, the number of patients are to be included here, the names being shown in A. F. A. 36.

_____ Signature of Commander.

8th April 1916 Date of Despatch.

For information of the A.G.'s Office at the Base.

Officers and men who have become casuals, been transferred or joined since last report.

Place B.E.F.   Date 28. 4. 16

Regtl. Number	Rank	Name	Corps	Nature of casualty, or name of unit from or to which transferred	Date of being struck off or coming on the ration return	Remarks*
		(Battle Casualties.)				
		Nil.				

FIELD RETURN.

* State whether absence is of a permanent or temporary nature, adding, in the case of casuals from wounds or disease, any available information for communication to the relatives.

Perforated Sheet giving detail of personnel and horses wanting to complete, shown on Army Form B. 213.

Number of Report _____

Detail of Wanting to Complete.	Drivers.						Gunners	Smith Gunners	Range Takers	Farriers		Shoeing, or Shoeing and Carriage Smiths	Cold Shoers	Wheelers			Saddlers or Harness Makers	Blacksmiths	Bricklayers and Masons	Carpenters and Joiners	Fitters & Turners (R. E.)		Fitters			Plumbers	Electricians		Signalmen	Engine Drivers		Air Line Men	Permanent Line Men	Operators, Telegraph	Cablemen	Brigade Section Pioneers	General-duty Pioneers	Signallers	Instrument Repairers	Motor Cyclists	Motor Cyclist Artificers	Telephonists	Clerks	Machine Gunners	Armament Artificers				Storemen	Privates	W.O.'s and N.C.O.'s (by ranks) not included in trade columns.	TOTAL to agree with Other Ranks wanting to complete		Horses				
	R.A.	R.E.	A.S.C.	Car	Lorry	Steam				Serjeants	Corporals			R.A.	H.T.	M.T.					Wood	Iron	R.A.	Wireless		Ordinary	W.T.		Loco.	Field																Fitters	Range Finders	Armourers					Officers	Other Ranks	Riding	Draught	Heavy Draught	Pack
CAVALRY																																																									
R. A.																																																									
R. E.																																																									
INFANTRY																																															631			R.C.M.		6			
R. A. M. C.																																																									
A. O. C.																																																									
A. V. C.																																																									

Remarks :—

Signature of Commander.

Unit.

Formation to which attached.

Date of Despatch.

[P.T.O.

(26149.) Wt. W. 10698/4046. 500,000. 10/15. M.R.Co., Ltd. Forms/B. 213/6.

FIELD RETURN.

Army Form B. 213.

No. of Report

(To be furnished by all arms, services and departments (except A.S.C. units) to the A. G.'s Office at the Base in accordance with Field Service Regulations, Part II.)

RETURN showing numbers RATIONED by, and Transport on charge of, O'ic B' Durham Cycle Regt at C6 6 6 on 5th May 1916 Date.

DETAIL	Personnel			Animals									Guns, carriages, and limbers, and transport vehicles.												REMARKS
	Officers	Other ranks	Natives	Horses				Mules		Camels	Oxen		Guns, carriages and limbers, showing description	Ammunition wagons and limbers	Machine guns	Aircraft, showing description	Horsed		Motor Cars	Tractors	Lorries, showing description	Trucks, showing description	Trailers	Motor Bicycles	Bicycles	
				Riding	Draught	Heavy Draught	Pack	Large	Small								4 Wheeled	2 Wheeled								
Effective Strength of Unit																										
Details, by Arms attached to unit as in War Establishment:—																										Not gathered with detail
R.A.M.C.	1	1																								2nd Corp Cyclists
Armoured		5																								Div. Cyclists + ditching
																										+ Drainage
																										Bn. Cyclists
																										Reg. Orders
																										M.C.Co. Relief
Total																										Orderly Clerk
																										C.E. 6
War Establishment																										Temp Carried 67
Wanting to complete																									33	
(Detail of Personnel and Horses below)																										
Surplus																									85	11
*Attached (not to include the details shown above)																										
Civilians:—																										Officers
Employed with the Unit																										P.B.sers
Accompanying the Unit																										Cases
TOTAL RATIONED ...																										Corp

* In the case of field ambulances, hospitals or depots, the number of patients are to be included here, the names being shown in A.F.A. 36.

Signature of Commander.

5th May 1916 Date of Despatch.

For information of the A.G.'s Office at the Base.

Officers and men who have become casuals, been transferred or joined since last report.

Place __B.E.F.__ Date __5-5-16__

Regtl. Number	Rank	Name	Corps	Nature of casualty, or name of unit from or to which transferred	Date of being struck off or coming on the ration return	Remarks*
		(Battle Casualties	Nil)			

* State whether absence is of a permanent or temporary nature, adding, in the case of casuals from wounds or disease, any available information for communication to the relatives.

Perforated Sheet giving detail of personnel and horses wanting to complete, shown on Army Form B. 213.

Number of Report _____

Remarks :—

Signature of Commander.

Unit.

Formation to which attached.

Date of Despatch.

5ᵗʰ May 1916

(26149.) Wt. W. 10698/4046. 500,000. 10/15. M.R.Co., Ltd. Forms/B. 213/6.

[P.T.O.

Army Form B. 213.

FIELD RETURN.

(To be furnished by all arms, services and departments (except A.S.C. units) to the A. G.'s Office at the Base in accordance with Field Service Regulations, Part II.)

No. of Report _____

Date _____

RETURN showing numbers RATIONED by, and Transport on charge of, _____ at _____

DETAIL	Personnel			Horses				Mules		Camels	Oxen	Guns, carriages and limbers, showing description	Ammunition wagons and limbers	Machine guns	Aircraft showing description	Horsed		Motor Cars	Tractors	Mechanical			Motor Bicycles	Bicycles	REMARKS
	Officers	Other ranks	Natives	Riding	Draught	Heavy Draught	Pack	Large	Small							4 Wheeled	2 Wheeled			Lorries, showing description	Trucks, showing description	Trailers			
Effective Strength of Unit	35	936		13	16	10	4	10	5					4		14	5							8	
Details, by Arms attached to unit as in War Establishment:— RAMC	1	5																							
Armourer		1																							
Total	35	942		13	16	10	4	10	5					4		14	3							6	
War Establishment	35	987		14	16	10	4	10	5					4		14	3							6	
Wanting to complete (Detail of Personnel and Horses below)		45		1																					
Surplus																									
Attached (not to include the details shown above)		7																							
Civilians:— Employed with the Unit																									
Accompanying the Unit																									
TOTAL RATIONED ...	36	945		13	16	10	4	10	5																

* In the case of field ambulances, hospitals or depots, the number of patients are to be included here, the names being shown in A. F. A. 36.

_____ Signature of Commander.

_____ Date of Despatch.

For information of the A. G.'s Office at the Base.

Officers and men who have become casuals, been transferred or joined since last report.

Place _B E F_   Date _12th May 1916_

Regtl. Number	Rank	Name	Corps	Nature of casualty, or name of unit from or to which transferred	Date of being struck off or coming on the ration return	Remarks*
		Battle Casualties				
		Nil				
		See Daily Casualty Report				

* State whether absence is of a permanent or temporary nature, adding, in the case of casuals from wounds or disease, any available information for communication to the relatives.

Number of Report _____

Detail of Wanting to Complete.	Drivers.					Gunners	Smith Gunners	Range Takers	Farriers				Wheelers			Saddlers or Harness Makers	Blacksmiths	Bricklayers and Masons	Carpenters and Joiners	Fitters & Turners (R.E.)		Fitters				Electricians			Engine Drivers														Armament Artificers					Storemen	Privates	W.O's. and N.C.O's (by ranks) not included in trade columns.	TOTAL, wanting to agree with		Horses				

(sub-column headers, left to right: R.A. | R.E. | A.S.C. | Car | Lorry | Steam | Gunners | Smith Gunners | Range Takers | Serjeants | Corporals | Shoe-ing, or Shoeing and Carriage Smiths | Cold Shoers | R.A. | H.T. | M.T. | Saddlers or Harness Makers | Blacksmiths | Bricklayers and Masons | Carpenters and Joiners | Wood | Iron | R.A. | Wireless | Plumbers | Ordinary | W.T. | Signalmen | Loco. | Field | Air Line Men | Permanent Line Men | Operators, Telegraph | Cablemen | Brigade Section Pioneers | General-duty Pioneers | Signallers | Instrument Repairers | Motor Cyclists | Motor Cyclist Artificers | Telephonists | Clerks | Machine Gunners | Fitters | Range Finders | Armourers | Storemen | Privates | W.O's and N.C.O's | Officers | Other Ranks | Riding | Draught | Heavy Draught | Pack)

CAVALRY					
R.A.					
R.E.					
INFANTRY				45	2451
R.A.M.C.					
A.O.C.					
A.V.C.					

Signature of Commander. _____

Unit.

Formation to which attached.

Date of Despatch.

Remarks :—

I.P.T.O.

FIELD RETURN.

Army Form B. 213.

No. of Report _____

(To be furnished by all arms, services and departments (except A.S.C. units) to the A. G.'s Office at the Base in accordance with Field Service Regulations, Part II.)

RETURN showing numbers RATIONED by, and Transport on charge of, _____ at _____ Date _____

DETAIL	Personnel			Animals									Guns, carriages, and limbers, and transport vehicles.														
	Officers	Other ranks	Natives	Horses			Mules		Camels	Oxen			Guns, carriages and limbers, showing description	Ammunition wagons and limbers	Machine guns	Aircraft, showing description	Horsed		Mechanical					Motor Bicycles	Bicycles
				Riding	Draught	Heavy Draught	Pack	Large	Small								4 Wheeled	2 Wheeled	Motor Cars	Tractors	Lorries, showing description	Trucks, showing description	Trailers		
Effective Strength of Unit															4										6
Details, *by Arms* attached to unit as in War Establishment:—																									
Total																									
War Establishment														4			14	4	14 3						
Wanting to complete																	14 3		14 3						
(Detail of Personnel and Horses below)																									
Surplus																									
Attached (not to include the details shown above)																									
Civilians:—																									
Employed with the Unit																									
Accompanying the Unit																									
TOTAL RATIONED ...																									

REMARKS

* In the case of field ambulances, hospitals or depots, the number of patients are to be included here, the names being shown in A. F. A. 36.

_____ Signature of Commander.

_____ Date of Despatch.

Officers and men who have become casuals, been transferred or joined since last report.

Place _____ B E F _____   Date _____ 19ᵗʰ May 1916 _____

Regtl. Number	Rank	Name	Corps	Nature of casualty, or name of unit from or to which transferred	Date of being struck off or coming on the ration return	Remarks*
		(Battle Casualties A.C)				
		"a Dup Casualty Report				

* State whether absence is of a permanent or temporary nature, adding, in the case of casuals from wounds or disease, any available information for communication to the relatives.

Perforated Sheet giving detail of personnel and horses wanting to complete, shown on Army Form B. 213.

Number of Report _____

Detail of Wanting to Complete.

Drivers.
- R.A.
- R.E.
- A.S.C.
- Car
- Lorry
- Steam

Gunners
Smith Gunners
Range Takers

Farriers
- Sergeants
- Corporals
- Shoeing, or Shoeing and Carriage Smiths
- Cold Shoers

Wheelers
- R.A.
- H.T.
- M.T.

Saddlers or Harness Makers
Blacksmiths
Bricklayers and Masons
Carpenters and Joiners

Fitters & Turners (R.E.)
- Wood
- Iron
- R.A.

Fitters
- Wireless

Plumbers

Electricians
- Ordinary
- W.T.
- Signalmen

Engine Drivers
- Loco.
- Field

Air Line Men
Permanent Line Men
Operators, Telegraph
Cablemen
Brigade Section Pioneers
General-duty Pioneers
Signallers
Instrument Repairers
Motor Cycle's
Motor Cyclist Artificers
Telephonists
Clerks
Machine Gunners

Armament Artificers
- Fitters
- Range Finders
- Armourers

Storemen
Privates

W.O's. and N.C.O's (by ranks) not included in trade columns.

TOTAL wanting to complete with
- Officers
- Other Ranks

Horses
- Riding
- Draught
- Heavy Draught
- Pack

CAVALRY
R.A.
R.E.
INFANTRY
R.A.M.C.
A.O.C.
A.V.C.

Remarks :—

_____ Signature of Commander.

_____ Unit.

_____ Formation to which attached.

_____ Date of Despatch.

[P.T.O.

(26149.) Wt. W. 10698/4046. 500,000. 10/15. M.R.Co., Ltd. Forms/B. 213/6.

FIELD RETURN.

Army Form B. 213.

To be made up to and for Sunday in each week.

No. of Report

(To be furnished by all arms, services, and departments (except A.S.C. units) to the A. G.'s Office at the Base in accordance with Field Service Regulations, Part II.

RETURN showing numbers
(a) Effective strength of Unit.
(b) Rationed by Unit.

of 9th Durham L.I. &c. at 6 6 7 — 26 March 1916 Date.

DETAIL	Personnel			Animals									Guns, carriages, and limbers and transport vehicles										REMARKS
	Officers	Other ranks	Natives	Horses			Mules		Camels	Oxen		Guns, carriages and limbers, showing description	Ammunition wagons and limbers	Machine guns	Aircraft, showing description	Horsed		Motor Cars.	Tractors	Lorries, showing description	Trucks, showing description	Trailers	Motor Bicycles	Bicycles	
				Riding	Draught	Heavy Draught	Pack	Large	Small								4 wheeled	2 wheeled								
Effective Strength of Unit	35	999		4	15	9	4	11	5					4			4	3							9	
Details, by Arms attached to unit as in War Establishment:— R.A.M.C.	1	5																								
Armourer		1																								
Total	36	1005		4	15	9	4	11	5					4			4	3							9	
War Establishment	35	989		4	15	9	4	11	5					4			4	3							9	
Wanting to complete (Detail of Personnel and Horses below)																										
Surplus	1	16																								
*Attached (not to include the details shown above)		2																								
Civilians:— Employed with the Unit Accompanying the Unit																										
TOTAL RATIONED...	36	1025		4	15	9	4	11	5					4			4	3							9	

* In the case of field ambulances, hospitals or depots, the number of patients are to be included here, the names being shown in A. F. A. 36.

Signature of Commander.

26 March 1916

Date of Despatch.

For information of the A.G.'s Office at the Base.

Officers and men who have become casuals, been transferred or joined since last report.

Place _BEF_   Date _26. 5. 16_

Regtl. Number	Rank	Name	Corps	Nature of casualty, or name of unit from or to which transferred	Date of being struck off or coming on the ration return	Remarks*
		Battle Casualties —			Nil	
		See Daily Casualty Report				

* State whether absence is of a permanent or temporary nature, adding, in the case of casuals from wounds or disease, any available information for communication to the relatives.

Perforated Sheet giving detail of personnel and horses wanting to complete, shown on Army Form B. 213.

Number of Report

Detail of Wanting to Complete	Drivers						Farriers					Wheelers									Fitters & Farriers (R.E.)		Fitters		Electricians			Engine Drivers														Armament Artificers						W.O's. and N.C.O's. (by ranks) not included in trade columns	TOTAL to agree with Other Ranks wanting to complete			Horses			
	R.A.	R.E.	A.S.C.	Car	Lorry	Steam	Gunners	Smith Gunners	Range Takers	Serjeants	Corporals	Shoeing, or Shoeing and Carriage Smiths	Cold Shoers	R.A.	H.T.	M.T.	Saddlers or Harness Makers	Blacksmiths	Bricklayers and Masons	Carpenters and Joiners	Wood	Iron	R.A.	Wireless	Plumbers	Ordinary	W.T.	Signalmen	Loco.	Field	Air Line Men	Permanent Line Men	Operators, Telegraph	Cablemen	Brigade Section Pioneers	General-duty Pioneers	Signallers	Instrument Repairers	Motor Cyclists	Motor Cyclist Artificers	Telephonists	Clerks	Machine Gunners	Fitters	Range Finders	Armourers	Storemen	Privates		Officers	Other Ranks	Riding	Draught	Heavy Draught	Pack
CAVALRY																																																						
R.A.																																																						
R.E.																																																						
INFANTRY																																													Nil										
R.A.M.C.																																																						
A.O.O.																																																						
A.V.C.																																																						

Remarks :—

Signature of Commander.

O. 9th Northumbrian Cyclist Infantry

Unit.

151 Inf. Bde. 50th Div. Northn Div. Formation to which attached.

26th May 1916 Date of Despatch.

(B 99511.) Wt. W15519/M149. 1,000,000. 1/16. J. P. & Co., Ltd. Forms/B. 213/7.

[P.T.O.

WAR DIARY
or
INTELLIGENCE SUMMARY.

(Erase heading not required.)

Instructions regarding War Diaries and Intelligence
Summaries are contained in F. S. Regs., Part II.
and the Staff Manual respectively. Title pages
will be prepared in manuscript.

9th Bn. Durham L. I.

Vol. XI

Place	Date	Hour	Summary of Events and Information	Remarks and references to Appendices
	1/6/16		Enemy rather quiet on our immediate front but have initiated a terrific bombardment firing chiefly on our left about HOOGE & MOUNT SORREL. 2 wounded. The bombardment to our left died away during the day. Fighting commenced into fury about 8 p.m. on the right of my brigade Rockets fired Flares & magnificent.	
	2/6/16		This morning. Heavy bombardment from down enemy's front & burst heart by our engrs shipping & wounded our elite fighting on our left my vicinity. Relieved by 8th D.L.I. & proceed to Kent Billets a farm. Divisional Reserve, where we relieved another high...... ? Relieved 6th D.L.I. on left int. sect, Sanctuary on our left 5th Border Regt on right	
	8/6/16	8½	1 man wounded.	
	14/6/16		Had best of luck this trip although the enemy shored signs of activity with Trench Mortars, minnenwerfer etc. We only had 1 man wounded in 124... Relieved by 6th D.L.I. at Ridgwood forming Brigade Reserve. Rest Reserve. Heavy working parties nightly	2 wounded
	15th	"		1 man wounded, 2 wounded
	16th	"		1 man wounded, 1 man died of wounds
	17	"		2 men wounded
	18	"		

1577   Wt. W10791/1773   500,000   1/15   D. D. & L.   A.D.S.S./Forms/C. 2118.

Army Form C. 2118.

WAR DIARY
OR
INTELLIGENCE SUMMARY.

(Erase heading not required.)

Instructions regarding War Diaries and Intelligence
Summaries are contained in F. S. Regs., Part II.
and the Staff Manual respectively. Title pages
will be prepared in manuscript.

9th Bn Durham L.I.

Place	Date	Hour	Summary of Events and Information	Remarks and references to Appendices
	19/6/16		Still in Bde Reserve, strong working parties furnished, 2 men wounded	
	20/6		Relieved 6th D.L.I. in left sub-sector. 29th Canadians on our left - 5th Border on the right. 2 men wounded	
	21/6		Enemy trench mortar fire Bombs, 5 casualties all wounded, 2/Lt Hall & Stronghan doing away the casualties	
	22/6		Enemy trench mortar. 2 casualties	
	23/6		" " " " 2 casualties	
	24/6		Enemy active, by no strong our front, which brought moment retaliation only. 1 killed 9 wounded	
	25/6		Still much activity on our front. Enemy firing steadily all day assisted by trench mortar batteries. Wire badly cut up & parapets badly damaged, our team's & machine guns mostly firing, many necessary repairs 2/Lt Hartworth died of wounds received from a H.E. fair bomb. 5 other ranks wounded	
	26/6		Enemy intermittent. Our guns answering steadily. 1 casualty. (wounded)	
	27/6		Relieved by 8th D.L.I. opposite to LA CLYTTE & farm. Normal reserve have furnished strong working parties of 500 each night - casualties have remained. Received our time	
	28/6 29/6		of guns a share of the Hugh Bairde in full swing.	

1577 Wt. W10791/1773 500,000 1/15 D. D. & L.   A.D.S.S./Forms/C. 2118.

Army Form C. 2118.

WAR DIARY
or
INTELLIGENCE SUMMARY.

(Erase heading not required.)

Instructions regarding War Diaries and Intelligence
Summaries are contained in F. S. Regs., Part II.
and the Staff Manual respectively. Title pages
will be prepared in manuscript.

9th Bn Durham L.I. 9.

Place	Date	Hour	Summary of Events and Information	Remarks and references to Appendices
	3/6		Still in Divisional Reserve, 500 working party, More here & very uncertain Pozic, tomorrow still in Bri. Reserve	

J.A. Armand Leodge Lt Col O.C.
9th Bn Durham L.I. 9.

1577 Wt.W10791/1773 500,000 1/15 D. D. & L.   A.D.S.S./Forms/C. 2118.

Army Form C. 2118.

50

WAR DIARY
or
INTELLIGENCE SUMMARY

(Erase heading not required.)

Instructions regarding War Diaries and Intelligence Summaries are contained in F. S. Regs., Part II. and the Staff Manual respectively. Title Pages will be prepared in manuscript.

Place	Date	Hour	Summary of Events and Information	Remarks and references to Appendices

Vol 12

9th Bn. Durham L.I.
War Diary.
July. 1916.
Volume No. 12.

2449 Wt. W14957/M90 750,000 1/16 J.B.C. & A. Forms/C.2118/12.

FIELD RETURN.

Army Form B. 213.

To be made up to and for Sunday in each week.

No. of Report

(To be furnished by all arms, services, and departments (except A.S.C. units) to the A. G.'s Office at the Base in accordance with Field Service Regulations, Part II.)

RETURN showing numbers {(a) Effective strength of Unit. (b) Rationed by Unit.} of _____ at _____ Date. _____

DETAIL	Personnel			Horses			Mules			Camels	Oxen	Guns, carriages, and limbers showing description	Ammunition wagons and limbers	Machine guns	Aircraft showing description	Horsed 4-wheeled	Horsed 2-wheeled	Motor Cars	Tractors	Lorries, showing description	Trucks, showing description	Trailers	Motor Bicycles	Bicycles	REMARKS
	Officers	Other ranks	Natives	Riding	Draught	Heavy Draught	Pack	Large	Small																
Effective Strength of Unit	33	890		14	19	0	4	11	5					4		14	3							9	
Details, by Arms attached to unit as in War Establishment: RAMC Armourer Corps	1 1	5 1																							
Total	34	890		14	19	0	4	11	5					4		14	3							9	
War Establishment	35	887		14	19	0	4	11	5					4		14	3							9	
Wanting to complete	1																								
Surplus (Detail of Personnel and Horses below)		3																							
*Attached (not to include the details shown above)		2																							
Civilians:— Employed with the Unit Accompanying the Unit																									
TOTAL RATIONED...	26	903		14	19	0	4	11	5					4											

Signature of Commander.

_____ Date of Despatch.

* In the case of field ambulances, hospitals or depots, the number of patients are to be included here, the names being shown in A. F. A. 36.

For information of the A.G.'s Office at the Base.

Officers and men who have become casuals, been transferred or joined since last report.

Place _C.E.F_   Date _2nd June 1916_

Regtl. Number	Rank	Name	Corps	Nature of casualty, or name of unit from or to which transferred	Date of being struck off or coming on the ration return	Remarks*
		Battle Casualties				
A 3133	Pte	McKenzie J		Killed in Action	27-5-16	Ravenswood Militia Cemetery (Plot 28) N.5.a.5.5
" 3197	"	Gleason J	Slight Wound Head		28-5-16	Philadelphia
C 1151	"	Redden E		Killed in Action	29-5-16	Ravenswood Militia Cemetery N.5.a.5.5
" 4133	"	McCall E		Wounded	"	To Hospital
4022	"	Coulson J		"	"	"
B 1826	"	Smith W	Shell Shock Deafness		30-5-16	Still at duty
" 4987	"	Ould N		Wounded Knee	"	"
" 1059	"	Johnson J		"	"	To Hospital
" 1943	"	Napier J		Shell Shock	"	"
C 7938	Bglr	Carr A E		Wounded Wrist	31-5-16	Still at duty
D 2145	L/C	Hodgson M		Wounded	"	To Hospital
C 995	"	Ferguson A		Killed in Action	"	Ravenswood Militia Cemetery Plot 28 N.5.a.5.5
D 7980	Pte	Smith T		Wounded	"	To Hospital
B 4193	"	Dodsworth W		"	1-6-16	" "
C 1250	"	Forster J W	Wounded in Eye		"	Still at Duty
	Lieut	Palmer E C	Wounded in Arm		1-6-16	To Hospital
	"	Mercer A J	"		2-6-16	"

* State whether absence is of a permanent or temporary nature, adding, in the case of casuals from wounds or disease, any available information for communication to the relatives.

Perforated Sheet giving detail of personnel and horses wanting to complete, shown on Army Form B. 213.

Number of Report ——————

Detail of Wanting to Complete	Drivers						Gunners	Smith Gunners	Range Takers	Farriers				Wheelers				Saddlers or Harness Makers	Blacksmiths	Bricklayers and Masons	Carpenters and Joiners	Fitters & Turners (R. E.)		Fitters			Plumbers	Electricians			Engine Drivers			Air Line Men	Permanent Line Men	Operators, Telegraph	Cablemen	Brigade Section Pioneers	General-duty Pioneers	Signallers	Instrument Repairers	Motor Cyclists	Motor Cyclist Artificers	Telephonists	Clerks	Machine Gunners	Armament Artificers			Armourers	Storemen	Privates	W.O.'s and N.C.O.'s (by ranks) not included in trade columns	TOTAL to agree with wanting to complete		Horses				
	R.A.	R.E.	A.S.C.	Car	Lorry	Steam				Serjeants	Corporals	Shoeing, or Shoeing and Carriage Smiths	Cold Shoers	R.A.	H.T.	M.T.						Wood	Iron	R.A.	Wireless		Ordinary	W.T.	Signalmen	Loco.	Field																Fitters	Range Finders				Officers	Other Ranks		Officers	Riding	Draught	Heavy Draught	Pack
CAVALRY																																																										
R.A.																																																										
R.E.																																																										
INFANTRY																																																										
R.A.M.C.																																																										
A.O.C.																																																										
A.V.C.																																																										

Remarks :—

Signature of Commander.

Unit ——————

Formation to which attached. ——————

Date of Despatch. ——————

2nd June 1916

(B 99511.) Wt. W15500/M149. 1,000,000. 1/16. J. P. & Co., Ltd. Forms/B. 213/7.

[P.T.O.

Army Form B. 213.

FIELD RETURN.

(To be furnished by all arms, services and departments (except A.S.C. units) to the A. G.'s Office at the Base in accordance with Field Service Regulations, Part II.)

RETURN showing numbers RATIONED by, and Transport on charge of_____ at _____ Date._____

No. of Report _____

Guns, carriages, and limbers, and transport vehicles.

DETAIL	Personnel: Officers	Other ranks	Natives	Horses: Riding	Draught	Heavy Draught	Pack	Mules: Large	Small	Camels	Oxen	Guns, carriages and limbers, showing description	Ammunition wagons and limbers	Machine guns	Aircraft, showing description	Horsed: 4 Wheeled	2 Wheeled	Motor Cars	Tractors	Lorries, showing description	Trucks, showing description	Trailers	Motor Bicycles	Bicycles.	REMARKS
Effective Strength of Unit				14	14	9	4	11	5					4		14	3							9	
Details, by Arms attached to unit as in War Establishment:—	1	5																							
	1	1																							
Total	41	986		14	14	9	4	11	5					4		14	3							9	
War Establishment	35	987		14	14	9	4	11	5					4		14	3							9	
Wanting to complete (Detail of Personnel and Horses below)		1																			1				
Surplus	6																								
*Attached (not to include the details shown above)		2																							
Civilians:— Employed with the Unit, Accompanying the Unit																									
TOTAL RATIONED...	35	890		14	17	9	4	11	5																

* In the case of field ambulances, hospitals or depots, the number of patients are to be included here, the names being shown in A. F. A. 36.

Signature of Commander.

_____ Date of Despatch.

Officers and men who have become casuals, been transferred or joined since last report.

Place **B.E.F.**   Date **9ᵗʰ June 1916.**

Regtl. Number	Rank	Name	Corps	Nature of casualty, or name of unit from or to which transferred	Date of being struck off or coming on the ration return	Remarks*
1585	Pte		Battle Casualties			
1565	Pte	Skidmore *N*	(Bee King Section)	Wounded	5-6-16	to Hospital
2132	"	Moore *J*	"	Killed in Action	6-6-16	Buried. Ridgewood (Sh. 28). N.5.a.5.5

Perforated Sheet giving detail of personnel and horses wanting to complete, shown on Army Form B. 213.

Number of Report _____

Detail of Wanting to Complete.						
CAVALRY						
R. A.						
R. E.						
INFANTRY						
R. A. M. C.						
A. O. C.						
A. V. C.						

Drivers: R.A., R.E., A.S.C., Car, Lorry, Steam
Gunners
Smith Gunners
Range Takers
Farriers: Serjeants, Corporals, Shoeing, or Shoeing and Carriage Smiths, Cold Shoers
Wheelers: R. A., H. T., M. T.
Saddlers or Harness Makers
Blacksmiths
Bricklayers and Masons
Carpenters and Joiners
Fitters & Turners (R. E.): Wood, Iron
Fitters: R. A., Wireless
Plumbers
Electricians: Ordinary, W. T.
Signalmen
Engine Drivers: Loco., Field
Air Line Men
Permanent Line Men
Operators, Telegraph
Cablemen
Brigade Section Pioneers
General-duty Pioneers
Signallers
Instrument Repairers
Motor Cyclie's
Motor Cyclist Artificers
Telephonists
Clerks
Machine Gunners
Armament Artificers: Fitters, Range Finders, Armourers
Storemen
Privates

W.O's. and N.C.O's (by ranks) not included in trade columns.

TOTAL: Officers, Other Ranks wanting to agree with to complete

Horses: Riding, Draught, Heavy Draught, Pack

Remarks:—

_____ Signature of Commander.

_____ Unit.

_____ Formation to which attached.

_____ Date of Despatch.

(26149.) Wt. W. 10698/4046. 500,000. 10/15. M.R.Co., Ltd. Forms/B. 213/6. [P.T.O.

FIELD RETURN.

Army Form B. 213.

No. of Report.

(To be furnished by all arms, services and departments (except A.S.C. units) to the A. G.'s Office at the Base in accordance with Field Service Regulations, Part II.)

RETURN showing numbers RATIONED by, and Transport on charge of, _____ at _____ Date _____ 16th June 1916.

DETAIL	Personnel			Animals									Guns, carriages, and limbers, and transport vehicles.													REMARKS
	Officers	Other ranks	Natives	Horses				Mules		Camels	Oxen	Guns, carriages and limbers, showing description	Ammunition wagons and limbers	Machine guns	Aircraft, showing description	Horsed		Motor Cars	Tractors	Mechanical			Trailers	Motor Bicycles	Bicycles	
				Riding	Draught	Heavy Draught	Pack	Large	Small							4 Wheeled	2 Wheeled			Lorries, showing description	Trucks, showing description					
Effective Strength of Unit	42	1917		14	14	9	4	11	5					4		14	3								9	
Details, by Arms attached to unit as in War Establishment:— R.A.M.C.	1	5																							
Horses	1	1																							
Total	42	1903		14	14	9	4	11	5					4		14	3				3				9	
War Establishment	35	917		14	14	9	4	11	5					4		14	3								9	105
Wanting to complete (Detail of Personnel and Horses below)																										
Surplus	7	16																								
Attached (not to include the details shown above)		2																								
Civilians:— Employed with the Unit Accompanying the Unit																										
TOTAL RATIONED ...	35	900		14	14	9	4	11	5																	

* In the case of field ambulances, hospitals or depots, the number of patients are to be included here, the names being shown in A. F. A. 36.

_____ Signature of Commander.

_____ Date of Despatch.

Officers and men who have become casuals, been transferred or joined since last report.

Place _____ B. E. F. _____ Date _____ 16th June 1916.

Regtl. Number	Rank	Name		Corps	Nature of casualty, or name of unit from or to which transferred	Date of being struck off or coming on the ration return	Remarks*
				Battle Casualties			
C. 1973	Pte	Lockey	W	9th D.L.I.	Wounded	8/6/16.	to hospital
A 2296		Cowell	A	"	"	12/6/16	"

* State whether absence is of a permanent or temporary nature, adding, in the case of casuals from wounds or disease, any available information for communication to the relatives.

Perforated Sheet giving detail of personnel and horses wanting to complete, shown on Army Form B. 213.

Number of Report _____

Detail of Wanting to Complete.																																																															

Horses: Peck, Heavy Draught, Draught, Riding

TOTAL to agree with wanting to complete: Officers, Other Ranks

W.O's and N.C.O's (by ranks) not included in trade columns.

Privates
Storeman
Armourers
Armament Artificers: Range Finders, Fitters
Machine Gunners
Clerks
Telephonists
Motor Cyclist Artificers
Motor Cycle's
Instrument Repairers
Signallers
General-duty Pioneers
Brigade Section Pioneers
Cablemen
Operators, Telegraph
Permanent Line Men
Air Line Men
Engine Drivers: Field, Loco.
Signalmen
Electricians: W.T., Ordinary
Plumbers
Fitters: Wireless, R.A.
Fitters & Turners (R.E.): Iron, Wood
Carpenters and Joiners
Bricklayers and Masons
Blacksmiths
Saddlers or Harness Makers
Wheelers: M.T., H.T., R.A.
Cold Shoers
Shoeing, or Shoeing and Carriage Smiths
Farriers: Corporals, Serjeants
Range Takers
Smith Gunners
Gunners
Drivers: Steam, Lorry, Car, A.S.C., R.E., R.A.

CAVALRY
R. A.
R. E.
INFANTRY
R. A. M. C.
A. O. C.
A. V. C.

Signature of Commander. _____ Unit.

Formation to which attached. _____

Date of Despatch. _____

9th Bn. The Durham Light Infantry
151st Infy. Bde. 50 Divn. 2 Corps

Remarks :—

[P.T.O.

(26149.) Wt. W. 10698/4046. 500,000. 10/15. M.R.Co., Ltd. Forms/B. 213/6.

FIELD RETURN.

Army Form B. 213.

To be made up to and for Sunday in each week.

No. of Report _____

(To be furnished by all arms, services, and departments (except A.S.C. units) to the A. G.'s Office at the Base in accordance with Field Service Regulations, Part II.)

RETURN showing numbers at _____ 13 E.I. _____ Date. 23rd June 1916.

(a) Effective strength of Unit.
(b) Rationed by Unit.

DETAIL	Personnel			Animals								Guns, carriages, and limbers and transport vehicles												REMARKS
	Officers	Other ranks	Natives	Horses			Mules		Camels	Oxen		Guns, carriages and limbers, showing description	Ammunition wagons and limbers	Machine guns	Aircraft, showing description	Horsed		Motor Cars.	Tractors	Mechanical			Motor Bicycles	Bicycles	
				Riding	Draught	Heavy Draught	Pack	Large	Small							4 wheeled	2 wheeled			Lorries, showing description	Trucks, showing description	Trailers			
Effective Strength of Unit	40	857		14	14	9	4	11	5					4		14	3							9	
Details, by Arms attached to unit as in War Establishment:— RMC	1	5																							
Mercury	1																								
Total	41	862		14	14	9	4	11	5					4		14	2							9	
War Establishment	35	862		14	14	9	4	11	5					4		14	8							9	
Wanting to complete														1											
Surplus (Detail of Personnel and Horses below)	6	6																							
*Attached (not to include the details shown above)		2																							
Civilians:— Employed with the Unit																									
Accompanying the Unit																									
TOTAL RATIONED	32	875		14	14	9	4	11	5																

* In the case of field ambulances, hospitals or depots, the number of patients are to be included here, the names being shown in A. F. A. 36.

Signature of Commander. _____

23rd June 1916. Date of Despatch.

For information of the A.G.'s Office at the Base.

Officers and men who have become casuals, been transferred or joined since last report.

Place .B.E.F.   Date 23rd June 1916

Coy	Regtl. Number	Rank	Name		Corps	Nature of casualty, or name of unit from or to which transferred	Date of being struck off or coming on the ration return	Remarks*
			Battle Casualties					
B	1653	Pte	Holden	G	9th D L I	Wounded	17-6-16	to hospital
A	2596	"	Keating	E		"	"	"
"	4710	"	Wheale	W		"	"	"
C	2688	"	Weatheral	G		"	18-6-16	"
D	1071	"	Robson	A		"	19-6-16	"
"	2485	"	Strong	J		"	"	"
"	4219	"	Carter	J		"	18-6-16	At duty
"	4081	"	Craig	J		"	20-6-16	to hospital
"	4131	"	Potts	J		"	"	"
		2/Lieut	H Hall			"	21-6-16	"
		2/Lieut	H. Strachan			"	"	"
C	1616	Pte	Mohan	J		Shell Shock	"	At duty
"	1731	Sgt	Wheatley	W		Wounded	"	to hospital
"	1653	L/C	Robinson	C		"	"	At duty

* State whether absence is of a permanent or temporary nature, adding, in the case of casuals from wounds or disease, any available information for communication to the relatives.

Perforated Sheet giving detail of personnel and horses wanting to complete, shown on Army Form B. 213.

Number of Report

Horses — Pack / Heavy Draught / Draught / Riding

TOTAL wanting to complete to agree with Other Ranks / Officers

W.O.'s and N.C.O.'s (by ranks) not included in trade columns

Privates
Storeman
Armourers
Armament Artificers — Range Finders / Fitters
Machine Gunners
Clerks
Telephonists
Motor Cyclist Artificers
Motor Cyclists
Instrument Repairers
Signallers
General-duty Pioneers
Brigade Section Pioneers
Cableman
Operators, Telegraph
Permanent Line Men
Air Line Men
Engine Drivers — Field / Loco.
Signalmen
Electricians — W. T. / Ordinary
Plumbers
Fitters — Wireless / R. A.
Fitters & Turners (R. E.) — Iron / Wood
Carpenters and Joiners
Bricklayers and Masons
Blacksmiths
Saddlers or Harness Makers
Wheelers — M. T. / H. T. / R. A.
Cold Shoers
Farriers — Shoeing, or Shoeing and Carriage Smiths / Corporals / Sergeants
Range Takers
Smith Gunners
Gunners
Drivers — Steam / Lorry / Car / A.S.C. / H.B. / R.A.

Detail of Wanting to Complete

CAVALRY
R. A.
R. E.
INFANTRY
R. A. M. C.
A. O. C.
A. V. C.

Remarks:—

30 Armourers are required please

B. G. Brown *Lt. Adjt.* 9.6.06

Signature of Commander.

9th Bn. The Durham Light Infantry

Unit.

151 Inf. Bde, 50th Divn. I Corps.

Formation to which attached.

23rd June 1916

Date of Despatch.

(B 99511.) Wt. W15519/M149. 1,000,000. 1/16. J. P. & Co., Ltd. Forms/B. 213/7.

[P.T.O.

FIELD RETURN.

(To be furnished by all arms, services, and departments (except A.S.C. units) to the A. G.'s Office at the Base in accordance with Field Service Regulations, Part II.)

To be made up to and for Sunday in each week.

No. of Report

RETURN showing numbers   (a) Effective strength of Unit.
     (b) Rationed by Unit.

Date. 30th June 1916

Detail	Personnel			Animals									Guns, carriages, and limbers and transport vehicles						Mechanical					Remarks
	Officers	Other ranks	Natives	Horses Riding	Draught	Heavy Draught	Mules Pack	Baggage	Small	Camels	Oxen		Guns, carriages, limbers, showing description	Ammunition wagons and limbers	Machine guns	Aircraft, showing description	Horsed 4 wheeled	2 wheeled	Motor Cars	Tractors	Lorries, showing description	Trucks, showing description	Trailers	Motor Bicycles	Bicycles	
Effective Strength of Unit	41	950		14	-	9	4	29	5						6		14	3							9	
Details, by Arms attached to unit as in War Establishment. Corps Rank Armourers	1	3 1																								
Total	42	936		14	-	9	4	29	5						6		14	3							9	
War Establishment	35	927		14		9	4	29	5						6		14	3							9	
Wanting to complete		1																								
Surplus	7																									
*Attached (not to include the details shown above)		2																								
Civilians:— Employed with the Unit Accompanying the Unit																										
TOTAL RATIONED...	31	875		14	-	9	4	29	5						6		14	3							9	

* In the case of field ambulances, hospitals or depots, the number of patients are to be included here, the names being shown in A. F. A. 36.

Signature of Commander. A.G. Brown Lt Adjt for O.C.

Date of Despatch. 30th June 1916

For information of the A.G.'s Office at the Base.

Officers and men who have become casuals, been transferred or joined since last report.

Place ___B.E.F_____   Date __30th June 1916__

Regtl. Number	Rank	Name		Corps	Joint	Nature of casualty, or name of unit from or to which transferred	Date of being struck off or coming on the ration return	Remarks*
		Battle Casualties						
D. 2964	Pte	Foster	J	9th D.L.I.		Wounded	23-6-16	To Hospital
A. 2792	"	Borrowdale	J	"		"	24-6-16	"
" 2797	"	Adams	J	"		Killed in Action	"	Buried RIDGEWOOD N.5.a.5.5 (Sheet 28)
" 4246	"	Gair	E	"		Wounded	"	To Hospital
" 2193	"	Storrie	S.J.	"		"	"	Still at duty
B. 5019	"	Kennedy	G	"		"	"	To Hospital
" 2573	"	Forbes	R	"		"	"	"
" 1745	"	Skelton	J	"		"	"	"
D. 3284	"	Learmouth	L	"		"	"	"
" 5059	"	Bellerby	H	"		"	"	"
" 3218	"	Egan	J	"		"	"	"
	2/Lieut	Ashworth	J.F.G			Died of Wounds	25-6-16	Buried LA CLYTTE N.7.c.8.7½ (Sheet 28)
C. 1438	Sgt	Hamilton	J	"		Wounded	"	To Hospital
" 1552	Pte	Ramsay	W.B.	"		"	"	"
" 2447	"	Lugsden	N	"		"	"	"
" 2947	"	Pharoah	J	"		"	"	"
" 2994	L/C	Charlton	J	"		"	26-6-16	Still at duty

* State whether absence is of a permanent or temporary nature, adding, in the case of casuals from wounds or disease, any available information for communication to the relatives.

Perforated Sheet giving detail of personnel and horses wanting to complete, shown on Army Form B. 213.

Number of Report _____

Detail of Wanting to Complete	Drivers					Gunners	Smith Gunners	Range Takers	Farriers			Wheelers				Saddlers or Harness Makers	Blacksmiths	Bricklayers and Masons	Carpenters and Joiners	Fitters & Turners (R.E.)		Fitters			Plumbers	Electricians		Signalmen	Engine Drivers		Air Line Men	Permanent Line Men	Operators, Telegraph	Cablemen	Brigade Section Pioneers	General-duty Pioneers	Signallers	Instrument Repairers	Motor Cyclists	Motor Cyclist Artificers	Telephonists	Clerks	Machine Gunners	Armament Artificers				Armourers	Storemen	Privates	W.O.'s and N.C.O.'s (by ranks) not included in trade columns	TOTAL to agree with wanting to complete		Horses				
	R.A.	R.E.	A.S.C.	Car	Lorry	Steam				Serjeants	Corporals	Shoeing, or Shoeing and Carriage Smiths	Cold Shoers	R.A.	H.T.	M.T.					Wood	Iron	R.A.	Wireless		Ordinary	W.T.		Loco.	Field														Fitters	Range Finders	Armourers						Officers	Other Ranks	Riding	Draught	Heavy Draught	Pack
CAVALRY																																																									
R.A.																																																									
R.E.																																																									
INFANTRY																																																									
R.A.M.C.																																																									
A.O.C.																																																									
A.V.C.																																																									

Remarks :— 3 C Musicians required

Signature of Commander. _____

Unit. _____ 4th Bn. The Durham Light Infantry

Formation to which attached. _____ 151 Infy Bde. 50th Division. 8 Corps.

Date of Despatch. _____ 30th June 1916

[P.T.O.

(B 99511.) Wt. W15519/M149. 1,000,000. 1/16. J. P. & Co., Ltd. Forms/B 213/7.

WAR DIARY
or
INTELLIGENCE SUMMARY.

(Erase heading not required.)

Instructions regarding War Diaries and Intelligence Summaries are contained in F. S. Regs., Part II. and the Staff Manual respectively. Title pages will be prepared in manuscript.

Place	Date	Hour	Summary of Events and Information	Remarks and references to Appendices
	1/7/16		Still in Divisional Reserve. Normal working Parties.	
	2/7/16		Relieve 6th Bn D.L.I. in left sub-sector, Lancashire & left Potteries Post. Rifles	
	3/7/16		Enemy fairly lively with Trench Mortars, Bombs & large Minniefrence. Able to work by keeping snipers with att. there are mostly able to avoid the large bombs, they amusing themselves playing these large Rum-Jars & Bombs. deep normal the trenches & parapets staying.	
	4/7/16		Enemy's activity much the same, 2 casualties all wounded	
	5 "		" " " " 5 " " "	
	6/7/16		" " " " 3 " " "	
	7/7/16		Enemy much quieter today	1 " "
	8/7/16		Relieved by 6th Bn D.L.I. & proceeded to Ridgewood from Brigade Reserve.	
	9/7/16		Bee Reserve at Ridgewood furnished any available man for work under R.E. the following evacuation resumed, 12. 1 Killed & 3 wounded, 13th 1 wounded	
	12/7/16		Relieved by 6th D.L.I. from Bee Reserve proceeded to Pit Breuer at La Blyfte. 1 man wounded	
	13+14/7/16		In Divisional Reserve furnishing strong working parties nightly under R.E.	
	16/7/16		16th 1 man killed, 1 wounded. 17th 1 wounded, 18th 2 wounded	
	18/7/16			
	19/7/16		Division taking over more frontage, 9th Bn D.L.I. proceeded to E & F Trenches KEMMEL	

Instructions regarding War Diaries and Intelligence
Summaries are contained in F. S. Regs., Part II.
and the Staff Manual respectively. Title pages
will be prepared in manuscript.

WAR DIARY
or
INTELLIGENCE SUMMARY.

(Erase heading not required.)

Place	Date	Hour	Summary of Events and Information	Remarks and references to Appendices
	20/7/16		Sector. This portion of line was held by one Brigade in June & July 1915, so ground is rather familiar to many. Brown Regt on our Right, 5th Bn Durham L.I. on our Left	
	21/7/16		Enemy's Snipers very active showing things very natural. " " he fed rounds of 5.9 & Shrapnel we put over by Enemy on 2 Coy? " " " he fed rounds of 5.9 & Shrapnel we put over by Enemy on our Left. Enemies 8 men wounded. 6th Dr.L.I. behind 5th Durham on our Left.	
	22/7/16		Local activity of Enemy & ourselves.	
	23/7/16		Gas map R.H & S trenches 8.8 & D.L.I a conducted on the ... Frontage junction ... E.1. (Bruce Ridge) ... & D. 4 & 5. from 5th Brown Regiment who were relieved from Line, Lt. Smith Andrews on our Right; Officers Relief, consisting of 2/Lt D.A. Brown & Capt Kelly & Pte Pearson, went out & recovered ... to them & handed a dig ... it is presumed they were instructed by Enemy, who were variant in this Particulars spent a few days ... admitted by ... party taken ... not ... ... & other ... In Branch of ... but ... not ...	
	24/7/16		Enemy active with 5.9 which he has distributed pretty freely between front supports two of Pte Briggs, Foster & Thompson, wounded & 1 man wounded.	
	26/7/16		Enemy Pte Young active with Trench Mortar, Machine Gun & S.9. 1 man killed & 4 wounded	

1577 Wt. W10791/1773 500,000 1/15 D. D. & L. A.D.S.S./Forms/C. 2118.

9th Bn McLean's S.D.

Army Form C. 2118.

WAR DIARY

or

INTELLIGENCE SUMMARY.

(Erase heading not required.)

Instructions regarding War Diaries and Intelligence Summaries are contained in F. S. Regs., Part II. and the Staff Manual respectively. Title pages will be prepared in manuscript.

Place	Date	Hour	Summary of Events and Information	Remarks and references to Appendices
	28/1/16		Had a fairly quiet day but except 9 pm or later received some attention from Enemy, 2 other ranks wounded, from 33 - 26. had several men ght-through this well have but otherwise uninjured. This happened in Bull Ring which is explained; relieved by 5th Border Regiment & moved into Brigade Reserve near Kemmel Hill.	
	29/1 and 31/1/16		While in Brigade Reserve. Bivouaced in a subsequent place of security, stores are busy carrying them here by here a new new of carrying behind Enemy's lines from here, working parties of 200 nightly.	

S.G. French Lt & Adjutant for O.C.
9th Bn Durham L.I.

1577 Wt. W10791/1773 500,000 1/15 D. D. & L. A.D.S.S/Forms/C. 2118.

File War Diary

SPECIAL ORDER OF THE DAY

BY

GENERAL SIR DOUGLAS HAIG,

G.C.B.,   K.C.I.E.,   K.C.V.O.,   A.D.C.

Commander-in-Chief, British Armies in France.

The following telegrams are published for the information of all ranks :—

I. GENERAL SIR DOUGLAS HAIG,
G.H.Q., B.E.F.

July 27th.

Management Committee General Federation Trade Unions representing over a million British workers, send sincere congratulations to you, to your Staff, and to your heroic soldiers on success achieved since July first.   Also wishes speedy recovery to wounded and expresses deepest sympathy with relatives of those who died in defence of honour and civilization.

APPLETON,
Secretary.

II. SECRETARY GENERAL FEDERATION TRADE UNIONS.

July 27th.

Your inspiriting message has appealed to us all.   On behalf of my Staff, the Army in France and myself I beg to express to the members of the General Federation of Trade Unions our warmest thanks for their kindness in congratulating the British Army in France on its success.   All ranks realise how much this success is due to the patriotism, self denial and whole-hearted co-operation of their brother workmen at home.

DOUGLAS HAIG.

General Headquarters,
29th July, 1916.

Commanding-in-Chief,
British Armies in France.

ARMY PRINTING AND STATIONERY SERVICES A—7/16

War Diary

SPECIAL ORDER OF THE DAY

BY

GENERAL SIR DOUGLAS HAIG,

G.C.B., K.C.I.E., K.C.V.O., A.D.C.

Commander-in-Chief, British Armies in France.

The following telegrams, sent on the occasion of the celebration of the French National Fête on July 14th, are published for the information of all ranks :—

I. MONSIEUR POINCARÉ, PRESIDENT OF THE FRENCH REPUBLIC.

14th July.

The British Army, fighting by the side of the brave soldiers of France in the bitter struggle now proceeding, expresses on the occasion of this great anniversary its admiration for the results achieved by the French Army and its unshakeable confidence in the speedy realization of our common hopes.

SIR DOUGLAS HAIG.

II. GENERAL SIR D. HAIG, COMMANDER-IN-CHIEF, BRITISH ARMIES IN FRANCE.

14th July.

I thank you, my dear General, for the good wishes which you have expressed towards France, and beg you to convey to the brave British Army my lively admiration of the fine successes which it has just achieved and which only this morning have been so brilliantly extended. They have produced a deep impression on the hearts of all Frenchmen. Those of your magnificent troops who have to-day paraded in the streets of Paris, in company with those of our Allies, received throughout their march a striking proof of the public sentiment. I am glad to have this opportunity of sending you—to you personally and to your troops—my warm congratulations.

POINCARÉ.

General Headquarters,
18th July, 1916.

Commanding-in-Chief,
British Armies in France.

ARMY PRINTING AND STATIONERY SERVICES A—7/16.

SPECIAL ORDER OF THE DAY

BY

GENERAL SIR DOUGLAS HAIG,

G.C.B., K.C.I.E., K.C.V.O., A.D.C.
Commander-in-Chief, British Armies in France.

The following telegrams are published for the information of all ranks :—

I. GENERAL SIR DOUGLAS HAIG, COMMANDER-IN-CHIEF, BRITISH ARMIES IN FRANCE.

16th July.

    The continued successful advance of my troops fills me with admiration, and I send my best wishes to all ranks. The Emperor of Russia has asked me to convey his warm congratulations to the troops upon the great success they have achieved.

GEORGE, R.I.

II. HIS MAJESTY THE KING,
      BUCKINGHAM PALACE, LONDON.

17th July.

    The British Armies in France offer most respectful and grateful thanks for this further mark of your Majesty's gracious appreciation of what they have achieved.

    They also respectfully beg that their grateful acknowledgment may be conveyed to the Emperor of Russia for His Majesty's congratulations.

SIR DOUGLAS HAIG.

III. GENERAL SIR D. HAIG, COMMANDER-IN-CHIEF, BRITISH ARMIES IN FRANCE.

14th July, 1916.

    I have heard with great joy of the new successes just won by the British Army. The French Armies applaud the progress which is effected every day by our gallant comrades. I am glad to voice their feelings in offering to the Commanders and soldiers of your armies, and in particular to you, my dear General, my very cordial felicitations.

GENERAL JOFFRE.

IV. GENERAL JOFFRE, COMMANDER-IN-CHIEF OF THE FRENCH ARMIES.

15th July.

    Sincere thanks from myself and all ranks under my command for your very kind telegram.

    We cordially appreciate the felicitations of our brave Allies whose steadfast courage and endurance in the long struggle at Verdun gave us time to prepare for the combined offensive which has begun so well on both sides of the Somme. Your splendid artillery continues to give us valuable assistance.

GENERAL HAIG.

V. GENERAL SIR D. HAIG, Commander-in-Chief, British Armies in France.

(Translation.)

14th July.

The unbroken success of the offensive of the British Armies under your command confirms our unshakeable faith in the power and genius of the British people.

All honour to England in her greatness, to her King, her Armies and her Fleet! They have won immortality in a heroic contest.

PRESIDENT of the ASSEMBLY of ZEMSTVOS OF THE GOVERNMENT of SAMARA.

VI. PRESIDENT of the ASSEMBLY of ZEMSTVOS, SAMARA, RUSSIA.

14th July.

I beg you to convey to the Zemstvos of Samara on behalf of the British Army under my command our warm appreciation of your inspiriting message. On our side we have watched with admiration the great feats of the Russian Armies and Navy and the heroic determination of the Russian Emperor and his people. United in a great cause we shall march together with unshakeable confidence to the final triumph.

SIR DOUGLAS HAIG.

General Headquarters,
17th July, 1916.

Commanding-in-Chief,
British Armies in France.

ARMY PRINTING AND STATIONERY SERVICES A—7/16

FIELD RETURN.

To be made up to and for Sunday in each week.

No. of Report _____

(To be furnished by all arms, services, and departments (except A.S.C. units) to the A. G.'s Office at the Base in accordance with Field Service Regulations, Part II.)

RETURN showing numbers { (a) Effective strength of Unit. (b) Rationed by Unit. }

_____ at _____ Date. _____

DETAIL	Personnel			Animals									Guns, carriages, and limbers and transport vehicles				Horsed		Motor Cars	Tractors	Mechanical				Motor Bicycles	Bicycles	REMARKS
	Officers	Other ranks	Natives	Horses				Mules		Camels	Oxen		Guns, carriages, limbers, showing description	Ammunition wagons and limbers	Machine guns	Aircraft, showing description	4 wheeled	2 wheeled			Lorries, showing description	Trucks, showing description	Trailers			
				Riding	Draught	Heavy Draught	Pack	Large	Small																	
Effective Strength of Unit																										
Details, by Arms attached to unit as in War Establishment																										
Total																										
War Establishment																										
Wanting to complete (Detail of Personnel and Horses below)																										
Surplus																										
*Attached (not to include the details shown above)																										
Civilians:— Employed with the Unit. Accompanying the Unit																										
TOTAL RATIONED...																										

* In the case of field ambulances, hospitals or depots, the number of patients are to be included here, the names being shown in A.F.A. 36.

_____ Signature of Commander.

_____ Date of Despatch.

Perforated Sheet giving detail of personnel and horses wanting to complete, shown on Army Form B. 213.

Number of Report

| Horses — Pack |
| Horses — Heavy Draught |
| Horses — Draught |
| Horses — Riding |
| TOTAL wanting to agree with complete — Other Ranks |
| TOTAL wanting to agree with complete — Officers |
| W.O.s and N.C.O.s (by ranks) not included in trade columns |
| Privates |
| Storemen |
| Armourers |
| Armament Artificers — Range Finders |
| Armament Artificers — Fitters |
| Machine Gunners |
| Clerks |
| Telephonists |
| Motor Cyclist Artificers |
| Motor Cyclists |
| Instrument Repairers |
| Signallers |
| General-duty Pioneers |
| Brigade Section Pioneers |
| Cablemen |
| Operators, Telegraph |
| Permanent Line Men |
| Air Line Men |
| Engine Drivers — Field |
| Engine Drivers — Loco. |
| Signalmen |
| Electricians — W. T. |
| Electricians — Ordinary |
| Plumbers |
| Fitters — Wireless |
| Fitters — R.A. |
| Fitters & Turners (R. E.) — Iron |
| Fitters & Turners (R. E.) — Wood |
| Carpenters and Joiners |
| Bricklayers and Masons |
| Blacksmiths |
| Saddlers or Harness Makers |
| Wheelers — M. T. |
| Wheelers — H. T. |
| Wheelers — R. A. |
| Cold Shoers |
| Shoeing, or Shoeing and Carriage Smiths |
| Farriers — Corporals |
| Farriers — Serjeants |
| Range Takers |
| Smith Gunners |
| Gunners |
| Drivers — Steam |
| Drivers — Lorry |
| Drivers — Car |
| Drivers — A.S.O. |
| Drivers — R.E. |
| Drivers — R.A. |

Detail of Wanting to Complete

CAVALRY
R.A.
R.E.
INFANTRY
R.A.M.C.
A.O.C.
A.V.C.

Signature of Commander.

Unit.

Formation to which attached.

Date of Despatch.

Remarks:

[P.T.O.]

(B 99511.) Wt. W15519/M149. 1,000,000. 1/16. J. P. & Co., Ltd. Form/B 213/7.

FIELD RETURN.

Army Form B. 213.
Field Service Regulations, Part II.

Date.

No. of Report.

(To be furnished by all arms, services and departments (except A.S.C. units) to the A.G.'s Office at the Base in accordance with Field Service Regulations, Part II.)

RETURN showing numbers RATIONED by, and Transport on charge of, _____ at _____

DETAIL	Personnel			Animals										Guns, carriages, and limbers, and transport vehicles.												REMARKS
	Officers	Other ranks	Natives	Horses				Mules		Camels	Oxen			Guns, carriages and limbers, showing description	Ammunition wagons and limbers	Machine guns	Aircraft, showing description	Horsed		Motor Cars	Tractors	Mechanical			Motor Bicycles	Bicycles	
				Riding	Draught	Heavy Draught	Pack	Large	Small									4 Wheeled	2 Wheeled			Lorries, showing description	Trucks, showing description	Trailers			
Effective Strength of Unit																											
Details, by Arms attached to unit as in War Establishment:—	1	5		9	4	26	5									6										9	
	1																										
Total	12		9	4	26	5										6											
War Establishment	12		9	4	26	5																					
Wanting to complete (Detail of Personnel and Horses below)																6										9	
Surplus																											
Attached (not to include the details shown above)																											
Civilians:— Employed with the Unit Accompanying the Unit																											
TOTAL RATIONED ...	12		9	4	26	5																					

* In the case of field ambulances, hospitals or depots, the number of patients are to be included here, the names being shown in A. F. A. 36.

Signature of Commander.

Date of Despatch.

Officers and men who have become casuals, been transferred or joined since last report.

Place _B.E.F._   Date _14th July 1916_

Regtl. Number	Rank	Name	Corps	Nature of casualty, or name of unit from or to which transferred	Date of being struck off or coming on the ration return	Remarks*
		Battle Casualties.				
A 996	Pte	Swanston M.	Wounded Slight	Head	6-7-16	Still at duty
" 1878	"	Cassidy J	" "	Hand	"	" " "
B 9503	"	Forbes J	" "	Head	"	To Hosp.
C 4502	"	Beck A.H.	"		7-7-16	" "
B 4509	"	Alexander J	" Severe		10-7-16	" "
" 3070	"	Satherly W	"		"	" "
A 3036	"	Martin J	Killed in Action		"	Wife commons at V² on S.O. (Suttherd)
D 4707	"	Beeston J.C.	Wounded		"	To Hosp.
A 3020	"	Thompson J	"		13-7-16	" "

PUBLIC RECORD OFFICE

Perforated Sheet giving detail of personnel and horses wanting to complete, shown on Army Form B. 213.

Number of Report

Detail of Wanting to Complete.	Drivers.							Gunners	Smith Gunners	Range Takers	Farriers			Cold Shoers	Wheelers				Saddlers or Harness Makers	Blacksmiths	Bricklayers and Masons	Carpenters and Joiners	Fitters & Turners (R. E.)		Fitters				Plumbers	Electricians			Engine Drivers			Air Line Men	Permanent Line Men	Operators, Telegraph	Cablemen	Brigade Section Pioneers	General-duty Pioneers	Signallers	Instrument Repairers	Motor Cycle's	Motor Cyclist Artificers	Telephonists	Clerks	Machine Gunners	Armament Artificers			Armourers	Storemen	Privates	W.O's. and N.C.O's (by ranks) not included in trade columns.	TOTAL, to agree with wanting to complete			Horses				
	R.A.	R.E.	A.S.C.	Car	Lorry	Steam					Corporals	Serjeants	Shoeing, or Shoeing and Carriage Smiths		R.A.	H.T.	M.T.					Wood	Iron	R.A.	Wireless	Ordinary	W.T.		Signalmen	Loco.	Field																Fitters	Range Finders					Officers	Other Ranks		Riding	Draught	Heavy Draught	Pack
CAVALRY																																																											
R. A.																																																										
R. E.																																																										
INFANTRY																																																										
R. A. M. C.																																																										
A. O. C.																																																										
A. V. C.																																																										

Remarks :—

Signature of Commander

Unit

Formation to which attached.

Date of Despatch.

[P.T.O.

(26149.) Wt. W.10698/4046. 500,000. 10/15. M.R.Co., Ltd. Forms/B. 213/6.

Army Form C. 2118.

WAR DIARY

or

INTELLIGENCE SUMMARY

(Erase heading not required.)

Vol 13

War Diary

1/9th Battⁿ the Durham Light Infantry.

August. 1916

Volume No 7

Place	Date	Hour	Summary of Events and Information	Remarks and references to Appendices

2449 Wt. W14957/M90 750,000 1/16 J.B.C. & A. Forms/C.2118/12.

Army Form C. 2118.

WAR DIARY
or
INTELLIGENCE SUMMARY.
(Erase heading not required.)

9th Bn DURHAM LIGHT INFANTRY
AUGUST 1916
Vol. 17

Instructions regarding War Diaries and Intelligence Summaries are contained in F. S. Regs., Part II. and the Staff Manual respectively. Title pages will be prepared in manuscript.

Place	Date	Hour	Summary of Events and Information	Remarks and references to Appendices
	1/9/16		Relieved 5th Borders in Right-Sub-Sector of Kemmel Area. S.P. I.7.8 in on left. Battln frontline 174 on right.	
		9am	Enemy fairly quiet, 1 man wounded	
		3pm	Enemy kept quiet, at about 3.pm they commenced an organised strafe in our front which they kept up until 6.pm minnenwerfer, 5.9, shrapnel, Rifle Grenades etc, this was not on very heavy did considerable damage to our trenches, casualties, rather light. considering, 1 man killed & 6 wounded, our artillery, Field & Heavy with Stokes Guns etc retaliated. Had last very much quieter today, 1 man wounded.	
		4th		
		5th	Three to 6 oclock pm been a furious line of enemy to strafe but Trench Artillery but today was on short, Our Artillery, Heavy & Field Stokes Guns Mortars etc. stopped enemy very heavy during his usual period of activity. retaliation by enemy was weak. Our Artillery did considerable damage to enemys front support & reserve lines, 4 men wounded & 2 officers. ... & miracleous escape being shot through his steel helmet, which deflected bullet very slightly grazed his head, these steel helmets are very valuable sharp ... serial men during this time. ...	
		6th	Enemy first strafing today not all, evidently yesterday did him some good, 1 man killed.	

WAR DIARY
or
INTELLIGENCE SUMMARY.
(Erase heading not required.)

Instructions regarding War Diaries and Intelligence Summaries are contained in F. S. Regs., Part II. and the Staff Manual respectively. Title pages will be prepared in manuscript.

Place	Date	Hour	Summary of Events and Information	Remarks and references to Appendices
	7/8/16		Fairly quiet from day break until afternoon when Enemy opened out again with the usual supply of Bombs, Shells, Rifle Grenades, our Artillery quickly took him to task the from quietened down. Very little damage done, 1 Officer & 2 men wounded. Reinforcements came from Somme (562 A? A?).	
	8/8/16		On the front Ring to 10th Royal Warwick Regt. who have just come from Somme, still same old game, except that Enemy opened out a bit earlier today & was closed up by our Gunners pretty quickly, but not before he had done damage to Trenches, 2 men killed, 6 wounded. Relieved by 7th E. Lancs Regt. 57 Inf? Bde, in Trenches A. 2, 4 & 5, afterwards to Dranoutre Huts. This relief witnessed state from throwing from line in preparation the trip South of our front Infantry Operations in Somme Valley.	
LOCRE. BERTHEN.	9/8/16		Moved from Doncaster Huts to old billets of April at BERTHEN.	
PROUVILLE.	11/9/16		Moved to PROUVILLE. Entrained GODEWAERSVELDE — detrained CANDAS. A long train journey. Marched from CANDAS to PROUVILLE — about ten kilometres — arrived 2AM on 12th.	
MENACOURT.	15/8/16.		Marched to Hyracourt — about ten miles.	
RAINEVILLE.	16/8/16.		Marched to RAINEVILLE — about ten miles.	
RAIZEUX.	17/8/16.		Marched to RAIZEUX — about eight miles. The Brigadier complimented the left on being	

1577 Wt. W10791/1773 500,000 1/15 D. D. & L.   A.D.S.S./Forms/C. 2118.

Army Form C. 2118.

WAR DIARY

or

INTELLIGENCE SUMMARY.

(Erase heading not required.)

Instructions regarding War Diaries and Intelligence
Summaries are contained in F. S. Regs., Part II.
and the Staff Manual respectively. Title pages
will be prepared in manuscript.

Place	Date	Hour	Summary of Events and Information	Remarks and references to Appendices
RAIZEUX.	17–27		Held marching Kt. in the Brigade.	
			ℒ training. We are billeted(?) in a wood; in few tents for officers – men in bivouacs made of waterproof sheets, and branches and brushwood. The whole division is in village quite close.	
	28		The Corps Commander (III Corps) should have inspected the whole Division Today, but the parade was cancelled owing to weather.	
	30		Brigade Practice Assault. It came on to pour and operations were stopped. The men got very wet before we got back to the woods (but the ℒ made hut makes an excellent drying place and there is a good fire there.	

R. Boyle, Jones, Colonel, OC

fm. OC
/ gE Batt: the Hull.L.L.I

9th. DURHAM LIGHT INFANTRY

151st. INFANTRY BRIGADE

S E P T E M B E R   1 9 1 6 .

Army Form C. 2118.

$\frac{151}{50}$.

WAR DIARY

or

INTELLIGENCE SUMMARY

~~(Erase heading not required.)~~

Instructions regarding War Diaries and Intelligence
Summaries are contained in F. S. Regs., Part II.
and the Staff Manual respectively. Title Pages
will be prepared in manuscript.

Place	Date	Hour	Summary of Events and Information	Remarks and references to Appendices

VOL 14

9" Bn. Durham L.I.

September. 1916.

Volume N.° 14.

2449 Wt. W14957/M90 750,000 1/16 J.B.C. & A. Forms/C.2118/12.

Army Form C. 2118.

WAR DIARY
or
INTELLIGENCE SUMMARY.

(Erase heading not required.)

Instructions regarding War Diaries and Intelligence Summaries are contained in F. S. Regs., Part II. and the Staff Manual respectively. Title pages will be prepared in manuscript.

Place	Date	Hour	Summary of Events and Information	Remarks and references to Appendices
	1-9. 9.16		Remained in DARIEUX WOOD, in Corps Reserve. Bn & Company Training. Carried out a men from getting very fit after 16 months of continuous Trench Work. All ranks are enjoying being away from the front & taking part in the great formed offensive.	
	10th		Bn moved by march route to BECOURT. WOOD N of ALBERT.	
	11–13th		Still in Bivouacs at BECOURT, being working parties furnished	
	14th	7. pm	Bn Left BECOURT. WOOD & marched to MAMETZ WOOD where they bivouaced in S.W. corner of WOOD. The Division is expected to attack on N & a Bn is in the Divisional Reserve.	
	15th	6.30 AM	Bn moved from S.W. corner to N.W. corner of MAMETZ WOOD.	
	"	12 m	Became attached to 149 Infantry Brigade & moved 2 Companies to Price Shunk & 2 Companies to PRICES QUARRY. Bn HQ at QUARRY. Ry Map FRANCE SHEET 57c S.W. S.8.d.9.9	
	"	3. PM	Bn moved forward to HOOK Trench. S.3.a.9.9. to S.3.c.7.8. with Bn HQ Coy in & CLARKS TRENCH. S.3.c.0.9 with men to carry out an attack at 6.p.m on the STARFISH and PRUE LINES. This attack was cancelled. At 9.30pm the 70th in conjunction with the 5th Border Regt & 6th D.L.I. was to attack the German STARFISH & PRUE LINES. the 5th Border Regt & 6th D.L.I. troop late in starting, our Bn was met with heavy machine gun and	

1577 Wt. W10791/1773 500,000 1/15 D. D. & L. A.D.S.S./Forms/C. 2118.

WAR DIARY

or

INTELLIGENCE SUMMARY.

(Erase heading not required.)

Instructions regarding War Diaries and Intelligence Summaries are contained in F. S. Regs., Part II. and the Staff Manual respectively. Title pages will be prepared in manuscript.

Place	Date	Hour	Summary of Events and Information	Remarks and references to Appendices
			and rifle fire from both flanks. Part of the first 2 waves crossed the STARFISH LINE and pushed on to about 30x from PRUE TRENCH and dug in. Here there small parties were all killed with exception of one wounded man who crawled back. These strikes entered the O STARFISH LINE were excited and no front line dug deep in on a line M.34 C.2.6 ✗ M.34.C.S.4 and consolidated a line there.	
	16/9/16	9.30 a.m.	The Pos. in conjunction with the 6th Border Regiment consolidated STARFISH LINE but was again held up by heavy Machine Gun fire from front & flanks	
	17/9/16	10.30 p.m.	Two parties of 50 men each under the Command of 2/Lt Thompson attempted to gain the STARFISH TRENCH but was held up by Machine Gun & Rifle fire. These parties established a series of posts in shell holes about 100x in front from lines.	
	18/9/16	5.30 a.m.	Captain OSWELL's Company of the 8th D.L.I. and a party of 100 men of the 9th D.L.I. advanced STARFISH TRENCH but was met by heavy Machine Gun & Rifle fire & were unable to gain the Objective. At 5 p.m. the Pos. was relieved by the 8th D.L.I. & withdrawn to CLARK TRENCH	
	19/9/16		Remained in Clark's Trench in Reserve, the Casualties during these operations	

1577 Wt. W10791/1773 500,000 1/15 D. D. & L. A.D.S.S./Forms/C. 2118.

Army Form C. 2118.

WAR DIARY
or
INTELLIGENCE SUMMARY

(*Erase heading not required.*)

Instructions, regarding War Diaries and Intelligence
Summaries are contained in F.S. Regs., Part II.
and the Staff Manual respectively. Title Pages
will be prepared in manuscript.

Place	Date	Hour	Summary of Events and Information	Remarks and references to Appendices
			Casualties from 15th to 27th:– Killed Chaplain R. RUTHERFORD. 2/Lt E.A. WALTON. 2/Lt A. LAWSON	
			Died of Wounds. 2/Lt J.H.TYTLER. & 9 Officers wounded. Other Ranks Killed 43. Missing	
			27. Wounded 219. Total of 303 :– Total of 449 other things when counting – death.	
	20/7/16		Still in Bivouac at CLARK'S STREET.	
	21st	6 pm	Moved to S.W. Corner of MAMETZ WOOD, in Divisional Reserve. 23 Reinforcements arrived.	
	22nd - 24th		At MAMETZ WOOD Reorganising Bn: & furnishing strong working parties at night.	
	25th		Moved into Divisional Support in O.G.LINE (Dag綦men line)	
	26 & 27th		Still in O.G. Line, furnishing strong working parties daily.	
	28th		Relieved 4th EAST YORKS, & took life M 28.a.6.5 & M.28.d.8.8.5, which was completed by 10.0.a.m, during the night. Dug a fire trench from M.22.a.1.3 & M.12.c.7.3 and a communication trench from M.22.a.1.3 – Front trench line M.28.a.9.6. the fire trench was christened BLAYDON TRENCH and the communication trench SHOPWELL AVENUE. A draft of 19 Reinforcements arrived at about 7 pm containing 11 2 officers & from 2 53 other ranks.	
	29th	7.30 am	A party of Bombers under 2/Lt Inram, & simultaneously a party of 50 men under 2/Lt W.F. SCOTT. attempted to effect a lodgement about M. 22.t. but a M. 22. B.1.1. Both parties were met by heavy machine gun & rifle fire & had to retire, a German sniper & the 20th Bavarian Reg–190 Certificate M.Dy. Bombers in the act of crying from a shell hole about M.22.a.1½.3.	

2449 Wt. W14957/M90 750,000 1/16 J.B.C. & A. Form/C.2118/12.

WAR DIARY
or
INTELLIGENCE SUMMARY.

(Erase heading not required.)

Instructions regarding War Diaries and Intelligence Summaries are contained in F. S. Regs., Part II. and the Staff Manual respectively. Title pages will be prepared in manuscript.

Place	Date	Hour	Summary of Events and Information	Remarks and references to Appendices
28th			Intelligence Reports:- From 9 am 28th to 9 am 29th:-	

Last night a hostile patrol working from M.22.c.1.3 to M.22.c.7.3 of a Communication Trench from M.22.a.1.3 to M.28.a.9.6. The Fire Trench sharp cursed BLAYDON TRENCH and the C.T. CHOPWELL AVENUE. It is reported that the fire trench was not along in the front ordered, but the officer in charge of the work was wounded, when proceeding to the site, and the party was very much hampered by Artillery and rifle fire. No work advanced Posts at M.22.d.D.5. and M.22.d.2.8. No did not get Trench with the 8th D.L.I. At 7.30 am Friday a party of Bombers under an officer worked forward along the tramline and endeavoured to effect a lodgement at M.22.c.2.2. At the same time a party of men an officer worked forward & endeavoured to effect a lodgement at M.22.c.1.1. Both parties were driven back & not by heavy machine gun and rifle fire & had to retire. The officers report the line was very strongly held they had about 30 gunners a heard them work but the above, some of the hottest were in the Bn were killed. A prisoner was captured in a shell hole at M.22.a.1.2.3. he was Bn was killed. A sniper was about two his left when captured. Rutherford Alley from M.28.c.1.2. was cut through from line at M.28.a.9.6. Block built in CRESCENT ALLEY

WAR DIARY
or
INTELLIGENCE SUMMARY
(Erase heading not required.)

Oct 2.9

Bthunen E.

Instructions regarding War Diaries and Intelligence Summaries are contained in F. S. Regs., Part II. and the Staff Manual respectively. Title Pages will be prepared in manuscript.

Place	Date	Hour	Summary of Events and Information	Remarks and references to Appendices
			ALLEY at M. 28. b. 3. 8. The front line of wire about 100 x in front of Enemy's Trench (FLERS LINE) is badly damaged and of no account. The second line of wire about 10 x in front of this trench is very little damaged a no gaps noticeable. There is a similar gaps marks at M. 22. b. 0. 1. The enemy has thrown up (a lot more earth in front of this parapet during the night. The enemy's battery was active throughout the night. PRUE Trench & CRESCENT ALLEY are under intermittent bombardment the whole by 7. 7 C M a 15 C M. Our men who dug CHOPWELL AVENUE came under heavy shelling throughout the night. Among a large amount of other enemy material in the trench has been found a FISH TAIL trench machine & a box of FISH TAIL bombs. Also an telephonic communication with BLAYDON TRENCH.	
29th			Intelligence Report from 9 am 29th 9 am 30th :- At 6.15 p.m. a Daring Officers patrol endeavoured to effect a Lodgement at M. 22 & 9.1. They found the forward line manned & strongly wired. Is it A Sentry sounded German alarm of the Q16. BAVARIAN RESERVE REGT. who had been shot by one of our snipers was captured by a patrol at M. 22. c. 3. 5. Two fire trench into dug from M. 22. a. 8. 1 to M. 22. C. 8. 9. Germans made a bombing attack on this trench at 5. am this morning but were driven off. An enemy relief took place at about 6. am this morning of the line from about M. 23. C. 0. 7. - M. 22. S. 4. 1. One company (with two Lewis guns) S. 4. 1. He was particularly exposed at M. 22. b. 4. 1 & we this morning of the line a inflicted very heavy casualties. Opened rapid fire & fire a inflicted very heavy casualties.	

2449 Wt. W14957/M90 750,000 1/16 J.B.C. & A. Forms/C.2118/12.

WAR DIARY

or

INTELLIGENCE SUMMARY

(Erase heading not required.)

Instructions regarding War Diaries and Intelligence Summaries are contained in F. S. Regs., Part II. and the Staff Manual respectively. Title Pages will be prepared in manuscript.

Place	Date	Hour	Summary of Events and Information	Remarks and references to Appendices
	30/9/16		Still holding front line, a congratulatory Telegram was Received from Divisional Commander endorsed by Brigadier General happy to forward:- "G.O.C. L.M. Wishes his congratulation conveyed to H.Q. and F.B. for the gallant work during the last 48 hours AAA. C.O.C. D.G. also adds warmest congratulations on the front." The following casualties occurred between 28th & 30th:- 28th 1 Officer wounded, O.R. Killed 5, Wounded 6, Missing 2. 29th 1 " Wounded, 2 Lieut. W.E.O. Scott Missing believed Killed, O.R. 1. Killed, 6 Wounded 30th Other Ranks, 2 Wounded.	

J.C. Cracall. Lieut Col. O.C.
9th Bn. Durham L. I.

2449 Wt. W14957/M90 759,000 1/16 J.B.C. & A. Forms/C.2118/12.

Army Form C. 2118.

WAR DIARY
or
INTELLIGENCE SUMMARY
(Erase heading not required.)

9ᵗʰ D.L.I.

Instructions regarding War Diaries and Intelligence Summaries are contained in F.S. Regs., Part II. and the Staff Manual respectively. Title Pages will be prepared in manuscript.

Place	Date	Hour	Summary of Events and Information	Remarks and references to Appendices

The C.T. CHOPWELL AVENUE was continued to this trench. BLAYDON TRENCH was improved & C.T's deepened. Trench tramway dug from Bn. H.Q. from M.28.d.1.8 to M.28.a.8.9. At the HOT FUNCK MORTAR was fired at M.22.d.1.3. To front work was obtained. R.E. done on enemy wire or trenches during last 48 hours. The machine guns at M.22.b.2.1 were very active during the night. A machine gun fired on our stragglers from M.28.b.62.0. The enemy shelled BLAYDON TRENCH heavily from 6 pm to 6.30 pm with 4.7 C.M. shells. The white area between PRUE TRENCH & BLAYDON TRENCH was intermittently shelled throughout the day & night. On our artillery S.M. heavy & fired S.M.G. firing 6.30 pm. It is estimated that our F.O.O. located to the rear Fire Trench about M.22.a.5.7 working the wire cutting of FLERS LINE wire. The enemy were decreasing up large numbers of minenwerfer during the night. & fired a number of bombs into the Tom line at intervals. He was intermittently very nervous. By about 6.30 pm 8ᵗʰ D.L.I. had relieved us, all companies moving into PRUE TRENCH & STARFISH LINE. Bn. H.Q. O.C. same place.

B.C. Evans Lieut Col. O.C.
9ᵗʰ Bn. Durham L.I.

2449 Wt. W14957/M90 750,000 1/16 J.B.C. & A. Forms/C.2118/12.

WAR DIARY

OCTOBER. 1916.

9th Durham Light Infantry

Vol. 4.

WAR DIARY
or
INTELLIGENCE SUMMARY
(Erase heading not required.)

Instructions regarding War Diaries and Intelligence Summaries are contained in F. S. Regs. Part II. and the Staff Manual respectively. Title Pages will be prepared in manuscript.

Place	Date	Hour	Summary of Events and Information	Remarks and references to Appendices
	1.10.16	3.15pm	After an intense bombardment the 50th Div. in conjunction with the 47th on our right and 23rd on our left attacked the FLERS LINE. 151st I.B. leads the attack, 149 I.B. in support, 150 I.B. in reserve. 151st I.B. weapons attacked as follows: right Bn 6 D.L.I (covered by 9 D.L.I) centre Battalions of Border Regt. and 8 D.L.I combined, left Bn 5th N.F attacked to 151 I.B. (covered by 6 N.F in close support).

Objectives – Two lines of trenches between M.22.b.3.4 and M.21.b.8.4 (FLERS LINE)
objectives of right Bn (6 D.L.I – covered by 9 D.L.I) M.22.b.3.1
1st objective
M.22.a.7½.0

2nd objective
M.22.b.3.4
to
M.22.a.7½.3½. | |
| | 2.10.16 | 1 Apm | Owing to heavy machine gun fire from our right flank we were only able to reach our first objective. But by 1 Apm we had gained the second objective also, that is 6 D.L.I and 9 D.L.I. Attack was established in first objective at M.22.b.3.4 and in second objective at M.22.b.3.4. As the 47th Div. did not gain their objective on our immediate right and the enemy ... to holding the trenches strongly. ... | |

WAR DIARY
or
INTELLIGENCE SUMMARY
(Erase heading not required.)

Instructions regarding War Diaries and Intelligence Summaries are contained in F. S. Regs., Part II. and the Staff Manual respectively. Title Pages will be prepared in manuscript.

Place	Date	Hour	Summary of Events and Information	Remarks and references to Appendices
	1/2.		In a severe nature bazed round our block now to/left flank for 24 hours (but all attempts to eject us were repulsed.) On our gaining hold on our first and Second Objectives touch was immediately established with the 5 Flanders and @ J.1.1 now left. RUTHERFORD ALLEY was continued right through to the second objective. A.E.R. Heslop, O.C. B. Coy. was wounded while working in it. the enemy had a very rough time between M.22.b.4.1 and M.22.b.6.0. He was especially exposed in this trench here and we led/trained to this portion, two Stokes guns, one	
	2.	7-9 AM	2" mortar, heavier guns, Vickers guns. Our snipers alone claimed 30 hits between 7 AM - 9 AM. We captured early on 2nd Oct. 4 unwounded and 6 wounded prisoners, all 17 Res. Bav. Regt., in the Second Objective. Our patrols were unable to push far forward as enemy was shifting from the direction of the STARS. We endeavoured to push determinedly. Sharp fighting continued throughout today.	
	2.		out our block to M.22.b.4½.½ and M.22.b.5.4. respectively. The enemy however was in such strength and was fighting so determinedly that inspite of the gallantry of our flankers we were unable to make progress.	
	6.3pm		The enemy attempted a strong	

2449 Wt. W14957/M90 750,000 1/16 J.B.C. & A. Forms/C.2118/12.

Army Form C. 2118.

WAR DIARY
or
INTELLIGENCE SUMMARY

(Erase heading not required.)

Instructions regarding War Diaries and Intelligence
Summaries are contained in F. S. Regs., Part II.
and the Staff Manual respectively. Title Pages
will be prepared in manuscript.

Place	Date	Hour	Summary of Events and Information	Remarks and references to Appendices
	2.	8pm	Counter attack on our right. Blocks. He had assembled a large number of troops to take part in this attack. We brought fire from Artillery, Stokes Guns, Machine Guns, Lewis guns and rifles broke up his attack.	
	2/3		The enemy again this afternoon tried to meet but our blacks LMG were driven in to the trenches. We had to fight throughout the evening we were unable to push forward any patrols but everything on the North front was particularly quiet. During the night the C.T. from North Durham trench to the front line was deepened and widened.	
	2/3		Enemy Artillery was active throughout today and night. He did not however attempt to retake our captured lines - perhaps he was content to let our own Heavy Artillery do this - . He shelled BLAYDON TRENCH, NORTH DURHAM TRENCH, RUTHERFORD ALLEY between M. 28. a. 9. 6 and NORTH DURHAM TRENCH.	
	3.	About 5.30am	We were relieved about 5.30am by 7 N.F. The relief took some 8 hours to come from PRUE TRENCH to the captured lines owing to the weather. Our weary men arrived back in PRUE TRENCH about 6.30am.	Lt. Heslop wounded on night of 1st. TOTAL CASUALTIES 1st 3rd OCT. 2 O.R. killed 2 missing, 45 wounded.

WAR DIARY
or
INTELLIGENCE SUMMARY
(Erase heading not required.)

9 Durham Light Inf

Instructions regarding War Diaries and Intelligence Summaries are contained in F. S. Regs., Part II. and the Staff Manual respectively. Title Pages will be prepared in manuscript.

758

Place	Date	Hour	Summary of Events and Information	Remarks and references to Appendices
			TOTAL CASUALTIES. 2nd Oct. 2 killed, 17 missing, 3 wounded. 3rd — 2 missing.	
	3 Oct.	11 am.	Bn. left PRUE TRENCH and returned to BECOURT WOOD).	
	4 Oct.	12 noon	Bn. left BECOURT WOOD), arrived HENENCOURT WOOD), for a few days' rest about 5.30 p.m.	
	5 Oct. to 10 Oct.		Battalion training, refitting, and reorganising, to enter the Battle again.	
	11 Oct. to 13 Oct.		Battalion received sudden orders to move up to S.W. corner of MAMETZ WOOD) to a tent camp and arrived there very weary about 9 p.m. Battalion working on roads round CONTALMAISON.	
	14 Oct.	4 p.m.	Battalion returned to HENENCOURT WOOD) (the same position as before.	
	15 Oct. to 22 Oct.		training. We have started a band which promises to be a great success. Drafts (both officers and men continually arrive.	
	23 Oct.		Battalion moved back once more to the Battle. March from HENENCOURT to BECOURT WOOD) and eventually pitch tents on about X.26.a (57.3).	
	24 Oct.		Same place. Battalion is now at full strength with 41 officers and 1011 other ranks	

2449 Wt. W14957/M90 750,000 1/16 J.B.C. & A. Forms/C.2118/12.

WAR DIARY
or
INTELLIGENCE SUMMARY
(Erase heading not required.)

Instructions regarding War Diaries and Intelligence Summaries are contained in F. S. Regs., Part II. and the Staff Manual respectively. Title Pages will be prepared in manuscript.

Place	Date	Hour	Summary of Events and Information	Remarks and references to Appendices
	24th Oct.		These 32 Officers and 890 other ranks are actually with the Battalion, the others being employed away.	
	25 Oct		Battalion received orders to move into (relief) at BAZENTIN LE GRAND and relieve a unit of 9 Division there. We eventually, after much marching and counter-marching arrived at N.E. corner of MAMETZ WOOD and relieved 7 KOSB there. 50th Division relieved 9th Division, in the front line with 150 & 149 I.B.; 151 I.B. in Reserve	
	26 Oct		Same place. Colonel and Coy Commanders made a reconnaissance of the front held by the Division - that is EAUCOURT L'ABBAYE and travelled on either side.	
	27 Oct.		Same place. Whole Battalion at work on the roads from HIGH WOOD to BAZENTIN LE PETIT. The weather is vile and the mud awful.	
	28th-31		Same place. Working parties every day. In spite of wretched weather and very poor shelters (tents and dugouts - both soaking inside) the spirits of the men are high and their keenness undiminished. There is every prospect of being in the Battle again in the course of the next few days.	759- / 48
			R. Floyd Stone Captain and Adjutant.	
			9 Batt: the Durham Light Infantry. 31.10.16	

760-
85

WAR DIARY.

9'ᵗʰ Bᴺ. Durham L.I.

November 1916.

Volume 20.

WAR DIARY
or
INTELLIGENCE SUMMARY
(Erase heading not required.)

9. D. L. I.
VOL: 20.

Instructions regarding War Diaries and Intelligence Summaries are contained in F. S. Regs., Part II and the Staff Manual respectively. Title Pages will be prepared in manuscript.

Place	Date	Hour	Summary of Events and Information	Remarks and references to Appendices
Map 57.C.S.N 1/20000	1.11.16 ? 2.11.16		N.E. corner of MAMETZ WOOD. Working parties ? whole Battalion on cleaning out and repairing RUTHERFORD ALLEY.	761.
	3		Battalion moved up to front line and taken over trenches from 5th Yorks. Companies left here about 2 p.m and relief was reported complete at 9 p.m - very good considering the [illegible] the ground and trenches. Battalion disposed as follows: B.Coy in front line: 4 Posts in MAXWELL TRENCH (the jumping-off trench), remainder in SNAG and TAIL TRENCHES. MAXWELL TRENCH 57. C. S. N. M.17.C.1.8 - 5.8. TAIL — M.17.C.1.8 - 4.4. SNAG — M.17.C.4.4 - 7.5. A.Coy in ABBAYE LANE (about M.23.A.) C & D Coys in FLERS SWITCH (about M.29.B.) Bn H.Q. at M.22.d.4.2	
	4.		Nothing of much importance happened. The day was spent in preparing for the morrow. The front line and the enemy's line were carefully observed by all our officers and the ground studied. The BUTTE DE WARLENCOURT stands out very prominently and can be seen very clearly from everywhere round here. We are to attack at 9.10 A.M. tomorrow. The attack will be made as follows:-	

WAR DIARY

or

INTELLIGENCE SUMMARY

(Erase heading not required.)

Instructions regarding War Diaries and Intelligence Summaries are contained in F. S. Regs., Part II. and the Staff Manual respectively. Title Pages will be prepared in manuscript.

Place	Date	Hour	Summary of Events and Information	Remarks and references to Appendices
	4		A.B. and C. Coys. will attack in 4 waves - 30 paces between waves. I.e. 3 Coys. in line (9 Coys. in column of platoons. D.Coy. is left in support. Objective of the Battalion is M.17.A.3.8 to M.16.B.9.8. This objective includes the famous BUTTE DE WARLEN COURT and the QUARRY (M.17.A.0.6) The Jumping off trench before A.B. and C. are to assemble is MAXWELL TRENCH. D.Coy. is to be in the TAIL and move forward to MAXWELL TRENCH or sooner this is vacated by A.B. and C. Bn H.Q. move forward to M.17.C.3½.4. — about the place where there are some dugouts — We shall have a dugout with 6 D.L.I.	762 -
	4/5		The night of 4/5 was somewhat disturbed and the enemy on two occasions put heavy barrage of MAXWELL TRENCH and THE TAIL. By 6 A.M. on 5th all Companies were in their correct positions and Bn H.Q. had moved forward.	
	5		9.10 A.M. A.B.C. Coys. crept forward under the artillery barrage and assaulted the enemy trenches. The assault was entirely successful. By 10.30 A.M. we had taken the QUARRY and had penetrated	

WAR DIARY
or
INTELLIGENCE SUMMARY

(Erase heading not required.)

Instructions regarding War Diaries and Intelligence Summaries are contained in F. S. Regs., Part II. and the Staff Manual respectively. Title Pages will be prepared in manuscript.

Place	Date	Hour	Summary of Events and Information	Remarks and references to Appendices

the GIRD LINE - our objective. A post was established on the BAPAUME ROAD at M. 16.8.9.8.   A machine gun in the dugout on M.E. Side of the BUTTE held up our advance somewhat and we attempted many times to find the dugout. Telephonic communication with the QUARRY established.

GIRD FRONT LINE from M.11.C.2.1. to M.17.A.4.7 with a post in GIRD SUPPORT LINE at M.11.C.4.½.

The enemy still had a post on North side of BUTTE. We held BUTTE ALLEY also to QUARRY strongly. Telephone communication with the QUARRY still holding.

On our right the 6 J.21 had been held up by machine gun fire and could not advance much beyond MAXWELL TRENCH, independent whatever states that our assault was very finely carried out and that our men could be seen advancing ... steadily. They passed right over the BUTTE and straight on to the GIRD LINE when our artillery directed were immediately put out.

2449 Wt. W14957/M90 750,000 1/16 J.B.C. & A. Forms/C.2118/12.

WAR DIARY
or
INTELLIGENCE SUMMARY
(Erase heading not required.)

Instructions regarding War Diaries and Intelligence Summaries are contained in F. S. Regs., Part II. and the Staff Manual respectively. Title Pages will be prepared in manuscript.

Place	Date	Hour	Summary of Events and Information	Remarks and references to Appendices
				764

From noon up to 3pm the position remained unchanged - the enemy delivered several determined assaults on the GIRD LINE but there were all repulsed. Fighting still continued in the BUTTE where we tried to capture the fortified dugout on North side. At about 3 p.m. the Enemy strongly reinforced again counterattacked and at 3.20 pm we repulsed as follows

"we have been driven out of GIRD FRONT LINE and I believe my posts there were captured. I have tried to get back but the enemy is in considerable force and is still counter attacking. It is taking me all my time to hold BUTTE ALLEY. Please ask artillery to shell area N.9 BAPAUME road in M.16.d) and M.11.c as Germans are in considerable force there. Enemy is holding GIRD FRONT LINE strongly my right. In my opinion anything advance to the right of the BUTTE would meet with success. I have a small post in a Shell hole at the N.W. Corner of the BUTTE but the enemy still hold most of the BUTTE on the NORTH side. I am not going to make another effort to capture the post."

Desperate hand to hand fighting continued all afternoon and at 7.15 pm

WAR DIARY

or

INTELLIGENCE SUMMARY

(Erase heading not required.)

Instructions regarding War Diaries and Intelligence Summaries are contained in F. S. Regs., Part II and the Staff Manual respectively. Title Pages will be prepared in manuscript.

76

Place	Date	Hour	Summary of Events and Information	Remarks and references to Appendices
	5.	7.10?	The follow message was sent back to the Brigade. "We are holding BUTTE ALLEY from M.17.A.5.5 to M.17.A.3.9. We have beaten N. side of BUTTE at M.17.A.3.9. The enemy still have a post in NORTHERN slope of BUTTE but are failing to scupper this. We are now endeavouring to establish a post in GIRD FRONT LINE at M.17.A.7.6. and another at M.17.A.3.8. Germans are still attacking and a good deal of hand (close) fighting is taking place. We killed large numbers of the enemy in the BUTTE and in the 2 QARRY and any to heavy the could not take so many prisoners were night otherwise. A further Battalion were attacked to here I could probably take the GIRD front line from M.17.A.7.7 to M.17.6.3.4. The work on the C.T. to BUTTE is progressing." At 12.20 AM, we had to report as follows. "We have been driven out of BUTTE ALLEY by a strong counter attack and 9.D.L.I. and 6.D.L.I. are now in MAXWELL TRENCH. Enemy was in great force and we cannot get back to BUTTE ALLEY. All our posts (were captured or driven back)"	
	6.			

2449   Wt. W14957/M90 750,000 1/16 J.B.C. & A. Forms/C.2118/12

Army Form C. 2118.

WAR DIARY
or
INTELLIGENCE SUMMARY
(Erase heading not required.)

Place	Date	Hour	Summary of Events and Information	Remarks and references to Appendices
			The enemy counter attack was delivered from the front (turn to GIRD LINE) then to left flank (turn to direction g.m. 16.6.8.9) and from the right flank (from GIRD LINE. The Germans still holding out in the BUTTE dugout came out and advanced over the BUTTE. The enemy advanced throwing bombs.	
			Apart) About 20 Germans worked round our left flank and attacked to 2 officers of the Coy. The enemy were in great strength. this attack was perfectly organised and was pushed with great energy and determination. but after a desperate stand they were driven out then resisted heroically but after a desperate stand they were driven out to the same (back to MAXWELL TRENCH, so that by 1 p.m. or 6t we were in the same	
6. 11am.			position as on the morning of 5th Prior to the assault. We had killed great numbers of Germans and sent down 7 prisoners of –179 Infantry Regiment (SAXONS). The rest of the night was spent in clearing out wounded. The day 16th passed uneventfully except for very heavy enemy shelling. At 4 p.m. we bombarded intended our weary men in	
4pm.				

WAR DIARY
or
INTELLIGENCE SUMMARY

(Erase heading not required.)

767—

Place	Date	Hour	Summary of Events and Information	Remarks and references to Appendices
	6.	11 P.M.	MAXWELL TRENCH: By about eleven o'clock we were relieved by S.D.L.I. (150 I.B.) and the Battalion returned to camp at N.E. corner of MAMETZ WOOD, reaching here	
	7.		about 3 A.M. Our casualties were heavy and are as follows:-	
			Officers:	
			CAPT. J.D. RICKABY - wounded.	
			CAPT. T. HARKER -	
			2 Lieut. T.E. COULSON. - Missing.	
			— N.E. MEIKLE. - wounded.	
			— N. WALTON. - wounded.	
			— C.E. HIGGINBOTTOM - Killed.	
			— H.V. CHISHOLM - missing.	
			— N. KELLY. - wounded.	
			— S.T. PAXTON. - Killed.	
			— N. MANNERS - missing.	
			— S.F. PLASKITT. - missing.	
			2 Lieut. A.L.L. POTTS - missing.	
			— J.T. GREEN - missing.	
			— J.A. HONE - missing.	
			— F.A. BLACK	
			— J.A. BLACKETT - wounded.	
			OTHER RANKS.	
			KILLED. WOUNDED. MISSING.	
			30. 200. 161.	

WAR DIARY
or
INTELLIGENCE SUMMARY

(Erase heading not required.)

Instructions regarding War Diaries and Intelligence Summaries are contained in F. S. Regs, Part II. and the Staff Manual respectively. Title Pages will be prepared in manuscript.

768.8/3

Place	Date	Hour	Summary of Events and Information	Remarks and references to Appendices
MAMETZ Wood	7-15		In Camp at MAMETZ Wood. Daily working parties - building huts, mending roads etc.	
	16.		Battalion (less a working party of 100 which went to MEAULTE to unload ammunition at the siding on the Railway - tent camp) proceeded to MILLENCOURT. Excellent tent camp and billety accommodation. Relieved at MAMETZ Wood by 1st Bn S.W.B., 1st Division.	
		16-30	In Camp at MILLENCOURT. Drafts of 8 officers and 219 other ranks joined the Battalion. Company and Battalion training in working parties every Wednesday and Saturday.	
			Extract from the London Gazette dated November 25th 1916. "The Victoria Cross - Lieutenant (Temp. Lieutenant Colonel) Roland Boys Bradford M.C., late Durham Light Infantry. For most conspicuous bravery and good leadership in attack, whereby he saved the situation on the right flank of the Brigade and of the Division."	

WAR DIARY Vol. 17

9th Bn. Durham Light
Infantry.

Nov. 30th to Dec. 31st 1916.

Volume II.

WAR DIARY
or
INTELLIGENCE SUMMARY
(*Erase heading not required.*)

Instructions regarding War Diaries and Intelligence
Summaries are contained in F. S. Regs., Part II.
and the Staff Manual respectively. Title Pages
will be prepared in manuscript.

Place	Date	Hour	Summary of Events and Information	Remarks and references to Appendices
WARLOY	1.12.16		Battalion moved from MILLENCOURT into billets at WARLOY for training. 7th Connaught Highlanders took over our comds at MILLENCOURT. We took over billets at WARLOY from the 12th Highland Light Infantry were mostly broken down barns.	
	2		Battalion Rest to enable all ranks to get settled down in billets, which	
	3-10		Platoon Training.	
		10AM	Battalion Inter Company Football League commenced under the control of 2Lt CH WADE.	
			Gen: Grenadfr(?) Lieutenany ICB, DSO. inspected the Brigade at WARLOY or the 5th Dec.	
	11-19		Company Training	
			Brigade Football League commenced on the 13th	
	13		1st match 151st M.G.C. 1 goal v 9th DLI NIL	
	18		2nd match 151st T.M.B. 2 goals v 9th DLI 6 goals.	
	20		20 Box details arrived from the Base.	
			Battalion training in night operations. Digging a jumping off trench	
	1		Battalion Training	
	24	2.PM	Brigade Cross Country Run, WARLOY–HENENCOURT–BAIZIEUX–WARLOY	
	24		9th DLI team won easily.	
	25-26		Battalion Football League. Headquarters left the Line on the end of the tournament	

WAR DIARY

or

INTELLIGENCE SUMMARY

(Erase heading not required.)

Instructions regarding War Diaries and Intelligence
Summaries are contained in F. S. Regs., Part II.
and the Staff Manual respectively. Title Pages
will be prepared in manuscript.

Place	Date	Hour	Summary of Events and Information	Remarks and references to Appendices
WARLOY	26		Brigade Training. Colonel & Brigade Platoon	
	27		" Attack on VADENCOURT WOOD	
ALBERT	28	12.30 PM	Battalion moved to ALBERT	
			Quiet days in good billets	
	29	3 PM	Convent in Circle a Hall	
	30	9 AM	Battalion moved to Sub 2 (57.S.W.S.8&99.) BAZENTIN LE PETIT.	
BAZENTIN LE PETIT	31		British Artillery kept up a steady bombardment all day	
			a few enemy shells were... still quiet.	
			Enemy shelled the camp and the surrounding country, one shell which killed one	
		12 noon	... final orders a hot ...	
		4 PM	The Battalion moved off to the front line and took over trenches from the 1st Royal North Staves. Relief was ... quickly and was completed at 7.30 PM.	
			Companies disposed as follows:-	
			Frontage:—	
			A Coy M24 6.58 to N19 a 5.9 (inclusive)	
			C Coy N19 a 5.9 (exclusive) to N19 d 4.9.	
			D Coy N19 central	
			B Coy N19 d 2.10 to IN19 d 2.7	
			Support	
			Reserve	
FACTORY CORNER Sh 57c SW N19c7/22				

WAR DIARY

or

INTELLIGENCE SUMMARY

(Erase heading not required.)

Instructions regarding War Diaries and Intelligence Summaries are contained in F. S. Regs., Part II. and the Staff Manual respectively. Title Pages will be prepared in manuscript.

Place	Date	Hour	Summary of Events and Information	Remarks and references to Appendices
	31		The line consisted of a series of 16 posts which were in a very damp and muddy condition. The shelters were very small. The 2nd Australians were on our left, and the 5th Northumberland Fusiliers were on our right, opposite LE BARQUE. The line was immediately	

(signature)
2/Lieut.
2nd ....
q..... J.I.

WAR DIARY.

9TH BN. THE DURHAM LIGHT INFANTRY.

JANUARY 1917.

VOLUME NO. II.

WAR DIARY
or
INTELLIGENCE SUMMARY

(*Erase heading not required.*)

Instructions regarding War Diaries and Intelligence
Summaries are contained in F. S. Regs., Part II.
and the Staff Manual respectively. Title Pages
will be prepared in manuscript.

Place	Date	Hour	Summary of Events and Information	Remarks and references to Appendices
BAZENTIN LE PETIT	31.12.16 1.1.17		The Battalion moved to the front line trenches and relieved the 1st Bar. Roy of North [Lancs] Regt. (Shree 57 & 58.- M 24 & , N 19 a & b.) A and C Companies manned the left & right front line sector respectively. Battalion Headquarters - FACTORY CORNER N.19.c.5.2. D Coy. was in Support , B Coy. in Reserve. Capt. CARMICHAEL wounded, to Hospital The whole line consisted of a line of 16 Posts in an old trench at (from 20 to 80 yards intervals.)	
FACTORY CORNER	3.1.17		1 killed in action 1 wounded to Hospital	
BAZENTIN LE PETIT	4th/5th 4 7		Battalion relieved by the 8th D.L.I. and moved to Cars Schi. BAZENTIN LE PETIT Capt. R.Boydston and Capt. A.C.Scott (RAMC) awarded the Military Cross. Major E.E.Crowel to duty at 151 at Infy Brigade training Camp BAIZIEUX to command.	
	8th/9th		The Battalion moved to the Support Trenches and there relieved the 6th D.L.I.	
SUPPORT TRENCHES	9		Battalion Headquarters M.30.c.30. 124 Reinforcements arrived at BAIZIEUX from the Base. 2 men killed in action , 3 wounded to Hospital 3 men killed in action , 7 wounded to Hospital	
	10		5 Officers, 2 Lt. J. Hall , D Stephenson , L. Burton , AW.Bell , and A.T.Bates, joined unit.	
	11		11 Reinforcements and to Base details also joined the Battalion.	

Army Form C. 2118.

WAR DIARY

or

INTELLIGENCE SUMMARY.

(*Erase heading not required.*)

Instructions regarding War Diaries and Intelligence Summaries are contained in F. S. Regs., Part II. and the Staff Manual respectively. Title pages will be prepared in manuscript.

(2)

Place	Date	Hour	Summary of Events and Information	Remarks and references to Appendices
SUPPORT TRENCHES	12th/13th		The Battalion was relieved in the Support trenches by the 8th DLI and proceeded to HIGH WOOD WEST CAMP. One man killed in Action.	
HIGH WOOD WEST CAMP	15	15	8 Reinforcements joined the Battalion from the BAIZIEUX Training Camp	
		16	The enemy shelled the Camp, one shell falling in a hut occupied by men of B Company. Killed in Action. Casualties: 8 men. 16 men wounded to hospital. 5 men on Duty.	
			Draft of 74 reinforcements joined the Battalion from the BAIZIEUX Training Camp.	
	16/9		The Battalion proceeded to the Front Line trenches and relieved the 6th DLI. B Company occupied the left & front, right & " " " " " D " " " " A " " " " C " " " " Support Dugouts in Rear. Battalion Headquarters at FACTORY CORNER.	

A5834 Wt. W4973 M687 750,000 8/16 D. D. & L. Ltd. Forms/C.2118/13.

WAR DIARY
or
INTELLIGENCE SUMMARY.

(Erase heading not required.)

Instructions regarding War Diaries and Intelligence Summaries are contained in F. S. Regs. Part II. and the Staff Manual respectively. Title pages will be prepared in manuscript.

Place	Date	Hour	Summary of Events and Information	Remarks and references to Appendices
FRONT SYSTEM OF TRENCHES	18		The enemy shelled very heavily during the relief. Casualties:- One man killed in action. 2 Lt T Hall wounded to hospital. Lt Col R.B. Bradford V.C., M.C. wounded to Duty. Capt J.A.C. Scott M.C. (R.A.M.C.) wounded to hospital. 4 men wounded to hospital.	
	20		"Casualties":- One man killed in action 6 men wounded to hospital	
	20/21		Casualties:- 2 Lt D. STEPHENSON wounded to hospital The Battalion was relieved by the 8th D.L.I. and proceeded to Camp Site 1 BAZENTIN LE PETIT.	
BAZENTIN LE PETIT	21		A Reinforcements joined the Battalion	
	22 and 23		Battalion Training in Bombing. Each Officer and man threw two live grenades.	
	24		36 joined the Battalion. 2 Lt E.S. GIBSON, 2 Lt G.F. BOLAM, 2 Lt J.R. THOMPSON.	
	24		The Battalion proceeded to the Support trenches and relieved the 6th D.L.I.	

A5834 Wt. W4973 M687 750,000 8/16 D. D. & L. Ltd. Forms/C.2118/13.

WAR DIARY

or

INTELLIGENCE SUMMARY.

(Erase heading not required.)

Instructions regarding War Diaries and Intelligence
Summaries are contained in F. S. Regs., Part II.
and the Staff Manual respectively. Title pages
will be prepared in manuscript.

(4)

Place	Date	Hour	Summary of Events and Information	Remarks and references to Appendices
SUPPORT TRENCHES	25 26		Enemy Artillery inactive during the greater part of the time in Support.	
	26/27		The Battalion was relieved by the 61st Australian Infantry Battalion, and moved to Camp Site 4, BAZENTIN LE PETIT.	
Camp Site 4 BAZENTIN LE PETIT	27	9.30am	The Battalion moved to Camp 'C', BECOURT.	
BECOURT	28		Rest.	
	29	1.45PM	The Battalion moved to RIBEMONT, via ALBERT. Some of the billets were very poor and overcrowded. Short route marches were carried out by the Companies.	
RIBEMONT	30		Training Area allotted. Training by Companies was carried out from 9.45 AM to 1 PM. Major E.G.Crowd returned to duty from BAIZIEUX Training Camp. 66 reinforcements joined the Battalion from BAIZIEUX Training Camp.	
	31			

W.Wylie
2nd Lt
9/A DLI

A5834 Wt.W4973 M687 750,000 8/16 D. D. & L. Ltd. Forms/C.2118/13.

Army Form C. 2118.

WAR DIARY

or

INTELLIGENCE SUMMARY.

(Erase heading not required.)

Instructions regarding War Diaries and Intelligence Summaries are contained in F. S. Regs., Part II. and the Staff Manual respectively. Title pages will be prepared in manuscript.

Place	Date	Hour	Summary of Events and Information	Remarks and references to Appendices
				Vol 19

WAR DIARY.

9TH BN. THE DURHAM LIGHT INFANTRY.

FEBRUARY 1917.

VOLUME 23.

A5834   Wt. W4973 M687 750,000 8/16 D. D. & L. Ltd. Forms/C.2118/13.

WAR DIARY
or
INTELLIGENCE SUMMARY.

(Erase heading not required.)

Instructions regarding War Diaries and Intelligence Summaries are contained in F. S. Regs., Part II. and the Staff Manual respectively. Title pages will be prepared in manuscript.

Place	Date	Hour	Summary of Events and Information	Remarks and references to Appendices
RIDEMONT	1.2.17		Training was carried out by Companies in the Training Area.	
			85 OR reinforcements proceeded from the 73/Ailleux Training Camp to the PONT REMY Musketry School where 2/Lt HAMPTON is.	
			Training carried out on Rifle Range and Training Area.	
	2.2.17		Training	
	3.2.17		Training: Battalion Drill.	
			Rewards: <u>The Distinguished Conduct Medal</u>	
			2042 Sgt J.W. Goffin.	
			2248 Sgt W. Craig.	
	4.2.17		Church Parade.	
			Lieut. Colonel R.B. Bradford presented the Gold Medals to the winning team (Headquarters) of the Battalion Football League, commenced at WARLOY and Silver Medals to the 'Runners up' (D Company)	
			Football:- 9th DURHAM LIGHT INFANTRY versus 2nd Bn. GRENADIER GUARDS	
			NIL. 3 goals.	
			GRENADIER GUARDS' TEAM	
			Cpl COOPER Sgt CARTWRIGHT (Aston Villa) Cpl HURLEY (Army Football Club)	
			Pte CHEMALT Pte COX Pte HILL (Wednesfield Rangers)	
			Pte HARGRAVES (Burton United)	
			Sgt BUCHAN (Sunderland) Sgt NEALE (Birmingham) L/Lawrence Sgt BETTS	

A5834 Wt.W4973 M687 730,000 8/16 D. D. & L. Ltd. Forms/C.2118/13.

WAR DIARY
or
INTELLIGENCE SUMMARY.
(Erase heading not required.)

Instructions regarding War Diaries and Intelligence Summaries are contained in F. S. Regs., Part II. and the Staff Manual respectively. Title pages will be prepared in manuscript.

Place	Date	Hour	Summary of Events and Information	Remarks and references to Appendices
RIBEMONT Sh.62D	6.2.17		Training: Lecture by Major E.G. Crouch at Bn H.Q.	
	6.2.17	12.15PM	Brigade Route March, Route Baizieux — Franvillers — Ribemont.	5 Officers and 14 Other Ranks of 2/6 South Staffordshire Regt (59th Division) attached for instruction in billets and huts recently
	7.2.17 to 9.2.17		Training: hard frost is still prevailing.	
	9.2.17		5 Officers and 14 Other Ranks of 2/6 South Staffordshire Regt (59th Division) attached for instruction.	
	10.2.17	10AM	The Battalion marched to Hamel and took over billets and huts recently was vacated by the French. The huts were capable of holding 100 men.	
HAMEL	11.2.17		Church Parades. Rest.	
	12.2.17		The Battalion marched from Hamel to Foucaucourt. The 50th Division relieved the 35th and 36th French Divisions on the night of the British Line. The French soldiers showed much interest in the passing columns of British troops.	
FOUCAUCOURT Sh.62C	13.2.17		Rest	

WAR DIARY

or

INTELLIGENCE SUMMARY.

(Erase heading not required.)

Instructions regarding War Diaries and Intelligence Summaries are contained in F. S. Regs., Part II. and the Staff Manual respectively. Title pages will be prepared in manuscript.

Place	Date	Hour	Summary of Events and Information	Remarks and references to Appendices
FOUCAUCOURT LL62c	14.2.17		Good training areas having been located, training was resumed. Companies etc. carried out short route marches. Rewards:-	
			The CROIX DE GUERRE	
			1106 9/RSM T. SORDY	
	15.2.17		Thaw set in. Training carried out. Several Officers visited the line	
	16.2.17		Training great attention being given to Bombing work. A pleasant afternoon was passed on the Recreation Ground. Inter Platoon football 'knock-out' Competition commenced. 1st two matches played. A Comic Costume Parade caused much amusement.	
	17.2.16		Training. Battalion Canteen opened with good results. 40 Other Ranks of the 149th Infantry Bde and 20 Other Ranks of the 6th BORDER REGT. Enlisted with the Battalion.	

A5834 Wt. W4973 M687 750,000 8/16 D. D. & L. Ltd. Forms/C.2118/13.

WAR DIARY
or
INTELLIGENCE SUMMARY.

(*Erase heading not required.*)

Instructions regarding War Diaries and Intelligence Summaries are contained in F. S. Regs. Part II. and the Staff Manual respectively. Title pages will be prepared in manuscript.

Place	Date	Hour	Summary of Events and Information	Remarks and references to Appendices
FOUCAUCOURT	18.2.17		Training Carried out.	
	19		Training — 300 rifle grenades were fired on the bombing pit.	
	19/20		The Battalion moved to the Support Trenches at BERNY with Bn HQ at N.32.d.8.3. and relieved 4 EAST YORKS. The trenches were in a very wet condition. Dugouts — generally good	
BERNY N32D	21		Work on clearing of trenches. 13 reinforcements joined unit. Slight enemy shelling. Enemy sniper active. We captured a German Sergeant Major on the N W corner of BERNY. He was very clean, having just returned from a Trench Mortar course and had apparently lost his way in the mist. He belonged to the 4th Inf Regt. (221 Division) 2nd Lt A.W. BELL wounded to hospital.	
	22			
	23		Enemy reported retiring further North. Pys reported renewed	

A3834 Wt. W4973 M687 759,000 8/16 D.D. & L. Ltd. Forms/C.2118/13.

Army Form C. 2118.

WAR DIARY
or
INTELLIGENCE SUMMARY.

(Erase heading not required.)

Instructions regarding War Diaries and Intelligence Summaries are contained in F. S. Regs., Part II. and the Staff Manual respectively. Title pages will be prepared in manuscript.

Place	Date	Hour	Summary of Events and Information	Remarks and references to Appendices
BERNY	23		Casualties:- 2 men killed in Action 1 men wounded to hospital	
	23/24		Battalion moved into the front line & and relieved the 8th DLI who occupied the trenches in the Support line vacated by us. Battalion HQ — T9c38. Line extended from T9c59 to T14b78. Trenches were very muddy & in some places impassable. 5th Border Regt on our left 61st Division on our right Relief were steady	
FRONT LINE	25		2 Lt GREENLAND found mine one slesomente wounded to hospital Enemy snipers very active. Our artillery shelled enemy trenches heavily on our right.	
	26		2 Lt I.M. HERRING wounded to hospital. 2 Other Ranks " "	
		11PM 26 2AM 27.2.17	6 patrols were sent out to ascertain whether the enemy had evacuated his trenches but all found them occupied and returned.	

A5834 Wt. W4973 M687 750,000 8/16 D. D. & L. Ltd. Forms/C.2118/13.

Army Form C. 2118.

WAR DIARY

or

INTELLIGENCE SUMMARY.

(Erase heading not required.)

Instructions regarding War Diaries and Intelligence Summaries are contained in F. S. Regs., Part II. and the Staff Manual respectively. Title pages will be prepared in manuscript.

Place	Date	Hour	Summary of Events and Information	Remarks and references to Appendices
	27		Lt. Col. R.D.BRADFORD V.C., M.C. left Bottn. to attend a Senior Officers Conference at FLIXECOURT. MAJOR E.G. CROUCH assumed command.	
	28		Both hostile and British artillery kept up a steady bombardment. Great activity was noticed in the front line by the 8th Dvn. The Battalion was relieved and moved to Reserve in the CAMP DES POMMIERS, FOUCAUCOURT.	
FOUCAUCOURT	28		4 Officers joined unit and posted as under:- 2 Lt. H. HALL to D Coy 2 Lt. J.F. CAWTHORN to B " 2 Lt. D.S PARFETT to B " 2 Lt. H.C.B. PLUMMER to C " Day devoted to rest and general cleaning of clothing and equipment.	

W.S.Wylie
2nd Lt/Adj
9th D.L.I.

A5834 Wt. W4973 M687. 750,000 8/16. D. D. & L. Ltd. Forms/C.2118/13.

Army Form C. 2118.

WAR DIARY

or

INTELLIGENCE SUMMARY.

(Erase heading not required.)

Instructions regarding War Diaries and Intelligence
Summaries are contained in F. S. Regs., Part II.
and the Staff Manual respectively. Title pages
will be prepared in manuscript.

Place	Date	Hour	Summary of Events and Information	Remarks and references to Appendices

WE 20

9TH BN. DURHAM LIGHT INFANTRY.

MARCH. 1917.

VOLUME 24.

A5834 Wt. W4973 M687 730,000 8/16 D. D. & L. Ltd. Forms/C.2118/13.

WAR DIARY
or
INTELLIGENCE SUMMARY.

(Erase heading not required.)

9th Battalion The Durham Light Infantry.

March 1917.

Volume XXIV

Instructions regarding War Diaries and Intelligence Summaries are contained in F. S. Regs., Part II. and the Staff Manual respectively. Title pages will be prepared in manuscript.

Place	Date 1917 March	Hour	Summary of Events and Information	Remarks and references to Appendices
FOUCAUCOURT	1		Major E.G. Crouch took over temporary command of 6th D.L.I. The Battalion carried out training and bathing during the day.	
	2		Training. A party of 2 Officers and 70 Other Ranks moved to the Support Line. Training in Bombing both during the morning.	
	3		Preparing to move to the trenches during afternoon. Battalion moved to the front line trenches and relieved the 8th D.L.I. Relief was reported soon after 10 P.M.	
	3/4		B attalion HQ - T.9.c.3.8. LL 6.2.Q.SW. Battalion Headquarters were under observation which prohibited much movement during the day. Frontage T.9.d. 5.9. to T.14.d.7.8. 'A' 'B' and 'C' Companies again occupied the front line. 'D' Coy was in Support. The 2 Officers and 70 Other Ranks who moved to Support at BERNY on 2nd. moved up to the front line at 10 P.M. in readiness to raid the enemy's trenches before dawn. 61st Division were on our right and the 6th D.L.I on the left.	

1577   Wt. W10791/1773   500,000   1/15   D. D. & L.   A.D.S.S./Forms/C. 2118.

Army Form C. 2118.

WAR DIARY
or
INTELLIGENCE SUMMARY.

(Erase heading not required.)

Instructions regarding War Diaries and Intelligence Summaries are contained in F. S. Regs., Part II. and the Staff Manual respectively. Title pages will be prepared in manuscript.

Place	Date	Hour	Summary of Events and Information	Remarks and references to Appendices
FRONT SYSTEM OF TRENCHES	4 1917	2.35 AM	A party of 2 Officers (2 Lt J.R.THOMPSON and 2 Lt J.T.BAILES) and 70 Other Ranks left our line at T.9.c.3.0. with the intention of raiding the enemy's trenches on the Northern edge of DRAGON WOOD. The party crossed No Man's Land without being noticed. Zero Hour was at 3.45 AM. At this time the party had just reached the Sunken Road at T.15.a.5.5.; artillery and machine Guns opened with deadly accuracy on the boundaries of the portion to be raided. The noise drowned any sound which the raiding party might have made as they rapidly cut a way through the wire obstacles and stealthily crossed the remaining 15 yards. They entered the enemy's trench at T.15.a.55.40. without being observed. The party broke away then, half going to the right and half to the left. One German was found on sentry duty and five others were taken, some of whom were found in a dugout.	

A5834 Wt. W4973 M687 750,000 8/16 D.D. & L. Ltd. Forms/C.2118/13.

Army Form C. 2118.

WAR DIARY
or
INTELLIGENCE SUMMARY.
(Erase heading not required.)

Instructions regarding War Diaries and Intelligence Summaries are contained in F. S. Regs., Part II. and the Staff Manual respectively. Title pages will be prepared in manuscript.

Place	Date	Hour	Summary of Events and Information	Remarks and references to Appendices
	1917 March		At 3.55 AM the party withdrew and rapidly made their way along the tape which had been laid on the outward journey, entering our trench at the starting point.	
			Casualties—Nil.	
			The 6 prisoners revealed a certain amount of valuable information. They belonged to the 3rd Coy. 1st Battalion 104th Grenadier Regt, 11th Division.	
			The enemy trench was deep, trench boarded, deep and well revetted. No hostile Artillery or Machine Guns replied.	
			At dawn this morning stretcher bearers were observed behind the enemy's line carrying wounded, which pointed to the fact that our artillery must have inflicted severe losses upon the enemy.	
			Major E.G. Crouch had returned a few hours prior to the Raid, from the 6th D.L.I. and instrumental to a marked degree was in bringing about its success.	
	4/5		The relief of the Division by the 59th Division commenced.	
			5 Officers and 152 Other Ranks of the 5th NORTH STAFFORDSHIRE REGt relieved the same number of our Officers and men.	
			These remained under our command until the remainder of the 5th Bn N. Staffs. Regt had relieved the Battalion on the night of the 6th/7th.	

A5834 Wt. W4973 M687 750,000 8/16 D.D. & L. Ltd. Forms/C.2118/13.

Army Form C. 2118.

WAR DIARY

or

INTELLIGENCE SUMMARY.

(Erase heading not required.)

Instructions regarding War Diaries and Intelligence
Summaries are contained in F. S. Regs., Part II.
and the Staff Manual respectively. Title pages
will be prepared in manuscript.

Place	Date 1917 March	Hour	Summary of Events and Information	Remarks and references to Appendices
	5		Our artillery shewed activity during the day. The enemy heavy artillery shewed more activity than usual.	
	6		Quiet day.	
	6/7		The Battalion was relieved by the 5th Bn. The North Staffordshire Regt. in the right sub-section and moved into billets in FOUCAUCOURT.	
FOUCAUCOURT	7		Headquarters in the dugouts under the Chateau which had been ruined by shell fire. The morning was devoted to cleaning up clothing and equipment and packing up in preparation for a move.	
MERICOURT SUR SOMME		2PM	The Battalion moved to MERICOURT—SUR—SOMME via PROYART. A,B, and D Companies occupied huts in the Camp in R.1.c. "C" Coy and Details were billetted in the village. Headquarters in the village at Q.6.c.2.7. Lt. Colonel R.B. Bradford V.C., M.C. rejoined the Battalion from the Senior Officer's Conference, FLIXECOURT. One Officer, 2/Lt. A.C.L. Crosby, and 12 Other Ranks joined the Battalion.	

A 3834 Wt. W4973 M687 750,000 8/16 D. D. & L. Ltd. Forms/C.2118/13.

Army Form C. 2118.

WAR DIARY

or

INTELLIGENCE SUMMARY.

(Erase heading not required.)

Instructions regarding War Diaries and Intelligence Summaries are contained in F. S. Regs., Part II. and the Staff Manual respectively. Title pages will be prepared in manuscript.

Place	Date	Hour	Summary of Events and Information	Remarks and references to Appendices
	1917			
	8		Rest.	
	9		A new Training Area having been found work was started on Bombing Pits, Rifle Range and Assault Course. These were completed and ready for use within a few days.	
	10		Bathing at MORCOURT. Three Reading Rooms established, one for Sergeants, one for Corporals and one for Privates.	
	11	AM	Divine Services.	
		PM	Holiday.	
	12		A Training Programme revised, and hard training immediately got under way. Joined Unit — 1 Officer Capt. L.A. Ramsay 8 Other Ranks.	
	13		Training.	
	14		Training: Demonstration and Practice in New Attack Formations.	

A5834 Wt. W4973 M687 750,000 8/16 D. D. & L. Ltd. Forms/C.2118/13.

WAR DIARY

or

INTELLIGENCE SUMMARY.

(Erase heading not required.)

Instructions regarding War Diaries and Intelligence Summaries are contained in F. S. Regs., Part II. and the Staff Manual respectively. Title pages will be prepared in manuscript.

Place	Date	Hour	Summary of Events and Information	Remarks and references to Appendices
	1917 Mar. 15		Training: Special attention given to New Attack formation, and Bombing. Lt. and Q.M. W.H. Roberton joined Unit.	
	16		Training: Attack formation. Awards. Military Medal - 1739 Cpl W.C.Guy and 7763 Pte D.Varty.	
	17		Training: Demonstration Raid by D'Company. 2 Lt. A. Braithwaite and Lt. E.D. Brown joined Unit.	
	18		Divine Service.	
	19	3 PM	Rest. Battalion Open-Air Concert. Exceptional talent was brought to light. The Platoon football Matches are being played each afternoon.	
		2.30 PM to 5 PM	Training. Football and Boxing Competitions.	
	20		Training: Battalion attack on a system of trenches.	
	21	2.30 PM TO 5 PM	Training: Aldershot Attack. C'Coy on the Rifle Range. Boxing and Football Competitions.	

A5834 Wt. W4973 M687 750,000 8/16 D. D. & L. Ltd. Forms/C.2118/13.

Army Form C. 2118.

WAR DIARY
or
INTELLIGENCE SUMMARY.

(Erase heading not required.)

Instructions regarding War Diaries and Intelligence
Summaries are contained in F. S. Regs., Part II.
and the Staff Manual respectively. Title pages
will be prepared in manuscript.

Place	Date 1917 March.	Hour	Summary of Events and Information	Remarks and references to Appendices
	22	3PM at MORCOURT 6PM	Training : 'B' Coy on the Range. Football — 151st Bde. Hqrs. NIL v 9th D.L.I. 2 Goals. 7th Durham Light Infantry sent a Concert Party to entertain the Battalion & very enjoyable evening was passed. Training 'D' Coy on Range Inter-Platoon football Competition continued	
	23			
	24		Training : 'A' Coy on Rifle Range : Live Grenade throwing.	
	25	3PM	Divine Service Pierrot 'The Green Diamonds Ragtime Troupe' gave a splendid performance on the 'Bankside', MERICOURT to a large audience. Brigade Boxing Tournament at MORCOURT. 2720 L/Cpl Reid won the Middleweight Championship. Inter-Platoon football Competition continued.	
	26		Brigade Scheme ordered but postponed on account of bad weather. Instruction carried out indoors.	

A5834 Wt. W4973 M687 759,000 8/16 D. D. & L. Ltd. Forms/C.2118/13.

Army Form C. 2118.

WAR DIARY

or

INTELLIGENCE SUMMARY.

(Erase heading not required.)

Instructions regarding War Diaries and Intelligence
Summaries are contained in F. S. Regs., Part II.
and the Staff Manual respectively. Title pages
will be prepared in manuscript.

Place	Date 1917 March	Hour	Summary of Events and Information	Remarks and references to Appendices
	27		Training. Blankets disinfected at Divisional Laundry.	
		3 PM	Football — Brigade Championship 8th D.L.I. NIL versus 9th D.L.I. NIL.	
	28	12 noon	Reinforcements:- One Officer (Capt. R.H. Guest-Williams) and 176 other Ranks joined Unit. Brigade inspected by Lieut General Sir W.P. Pulteney, K.C.B., K.C.M.G., D.S.O., Commanding III Army Corps. He thanked the Officers, N.C.Os. and men of the 151st Infantry Brigade for the good work they had done on the Somme while under his Command, and hoped they would be as successful in the XVIII Corps, to which they were going, as they had been in the III Corps. After wishing all good luck the Brigade marched past in Column 8 Route.	
		11.0 AM	Football — Brigade Championship replayed. 8th D.L.I. NIL versus 9th D.L.I. 1 Goal.	
		4.0 PM	Divisional Championship Semi-Final. 5th D.L.I. (150th Inf. Bde.) 4 Goals versus 9th D.L.I. (151st Inf. Bde.) NIL.	

A5834 Wt. W4973 M68; 750,000 8/16 D. D. & L. Ltd. Forms/C.2118/13.

Army Form C. 2118.

WAR DIARY

or

INTELLIGENCE SUMMARY.

(Erase heading not required.)

Instructions regarding War Diaries and Intelligence
Summaries are contained in F. S. Regs., Part II.
and the Staff Manual respectively. Title pages
will be prepared in manuscript.

Place	Date 1917 March	Hour	Summary of Events and Information	Remarks and references to Appendices
	29		Route March and Instruction in Bivouacing.	
			Football — Platoon Tournament continued.	
	30		The First Line Transport marched to St. GRATIEN and billetted there for the night.	
			Billeting Party under Major E. G. Croch proceeded to NAOURS by Motor Lorry.	
			Route March by Companies.	
			300 Live Grenades thrown on the Bombing Pits.	
			The 'Green Diamonds' gave a very entertaining concert.	
	31	6 P.M.	The Battalion moved by Motor Lorry from MERICOURT – SUR – SOMME to TALMAS via AMIENS and the marched to NAOURS.	
			Billets — good. Battalion Headquarters in the Convent.	
			Roads — very wet and muddy.	
			The First Line Transport marched from St. GRATIEN to NAOURS.	

A5834 Wt. W4973 M687 750,000 8/16 D. D. & L. Ltd. Forms/C.2118/13.

WAR DIARY (Vol 21

9th Bn Durham L.I.

VOLUME No 25.

for

APRIL, 1917

WAR DIARY

or

INTELLIGENCE SUMMARY.

(Erase heading not required.)

Instructions regarding War Diaries and Intelligence Summaries are contained in F. S. Regs., Part II. and the Staff Manual respectively. Title pages will be prepared in manuscript.

Place	Date	Hour	Summary of Events and Information	Remarks and references to Appendices
NAOURS	1	11 AM	Divine Service.	
			Rest.	
	2	8.20 a.m.	The Battalion marched to GÉZAINCOURT	
			Billets poor	
			During the march the Battalion Signallers kept touch with the Signalling of Brigade Headquarters and other Battalions by flag.	
GÉZAINCOURT	3	7AM	The Battalion marched to SIBIVILLE and billetted there.	
			'A' Company were billetted in SÉRICOURT	
			Dinner was cooked and served on the march.	
			Signallers maintained communication with other Units as on the 2nd April.	
SIBIVILLE	4	8AM	The Battalion marched to CROIX.	
			Billets good.	
			Awards:- Military Cross – 2 Lr. J.R.THOMPSON	
			Distinguished Conduct Medal — No. 1434 Sgt. D. SHEPHARD	
CROIX	5		Light Training	
	6		Training: Battalion Drill	
	7	10.30 a.m.	The Battalion marched to AVERDOINGT.	
			Signallers maintained communication as on previous marches.	

A5834 Wt. W4973 M687 750,000 8/16 D. D. & L. Ltd. Forms/C.2118/13.

WAR DIARY
or
INTELLIGENCE SUMMARY.
(Erase heading not required.)

Instructions regarding War Diaries and Intelligence Summaries are contained in F. S. Regs., Part II. and the Staff Manual respectively. Title pages will be prepared in manuscript.

Place	Date	Hour	Summary of Events and Information	Remarks and references to Appendices
AVERDOINGT	April 1917 8.	11AM	The Battalion marched to IZEL-LEZ-HAMEAU.	
	9		Training: 7 mile Route march by Platoons.	
	10		Battalion suddenly ordered to move to AGNEZ-LES-DUISANS. Left AVERDOINGT at 2PM. Billeted in Prison Huts.	
	11	7PM	Suddenly ordered up the line. Marched in blinding snowstorm to reserve line NE of BEAURAIN'S.	
	12 & 13	3PM	The Battalion proceeded to the front line captured a few hours previously. Took over from 8th Rifle Brigade. 56th Division on right. 29th left with gaps in between. Casualties:- Due to Machine-gun fire & heavy shelling. Killed in Action 2/Lt R. GREENLAND. O.R. 13. Wounded to Hospital:- 2/Lt J.F. CAWTHORN. " J.T. BAILES OR 39. " W.G. WYLIE " W.R.S. CATCHESIDE (returned to duty 13/4/17) Shell Shock:-	
	14		At night, advanced line 300 yds.	
	15	2AM	Relieved by 6th N.Fs. marched to Caves at RONVILLE. Casualties- 14th/4/17 Killed in Action 2/Lt R.N. BELL. O.R.4. Wounded to Hospital: Other Ranks 8. Missing:- 2.	

A5834 Wt.W4973 M687 750,000 8/16 D. D. & L. Ltd. Forms/C.2118/13.

WAR DIARY

or

INTELLIGENCE SUMMARY.

(Erase heading not required.)

Instructions regarding War Diaries and Intelligence Summaries are contained in F. S. Regs., Part II. and the Staff Manual respectively. Title pages will be prepared in manuscript.

Place	Date	Hour	Summary of Events and Information	Remarks and references to Appendices
RONVILLE	April 1917 16th		In Camp. Church Parade 4 pm. Impromptu Concert in evening	
	17th		Training programme	
	18th		Training under Coy arrangements	
	19th		Training. Working Parties	
	20th		Working Party BEAURAIN ? Working Party. Rumaucourt Baths	
	21st		Working Party. Rumaucourt Baths.	
	22nd		Church Parade. Baths. In evening "GREEN DIAMONDS" Concert in upon an	
	23rd 7 Am		Left Ronville & marched to the HARP where Battn halted till Midday, When suddenly received its proceed at once to NEPAL trenches in support to 150 Inf Brigade who were being counter-attacked by enemy along bed of COJEUL RIVER. On the way further orders were received that we were to move to the front line & be in readiness to attack at 6 pm (Zero hour) The companies moved up to form lines by section at 25 paces distance. Dispositions as follows 2 Coys in first wave & 2 in the 2nd the 3rd Barrain were on our right with the 6th BORDER Regt in between. The 15th Div were on our left. At 6pm Artillery barrage came down & the Coys moved forward our men making good progress. The Coys carried the first trench by storm making considerable	

(A7092). Wt. W12859/M1393. 750,000. 1/17. D. D. & L., Ltd. Forms/C.2118/14.

WAR DIARY

or

INTELLIGENCE SUMMARY.

(Erase heading not required.)

Instructions regarding War Diaries and Intelligence
Summaries are contained in F. S. Regs., Part II.
and the Staff Manual respectively. Title pages
will be prepared in manuscript.

Place	Date	Hour	Summary of Events and Information	Remarks and references to Appendices
	April 1917 23		Capture & firing on the retreating enemy not one of whom escaped. Without pausing the advance continued for several hundred yards when further enemy machine guns were encountered & several played on us from the North side of the COJEUL RIVER. After a short struggle — before our men were, their Lewis Guns, rifle grenades & rifles these were overcome and the enemy abandoning their position were either killed or captured. On arrival at the objective & partly consolidated trench was found lightly held by the enemy. This was immediately occupied by all four Companies & the work of consolidation commenced. Throughout the attack all ranks showed determination & enthusiasm the line ran from O.20.c.6.6 to road at O.20.a.8.5. We advanced 1600 yds on a 500 yd frontage. Both flanks were held up & we did not get in touch until the 25th when the 16th & 30th Division attacked Battalion HQ were in old German trench at O.19.a.1.2. Our casualties were slight. The enemy losses Our artillery barrage was particularly good but slow	MAP REF'R Sheet 51 SW

WAR DIARY

or

INTELLIGENCE SUMMARY.

(Erase heading not required.)

Instructions regarding War Diaries and Intelligence Summaries are contained in F. S. Regs., Part II. and the Staff Manual respectively. Title pages will be prepared in manuscript.

Place	Date	Hour	Summary of Events and Information	Remarks and references to Appendices
	April 1917	23	Several prisoners were captured and the graves were strewn with large numbers of dead & dying. Their morale seemed good & they all belonged to the 14 ... I.B.	
			Captured	
			Colonel.	
			M.O & 4 Officers	
			In addition to these 200 O.Rs were captured	
			Material :	
			3 guns (calibre not determined)	
			1 new gas appliance	
			1000 picks & shovels	
			1 Very pistol	
			11 Machine Guns (in addition not collected)	
			14 Fish-tail trench Mortars	
			Large quantities of S.A.A. equipment, grenades etc.	

Army Form C. 2118.

WAR DIARY
or
INTELLIGENCE SUMMARY.

(Erase heading not required.)

Instructions regarding War Diaries and Intelligence Summaries are contained in F. S. Regs., Part II. and the Staff Manual respectively. Title pages will be prepared in manuscript.

Place	Date	Hour	Summary of Events and Information	Remarks and references to Appendices
	Apl 1917	23		

Casualties. Officers

2/Lt J. Belfield } Wounded 15 Mortar
2/Lt L. Wheatley }
2/Lt A. B. Crosby :- Wounded to Hospital; since died of wounds
Lieut J. D. Brown   Wounded to Hospital 24/4/17
Capt. E. Gibson Wounded :- to Hospital 29/4/17
2/Lt L. D. Jordan : Wounded-still at duty.

Other Ranks

Wounded — 92.
Killed in Action — 20.
Missing — 3

The enemy had a large number of Machine Guns which gave a certain amount
of trouble. At the commencement of the attack we were led up from their front line.
Our guns engaged the machine gun lines taking the enemy's attention off the Rifle
Grenadiers who crept up & opened fire. The this enabled the left Coy to work round the
flank & the advance continued, several prisoners being captured. Dug-outs were bombed
& after a few minutes the advance was ... continued to the final objective. Here opposition
was overcome in the same way. The men then ... fired as they advanced on the
retiring enemy thus causing many casualties. Even then were mowed ... until ...
to ... than the Germans threw down their arms.

A.5834 Wt. W.4973/M687 750,000 8/16 D. D. & L. Ltd. Forms/C.2118/13.

WAR DIARY

or

INTELLIGENCE SUMMARY.

(Erase heading not required.)

Instructions regarding War Diaries and Intelligence
Summaries are contained in F. S. Regs., Part II
and the Staff Manual respectively. Title pages
will be prepared in manuscript.

Place	Date	Hour	Summary of Events and Information	Remarks and references to Appendices
	24/9/17		Spent in consolidating the position. Brigade relieved for supports. Rations brought up on pack mules to Batt HQ. Large quantities of German bread found & used. Battalion had a quiet day being shelled at intervals. 1 OR casualty.	
		Before dawn	TMS came up & got into position.	
		12 noon	"B" Battalion N.F's attached at 1 Coy of 5th BORDER Regt. This later placed on "A" & "B" Coy One Coy of Northumberland Fusiliers on the R. flank next to the Coy of BORDER Regt 3 Coys N.F. Regt in support. Reinforced by machine gun from 151 M.G.Coy.	
		10 P.M	Rations brought up to front line on mules. 2 of transport wounded & 2 mules casualties.	
	25th	2 P.M	Enemy attempted a counter-attack on the left division. It was caught by our barrage & repulsed. Our part of line very heavily shelled. No casualties. All "stood to" ready for an enemy attack.	
			Trenches much improved & about five feet in depth.	
			Throughout the day weakening shelling. Casualties 7 Wounded 1 Missing	
	25/9/10		Relieved by Oxford & Bucks L.I. proceeded to AARP.	
	26	12 mdn	Marched to tents in the vicinity of the AARP.	
	27	9.30 A.m	Marched to Billets in ARRAS, preparing to entrain.	
			CITADEL. Officers in Billets	
		4 P.M	Moved to Station & after a long wait entrained at dusk. Arrived at WARLINCOURT HALTE about 3 A.m. Marched to WARLUZEL.	
	28/9/28			

(A7992). Wt. W12839/M1293. 750,000. 1/17. D.D. & L. Ltd. Forms/C.2118/14.

WAR DIARY

or

INTELLIGENCE SUMMARY.

(Erase heading not required.)

Instructions regarding War Diaries and Intelligence
Summaries are contained in F.S. Regs., Part II
and the Staff Manual respectively. Title pages
will be prepared in manuscript.

Place	Date	Hour	Summary of Events and Information	Remarks and references to Appendices
WARLUZEL	April 1917 28th		In very comfortable billets. Rest	
	29th		Rest. Church Parade	
	30th		Rest. Wash bottles disinfected. Ordered to march to BIENVILLERS–AU–BOIS.	

A. Marshall.
2 Lt. A/Adj. 9th R.I.F.

(A7092). Wt. W28839/M1293. 750,000. 1/17. D. D. & L., Ltd. Forms/C.2118/14.

157/50

Yo 22

WAR DIARY.

9th Bn. The Durh. L.I.

Volume XXVI.

MAY, 1917.

Army Form C. 2118.

WAR DIARY
or
INTELLIGENCE SUMMARY.
(Erase heading not required.)

MAY 1917 Volume XXVI

Instructions regarding War Diaries and Intelligence Summaries are contained in F. S. Regs., Part II. and the Staff Manual respectively. Title pages will be prepared in manuscript.

Place	Date 1917	Hour	Summary of Events and Information	Remarks and references to Appendices
WARLUZEL	May 1st		Marched to BIENVILLERS – AU – BOIS. Left at 12.45 pm, arrived B. 7pm. Billeted in Shell shattered houses. Warm weather	
	2nd		Ordered to leave for BAILLEULVAL. Marched from 4pm to 7.45pm. Billets fair. In support the big attack taking place on the morrow.	
BAILLEULVAL	3rd		Remained here all day. No orders. Baths.	
	4		Received orders to move back to WARLUZEL. Moved off at 4pm arrived in WARLUZEL at 7.45 pm. Very hot weather. When staff of steel helmes allowed to be worn at back of head on 9c of heat.	
WARLUZEL	5th		Rear. Baths. Impromptu Concert.	
	6th		Reveille 5am. Parade 9am & 10am. 11 Church Parades. 2pm declare Suttallian Corporals	
	7th		L/C. "Bombing". 5 PM. Sergeant's instruction under R.S.M. Training. Purposed issued. Training 7am – 12.30pm. Semi-final a	
	8th		Game played. Result of Final. Band 3 goals V Stretcher Bearers 2. Sep 1904. Range phosphorus candlelit training. Route Marche in afternoon	
	9th		New football competition started. Range. Field firing Scheme. All advanced as in a trench attack. Fire line from lip. When lied up Rifle Grenades used. Bombin attack organized. Machine Gun fire overhead fire. Runner served on the Range at LUCHEUX. Back in billets 9 pm	
	10th		All enjoyed days outing. Training 9 – 1pm. Y-collar hateben in afternoon	
	11th		Training 7.12.30. football	

(A7092). We. W12859/M1293. 75,000. 1/17. D. D. & L., Ltd. Forms/C2118/14.

Army Form C. 2118.

(2)

WAR DIARY
or
INTELLIGENCE SUMMARY.

(Erase heading not required.)

Instructions regarding War Diaries and Intelligence Summaries are contained in F. S. Regs., Part II. and the Staff Manual respectively. Title pages will be prepared in manuscript.

Place	Date 1917	Hour	Summary of Events and Information	Remarks and references to Appendices
MARŒUIL	12		Training. B Coy on Range. Football.	
	13		Divine Service. Football	
	14		Range at LOCHEUX. Field firing when Company Arrangements. Programme of work for the week issued.	
	15		Training attack in the Open. Corps Commander replied no at Gournay.	
	16		Training. Football Competition.	
	17		Raining. Route March. Church Parade in afternoon. Indoor Shows.	
	18		Transferred to VII Corps	
	19		Moved to MONCHY-AU-BOIS. Bivouacs.	
	20		Training — In Corps reserve.	
	21		"Attack in the Open". Church Parades. Baths (Russian)	
	22		Brigade Scheme. Nignt Operation. Russian Baths.	
	23		Resting.	
ST AMAND	23		Marched 15 move back to ST AMAND. In Billets. Van	
	24		War orders to proceed to HEBEUTERNE. Cancelled. Route March.	
	25		Training.	
	26		Training. Attack on System of Trenches.	
	27		Training. Attack on System of Trenches. Umpires used at Training Area. Res. Concert by Divn Orchestra, in Cinema Hall	

(A7094). Wt. W1250/M1293. 750,000. 1/17. D. D. & L., Ltd. Forms/C.2118/14.

WAR DIARY
or
INTELLIGENCE SUMMARY.

(Erase heading not required.)

Instructions regarding War Diaries and Intelligence Summaries are contained in F. S. Regs., Part II. and the Staff Manual respectively. Title pages will be prepared in manuscript.

Place	Date 1917	Hour	Summary of Events and Information	Remarks and references to Appendices
ST AMAND	28		Monday "Attack in Open" + Supervision of Trench Training in Monchy area. Gunners arrived in "Green Diamond Orchard" Back in Billets 5.30 p.m.	
	3 ½		Tuesday Training. Organizing Battn. 6 p.m. Bath	
	30	7.30 p.m/9.30 p.m	Inoculation	
	3 Oct		Training in rifle, wiring, Day & Night Patrols, Lewis Guns	
	30		Honours & Awards.	
			MILITARY CROSS.—	
			Capt. M. Feeley. 2/Lts. H. Hall. M.O.B. Thompson. W.H. Wylie	
			Bar to Military Cross.	
			Major J.R.E. Scott. (RAMC) Major C. Bowdery	
			CROIX DE GUERRE.—	
			Capt. J.A.E. Scott	
			Dist. Conduct Medal. —	
			Sgt. A. Caldwell	
			Medaille Militaire	
			335899 Pte. H. Sanderson	

(A7092.) Wt. W12839/M1293. 759,000. 1/17. D. D. & L., Ltd. Forms/C.2118/14.

WAR DIARY
or
INTELLIGENCE SUMMARY.
(*Erase heading not required.*)

Instructions regarding War Diaries and Intelligence Summaries are contained in F. S. Regs. Part II. and the Staff Manual respectively. Title pages will be prepared in manuscript.

Place	Date	Hour	Summary of Events and Information	Remarks and references to Appendices
	1917 May		Missing Medal -	
			Sgts Waugh E, Gibson J, Shirley W, Greenwood J, Goffin W.	
			Appleby J	
			Cpls Bilton J. Vasey J (1435)	
			L/C.B. Brello (325429) 325226 L/C Jones J 325281 Henson M	
			L/C Bell E.R. (325389) 325146 L/C Kenny C. 325330 L/C Reid G.S.	
			325972 L/C Burton R.S. 325022 L/C Willson J	
			Privates - 325387 Bryant C 325752 Adamson J	
			325357 Searle J10 326464 Warren R.	
			Born Kith/h	
			325464 A/Sgt Marsh J.E. 325084 A/C Bee J	
			E.A.Marshall 2/Lt	
			A/Adjt 9th 10 L.9	

Army Form C. 2118.

WAR DIARY

or

INTELLIGENCE SUMMARY.

(Erase heading not required.)

Instructions regarding War Diaries and Intelligence Summaries are contained in F. S. Regs., Part II. and the Staff Manual respectively. Title pages will be prepared in manuscript.

Place	Date	Hour	Summary of Events and Information	Remarks and references to Appendices
				Vol 23

WAR DIARY.

9th Bn. The Durham Light Infantry, T.F.

June, 1917.

Volume 27.

2353 Wt. W3344/1454 700,000 5/15 D. D. & L.   A.D.S.S./Forms/C. 2118.

Army Form C. 2118.

WAR DIARY
or
INTELLIGENCE SUMMARY.

(Erase heading not required.)

JUNE 1917. VOL. XXVII

Instructions regarding War Diaries and intelligence Summaries are contained in F. S. Regs., Part II. and the Staff Manual respectively. Title pages will be prepared in manuscript.

Place	Date 1917	Hour	Summary of Events and Information	Remarks and references to Appendices
ST AMAND	June 1		Training ST AMAND	
	2nd		Range SOUASTRE. Running out.	
	3rd		Divine Services. Baths	
	4th		Training ST AMAND	
	5th		Brigade Field Day. Battalion attacked & captured village of	
	6th		FONQUEVILLERS. Running out. Battalion marched past in "Column"	
	6th		Training	
			BIRTHDAY HONOURS:- Distinguished Service Order, Major F.G. Crouch	
			Military Cross, Reg. Serg. Major T. Sordy	
	7th		Demonstration "Raid" by "D" Coy. Practice throwing live grenades	
	8th		Training. Rifle Range SOUASTRE.	
	9th		Training. B" Scale. Afternoon. Sports - Heats run.-	
	10th		Divine Service. Sports.	
	11th		Baths. Training in being	
			Demonstration "Raid" by D Company at night.	
	12th		Throwing Live Bomb Covered by Green Diamonds.	
	13th		Honours and Awards	
			Mentioned in Despatches.	
			Major Crouch, F.G., Lieut Craddock, Lieut Fisher, Lieut Hampton 2nd Lt Coulson	

Army Form C. 2118.

WAR DIARY

or

INTELLIGENCE SUMMARY.

(*Erase heading not required.*)

Instructions regarding War Diaries and Intelligence
Summaries are contained in F. S. Regs., Part II.
and the Staff Manual respectively. Title pages
will be prepared in manuscript.

Place	Date 1917	Hour	Summary of Events and Information	Remarks and references to Appendices
ST AMAND	14th		Training. ST AMAND	
	15th		Divs Bomb Throwing and Training ST AMAND	
	16th		Marched to HENIN-SUR-COJEUL. Lr Leroraas	
HENIN-SUR- COJEUL.	17th		Rested after march. Church Parades. Cricket started. Officers had Sergeants	
	18th		Baths Drill. Baths at NEUVILLE-MITTSSE. Cricket teams started	
	19th		Baths Drill. Supplied 140 men to carry gas projectors at night	
	20th		Training. Similar carrying parties at night	
	21st		A Company carried out firing on Rifle Range. Remainder Drill. Same carrying parties same required	
	20th		Training. Both carrying and finding parties were supplied at night. 2nd Lt CJ Bevan and W/Pl Faskby were killed and two wounded by a Leithhal grenades.	
	23 63		Light training after heavy night work. C Company below the Range. Mar 36 "Lancashire" was obstacles and sent them up to front line at night	
	24th		to Company fired on Rifle Range. Church parades at noon. Marched to camp at BOISLEUX-AU-MONT. In Bell Tents.	
BOISLEUX- AU-MONT	25th		Training near camp	
	26th		Baths Drill in morning. Inspection by G.O.C 50th Division and "March Past" in afternoon.	

(A7092). Wt. W12850/M293. 750,000. 1/17. D. D. & L, Ltd. Forms/C.2118'14.

Army Form C. 2118.

WAR DIARY

or

INTELLIGENCE SUMMARY.

(Erase heading not required.)

Instructions regarding War Diaries and Intelligence
Summaries are contained in F. S. Regs., Part II.
and the Staff Manual respectively. Title pages
will be prepared in manuscript.

Place	Date 1917 June	Hour	Summary of Events and Information	Remarks and references to Appendices
BOISLEUX- AU-MONT.	27th		Training.	
	28th		Baths at BOISLEUX-AU-MONT. Shot Training	
	29th		Training. Reconnaisance of front line by C.O. & Coy Commanders	
	30th		Training. Reconnaisance of front line by Bn. Scouts & of approaches by transport Sergeant & W.O.O	

C H R Geary
2nd Lt. & 2/01

9th E.L.I.

— WAR DIARY — 9a24

9TH DURHAM LIGHT INFTY

JULY 1917

VOLUME No XXVIII

Army Form C. 2118.

Instructions regarding War Diaries and Intelligence
Summaries are contained in F. S. Regs., Part II.
and the Staff Manual respectively. Title pages
will be prepared in manuscript.

WAR DIARY

or

INTELLIGENCE SUMMARY.

(Erase heading not required.)

9th Bn DURHAM LIGHT INFANTRY
JULY 1917 VOLUME II XXVIII

Place	Date July	Hour	Summary of Events and Information	Remarks and references to Appendices
BOISLEUX - AU - MONT.	1.		Short Training. Church Parades. Games. Open air concert	
HENIN - SUR - COJEUL	2.		Short Training in morning. Marched forward to Camp at HENIN.	
	3.		Preparation for Trenches. Moved up at 9 P.M. Relief Dipails in camp. Successful Relief over by 11.30pm	
TRENCHES	4.		Trenches fairly comfortable but very incomplete and quiet on the whole. Work indefinite by day but carried on strenuously at night. There were wounded + two of whom were killed.	
Opp. Vis-EN-ARTOIS RAM R.1 of EUX. Bn HR. at O.19.a.2.14. Front line from O.2.6.a.4.5.	5.		Rather more... Pack Ponies. Enemy artillery action especially at night when the snipers great use of Mishkaila. Enemy patrol active + reports great use of ours. Very quiet	
O.2.0.a 8.5. 14.9 Inf. Bn. on our Right 5th BORDERS 8th D.L.I. on left	6.		took day night again with enemy action.	
	7.		Heavy enemy artillery fire early in the morning. Relieved by 6th ~~D.L.I.~~ Relief completed by 1 A.M. 8th Provided working parties during night 7/8. Very fatiguing days work through a hot though quiet through all the trenches	1 killed 1 wounded
We relieved 8th D.L.I. B coy in care at MARLIERE 8th D.L.I. reinforced Bn in support to 6th D.L.I. Other three coys in trenches	8.		with enemy bombers at night 3 men wounded. Large working parties at night.	

(A.7093). Wt. W.12859/M.1293. 750,000. 1/17. D. D. & L., Ltd. Forms/C.2118-14.

Army Form C. 2118.

(2)

WAR DIARY
or
INTELLIGENCE SUMMARY.
(Erase heading not required.)

Instructions regarding War Diaries and Intelligence Summaries are contained in F. S. Regs., Part II. and the Staff Manual respectively. Title pages will be prepared in manuscript.

Place	Date	Hour	Summary of Events and Information	Remarks and references to Appendices
	9th		Cleaning up and starting fatigue duty, and large working parties supplied at night to carry to front line.	
	10th		Same work on for Bn. Band gave a concert in camp to "B" Coy — only just over a mile from the front line!	
150 Bde on our Right.	11th		Relieved 6th D.L.I. in front line. Relief done early. Three Coys in front line and one (D) in support.	
	12th		Bn. furnished large working parties to R.E. for work in support and shelters in support trenches. Carried on the work. Active bombing all of away in front of the posts.	
	13th		Kin. was locate enemy beyond his trenches. Artillery bombarded & shelled enemy advanced out, and an officers patrol moved out to occupy. They were found to be unoccupied. As soon as it was dark by the enemy were found by day and night, and in addition working parties were employed, and the line of forward posts.	
	14th		The front line was connected to front line by a L.T. post connected to front line by a L.T. Almost two men required for working parties. Were relieved by 6th D.L.I. just before leaving for Boethe Bois of 10 raided one of "A" Coys posts.	
	15th		...relief took place	

(A7092) Wt. W12839/M1293. 75v,000. 1/17. D. D. & L., Ltd. Forms/C2118/14.

WAR DIARY
or
INTELLIGENCE SUMMARY.

(Erase heading not required.)

Instructions regarding War Diaries and Intelligence Summaries are contained in F. S. Regs., Part II. and the Staff Manual respectively. Title pages will be prepared in manuscript.

③

Place	Date	Hour	Summary of Events and Information	Remarks and references to Appendices
			They are driven off without casualties to us and left at least one dead, from whom identifications were obtained. On completion of relief, Bn. went into 'Bde. Reserve at NEUVILLE VITASSE, after rough time, except to 4th "A" platoons Total casualties for 12 days:- 1 killed, 9 wounded including 1 Officer slightly wounded	
NEUVILLE VITASSE.	16th		Major F.C. Howell DSO. takes over temporary command of 5th Borders.	
	17th		Bn. Bathed at NEUVILLE VITASSE. Party of 300 proceeded to Front Line and dug a new Assembly Trench into the COJEUL VALLEY were complimented on work done by Bn. in Front Line and by Brigade Commander (Attached letters from 8th Bn.)	
	18th		Rest to working party. Training to remainder.	
	19th		Coys. etc. under their own Coms. Ors. for Training. Marched to new Camp in afternoon and became Divisional Reserve for 8 days. Bn. was relieved by 149 Inf. Bde.	
MERCATEL.	20th		Training. B Company moved forward to carry out work on Trench Tram Line in COJEUL VALLEY for two days.	

A5834   Wt. W.4973 M687   750,000   8/16   D. D. & L. Ltd.   Forms/C.2118/13.

WAR DIARY

or

INTELLIGENCE SUMMARY.

(Erase heading not required.)

④

Instructions regarding War Diaries and Intelligence
Summaries are contained in F. S. Regs. Part II.
and the Staff Manual respectively. Title pages
will be prepared in manuscript.

Place	Date	Hour	Summary of Events and Information	Remarks and references to Appendices
	21st		A Coy carried out firing on the Rifle Range finishing up with field firing deleve during all arms. C & D Coys carried out training	
	22nd		D Coy made Concentras at HAVIN. Church Parades with C & D Z.I. Baths for A, C Coys and Details. B Coy returned from work at COEUVE VALLEY after completing Tron Line as far as Reserve Trench.	
	23rd		Training.	
	24th		C Coy on Range in morning and B in afternoon. Similar brackets were fired Pt WOODRIELD wounded by premature burst of Rifle Grenade. Baths for B & D Coys and Details at Hockey and won.	
	25th		W.F. Details at Hockey and won.	
	26th		"B" Coy carried out firing on Range. A Coy constructed 200 line "Concertinas" at HAVIN. C.O. and Lieut Condon and Moved up into front line. Day night Relief which we see 6yo. at 6 A.M. Very successful. Relieved 4th Yorks. in Rght Bde Sector. The 6and Inf Bdr. 5th BORDRS. on our left	
TRENCHES N/ 1st			Yorks. in Rght Bde Sector. The 6and Inf Bdr. 5th BORDRS. on our left	
H.Q. N. 36. d. 4.0 A Coy in SUPPORT. FRONTAGE				

WAR DIARY
or
INTELLIGENCE SUMMARY.

(Erase heading not required.)

Instructions regarding War Diaries and Intelligence Summaries are contained in F. S. Regs., Part II. and the Staff Manual respectively. Title pages will be prepared in manuscript.

Place	Date	Hour	Summary of Events and Information	Remarks and references to Appendices
Right Flank O.3.d.6.7. Lijssenhoek 0.25.d.9.4.	28th		Enemy active at night with liebrads, some of which contained their own gas. Two breastworks from gas. One of whom died later. Prisoner. Enemy's patrolling also active but carried out.	
	29th		Enemy's activity at night & succeeding. Night patrol under wire, repulsed. Enemy's patrols & night firing enemy in strength, putting up wire. During continued.	
	30th		On night 29/30 enemy was exceptionally active with their trench mortars. A patrol under with HMs encountered an enemy patrol of equal strength, but bombed it scattering one Man. Who rifle relief which followed another Bosch was wounded before our Patrol withdrew. On returning later no trace of enemy wounded could be found.	
	31st		Were relieved by 6th D.C. commencing 8 pm. On completion of succeeding relief we became Bde Support with HQ. in the WASH. (N.29.d.9.4.)	

WAR DIARY

or

INTELLIGENCE SUMMARY.

(Erase heading not required.)

Instructions regarding War Diaries and Intelligence Summaries are contained in F. S. Regs., Part II. and the Staff Manual respectively. Title pages will be prepared in manuscript.

Place	Date	Hour	Summary of Events and Information	Remarks and references to Appendices

We had been holding a large frontage which to some extent accounted for the slight casualties we suffered considering the activity of the enemy.

TOTAL CASUALTIES

3 Killed
1 Died - Gas
4 Gassed
7 Wounded (3 still at duty)

mainly

The Trenches were ~~rough~~ in good condition and

The weather was ~~rough~~ fine.

On 31st July we supplied 250 men for working parties in throat system for dug-outs and carrying work.

A.H. Capel
Lieut Col
2nd R.B.

A5834 Wt.W4973/M687 750,000 8/16 D. D. & L. Ltd. Forms/C.2118/13.

WAR DIARY.

9th Bn. Durham Light Infantry

August, 1917.

VOLUME XXIX

Army Form C. 2118.

WAR DIARY
or
INTELLIGENCE SUMMARY.
(Erase heading not required.)

9th Bn. The DURHAM LIGHT INFANTRY.
August 1917.   VOLUME XXIX.

Instructions regarding War Diaries and Intelligence
Summaries are contained in F. S. Regs., Part II.
and the Staff Manual respectively. Title pages
will be prepared in manuscript.

Place	Date	Hour	Summary of Events and Information	Remarks and references to Appendices
TRENCHES. In support H.Q. N.29.b.9.4. (Sh.51 A Sw.)	1st		Three days in FRONT TR. & FRONT LOOP, & Bn. & Bn. H.Q. at MESS. Comfortable Trenches, but had weather. Provided 200 men for various work of night.	
	2nd		Bad weather continues. Same working Parties with the addition of 40 men for Trench Digging.	
	3rd		Same as for 1st. Enemy occasionally shelled Trenches. 2nd W.R.S. Staple side badly injured on a Working Party.	
Front Line.	4th		Moved up in the morning to Front Line where we relieved the 6th D.L.I. Still very muddy. This Sector had quietened down considerably in last 4 days. "B" Coy in Support.	
	5th		Everyone worked at improving general condition of Trenches.	
	6th		5th BORDERS on our Left took over the Frontage of our Left & (another Coy.) while we took over the whole frontage of 13th Durhams. New Trenches taken over very good and comfortable in support. "A" Coy. now in daylight reliefs.	
	7th		N.F.5 on our Right. Very successful. Enemy still quiet. Usual work on wire and Trenches carried out.	

A 5834   Wt. W4973 M68/ 750,000   8/16   D. D. & L. Ltd.   Forms/C.2118/13.

WAR DIARY

or

INTELLIGENCE SUMMARY.

(Erase heading not required.)

Instructions regarding War Diaries and Intelligence
Summaries are contained in F. S. Regs. Part II.
and the Staff Manual respectively. Title pages
will be prepared in manuscript.

Place	Date Aug.	Hour	Summary of Events and Information	Remarks and references to Appendices
HÉNIN	8		Successfully relieved in afternoon by 6th D.L.I. West side Reserve in our old lines near HÉNIN very heavy rain. Casualties for last tour - Nil. Were worried by new gas at night, but otherwise the time was peaceful. "A" Coy remained	2
"CONCRETE TR."	9th		left to a Reserve Avg to 6th D.L.I. Rested. — AWARD. Sergt. A. GILLINGS No. 325073 — Military Medal	
	10th		2½ hours Training in morning supplied 6 Parties of 50 men at night to bury a cable 6 ft deep between Rev Support Trenches Work very heavy, but accomplished satisfactorily.	
	11th		Rest & Baths. Supplied 30 Men for Haymaking at FRUIKERS' AYETTE.	
	12th		Supplied over 200 Men for various work Rendindie - Check Parades.	
	13th		Moved to old camp near MERCATEL where we relieved 6th NF. Almost whole Bn with an Working Parties "A" Coy relieved.	
	14th		Men return from work. "A" & "B" Coys carried out firing on Range "D" & "C" Coy. — Training in Camp.	
	15th		Training in Camp.	
	16th		Training "A" Coys. officer, off, directed to Lew Bomb throwing Baths tuber "A" & "B" Coys. Special instruction in Bayonet Fighting during Training	

A5834 Wt.W4973 M687. 750,000 8/16 D. D. & L. Ltd. Forms/C.2118/13.

WAR DIARY
or
INTELLIGENCE SUMMARY.
(Erase heading not required.)

Instructions regarding War Diaries and Intelligence Summaries are contained in F. S. Regs., Part II. and the Staff Manual respectively. Title pages will be prepared in manuscript.

Place	Date	Hour	Summary of Events and Information	Remarks and references to Appendices
	17th		Training in Camp. "C" & "D" Coys. carried out firing on Range. Balts at NEUFMARVITASSE for C & D Coys.	
	18.		Training. 28 Officers & 60 O.R. sent to Corps Horse Show at BAILLEULVAL. Honours & Awards. PTE INNES — MILITARY MEDAL	
	19th		Church Parades. 6 mile Route March for Br. ranks officers & C.S.N.s who attended a lecture by Commanding Officer on Trench Warfare.	
TRENCHES. Bn H.Q. G19.a.3.4. Front line G26.o.3.5. & COTEVER.	20th		Morning spent in preparation for Trenches. Afternoon Relief of 5th D.L.I. in Trenches opposite H.S. FM ARTOIS. 5th BORDERS on Left and 149th Inf Bde on Right. Successful relief except for 6 casualties caused by 1 shell. Night spent in improving Trenches.	
	21st		Situation quieter than usual on this front. All ranks hard at work by night in patrolling, and wiring or working in Trenches &	
	22nd		Usual work about. Weather still fine.	
	23rd		A little Rain, and several intermittent Artillery activity.	
			Supplied 324 Men for various work throughout the day and night.	

A5834 Wt.W4473 M687 750,000 8/16 D. D. & L. Ltd. Forms/C.2118/13.

WAR DIARY

or

INTELLIGENCE SUMMARY.

(Erase heading not required.)

Instructions regarding War Diaries and Intelligence Summaries are contained in F. S. Regs., Part II. and the Staff Manual respectively. Title pages will be prepared in manuscript.

Place	Date Hour	Summary of Events and Information	Remarks and references to Appendices
SUPPORT R.Hq. N.24.c.s.7.	24th (cont.)	Relieved by 6th D.L.I. in evening. Brigading at 5 P.M. After relief went into support with mol.By. (?3) in NARENTEE caves and Hill. Stood in FGRET, KIOT? DUGR.TRENCHES.	4.
	25th	Successful Tour in Front Line. Casualties 3 killed, 3 wounded. Same working Parties. Frey Men working at night. Afternoons spent in cleaning up and Musketry training.	
	26th	Same work. Concert in NARENTEE Caves 20th Band.	
	27th	Similar working Parties. Heavy Rain. 1 Man wounded.	
	28th	Fine & windy. 45 Men on working Parties. Relieved by 8th D.L.I. in support and moved forward to relieve 6th D.L.I. in Front line.	
FRONT LINE.	29th	Successful relief completed soon after 8 P.M. Work directed to Revetting Front Line Ports, and completing Blue.	
	30th	Same work all night - Enemy quiet - 1 Man wounded - Rain.	
	31st	Continued same work - Nothing unusual.	

CHRgee Lieut
adj. 9th Durham Lght Infantry

A5834   Wt. W4973 M687   750,000   8/16.   D. D. & L. Ltd.   Forms/C.2118/13.

WAR DIARY.

Vol 26

Volume —

XXX

Army Form C. 2118.

WAR DIARY

or

INTELLIGENCE SUMMARY.

(Erase heading not required.) September 1917   9th Bn. The Durham Light Infantry   VOLUME XXX

Instructions regarding War Diaries and Intelligence Summaries are contained in F.S. Regs., Part II. and the Staff Manual respectively. Title pages will be prepared in manuscript.

Place	Date	Hour	Summary of Events and Information	Remarks and references to Appendices
Bn H.Q. N.21.a.	1st		Relieved by 6th D.L.I. in afternoon and moved into Bde. Reserve. Camp relieved NEUVILLE VITASSE. Scattered dugouts, but food accommodation	
	2nd		Baths for B.C. & D Coys at NEUVILLE VITASSE, and for A Coy & Details at MERCATEL. Rest and clean up.	
	3rd		Each Coy sent for 3 mile march with Batt. Band. Practice in the Attack on Trenches	
	4th		Further practice in the attack by A, B & C Coys. D Coy marched 9 miles	
	5th		Training in morning. In afternoon 6th N.F.s relieved us, and we moved into SUBEAU LINES (Winter Camp) near BOISLEUX – AU – MONT.) Good accommodation	
Bn H.Q. S.11.a.	6th		Conference about a forthcoming Raid in morning. Battn for A & B Coys at BOISLEUX – AU – MONT. Practice in the Attack over Replica of Enemy Trenches in S.C.B. during afternoon.	
	7th		Baths for C & D Coys in morning. The Battalion carried out further practice over Replica of Enemy Trenches in afternoon.	
	8th		All Coys carried out 1½ hrs firing on MEN IN RANGE, and also carried out practice over their portion of the Enemy Trenches to be raided.	
	9th		Church Parade in morning. The Battalion walked over Replica	

A5834 Wt.W4973 M687 730,000 8/16 D.D. & L. Ltd. Forms/C.2118/13.

d

WAR DIARY

or

INTELLIGENCE SUMMARY.

(Erase heading not required.)

Instructions regarding War Diaries and Intelligence Summaries are contained in F. S. Regs., Part II. and the Staff Manual respectively. Title pages will be prepared in manuscript.

Place	Date	Hour	Summary of Events and Information	Remarks and references to Appendices
	10th		in the afternoon. Training near Camp.	
	11th		The Battalion carried out a practice attack on Replica with the Army Corps, Divisional and Brigade Commanders watching.	
	12th		Battalion Drill throughout the Morning. Church Parade with 5th BORDER Regt. in Evening.	
HENIN	13th		Moved forward to HENIN Res. Camps and carried out training on the way. All Coys. practised the attack, and fired on HENIN RANGE.	
	14th		Preparation for the Line in the morning. "A" & "C" Coys. Artillery FRONT LINE opposite CHÉRISY in afternoon moved up into the line.	
Bn. HQ. N.25.d.5.9.	15th		Quiet morning. At 4.0 P.M. heavy creeping barrage came down and "A" & "C" Coys. raided the German Front and Support Line in front of CHÉRISY. "A" was Left Coy, "C" Coy. and "B" Right Coy. "C"ents and with a WIRA HALL and with 25 INNIN covered Patrol each 1 & OR. made a complete surprise to Enemy. About 70 Germans were killed and 25 Prisoners brought Back. 11 dugouts were blown in & and 1 Machine Gun brought back. Raiders remained	

A5834 Wt.W4973 M687 750,000 8/16 D. D. & L. Ltd. Forms/C.2118/13.

Army Form C. 2118.

WAR DIARY
or
INTELLIGENCE SUMMARY.
(Erase heading not required.)

Instructions regarding War Diaries and Intelligence
Summaries are contained in F. S. Regs., Part II.
and the Staff Manual respectively. Title pages
will be prepared in manuscript.

Place	Date	Hour	Summary of Events and Information	Remarks and references to Appendices
			in Filing Trenches for half an hour before returning. A hostile counter attack was repulsed. Raid a great success. Congratulations from all sides. Casualties both H. HHH killed 9 7 O.R. killed	
HENIN.	16th		Raiders were relieved by 8th D.L.I. shortly after return and came back to Bde. Res. Camp near HENIN.	
	17th		2 Off. 10 O.R. wounded to Hospital 3 Off. & 8 O.R. wounded at Duty Rest & Batho at NEUVILLE VITASSE. Relieved 6th D.L.I. in Right Front Subsection with H.Q. in HENIN. R. flank "A Right Front, "D" Centre, and "B" Left. Coy. "C" in Support.	
H.Q. N.36. C.u.o.	18.		Very quiet alert completed by 5 P.M. Trenches in good condition and dry. Provided 8 groups of 9 O.R. for work at wiring. Flank party quiet except for details at wiring and making dummy work done daily at wiring and making dummy positions, which attracted Enemy fire.	
	19. 20.		Same work carried out. Heavy Shelling of Centre Coy. by Hy 5"9 & 4.2 shells.	

Army Form C. 2118.

WAR DIARY
or
INTELLIGENCE SUMMARY.
(Erase heading not required.)

Instructions regarding War Diaries and Intelligence
Summaries are contained in F. S. Regs., Part II.
and the Staff Manual respectively. Title pages
will be prepared in manuscript.

Place	Date	Hour	Summary of Events and Information	Remarks and references to Appendices
Bn HQ. NEST. N.3.a.5.3.	21st		Relieved by the D.C.I. during afternoon. Became support Bn. with H.Q. at NEST & Coy at NEST and BANK and three Coys in FGRBT KGRBT LOOP, CUCKOO. Accommodation good. 50 Men were supplied to carry T.M. ammunition and three groups for work in HINDENBURG TUNNEL.	
	22nd		Weather still fine. Unsuccessful raid on left would be early seen similar work. 117 Men from Trenches had Baths at NESTIN and stayed at detail Camp for the night and came up to SUPPORT again the following day.	
	23.		148 Men supplied for various work. 100 Men had Baths.	
	24th		Weather still fine. Same work. Remainder went out for Baths.	
	24th		Relieved the 6th D.C.I. in the Right Front sub-section. Heavy shelling before Relief. Relief complete by 11.20 P.M.	
	25th		Left Front Coy (B Coy) heavily shelled especially HORSESHOE POST. 1 Man killed and 4 wounded. Faces were found of Enemy Patrol near our Gut line by night. Hard work done by day and night on Trenches.	
	27th		Wt 10-15 T.M. Emplt GIBSON and 2 O.R. of 3rd Coy raided the	

Army Form C. 2118.

WAR DIARY

or

INTELLIGENCE SUMMARY.

(Erase heading not required.)

Instructions regarding War Diaries and Intelligence
Summaries are contained in F. S. Regs., Part II.
and the Staff Manual respectively. Title pages
will be prepared in manuscript.

Place	Date	Hour	Summary of Events and Information	Remarks and references to Appendices
	28		Enemy raid about V.1.b. 55.65. Enemy was driven back by means of Mills. Raid successful 6 Enemy killed, and one wounded prisoner brought back. Our casualties were 1 slightly wounded by our own Artillery. Heavy shelling of front line at 6.0 A.M. One Man wounded. Lt. Colonel R. B. Bradford. V.C., M.C. took over command of the Brigade in the absence of the Brigadier General, and Major F.E. Couch D.S.O. assumed command of the Battalion.	
KIRKHAM LINES S.II.a.	29.		Relieved by 4th N.F. in afternoon. Camp at Bretlan Lines again.	
	30.		Battns. 'A''B'&'C' Coys. Church Parades in morning. 'D' Coy. provided 46 Men for working Parties.	

A5834 Wt. W4973/M687 750,000 8/16 D. D. & L. Ltd. Forms/C.2118/13.

Alee Cox
Adjutant
9th Bn. The Durham Light Infantry

WAR DIARY.

9th Durham Light Infantry

October, 1917.

$$\overline{\times \overline{XXI}}.$$

Volume

Army Form C. 2118.

WAR DIARY
or
INTELLIGENCE SUMMARY.
(Erase heading not required.)

9th Battalion THE DURHAM LIGHT INFANTRY   VOLUME XXXI   Page 1.

Instructions regarding War Diaries and Intelligence Summaries are contained in F. S. Regs., Part II. and the Staff Manual respectively. Title pages will be prepared in manuscript.

Place	Date	Hour	Summary of Events and Information	Remarks and references to Appendices
DURHAM LINES BOISLEUX-AU-MONT. (S–11 a)	October 1.		Training carried out in the morning. Lecture in afternoon by the acting Brigadier on "French to French Attack". Baths for Bn. Corporals & details.	
	2.		An advance party proceeded to GOMIECOURT, consisting of 1 platoon of A Coy. 2/Lt T.F. Molyneux ? Corps Cyclists rejoined unit. 2/Lt BRAITHWAITE to R.F.C. The following awards have been made by the Corps Commander for acts of gallantry in the field Sept 15th:—	

325086 Cpl J. BEE   2nd Bar to Military Medal.
325417 Sgt J. MARSH   "   "   "   "   —
325212 Sgt W. GOFFIN   Bar to Military Medal.
325389 Cpl J.R. BELL   "   "   "   "   —

MILITARY MEDALS :—

325873 Pte E. HINDMARSH.	325757 Sgt W. CHAPMAN	
325171 Cpl T. WILLIAMS	325915 Pte H. WILKINSON	24787 Pte T. JACKSON
325068 L/Cpl F. ASHARD.	325945 L/Cpl B. NIMMO	325505 Cpl J.T. CROZIER
325637 " E. GILL	325096 " H. FAIRMINGTON	325078 Sgt R. STARK
325329 " R. POSKETT	325217 Pte J. WAITT	325262 Cpl W. PARK.

A5834 Wt. W4973 M687 750,000 8/16 D. D. & L. Ltd. Forms/C.2118/13.

WAR DIARY

or

INTELLIGENCE SUMMARY.

(Erase heading not required.)

Instructions regarding War Diaries and Intelligence Summaries are contained in F. S. Regs., Part II. and the Staff Manual respectively. Title pages will be prepared in manuscript.

Place	Date	Hour	Summary of Events and Information	Remarks and references to Appendices
GOMIECOURT	3rd		Training.	
	4th		Bn. moved to GOMIECOURT.	
	5th		Short Training.	
	6th		Corps Commander conferred the Military Medal for gallantry in the Field on 325075 Pte Abiell & 325362 L/Corporal P.D Coy.	
			Short Training. Draft of 20 O.R. arrived from the base	
	7th		Bn Drill & Divine Service.	
	8th		Bn Drill	
			The King conferred the Indelting Cross on the following	
			CAPT. F.C. PALMER; CAPT. T.HARKER; CAPT. J.D. INNES; CAPT. C.H. MARSHALL,	
			325372 C.S.M. E. MADDISON.	
			Military Medal to 27629 Cpl R. Williams.	
	9.		Commel Parade.	
	10.		Tactical Exercise & Inspection by Lt.Gen. AA.LDANE C.B. D.S.O commanding the 6th Corps. Also a presentation of Medal Ribbons by Corps Commander.	
	11		Training Draft of 70 O.R. arrived from 7/D.L.I.	
			Coys. Reorganised on 4 Platoon System again.	
	12.		Rained all day. Training in tents.	
			Short Training. 2/Lt E.s Gibson awarded the Military Cross.	
	13		Bn. on the range. Divine Service. Advance party proceeded to ESQUELBEQ.	
	14.		2/Lt F.L. PARKINSON 2/Lt R.C. MUIR- MACKENZIE } att. 151 TMB, awarded Military Cross.	
	15th		Bombing and short Training.	
	16th		Preparation for moving North. Bombing. Football	

(A7994) Wt. W28811/M1253. 750,000. 1/17. D.D. & L. Ld. Forms/C2118/14.

WAR DIARY
or
INTELLIGENCE SUMMARY.

(Erase heading not required.)

Instructions regarding War Diaries and Intelligence Summaries are contained in F. S. Regs., Part II. and the Staff Manual respectively. Title pages will be prepared in manuscript.

Place	Date	Hour	Summary of Events and Information	Remarks and references to Appendices
GOMIECOURT	17th		The Battalion entrained at BAPAUME in the morning. Arrived at ESQUELBECQ in the evening at 11.30 P.M. Marched 4 miles to billets in pouring rain. Small accommodation in billets.	
PADDE VEDTH	18th		Coys. at the disposal of their Commanders.	
	19th		Battalion Route March of 10 miles.	
	20		Marched to ARNEKE to good billets. Lt Col. R. B. Bradford, V.C., M.C. rejoined Unit after short Paris Leave.	
ARNEKE.				
PROVEN.	21st		Marched to camp near PROVEN. Muddy camp.	
(PITHEC OT B/E)	22nd		Marched to SUTTON CAMP, about 1½ miles nearer PROVEN. Coys. at the disposal of their Commanders.	
	23rd		Training and short Route March by Coys. in morning. Football in afternoon.	
	24th		Entrained at PROVEN at 8.0 A.M. and detrained at BUYSINGHE at 9.0 A.M.	
SARAGOSSA FM. Camp.	25th		Camp at SARAGOSSA Farm was very poor and not vacated till 5.0 P.M. Supplied 200 Men to carry up French Boards and 250 for rations & stores. 150 Men carried up LoF Ka and a further 50 rations. Key not 5 Men killed, 5 wounded to hospital. 2 Lt ROWLANDS & 4 O.R. wounded at duty.	
	26th		BELIZEELE The billets left to Div Depot Bn at BELIZEELE be supplied The billets left to carry French Boards up, 150 Men for stores and 80 200 Men to carry Men to move some guns forward. One Man wounded.	

WAR DIARY

or

INTELLIGENCE SUMMARY.

(Erase heading not required.)

Instructions regarding War Diaries and Intelligence
Summaries are contained in F. S. Regs., Part II.
and the Staff Manual respectively. Title pages
will be prepared in manuscript.

Place	Date	Hour	Summary of Events and Information	Remarks and references to Appendices
	27ᵗʰ		"A" & "B" Coy. worked under 447ᵗʰ Field Coy. R.E. and "B" & "C" Coy. under 446ᵗʰ H.A.Coy. Trench Boards were carried up to the Line and laid.	
			Casualties :- 2 O.R. Killed, 18 O.R. wounded by aeroplane bombs.	
			"B" Coy. provided working party of 20 Men at BOESINGHE DUMP.	
MARSOUIN FARM.	28ᵗʰ		Bn. moved up to MARSOUIN FARM Camp in afternoon, same working Parties were provided. Casualties 2nd Lt. J. DICK Killed, 7 O.R. Killed and 20 O.R. wounded.	
	29ᵗʰ		Light Training No working Parties.	
	30ᵗʰ		Light Training	
	31ˢᵗ		Practice Attack carried out near ELVERDINGHE in morning	
HULL'S FARM			Bn. moved back to HULL'S FARM in afternoon.	
			by skeleton corps.	
			Comfortable Camp	

M.C. ... Coy
Adjutant.

Lieut Colonel,
Comdg. 9ᵗʰ Bn. K.R.L.

(A7092.) Wt. W12850/M1293 750,000. 1/17. D. D. & L., Ltd. Forms/C.2118/4.

Vol 28

WAR DIARY

9th Bn the Durham Light Infy.

November, 1917.

Volume — XXXII

Army Form C. 2118.

WAR DIARY
or
INTELLIGENCE SUMMARY.

(Erase heading not required.)

Instructions regarding War Diaries and Intelligence Summaries are contained in F. S. Regs., Part II. and the Staff Manual respectively. Title pages will be prepared in manuscript.

9th Battalion. The Durham Light Infantry.
VOLUME XXXII.
Page 1.

Place	Date	Hour	Summary of Events and Information	Remarks and references to Appendices
	NOVEMBER			
WILES FARM.	1st		Coy Commanders' Conference in morning. Training. Moved back to MARSOUIN FARM. Coy in afternoon. Supplied 47 Men from Hly for Bde. Burying Party.	
MARSOUIN FARM.	2nd		Whole day spent in issuing stores and preparing for the Line. More cancelled at 4.0 P.M.	
	3rd		Conference of officers in morning. Training. Frey Horn in the Bn. attended at Div. Lock office for foot-att. and clean socks.	
LINE	4th		Light training and preparation. Moved up to the front line in evening. H.Q. EGYPT HOUSE. Twilight relief of 6th 2x1 "B" "D" Coys in front line. 9th DLI on our right.	
	5th		Heavy damage on our front line and supports. Colonel Bradford V.C. M.C. wounded in sleek – still at duty.	
	5th		Mutual intense shelling in morning and evening. Colonel Bradford V.C. M.C. appointed to command a Brigade in consequence. Major S.Aug 9th Border Regt comes to command until Major Gibson D.S.O. returns from leave.	
	6		Coy very heavily shelled all morning. Was relieved by 8th Suffolk Regt by 8.0 P.M. and Men so side-stepped and relieved	

(A7090). Wt. W12839/M12893. 750,000. 1/17. D. D. & L., Ltd. Forms/C.2118/14.

WAR DIARY

or

INTELLIGENCE SUMMARY.

(Erase heading not required.)

Instructions regarding War Diaries and Intelligence Summaries are contained in F. S. Regs., Part II. and the Staff Manual respectively. Title pages will be prepared in manuscript.

Place	Date	Hour	Summary of Events and Information	Remarks and references to Appendices
June	6th		8th D.L.I. in Right sector and 8th Border Regt in support with Bn. H.P. near PASCAL FARM. Quiet relief.	
	7th		Comparatively quiet day. Unsuccessful raid and short relief by 8th D.L.I. in evening.	
SARAGOSSA CAMP.	8th		Arrived back in SARAGOSSA Camp by midnight. Rest. Light training and inspections. Bn paraded in afternoon and Brig. Gen. R.B. Bradford V.C., H.C. made a farewell speech and shook hands with every Man.	
	9th		Light training and Baths. Part of Transport proceeded to Rest area.	
	10th		Bn entrained at FYFERDINRTE at 11.30 AM and detrained at 10.17PM. Billeted at MOURLE in very good barns etc.	
MOURLE	11th		Rest. Church Parade by Coys. Stragglers reported from Div. Depot.	
	12th		Training near billets.	
	13th		Training. Baths and Kit inspection by C.O.	
	14th		Training on "E" Area, 2½ miles from billets.	
	15th		Training near billets and municipal Range practice. Concert.	
	16th		Battalion Drill and Battalion in attack in "D" Area.	

(A7093) Wt. W12839/M1293. 750,000. 1/17. D. D. & L., Ltd. Forms/C-2118-14.

WAR DIARY
or
INTELLIGENCE SUMMARY.
(Erase heading not required.)

Instructions regarding War Diaries and Intelligence Summaries are contained in F. S. Regs., Part II. and the Staff Manual respectively. Title pages will be prepared in manuscript.

Place	Date	Hour	Summary of Events and Information	Remarks and references to Appendices
	17th		Training near billets.	
	18th		Church Parade. Baths at HOUXLE.	
	19th		Range from 11 am - 3 P.M. Tea on Range and Dinner on 2hr.	
	20th		Training near billets.	
	2.30		Company training on "D" Area.	
	22nd		Training on Miniature Range near billets and Platoon Training Rifle Grenade firing and Lewis Gun practice.	
	23rd		Battalion in the Attack on "D" Area. Major F.G. lunch D.S.O. returned.	
	24th		Bde Field day. Some open attack.	
	26th		Bn carried out practices 16, 27, 9 on "B" Range from 8 - 11 am. Very cold and a bad day for shooting.	
			HONOURS AND REWARDS	
			The following have been awarded the M.M.	
			L/C Davidson R. 325294 Pte Vallans, T. 348038	
			L/C Wilkinson J. 327220. Pte Anderson, W. 325211.	
			L/C Varg, J. 325736. Pte Grundy, J. 273099.	
			L/C Booth, B. 327247	
	2/5		Guard Course and Practice in Advance and Rear Guards.	

WAR DIARY

or

INTELLIGENCE SUMMARY.

(Erase heading not required.)

Instructions regarding War Diaries and Intelligence Summaries are contained in F. S. Regs., Part II. and the Staff Manual respectively. Title pages will be prepared in manuscript.

Place	Date	Hour	Summary of Events and Information	Remarks and references to Appendices
	27th		Divine Service, Final of Bde Football Competition. — 9th R.I. rif. 6 R.I. rif.	
	28th		Training near Sillack	
	29th		Training on "D" Area. Inter unit digging tous batch h.g. & n.c.o. in gun & final of Divisional Football Competition.	
	30th		Training in local parade grounds.	

91 29

WAR DIARY.

9th Bn. The Durham Light Infantry.

December, 1917

Volume No. XXXIII

WAR DIARY

or

INTELLIGENCE SUMMARY.

(Erase heading not required.)

Instructions regarding War Diaries and Intelligence
Summaries are contained in F. S. Regs., Part II.
and the Staff Manual respectively. Title pages
will be prepared in manuscript.

Place	Date December	Hour	Summary of Events and Information	Remarks and references to Appendices
MOULLE	1st		Range firing in morning. Complete identification practices.	
	2nd		Church Parades. Commanding Officer's Rifle for volunteer 23.	
	3rd		Company Training "B" Rifle Butts attend instruction in Lewis M.J.	
	4th		Officers and Sergeants attended lecture and demonstration by Met. N.F.F.P. of Y.M.C.A. Remainder went for Route March under C.O.	
	5th		Coys in attack practice. Officers & N.C.O.s examined ground for practise attack outlined 1—0 by 6th D.L.I. In relay of first effort Football Competition. Box Respirators tested.	
	6th		Coys to attack outlined area. Bn Sports.	
	7th		Range firing and Training team Gun firing practise.	
	8th		Training near billets. Major P. Pattison, 7 D.L.I., appointed 2nd in Command.	
	9th		Church Parades. C.O. and Coy Commanders went up by bus to visit front line and stayed one night in POPERINGHE. Rain scouts made to specimen consolidated still hole.	
	10th		Bn practised consolidating in depth & to shell hole positions in "V" Training Area.	
	11th		Went Training near billets and inspection for move forward by motor route to new camp.	

WAR DIARY
or
INTELLIGENCE SUMMARY.
(Erase heading not required.)

Instructions regarding War Diaries and Intelligence Summaries are contained in F. S. Regs., Part II. and the Staff Manual respectively. Title pages will be prepared in manuscript.

Place	Date	Hour	Summary of Events and Information	Remarks and references to Appendices
TORONTO CAMP BRANDHOEK	12th		Finished at WATTEN at 9 a.m. and detrained at BRANDHOEK at 2.0 P.M. Good Hut Camp near BRANDHOEK. Part of Transport came by train.	
	13th		Short Training near Camp. Bn was detailed as Brks works Bn during tour.	
	14th		Supplied 235 Men for various work under 14th Div. Remainder worked on various work at huts in the Camp.	
	15th		Supplied 325 Men for similar work.	
	16th		Same work. Voluntary Church service in Y.M.C.A. in Evening.	
	17th		Supplied 300 Men.	
	18th		Supplied 315 Men.	
	19th		Similar working Parties.	
	20th		Three Coys worked under 8th Div on Road in forward area. Hard front Undered work. Party left Camp at 5.0 AM & returned at 1.30PM.	
	cont.		A Coy were inspected by the C.O. and then marched to see a model of the Forward Area, near POPERINGHE. B & C Coys went out on work on Road. B & C Coys were inspected by 2nd Div Command and then marched to see model.	

(A7092). W. W2859/M1293. 750,000. 1/17. D. D. & L., Ltd. Forms/C.2118/14.

WAR DIARY

or

INTELLIGENCE SUMMARY.

(Erase heading not required.)

Instructions regarding War Diaries and Intelligence
Summaries are contained in F. S. Regs., Part II.
and the Staff Manual respectively. Title pages
will be prepared in manuscript.

Place	Date	Hour	Summary of Events and Information	Remarks and references to Appendices
TORONTO CAMP.	22nd		B, C & ½ A Coy sent forward for same work. D Coy see inspection and marched to the Model.	
	23rd		C D & ½ A Coy sent out on work. Training and work on camp for remainder.	
	24th		A B & D Coy made up the working Party. Remainder had baths and carried out Training. Band played Cards at night.	
	25th		No work. Church Services at 10.0 A.M. Whole Bn had dinner in three sittings from 12.30 P.M. till 3.0 P.M. Officers dinner in the Y.M.C.A. concert in Y.M.C.A. from 3.45 – 6.0 P.M. Officers dinner in evening two.	
	26th		A, C & D Coy out on work. Remainder worked at revetting huts.	
	27th		B, D and ½ A Coy. sent out on work. Remainder carried out training and work on the Camp.	
	28th		A & B Coy. were located at Army Belering station. All had then first batted before going to forward area.	

Army Form C. 2118.

WAR DIARY
or
INTELLIGENCE SUMMARY.

(Erase heading not required.)

Instructions regarding War Diaries and Intelligence
Summaries are contained in F. S. Regs., Part II.
and the Staff Manual respectively. Title pages
will be prepared in manuscript.

Place	Date	Hour	Summary of Events and Information	Remarks and references to Appendices
ToRoNTo CAMP.	29th		Bath parades to WHITBY camp POTIJZE; Details to RIDGE Camp. BRANDHOEK	
WHITBY CAMP	30th		Training near camp. Reft. washing out inspection. Move to SEINE SUPPORT at 4.30 p.m.	
SEINE	31st		Casualties 1 O.R. killed 1 O.R. wounded.	

P.G. Wilson
Major
9th Durham Light Infy

(A7592) Wt. W12859/M1293. 750,000. 1/17. D. D. & L., Ltd. Forms/C2118/14

WAR DIARY.

9th Bn. The Durham Light Infantry

January, 1918.

Volume — XXXIV.

Army Form C. 2118.

9th Battn. Durham Light Infantry
VOLUME XXXIV   Page 1.

WAR DIARY
or
INTELLIGENCE SUMMARY.

(Erase heading not required.)

Instructions regarding War Diaries and Intelligence Summaries are contained in F.S. Regs., Part II. and the Staff Manual respectively. Title pages will be prepared in manuscript.

Place	Date Jan 1918	Hour	Summary of Events and Information	Remarks and references to Appendices
SEINE Sh 28	1st		Quiet morning. Relieved 7th N.F. in Right Front Subsector commencing at 5.0 p.m. Relief completed by 8.0 p.m. with 4 then wounded. H.Q. at HAMBURG. Frontage from PASSCHENDAELE-MOORSLEDE Road to TIBER COPSE inclusive. 49th Div. on Right and 3rd Border Regt. on Left. Irregular outpost line held by 3 coys with D Coy in close support. Ground covered by Bn. H.Q. & 9 Lewis.	
HAMBURG	2nd		Intermittent shelling. Two wounded. Work done in wiring and making covered dumps in Forward Area. Active Patrolling.	
	3rd		On O.P. made 9 Lewis lines watched all day without seeing movement. Spthby patrol went out 700x and located three enemy posts & returned safely. Enemy occupying GASOMETERS.	
	4th		More work in wiring posts. organization of front line undertaken and two new posts made. Another fighting patrol starts to secure identification. 2 O.R. wounded. Were relieved by 20th Royal Fusiliers and moved back to MIZZAR CAMP POTIJZE. Very low relief. Heavy shelling.	
POTIJZE	5th		NEW YEARS HONOURS M.C. Lieut E.T. HAMPTON M.C. R.Q.M.S. TAYLOR.	

(B7093). Wt. W12839/M1293. 79,000. 1/17. D. D. & L. Ltd. Forms/C.2118/14.

WAR DIARY

or

INTELLIGENCE SUMMARY.

(Erase heading not required.)

Instructions regarding War Diaries and Intelligence Summaries are contained in F. S. Regs., Part II. and the Staff Manual respectively. Title pages will be prepared in manuscript.

Place	Date	Hour	Summary of Events and Information	Remarks and references to Appendices
POTIJZE	6th		Moved back to EECKE in Corps Reserve. Transport by Road and Personnel by Bus. Good billets.	
	7th		Coys. under Commanders for clearing up etc. Coys. at the disposal of their Commanders.	
	8th		Training for 4 hours in morning and 1 hour at night.	
	9th		Baths at SHERWOOD.	
	10th		Training at SHERWOOD & Training Throw.	
	11th		Training in morning and inspection by B.G.C. in organisation and administration.	
	12th		Company Training and inspection of Lewis Guns.	
	13th		Church Parade. Collection at 1 o/f realised 145 fr. for the men's Recreation Room fund.	
	14th		Coy. Training. All Ranks had Box Respirators tested in a Gas chamber. Baths for details. The Transport are inspected by A.D.V.S. 5th Divn & prizes awarded for the best Horsemanship in the Bn. Coy. and rugs for Officers chargers.	

(A7992). Wt. W2839/M1293. 750,000. 1/17. D. D. & L., Ltd. Forms/C.2118/44.

WAR DIARY

or

INTELLIGENCE SUMMARY.

(Erase heading not required.)

Instructions regarding War Diaries and Intelligence Summaries are contained in F. S. Regs., Part II. and the Staff Manual respectively. Title pages will be prepared in manuscript.

Place	Date	Hour	Summary of Events and Information	Remarks and references to Appendices
	15th		Training in Billets. Snow & Rain.	
	16th		Company Training. Lecture on "Submarine Warfare".	
	17th		Entrained at CAESTRE at 8.0 A.M. after a long wait. Arrived at and marched to Billets at BOISDINGHEM	
BOISDINGHEM. V.4. 51 2/a S.E.	18th		REVEILLE at 11.0 P.M. and marched to Billets at BOISDINGHEM	
	19th		Rest and clean up. Lewis Gun practice.	
	20th		Coy. Training. Lewis Gun & practice Revolver firing	
	21st		"A" Range near MOYELLE. Dinners out. hot day.	
	22nd		A & B Coys in Coy in attack & L.T.B Coys carried out wiring & digging	
	23rd		L.T.B. in Attack & A & B in wiring and digging.	
	24th		"A" Range soon and by Coy. in succession. Battn at ACQUIN.	
	25th		Battalion in attack on "model" of PASSCHENDAELE RIDGE.	
	26th		Work on "Model". Battalion Drill.	
			Bn. Field days on "model." The Battn counter attacked	

Signature

(B7093). Wt. W12859/M1203/750,000. 1/17. D. D. & L., Ltd. Forms/C.2118/14.

Army Form C. 2118.

WAR DIARY
or
INTELLIGENCE SUMMARY.
(Erase heading not required.)

Instructions regarding War Diaries and Intelligence Summaries are contained in F. S. Regs., Part II. and the Staff Manual respectively. Title pages will be prepared in manuscript.

Page 4.

Place	Date	Hour	Summary of Events and Information	Remarks and references to Appendices
	27th		Church Parade. Anzac.	
	28th		Baths and shot training. Transport moved forward towards BRANDHOEK.	
	29th		Company Training & preparation for the move. Bn to become a Pioneer Bn.	
	30th		Bn paraded at 8.0 a.m. & march to WIZERNES. Entrained at 11.0 a.m. Arrived BRANDHOEK at 5.0 p.m. Occupied old camp i.e.	
TORONTO CAMP.			TORONTO CAMP.	
BRANDHOEK	31st		Shot training & refitting etc.	

M.R. Gurney Lt Col
Adjutant
9th D.L.I.

(A7092) Wt. W12889/M1293. 750,000. 1/17. D. D. & L., Ltd. Forms/C.2118/14.

Lightning Source UK Ltd.
Milton Keynes UK
UKHW051354060622
403988UK00003B/8

9 781474 528078